WORDSWORTH CLASSICS
OF WORLD LITERATURE

General Editor: Tom Griffith

THE HEART OF
THE ANTARCTIC

SOUTH

SHACKLETON

The Heart of
the Antarctic
and
South

❖

*with an introduction
by Beau Riffenberg*

**WORDSWORTH CLASSICS
OF WORLD LITERATURE**

In loving memory of
MICHAEL TRAYLER
the founder of Wordsworth Editions

I

For customers interested in other titles from
Wordsworth Editions visit out website at
www.wordsworth-editions.com

For our latest list and a full mail order service contact
Bibliophile Books, 5 Thomas Road, London E14 7BN
Tel: +44 0207 515 9222
Fax: +44 0207 538 4115
e-mail: orders@bibliophilebooks.com

This edition published 2007 by Wordsworth Editions Limited
8B East Street, Ware, Hertfordshire SG12 9HJ

ISBN 978 1 84022 616 4

Typeset in Great Britain by Chrissie Madden
Printed and bound by Clays Ltd, St Ives plc

CONTENTS

ILLUSTRATIONS

INTRODUCTION

Early on the morning of 9 January 1909, after 50 hours held inside a small tent by a howling gale, four ragged explorers – Jameson Adams, Eric Marshall, Frank Wild, and their leader, Ernest Shackleton – broke camp and began a final push across the barren, endless wastes of the Antarctic Plateau. Carrying little more than some biscuits and chocolate in their pockets, a flag on a bamboo pole, and a camera, for five hours they marched as hard as their drained physical condition would allow. Then, having reached 88° 23' S – only 97 geographical miles from the South Pole and 366 miles farther south than any man had previously been – they planted the Union Jack, took possession of the area in the name of King Edward VII, and snapped two photographs.

Their nearly exhausted food supply prevented them from pushing any closer to their original goal of the South Pole, and the four men were left with no alternative but to turn north. 'All' that remained now was to retrace their tortuous steps of the previous months and cover the more than 700 miles to their base. It was a daunting task, and one for which the probability of success was low due to them already having suffered weeks of short rations, continuous exposure to the terrible cold and wind of the Antarctic Plateau, and extreme altitude sickness and dehydration. In fact, Adams later stated with the utmost certainty: 'If we'd gone on one more hour, we shouldn't have got back.'[1] Nevertheless, they somehow overcame innumerable obstacles as well as periods in which they ran out of food, to return alive, the journey becoming one of the most remarkable adventures in the history of exploration. During it, each man at different times came to the fore, showing a mettle that allowed him to help save his comrades, and that raised each of them into the pantheon of polar heroes.

But Shackleton's farthest south and his courage and determination on the return from it are not the primary reasons he is revered today as one of the greatest figures from the 'Heroic Age' of polar exploration. Rather, in recent years his legend has grown because of his *next* expedition. Whereas few books have concentrated on that earlier venture – which was named the British Antarctic Expedition – television, cinema, and a multitude of books have told the tale of the Imperial Trans-Antarctic Expedition (ITAE), which Shackleton planned as the first crossing of the Antarctic continent. Thus, it is widely known that his ship *Endurance* was trapped and later crushed in the ice of the Weddell Sea before his party could be landed, leaving the men in a seemingly hopeless situation. It is also common knowledge that in the following months, stranded on the floating ice, Shackleton – usually known simply as 'The Boss' – proved beyond doubt his marvellous leadership capabilities, as he held his party together before taking to boats and bringing everyone safely to Elephant Island. And the stories of his subsequent open-boat journey to South Georgia, his crossing of that island's mountain chain, and the eventual rescue of the party left behind, have now been repeated until they are burnt into the collective imagination of the English-speaking world.

And yet the many recountings of the ITAE have tended to reflect other people's viewpoints, interpretations, and opinions. It has not been always been easy to find Shackleton's own telling of his adventures. But now his official accounts of the events on *both* of his great expeditions have been combined in this one volume. Compiled here are Shackleton's most significant geographical accomplishments, his greatest deeds, his most momentous decisions, and a picture of his growth into one of the icons of his age and of the British Empire.

But what set the stage for these achievements and for the man who consequently gained such fame? Shackleton's career as an explorer did not spring, like Athene from Zeus, into a fully-grown form. Instead, it took a rather circuitous route to greatness, with chances of its being derailed several times along the way.

It all began in February 1874 in Kilkea, County Kildare, some 30 miles from Dublin, when Shackleton became the second child and eldest son of an Anglo-Irish family. When Shackleton was 10, his father moved the family to Croydon, and later Sydenham, to establish a medical practice. But pursuing a similar professional career was not for young Ernest, who from an early age dreamed instead about a life at sea. At 16 he finally persuaded his parents to let him live those dreams, and he left Dulwich College to join the three-masted sailing ship *Hoghton Tower* as an apprentice. It was the start of a decade in the merchant marine, during which he moved from sail to steam, and from hauling cargoes of nitrates from Chile to serving as an officer aboard the plush mail and passenger ships of the Union-Castle Line.

However, the stability of a respectable job that might see him rise slowly but surely to command of his own ship was not enough for Shackleton. Throughout his life, he was driven by the need to test himself, and by the beginning of the twentieth century his position with Union-Castle no longer served as a proving-ground for the fulfilment of the challenge he sought. Moreover, Shackleton was at heart a nomad, a man who required a spiritual freedom greater than most, and therefore the far-off, unknown reaches of the Earth had an irresistible pull that could never be matched by plying the well-known route back and forth between Southampton and the Cape Colony.

Even so, the possibility of such significant changes might still have come to naught had it not been for Emily Dorman, an attractive, talented woman six years Shackleton's senior, whom he had courted for several years. Emily's father was protective of her, and Shackleton knew that he needed to be more than a simple sailor to impress him and win his daughter's hand. So, seeing in exploration both a way to fulfil his desire for challenge and a path to fame and fortune, which in turn would lead to Emily, he applied to join an expedition to the least-known place on Earth – the Antarctic.

At the beginning of the twentieth century, the geography of Antarctica was still a mystery. No one knew for certain if it was a continent, a set of ice-covered islands, or one massive ice shelf. In fact, in 1896, the Sixth International Geographical Congress in London had passed a resolution stating that the exploration of the unknown Antarctic was the greatest piece of geographical investigation remaining and that it should be explored before the turn of the century. Two expeditions wintered in the Antarctic in the next several years, but the dawn of the twentieth century saw the preparation of the most extensive scientific and geographical effort yet. Named the British National Antarctic Expedition, it was brought into existence by Sir Clements Markham, the president of the Royal Geographical Society, and led by Markham's protégé, a Royal Navy commander named Robert Falcon Scott. Most of the officers and sailors were drawn from the Royal Navy, but to his eternal delight Shackleton was named the third officer.

Early in 1902, the expedition ship *Discovery* anchored safely off a place that Scott named Hut Point. It was on a southern cape of Ross Island, at the southern end of McMurdo Sound, which lies at the base of the great Ross Sea. The party built a hut there, but used it for work while living aboard the ship, all the while carrying out scientific studies and geographical investigations. Then, in November 1902, the most publicised part of expedition began, when Scott and two companions – Shackleton and Dr Edward Wilson – left with a team of 19 dogs to try to conquer the South Pole. They were the first men to sledge far out onto the Great Ice Barrier (now known as the Ross Ice Shelf), where deep crevasses, steep ridges, and heavy snow made conditions much worse than they had expected. Moreover, none of them had mastered the art of driving dogs, which, combined with not having appropriate food for the animals, led to a lack of efficiency. Soon the men had to join the dogs in harness themselves and begin man-hauling. For more than a month they relayed, dragging part of the load forward and then returning for the rest, making only one mile south for every three travelled. Through it all, they suffered painfully from overwork, lack of food, snowblindness, and, as of December, from scurvy. On 30 December, they reached a farthest south at 82° 17' S (463 geographic miles from the South Pole). But, with dwindling supplies, they were forced to turn for home or risk never making it back.

The journey north was a misery. The dogs died one by one, and the scurvy-ridden men had to man-haul their sledges without any other help whatsoever. Shackleton particularly suffered; he was short of breath and spat blood in coughing fits. For a while he was given the only remaining pair of skis, while Scott and Wilson pulled the sledge. Then Wilson's eyesight began to fail, and the weather, which had been glorious on the way out, turned ugly.

end of para 2 on this page: strictly speaking, hadn't they <u>already</u> risked never making it back? Surely carrying on meant not the risk, but the certainty, of never making it back?

But still they struggled on. One night, as a blizzard roared and Shackleton lay gasping for breath in the tent, he heard Wilson tell Scott that he did not expect him to last the night. That made him determined, Shackleton later said, to pull through, and somehow he did. On 3 February 1903, against all odds, the three men staggered into the base at Hut Point.

When autumn came and it became obvious that *Discovery* would remain trapped in the ice where she was anchored, Scott decided to remain in the Antarctic another year rather than abandon the ship. However, he sent a number of men back to England on a relief ship, including, for medical reasons but very much against his will, Shackleton. The junior officer was humiliated by being 'invalided' home, resulting in a deep desire to prove that that he should not have been sent back early. Together with his belief that a successful attempt on the South Pole could gain him fame and fortune, this led to his growing desire to command his own expedition. After his return to England, Shackleton married Emily, went through a series of jobs, and even stood for Parliament. But thoughts of going back to the Antarctic were never far from his mind, and in February 1907 his employer, the wealthy Scottish industrialist William Beardmore, guaranteed him a loan of £7000 towards his dream. It was not much, but it allowed Shackleton to sweep into action and begin initiating his Antarctic plans. Unlike previous expeditions, where science was a key objective, Shackleton's unabashed purpose was to reach the South Pole, and within days he announced that his grandly named 'British Antarctic Expedition' would begin the attempt that very year.

That point is where the first book in this volume, *The Heart of the Antarctic*, begins. It tells of Shackleton's preparations, his recruitment of shore party and ship's personnel, his decisions to use ponies and a motor-car as modes of transport, the departure of the expedition ship *Nimrod* first from England and then from New Zealand, and thence the numerous glorious achievements of the expedition in the far south. Widely considered one of the classics of polar literature, it is one of the most compelling narratives ever produced about the Antarctic. The account of the journey towards the South Pole was taken virtually verbatim from Shackleton's sledging diary, and the anxiety, the disappointment, and the triumph so apparent because of the day-to-day recording of events and emotions lend an immediacy to a text that otherwise might have been difficult to replicate.

At few points is this more obvious than in the days surrounding the four men's realisation that they would not be able to attain the Pole and their subsequent decision to change their goal to coming within 100 miles of it. Throughout the expedition, all of the men had recorded their distances in statute miles, rather than in geographical (or nautical) miles, as were commonly used at sea or by some other explorers, such as Scott or Roald Amundsen. The statute mile, which is still a common measurement in Britain or the United States, is 5,280 feet. However, the geographical or nautical mile – which is based on one-sixtieth of a degree, or one minute, of latitude – is 6,080 feet, or 1½ statute miles. So when Shackleton's party decided they needed to reach a point within 100 miles of the Pole, that meant at least 88° 20' S. Conveniently ignored – particularly for later public consumption – was that this distance was, in fact, 115 statute miles from the Pole. But for a number of days, all distances in each of the men's diaries suddenly changed to degrees, minutes, and geographical miles. Then, once the farthest south had been reached and they turned for home, distances again reverted, as the reader will see, to statute miles.

But it is not only the parts of the book based on Shackleton's diary that have such vitality and immediacy. The rest of the book has a pace and verve of equal vigour, and the reader can almost feel the intensity of the story as it poured from Shackleton's lips to be transcribed. With both Shackleton and his publisher, William Heinemann, anxious to complete the book hastily in order to benefit from a frenzy of 'Shackleton-mania' that followed the expedition's return, Shackleton hired Edward Saunders, a former reporter for the *Lyttelton Times*, as an amanuensis. Shackleton had a natural gift for the English language when speaking, and he dictated much of the text to Saunders as they sailed from Australia to England after the expedition and then in the first months back in Britain. To this already impressive tale, Saunders added a taut, vivid, forceful style that preserved yet improved upon Shackleton's literary skills. Not the average ghost-writer, Saunders contributed so mightily to the final product that Shackleton wanted him acknowledged on the title page. Saunders, however, refused, commenting afterwards that the it 'should stand without any attempt being made to explain just how [it was] produced.' [2]

Clearly, the text stood very well on its own. In reviewing it, *The Manchester Guardian* praised *The Heart of the Antarctic* as the 'best book of Polar travel which has ever been written.' [3] When the two-volume first edition was abridged into one volume as the 'Popular edition' the following year, the tributes to it were just as effusive. The obvious reason for this was that the Popular edition – which is the one that is reproduced here – was not an overall tightening of the first edition, which could change the literary style, but was abridged by cutting out entire swathes of material. There were four elements that were thus taken out of the first edition, two of which – Hugh Robert Mill's historical introduction and the majority of the scientific appendices – formed no real part of the basic narrative. The third section received slightly different treatment in that it compressed five chapters covering the preparations and depot-laying for, and the initial stages of, the Southern Journey. These were turned into one chapter, in this volume entitled 'The Southern Journey'. The final section removed for the Popular edition consisted of eight chapters entitled 'Professor David's Narrative' – or 'Professor David's Narrative (Continued)' – which told the story of the Northern Party's attempt to reach the South Magnetic Pole.

Due to this excising, the tale of the Northern Party tends to be less familiar than Shackleton's own story, although it was equally remarkable and, during its final stages, every bit as fraught with potential for disaster. Yet, like the Southern Party, its three members managed to scrape through – just.

The Northern Party consisted of Professor T. W. Edgeworth David, a renowned geologist from the University of Sydney whose late joining of the expedition had given it instant scientific credibility; Douglas Mawson, a geologist at the University of Adelaide (although officially the expedition's physicist), who would become one of the greatest figures in the history of Antarctic exploration; and Scottish surgeon Alistair Mackay. The South Magnetic Pole (which wanders as the Earth's magnetic field shifts slightly) lay at an undetermined point in the interior to the north-northwest of Ross Island. The three men left the base at Cape Royds in early October 1908 and began man-hauling up the coast of Victoria

Land. Forced to relay their sledges due to the weight of their supplies, they made slow progress as they continued to search for a way through the mountains that stood sentinel for that section of the Antarctic Plateau.. In early November they passed over the Nordenskjöld Ice Barrier, and on 1 December they reached the massive Drygalski Ice Tongue, which took 10 days to cross. The surface of the Drygalski, according to Professor David, 'was formed of jagged surfaces of ice very heavily crevassed, and projecting in the form of immense séracs separated from one another by deep undulations or chasms. It at once suggested to my mind some scaly dragon-like monster.'[4]

Once past the Drygalski Ice Tongue, the three began their ascent up a series of glaciers towards the Antarctic Plateau. A month later, on 16 January 1907, their trek inland culminated at 72° 15' S, 155° 16' E, when Mawson calculated they had reached the Magnetic Pole. Like their comrades almost a thousand geographic miles to the south, they claimed the region, took a picture of themselves, and then turned to race back towards the coast, hoping to reach it in time to meet *Nimrod*. The expedition ship, returning from New Zealand, did not have the coal to conduct an extensive search and still make it back to civilisation, so the captain had decided to make just one pass along Victoria Land looking for the party. If they were not found, he would then leave them to their fate. David, Mawson, and Mackay successfully retraced their steps towards the coast until blundering into a terribly crevassed and dangerous area in the final stages of the descent from the Plateau. Camped near the shore in early February, they were almost left behind after *Nimrod* passed them during a blizzard. Fortunately, John King Davis, the first mate, convinced the captain to return for one last look. With bad grace the captain sailed back the way he had come, and there, in a small inlet, were the three explorers – saved at last.

The Northern Party's journey made David and Mawson heroes to their countrymen in Australia when they returned, and Mawson's newly established reputation helped pave the way for his great scientific effort, the Australasian Antarctic Expedition (1911–14). But few explorers ever became more popular with the public of Britain and the British Empire than Shackleton.

Almost immediately upon arriving in New Zealand, he found himself in the role of imperial hero, his achievements spurring a wave of patriotic fervour and public adoration and helping to serve as an antidote to the national doubts induced by Britain's loss of economic and technological supremacy in Europe and the Empire's military débâcle in the South African War. 'So long as Englishmen are prepared to do this kind of thing,' proclaimed a writer for *The Sphere*, 'I do not think we need to lie awake all night every night dreading the hostile advance of the "boys of the dachshund breed".'[5]

Shackleton was, in fact, just what the public and the press wanted. Not only was he handsome, charismatic, direct, and a remarkable speaker, his story was one of endurance, determination, and raw courage, ending with triumph against the odds. It could not have been a more potent combination, and Shackleton the showman appealed to men and women alike, from flower-sellers and rag-and-bone men to captains of industry and Members of Parliament. When, in the same week in November 1909 that *The Heart of the Antarctic* was published, it was announced that Shackleton would receive a knighthood, the *Daily Mirror* recorded that 'It is safe to say that none of the honours will be more popular with the general public.'[6]

The world seemed to be at Shackleton's feet, but it was at this point that Scott announced his own forthcoming attempt on the South Pole. Having just returned home, Shackleton had not yet formulated any new plans – and he had promised Emily that he would not go again – so he had to accede publicly to Scott's efforts or play the part of the churl. Shackleton instead threw himself into a series of lectures to pay off the debts of his expedition and a succession of money-making ventures that he hoped would gain him a fortune – although none ever did. But although he held the Antarctic at arm's length, it was not out of his system, and before too long he commandeered Mawson's plans for an expedition to the area of unknown coastline south of Australia. Shackleton convinced Mawson that he could gain financing that the Australian could not, so Mawson agreed for Shackleton to become leader of the expedition, while his own role was reduced to chief scientist. But that region, although offering great opportunities for scientific investigation, was too far from the Pole and from adventures that might excite the public to remain of interest to Shackleton for long. Within a period of months, he renounced command of the expedition, leaving Mawson to continue his pursuit of launching it.

Upon the announcement in 1912 that Amundsen had reached the Pole, it was immediately apparent to Shackleton what task he had left to focus upon. 'The discovery of the South Pole will not be the end of Antarctic exploration,' he had told the *Daily Mail* the previous year when Amundsen's plans had first come to light, indicating that the next great work in the south would be 'a transcontinental journey from sea to sea, crossing the Pole.'[7] Now the key piece of information was to find out what had happened to Wilhelm Filchner's expedition, which had left Bremerhaven for the Weddell Sea in May 1911 with vague hopes of crossing to the Ross Sea using horse-drawn sledges. In fact, although discovering the Filchner Ice Shelf at the base of the Weddell Sea, Filchner's plan had gone awry when a large tabular iceberg upon which he started to build his base broke free from the ice shelf and drifted north. Soon thereafter the expedition ship, *Deutschland*, was solidly beset in the ice and began drifting north herself. By the time the ship was freed, Filchner had decided to abandon his futile efforts and sailed north to South Georgia.

When Filchner's lack of success became public knowledge, the way was open for Shackleton to pursue a plan based to a great extent on the proposals of the Scottish oceanographer William Speirs Bruce. In 1908, Bruce had been unable to gain funding for his ideas, and he now willingly allowed his scheme to be taken over by Shackleton. Throughout much of 1913, while the British public mourned for the loss of Captain Scott, and much of the polar establishment seemed to think that any British role in Antarctic exploration had come to a close, Shackleton developed his plans for the Imperial Trans-Antarctic Expedition. These were made public in a letter to *The Times* on 29 December 1913.

Mentioned briefly by Shackleton in the Preface of *South*, these plans included a party of 12 being landed from the ship *Endurance* at Vahsel Bay, which Filchner had discovered at the base of the Weddell Sea. Six of these men would then make the 1800-mile crossing to the Ross Sea region, reaching the South Pole on the way and continuing along the route that Shackleton had established during his first expedition before eventually emerging at McMurdo Sound. The crossing would be possible only with the assistance of a second team, which would lay a series of depots from Ross Island to the base of the Beardmore Glacier, the mammoth river of ice that Shackleton had pioneered – and Scott had followed – as the route to the Pole. The Ross Sea party, as this second group was called, would reach the Antarctic aboard the ship *Aurora*, which in 1914 Shackleton purchased from Mawson, after the latter's return from his own expedition.

After a brief Preface, *South* begins with the departure of *Endurance* from South Georgia on her way to the Weddell Sea. Although most of the book is dedicated to the popular tale of the events in the Weddell Sea, Elephant Island, South Georgia, and Shackleton's eventual rescue of his men, the final six chapters cover the less-known Ross Sea party. Having set up their base at Scott's old Cape Evans hut, 10 men were left in conditions equally unpleasant as those that faced Shackleton, when *Aurora*, anchored off of Ross Island with most of the party's provisions, was blown north by a gale into the Ross Sea and unable to return. This left the unfortunate men to fend for themselves for more than a year and a half before *Aurora* – having eventually been able to limp into New Zealand – was refitted and, under the command of John King Davis, returned to rescue the survivors. In the meantime, facing all manner of challenges from nature, lack of food and equipment, and scurvy, the party had successfully laid the depots for Shackleton's proposed crossing. Three of the men died – one from scurvy and two disappearing on shifting sea ice – before the others made it back to Cape Evans. As it turned out, all had been for naught, as Shackleton had not even disembarked on the other side of the continent.

Due in part to Shackleton's participation in the rescue of the Ross Sea party and his subsequent service in the First World War, *South* did not appear with nearly the rapidity as had *The Heart of the Antarctic*. Again he worked with Edward Saunders on the book, dictating parts of the text to him during a three-week period in Wellington and Sydney in 1917 after having travelled to McMurdo Sound aboard *Aurora* to rescue his remaining men. The way Shackleton and Saunders worked together was commented upon by Shackleton's long-time confidante Leonard Tripp, a Wellington attorney who was there when Shackleton dictated to Saunders the story of the crossing of South Georgia. 'Shackleton walked up and down the room smoking a cigarette, and I was absolutely amazed at his language,' Tripp later recalled. 'He very seldom hesitated, but every now and then he would tell Saunders to make a mark, because he had not got the right word; but that was only occasionally. I watched him, and his whole face seemed to swell, and I could see the man was suffering. After about half an hour he turned to me and with tears in his eyes he said, "Tripp, you don't know what I've been through, and I am going through it all again . . . ".'[8]

Shackleton had not kept a full diary as he had on his sledging journey, so much of what he told Saunders was based on memory, but he also gave him a number of expedition documents, including a copy of Captain Worsley's diary. It was approximately a year later that Saunders finally sent Shackleton the manuscript of *South*, and the final edit of the text was done by Leonard Hussey, one of the men who had remained on Elephant Island under the command of Frank Wild when Shackleton had sailed to South Georgia. Again Shackleton suggested acknowledging Saunders' contribution, offering to name him as the editor of the book in the Preface. However, once again Saunders declined the recognition.

When it finally appeared in November 1919, *South* proved a much briefer account than *The Heart of the Antarctic*, comprising only one volume. In addition, the first impression was printed on a much lower quality paper, and there was no opulent, special limited edition published in full vellum, as there had been for *The Heart of the Antarctic*. But it did have the decided advantage of being illustrated by both the remarkable photographs of Frank Hurley, a member of the expedition who has long been considered one of the two greatest Antarctic photographers (along with Herbert Ponting of Scott's last expedition), and the drawings of George Marston, who had been with Shackleton on both *Nimrod* and *Endurance*. When it appeared, *South* received reviews that were equally glowing as those for *The Heart of the Antarctic*, and the passage of time has confirmed Shackleton's second account – like its predecessor – as one of the finest works of Antarctic literature. Unfortunately for Shackleton, he did not benefit from any sales because he was forced to assign the rights to the book to creditors who had contributed to the outfitting of *Aurora*.

Being shorter than *The Heart of the Antarctic* to start with, *South* was not edited nearly so much when the 'Cheap edition' (as it was called at the time) appeared in September 1921. This had a slightly different sub-title than *The Story of Shackleton's Last Expedition, 1914–1917*, which had appeared on the first edition. With Shackleton sailing from London that very month on the hastily cobbled together Shackleton-Rowett Antarctic Expedition, the original sub-title was now inaccurate, so it was replaced with *The Story of Shackleton's 1914–1917 Expedition*.

Shackleton's actual last expedition had begun as a scheme after the First World War to search for new lands in the Arctic. However, when the Canadian government withdrew the support Shackleton had been counting on, he decided instead to turn to the south. John Quiller Rowett, who had attended Dulwich College with him, agreed to provide the necessary funds. Unlike Shackleton's earlier expeditions, there was no one glorious primary goal for the expedition. Rather, in his various proposals he included circumnavigating Antarctica in a search for doubtful and poorly mapped islands, conducting comprehensive ship-based scientific research, charting some 2000 miles of Antarctic coastline, investigating sealing and whaling grounds, making the first use of an aeroplane in the Antarctic, and even visiting the islands of the South Pacific in order to determine how they had been settled. Underneath the surface, the expedition felt very much like simply the opportunity for Shackleton to revisit the Antarctic while accompanied by cronies from *Endurance*.

With preparations being completed in only three months, the expedition ship *Quest* sailed to Rio de Janeiro, where a major refit was required. The tiny vessel then headed towards South Georgia, but was plagued by boiler problems. They arrived at Grytviken, an old whaling station on South Georgia, on 4 January 1922, but in the small wee hours of the next morning Shackleton suffered a heart attack and died. Wild took over as leader, and one of his first decisions was to send Shackleton's body back to England for burial.

Wild then sailed south, but continuing problems with the ship, bad weather, and a shortage of coal forced the expedition to return to South Georgia three months later. There the men found Leonard Hussey, who had been detailed to accompany Shackleton's body home. When he had reached Montevideo, Hussey had received a message from Emily Shackleton. She had had no doubt that the wandering soul who was her husband should be buried not in England but in South Georgia, the wild island that had meant so much to him and his career. So Hussey had escorted 'The Boss' back to Grytviken, where he was buried in a small Norwegian whalers' cemetery.

More than eight decades later, tourists to South Georgia now make a visit to Shackleton's grave their highest priority, forcing their way through the tussock grass and carefully stepping over the lounging elephant seals that keep the dead company. There, homage is paid to the man who, despite not having fully achieved any of the basic objectives of his expeditions, had the vision, bravery, determination, and strength to open up the interior of Antarctica for all those who followed. Even more, however, Shackleton showed the flame of leadership as few others ever did in the entire history of exploration. It is this for which he is justly most remembered, and nowhere do Shackleton's leadership skills, his passion, his endurance, and his greatness come through more clearly than in the two accounts in this volume.

BEAU RIFFENBURGH
Scott Polar Research Institute

References:
1 Jameson Adams, interview with James Fisher, 5 October 1955; SPRI MS 1456/63
2. Edward Saunders, letter to L. Tripp, 10 August 1922; Alexander Turnbull Library
3. Quoted in Roland Huntford, *Shackleton*, page 318
4. T. W. Edgeworth David, Professor David's Narrative, in *The Heart of the Antarctic*, volume 2, page 130
5. *The Sphere*, 3 April 1909, page 14
6. *Daily Mirror*, 8 November 1909
7. *Daily Mail*, 11 March 1911
8. Quoted in H. R. Mill, *The Life of Sir Ernest Shackleton*, page 245

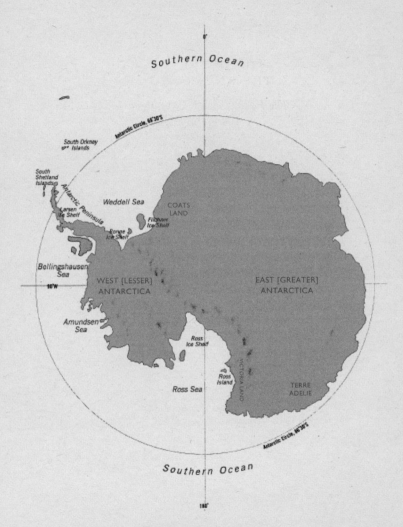

The Antarctic today

THE HEART OF
THE ANTARCTIC

The Farthest South Expedition
1907–1909

The scientific results of the expedition cannot be stated in detail in a single volume. Some of the more important features of the geographical work were as follows.

We passed the winter of 1908 in McMurdo Sound, twenty miles north of the *Discovery* winter quarters. In the autumn a party ascended Mount Erebus and surveyed its various craters. In the spring and summer of 1908 to 1909, three sledging parties left winter quarters; one went south and attained the most southerly latitude ever reached by man, and another reached the South Magnetic Pole for the first time; while a third surveyed the mountain ranges west of McMurdo Sound.

The Southern Sledge-Party planted the Union Jack in latitude 88° 23' South, within one hundred geographical miles of the South Pole. This party of four ascertained that a great chain of mountains extends from the 82nd parallel, south of McMurdo Sound, to the 86th parallel, trending in a south-easterly direction; that other great mountain ranges continue to the south and south-west, and that between them flows one of the largest glaciers in the world, leading to an inland plateau, the height of which, at latitude 88° South, is over 11,000 ft. above sea level. This plateau presumably continues beyond the geographical South Pole, and extends from Cape Adare to the Pole.

The journey made by the northern party resulted in the attainment of the South Magnetic Pole, the position of which was fixed, by observations made on the spot and in the neighbourhood, at latitude 72° 25' South, longitude 155° 16' East. The first part of this journey was made along the coastline of Victoria Land, and many new peaks, glaciers, and ice tongues were discovered, in addition to a couple of small islands. The whole of the coast traversed was carefully triangulated, and the existing map was corrected in several respects.

The survey of the western mountains by the western party added to the information of the topographical details of that part of Victoria Land, and threw some new light on its geology.

The discovery of forty-five miles of new coastline extending from Cape North, first in a south-westerly and then in a westerly direction, was another important piece of geographical work.

I should like to tender my warmest thanks to those generous people who supported the expedition in its early days. Miss Dawson Lambton and Miss E. Dawson Lambton made possible the first steps toward the organisation of the expedition, and assisted afterward in every way that lay in their power. Mr William Beardmore (Glasgow), Mr G. A. McLean Buckley (New Zealand), Mr Campbell McKellar (London), Mr Sydney Lysaght (Somerset), Mr A. M. Fry (Bristol), Colonel Alexander Davis (London), Mr H. H. Bartlett (London), and other friends contributed liberally toward the cost of the expedition.

I also wish to thank those friends who guaranteed a large part of the necessary expenditure, and the Imperial Government for the grant of £20,000, which enabled me to redeem those guarantees.

Overseas Britain showed a sympathetic interest. I am indebted to the Government of the Commonwealth of Australia for a contribution of £5000. The New Zealand Government gave me £1000; and also agreed to pay half the cost of towing the Nimrod as far as the Antarctic Circle. Indeed the kindness and generosity of Australasians will remain one of the happiest memories of the 'British Antarctic Expedition, 1907. My indebtedness to various firms in the matter of supplies has been acknowledged in Chapter 8.

I have drawn on the diaries of various members of the expedition to supply information regarding events that occurred while I was absent on journeys. Professor T. W. Edgeworth David narrates the incidents of the northern journey.

In regard to the management of the affairs of the expedition during my absence in the Antarctic, I would like to acknowledge the work done for me by my brother-in-law, Mr Herbert Dorman, of London; by Mr J. J. Kinsey, of Christchurch, New Zealand; and by Mr Alfred Reid, the manager of the expedition, whose work throughout has been as arduous as it has been efficient.

Finally, let me say that to the members of the expedition, whose work and enthusiasm have been the means of securing the measure of success recorded in these pages, I owe a debt of gratitude that I can hardly find words to express. I realise very fully that without their faithful service and loyal cooperation under conditions of extreme difficulty success in any branch of our work would have been impossible.

ERNEST H. SHACKLETON

PREFACE TO SECOND EDITION

The publication of this edition of *The Heart of the Antarctic* calls for a word or two from me.

Owing to the necessity of recording all that occurred during our stay in the Antarctic and the inclusion of much scientific matter, the first edition attained proportions that made it not only expensive to publish, but placed the book out of reach of the ordinary reader.

In this edition the narrative embraces all matters of general public interest. Judging by the way in which the public has shown its interest in the doings of the Expedition, I feel that the time has come for the issue of an account of our Work in Antarctic, less bulky in form and at a lower price.

I hope that the following pages will convey to readers a good idea of the work of our Expedition in the Far South: and, as a last word, I wish to thank all English-speaking people all the world over for the keen interest taken in the efforts of our members to extend the general knowledge of that portion of the Imperial Dominion round about the Pole.

E. H. S.

CHAPTER I

The expedition

Inception and preparation: Food supply: Equipment: The Nimrod:
*Hut for winter quarters: Clothing: Ponies, dogs, and motorcar: Scientific
instruments: Miscellaneous articles of equipment*

Men go out into the void spaces of the world for various reasons.
Some are actuated simply by a love of adventure, some have the
keen thirst for scientific knowledge, and others again are drawn
away from the trodden paths by the 'lure of little voices', the
mysterious fascination of the unknown. I think that in my own
case it was a combination of these factors that determined me to
try my fortune once again in the frozen south. I had been invalided
home before the conclusion of the *Discovery* expedition, and I had
a very keen desire to see more of the vast continent that lies amid
the Antarctic snows and glaciers. Indeed the stark polar lands grip
the hearts of the men who have lived on them in a manner that can
hardly be understood by the people who have never got outside
the pale of civilisation. I was convinced, moreover, that an expedition on the lines I had in view could justify itself by the results of
its scientific work. The *Discovery* expedition had brought back a
great store of information, and had performed splendid service in
several important branches of science. I believed that a second
expedition could carry the work still further. The *Discovery* expedition had gained knowledge of the great chain of mountains
running in a north and south direction from Cape Adare to
latitude 82° 17' South, but whether this range turned to the south-
east or eastward for any considerable distance was not known, and
therefore the southern limits of the Great Ice Barrier plain had not
been defined. The glimpses gained of King Edward VII Land from
the deck of the *Discovery* had not enabled us to determine either its
nature or its extent, and the mystery of the Barrier remained
unsolved. It was a matter of importance to the scientific world that

information should be gained regarding the movement of the ice
sheet that forms the Barrier. Then I wanted to find out what lay
beyond the mountains to the south of latitude 82° 17' and whether
the Antarctic continent rose to a plateau similar to the one found
by Captain Scott beyond the western mountains. There was much
to be done in the field of meteorology, and this work was of
particular importance to Australia and New Zealand, for these
countries are affected by weather conditions that have their origin
in the Antarctic. Antarctic zoology, though somewhat limited, as
regarded the range of species, had very interesting aspects, and I
wanted to devote some attention to mineralogy, apart from general geology. The aurora australis, atmospheric electricity, tidal
movements, hydrography, currents of the air, ice formations and
movements, biology and geology, offered an unlimited field for
research, and the dispatch of an expedition seemed to be justified on
scientific grounds quite apart from the desire to gain a high latitude.

The difficulty that confronts most men who wish to undertake
exploration work is that of finance, and in this respect I was rather
more than ordinarily handicapped. The equipment and dispatch
of an Antarctic expedition means the expenditure of very many
thousands of pounds, without the prospect of any speedy return,
and with a reasonable probability of no return at all. I drew up my
scheme on the most economical lines, as regarded both ship and
staff, but for over a year I tried vainly to raise sufficient money
to enable me to make a start. I secured introductions to wealthy
men, and urged to the best of my ability the importance of the
work I proposed to undertake, but the money was not forthcoming, and it almost seemed as though I should have to abandon
the venture altogether. I persisted, and toward the end of 1906 I
was encouraged by promises of support from one or two personal
friends. Then I made a fresh effort, and on February 12, 1907, I had
enough money promised to enable me to announce definitely that
I would go south with an expedition. As a matter of fact, some of
the promises of support made to me could not be fulfilled, and I
was faced by financial difficulties for some time; but when the
Governments of Australia and New Zealand came to my assistance, the position became more satisfactory.

In the *Geographical Journal* for March 1907 I outlined my plan of
campaign, but this had to be changed in several respects at a later

date owing to the exigencies of circumstances. My intention was that the expedition should leave New Zealand at the beginning of 1908, and proceed to winter quarters on the Antarctic continent, the ship to land the men and stores and then return. By avoiding having the ship frozen in, I would render the use of a relief ship unnecessary, as the same vessel could come south again the following summer and take us off. 'The shore party of nine or twelve men will winter with sufficient equipment to enable three separate parties to start out in the spring,' I announced. 'One party will go east, and, if possible, across the Barrier to the new land known as King Edward VII Land, follow the coastline there south, if the coast trends south, or north if north, returning when it is considered necessary to do so. The second party will proceed south over the same route as that of the southern sledge party of the *Discovery;* this party will keep from fifteen to twenty miles from the coast, so as to avoid any rough ice. The third party will possibly proceed westward over the mountains, and, instead of crossing in a line due west, will strike toward the magnetic pole. The main changes in equipment will be that Siberian ponies will be taken for the sledge journeys both east and south, and also a specially designed motorcar for the southern journey . . . I do not intend to sacrifice the scientific utility of the expedition to a mere record-breaking journey, but say frankly, all the same, that one of my great efforts will be to reach the southern geographical pole. I shall in no way neglect to continue the biological, meteorological, geological and magnetic work of the *Discovery*.' I added that I would endeavour to sail along the coast of Wilkes Land, and secure definite information regarding that coastline.

The program was an ambitious one for a small expedition, no doubt, but I was confident, and I think I may claim that in some measure my confidence has been justified. Before we finally left England, I had decided that if possible I would establish my base on King Edward VII Land instead of at the *Discovery* winter quarters in McMurdo Sound, so that we might break entirely new ground. The narrative will show how completely, as far as this particular matter was concerned, all my plans were upset by the demands of the situation. The journey to King Edward VII Land over the Barrier was not attempted, owing largely to the unexpected loss of ponies before the winter. I laid all my plans very carefully, basing them on experience I had gained with the *Discovery* expedition, and in the fitting out of the relief ships *Terra Nova* and *Morning,* and the Argentine expedition that went to the relief of the Swedes. I decided that I would have no committee, as the expedition was entirely my own venture, and I wished to supervise personally all the arrangements.

When I found that some promises of support had failed me and had learned that the Royal Geographical Society, though sympathetic in its attitude, could not see its way to assist financially, I approached several gentlemen and suggested that they should guarantee me at the bank, the guarantees to be redeemed by me in 1910, after the return of the expedition. It was on this basis that I secured a sum of £20,000, the greater part of the money necessary for the starting of the expedition, and I cannot express too warmly my appreciation of the faith shown in me and my plans by the men who gave these guarantees, which could be redeemed only by the proceeds of lectures and the sale of this book after the expedition had concluded its work. These preliminary matters settled, I started to buy stores and equipment, to negotiate for a ship, and to collect around me the men who would form the expedition.

The equipping of a polar expedition is a task demanding experience as well as the greatest attention to points of detail. When the expedition has left civilisation, there is no opportunity to repair any omission or to secure any article that may have been forgotten. It is true that the explorer is expected to be a handy man, able to contrive dexterously with what materials he may have at hand; but makeshift appliances mean increased difficulty and added danger. The aim of one who undertakes to organise such an expedition must be to provide for every contingency, and in dealing with this work I was fortunate in being able to secure the assistance of Mr Alfred Reid, who had already gained considerable experience in connection with previous polar ventures. I appointed Mr Reid manager of the expedition, and I found him an invaluable assistant. I was fortunate, too, in not being hampered by committees of any sort. I kept the control of all the arrangements in my own hands, and thus avoided the delays that are inevitable when a group of men have to arrive at a decision on points of detail.

The first step was to secure an office in London, and we selected a furnished room at 9 Regent Street, as the headquarters of the expedition. The staff at this period consisted of Mr Reid, a district messenger and myself, but there was a typewriting office on the same floor, and the correspondence, which grew in bulk day by day, could be dealt with as rapidly as though I had employed stenographers and typists of my own. I had secured estimates of the cost of provisioning and equipping the expedition before I made any public announcement regarding my intentions, so that there were no delays when once active work had commenced. This was not an occasion for inviting tenders, because it was vitally important that we should have the best of everything, whether in food or gear, and I therefore selected, in consultation with Mr Reid, the firms that should be asked to supply us. Then we proceeded to interview the heads of these firms, and we found that in nearly every instance we were met with generous treatment as to prices, and with ready cooperation in regard to details of manufacture and packing.

Food supplies

Several very important points have to be kept in view in selecting the food supplies for a polar expedition. In the first place the food must be wholesome and nourishing in the highest degree possible. At one time that dread disease scurvy used to be regarded as the inevitable result of a prolonged stay in the ice-bound regions, and even the *Discovery* expedition, during its labours in the Antarctic in the years 1902–4, suffered from this complaint, which is often produced by eating preserved food that is not in a perfectly wholesome condition. It is now recognised that scurvy may be avoided if the closest attention is given to the preparation and selection of food stuffs on scientific lines, and I may say at once that our efforts in this direction were successful, for during the whole course of the expedition we had not one case of sickness attributable directly or indirectly to the foods we had brought with us. Indeed, beyond a few colds, apparently due to germs from a bale of blankets, we experienced no sickness at all at the winter quarters.

In the second place the food taken for use on the sledging expeditions must be as light as possible, remembering always that extreme concentration renders the food less easy of assimilation and therefore less healthful. Extracts that may be suitable enough for use in ordinary climates are of little use in the polar regions, because under conditions of very low temperature the heat of the body can be maintained only by use of fatty and farinaceous foods in fairly large quantities. Then the sledging foods must be such as do not require prolonged cooking, that is to say, it must be sufficient to bring them to the boiling point, for the amount of fuel that can be carried is limited. It must be possible to eat the foods without cooking at all, for the fuel may be lost or become exhausted.

More latitude is possible in the selection of foods to be used at the winter quarters of the expedition, for the ship may be expected to reach that point, and weight is therefore of less importance. My aim was to secure a large variety of foods for use during the winter night. The long months of darkness impose a severe strain on any men unaccustomed to the conditions, and it is desirable to relieve the monotony in every way possible. A variety of food is healthful, moreover, and this is especially important at a period when it is difficult for the men to take much exercise, and when sometimes they are practically confined to the hut for days together by bad weather.

All these points were taken into consideration in the selection of our food stuffs. I based my estimates on the requirements of twelve men for two years, but this was added to in New Zealand when I increased the staff. Some important articles of food were presented to the expedition by the manufacturers: and others, such as the biscuit and pemmican, were specially manufactured to my order. The question of packing presented some difficulties, and I finally decided to use 'Venesta' cases for the food stuffs and as much as possible of the equipment. These cases are manufactured from composite boards prepared by uniting three layers of birch or other hard wood with waterproof cement. They are light, weatherproof, and strong, and proved to be eminently suited to our purposes. The cases I ordered measured about two feet six inches by fifteen inches, and we used some 2500 of them. The saving of weight, as compared with an ordinary packing case, was about four pounds per case, and we had no trouble at all with breakages, in spite of the rough handling given our stores in the process of landing at Cape Royds after the expedition had reached the Antarctic regions.

I decided to take food supplies for the shore party for two years; and some additions were made after the arrival of the *Nimrod* in New Zealand.*

I arranged that supplies for thirty-eight men for one year should be carried by the *Nimrod* when the vessel went south for the second time to bring back the shore party. This was a precautionary measure in case the *Nimrod* should get caught in the ice and be compelled to spend a winter in the Antarctic, in which case we would still have had one year's provisions in hand.

Equipment

After placing some of the principal orders for food supplies, I went to Norway with Mr Reid in order to secure the sledges, fur boots and mits, sleeping bags, ski, and some other articles of equipment. I was fortunate, on the voyage from Hull to Christiania, in making the acquaintance of Captain Pepper, the commodore captain of the Wilson Line of steamers. He took a keen interest in the expedition, and he was of very great assistance to me in the months that followed, for he undertook to inspect the sledges in the process of manufacture. He was at Christiania once in each fortnight, and he personally looked to the lashings and seizings as only a sailor could. We arrived at Christiania on April 22, and then learned that Mr C. S. Christiansen, the maker of the sledges used on the *Discovery* expedition, was in the United States. This was a disappointment, but after consultation with Scott-Hansen, who was the first lieutenant of the *Fram* on Nansen's famous expedition, I decided to place the work in the hands of Messrs. L. H. Hagen and Company. The sledges were to be of the Nansen pattern, built of specially selected timber, and of the best possible workmanship. I ordered ten twelve-foot sledges, eighteen eleven-foot sledges and two seven-foot sledges. The largest ones would be suitable for pony haulage. The eleven-foot ones could be drawn by either ponies or men, and the small pattern would be useful for work around the winter quarters and for short journeys such as the scientists of the expedition were likely to undertake. The timbers used for the sledges were seasoned ash and American hickory, and in addition to Captain Pepper, Captain Isaachsen and Lieutenant Scott-Hansen, both experienced Arctic explorers, watched the work of construction on

* See page 29.

my behalf. Their interest was particularly valuable to me, for they were able in many little ways hardly to be understood by the lay reader to ensure increased strength and efficiency. I had formed the opinion that an eleven-foot sledge was best for general work, for it was not so long as to be unwieldy, and at the same time was long enough to ride over sastrugi and hummocky ice. Messrs. Hagen and Company did their work thoroughly well, and the sledges proved all that I could have desired.

The next step was to secure the furs that the expedition would require, and for this purpose we went to Drammen and made the necessary arrangements with Mr W. C. Möller. We selected skins for the sleeping bags, taking those of young reindeer, with short thick fur, less liable to come out under conditions of dampness than is the fur of the older deer. Our furs did not make a very large order, for after the experience of the *Discovery* expedition I decided to use fur only for the feet and hands and for the sleeping bags, relying for all other purposes on woollen garments with an outer covering of windproof material. I ordered three large sleeping bags, to hold three men each, and twelve one-man bags. Each bag had the reindeer fur inside, and the seams were covered with leather, strongly sewn. The flaps overlapped about eight inches, and the head of the bag was sewn up to the top of the fly. There were three toggles for fastening the bag up when the man was inside. The toggles were about eight inches apart. The one-man bags weighed about ten pounds when dry, but of course the weight increased as they absorbed moisture when in use.

The foot gear I ordered consisted of eighty pairs of ordinary finnesko, or reindeer fur boots, twelve pairs of special finnesko and sixty pairs of ski boots, of various sizes. The ordinary finnesko is made from the skin of the reindeer stag's head, with the fur outside, and its shape is roughly that of a very large boot without any laces. It is large enough to hold the foot, several pairs of socks, and a supply of sennegrass, and it is a wonderfully comfortable and warm form of foot gear. The special finnesko are made from the skin of the reindeer stag's legs, but they are not easily secured, for the reason that the native tribes, not unreasonably, desire to keep the best goods for themselves. I had a man sent to Lapland to barter for finnesko of the best kind, but he only succeeded in getting twelve pairs. The ski boots are made of soft leather, with the upper coming right round under the sole, and a flat piece of leather sewn on top of the upper. They are made specially for use with skis, and are very useful for summer wear. They give the foot plenty of play and do not admit water. The heel is very low, so that the foot can rest firmly on the ski. I bought five prepared reindeer skins for repairing, and a supply of repairing gear, such as sinew, needles, and waxed thread.

I have mentioned that sennegrass is used in the finnesko. This is a dried grass of long fibre, with a special quality of absorbing moisture. I bought fifty kilos (110.25 lb.) in Norway for use on the expedition. The grass is sold in wisps, bound up tightly, and when the finnesko are being put on, some of it is teased out and a pad placed along the sole under the foot. Then when the boot has been pulled on more grass is stuffed around the heel. The grass absorbs the moisture that is given off from the skin, and prevents the sock freezing to the sole of the boot, which would then be difficult to remove at night. The grass is pulled out at night, shaken loose, and allowed to freeze. The moisture that has been collected congeals in the form of frost, and the greater part of it can be shaken away before the grass is replaced on the following morning. The grass is gradually used up on the march, and it is necessary to take a fairly large supply, but it is very light and takes up little room.

I ordered from Mr Möller sixty pairs of wolfskin and dogskin mits, made with the fur outside, and sufficiently long to protect the wrists. The mits had one compartment for the four fingers and another for the thumb, and they were worn over woollen gloves. They were easily slipped off when the use of the fingers was required, and they were hung round the neck with lampwick in order that they might not get lost on the march. The only other articles of equipment I ordered in Norway were twelve pairs of skis, which were supplied by Messrs. Hagen and Company. They were not used on the sledging journeys at all, but were useful around the winter quarters. I stipulated that all the goods were to be delivered in London by June 15, 1907.

The *Nimrod*

Before I left Norway I paid a visit to Sandyfjord in order to see whether I could come to terms with Mr C. Christiansen, the owner of the *Bjorn,* a ship specially built for polar work,

which would have suited my purposes most admirably. She was a
new vessel of about 700 tons burthen and with powerful triple-
expansion engines, better equipped in every way than the forty-
year-old *Nimrod,* but I found that I could not afford to buy her,
much as I would have wished to do so.

When I returned to London I purchased the *Nimrod,* which was
then engaged on a sealing venture, and was expected to return to
Newfoundland within a short time. The ship was small and old,
and her maximum speed under steam was hardly more than six
knots, but on the other hand, she was strongly built, and quite
able to face rough treatment in the ice. Indeed, she had already
received a good many hard knocks in the course of a varied career.
She was inspected on my behalf and pronounced sound, and,
making a fairly rapid passage, arrived in the Thames on June 15.
I must confess that I was disappointed when I first examined
the little ship, to which I was about to commit the hopes and
aspiration of many years. She was much dilapidated and smelled
strongly of seal oil, and an inspection in dock showed that she
required caulking and that her masts would have to be renewed.
She was rigged only as a schooner and her masts were decayed, and
I wanted to be able to sail her in the event of the engine breaking
down or the supply of coal running short. I had not then become
acquainted with the many good qualities of the *Nimrod,* and my
first impression hardly did justice to the plucky old ship.

I proceeded at once to put the ship in the hands of Messrs. R.
and H. Green, of Blackwall, the famous old firm that had built so
many of Britain's 'wooden walls', and that had done fitting and
repair work for several other polar expeditions. She was docked
for the necessary caulking, and day by day assumed a more
satisfactory appearance. The signs of former conflicts with the ice
floes disappeared, and the masts and running gear were prepared
for the troubled days that were to come. Even the penetrating
odour of seal oil ceased to offend after much vigorous scrubbing
of decks and holds, and I began to feel that after all the *Nimrod*
would do the expedition no discredit. Later still I grew really
proud of the sturdy little ship.

Quarters were provided on board for the scientific staff of the
expedition by enclosing a portion of the after hold and constructing cabins which were entered by a steep ladder from the

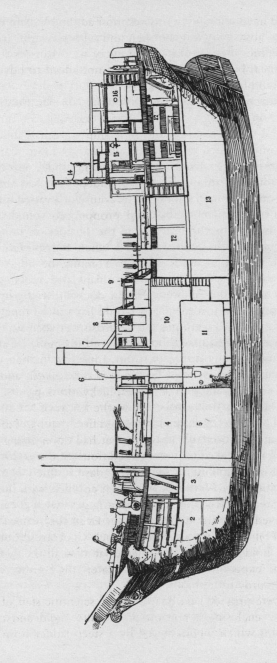

INTERIOR OF NIMROD

1 Forecastle 2 Stores 3 Chain Locker 4 Fore Hold 5 Lower Hold 6 Stoke Hold 7 Carpenter's Shop
8 Cook's Galley 9 Engine Room 10 Boiler 11 Boiler 12 After Hold 13 Lower Hold 14 After Bridge
15 Officers' Quarters 16 Captain 17 Oyster Alley

deck house. The quarters were certainly small; for some reason not on record, they were known later as 'Oyster Alley'.

As the *Nimrod,* after landing the shore party with stores and equipment, would return to New Zealand it was necessary that we should have a reliable hut in which to live during the Antarctic night until the sledging journeys commenced in the following spring.

The hut

The hut would be our only refuge from the fury of the blizzards, and in it would be stored many articles of equipment as well as some of the food. A hut measuring (externally) thirty-three feet by nineteen feet by eight feet to the eaves was specially constructed, to my order, by Messrs. Humphreys of Knightsbridge. After being erected and inspected in London, it was shipped in sections.

It was made of stout fir timbering of best quality in walls, roofs, and floors, and the parts were all morticed and tenoned to facilitate erection in the Antarctic. The walls were strengthened with iron cleats bolted to main posts and horizontal timbering, and the roof principals were provided with strong iron tie rods. The hut was lined with match boarding, and the walls and roof were covered externally first with strong roofing felt, then with one-inch tongued and grooved boards, and finally with another covering of felt. In addition to these precautions against the extreme cold the four-inch space in framing between the match boarding and the first covering of felt was packed with granulated cork, which assisted materially to render the wall non-conducting. The hut was to be erected on wooden piles let into the ground or ice, and rings were fixed to the apex of the roof so that guy ropes might be used to give additional resistance to the gales. The hut had two doors, connected by a small porch, so that ingress and egress would not mean the admission of a draft of cold air; and the windows were double, in order that the warmth of the hut might be retained. There were two louvre ventilators in the roof, controlled from the inside. The hut had no fittings, and we took little furniture. I proposed to use cases for the construction of benches, beds, and other necessary articles of internal equipment. The hut was to be lit with acetylene gas, and we took a generator, the necessary piping, and a supply of carbide.

The cooking range we used in the hut was manufactured by Messrs. Smith and Wellstrood, of London, and was four feet wide by two feet four inches deep. It had a fire chamber designed to burn anthracite coal continuously day and night and to heat a large superficial area of outer plate, so that there might be plenty of warmth given off in the hut. The stove had two ovens and a chimney of galvanised steel pipe, capped by a revolving cowl. It was mounted on legs.

Clothing

Each member of the expedition was supplied with two winter suits made of heavy blue pilot cloth, lined with Jaeger fleece. A suit consisted of a double-breasted jacket, vest and trousers, and weighed complete fourteen and three-quarter pounds. The underclothing was secured from the Dr Jaeger Sanitary Woollen Company.

An outer suit of windproof material is necessary in the polar regions, and I secured twenty-four suits of Burberry gaberdine, each suit consisting of a short blouse, trouser overalls and a helmet cover. For use in the winter quarters we took four dozen Jaeger camelhair blankets and sixteen camelhair triple sleeping bags.

Ponies. dogs, and motorcar

I decided to take ponies, dogs, and a motorcar to assist in hauling our sledges on the long journeys that I had in view, but my hopes were based mainly on the ponies. Dogs had not proved satisfactory on the Barrier surface, and I had not expected my dogs to do as well as they actually did. I felt confident, however, that the hardy ponies used in Northern China and Manchuria would be useful if they could be landed on the ice in good condition. I had seen these ponies in Shanghai, and I had heard of the good work they did on the Jackson-Harmsworth expedition. They are accustomed to hauling heavy loads in a very low temperature, and they are hardy, sure footed, and plucky. I noticed that they had been used with success for very rough work during the Russo-Japanese War, and a friend who had lived in Siberia gave me some more information regarding their capabilities.

I therefore got into communication with the London manager of the Hong Kong and Shanghai Bank (Mr C. S. Addis), and he was able to secure the services of a leading firm of veterinary surgeons in Shanghai. A qualified man went to Tientsin on my behalf, and from a mob of about two thousand of the ponies, brought down for sale from the northern regions, he selected fifteen of the little animals for my expedition. The ponies chosen were all over twelve and under seventeen years of age, and had spent the early part of their lives in the interior of Manchuria. They were practically unbroken, about fourteen hands high, and of various colours. They were all splendidly strong and healthy, full of tricks and wickedness, and ready for any amount of hard work over the snow fields. The fifteen ponies were taken to the coast and shipped by direct steamer to Australia. They came through the test of tropical temperatures unscathed, and at the end of October 1908 arrived in Sydney, where they were met by Mr Reid and at once transferred to a New Zealand-bound steamer. The Colonial Governments kindly consented to suspend the quarantine restrictions, which would have entailed exposure to summer heat for many weeks, and thirty-five days after leaving China the ponies were landed on Quail Island in Port Lyttelton, and were free to scamper about and feed in idle luxury.

I decided to take a motorcar because I thought it possible, from my previous experience, that we might meet with a hard surface on the Great Ice Barrier, over which the first part, at any rate, of the journey towards the south would have to be performed. On a reasonably good surface the machine would be able to haul a heavy load at a rapid pace. I selected a 12–15 horsepower New Arrol-Johnston car, fitted with a specially designed air-cooled four cylinder engine and Simms Bosch magneto ignition. Water could not be used for cooling, as it would certainly freeze. Round the carburettor was placed a small jacket, and the exhaust gases from one cylinder were passed through this in order that they might warm the mixing chamber before passing into the air. The exhaust from the other cylinders was conveyed into a silencer that was also to act as a foot warmer. The frame of the car was of the standard pattern, but the manufacturers had taken care to secure the maximum of strength, in view of the fact that the car was likely to experience severe strains at low temperature. I ordered a good supply of spare parts in order to provide for breakages, and a special non-freezing oil was prepared for me by Messrs. Price and Company. Petrol was taken in the ordinary tins. I secured wheels of several special patterns as well as ordinary wheels with rubber tyres, and I had manufactured wooden runners to be placed under the front wheels for soft surfaces, the wheels resting in chocks on top of the runners. The car in its original form had two bracket seats, and a large trough behind for carrying stores. It was packed in a large case and lashed firmly amidships on the *Nimrod*, in which position it made the journey to the Antarctic continent in safety.

I placed little reliance on dogs, as I have already stated, but I thought it advisable to take some of these animals. I knew that a breeder in Stewart Island, New Zealand, had dogs descended from the Siberian dogs used on the Newnes-Borchgrevink expedition, and I cabled to him to supply as many as he could up to forty. He was only able to let me have nine, but this team proved quite sufficient for the purposes of the expedition, as the arrival of pups brought the number up to twenty-two during the course of the work in the south.

Scientific instruments

The equipment of a polar expedition on the scientific side involved the expenditure of a large sum of money and I felt the pinch of necessary economies in this branch. I was lent three chronometer watches by the Royal Geographical Society. I bought one chronometer watch, and three wardens of the Skinners' Company gave me one which proved the most accurate of all and was carried by me on the journey toward the Pole.

The Geographical Society was able to send forward an application made by me for the loan of some instruments and charts from the Admiralty, and that Department generously lent me the articles contained in the following list:

3 Lloyd-Creak dip circles.
3 marine chronometers.
1 station pointer, 6 ft.
1 set of charts, England to Cape and Cape to New Zealand.
1 set of Antarctic charts.
1 set of charts from New Zealand through Indian Ocean to Aden.

1 set of charts, New Zealand to Europe *via* Cape Horn.
12 deep-sea thermometers.
2 marine standard barometers.
1 navy-pattern ship's telescope.
1 ship's standard compass.
2 azimuth mirrors (Lord Kelvin's type).
1 deep-sea sounding machine.
3 heeling error instruments.
1 3-in. portable astronomical telescope.
1 Lucas deep sea sounding machine.

I placed an order for further scientific instruments with Messrs. Cary, Porter and Company, Limited, of London.

Amongst other instruments that we had with us on the expedition was a four-inch transit theodolite, with Reeve's micrometers fitted to horizontal and vertical circles. The photographic equipment included nine cameras by various makers, plant for the darkroom, and a large stock of plates, films, and chemicals. We took also a moving picture camera in order that we might place on record the curious movements and habits of the seals and penguins, and give the people at home a graphic idea of what it means to haul sledges over the ice and snow.

Miscellaneous

The miscellaneous articles of equipment were too numerous to be mentioned here in any detail. I had tried to provide for every contingency, and the gear ranged from needles and nails to a Remington typewriter and two Singer sewing machines. There was a gramophone to provide us with music, and a printing press, with type, rollers, paper, and other necessaries, for the production of a book during the winter night. We even had hockey sticks and a soccer ball.

CHAPTER 2

The staff of the expedition

The members of the expedition: Nimrod *leaves East India Docks, July 30: In the Solent, August 3–5*

The *personnel* of an expedition of the character I proposed is a factor on which success depends to a very large extent. The men selected must be qualified for the work, and they must also have the special qualifications required to meet polar conditions. They must be able to live together in harmony for a long period without outside communication, and it must be remembered that the men whose desires lead them to the untrodden paths of the world have generally marked individuality. It was no easy matter for me to select the staff, although over four hundred applications arrived from persons wishing to join the expedition. I wanted to have two surgeons with the shore party, and also to have a thoroughly capable biologist and geologist, for the study of these two branches of science in the Antarctic seemed to me to be of especial importance. After much consideration I selected eleven men for the shore party. Three of them only, Adams, Wild, and Joyce, had been known to me previously, while only Wild and Joyce had previous experience of polar work, having been members of the *Discovery* expedition. Every man, however, was highly recommended, and this was the case also with the officers whom I selected for the *Nimrod*.

THE MEMBERS OF THE EXPEDITION
SHORE PARTY

ERNEST H. SHACKLETON, commander.

PROFESSOR T. W. EDGEWORTH DAVID, F.R.S., director of the scientific staff.

LIEUTENANT J. B. ADAMS, R.N.R., meteorologist.

SIR PHILIP BROCKLEHURST, Bart., assistant geologist.

BERNARD DAY, motor expert.

ERNEST JOYCE, in charge of dogs, sledges, etc.
DR A. F. MACKAY, surgeon.
DOUGLAS MAWSON, D.Sc., B.E., physicist.
BERTRAM ARMYTAGE, in charge of ponies.
DR E. MARSHALL, surgeon, cartographer.
G. E. MARSTON, artist.
J. MURRAY, biologist.
RAYMOND PRIESTLEY, geologist.
W. ROBERTS, cook.
F. WILD, in charge of provisions.

Before leaving New Zealand I was able to add to the strength of the staff:

Professor Edgeworth David, F.R.S., of Sydney University, consented to accompany us as far as the winter quarters, with the idea of returning in the *Nimrod,* but I persuaded him eventually to stay in the Antarctic, and his assistance in connection with the scientific work, and particularly the geology, was invaluable.

Dr Mawson (lecturer in mineralogy, etc., at the Adelaide University) joined us as physicist.

SHIP'S STAFF

LIEUTENANT R. G. ENGLAND, R.N.R., captain.
JOHN K. DAVIS, chief officer, later captain.
A. L. A. MACKINTOSH, second officer.
A. E. HARBOURD, auxiliary second officer.
H. J. L. DUNLOP, chief engineer.
W. A. R. MICHELL, surgeon.
ALFRED CHEETHAM, third officer and boatswain.
W. D. ANSELL, steward.
J. MONTAGUE, cook.
E. ELLIS ⎫
H. BULL ⎪
S. RICHES ⎬ A.B.s.
J. PATON ⎪
W. WILLIAMS ⎭
G. BILSBY, carpenter

[LIEUTENANT F. P. EVANS, R.N.R., was appointed captain for the second voyage to the Antarctic.]

The work of preparation made rapid progress, and as the end of July approached the stores and equipment were stowed away on board the *Nimrod* in readiness for the voyage to New Zealand. The final departure for the south was to be made from Lyttelton, at which I felt sure, from former experience, that I should receive every assistance from the authorities.

Early in July we exhibited at a room in Regent Street samples of our stores and equipment, and some thousands of people paid us a visit. The days were all too short, for scores of details demanded attention; but there were no delays, and on July 30, 1907, the *Nimrod* sailed from the East India Docks on the first stage of the long journey to New Zealand. Most of the members of the shore staff, including myself, intended to make this journey by mail steamer, but I left the docks with the *Nimrod,* intending to travel as far as Torquay.

We anchored for the first night at Greenhithe. Next morning, after landing Mr Reid at Tilbury in order that he might return to London for letters, we proceeded on our way down channel. When Mr Reid reached London, he found a telegram from the King's equerry, commanding the *Nimrod* to visit Cowes in order that their Majesties the King and Queen might inspect the ship and equipment on Sunday, August 4. Mr Reid had some difficulty in delivering this message to me, but the Admiral superintendent at Sheerness kindly despatched a tug which overtook the *Nimrod* off Ramsgate. On August 1 we stopped for an hour off Eastbourne to enable some supporters of the expedition to pay us a farewell visit, and then proceeded to the Solent, where we anchored.

CHAPTER 3

Royal visit to the *Nimrod*

In the Solent: The Nimrod *visited by Royal Party: Her Majesty Queen Alexandra presents a Union Jack to the Commander of the Expedition, Torquay, August 6:* Nimrod *arrives: August 7, The* Nimrod *sails for Lyttelton, via St. Vincent and Cape Town: Arrival at Lyttelton, November 23, 1907*

Cowes, *Aug.* 4.

Their Majesties King Edward and Queen Alexandra, their Royal Highnesses the Prince of Wales, the Princess Victoria, Prince Edward and the Duke of Connaught, came on board and inspected the *Nimrod*, an honour which was greatly appreciated by the members of the expedition.

The royal party showed much interest in some of the equipment for the southern journey. The picture* shows His Majesty the King examining the sledges, etc.

Her Majesty Queen Alexandra graciously entrusted me with a Union Jack to be carried on the southern journey; His Majesty King Edward graciously conferred on me the Victorian Order.

The *Nimrod* sailed for Torquay early on the following morning, and arrived there on August 6. We drank success to the expedition at a farewell dinner that evening, and on the morning of Wednesday, August 7, the ship sailed for New Zealand, and after calling at St. Vincent and Cape Town, arrived at Lyttelton on November 23, the voyage having occupied three months and a half. Mr Reid reached Australian waters a month ahead of the *Nimrod*, in order to make the necessary arrangements and meet the Manchurian ponies, and I arrived early in December to arrange for leaving Lyttelton on January 1, 1908.

* Not reproduced in this edition.

CHAPTER 4

Lyttelton to the Antarctic Circle
Final preparations at Lyttelton: Enthusiastic send-off: In tow
of the Koonya *for 1510 miles: Getting through the pack ice:*
Ross Sea reached January 17

The final preparations at Lyttelton during the month of December involved a great deal of work, but by December 31 all was in readiness for a start on New Year's Day.

The Postmaster-General of the Dominion had printed off for us a small issue of special stamps, and had constituted me a postmaster during my stay in the Antarctic.

The ponies were enjoying their holiday on Quail Island, and it was necessary that they should be broken to handling and sledge hauling. Mr C. Tubman undertook this work, with the assistance of Dr Mackay, and there were some exciting moments on the island. All the ponies had names, and we finally took away from New Zealand ten animals known as 'Socks', 'Queen', 'Grisi', 'Chinaman', 'Billy', 'Zulu', 'Doctor', 'Sandy', 'Nimrod', and 'Mac' respectively.

The quarters of the scientific staff on board the *Nimrod* were certainly small, in fact there was just room for the bunks and nothing else. As the day of departure approached and the scientists brought their personal belongings, Oyster Alley reached a state of congestion that can hardly be imagined.

The ponies were to be carried on deck, and ten stout stalls were built for them. The motorcar was enclosed in a large case and made fast with chains on the after hatch whence it could be transferred easily on to the ice when the occasion arose. The deck load was heavy and included cases of maize, tins of carbide for the manufacture of acetylene gas, a certain quantity of coal and the sledges. The *Nimrod* was low in the water as a result, and when we left Lyttelton the little ship had only three feet six inches of freeboard. Some live sheep presented to us by New Zealand farmers were placed on board the *Koonya,* the steamer which was to tow the *Nimrod* to the south. Messrs. Nathan and Co., of Wellington, presented the expedition with sixty-eight cases of 'Glaxo' dried milk, 192 lb. of New Zealand butter, and two cases of New Zealand cheese. Several other acceptable gifts were received before we sailed.

I had been anxious to have the *Nimrod* towed south in order to save coal. The ship could not take in a large quantity of coal after our provisions and equipment had been placed on board, for she was considerably overloaded, and it was important that there should be enough coal to take the ship through the ice and back to New Zealand, and also to provide for the warming of the hut during the winter. The Government of the Dominion consented to pay half the cost of the tow, and Sir James Mills, chairman of the Union Steamship Company, offered to pay the other half. The *Koonya,* a steel-built steamer of about 1100 tons, was chartered and placed under the command of Captain F. P. Evans. The wisdom of this selection was proved by after events. The pressure of work at this time was tremendous, and I owed a very great deal to the assistance and advice I received from Mr J. J. Kinsey, of Christchurch. Before my departure I placed the conduct of the affairs of the expedition in New Zealand in his hands.

December 31, 1907. The stores and equipment were now on board and were as complete as we could make them, and I had written my final letters, both business and personal. The ponies and the dogs were to be placed on board the *Nimrod* early the following morning.

January 1, 1908, arrived at last! Warm, fine, and clear broke the morning of our last day in civilisation. Before sunset we were to sever all ties with the outer world and more than a year must elapse ere we could look again on the scenes familiar to ordinary daily life. For me this day brought a feeling of relief, after all the strenuous work of the previous year, though the new work I was entering upon was fraught with more anxiety and was more exacting than any that had gone before. We all looked forward eagerly to our coming venture, for the glamour of the unknown was with us and the South was calling.

My personal belongings were gathered out of the chaos of papers and odds and ends in my office at the hotel; I knew that the legacy of unanswered letters, requests for special stamps, and the hundred and one things that collect under such circumstances would be faithfully administered by Mr Reid. Orders had been given to Captain England to have all in readiness for casting off at 4 p.m., and early in the afternoon most of us were on board. It was Regatta day and Lyttelton was crowded with holiday makers, many thousands of whom had come to see the *Nimrod*. All day the deck of our little vessel was thronged by the general public, who evinced the greatest interest in everything connected with the ship and her equipment. Naturally the ten ponies, now safely housed in their stalls on the forward deck, were a special attraction. Our nine dogs also claimed a share of attention, although it was a gymnastic feat to climb through the supports of the pony structure, stretching across the decks, in order to reach the forecastle, where the dogs lay panting in the hot sun. To the uninitiated the number and size of the beams belonging to the pony structure seemed excessive, but we knew we might encounter heavy weather which would tax their strength to the utmost. The *Nimrod* was deep in the water, for every available corner had been stowed with stores and coal and, if we could have carried it, we would have added at least another fifty tons to our two hundred and fifty; but the risk was too great. Indeed I was somewhat anxious as to the weather she might make, though I knew she was a good sea boat and had great confidence in her. There were many whose criticisms were frankly pessimistic as to our chances of weathering an Antarctic gale; and as I stood on deck I could hear the remarks of these Job's comforters. Such criticisms, however, did not disturb us, for we had confidence in the ship.

Oyster Alley was crammed with the personal belongings of at least fourteen of the shore party; it was the temporary resting place for many of the scientific instruments, so that both ingress and egress were matters of extreme difficulty. The entrance to this twentieth-century Black Hole was through a narrow doorway and down a ladder, which ushered one into almost complete darkness, for the doorway was practically filled up with cases, and the single narrow deck light generally covered by the feet of sightseers. The shore party's fourteen bunks were crammed with luggage, which also occupied the whole of the available floor space. It was in this uncomfortable place that the spirit of romance, the desire for the wind-whitened Southern Seas, and the still whiter wastes of the silent Antarctic, grew stronger in the heart of George Buckley, as he sat there talking over the days and doings before us, longing for a share in the work, even though he might only go as far as the Antarctic circle. He knew that time would not permit him to do more than this. Suddenly he jumped up, came to me, and asked if I would take him as far as the ice. I was only too glad to consent, for his interest in the expedition showed that his heart was in our venture, and his personality had already appealed to us all. It was 2 p.m. when the decision was made, and the *Nimrod* was to sail at 4 p.m. He managed to catch a train to Christchurch, dashed into his club, gave his power of attorney to a friend; slung his toothbrush and some underclothing into a bag; struggled through one seething crowd at Christchurch Station and another at the wharf, and arrived on board the *Nimrod,* a few minutes before sailing time equipped for the most rigorous weather in the world with only the summer suit he was wearing: surely a record in the way of joining a Polar expedition!

Time was passing quickly, it was nearing four o'clock and all our party were on board save Professor David. I had seen him earlier in the afternoon, struggling along the crowded wharf, bending under the weight of one end of a long iron pipe, a railway porter attached to the other. This precious burden, he had informed me, when it was safely on board, was part of the boring gear to be used in obtaining samples of ice from the Great Ice Barrier; he had found it at the railway station, where it had been overlooked. Doubtless he was having a last skirmish round in case there was anything else that had been left, and just as I was getting anxious, for I did not want to delay the departure of the ship, he appeared. His arms were filled with delicate glass apparatus and other scientific paraphernalia. As he was gingerly crossing the narrow gangway he was confronted by a stout female, of whom the Professor afterwards said: 'She was for the shore, let who would be for the Pole.' They met in the middle of the gangway. Hampered by the things he was carrying, the Professor could not move aside; he was simply charged down by superior weight, and clutching his precious goods, fell off the gangway on to the heads of some of our party. Wonderful to relate nothing was broken.

At one minute to four orders were given to stand by the engines, at 4 p.m. the lines were cast off from the wharf and the *Nimrod* moved slowly ahead. Cheer after cheer broke from the watching thousands as we moved towards the harbour entrance, with the Queen's flag flying at the fore and our ensign dipping farewell at the stern. The cheering broke out afresh as we passed the United States magnetic survey ship *Galilee*. She also was engaged in a scientific mission, but her lines were laid in warmer climes and calmer seas. Hearty as was this send off, it seemed mild compared to that which we received on passing the pier-head lighthouse. The air trembled with the crash of guns, the piercing steam whistles and sirens of every steamship in the port; and a roar of cheering from the throats of the thirty thousand people who were watching the little black-hulled barque moving slowly towards the open sea. With our powerful ally, the *Koonya,* steaming in front, and on each side passenger boats of the Union Company carrying some six or seven thousand persons, we passed down the Roads, receiving such a farewell and 'Godspeed' from New Zealand as left no man of us unmoved. The farewells were not over, for we were to receive one more expression of goodwill, and one that came nearer to the hearts of those of us who were sailors than any other could. Lying inside the Heads were three of His Majesty's ships of the Australian Squadron, the flagship *Powerful,* the *Pegasus* and the *Pioneer.* As we steamed past the last-named her crew mustered on the forecastle head and gave us three hearty cheers; we received the same from the *Pegasus* as we came abeam of her, our party of thirty-nine returning the cheers as we passed each ship in turn. Then we drew abreast of the flagship and from the throats of the nine hundred odd bluejackets on board her we got a ringing farewell, and across the water came the sound of her band playing 'Hearts of oak are our ships', followed by 'Auld Lang Syne'. We responded with three cheers and gave another cheer for Lady Fawkes, who had taken a kindly interest in the expedition.

Shortly after passing the *Powerful,* we stopped to pick up our tow-line from the *Koonya,* but before doing this we transferred to the tug-boat *Canterbury* the few personal friends who had accompanied some of the members of the expedition down the harbour. We then came close up to the stern of the *Koonya* and hauled in the 4-in. wire cable she was to tow us with. A 4-in. wire is measured not as 4 in. diameter, but 4 in. circumference, and is made of the finest steel. We passed a shackle through the eye at the end of this wire and shackled on to the free ends of both our chain cables. We then let out thirty fathoms of each cable, one on each side of the bow, and made the inner ends fast round the foremast in the 'tween decks. This cable acted as a 'spring', to use a nautical term; that is to say, it lessened the danger of the wire snapping if a sudden strain were put upon it, for the cable hung down in the water owing to its weight, even when the ship was being towed at seven or eight knots. This operation being completed we signalled the *Koonya* to go ahead and we were soon in the open sea. There was a slight breeze and a small choppy sea. Before we had been under way for an hour water began to come in at the scupper holes and through the wash ports. This looked ominous to us, for if the *Nimrod* was going to be wet in such fine weather, what was she going to be like when we got a southerly gale! She moved through the water astern of *Koonya* like a reluctant child being dragged to school; she seemed to have no vitality of her own. This was due to her deeply loaded condition, and more especially to the seven tons of cable and the weight of the wire on her bows dragging her nose down into the sea. No Antarctic exploring ship had been towed to the ice before, but it meant the saving of coal to us for a time when the tons saved in this manner might prove the salvation of the expedition.

Night came down on us, and the last we saw of New Zealand was a bold headland growing fainter and fainter in the gathering gloom. The occupants of Oyster Alley, after a somewhat sketchy meal in the wardroom, were endeavouring to reduce the chaos of their quarters into some sort of order. The efforts of some of the scientific staff were interrupted at times by sudden attacks of sea-sickness, and indeed one would not have been surprised if the seafaring portion of the staff had also succumbed, for the atmosphere of the alley, combined with the peculiar motion of the ship, was far from pleasant. A few of the members of the party preferred to sleep on deck in any odd corner they could find, and one man in particular was so overcome by the sea that for three days and nights he lay prostrate amongst the vegetables and cases of butter and carbide, on the unused fore bridge of the ship. He seemed to recover at mealtimes, and as his lair was just above the galley, he simply appeared from under his sodden blankets, reached down his hand, and in a plaintive voice asked for something to fill the yawning cavern that existed in his interior. Professor David was given Dr Michell's cabin, the latter taking up his abode in Oyster Alley. The cabin measured about 5 ft. 10 in. by 3 ft., and as the Professor had nearly a quarter of a ton of scientific instruments, books, and cameras, one can imagine that he had not much room for himself. The wardroom of the *Nimrod* was about 12 ft. long and 8 ft. broad, and as there were twenty-two mouths to feed there three times a day, difficulties were present from the beginning of the voyage. Dunlop's cabin came into service as the largest overflow dining room, for it accommodated three people. Davis and Mackintosh each found room for another hungry explorer in his cabin. When the food arrived it was passed along to the outside dining rooms first. Then people in the main room were served. All went well that first night out, for there was comparatively little movement, but later on the story of an ordinary meal became a record of adventure. I took up my quarters in the captain's cabin, and fluctuated between the bunk and the settee for a resting place, until the carpenter made me a plank bed about four inches off the deck. We did not know that we were not to take our clothes off for the next two weeks, but were to live in a constant state of wetness, wakefulness, and watchfulness until the *Nimrod* arrived in the neighbourhood of the winter quarters.

Bad weather was not long delayed. As the night of January 1 wore on, the wind began to freshen from the south-west, and the following morning the two vessels were pitching somewhat heavily and steering wildly. The *Koonya* signalled us to veer, that is, to slack out thirty more fathoms on each of our two cables, and with great difficulty we managed to do this. The ship was pitching and rolling, flinging the cables from one side of the deck to the other, and with our forty-year-old windlass it was no light task to handle the heavy chains. Then I felt one of the first real pinches of the stringent economy that had to be practised from the inception of the expedition. How I wished for the splendid modern gear of the *Discovery*, the large, specially-built vessel that we had on the previous expedition. During the afternoon the wind and sea increased greatly, and the *Nimrod* pitched about, shifting everything that could be moved on deck. The seas began to break over her, and we were soon wet through, not to be properly dry again for the next fortnight. The decks were flooded with heavy seas, which poured, whitecapped, over the side, and even the topsail yards were drenched with the spray of breaking waves. Lifelines were stretched along the deck, and it was a risky thing to go forward without holding on.

Our chief anxiety was the care of the ponies, and looking back now to those days, it remains a matter of wonder to me how they survived the hardships that fell to their lot. That night I arranged for a two-hour watch, consisting of two members of the shore staff, to be always in attendance on the ponies. The pony shelter had five stalls on the port side and five on the starboard side of the deck, with the fore hatch between them. The watch keepers named this place 'The Cavalry Club', and here in the bleak and bitter stormy nights, swept off their feet every now and then by the seas washing over the fore hatch, the members of the shore party passed many a bad quarter of an hour. They bore all the buffeting and discomfort cheerfully, even as those men of old, who 'ever with a frolic welcome took the thunder and the sunshine.' Night in the pony stables was a weird experience with inky blackness all round, save only where the salt-encrusted hurricane lamp, jerking to and fro, made a glimmer of light. The roar of the tempest rose into a shriek as the wind struck the rigid rigging, the creaking and swaying of the roof of the stable and the boat skids, which partly rested their weight on it, seemed to threaten a sudden collapse with each succeeding and heavier roll, and the seas crashed dully as they fell on board. The swirling waters, foam-white in the dim rays of the lamp, rushed through the stable and over the hatch, and even from the bridge far aft, we could hear the frightened whinnies of the animals, as they desperately struggled to keep their feet in the water that flooded the rolling stables. Every now and then some wave, larger and fiercer than the one before, would sweep the decks, tear the mats from under the feet of the ponies, and wash the watch keepers almost under the struggling beasts. When the bulk of the water had passed, the mats were nailed down again with difficulty, and the two watchers resumed their seats on a bag of fodder that had been fastened to the hatch. One can imagine that after a two-hours' watch a rest was welcome.

Oyster Alley was wet enough, and the beds were soaking, while the atmosphere was thick and heavy; but these conditions did not prevent the wearied men from falling asleep after wedging themselves into their bunks, lest some extra heavy lurch should send them to keep company with the miscellaneous collection of articles careering up and down the deck of the 'Alley'.

All during our second night out the weather was so bad, that we kept going slow, having requested the *Koonya* to slacken speed late in the afternoon. Next morning found us plunging, swerving, and rolling in a high sea, with a dull grey stormy sky overhead, and apparently no prospect of the weather becoming settled. We were moving little more than a mile an hour towards the south, and the ship seemed to be straining herself on account of the heavy pull on her bows, and the resulting lack of buoyancy. The weather moderated somewhat in the afternoon, and we signalled the *Koonya* to 'increase speed'. By midnight the improvement in the weather was much more marked. The following morning, January 4, we set loose the carrier pigeon which one of the New Zealand sailors had brought with him. We attached a message to the bird, briefly describing our passage so far, and hoped it would safely accomplish the three hundred odd miles to the land. On releasing our messenger it made one or two wide circles round the ship, and then set off in a beeline towards its home. We wondered at the time whether any of the albatrosses, which were now fairly numerous about our stern, especially at meal times, would attack the stranger, and we heard afterwards that the pigeon had not reached its home.

The hope that we were going to keep finer weather was dispelled in the afternoon, for the wind began to increase and the rising sea to break on board again, and within a couple of hours we were bearing the full brunt of another furious gale. The sea-going qualities of the *Nimrod* were severely taxed, but the little vessel rose to the occasion. As the gale increased in vehemence, she seemed to throw off the lethargy, one might almost say the sulkiness, which possessed her when she found herself outward bound at the end of a tow line, for the first time in her strenuous life of forty years. Now that the tow line, in the fury of the gale, was but of little use save to steady us, the *Nimrod* began to play her own hand. It was wonderful to see how she rose to the largest oncoming waves. She was flung to and fro, a tiny speck in this waste of waters, now poised on the summit of a huge sea, whence we got almost a bird's-eye view of the gallant *Koonya* smashing into the turmoil ahead; now dipping into the wave valleys, from which all we could discern of our consort was in very truth 'just a funnel and a mast lurching through the spray'.

As the afternoon wore on, those of us who were not still in the clutches of seasickness watched the grandeur of the gale. I shall always remember Buckley, who stood for hour after hour on the *Nimrod*'s poop, revelling in the clash and strife of the elements. Keen yachtsman that he was, his admiration was aroused by the way the two ships battled with the storm. Professor David, also, hanging to the dripping rails, was fascinated by the wild scene, and between the gusts we spoke of many things. Somehow or another the conversation turned to one's favourite poets, and it is but natural that, under these circumstances of stress and strain, Browning's verse was often the subject of conversation. Night drew on, sullen and black, our only light the lamp we steered by on the *Koonya*'s mast. We could imagine the stalwart figure of that splendid seaman, Captain Evans, as he stood on his spray-drenched bridge, alert, calm, and keen, doing his best to ease the little ship astern. We had nothing but admiration for the consummate seamanship that anticipated our every need and wish. All that night it blew harder than ever; on the morning of the 5th, I told Captain England to signal the *Koonya* and ask her to pour oil on the water in the hope that it might help us. To a certain extent I think it did, but not enough to prevent the heaviest seas from breaking on board. I thought that the gale had reached its height on the previous day, but certainly this evening it was much stronger. The *Nimrod* rolled over fifty degrees from the perpendicular to each side; how much more than that I cannot say, for the indicator recording the roll of the ship was only marked up to fifty degrees, and the pointer had passed that mark. Let the reader hold a pencil on end on a table, and then incline it fifty degrees one way, and back again till it reaches fifty degrees on the other side, and he will realise the length of arc through which the masts and deck of the *Nimrod* swung. It was only natural, under these circumstances, that the sturdy little ponies had their strength taxed to the utmost to keep their footing at all. It was impracticable to sling them, for they were only half broken, and the attempt to put a sling under one drove it nearly crazy with fright. All we could do was to try and soothe them, and the animals evidently appreciated the human voice and touch. Buckley had a wonderful way with them, and they seemed to understand that he was trying to help them.

Occasionally there were clear patches of sky to the south and east between the squalls. We had sleet for the first time on January 5, and the wind, ranging between west, south, and south-west, was chilly for the height of summer, the temperature being about 46° F. We passed large masses of floating kelp which may have torn from the islands to the south-west of us, for at noon on January 5 we were still north of the fiftieth parallel, a latitude corresponding to the South of England. Our course lay practically south, for I wanted to enter the pack ice somewhere about the 178th meridian east, previous experience having shown that the pack is less dense about that meridian than it is further west. About 9 p.m. that night, during an extra heavy roll, one of the ponies slipped down in its stall, and when the ship rolled the opposite way, turned right over on its back, as it could not regain its footing. We tried everything in our power to get the poor beast up again, but there was no room to work in the narrow stall, and in the darkness and rushing water it would have been madness to have tried to shift the other ponies out of the adjacent stalls in order to take down the partition, and so give the poor animal room to get up itself. We had perforce to leave it for the night, trusting that when daylight came the weather might have moderated, and that with the light we might be able to do more. It speaks wonders for the vitality of the animal that in spite of its cramped position and the constant washing of the cold seas over it during the whole night, it greedily ate the handfuls of hay which were given it from time to time. Every now and then the pony made frantic efforts to get on to its feet again, but without avail, and before the morning its struggles grew weaker and weaker. The morning of January 6 broke with the gale blowing more strongly than ever. There was a mountainous sea running, and at ten o'clock, after having made another futile attempt to get 'Doctor', as he was called, on his legs, and finding that he had no strength of his own, I had regretfully to give orders to have him shot. One bullet from a heavy service revolver ended his troubles. During the morning the gale moderated somewhat, and at noon we were in latitude 50° 58' South, and longitude 175° 19' East.

During the afternoon of January 6, the wind increased again, the squalls being of hurricane force, and the wind shifting to between west and north-west. The *Koonya* ahead was making bad weather of it, but was steaming as fast as practicable, for with the wind and sea coming more abeam she was able to make better headway than when she was plunging into a head sea with the weight and bulk of the towing cable and the *Nimrod* astern of her, factors in the situation that made the handling of the steamer very difficult. The temperature of the air that day was up to 49° F., but the sea temperature had dropped to 44°. This continuous bad weather was attributed by some on board to the fact that we had captured an albatross on the second day out. It is generally supposed by seamen to be unlucky to kill this bird, but as we did it for the purposes of scientific collections and not with the wantonness of the 'Ancient Mariner', the superstitious must seek for some other reason for the weather. By this time most of the scientific staff had recovered from seasickness, so to employ their time when they were not on pony guard, meteorological observations were taken every hour. There sometimes was an inclination to obtain the temperature of the sea water from the never-failing stream which poured over the deck, but to the observers' credit this feeling was sternly suppressed, and the more legitimate and accurate, if less simple means, that of drawing it from over the side, was adopted. It is not at all an easy operation to draw water in this way from the sea when a ship is under way, and in our particular circumstances the observer often got premature knowledge of the temperature by the contents of the bucket, or the top of a sea, drenching him. On this day we began to feel the serious effects of the towing strain on the ship. For days the sailors' quarters below the foredeck had been in a state of constant wetness from the leaking of the foredeck, and the inhabitants of Oyster Alley had come to the conclusion that it might more suitably be named 'Moisture Alley'. But when Dunlop, the chief engineer, came on the poop bridge that afternoon and reported that the ship was making about three feet of water in an hour, matters assumed a more serious complexion. I had not expected that we would get off scot free, as the ship had to endure a very severe strain, and was old, but three feet of water in an hour showed that she was feeling the effects of the towing very much. It was necessary to rig the hand pump to help the steam pumps to keep the water under, and this became, as the Professor remarked, the occasion for an additional scientific instrument to be used by the shore party. A watch was set to use this pump, and two members of the staff worked it for two hours, or as long as occasion demanded, and at the end of that time were relieved by two more. The weather grew steadily worse, and by midnight the squalls were of hurricane force. Even the mastheads of the *Koonya* disappeared from view at times, and the light we were steering by would only be seen for a few seconds, and would then disappear behind the mounting wall of waters that separated the two ships. A moderate estimate of the height of the waves is forty-two feet. During the squalls, which were accompanied by hail and sleet, the tops of the seas were cut off by the force of the wind and flung in showers of stinging spray against our faces, drenching even the topsail yards of the *Nimrod*. Each green wave rushed at us as though it meant to swamp the ship, but each time the *Nimrod* rose bravely, and, riding over the seemingly overwhelming mass, steadied for a moment on the other side as it passed on, seething and white, baffled of its prey. All night there were squalls of terrific force, and the morning of January 7 brought no abatement of the storm. The seas now came on board with increasing frequency, finding out any odd article that had escaped our vigilance and survived the rolling of the ship. A sack of potatoes was washed on to the deck, and the contents were floating in two or three feet of water. But standing on the poop bridge I heard one of the crew, in no way disheartened, singing, as he gathered them up, 'Here we go gathering nuts in May'.

At noon we were in latitude 53° 26' South and longitude 127° 42' East. In the afternoon the weather moderated slightly, though there was a heavy, lumpy sea. Albatrosses were becoming much more numerous, especially the sooty species, the death of which, on Shelvoke's voyage, inspired Coleridge's memorable poem. I noticed one, flying low between the two ships, strike its wings against the wire tow-line, which had suddenly emerged from the waves owing to the lift of the *Koonya*'s stern upon a sea. The weather became fairly moderate during the night and remained so next morning, with the wind in the north-west. After the second day out we had shifted the dogs from the forecastle head to the fore bridge, and one of these, in its struggles to get down on to the main deck, strangled itself before we knew that it was in trouble.

There was constant rain during the morning of January 8, but it did not beat the sea down much, and during the evening, with the wind shifting to the south-south-west, the gale increased again. It was so bad, owing to the confused sea, that we had to signal the *Koonya* to heave to. We did this with the sea on our starboard quarter. Suddenly one enormous wave rushed at us, and it appeared as though nothing could prevent our decks being swept, but the ship rose to it, and missed the greater part, though to us it seemed as if the full weight of water had come on board. We clung tightly to the poop rails, and as soon as the water had passed over us we wiped the salt from our eyes and surveyed the scene. The sea had smashed in part of the starboard bulwarks and destroyed a small house on the upper deck, pieces of this house and the bulwarks floating out to the leeward; the port wash-port was torn from its hinges, so that water now surged on board and swept away at its own sweet will, and the stout wooden rails of the poop deck, to which we had been clinging, were cracked and displaced, but no vital damage was done. The look of disgust on the faces of the dripping pony watch keepers, as they emerged from the water-logged 'Cavalry Club', was eloquent of their feelings. The galley was washed out and the fire extinguished. This happened more than once, but so pluckily did the members of the cooking department work that never during the whole of this very uncomfortable time had we been without a warm meal. This means far more than one is apt to think, for the galley was only five feet square, and thirty-nine persons blessed with extremely hearty appetites had to be provided for.

In a large measure, this unbroken routine of hot meals, the three oases of what I might call pleasure in the daily desert of discomfort, was due to Roberts, who, besides being assistant zoologist to the expedition, was going to act as cook. Seeing that the ship's staff would have more work to do than they could well carry out in providing for the thirty-nine people on board, he volunteered the first day out to assist the ship's cook, and the result was that we were always provided with fresh bread and hot cocoa and tea. Montague, the ship's cook, was ever at work, though the galley was in a constant state of flood. The stewards, Handcock and Ansell, worked wonders in getting the food across the danger zone between the galley and the wardroom. Ansell, with ten plates in one hand, overlapping one another up his arm, would arrive safely at his destination, though his boots were often filled with water on the way aft. Of course there were times when he was not so successful, and he would emerge from a sea with his clothes, hair, and face plentifully sprinkled with food. As a rule the accidents occurred in the wardroom, after the arrival of the food. The tablecloth, after two or three days, assumed an *écru* colour, owing to the constant upsetting of tea and coffee. Some of the staff had perforce to take their meals standing, from lack of seating accommodation, and the balancing of a plate of soup when the ship was rolling heavily required skill and experience. The meal was generally accompanied by the spurting of seawater through the wardroom door, or through cracks in the skylight, and the water washed to and fro unheeded until the meal was ended, and the indefatigable Ansell turned his attention to it. It was in the wardroom that I salved a small wooden case from the water, and found that it contained a patent mixture for extinguishing fires. The rooms of the ship's officers, opening out of the wardroom, were in a similar state of dampness, and when an officer finished his watch and turned in for a well-earned sleep, he merely substituted for clothes that were soaked through, others which were a little less wet.

The water, however, did not damp the spirits of those on board, for nearly every night extempore concerts were held, and laughter and mirth filled the little wardroom. It is usual on Saturday nights at sea to drink the toasts, 'Absent Friends', and 'Sweethearts and Wives'. I was generally at this time in the after cabin or on the bridge, and if, as sometimes happened, I had forgotten that particular day, a gentle hint was conveyed to me by Wild or Dunlop starting a popular song, entitled 'Sweethearts and Wives', the chorus of which was heartily rendered by all hands. This hint used to bring my neglect to my mind, and I would produce the necessary bottle.

On January 10 we had a clear sky during the morning until about ten o'clock, and then, with a westerly wind, the breeze became heavier, and rain commenced. Most of us that day, taking advantage of the comparative steadiness of the ship, managed to wash our salt-encrusted faces and hair; we had become practically pickled during the past week. About midnight we had a light wind from the north-north-east, and the almost continuous rain of the previous twelve hours had flattened the sea considerably.

Saturday evening toast 'Sweethearts and wives'
[*Scott Polar Research Institute*]

At noon on January 11, we were in latitude 57° 38' South, and longitude 178° 39' West, and during the day the wind and sea increased again from the north-west. The nature of this particular sea made it necessary for us to keep the ship away, altering our course from south to south-east, and before midnight the gale had reached its now customary force and violence. As I was standing on the bridge at 2 a.m., peering out to windward through a heavy snow squall that enveloped us, I saw, in the faint light of breaking day, a huge sea, apparently independent of its companions, rear itself up alongside the ship. Fortunately only the crest of the wave struck us, but away went the starboard bulwarks forward and abreast of the pony stalls, leaving a free run for the water through the stables. When we left port it was our augean problem how best to clean out the stables, but after the first experience of the herculean waves, the difficulty was to try and stop the flushing of them by every sea that came on board forward, and now not only every wave that fell on board, but the swell of the ocean itself swept the stables clean. This particular sea shifted the heavy starboard whaleboat from its chocks, landing it almost amidships on top of the 'Cavalry Club'. It swept some of our bales of fodder down on to the main deck, where they mingled with the drums of oil and cases of carbide torn from their lashings. Our latitude at noon was 59° 8' South, and 179° 30' East. The squalls of sleet and snow gave place later to clearer weather with a mackerel sky, which was of special interest to the meteorologists, as indicating the trend of the upper currents of the air.

During the afternoon the strength of the expedition was increased by Possum, one of our dogs, giving birth to six fine puppies. The mother and family were found a warm bed on the engine-room skylight, where a number of our cases were stowed. We signalled the happy event to the *Koonya* by flags, and received Captain Evans' congratulations. Signalling by flags was necessarily a somewhat slow operation, especially as the commercial code of signals is not exactly adapted for this particular sort of information, and we could see by the length of time they took to verify each signal that they were at a loss as to the subject matter of our communication, the incident of a birth naturally being farthest removed from their thoughts at such a time. Whenever the weather moderated at all the two ships always held short conversations by flags, and the Commander of the *Koonya* used to make enquiries in particular about the health of the scientific staff.

January 13 brought with it a gentle breeze from the eastward, the heavy leaden sky broke into blue, flecked with light cirrus clouds, and the day seemed warmer and more pleasant than any we had experienced since we left Lyttelton, though the temperature of the air and sea water were down to 34° and 37° F respectively. The warm sun tempted those who had not before been much in evidence on to the poop deck, and the whole vessel began to look like a veritable Petticoat Lane. Blankets, coats, boots, bags that might once have been leather but which now looked like lumps of dilapidated brown paper; pajamas that had been intended to be worn when the owners first came aboard the *Nimrod;* books that had parted with their covers after sundry adventures in dripping

Oyster Alley, but whose leaves evinced the strongest disinclination to separate; pillows of pulp that had once been pillows of feathers; carpet slippers, now merely bits of carpet; in short, all the personal belongings of each member of the expedition, including their most sacred penates and lares, were lying in a heterogeneous mass on the poop deck, in order that they might dry. A few of us ventured on baths, but it was chilly work in the open air, with the temperature only two degrees above freezing point.

Some of our party, who were old sailors, had not much impedimenta to look after and to dry; the hard-won experience of early days have taught them the lesson that the fewer things you have to get wet, the fewer you have to get dry. Adams in particular observed this rule, for he wore the flannel trousers in which he came on board the ship at Lyttelton through all this weather, allowing them to dry on him after each successive wetting. He fondly clung to them throughout the period we were navigating in the ice, and while working the ship at winter quarters, and would doubtless have worn them on the ascent of Erebus if they had not practically come to pieces.

We were now keeping a sharp lookout for icebergs and pack; we had been steering a little more to the east, as I felt that our delay owing to bad weather would give us little time for navigation if we had to pass through much pack ice, and a few degrees more easting might perhaps give us a more open sea. The meeting with the pack ice was to terminate the *Koonya*'s tow, and that also meant our parting with Buckley, who had endeared himself to every man on board, from able seaman upwards, and had been of the greatest assistance to us in the matter of the ponies. It was due to his prompt action on one occasion that the life of 'Zulu' was saved. We decided to give a farewell dinner to our friend that night, and Marston designed special menu cards for the occasion. At noon that day we were in latitude 61° 29' South, longitude 179° 53' East. During the afternoon the weather kept fine and we set some square sail. Occasionally during the bad weather of the previous week we had put 'fore and afters' on to try and steady the ship, but the wind had carried them away. The *Koonya* had done the same, with a similar result. Our dinner that night was a great success, and it was early next morning before we turned in.

Next morning, January 14, we sighted our first iceberg, and

passed it at a distance of about two and a half miles. It had all the usual characteristics of the Antarctic bergs, being practically tabular in form, and its sides being of a dead white colour. The sight of this, the first sentinel of the frozen south, increased Buckley's desire to stay with us, and it was evident that the thought of leaving our little company was not a pleasant one to him. There was a remarkable belt of clouds across the sky during the morning, and their direction indicated the movement of the upper air, so the Professor and Cotton made several estimates of the height of this belt of cloud to try to determine the lower limit of the higher current. The mean measurements were taken, partly with a sextant and partly with an Abney level, to the edge of the belt of mackerel sky. The result of the observations was that the height of this belt was fixed at about thirteen thousand feet. The belt of cloud was travelling in an east-north-east direction at the rate of about fourteen miles an hour. The surface wind at this time was blowing lightly from the west. Our latitude at noon was 63° 59' South and the longitude 179° 47' West, so we had crossed the 180th meridian.

During the afternoon we passed two more icebergs with their usual tails of brash ice floating out to leeward. The sea had changed colour from a leaden blue to a greenish grey. Albatrosses were not nearly so numerous, and of those following the ship the majority were the sooty species. The Cape pigeon and Wilson's petrel were occasionally to be seen, also a small grey-coloured bird, which is generally found near the pack, but the name of which I do not know. We called them 'ice birds'. Another sign of the nearness of the ice was that the temperature of the air and water had dropped to 32° F. Everything pointed to our proximity to the pack, so we signalled the *Koonya* that we were likely to sight the ice at any moment. I also asked Captain Evans to kill and skin the sheep he was carrying for our supplies, as they would be much more easily transported when the time came to cast off. The weather remained fine with light winds during the night.

Next morning it was fairly thick with occasional light squalls of snow, and about 9 a.m. we saw the ice looming up through the mist to the southward. It seemed to stretch from south-west to south-east, and was apparently the forerunner of the pack. Now had come the time for the *Koonya* to drop us, after a tow of 1510 miles – a record in towage for a vessel not built for the purpose. Before the *Koonya* finally cast off from us, she had achieved another record, by being the first steel vessel to cross the Antarctic Circle.

About 10 a.m. I decided to send Captain England across to the *Koonya* with Buckley and the mail. Our letters were all stamped with the special stamp given by the New Zealand Government. The sea was rising again, and the wind increasing, so we lost no time in making the necessary communication by boat between the two ships. During a favourable roll the whale boat was dropped into the water, and Buckley, with his weekend handbag, jumped into her. We gave him three cheers as the boat pushed off on its boisterous journey to the *Koonya*. With his usual forethought, to make matters lighter for the boat's crew, Captain Evans had floated a line astern, attached to a life buoy, and after about twenty-five minutes' hard pulling against wind and sea, the buoy was picked up, and the boat hauled alongside the steamer. I was glad to see the boat coming back again shortly afterward, for the wind kept increasing and the sea was rising every moment, but in a lull, after pouring oil on the water, we hauled the boat up safely.

A thin line had been brought back from the *Koonya*, and at a signal from us Captain Evans paid out a heavier one, which we hauled on board. He then manoeuvred his ship, so as to get her as near as possible to us, in order that we might haul the carcasses of the sheep on board. Ten of these were lashed on the line, and by dint of pulling hard, we got them on board. Meanwhile the greater part of our crew were working the old-fashioned windlass, getting in slowly, link by link, the port towing cable, whilst the *Koonya* took in as much of her wire hawser as she conveniently could. Our heavy line was carried away, owing to a sudden strain, before we received the second instalment of water-logged mutton. Captain Evans brought the *Koonya* round our stern, and a heaving line, to which the sheep were attached, was thrown on board, but as soon as we began to haul on it, it broke, and we had the chagrin of seeing our fresh mutton floating away on the billows. It was lost to sight shortly afterward, but we could locate its position by the albatrosses hovering above, doubtless surprised and delighted with this feast.

About a quarter to one Captain Evans signalled that he was going to cut his hawser, for in the rising sea the two vessels were in dangerous proximity to each other. We saw the axe rise and fall, rise and fall again, and the tie was severed. The *Koonya's* work was done, and the *Nimrod* was dependent on her own resources at last. Our consort steamed round us, all hands on both ships cheering, then her bows were set north and she vanished into a grey, snowy mist, homeward bound. We spent a long afternoon struggling to get on board the one hundred forty fathoms of cable and thirty fathoms of wire that were hanging from our bows. The windlass was worked by means of levers, and all hands were divided into two parties, one section manning the port levers, the other the starboard. All that afternoon, and up to seven o'clock in the evening, they unremittingly toiled at getting the cable in link by link. At last we were able to proceed, and the ship's head was put due south. We prepared to work our way through the floating belt of pack that guards the approach to the Ross Sea. The weather had cleared, and we passed the ice which we had seen in the morning. It was a fairly loose patch of what appeared to be thick land ice. We gradually made our way through similar streams of ice and small hummocky bergs, most of them between forty and fifty feet in height, but a few reaching a hundred feet.

By 2 a.m. on the morning of January 16, the bergs were much more numerous; perhaps they could hardly be classed as bergs, for their average height was only about twenty feet, and I am of opinion, from what I saw later, that this ice originally formed part of an ice-foot from some coastline. None of the ice that we passed through at this time had the slightest resemblance to ordinary pack ice. About 3 a.m., we entered an area of tabular bergs, varying from eighty to one hundred and fifty feet in height, and all the morning we steamed in beautiful weather with a light northerly wind, through the lanes and streets of a wonderful snowy Venice. Tongue and pen fail in attempting to describe the magic of such a scene. As far as the eye could see from the crow's nest of the *Nimrod,* the great, white, wall-sided bergs stretched east, west, and south, making a striking contrast with the lanes of blue-black water between them. A stillness, weird and uncanny, seemed to have fallen upon everything when we entered the silent water streets of this vast unpeopled white city. Here there was no sign of life, except when one of the little snow petrels, invisible when flying across the glistening bergs, flashed for a moment into sight, as it came against the dark water, its pure white wings just skimming the surface. The threshing of our screw raised a small wave astern of the ship, and at times huge masses of ice and snow from the bergs, disturbed by the unaccustomed motion, fell thundering in our wake. Some of these bergs had been weathered into the fantastic shapes more characteristic of the Arctic regions, and from peak and spire flashed out the new-caught rays of the morning sun. Beautiful as this scene was, it gave rise to some anxiety in my mind, for I knew that if we were caught in a breeze amidst this maze of floating ice, it would go hard with us. Already an ominous dark cloud was sweeping down from the north, and a few flakes of falling snow heralded the approach of the misty northerly wind. I was unfeignedly thankful, when, about three in the afternoon, I saw from the crow's nest open water ahead. A few more turnings and twistings through the devious water lanes, and we entered the ice-free Ross Sea. This was the first time that a passage had been made into the Ross Sea without the vessel having been held up by pack ice. I think our success was due to the fact that we were away to the eastward of the pack, which had separated from the land and the Barrier, and had drifted in a north-west direction. All my experience goes to prove that the easterly route is the best. Behind us lay the long line of bergs through which we had threaded our way for more than eighty miles from north to south, and which stretched east and west for an unknown distance, but far enough for me to say without exaggeration that there must have been thousands of these floating masses of ice. Whence they had come was open to conjecture; it was possible for them to have drifted from a barrier edge to the eastward of King Edward VII Land. If that were so, the barrier must be much lower than the Great Ice Barrier, and also much more even in height, for the vast majority of the bergs we passed were not more than one hundred thirty feet high, and seemed to be of a fairly uniform thickness. The lights and shadows on the bergs to the eastward at times almost gave them the appearance of land, but as they were congregated most thickly in this direction, we did not venture to make closer acquaintance with them. Of one thing I am certain, this ice had not long left the parent barrier or coastline, for there was no sign of weathering or wind action on the sides; and if they had been afloat for even a short period they must infallibly have shown some traces of weathering, as the soft snow was at least fifteen to twenty feet thick. This was apparent when pieces broke off from the bergs, and in one or two cases, where sections had been sheared off the top of particular bergs, evidently by collision with their fellows. There were no indications or signs of embedded rocks or earthy material on the bergs, so I am led to believe that this great mass of ice must have been set free only a short time previously from some barrier edge at no great distance. Our latitude at noon on the 16th was 68° 6' South, and the longitude 179° 21' West.

Before we entered the actual line of bergs a couple of seals appeared on the floe-ice. I did not see them myself, but from descriptions I gathered that one was a crab-eater, and the other a Weddell seal. A few of the Adelie penguins were observed also, and their quaint walk and insatiable curiosity afforded great amusement to our people, the surprise of the birds on seeing the ship was so thoroughly genuine. Marston, our artist, whose sense of the ludicrous is very fully developed, was in ecstasies at their solemn astonishment and profound concern, and at the way they communicated their feelings to one another by flapping their makeshift wings, craning their necks forward with ruffled feathers, and uttering short squawks. Marston's imitation of the penguin was perfect, and he and the rest of us always responded eagerly to the call on deck whenever we were passing a group of these polar inhabitants.

When we were clear of the icebergs a distinct swell was felt coming from the south, and for once the movement of the ocean was welcome to us, for it showed that we might expect open water ahead. I was fairly confident that we had managed to elude the pack, and without doubt for a ship, well found and capable of fair speed, the passage between the bergs on the meridian down which we steered is preferable to the slower progress through the ordinary pack farther west. I doubt if I would, except under similar circumstances, when time and coal were very precious, risk an old vessel like the *Nimrod,* which steams but slowly in this labyrinth of heavy ice, but a faster vessel could make the passage with safety. It may be that in future seasons the Antarctic Ocean in this particular part will be found to be quite ice-free, and a later expedition may be able to work more to the eastward, and solve the riddle as to the existence of land in that neighbourhood.

It was fortunate that we cleared the ice that afternoon, for shortly afterward the wind increased from the north, and the weather became thick with falling snow. The temperature was just at freezing point, and the snow melted on the decks when it fell. Altogether about an inch of snow fell between 2 p.m. and midnight. We saw no ice until eight o'clock next morning (January 17), and then only one small berg. The wind shifted to the southeast, the sky cleared somewhat, and with an open horizon all round we observed no sign of ice at all.

CHAPTER 5

The attempt to reach King Edward VII Land
Disappearance of Barrier Inlet: Course to King Edward VII Land
blocked by ice: Course set for McMurdo Sound: Arrival at
Cape Royds, February 3

We were now in the Ross Sea, and it was evident that we had
avoided the main pack. Our position at noon (January 17) was 70°
43' South latitude, and 178° 58' East longitude. We were now
steering a little more westerly, so as to strike the Barrier well to the
east of Barrier Inlet, and also to avoid the heavy pack that previous
expeditions had encountered to the east of meridian 160° West
where the ice has always proved impenetrable. In the afternoon
the wind blew fresh, and the sky became overcast again, and snow
began to fall. This snow differed from that brought by the northerly wind; the northerly snow had consisted of flakes about a
quarter of an inch in diameter, while that now met with was
formed of small round specks, hard and dry, like sago – the true
Antarctic type. Birds now became more numerous. Large numbers
of Antarctic petrels circled around and around the ship. Their
numbers were so great that as the flights passed close by, the
whirring of the wings could be distinctly heard on board.

Toward evening we began to pass a number of small floe bergs
and pack ice. We could not see very far ahead, as the weather was
thick, so we steered more to the west to skirt this mass of ice.
One berg had evidently been overturned, and also showed signs
of having been aground. The Adelie penguins had become much
more numerous, and we saw an occasional seal, but too far off to
distinguish the species. During the early hours of January 18 we
passed a few large bergs, and as morning progressed the wind
increased, ranging between south by west and south by east. The
ship was pitching to a short sea, and as the water coming on board
froze on deck, and in the stables, we made shift to keep it out by

nailing canvas over the gaping holes in the bulwarks. Adams and
Mackay were engaged in this very chilly job; Adams, slung in a
rope over the side, every now and then got soaked up to the
middle when the ship dipped into the sea, and as the temperature
of the air was four degrees below freezing point, his tennis trousers
were not of much value for warmth in the circumstances. When
he got too cold to continue outside, Mackay took his place, and
between them they made a very creditable jury bulwark, which
prevented the bulk of the water rushing into the stable. The wind
continued with a force of about forty miles an hour, up till midday
of the 19th, when it began to take off a little, and the sky broke
blue to the north-east; the decks were thickly coated with soft ice,
and the freshwater pumps had frozen up hard.

We were now revelling in the indescribable freshness of the
Antarctic that seems to permeate one's being, and which must
be responsible for that longing to go again which assails each
returned explorer from polar regions. Our position at noon on
January 19 was latitude 73° 44' South and longitude 177° 19' East.
The wind had decreased somewhat by midnight, and though the
air remained thick and the sky overcast during the whole of
the 20th, the weather was better. We passed through occasional
masses of floating ice and large tabular bergs, and at noon were in
latitude 74° 45' South, longitude 179° 21' East.

On the 21st the weather grew clear, the temperature was somewhat higher, and the wind light. We observed small flights of snow
petrels and Antarctic petrels, and saw a single giant petrel for the
first time. There were also several whales spouting in the distance.
The same sort of weather continued throughout the day, and
similar weather, though somewhat clearer, was experienced on the
22nd. On the morning of the 23rd we saw some very large
icebergs, and toward evening these increased in number. They
were evidently great masses broken off the Barrier. Early in the
morning we passed a large tilted berg, yellow with diatoms. On
our port side appeared a very heavy pack, in which a number of
large bergs were embedded. Our course for these three days was
about due south, and we were making good headway under steam.

We were now keeping a sharp lookout for the Barrier, which
we expected to see at any moment. A light south-easterly wind
blew cold, warning us that we could not be very far away from

the ice sheet. The thermometer registered some twelve degrees of frost, but we hardly felt the cold, for the wind was so dry. At 9:30 a.m. on the 23rd a low straight line appeared ahead of the ship. It was the Barrier. After half an hour it disappeared from view, having evidently been only raised into sight as an effect of mirage, but by eleven o'clock the straight line stretching out east and west was in full view, and we rapidly approached it. I had hoped to make the Barrier about the position of what we call the Western Bight, and at noon we could see a point on our starboard, from which the Barrier dropped back. This was evidently the eastern limit of the Western Bight. Shortly after noon we were within a quarter of a mile of the ice face, and exclamations of wonder and astonishment at the stupendous bulk of the Barrier were drawn from the men who had not seen it before.

We slowly steamed along, noting the various structures of the ice, and were thankful that the weather promised to keep fine, for the inlet to which we were bound could not easily have been picked up in thick weather. The height of the Barrier about this point ranged from a hundred and fifty feet to two hundred feet. In the afternoon, about half past one, we passed an opening in the Barrier trending in a south-easterly direction, but its depth was only about three-quarters of a mile. The eastern point had the form of the bows of a gigantic man-of-war, and reached a height of about two hundred thirty feet. It was appropriately called 'The Dreadnought'.

As we steamed close in to the Barrier, watching carefully for any sign of an opening, we were able to observe accurately the various changes in the ice face. In places the wall was perfectly smooth, clean cut from the top to the water line, in other places it showed signs of vertical cracks, and sometimes deep caverns appeared, which, illuminated by the reflected light, merged from light translucent blue into the deepest sapphire. At times great black patches appeared on the sides of the Barrier in the distance, but as we neared them they were resolved into huge caverns, some of which cut the water line. One was so large that it would have been possible to have steamed the *Nimrod* through its entrance without touching either side or its top by mast or yard. Looking at the Barrier from some little distance, one would imagine it to be a perfectly even wall of ice; when steaming along parallel with it, however, the impression it gave was that of a series of points, each of which looked as though it might be the horn of a bay. Then when the ship came abeam of it, one would see that the wall only receded for a few hundred yards, and then new points came into view as the ship moved on. In some places a cornice of snow overhung the Barrier top, and again in others the vertical cracks had widened so that some portions of the ice wall seemed in immediate danger of falling. The vagaries of light and shadow made appearances very deceptive. One inlet we passed had the sides thrown up in little hummocks, not more than ten or fifteen feet high, but until we were fairly close these irregularities had the appearance of hills.

The weather continued fine and calm. During the voyage of the *Discovery* we had always encountered a strong westerly current along the Barrier, but there was absolutely no sign of this here, and the ship was making a good five knots. To the northward of us lay a very heavy pack, interspersed with large icebergs, one of which was over two miles long and one hundred fifty feet high. This pack ice was much heavier and more rugged than any we had encountered on the previous expedition. Evidently there must have been an enormous breaking away of ice to the eastward for as far as we could see from the crow's nest, to the north and east, this ice continued.

About midnight we suddenly came to the end of a very high portion of the Barrier, and found as we followed around that we were entering a wide shallow bay. This must have been the inlet where Borchgrevink landed in 1900, but it had greatly changed since that time. He describes the bay as being a fairly narrow inlet. On our way east in the *Discovery* in 1902 we passed an inlet somewhat similar, but we did not see the western end as it was obscured by fog at the time. There seemed to be no doubt that the Barrier had broken away at the entrance of this bay or inlet, and so had made it much wider and less deep than it was in previous years. About half a mile down the bay we reached fast ice. It was now about half past twelve at night, and the southerly sun shone in our faces. Our astonishment was great to see beyond the six or seven miles of flat bay ice, which was about five or six feet thick, high rounded ice cliffs, with valleys between, running in an almost east and west direction. About four miles to the south we saw the opening of a large valley, but could not say where it led. Due south of us, and rising to a height of approximately eight hundred feet, were steep and rounded cliffs, and behind them sharp peaks. The southerly sun being low, these heights threw shadows which, for some time, had the appearance of bare rocks. Two dark patches in the face of one of the further cliffs had also this appearance, but a careful observation taken with a telescope showed them to be caverns. To the east rose a long snow slope which cut the horizon at the height of about three hundred feet. It had every appearance of ice-covered land, but we could not stop then to make certain, for the heavy ice and bergs lying to the northward of us were setting down into the bay, and I saw that, if we were not to be beset, it would be necessary to get away at once. All around us were numbers of great whales showing their dorsal fins as they occasionally sounded, and on the edge of the bay ice half a dozen Emperor penguins stood lazily observing us. We named this place the Bay of Whales, for it was a veritable playground for these monsters.

We tried to work to the eastward so as once more to get close to the Barrier which we could see rising over the top of the small bergs and pack ice, but we found this impossible, and so struck northward through an open lead and came south to the Barrier again about 2 a.m. on the 24th. We coasted eastward along the wall of ice, always on the lookout for the inlet. The lashings had been taken off the motorcar, and the tackle rigged to hoist it out directly we got alongside the ice foot, to which the *Discovery* had been moored; for in Barrier Inlet we proposed to place our winter quarters.

I must leave the narrative for a moment at this point and refer to the reasons that made me decide on this inlet as the site for the winter quarters. I knew that Barrier Inlet was practically the beginning of King Edward VII Land, and that the actual bare land was within an easy sledge journey of that place, and it had the great advantage of being some ninety miles nearer to the South Pole than any other spot that could be reached with the ship. A further point of importance was that it would be an easy matter for the ship on its return to us to reach this part of the Barrier, whereas King Edward VII Land itself might quite conceivably be unattainable if the season was adverse. Some of my *Discovery* comrades had also considered Barrier Inlet a good place at which to winter. After thinking carefully over the matter I had decided in favour of wintering on the Barrier instead of on actual land, and on the *Koonya*'s departure I had sent a message to the headquarters of the expedition in London to the effect that, in the event of the *Nimrod* not returning at the usual time in 1908, no steps were to be taken to provide a relief ship to search for her in 1909, for it was only likely under those circumstances that she was frozen in; but that if she did not turn up with us in 1909, then the relief expedition should start in December of that year. The point to which they should first direct their search was to be Barrier Inlet, and if we were not found there, they were to search the coast of King Edward VII Land. I had added that it would only be by stress of the most unexpected circumstances that the ship would be unable to return to New Zealand.

However, the best laid schemes often prove impracticable in polar exploration, and within a few hours our first plan was found impossible of fulfilment. Within thirty-six hours a second arrangement had to be abandoned. We were steaming along westward close to the Barrier, and according to the chart we were due to be abreast of the inlet about 6 a.m., but not a sign was there of the opening. We had passed Borchgrevink's Bight at 1 a.m., and at 8 p.m. were well past the place where Barrier Inlet ought to have been. The Inlet had disappeared, owing to miles of the Barrier having calved away, leaving a long wide bay joining up with Borchgrevink's Inlet, and the whole was now merged into what we had called the Bay of Whales. This was a great disappointment to us, but we were thankful that the Barrier had broken away before we had made our camp on it. It was bad enough to try and make for a port that had been wiped off the face of the earth, when all the intending inhabitants were safe on board the ship, but it would have been infinitely worse if we had landed there whilst the place was still in existence, and that when the ship returned to take us off she should find the place gone. The thought of what might have been made me decide then and there that, under no circumstances, would I winter on the Barrier, and that wherever we did land we would secure a solid rock foundation for our winter home.

We had two strings to our bow, and I decided to use the second at once and push forward toward King Edward VII Land. Just after 8 a.m. on the 24th we turned a corner in the Barrier, where it receded about half a mile, before continuing to the eastward again. The line of its coast here made a right angle, and the ice sloped down to sea level at the apex of the angle, but the slope was too steep and too heavily crevassed for us to climb up and look over the surface if we had made a landing.

We tied the ship up to a fairly large floe, and I went down to England's cabin to talk the matter over. In the corner where we were lying there were comparatively few pieces of floe ice, but outside us lay a very heavy pack, in which several large bergs were locked. Our only chance was to go straight on, keeping close to the Barrier, as a lane of open water was left between the Barrier and the edge of the pack to the north of us. Sights were taken for longitude by four separate observers, and the positions calculated showed us we were not only well to the eastward of the place where Barrier Inlet was shown on the chart, but also that the Barrier had receded at this particular point since January 1902.

About nine o'clock we cast off from the floe and headed the ship to the eastward, again keeping a few hundred yards off the Barrier, for just here the cliff overhung, and if a fall of ice had occurred while we were close in the results would certainly have been disastrous for us. I soon saw that we would not be able to make much easting in this way, for the Barrier was now trending well to the north-east, and right ahead of us lay an impenetrably close pack, set with huge icebergs. By 10 a.m. we were close to the pack and found that it was pressed hard against the Barrier edge, and, what was worse, the whole of the northern pack and bergs at this spot were drifting in toward the Barrier. The seriousness of this situation can be well realised by the reader if he imagines for a moment that he is in a small boat right under the vertical white cliffs of Dover; that detached cliffs are moving in from seaward slowly but surely, with stupendous force and resistless power, and that it will only be a question of perhaps an hour or two before the two masses come into contact with his tiny craft between.

There was nothing for it but to retrace our way and try some other route. Our position was latitude 78° 20' South and longitude 162° 14' West when the ship turned. The pack had already moved inside the point of the cliff where we had lain in open water at eight o'clock, but by steaming hard and working in and out of the looser floes we just managed to pass the point at 11:20 a.m. with barely fifty yards of open water to spare between the Barrier and the pack.

I breathed more freely when we passed this zone of immediate danger, for there were two or three hundred yards of clear water now between us and the pack. We were right under the Barrier cliff, which was here over two hundred fifty feet high, and our course lay well to the south of west, being roughly south-west true; so as we moved south more quickly than the advancing ice we were able to keep close along the Barrier, which gradually became lower, until about three o'clock we were abreast of some tilted bergs at the eastern entrance of the Bay of Whales. There was a peculiar light which rendered distances and the forms of objects very deceptive, and a great deal of mirage, which made things appear much higher than they actually were. This was particularly noticeable in the case of the pack ice; the whole northern and western sea seemed crowded with huge icebergs, though in reality there was only heavy pack. The penguins that we had seen the previous night were still at the same place, and when a couple of miles away from us they loomed up as if they were about six feet high. This bay ice, on which many seals were lying, was cracking, and would soon float away, with one or two large icebergs embedded in it.

Skirting along the seaward edge we came to the high cliff of ice at the westerly end, and passed safely out of the bay at ten minutes to four. We then continued to the westward, still having the heavy pack to the north. One berg that we passed was a temporary resting place for hundreds of Antarctic and snow petrels, and these took flight as we approached. About 6 p.m. the pack ice seemed to loosen somewhat, and by half past seven, from the crow's nest, I could see a lead of open water to the north through the belt of pack, and beyond that there appeared to be a fairly open sea. About eight o'clock the ship's head was put north, and we soon gained a fairly open sea, occasionally having to make detours around the heavier packed floes, though we were able to push aside the lighter pieces. At midnight, our easterly progress was arrested by a line of thick conglomerated pack, and we had to steer north for nearly an hour before we could again set the course easterly. It is remarkable how limited one's horizon is at sea, for from the crow's nest, after passing this belt of pack, there appeared to be open water for an indefinite distance, yet by two o'clock we were up against the rigid ice again. Low pack ice is not visible at any great distance, and one could not trust an appearance of open water, even with the wide horizon obtained from the crow's nest. All night long we followed a zigzag course in the endeavour to penetrate to the east, at times steering due west, practically doubling on our tracks, before we could find an opening which would admit of our pursuing the direction we desired to follow. During the night it had been somewhat cloudy toward the south, but about 3 a.m. it became quite clear over the Barrier, and we saw to our disappointment that we had made hardly any progress to the eastward, for we were at that hour only just abeam of the Bay of Whales. About half past seven in the morning we passed a huge berg, nearly three miles in length and over two hundred feet in height, and at eight o'clock the sea became much more open; indeed, there was no ice in sight to the east at all. It was a bright, sunny morning, and things looked much more hopeful as I left the bridge for a sleep, after having been on deck all night.

When I came up again, just before noon on January 25, I found that my hopes for a clear run were vain. Our noon observations showed that we were well to the north of the Barrier, and still to the westward of the point we had reached the previous morning before we had been forced to turn around. The prospect of reaching King Edward VII Land seemed to grow more remote every ensuing hour. There was high hummocky pack interspersed with giant icebergs to the east and south of the ship, and it was obvious that the whole sea between Cape Colbeck and the Barrier at our present longitude must be full of ice. To the northward the strong ice blink on the horizon told the same tale. It seemed as if it would be impossible to reach the land, and the shortness of coal, the leaky condition of the ship, and the absolute necessity of landing all our stores and putting up the hut before the vessel left us made the situation an extremely anxious one for me. I had not expected to find Barrier Inlet gone, and, at the same time, the way to King Edward VII Land absolutely blocked by ice, though the latter condition was not unusual, for every expedition in this longitude up till 1901 had been held up by the pack; indeed Ross, in this locality, sailed for hundreds of miles to the northward along the edge of a similar pack on this meridian. It is true that we had steam, but the *Discovery,* or even the *Yermak,* the most powerful ice-breaker ever built, would have made no impression upon the cemented field of ice.

I decided to continue to try and make a way to the east for at least another twenty-four hours. We altered the course to the north, skirting the ice as closely as possible, and taking advantage of the slightest trend to the eastward, at times running into narrow culs-de-sac in the main pack, only to find it necessary to retrace our way again. The wind began to freshen from the west, and the weather to thicken. A little choppy sea washed over the edges of the floes, and the glass was falling. About five o'clock some heavy squalls of snow came down, and we had to go dead slow, for the horizon was limited at times to a radius of less than one hundred yards. Between the squalls it was fairly clear, and we could make out great numbers of long, low bergs, one of which was over five miles in length, though not more than forty feet high. The waves were splashing up against the narrow end as we passed within a couple of cables' length of the berg, and almost immediately afterward another squall swept down upon us. The weather cleared again shortly, and we saw the western pack moving rapidly toward us under the influence of the wind; in some places it had already met the main pack. As it was most likely that we would be caught in this great mass of ice, and that days, or even weeks, might elapse before we could extricate ourselves, I reluctantly gave orders to turn the ship and make full speed out of this dangerous situation. I could see nothing for it except to steer for McMurdo Sound, and there make our winter quarters. For many reasons I would have preferred landing at King Edward VII Land, as that region was absolutely unknown. A fleeting glimpse of bare rocks and high snow slopes was all that we obtained of it on the *Discovery* expedition, and had we been able to establish our winter quarters there, we could have added greatly to the knowledge of the geography of that region. There would perhaps have been more difficulty in the attempt to reach the South Pole from that base, but I did not expect that the route from there to the Barrier surface, from which we could make a fair start for the Pole, would have been impracticable. I did not give up the destined base of our expedition without a strenuous struggle, as the track of the ship given in the sketch map shows; but the forces of these uncontrollable ice packs are stronger than human resolution, and a change of plan was forced upon us.

After more trouble with the ice we worked into clearer water and the course was set for McMurdo Sound, where we arrived on January 29, and found that some twenty miles of frozen sea separated us from Hut Point. I decided to lie off the ice foot for a few days at least, and give Nature a chance to do what we could not do with the ship, that is, to break up the miles of ice intervening between us and our goal.

So far the voyage had been without accident to any of the staff, but on the morning of the 31st, when all hands were employed getting stores out of the after hatch, preparatory to landing them, a hook on the tackle slipped and, swinging suddenly across the deck, struck Mackintosh in the right eye. He fell on the deck in great pain, but was able, in a few minutes, to walk with help to England's cabin, where Marshall examined him. It was apparent that the sight of the eye was completely destroyed, so he was put under chloroform, and Marshall removed the eye, being assisted at the operation by the other two doctors, Michell and Mackay. It was a great comfort to me to know that the expedition had the services of thoroughly good surgeons. Mackintosh felt the loss of his eye keenly; not so much because the sight was gone, but because it meant that he could not remain with us in the Antarctic. He begged to be allowed to stay, but when Marshall explained that he might lose the sight of the other eye, unless great care were taken, he accepted his ill fortune without further demur, and thus the expedition lost, for a time, one of its most valuable members.

Whilst waiting at the ice, I thought it as well that a small party should proceed to Hut Point, and report on the condition of the hut left there by the *Discovery* expedition in 1904. I decided to send Adams, Joyce, and Wild, giving Adams instructions to get into the hut and then return the next day to the ship. They started off on their sixteen-mile march with plenty of provisions in case of being delayed, and a couple of spades. On their return, Adams reported that they had found the hut practically clear of snow, and the structure quite intact.

On February 3 I decided to wait no longer at the ice face, but to seek for winter quarters on the east coast of Ross Island. About four o'clock we got under way and started toward Cape Barne on the lookout for a suitable landing place. Steaming slowly north along the coast we saw across the bay a long, low snow slope, connected with the bare rock of Cape Royds, which appeared to be a likely place for winter quarters.

About eight o'clock I left the ship in a boat, accompanied by Adams and Wild. Proceeding toward the shore, we used the hand lead at frequent intervals until we came up against fast ice. This covered the whole of the small bay from the corner of Flagstaff Point (as we afterward named the seaward cliff at the southern end of Cape Royds) to Cape Barne to the southward. Close up to the Point the ice had broken out, leaving a little natural dock into which we ran the boat. Adams and I scrambled ashore, crossing a well-defined tide crack and going up a smooth snow slope, about fifteen yards wide, at the top of which was bare rock. Hundreds of Adelie penguins were moving to and fro on the top of the slope, and they greeted us with hoarse squawks of excitement.

A very brief examination of the vicinity of the ice foot was sufficient to show us that Cape Royds would be an excellent place at which to land our stores. We therefore shoved off again, and skirting along the ice foot to the south, sounded the bay and found that the water deepened from two fathoms close inshore to about twenty fathoms four hundred yards further south.

After completing these soundings we pulled out toward the ship, which had been coming in very slowly. We were pulling along at a good rate when suddenly a heavy body shot out of the water, struck the seaman who was pulling stroke, and dropped with a thud into the bottom of the boat. The arrival was an Adelie penguin. It was hard to say who was the most astonished – the penguin, at the result of its leap on to what it had doubtless thought was a rock, or we, who so suddenly took on board this curious passenger. The sailors in the boat looked upon this incident as an omen of good luck. There is a tradition amongst seamen that the souls of old sailors, after death, occupy the bodies of penguins, as well as of albatrosses; this idea, however, does not prevent the mariners from making a hearty meal off the breasts of the former when opportunity offers. We arrived on board at 9 p.m., and by 10 p.m. on February 3 the *Nimrod* was moored to the bay ice, ready to land the stores.

Immediately after securing the ship I went ashore, accompanied by the Professor, England, and Dunlop, to choose a place for building the hut. We passed the penguins, which were marching solemnly to and fro, and on reaching the level land, made for a huge boulder of kenyte, the most conspicuous mark in the locality. I thought that we might build the hut under the lee of this boulder, sheltered from the south-east wind, but the situation had its drawbacks, as it would have entailed a large amount of levelling before the foundation of the hut could have been laid. We crossed a narrow ridge of rock just beyond the great boulder, and, turning a little to the right up a small valley, found an ideal spot for our winter quarters. The floor of this valley was practically level and covered with a couple of feet of volcanic earth; at the sides the bedrock was exposed, but a rough eye measurement was quite sufficient to show that there would be not only ample room for the hut itself, but also for all the stores, and for a stable for the ponies. A hill right behind this little valley would serve as an excellent shelter to the hut from what we knew was the prevailing strong wind, that is, the south-easter. A glance at the illustrations will give the reader a much better idea of this place than will a written description, and he will see how admirably Nature had provided us with a protection against her own destructive forces.* A number of seals lying on the bay ice gave promise that there would be no lack of fresh meat.

With this ideal situation for a camp, and everything else satisfactory, including a supply of water from a lake right in front of our little valley, I decided that we could not do better than start getting our gear ashore at once. There was only one point that gave me any anxiety, and that was as to whether the sea would freeze over between this place and Hut Point in ample time for us to get across for the southern and western journeys in the following spring. It was also obvious that nothing could be done in the way of laying out depots for the next season's work, as directly the ship left we would be cut off from any communication with the lands to the south of us, by sea and by land, for the heavily crevassed glaciers fringing the coast were an effectual bar to a march with sledges. However, time was pressing, and we were fortunate to get winter quarters as near as this to our starting point for the south.

* These illustrations are not reproduced in this edition.

CHAPTER 6

The landing of stores and equipment
February 3–22, 1908
Blizzard in McMurdo Sound, February 18–21: Nimrod
sails for New Zealand, February 22

We returned to the ship to start discharging our equipment, and with this work commenced the most uncomfortable fortnight, and the hardest work, full of checks and worries, that I or any other member of the party had ever experienced. If it had not been for the wholehearted devotion of our party, and their untiring energy, we would never have got through the long toil of discharging. Day and night, if such terms of low latitudes can be used in a place where there was no night, late and early, they were always ready to turn to, in face of most trying conditions, and always with a cheerful readiness. If a fresh obstacle appeared there was no time lost in bemoaning the circumstance, but they all set to work at once to remove the obstruction. The first thing to be landed was the motorcar, and after that came the ponies, for it was probable that any day might see the breakup of the bay ice, and there being only two fathoms of water along the shore, as we had ascertained by sounding down the tide crack, the ship could not go very close in. It would have been practically impossible to have landed the ponies in boats, for they were only half broken in, and all in a highly strung, nervous condition. At 10:30 p.m. on February 3 we swung the motor over on to the bay ice, and all hands pulled it up the snow slope across the tide crack and left it safe on the solid ground. This done, we next landed one of the lifeboats, which we intended to keep down there with us. Joyce ran the dogs ashore and tied them up to rocks, all except Possum, who was still engaged with her little puppies. Then followed the foundation pieces of the hut, for it was desirable that we should be safely housed before the ship went north. Meanwhile, the carpenter was busily engaged in unbolting the framework of the pony stalls, and the animals became greatly excited, causing us a lot of trouble. We worked till 3 a.m., landing pony fodder and general stores, and then knocked off and had some cocoa and a rest, intending to turn to at 6 a.m.

We had hardly started work again when a strong breeze sprung up with drifting snow. The ship began to bump heavily against the ice foot and twice dragged her anchors out, so, as there seemed no possibility of getting ahead with the landing of the stores under these conditions, we steamed out and tied up at the main ice face, about six miles to the south, close to where we had lain for the past few days. It blew fairly hard all day and right through the evening, but the wind went down on the afternoon of the 5th, and we returned to the bay that evening.

We lost no time in getting the ponies ashore. This was by no means an easy task, for some of the animals were very restive, and it required care to avoid accident to themselves or to us. Some time before we had thought of walking them down over a gangplank on to the ice, but afterward decided to build a rough horse box, get them into this, and then sling it over the side by means of the main gaff. We covered the decks with ashes and protected all sharp projections with bags and bales of fodder. The first pony went in fairly quietly, and in another moment or two had the honour of being the pioneer horse on the Antarctic ice. One after another the ponies were led out of the stalls into the horse box and were slung over on to the ice. They all seemed to feel themselves at home, for they immediately commenced pawing at the snow as they are wont to do in their own faraway Manchurian home, where, in the winter, they scrape away the snow to get out the rough tussocky grass that lies underneath. It was 3:30 a.m. on the morning of the 6th before we got all the ponies off the ship, and they were at once led up on to the land. The poor beasts were naturally stiff after the constant buffeting they had experienced in their narrow stalls on the rolling ship for over a month, and they walked very stiffly ashore.

They negotiated the tide crack all right, the fissure being narrow, and were soon picketed out on some bare earth at the entrance to a valley which lay about fifty yards from the site of our hut. We thought that this would be a good place, but the selection was to cost us dearly in the future. The tide crack played an important part in connection with the landing of the stores. In the polar regions, both north and south, when the sea is frozen over, there always appears between the fast ice, which is the ice attached to the land, and the sea ice, a crack which is due to the sea ice moving up and down with the rise and fall of the tide. When the bottom of the sea slopes gradually from the land, sometimes two or three tide cracks appear running parallel to each other. When no more tide cracks are to be seen landwards, the snow or ice foot has always been considered as being a permanent adjunct to the land, and in our case this opinion was further strengthened by the fact that our soundings in the tide crack showed that the ice foot on the landward side of it must be aground. I have explained this fully, for it was after taking into consideration these points that I, for convenience sake, landed the bulk of the stores below the bare rocks on what I considered to be the permanent snow slope.

About 9 a.m. on the morning of February 6 we started work with sledges, hauling provisions and pieces of the hut to the shore. The previous night the foundation posts of the hut had been sunk and frozen into the ground with a cement composed of volcanic earth and water. The digging of the foundation holes, on which job Dunlop, Adams, Joyce, Brocklehurst, and Marshall were engaged, proved hard work, for in some cases where the hole had to be dug the bedrock was found a few inches below the coating of the earth, and this had to be broken through or drilled with chisel and hammer. Now that the ponies were ashore it was necessary to have a party living ashore also, for the animals would require looking after if the ship were forced to leave the ice foot at any time, and, of course, the building of the hut could go on during the absence of the ship. The first shore party consisted of Adams, Marston, Brocklehurst, Mackay, and Murray, and two tents were set up close to the hut, with the usual sledging requisites, sleeping bags, cookers, etc. A canvas cover was rigged on some oars to serve as a cooking tent, and this, later on, was enlarged into a more commodious house, built out of bales of fodder.

The first things landed this day were bales of fodder for the ponies, and sufficient petroleum and provisions for the shore party in the event of the ship having to put to sea suddenly owing to bad weather. For facility in landing the stores, the whole party was divided into two gangs. Some of the crew of the ship hoisted the stores out of the hold and slid them down a wide plank on to the ice, others of the ship's crew loaded the stores on to the sledges, and these were hauled to land by the shore party, each sledge having three men harnessed to it. The road to the shore consisted of hard, rough ice, alternating with very soft snow, and as the distance from where the ship was lying at first to the tide crack was nearly a quarter of a mile, it was strenuous toil, especially when the tide crack was reached and the sledges had to be pulled up the slope. After the first few sledge loads had been hauled right up on to the land, I decided to let the stores remain on the snow slope beyond the tide crack, where they could be taken away at leisure. The work was so heavy that we tried to substitute mechanical haulage in place of man haulage, but had to revert to our original plan, and all that morning we did the work by man haulage. During the lunch hour we shifted the ship about a hundred yards nearer the shore alongside the ice face, from which a piece had broken out during the morning, leaving a level edge where the ship could be moored easily.

Just as we were going to commence work at 2 p.m. a fresh breeze sprang up from the south-east, and the ship began to bump against the ice foot, her movement throwing the water over the ice. We were then lying in a rather awkward position in the apex of an angle in the bay ice, and as the breeze threatened to become stronger, I sent the shore party on to the ice, and, with some difficulty, we got clear of the ice foot. The breeze freshening, we stood out to the fast ice in the strait about six miles to the south and anchored there. It blew a fresh breeze with drift from the south-east all that afternoon and night, and did not ease up till the following afternoon. Thus, unfortunately, two valuable working days were lost.

When I went ashore I found that the little party left behind had not only managed to get up to the site of the hut all the heavy timber that had been landed, but had also stacked on the bare land the various cases of provisions which had been lying on the snow slope by the tide crack. We worked till 2 a.m. on the morning of the 9th, and then knocked off till 9 a.m. Then we commenced again, and put in one of the hardest day's work one can imagine, pulling the sledges to the tide crack and then hauling them bodily over. Hour after hour all hands toiled on the work, the crossing of the tide crack becoming more difficult with each succeeding sledge load, for the ice in the bay was loosening, and it was over floating, rocking pieces of floe with gaps several feet wide between them that we hauled the sledges. In the afternoon the ponies were brought into action, as they had had some rest, and their arrival facilitated the discharge, though it did not lighten the labours of the perspiring staff. None of our party were in very good condition, having been cooped up in the ship, and the heavy cases became doubly heavy to our arms and shoulders by midnight.

Next day the work continued, the ice still holding in, but threatening every minute to go out. If there had been sufficient water for the ship to lie right alongside the shore we would have been pleased to see the ice go out, but at the place where we were landing the stores there was only twelve feet of water, and the *Nimrod,* at this time, drew fourteen. We tried to anchor one of the smaller loose pieces of bay ice to the ice foot, and this answered whilst the tide was setting in. As a result of the tidal movement, the influx of heavy pack in the bay where we were lying caused some anxiety, and more than once we had to shift the ship away from the landing place because of the heavy floes and hummocky ice which pressed up against the bay ice. One large berg sailed in from the north and grounded about a mile to the south of Cape Royds, and later another about the same height, not less than one hundred fifty feet, did the same, and these two bergs were frozen in where they grounded and remained in that position through the winter. The hummocky pack that came in and out with the tide was over fifteen feet in height, and, being of much greater depth below water, had ample power and force to damage the ship if a breeze should spring up.

When we turned to after lunch, and before the first sledge load reached the main landing place, we found that it would be impossible to continue working there any longer, for the small floe which we had anchored to the ice had dragged out the anchor and was being carried to sea by the ebbing tide. Some three hundred and fifty yards further along the shore of the bay was a much steeper ice foot at the foot of the cliffs, and a snow slope narrower than the one on which we had been landing the provisions. This was the nearest available spot at which to continue discharging.

We hoped that when the ship had left we could hoist the stores up over the cliff; they would then be within a hundred yards of the hut, and, after being carried for a short distance, they could be rolled down the steep snow slope at the head of the valley where it was being built. All this time the hut party were working day and night, and the building was rapidly assuming an appearance of solidity. The uprights were in, and the brace ties were fastened together, so that if it came on to blow there was no fear of the structure being destroyed.

The stores had now to be dragged a distance of nearly three hundred yards from the ship to the landing place, but this work was greatly facilitated by our being able to use four of the ponies, working two of them for an hour, and then giving these a spell whilst two others took their place. The snow was very deep, and the ponies sank in well above the knees; it was heavy going for the men who were leading them. A large amount of stores was landed in this way, but a new and serious situation arose through the breaking away of the main ice foot.

On the previous day an ominous-looking crack had been observed to be developing at the end of the ice foot nearest to Flagstaff Point, and it became apparent that if this crack continued to widen, it would cut right across the centre of our stores, with the result that, unless removed, they would be irretrievably lost in the sea. Next day (the 10th) there was no further opening of the crack, but at seven o'clock that night another crack formed on the ice foot inside of Derrick Point where we were now landing stores. There was no immediate danger to be apprehended at this place, for the bay ice would have to go out before the ice foot could fall into the sea. Prudence suggested that it would be better to shift the stores already landed to a safer place before discharging any more from the ship, so at 8 p.m. on the 10th we commenced getting the remainder of the wood for the hut and the bales of cork for the lining up on to the bare land. This took till about midnight, when we knocked off for cocoa and a sleep.

We turned to at six o'clock next morning, and I decided to get the stores up the cliff face at Derrick Point before dealing with those at Front Door Bay, the first landing place, for the former ice foot seemed in the greater peril of collapse than did the latter. Adams, Joyce, and Wild soon rigged up a boom and tackle from the top of the cliff, making the heel of the boom fast by placing great blocks of volcanic rocks on it. A party remained below on the ice foot to shift and hook on the cases, whilst another party on top, fifty feet above, hauled away when the word was given from below, and on reaching the top of the cliff, the cases were hauled in by means of a guy rope. The men were hauling on the thin rope of the tackle from eight o'clock in the morning till one o'clock the following morning with barely a spell for a bit to eat.

We now had to find another and safer place on which to land the rest of the coal and stores. Further round the bay from where the ship was lying was a smaller bight where a gentle slope led on to bare rocks, and Back Door Bay, as we named this place, became our new depot. The ponies were led down the hill, and from Back Door Bay to the ship. This was a still longer journey than from Derrick Point, but there was no help for it, and we started landing the coal, after laying a tarpaulin on the rocks to keep the coal from becoming mixed with the earth. By this time there were several ugly looking cracks in the bay ice, and these kept opening and closing, having a play of seven or eight inches between the floes. We improvised bridges out of the bottom and sides of the motor-car case so that the ponies could cross the cracks, and by eleven o'clock were well under way with the work. Mackay had just taken ashore a load with a pony, Armytage was about to hook on another pony to a loaded sledge at the ship, and a third pony was standing tied to our stern anchor rope waiting its turn for sledging, when suddenly, without the slightest warning, the greater part of the bay ice opened out into floes, and the whole mass that had opened started to drift slowly out to sea. The ponies on the ice were now in a perilous position. The sailors rushed to loosen the one tied to the stern rope, and got it over the first crack, and Armytage also got the pony he was looking after off the floe nearest the ship on to the next floe. Just at that moment Mackay appeared around the corner from Back Door Bay with a third pony attached to an empty sledge, on his way back to the ship to load up. Orders were shouted to him not to come any further, but he did not at first grasp the situation, for he continued advancing over the ice, which was now breaking away more rapidly. The party working on the top of Derrick Point, by shouting and waving, made him realise what had occurred. He accordingly left his sledge and pony and rushed over toward where the other two ponies were adrift on the ice, and, by jumping the widening cracks, he reached the moving floe on which they were standing. This piece of ice gradually drew closer to a larger piece, from which the animals would be able to gain a place of safety. Mackay started to try and get the pony Chinaman across the crack when it was only about six inches wide, but the animal suddenly took fright, reared up on his hind legs, and backing toward the edge of the floe, which had at that moment opened to a width of a few feet, fell bodily into the ice cold water. It looked as if it was all over with poor Chinaman, but Mackay hung on to the head rope, and Davis, Mawson, Michell and one of the sailors who were on the ice close by rushed to his assistance. The pony managed to get his forefeet on to the edge of the ice floe. After great difficulty a rope sling was passed underneath him, and then by tremendous exertion he was lifted up far enough to enable him to scramble on to the ice. There he stood, wet and trembling in every limb. A few seconds later the floe closed up against the other one. It was providential that it had not done so during the time that the pony was in the water, for in that case the animal would inevitably have been squeezed to death between the two huge masses of ice. A bottle of brandy was thrown on to the ice from the ship, and half its contents were poured down Chinaman's throat. The ship was now turning around with the object of going bow on to the floe, in order to push it ashore, so that the ponies might cross on to the fast ice, and presently, with the engine at full speed, the floe was slowly but surely moved back against the fast ice. Directly the floe was hard up against the unbroken ice, the ponies were rushed across and taken straight ashore, and the men who were on the different floes took advantage of the temporary closing of the crack to get themselves and the stores into safety. I decided, after this narrow escape, not to risk the ponies on the sea ice again. The ship was now backed out, and the loose floes began to drift away to the west.

By 1 p.m. most of the ice had cleared out, and the ship came in to the edge of the fast ice, which was now abreast of Back Door Bay. Hardly were the ice anchors made fast before new cracks appeared, and within a quarter of an hour the ship was adrift again. As it was impossible to discharge under these conditions, the *Nimrod* stood off. We had now practically the whole of the wintering party ashore, so when lunch was over, the main party went on with the work at Derrick Point, refreshed by the hot tea and meat, which they had hastily swallowed.

I organised that afternoon a small party to shift the main stores into safety. We had not been long at work before I saw that it would need the utmost dispatch and our most strenuous endeavours to save the valuable cases; for the crack previously observed opened more each hour. Perspiration poured down our faces and bodies as we toiled in the hot sun. After two hours' work we had shifted into a place of safety all our cases of scientific instruments, and a large quantity of fodder, and hardly were they secured than, with a sharp crack, the very place where they had been lying fell with a crash into the sea. Had we lost these cases the result would have been very serious, for a great part of our scientific work could not have been carried out, and if the fodder had been lost, it would have meant the loss of the ponies also. The breaking of this part of the ice made us redouble our efforts to save the rest of the stores, for we could not tell when the next piece of ice might break off, though no crack was yet visible. The breaking up of the bay ice that morning turned out to be after all for the best, for I would not otherwise have gone on so early with this work. I ran up the hill to the top of Flagstaff Point to call the ship in, in order to obtain additional help from the crew; she had been dodging about outside of the point since one o'clock, but she was beyond hailing distance, and it was not till about seven o'clock that I saw her coming close in again. I at once hailed England and told him to send every available man ashore immediately. In a few minutes a boat came off with half a dozen men, and I sent a message back by the officer in charge for more members of the ship's crew to be landed at once, and only enough men left on board to steer the ship and work the engines. I had previously knocked off the party working on the hut, and with the extra assistance we 'smacked things about' in a lively fashion. The ice kept breaking off in chunks, but we had the satisfaction of seeing every single package safe on the rocks by midnight.

Our party then proceeded to sledge the heavier cases and the tins of oil at the foot of Derrick Point around the narrow causeway of ice between the perpendicular rocks and the sea to the depot at

Back Door Bay. I was astonished and delighted on arriving at the derrick to find the immense amount of stores that had been placed in safety by the efforts of the Derrick Point party, and by 1 a.m. on February 13 all the stores landed were in safety. About a ton of flour in cases remained to be hauled up, but as we already had enough ashore to last us for a year, and knowing that at Hut Point there were large quantities of biscuit left by the last expedition, which would be available if needed, we just rolled the cases on the ice foot into a hollow at the foot of the cliff, where they were in comparative safety, as the ice there would not be likely to break away immediately. We retrieved these after the ship left.

When making arrangements for the necessary equipment of the expedition, I tried to get the bulk of the stores into cases of uniform size and weight, averaging fifty to sixty pounds gross, and thus allow of more easy handling than would have been the case if the stores were packed in the usual way. The goods packed in Venesta cases could withstand the roughest treatment without breakage or damage to the contents. These Venesta cases are made of three thin layers of wood, fastened together by a patent process; the material is much tougher than ordinary wood, weighs much less than a case of the same size made of the usual deal, and being thinner, takes up much less room, a consideration of great moment to a Polar expedition. The wood could not be broken by the direct blow of a heavy hammer, and the empty cases could be used for the making of the hundred and one odds and ends that have to be contrived to meet requirements in such an expedition as this.

At 1 p.m. on the morning of February 13 I signalled the ship to come in and take off the crew, and a boat was sent ashore. There was a slight breeze blowing, and it took them some time to pull off to the *Nimrod,* which lay a long way out. We on shore turned in, and we were so tired that it was noon before we woke up. A glance out to sea showed that we had lost nothing by our sleep, for there was a heavy swell running into the bay and it would have been quite impossible to have landed any stores at all. In the afternoon the ship came in fairly close, but I signalled England that it was useless to send the boat. This northerly swell, which we could hear thundering on the ice foot, would have been welcome a fortnight before, for it would have broken up a large amount of fast ice to the south, and I could not help imagining that probably at this date there was open water up to Hut Point. Now, however, it was the worst thing possible for us, as the precious time was slipping by, and the still more valuable coal was being used up by the continual working of the ship's engines. Next day the swell still continued, so at 4 p.m. I signalled England to proceed to Glacier Tongue and land a depot there. Glacier Tongue is a remarkable formation of ice which stretches out into the sea from the south-west slopes of Mount Erebus. About five miles in length, running east and west, tapering almost to a point at its seaward end, and having a width of about a mile where it descends from the land, cracked and crevassed all over and floating in deep water, it is a phenomenon which still remains a mystery. It lies about eight miles to the northward of Hut Point, and about thirteen to the southward of Cape Royds, and I thought this would be a good place at which to land a quantity of sledging stores, as by doing so we would be saved haulage at least thirteen miles, the distance between the spot on the southern route and Cape Royds. The ship arrived there in the early evening, and landed the depot on the north side of the Tongue. The Professor took bearings so that there might be no difficulty in finding the depot when the sledging season commenced. The sounding at this spot gave a depth of 157 fathoms. From the seaward end of the glacier it was observed that the ice had broken away only a couple of miles further south, so the northerly swell had not been as far-reaching in its effect as I had imagined. The ship moored at the Tongue for the night.

During this day we, ashore at Cape Royds, were variously employed; one party continued the building of the hut, whilst the rest of us made a more elaborate temporary dwelling and cook house than we had had up to that time. The walls were constructed of bales of fodder, which lent themselves admirably for this purpose, the cook tent tarpaulin was stretched over these for a roof and was supported on planks, and the outer walls were stayed with uprights from the pony stalls. As the roof was rather low and people could not stand upright, a trench was dug at one end, where the cook could move about without bending his back the whole time. In this corner were concocted the most delicious dishes that ever a hungry man could wish for. Wild acted as cook till Roberts came ashore permanently, and it was a sight to

see us in the dim light that penetrated through the door of the
fodder hut as we sat in a row on cases, each armed with a spoon
manufactured out of tin and wood by the ever inventive Day,
awaiting with eagerness our bowl of steaming hoosh or rich
dark-coloured penguin breast, followed by biscuit, butter and jam;
tea and smokes ended up the meal, and, as we lazily stretched
ourselves out for the smoke, regardless of a temperature of 16 or 18
degrees of frost, we felt that things were not so bad.

The same day that we built the fodder hut we placed inside it
some cases of bottled fruit, hoping to save them from being
cracked by the severe frost outside. The bulk of the cases containing liquid we kept on board the ship till the last moment so
that they could be put into the main hut when the fire was lighted.
We turned in about midnight, and got up at seven next morning.
The ship had just come straight in, and I went off on board.
Marshall also came off to attend to Mackintosh, whose wound was
rapidly healing. He was now up and about. He was very anxious to
stay with us, but Marshall did not think it advisable for him to risk
it. During the whole of this day and the next, the 15th, the swell
was too great to admit of any stores being landed, but early on the
morning of the 16th we found it possible to get ashore at a small
ice foot to the north of Flagstaff Point, and here, in spite of the
swell, we managed to land six boatloads of fruit, some oil, and
twenty-four bags of coal. The crew of the boat, whilst the stores
were being taken out, had to keep to their oars, and whenever the
swell rolled on the shelving beach, they had to back with all their
might to keep the bow of the boat from running under the
overhanging ice foot and being crushed under the ice by the lifting
wave. Davis, the chief officer of the *Nimrod,* worked like a Titan.
A tall, red-headed Irishman, typical of his country, he was always
working and always cheerful, having no time limit for his work.
He and Harbourd, the second officer, a quiet, self-reliant man,
were great acquisitions to the expedition. These two officers were
ably supported by the efforts of the crew. They had nothing but
hard work and discomfort from the beginning of the voyage, and
yet they were always cheerful, and worked splendidly. Dunlop,
the chief engineer, not only kept his department going smoothly
on board but was the principal constructor of the hut. A great deal
of the credit for the work being so cheerfully performed was due

to the example of Cheetham, who was an old hand in the Antarctic, having been boatswain of the *Morning* on both the voyages she made for the relief of the *Discovery*. He was third mate and boatswain on this expedition.

When I had gone on board the previous day I found that England was still poorly and that he was feeling the strain of the situation. He was naturally very anxious to get the ship away and concerned about the shrinkage of the coal supply. I also would have been glad to have seen the *Nimrod* on her way north, but it was impossible to let her leave until the wintering party had received their coal from her. In view of the voyage home, the ship's main topmast was struck to lessen her rolling in bad weather. It was impossible to ballast the ship with rock, as the time needed for this operation would involve the consumption of much valuable coal, and I was sure that the heavy iron bark and oak hull, and the weight of the engine and boiler filled with water, would be sufficient to ensure the ship's safety.

We found it impossible to continue working at Cliff Point later on in the day, so the ship stood off whilst those on shore went on with the building of the hut. Some of the shore party had come off in the last boat to finish writing their final letters home, and during the night we lay to waiting for the swell to decrease. The weather was quite fine, and if it had not been for the swell we could have got through a great deal of work. February is by no means a fine month in the latitude we were in, and up till now we had been extremely fortunate, as we had not experienced a real blizzard.

The following morning, Monday, February 17, the sea was breaking heavily on the ice foot at the bottom of Cliff Point. The stores that had been landed the previous day had been hoisted up the overhanging cliff and now formed the fourth of our scattered depots of coal and stores. The swell did not seem so heavy in Front Door Bay, so we commenced landing the stores in the whale boat at the place where the ice foot had broken away, a party on shore hauling the bags of coal and the cases up the ice face, which was about fourteen feet high. The penguins were still around us in large numbers. We had not had any time to make observations on them, being so busily employed discharging the ship, but just at this particular time our attention was called to a couple of these birds which suddenly made a spring from the water and landed on their feet on the ice edge, having cleared a vertical height of twelve feet. It seemed a marvellous jump for these small creatures to have made, and shows the rapidity with which they must move through the water to gain the impetus that enables them to clear a distance in vertical height four times greater than their own, and also how unerring must be their judgment in estimation of the distance and height when performing this feat. The work of landing stores at this spot was greatly hampered by the fact that the bay was more or less filled with broken floes, through which the boat had to be forced. It was impossible to use the oars in the usual way, so, on arriving at the broken ice, they were employed as poles. The bow of the boat was entered into a likely looking channel, and then the crew, standing up, pushed the boat forward by means of the oars, the ice generally giving way on each side, but sometimes closing up and nipping the boat, which, if it had been less strongly built, would assuredly have been crushed. The Professor, Mawson, Cotton, Michell and a couple of seamen formed the boat's crew, and with Davis or Harbourd in the stern, they dodged the ice very well, considering the fact that the swell was rather heavy at the outside edge of the floes. When alongside the ice foot one of the crew hung on to a rope in the bow, and another did the same in the stern, hauling in the slack as the boat rose on top of the swell, and easing out as the water swirled downward from the ice foot. There was a sharp pointed rock, which, when the swell receded, was almost above water, and the greatest difficulty was experienced in preventing the boat from crashing down on the top of this. The rest of the staff in the boat and on shore hauled up the cases and bags of coal at every available opportunity. The coal was weighed at the top of the ice foot, and the bags emptied on to a heap which formed the main supply for the winter months. We had now three depots of coal in different places around the winter quarters. In the afternoon the floating ice at this place became impassable, but fortunately it had worked its way out of Back Door Bay, where, in spite of the heavy swell running against the ice foot, we were able to continue adding to the heap of coal until nearly eight tons had been landed. It was a dull and weary job except when unpleasantly enlivened by the imminent danger of the boat being caught between heavy pieces of floating ice and the solid ice foot. These masses of ice rose and fell on the swell, the water swirling around them as they became submerged, and pouring off their tops and sides as they rose to the surface. It required all Harbourd's watchfulness and speediness of action to prevent damage to the boat. It is almost needless to observe that all hands were as grimy as coal heavers, especially the boat's crew, who were working in the half-frozen slushy coal dust and sea spray. The Professor, Mawson, Cotton, and Michell still formed part of the crew. They had, by midnight, been over twelve hours in the boat, excepting for about ten minutes' spell for lunch, and after discharging each time had a long pull back to the ship. When each boatload was landed, the coal and stores had to be hauled up on a sledge over a very steep gradient to a place of safety, and after this was accomplished, there was a long wait for the next consignment.

Work was continued all night, though everyone was nearly dropping with fatigue; but I decided that the boat returning to the ship at 5 a.m. (the 18th) should take a message to England that the men were to knock off for breakfast and turn to at 7 a.m. Meanwhile Roberts had brewed some hot coffee in the hut, where we now had the stove going, and, after a drink of this, our weary people threw themselves down on the sleeping bags in order to snatch a short rest before again taking up the work. At 7 a.m. I went to the top of Flagstaff Point, but instead of seeing the ship close in, I spied her hull down on the horizon, and could see no sign of her approaching the winter quarters to resume discharging. After watching her for about half an hour, I returned to the hut, woke up those of the staff who from utter weariness had dropped asleep, and told them to turn into their bags and have a proper rest. I could not imagine why the ship was not at hand, but at a quarter to eleven Harbourd came ashore and said that England wanted to see me on board; so, leaving the others to sleep, I went off to the *Nimrod*. On asking England why the ship was not in at seven to continue discharging, he told me that all hands were so dead tired that he thought it best to let them have a sleep. The men were certainly worn out. Davis's head had dropped on the wardroom table, and he had gone sound asleep with his spoon in his mouth, to which he had just conveyed some of his breakfast. Cotton had fallen asleep on the platform of the engine room steps, whilst Mawson, whose lair was a little store-room in the engine room, was asleep on the floor. His long legs, protruding through the doorway, had found a resting place on the crosshead of the engine, and his dreams were mingled with a curious rhythmical motion which was fully accounted for when he woke up, for the ship having got under way, the up-and-down motion of the piston had moved his limbs with every stroke. The sailors also were fast asleep; so, in the face of this evidence of absolute exhaustion, I decided not to start work again till after one o'clock, and told England definitely that when the ship had been reduced in coal to ninety-two tons as a minimum I would send her north. According to our experiences on the last expedition, the latest date to which it would be safe to keep the *Nimrod* would be the end of February, for the young ice forming about that time on the sound would seriously hamper her getting clear of the Ross Sea. Later observations of the ice conditions of McMurdo Sound at our winter quarters showed us that a powerfully engined ship could have gone north later in the year, perhaps even in the winter, for we had open water close to us all the time.

About 2 p.m. the *Nimrod* came close in to Flagstaff Point to start discharging again. I decided that it was time to land the more delicate instruments, such as watches, chronometers, and all personal gear. The members of the staff who were on board hauled their things out of Oyster Alley, and, laden with its valuable freight, we took the whale boat into Front Door Bay. Those who had been ashore now went on board to collect their goods and finish their correspondence. During the afternoon we continued boating coal to Front Door Bay, which was again free of ice, and devoted our attention almost entirely to this work.

About five o'clock on the afternoon of February 18, snow began to fall, with a light wind from the north, and as at times the boat could hardly be seen from the ship, instructions were given to the boat's crew that whenever the *Nimrod* was not clearly visible they were to wait alongside the shore until the snow squall had passed and she appeared in sight again. At six o'clock, just as the boat had come alongside for another load, the wind suddenly shifted to the south-east and freshened immediately. The whaler was hoisted at once, and the *Nimrod* stood off from the shore, passing between some heavy ice floes, against one of which her propeller struck, but fortunately without sustaining any damage. Within half an hour it was blowing a furious blizzard, and every sign of land, both

east and west, was obscured in the scudding drift. I was aboard the
vessel at the time. We were then making for the fast ice to the
south, but the *Nimrod* was gaining but little headway against the
terrific wind and short rising sea; so to save coal I decided to keep
the engines just going slow and maintain our position in the sound
as far as we could judge, though it was inevitable that we should
drift northward to a certain extent. All night the gale raged with
great fury. The speed of the gusts at times must have approached a
force of a hundred miles an hour. The tops of the seas were cut off
by the wind, and flung over the decks, mast, and rigging of the
ship, congealing at once into hard ice, and the sides of the vessel
were thick with the frozen sea water. 'The masts were grey with
the frozen spray, and the bows were a coat of mail.' Very soon the
cases and sledges lying on deck were hard and fast in a sheet of solid
ice, and the temperature had dropped below zero. Harbourd, who
was the officer on watch, on whistling to call the crew aft, found
that the metal whistle stuck to his lips, a painful intimation of the
low temperature. I spent most of the night on the bridge, and
hoped that the violence of the gale would be of but short duration.
This hope was not realised, for next morning, February 19, at
8 a.m., it was blowing harder than ever. During the early hours of
the day the temperature was minus 16° F, and consistently kept
below minus 12° F. The motion of the ship was sharp and jerky,
yet, considering the nature of the sea and the trim of the vessel, she
was remarkably steady. To a certain extent this was due to the fact
that the main topmast had been lowered. We had constantly to
have two men at the wheel, for the rudder, being so far out of the
water, received the blows of the sea as they struck the quarter and
stern; and the steersman having once been flung right over the
steering chains against the side of the ship, it was necessary to have
two always holding on to the kicking wheel. At times there would
be a slight lull, the seas striking less frequently against the rudder,
and the result would be that the rudder well soon got filled with
ice, and it was found impossible to move the wheel at all. To
overcome this dangerous state of things the steersmen had to keep
moving the wheel alternately to port and starboard, after the ice
had been broken away from the well. In spite of this precaution,
the rudder well occasionally became choked, and one of the crew,
armed with a long iron bar, had to stand by continually to break

the frozen sea water off the rudder. In the blinding drift it was impossible to see more than a few yards from the ship, and once a large iceberg suddenly loomed out of the drift close to the weather bow of the *Nimrod;* fortunately the rudder had just been cleared, and the ship answered her helm, thus avoiding a collision.

All day on the 20th, through the night, and throughout the day and night of the 21st, the gale raged. Occasionally the drift ceased, and we saw dimly bare rocks, sometimes to the east and sometimes to the west, but the upper parts of them being enveloped in snow clouds, it was impossible to ascertain exactly what our position was. At these times we were forced to wear ship; that is, to turn the ship around, bringing the wind first astern and then on to the other side, so that we could head in the opposite direction. It was impossible in face of the storm to tack, *i.e.* to turn the ship's head into the wind, and around, so as to bring the wind on the other side. About midnight on the 21st, whilst carrying out this evolution of wearing ship, during which the *Nimrod* always rolled heavily in the trough of the waves, she shipped a heavy sea, and, all the release water ports and scupper holes being blocked with ice, the water had no means of exit, and began to freeze on deck, where, already, there was a layer of ice over a foot in thickness. Any more weight like this would have made the ship unmanageable. The ropes, already covered with ice, would have been frozen into a solid mass, so we were forced to take the drastic step of breaking holes in the bulwarks to allow the water to escape. This had been done already in the forward end of the ship by the gales we experienced on our passage down to the ice, but as the greater part of the weight in the holds was aft, the water collected toward the middle and stern, and the job of breaking through the bulwarks was a tougher one than we had imagined; it was only by dint of great exertions that Davis and Harbourd accomplished it. It was a sight to see Harbourd, held by his legs hanging over the starboard side of the *Nimrod,* and wielding a heavy axe, whilst Davis, whose length of limb enabled him to lean over without being held, did the same on the other side. The temperature at this time was several degrees below zero. Occasionally on this night, as we approached the eastern shore, the coast of Ross Island, we noticed the sea covered with a thick yellowish-brown scum. This was due to the immense masses of snow blown off the mountain sides out to sea, and this scum, to a certain extent, prevented the tops of the waves from breaking. Had it not been for this unexpected protection we would certainly have lost our starboard boat, which had been unshipped in a sea and was hanging in a precarious position for the time being. It was hard to realise that so high and so dangerous a sea could possibly have risen in the comparatively narrow waters of McMurdo Sound. The wind was as strong as that we experienced in the gales that assailed us after we first left New Zealand, but the waves were not so huge as those which had the whole run of the Southern Ocean in which to gather strength before they met us. At 2 a.m. the weather suddenly cleared, and though the wind still blew strongly and gustily, it was apparent that the force of the gale had been expended. We could now see our position clearly. The wind and current, in spite of our efforts to keep our position, had driven us over thirty miles to the north, and at this time we were abeam of Cape Bird. The sea was rapidly decreasing in height, and we were able to steam for Cape Royds.

We arrived there in the early morning, and I went ashore at Back Door Bay; after pushing the whale boat through pancake ice and slush, the result of the gale. Hurrying over to the hut I was glad to see that it was intact, and then I received full details of the occurrences of the last three days on shore. The report was not very reassuring as regards the warmth of the hut, for the inmates stated that, in spite of the stove being alight the whole time, no warmth was given off. Of course the building was really not at all complete. It had not been lined, and there were only makeshift protections for the windows, but what seemed a grave matter was the behaviour of the stove, for on the efficiency of this depended not only our comfort but our very existence. The shore party had experienced a very heavy gale indeed. The hut had trembled and shaken the whole time, and if the situation had not been so admirable I doubt whether there would have been a hut at all after the gale. A minor accident had occurred, for our fodder hut had failed to withstand the gale, and one of the walls had collapsed, killing one of Possum's pups. The roof had been demolished at the same time.

On going down to our main landing place, the full effect of the blizzard became apparent. There was hardly a sign to be seen of the greater part of our stores. At first it appeared that the drifting snow had covered the cases and bales and the coal, but a closer inspection showed that the real disappearance of our stores from view was due to the sea. Such was the force of the wind blowing straight on to the shore from the south that the spray had been flung in sheets over everything and had been carried by the wind for nearly a quarter of a mile inland, and consequently in places our precious stores lay buried to a depth of five or six feet in a mass of frozen sea water. The angles taken up by the huddled masses of cases and bales had made the surface of this mass of ice assume a most peculiar shape. We feared that it would take weeks of work to get the stores clear of the ice. It was probable also that the salt water would have damaged the fodder, and worked its way into cases that were not tin lined or made of Venesta wood, and that some of the things would never be seen again. No-one would have recognised the landing place as the spot on which we had been working during the past fortnight, so great was the change wrought by the furious storm. Our heap of coal had a sheet of frozen salt water over it, but this was a blessing in disguise, for it saved the smaller pieces of coal from being blown away.

There was no time then to do anything about releasing the stores from the ice; the main thing was to get the remainder of the coal ashore and send the ship north. We immediately started landing coal at the extreme edge of Front Door Bay. The rate of work was necessarily very slow, for the whole place was both rough and slippery from the newly formed ice that covered everything. Before 10 p.m. on February 22, the final boatload of coal arrived. We calculated that we had in all only about eighteen tons, so that the strictest economy would be required to make this amount spin out until the sledging commenced in the following spring. I should certainly have liked more coal, but the delays that had occurred in finding winter quarters, and the difficulties encountered in landing the stores, had caused the Nimrod to be kept longer than I had intended already. We gave our final letters and messages to the crew of the last boat, and said goodbye. Cotton, who had come south just for the trip, was among them, and never had we a more willing worker. At 10 p.m. the Nimrod's bows were pointed to the north, and she was moving rapidly away from the winter quarters with a fair wind. Within a month I hoped she would be safe in New Zealand, and her crew enjoying a well earned rest. We were all devoutly thankful that the landing of the stores had been finished at last, and that the state of the sea would no longer be a factor in our work, but it was with something of a pang that we severed our last connection with the world of men. We could hope for no word of news from civilisation until the *Nimrod* came south again in the following summer, and before that we had a good deal of difficult work to do, and some risks to face.

There was scant time for reflection, even if we had been moved that way. We turned in for a good night's rest as soon as possible after the departure of the ship, and the following morning we started digging the stores out of the ice, and transporting everything to the vicinity of the hut. It was necessary that the stores should be close by the building, partly in order that there might be no difficulty in getting what goods we wanted during the winter, and partly because we would require all the protection that we could get from the cold, and the cases, when piled around our little dwelling, would serve to keep off the wind. We hoped, as soon as the stores had all been placed in position, to make a start with the scientific observations that were to be an important part of the work of the expedition.

CHAPTER 7

Winter quarters at Cape Royds
Outside and inside

View from winter quarters over the Sound and the Western
Mountains: Field for scientific work: The hut completed
and out-buildings erected: Interior arrangements:
The bed question: Acetylene gas-plant

The next four or five days were spent in using pick and shovel and iron crowbars on the envelope of ice that covered our cases, corners of which only peeped out from the mass. The whole had the appearance of a piece of the sweet known as almond rock, and there was as much difficulty in getting the cases clear of the ice as would be experienced if one tried to separate almonds from that sticky conglomerate without injury. Occasionally the breaking out of a case would disclose another which could be easily extracted, but more often each case required the pick or crowbars. A couple of earnest miners might be seen delving and hewing the ice off a case, of which only the corner could be seen, and after ten minutes' hard work it would be hauled up, and the stencilled mark of its contents exposed to view. Brocklehurst took great interest in the recovery of the chocolate, and during this work took charge of one particular case which had been covered by the ice. He carried it himself up to the hut so as to be sure of its safety, and he was greeted with joy by the Professor, who recognised in the load some of his scientific instruments which were playing the part of the cuckoo in an old chocolate box. Needless to say Brocklehurst's joy was not as heartfelt as the Professor's.

After about four days' hard work at the Front Door Bay landing place, the bulk of the stores was recovered, and I think we may say that there was not much lost permanently, though, as time went on, and one or two cases that were required did not turn up, we used to wonder whether they had been left on board the ship, or lay buried under the ice. We do know for certain that our only case of beer lies to this day under the ice, and it was not until a few days before our final departure that one of the scientists of the expedition dug out some volumes of the Challenger reports, which had been intended to provide us with useful reading matter during the winter nights. A question often debated during the long, dark days was which of these stray sheep, the Challenger reports or the case of beer, any particular individual would dig for if the time and opportunity were available. In moving up the recovered stores, as soon as a load arrived within fifteen yards of the hut, where, at this time of the year, the snow ended, and the bare earth lay uncovered, the sledges were unpacked, and one party carried the stuff up to the south side of the hut, whilst the sledges returned to the landing place for more. We were now utilising the ponies every day, and they proved of great assistance in moving things to and fro. The stores on the top of the hill at Derrick Point were fortunately quite clear of snow, so we did not trouble to transport them, contenting ourselves with getting down things that were of immediate importance. Day by day we continued collecting our scattered goods, and within ten days after the departure of the ship we had practically everything handy to the hut, excepting the coal. The labour had been both heavy and fertile in minor accidents. Most of us at one time or another had wounds and bruises to be attended to by Marshall, who was kept busy part of every day dressing the injuries. Adams was severely cut in handling some iron-bound cases, and I managed to jam my fingers in the motorcar. The annoying feature about these simple wounds was the length of time it took for them to heal in our special circumstances. The irritation seemed to be more pronounced if any of the earth got into the wound, so we always took care, after our first experiences, to go at once to Marshall for treatment, when the skin was broken. The day after the ship left we laid in a supply of fresh meat for the winter, killing about a hundred penguins and burying them in a snow drift close to the hut. By February 28 we were practically in a position to feel contented with ourselves, and to look further afield and explore the neighbourhood of our winter quarters.

From the door of our hut, which faced the north-west, we commanded a splendid view of the sound and the western mountains. Right in front of us, at our door, lay a small lake, which came to be known as Pony Lake; to the left of that was another sheet of ice that became snow-covered in the autumn, and it was here in the dark months that we exercised the ponies, and also ourselves. Six times up and down the 'Green Park', as it was generally called, made a mile, and it was here, before darkness came on, that we played hockey and soccer. To the left of Green Park was a gentle slope leading down between two cliffs to the sea, and ending in a little bay known as Dead Horse Bay. On either side of this valley lay the penguin rookery, the slopes being covered with guano, and during the fairly high temperatures that held sway up to April, the smell from these deserted quarters of the penguins was extremely unpleasant. On coming out of the hut one had only to go around the corner of the building in order to catch a glimpse of Mount Erebus, which lay directly behind us. Its summit was about fifteen miles from our winter quarters, but its slopes and foothills commenced within three-quarters of a mile of the hut. Our view was cut off in all directions from the east to the south-west by the ridge at the head of the valley where the hut stood. On ascending this ridge, one looked over the bay to the south-east, where lay Cape Barne. To the right was Flagstaff Point, and to the left lay, at the head of the Bay, the slopes of Erebus. There were many localities which became favourite places for walks. Sandy Beach, about a mile away to the north-west of the hut, was generally the goal of anyone taking exercise, when the uncertainty of the weather warned us against venturing further afield, and while the dwindling light still permitted us to go so far. It was here that we sometimes exercised the ponies, and they much enjoyed rolling in the soft sand. The beach was formed of black volcanic sand, blown from the surrounding hills, and later on the pressed up ice, which had been driven ashore by the southward movement of the pack, also became covered with the wind-borne dust and sand. The coastline from Flagstaff Point right round to Horse Shoe Bay, on the north side of Cape Royds, was jagged and broken up. At some points ice cliffs, in others bare rocks, jutted out into the sea, and here and there small beaches composed of volcanic sand were interposed. Our local scenery, though not on a grand scale, loomed large in the light of the moon as the winter nights lengthened. Fantastic shadows made the heights appear greater and the valleys deeper, casting a spell of unreality around the place, which never seemed to touch it by day. The greatest height of any of the numerous sharp-pointed spurs of volcanic rock was not more than three hundred feet, but we were infinitely better off as regards the interest and the scenery of our winter quarters than the expedition which wintered in McMurdo Sound between 1901 and 1904. Our walks amongst the hills and across the frozen lakes were a great source of health and enjoyment, and as a field of work for geologists and biologists, Cape Royds far surpassed Hut Point. The largest lake, which lay about half a mile to the north-east, was named Blue Lake, from the intensely vivid blue of the ice. This lake was peculiarly interesting to Mawson, who made the study of ice part of his work. Beyond Blue Lake, to the northward, lay Clear Lake, the deepest inland body of water in our vicinity. To the left as one looked north, close to the coast, was a circular basin which we called Coast Lake, where, when we first arrived, hundreds of skua gulls were bathing and flying about. Following the coast from this point back toward winter quarters was another body of water called Green Lake. In all these various lakes something of interest to science was discovered, and though they were quite small, they were very important to our work and in our eyes, and were a source of continuous interest to us during our stay in the vicinity. Beyond Blue Lake, to the east, rose the lower slopes of Mount Erebus, covered with ice and snow. After passing one or two ridges of volcanic rocks, there stretched a long snow plain, across which sledges could travel without having their runners torn by gravel. The slope down to Blue Lake was picked out for skiing, and it was here, in the early days, when work was over, that some of our party used to slide from the top of the slope for about two hundred feet, arriving at the bottom in a few seconds, and shooting out across the frozen surface of the lake, until brought up by the rising slope on the other side. To the north of Clear Lake the usual hills of volcanic rock separated by valleys filled more or less with snow drifts, stretched for a distance of about a mile. Beyond this lay the coast, to the right of which, looking north, was Horse Shoe Bay, about four miles from our winter quarters; further to the right of the northern end of Cape Royds the slopes of Erebus were reached again. From the northern coast a good view could be obtained of Cape Bird, and from the height we could see Castle Rock to the south, distant about eighteen miles from the winter quarters. The walk from Hut Point to Castle Rock was familiar to us on the last expedition. It seemed much nearer than it really was, for in the Antarctic the distances are most deceptive, curiously different effects being produced by the variations of light and the distortion of mirage.

As time went on we felt more and more satisfied with our location, for there was work of interest for everyone. The Professor and Priestley saw open before them a new chapter of geological history of great interest, for Cape Royds was a happier hunting-ground for the geologist than was Hut Point. Hundreds of erratic boulders lay scattered on the slopes of the adjacent hills, and from these the geologists hoped to learn something of the past conditions of Ross Island. For Murray, the lakes were a fruitful field for new research. The gradually deepening bay was full of marine animal life, the species varying with the depth, and here also an inexhaustible treasure ground stretched before the biologist. Adams, the meteorologist, could not complain, for Mount Erebus was in full view of the meteorological station, and this fortunate proximity to Erebus and its smoke cloud led, in a large measure, to important results in this branch. For the physicist the structure of the ice, varying on various lakes, the different salts in the earth, and the magnetic conditions of the rocks claimed investigation, though, indeed, the magnetic nature of the rocks proved a disadvantage in carrying out magnetic observations, for the delicate instruments were often affected by the local attraction. From every point of view I must say that we were extremely fortunate in the winter quarters to which we had been led by the state of the sea ice, for no other spot could have afforded more scope for work and exercise.

Before we had been ten days ashore the hut was practically completed, though it was over a month before it had been worked up from the state of an empty shell to attain the fully furnished appearance it assumed after everyone had settled down and arranged his belongings. It was not a very spacious dwelling for the accommodation of fifteen persons, but our narrow quarters were warmer than if the hut had been larger. The coldest part of the house when we first lived in it was undoubtedly the floor, which was formed of inch tongue-and-groove boarding, but was not double lined. There was a space of about four feet under the hut at the north-west end, the other end resting practically on the ground, and it was obvious to us that as long as this space remained we would suffer from the cold, so we decided to make an airlock of the area under the hut. To this end we decided to build a wall round the south-east and southerly sides, which were to windward, with the bulk of the provision cases. To make certain that no air would penetrate from these sides we built the first two or three tiers of cases a little distance out from the walls of the hut, pouring in volcanic earth until no gaps could be seen, and the earth was level with the cases; then the rest of the stores were piled up to a height of six or seven feet. This accounted for one side and one end. On either side of the porch two other buildings were gradually erected. One, built out of biscuit cases, the roof covered with felt and canvas, was a storeroom for Wild, who looked after the issue of all food stuffs. The building on the other side of the porch was a much more ambitious affair, and was built by Mawson, to serve as a chemical and physical laboratory. It was destined, however, to be used solely as a storeroom, for the temperature within its walls was practically the same as that of the outside air, and the warm, moist atmosphere rushing out from the hut covered everything inside this storeroom with fantastic ice crystals.

The lee side of the hut ultimately became the wall of the stables, for we decided to keep the ponies sheltered during the winter. During the blizzard we experienced on February 18, and for the three following days, the animals suffered somewhat, mainly owing to the knocking about they had received whilst on the way south in the ship. We found that a shelter, not necessarily warmed to a high temperature, would keep the ponies in better condition than if they were allowed to stand in the open, and by February 9 the stable building was complete. A double row of cases of maize, built at one end to a height of five feet eight inches, made one end, and then the longer side of the shelter was composed of bales of fodder. A wide plank at the other end was cemented into the ground, and a doorway left. Over all this was stretched the canvas tarpaulin which we had previously used in the fodder hut, and with planks and battens on both sides to make it windproof, the stable was complete. A wire rope was stretched from one end to the other on the side nearest to the hut, and the ponies' head ropes were made fast to this. The first night that they were placed in the stable there

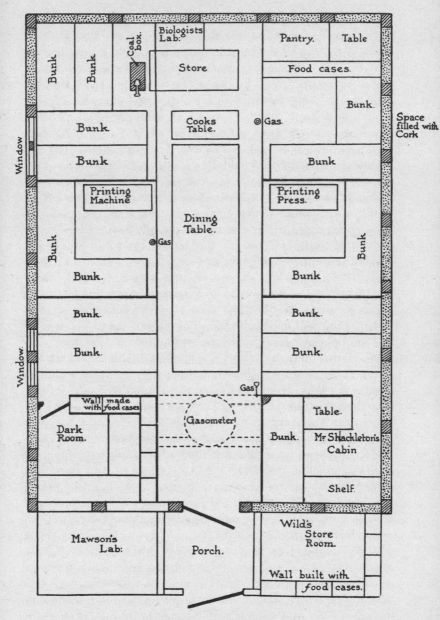

Plan of the hut at Winter Quarters

was little rest for any of us, and during the night some of the animals broke loose and returned to their valley. Shortly afterwards Grisi, one of the most high-spirited of the lot, pushed his head through a window, so the lower halves of the hut windows had to be boarded up. The first strong breeze we had shook the roof of the stable so much that we expected every moment it would blow away, so after the gale all the sledges except those which were in use were laid on the top of the stable, and a stout rope passed from one end to the other. The next snowfall covered the sledges and made a splendid roof, upon which no subsequent wind had any effect. Later, another addition was made to the dwellings outside the hut in the shape of a series of doghouses for those animals about to pup, and as that was not an uncommon thing down there, the houses were constantly occupied.

On the south-east side of the hut a storeroom was built, constructed entirely of cases, and roofed with hammocks sewn together. Here we kept the tool chest, shoemaker's outfit, which was in constant requisition, and any general stores that had to be issued at stated times. The first heavy blizzard found this place out, and after the roof had been blown off, the wall fell down, and we had to organise a party, when the weather got fine, to search for anything that might be lost, such as mufflers, woollen helmets, and so on. Some things were blown more than a mile away. I found a Russian felt boot, weighing five pounds, lying three-quarters of a mile from the crate in which it had been stowed, and it must have had a clear run in the air for the whole of this distance, for there was not a scratch on the leather; if it had been blown along the rocks, which lay in the way, the leather would certainly have been scratched all over. The chimney, which was an iron pipe, projecting two or three feet above the roof of the hut, and capped by a cowl, was let through the roof at the south-east end, and secured by numerous rope stays supporting it at every point from which the wind could blow.

We were quite free from the trouble of down drafts or choking with snow, such as had been of common occurrence in the large hut on the *Discovery* expedition. Certainly the revolving cowl blew off during the first blizzard, and this happened again in the second, so we took the hint and left it off for good, without detriment, as it happened, to the efficiency of the stove.

The dog kennels were placed close to the porch of the hut, but only three of the dogs were kept constantly chained up. The meteorological station was on the weather side of the hut on the top of a small ridge, about twenty feet above the hut and forty feet above sea level, and a natural path led to it. Adams laid it out, and the regular readings of the instruments began on March 22. The foundation of the thermometer screen consisted of a heavy wooden case resting on rocks. The case was three-quarters filled with rock, and around the outside were piled more blocks of kenyte; the crevices between them were filled with volcanic earth on to which water was poured, the result being a structure as rigid as the ground itself. On each side of the box a heavy upright was secured by the rocks inside the case and by bolts at the sides, and to these uprights the actual meteorological screen, one of the Stevenson pattern and of standard size, was bolted. As readings of the instruments were to be taken day and night at intervals of two hours, and as it was quite possible that the weather might be so thick that a person might be lost in making his way between the screen and the hut, a line was rigged up on posts, which were cemented into the ground by ice, so that in the thickest weather the observer could be sure of finding his way by following this very substantial clue.

The inside of the hut was not long in being fully furnished, and a great change it was from the bare shell of our first days of occupancy. The first thing done was to peg out a space for each individual, and we saw that the best plan would be to have the space allotted in sections, allowing two persons to share one cubicle. This space for two men amounted to six feet six inches in length and seven feet in depth from the wall of the hut toward the centre. There were seven of these cubicles, and a space for the leader of the expedition; thus providing for the fifteen who made up the shore party. The accompanying photographs will give an idea of the hut as finished. One of the most important parts of the interior construction was the darkroom for the photographers. We were very short of wood, so cases of bottled fruit, which had to be kept inside the hut to prevent them freezing, were utilised for building the walls. The darkroom was constructed in the left-hand corner of the hut as one entered, and the fruit cases were turned with their lids facing out, so that the contents could be removed without demolishing the walls of the building. These cases, as they

were emptied, were turned into lockers, where we stowed our
spare gear and so obtained more room in the little cubicles. The
interior of the dark room was fitted up by Mawson and the Professor. The sides and roof were lined with the felt left over after the
hut was completed. Mawson made the fittings complete in every
detail, with shelves, tanks, etc., and the result was as good as
anyone could desire in the circumstances.

On the other side of the doorway, opposite the darkroom, was
my room, six feet long, seven feet deep, built of boards and roofed,
the roof being seven feet above the floor. I lined the walls inside
with canvas, and the bed place was constructed of fruit boxes,
which, when emptied, served, like those outside, for lockers. My
room contained the bulk of our library, the chronometers, the
chronometer watches, barograph, and the electric recording thermometer; there was ample room for a table, and the whole made a
most comfortable cabin. On the roof we stowed those of our
scientific instruments which were not in use, such as theodolites,
spare thermometers, dip circles, etc. The gradual accumulation of
weight produced a distinct sag in the roof, which sometimes seemed
to threaten collapse as I sat inside, but no notice was taken, and
nothing happened. On the roof of the darkroom we stowed all our
photographic gear and our few cases of wine, which were only
drawn upon on special occasions, such as Midwinter Day. The
acetylene gas plant was set up on a platform between my room and
the darkroom. We had tried to work it from the porch, but the
temperature was so low there that the water froze and the gas would
not come, so we shifted it inside the hut, and had no further trouble.
Four burners, including a portable standard light in my room, gave
ample illumination. The simplicity and portability of the apparatus
and the high efficiency of the light represented the height of luxury
under polar conditions and did much to render our sojourn more
tolerable than would have been possible in earlier days. The particular form that we used was supplied by Mr Morrison, who had
been chief engineer on the *Morning* on her voyage to the relief of
the *Discovery*. The only objectionable feature, due to having the
generating plant in our living room was the unpleasant smell given
off when the carbide tanks were being recharged, but we soon got
used to this, though the daily changing always drew down strong
remarks on the unlucky head of Day – who had the acetylene plant

especially under his charge. He did not have a hitch with it all the time. Flexible steel tubes were carried from the tank, and after being wound around the beams of the roof, served to suspend the lights at the required positions.

A long ridge of rope wire was stretched from one end of the hut to the other on each side, seven feet out from the wall; then at intervals of six feet another wire was brought out from the wall of the hut, and made fast to the fore and aft wire. These lines marked the boundaries of the cubicles, and sheets of duck sewn together hung from them, making a good division. Blankets were served out to hang in the front of the cubicle, in case the inhabitants wanted at any time to 'sport their oak'. As each of the cubicles had distinctive features in the furnishing and general design, especially as regards beds, it is worthwhile to describe them fully. This is not so trivial a matter as it may appear to some readers, for during the winter months the inside of the hut was the whole inhabited world to us. The wall of Adams and Marshall's cubicle, which was next to my room, was fitted with shelves made out of Venesta cases, and there was so much neatness and order about this apartment that it was known by the address, 'No. 1 Park Lane'. In front of the shelves hung little gauze curtains, tied up with blue ribbon, and the literary tastes of the occupants could be seen at a glance from the bookshelves. In Adams's quarter the period of the French Revolution and the Napoleonic era filled most of his bookshelves, though a complete edition of Dickens came in a good second. Marshall's shelves were stocked with bottles of medicine, medical works, and some general literature. The dividing curtain of duck was adorned by Marston with life-sized coloured drawings of Napoleon and Joan of Arc. Adams and Marshall did Sandow exercises daily, and their example was followed by other men later on, when the darkness and bad weather made open air work difficult. The beds of this particular cubicle were the most comfortable in the hut, but took a little longer to rig up at night than most of the others. This disadvantage was more than compensated for by the free space gained during the day, and by permission of the owners it was used as consulting room, dispensary, and operating theatre. The beds consisted of bamboos lashed together for extra strength, to which strips of canvas were attached, so that each bed looked like a stretcher. The wall end rested on stout cleats screwed on to the side of the hut, the other ends on chairs, and so supported, the occupants slept soundly and comfortably.

The next cubicle on the same side was occupied by Marston and Day, and as the former was the artist and the latter the general handy man of the expedition, one naturally found an ambitious scheme of decoration. The shelves were provided with beading, and the Venesta boxes were stained brown. This idea was copied from 'No. 1 Park Lane', where they had stained all their walls with Condy's Fluid. Marston and Day's cubicle was known as 'The Gables', presumably from the gabled appearance of the shelves. Solid wooden beds, made out of old packing cases and upholstered with wood shavings covered with blankets, made very comfortable couches, one of which could be pushed during meal times out of the way of the chairs. The artist's curtain was painted to represent a fireplace and mantelpiece in civilisation; a cheerful fire burned in the grate, and a bunch of flowers stood on the mantelpiece. The dividing curtain between it and No. 1 Park Lane, on the other side of the cubicle, did not require to be decorated, for the colour of Joan of Arc, and also portions of Napoleon, had oozed through the canvas. In 'The Gables' was set up the lithographic press, which was used for producing pictures for the book which was printed at our winter quarters.

The next cubicle on the same side belonged to Armytage and Brocklehurst. Here everything in the way of shelves and fittings was very primitive. I lived in Brocklehurst's portion of the cubicle for two months, as he was laid up in my room, and before I left it I constructed a bed of empty petrol cases. The smell from these for the first couple of nights after rigging them up was decidedly unpleasant, but it disappeared after a while. Next to Brocklehurst's and Armytage's quarters came the pantry. The division between the cubicle and the pantry consisted of a tier of cases, making a substantial wall between the food and the heads of the sleepers. The pantry, bakery, and storeroom, all combined, measured six feet by three, not very spacious, certainly, but sufficient to work in. The far end of the hut constituted the other wall of the pantry, and was lined with shelves up to the slope of the roof. These shelves were continued along the wall behind the stove, which stood about four feet out from the end of the house, and an erection of wooden battens and burlap or sacking concealed the biological laboratory. The space taken up by this important department was four feet by four, but lack of ground area was made up for by the shelves, which contained dozens of bottles soon to be filled with Murray's biological captures.

Beyond the stove, facing the pantry, was Mackay and Roberts's cubicle, the main feature of which was a ponderous shelf, on which rested mostly socks and other light articles, the only thing of weight being our gramophone and records. The bunks were somewhat feeble imitations of those belonging to No. 1 Park Lane, and the troubles that the owners went through before finally getting them into working order afforded the rest of the community a good deal of amusement. I can see before me now the triumphant face of Mackay, as he called all hands around to see his design. The inhabitants of No. 1 Park Lane pointed out that the bamboo was not a rigid piece of wood, and that when Mackay's weight came on it the middle would bend and the ends would jump off the supports unless secured. Mackay undressed before a critical audience, and he got into his bag and expatiated on the comfort and luxury he was experiencing, so different to the hard boards he had been lying on for months. Roberts was anxious to try his couch, which was constructed on the same principle, and the audience were turning away disappointed at not witnessing a catastrophe, when suddenly a crash was heard, followed by a strong expletive. Mackay's bed was half on the ground, one end of it resting at a most uncomfortable angle. Laughter and pointed remarks as to his capacity for making a bed were nothing to him; he tried three times that night to fix it up, but at last had to give it up for a bad job. In due time he arranged fastenings, and after that he slept in comfort.

Between this cubicle and the next there was no division, neither party troubling about the matter. The result was that the four men were constantly at war regarding alleged encroachments on their ground. Priestley, who was long-suffering, and who occupied the cubicle with Murray, said he did not mind a chair or a volume of the *Encyclopedia Britannica* being occasionally deposited on him while he was asleep, but that he thought it was a little too strong to drop wet boots, newly arrived from the stables, on top of his belongings. Priestley and Murray had no floor space at all in their cubicle, as their beds were built of empty dog biscuit boxes. A division of boxes separated the two sleeping places, and the whole cubicle was garnished on Priestley's side with bits of rock, ice axes, hammers and chisels, and on Murray's with biological requisites.

Next came one of the first cubicles that had been built. Joyce and Wild occupied the 'Rogues' Retreat', a painting of two very tough characters drinking beer out of pint mugs, with the inscription *The Rogues' Retreat* painted underneath, adorning the entrance to the den. The couches in this house were the first to be built, and those of the opposite dwelling, The Gables, were copied from their design. The first bed had been built in Wild's storeroom for secrecy's sake; it was to burst upon the view of everyone, and to create mingled feelings of admiration and envy, admiration for the splendid design, envy of the unparalleled luxury provided by it. However, in building it, the designer forgot the size of the doorway he had to take it through, and it had ignominiously to be sawn in half before it could be passed out of the storeroom into the hut. The printing press and type case for the polar paper occupied one corner of this cubicle.

The next and last compartment was the dwelling place of the Professor and Mawson. It would be difficult to do justice to the picturesque confusion of this compartment; one hardly likes to call it untidy, for the things that covered the bunks by daytime could be placed nowhere else conveniently. A miscellaneous assortment of cameras, spectroscopes, thermometers, microscopes, electrometers, and the like lay in profusion on the blankets. Mawson's bed consisted of his two boxes, in which he had stowed his scientific apparatus on the way down, and the Professor's bed was made out of kerosene cases. Everything in the way of tin cans or plug-topped, with straw wrappers belonging to the fruit bottles, was collected by these two scientific men. Mawson, as a rule, put his possessions in his storeroom outside, but the Professor, not having any retreat like that, made a pile of glittering tins and coloured wrappers at one end of his bunk, and the heap looked like the nest of the Australian bower bird. The straw and the tins were generally cleared away when the Professor and Priestley went in for a day's packing of geological specimens; the straw wrappers were utilised for wrapping around the rocks and the tins were filled with paper wrapped around the more delicate geological specimens. The name given, though not by the owners, to this cubicle was 'The Pawn Shop', for not only was there always a heterogeneous mass of things on the bunks, but the wall of the darkroom and the wall of the hut at this spot could not be seen for the multitude of cases ranged as shelves and filled with a varied assortment of notebooks and instruments.

In order to give as much free space as possible in the centre of the hut we had the table so arranged that it could be hoisted up over our heads after meals were over. This gave ample room for the various carpentering and engineering efforts that were constantly going on. Murray built the table out of the lids of packing cases, and though often scrubbed, the stencilling on the cases never came out. We had no tablecloth, but this was an advantage, for a well-scrubbed table had a cleaner appearance than would be obtained with such washing as could be done in an Antarctic laundry. The legs of the table were detachable, being after the fashion of trestles, and the whole affair, when meals were over, was slung by a rope at each end about eight feet from the floor. At first we used to put the boxes containing knives, forks, plates, and bowls on top of the table before hauling it up, but after these had fallen on the unfortunate head of the person trying to get them down, we were content to keep them on the floor.

I had been very anxious as regards the stove, the most important part of the hut equipment, when I heard that, after the blizzard that kept me on board the *Nimrod,* the temperature of the hut was below zero, and that socks put to dry in the baking ovens came out as damp as ever the following morning. My anxiety was dispelled after the stove had been taken to pieces again, for it was found that eight important pieces of its structure had not been put in. As soon as this omission was rectified the stove acted splendidly, and the makers deserve our thanks for the particular apparatus they picked out as suitable for us. The stove was put to a severe test, for it was kept going day and night for over nine months without once being out for more than ten minutes, when occasion required it to be cleaned. It supplied us with sufficient heat to keep the temperature of the hut sixty to seventy degrees above the outside air. Enough bread could be baked to satisfy our whole hungry party of fifteen every day; three hot meals a day were also cooked, and water melted from ice at a temperature of perhaps twenty degrees below zero in sufficient quantity to afford as much as we required for ourselves, and to water the ponies twice a day, and all this work was done on a consumption not exceeding five hundredweight of coal per week. After testing the stove by running it on an accurately measured amount of coal for a month, we were reassured about our coal supply being sufficient to carry us through the winter right on to sledging time.

As the winter came on and the light grew faint outside, the hut became more and more like a workshop, and it seems strange to me now, looking back to those distant days, to remember the amount of trouble and care that was taken to furnish and beautify what was only to be a temporary home. One of our many kind friends had sent us a number of pictures, which were divided between the various cubicles, and these brightened up the place wonderfully. During our first severe blizzard, the hut shook and trembled so that every moment we expected the whole thing to carry away, and there is not the slightest shadow of a doubt that if we had been located in the open, the hut and everything in it would have been torn up and blown away. Even with our sheltered position I had to lash the chronometers to the shelf in my room, for they were apt to be shaken off when the walls trembled in the gale. When the storm was over we put a stout wire cable over the hut, burying the ends in the ground and freezing them in, so as to afford additional security in case heavier weather was in store for us in the future.

Divine service was held in the hut on Sundays during the winter months.

CHAPTER 8

Sledging equipment

Sledges: Cookers: Tents: Sleeping bags: Clothing: Ponies:
Dogs and food: Acknowledgment of supplies presented
to the expedition by various firms

I will now give some details of the sledging outfits used by the various expeditions that left our winter quarters. The first, and one of the most important of the items was, of course, the sledge, though, indeed, everything taken on a sledge journey is absolutely essential; one does not load up odds and ends on the chance of their proving useful, for the utmost reduction of weight compatible with efficiency is the first and last thing for the polar explorer to aim at.

The sledge which we used is the outcome of the experience of many former explorers, but it is chiefly due to Nansen that it has become the very useful vehicle that it is at the present day. On the *Discovery* expedition we had sledges of various lengths, seven feet, nine feet, eleven feet and twelve feet. Our experience on that occasion showed that the eleven-foot sledge was the best for all-round use, but I had taken with me a certain number of twelve-foot sledges as being possibly more suitable for pony traction. A good sledge for Antarctic or Arctic travelling must be rigid in its upright and cross bars, and yet give to uneven surfaces, so that in travelling over sastrugi the strain will not come on the whole of the sledge. A well-constructed sledge, travelling over an uneven surface, appears to have an undulating, snake-like movement, and the attainment of this suppleness without interfering with the strength of the structure as a whole is the main point to be aimed at; in our case there was nothing wanting in this respect. The wooden runners were about four inches wide and made of hickory, split from the tree with the grain of the wood and not sawn. Many pieces were inspected and rejected and only those passed as perfect were used. This method of preparing the runners, it can easily be seen, allows much greater scope for bending than would be the case if the wood were sawn regardless of the run of the grain. In pulling the sledge the direction of the grain on the snow surface has to be observed, and it is wonderful what a difference it makes whether one is pulling with or against the grain of the runner. The second point to consider is the height of the framework of the sledge above the surface of the snow. Naturally, with a low framework there is less chance of the sledgeload capsizing when passing over rough ground, and the aim of the explorer is therefore to keep the load as low as possible on the sledge. It has been found that a clearance of six inches is ample in all ordinary circumstances, so the uprights of our sledges were only about six inches high. These uprights were fastened at intervals into holes on the upper side of the runners, and instead of being fastened on the under-side of the latter, other holes were bored in the ridge of the upper side and raw hide lashings passed through them and through the upright. Cross-pieces were fastened by a sort of dovetailing process, supplemented by marlin lashings, and the angle made by the vertical upright and horizontal cross-piece was crossed by a short iron stay. This junction of cross-piece and upright was the only absolutely rigid part of the whole sledge. Every other portion of a good sledge gives somewhat as it takes up the various strains, and it entirely depends on good workmanship and sailorlike lashings whether, on the strain being removed, the sledge returns to its normal shape or is permanently distorted. Two long runners or bearers, about an inch square, rested on the uprights, and cross-pieces projecting the whole length of the sledge and fastened by extra strong marlin lashings, covered with leather to protect them from the chafing of the equipment stowed on top, formed a sort of platform on which the stores were placed. The fore end of the sledge had a bow of wood, forming practically a semicircle, the two ends being fastened to the slightly upturned ends of the runners. The upper bearers were pressed down, and also lashed to this bow. This upturning at the forward end of the sledge allowed for the meeting of unequal surfaces, and the shape of the bow was intended to prevent the ends of the sledge being driven into snow or ice obstructions. The rear end of the sledge was also slightly turned up, and the top bearers bent down and lashed to the bare ends. Of course, a bow was not necessary at that end. At each end of the sledge, made fast round the first two uprights and the last two on both sides, were two pieces of alpine rope, which combines strength with lightness. The bight of this rope was formed into a becket, and by this means a toggle attached to the sledge harness could readily be put in. When sledges are running in line, one behind the other, particular care has to be taken with these ropes, so that the tracks of the second sledge coincide with the first. By doing this the amount of friction on the runners of the second sledge is greatly reduced, for the forward sledge does practically all the work of breaking the trail, and the following ones run lightly over the made track. An eleven-foot sledge, fully loaded, is at its best working weight with about 650 lb. on it, but this by no means represents its actual strength capacity, for we tested ours most rigorously during the unloading of the ship, often placing over a thousand pounds' weight on a sledge without it sustaining the slightest damage. After our experience on the Barrier surface during the *Discovery* expedition, I had decided to dispense with metal runners, so only a few sets of detachable steel under runners were provided, to be used for work on ground bare of snow or on rough glacier ice. In order to fasten the stores on the sledge we riveted straps on to the bearers, and thus formed a handy and trustworthy means of fastening things with the least possible loss of time.

Another vitally important article of equipment for the polar explorer is the cooker and cooking stove. Here again we were indebted to the practical genius of Nansen, who designed the form of cooker that is now invariably used in polar work. The stove was the ordinary 'primus', burning kerosene, vaporised in the usual way. This stove is highly efficient, and, with strict economy, one gallon of oil will last three men for ten days, allowing three hot meals per day. This economy is due, in a large measure, to the qualities of the cooker. The form we used consisted of an outer cover of aluminium drawn out of one piece, inside which was a ring-shaped vessel so designed that the heated air could circulate around it. Inside this vessel was the centre cooking pot, and these pots were all mounted on a concave plate of aluminium which fitted over the top of the primus lamp. The middle cooker was first filled with snow or ice, pressed tightly down, the lid was put on and this vessel placed inside the outer, ring-shaped cooker, which was also filled with snow; over all this apparatus the aluminium outside cover was placed, inverted. The heated gases from the stove, after heating the bottom of the centre cooker, mounted into the space between the two vessels, and were then forced down the outside of the ring-shaped cooker by the cover, finally escaping at the lower edge. Experiments showed that about 92 percent of the heat generated by the lamp was used in the cooker, a most satisfactory result, for economy in fuel is of great importance when the oil has to be carried on sledges. I did not have draw-off taps on the cookers, but they were so arranged that the boiling pot in the centre lifted in and out easily. Such was the efficiency of the cooker and stove that, in a temperature of forty or fifty degrees below zero, the snow or ice, which would be at this temperature, could be melted and a hot meal prepared within half an hour from the time the cooker was first placed on the primus. The whole apparatus, including the primus, did not weigh more than fifteen pounds. When the cooker was empty after meals, our feeding utensils were placed inside. They consisted of pannikins and spoons only. They former were made of aluminium in pairs, and fitted one into another. The outer pannikin, for holding the hot tea or cocoa, was provided with handles, and the other fitted over the top of this and was used for the more solid food. There was no 'washing up' on the march, for spoons were licked clean and pannikins scraped assiduously when sledging appetites had been developed.

The next important item was the tent. The usual unit for sledging consists of three men, and our tents were designed to contain that number. The tent cloth was thin Willesden duck, with a 'snow cloth' of thicker material round the lower edge. This snow cloth was spread out on the ground and snow or ice piled on it so that the form of the tent was like that of an inverted convolvulus. Instead of a single tent pole we used five male bamboo rods, eight feet six inches in length, fastened together at one end in a cap, over which the apex of the tent fitted. The bamboos were stretched out, and the tent was slung over the top, with the door, which took the form of a sort of spout of Burberry material, on the lee side. This Burberry spout was loose and could be tied up by being gathered together when the occupants were inside the tent, or could be left open when desired. Inside the tent was placed on the snow a circle of thick Willesden waterproof canvas to protect the sleeping bags from actual contact with the ground. The material of which the tents were constructed appeared flimsy and the bamboos were light, but one could trust them with absolute confidence to encounter successfully the fiercest blizzards of this exceptionally stormy part of the world. There was no instance of damage to a tent owing to bad weather during the expedition.

The next important item of our equipment was the sleeping bag. It has been generally assumed by polar explorers, despite our experience with the *Discovery* expedition, that it is absolutely necessary for sledge travellers to wrap themselves up in furs. We have found this to be quite unnecessary, and I think that I am justified, from my experience during two expeditions in what is, undoubtedly, a more rigorous climate than exists in the north polar regions, in stating that, except for the hands and feet, in the way of personal clothing, and the sleeping bags for camping, furs are entirely unnecessary. Our sleeping bags were made of hides of young reindeer (fur inside). The term 'bag' literally describes this portion of the sledging gear. It is a long bag, with closely sewn seams, and is entered by means of a slit at the upper end. A large sleeping bag will hold three men. We were well supplied with one-man bags.

Having considered various parts of the equipment of a sledge party, we now come to the important item of food. The appetite of a man who has just come to camp after a five hours' march in a low temperature is something that the ordinary individual at home would scarcely understand, and, indeed, the sledger himself has moments of surprise when, after finishing his ration, he feels just about as hungry as when he started.

In selecting our supplies I had based my plans on previous experience; and, for the sledging journeys I had tried to provide the maximum amount of heat-giving and flesh-forming materials, and to avoid as far as possible foods containing a large amount of moisture, which means so much dead weight to be carried. Our cuisine was not very varied, but a voracious appetite has no nice discernment and requires no sauce to make the meal palatable; indeed, all one wants is more, and this is just what cannot be allowed if a party is to achieve anything in the way of distance whilst confined to a man haulage. It is hard for a hungry man to rest content with the knowledge that the particular food he is eating contains so much nourishment as is sufficient for his needs, if at the same time he does not feel full and satisfied after the meal and if, within an hour or so, the aching void again makes itself felt, and he has to wait another five hours before he can again temporarily satisfy the craving. One of the main items of our food supply was pemmican, which consisted of the finest beef powdered with 60 percent of fat added. This is one of the staple foods in polar work, and the fat has properties specially tending to promote heat. Our pemmican for use on the long sledge journeys was obtained from Messrs. Beauvais, of Copenhagen, and was similar to the pemmican we had on the *Discovery* expedition. Biscuits are a standard food also, and in this matter I had made a departure from the example of the previous expedition. We found then that the thin wholemeal biscuits which we used in sledging work were apt to break, and it was difficult to make out the exact allowance for each day, the result being that sometimes we used up our supply for the week too early. I secured thicker biscuits, but the principal change was in the composition itself. The Plasmon Company supplied a ton of the best wholemeal biscuit, containing 25 percent of plasmon; the plasmon tended to harden the biscuit, and, as is well known, it is an excellent food. These biscuits were specially baked, and, with an allowance of one pound for each man per day, were a distinct advance on the farinaceous food of the previous expedition. This allowance, I may mention, was reduced very considerably when food began to run short on the southern and northern journeys, but we had no fault to find with the quality of the biscuits. The addition of the plasmon certainly increased their food value. Tea and cocoa were selected as our beverages for use on the march. We used tea for breakfast and lunch, and cocoa, which tends to produce sleepiness, for dinner at night. Sugar is a very valuable heat-forming substance, and our allowance of this amounted to about a third of a pound for each man for a day. We also took chocolate, cheese, and oatmeal, so that, though there was not very much variety, we felt we were getting the most nutritious food possible. We had a much more varied selection of foods at the winter quarters, and the supplies taken on the sledging journeys would be varied to some extent according to the necessities of the occasion.

The following firms presented us with food stuffs, all of which proved entirely satisfactory: Messrs. J. and J. Colman, Ltd., of Norwich: 9 tons wheat flour, ½ ton self-raising flour, ½ ton wheatmeal, 100 lb. corn flour, 84 lb. best mustard, 1¾ gross mixed mustard; Messrs. Rowntree and Co., Ltd., York: 1700 lb. Elect cocoa (28 percent of fat), 200 lb. Queen's chocolate; Messrs. Alfred Bird and Sons, Ltd., Birmingham: 120 doz. custard, baking, egg, crystal jelly, and blancmange powders; Liebig's Extract of Meat Co., Ltd., London: 'Oxo', 'Service Oxo emergency food', 'Lemco', and Fray Bentos ox tongues; Evans, Sons, Lescher and Webb, Ltd., London: 27 cases Montserrat lime juice; Messrs. Lipton, Ltd.: 350 lb. Ceylon tea.

The clothing usually worn for sledging work consisted of thick Jaeger underclothing, heavy blue pilot cloth trousers, a Jaeger pajama jacket for coat, and over this as our main protection against cold and wind, the Burberry blouse and trousers.

On the hands we wore woollen gloves and then fur mits, and on the feet several pairs of heavy woollen socks and then finnesko. Anyone feeling the texture and lightness of the Burberry material would hardly believe that it answers so well in keeping out the cold and wind and affords a complete protection, during a blizzard, against the fine drifting snow that permeates almost everything.

The head gear was a matter on which there were marked differences of opinion, but the most general method of keeping head and ears warm was to wrap a woollen muffler twice around the chin and head, thus forming protection for the ears, which are the first parts of the body to show signs of frostbite; the muffler was then brought round the neck, and over the muffler was pulled a fleecy travelling cap, a woollen helmet, something like an old-time helmet without the visor. If a blizzard were blowing, the muffler was discarded, the helmet put on, and over this the Burberry helmet, which has a stiff flap in front that can be buttoned into a funnel shape. The sledge traveller thus equipped could be assured that his features and body would be exempt from frostbite under all ordinary circumstances. In very low temperatures, or with a moderately low temperature and a breeze, it was necessary, occasionally, to inspect each others' faces for the sign of frostbite; if the white patch denoting this was visible, it had to be attended to at once.

In considering the various methods of haulage in the Antarctic the experience of the National Antarctic Expedition proved of very great value. The equipment, as far as the sledges and harness, etc., were concerned, was excellent — but this expedition was dependent on dogs for haulage purposes, and the use of these animals on the Barrier was not at all successful. Only twenty dogs were taken with the *Discovery,* and the trouble they gave and their eventual collapse and failure are matters of common knowledge amongst those interested in Antarctic exploration. The knowledge I gained of the Barrier surface on that occasion suggested to me the feasibility of using ponies for traction purposes, for I had heard that in Siberia and Northern Manchuria ponies of a peculiarly hardy and sturdy stock did excellent work in hauling sledges and carrying packs over snow and ice at very low temperatures and under very severe weather conditions.

It seems to be generally assumed that a Manchurian pony can drag a sledge over a broken trail at the rate of twenty to thirty miles a day, pulling not less than twelve hundred pounds. It was a risk to take ponies from the far north through the tropics and then across two thousand miles of stormy sea on a very small ship, but I felt that if it could be done it would be well worth the trouble, for, compared with the dog, the pony is a far more efficient animal, one pony doing the work of at least ten dogs on the food allowance for ten dogs, and travelling a longer distance in a day.

We established ourselves at the winter quarters with eight ponies, but unfortunately we lost four of them within a month of our arrival. The loss was due, in the case of three of the four, to the fact that they were picketed when they first landed on sandy ground, and it was not noticed that they were eating the sand. I had neglected to see that the animals had a supply of salt given to them, and as they found a saline flavour in the volcanic sand under their feet, due to the fact that the blizzards had sprayed all the land near the shore with sea water, they ate it at odd moments. All the ponies seem to have done this, but some were more addicted to the habit than the others. Several of them became ill, and we were quite at a loss to account for the trouble until Sandy died. Then a post-mortem examination revealed the fact that his stomach contained many pounds of sand, and the cause of the illness of the other ponies became apparent. We shifted them at once from the place where they were picketed, so that they could get no more sand, and gave them what remedial treatment lay in our power, but two more died in spite of all our efforts. The loss of the fourth pony was due to poisoning. The Manchurian ponies will eat anything at all that can be chewed, and this particular animal seems to have secured some shavings in which chemicals had been packed. The post-mortem examination showed that there were distinct signs of corrosive poisoning. The losses were a matter of deep concern to us.

We were left with four ponies, Quan, Socks, Grisi, and Chinaman, and it is a rather curious fact that the survivors were the white or light-coloured animals, while disaster had befallen all the dark animals. The four ponies were very precious in our eyes, and they were watched and guarded with keen attention.

During the winter months those of us who generally took the ponies out for exercise got to learn the different traits and character of each individual animal. Every one of them seemed to possess more cunning and sense than the ordinary broken-in horse at home, and this cunning, when put into practice to gain any end of their own, was a constant source of petty annoyance to us. Quan was the worst offender, his particular delight being to bite through his head rope and attack the bales of fodder stacked behind him; then, when we put a chain on to prevent this, he deliberately rattled it against the side of the hut, which kept us awake. He had at first suffered from eating sand, and we had to use great care to prevent him getting at it again, he being greatly addicted to the practice; if he were given the smallest opportunity down would go his head and he would be crunching a mouthful of the loose volcanic material.

Grisi was our best-looking pony, with a very pretty action and in colour a dapple grey; his conduct in the stables, however, was not friendly to the other ponies and we had to build him a separate stall in the far corner, as on the slightest provocation he would lash out with his hind feet. Socks was a pretty little pony, shaped something like a miniature Clydesdale, very willing to work and always very fiery. The last of our remaining ponies, Chinaman, was a strong beast, sulky in appearance, but in reality one of the best of the horses; he also had a penchant for biting through his lead rope, but a chain stopped this. When we first landed we had an idea of not building a stable, as information from people in Siberia suggested that the ponies were able to resist cold unsheltered, but after the first blizzard it was quite obvious that if they were to keep any sort of condition it would be necessary to stable them. A little army of pups used to sleep in the stables during the cold weather, and if by any means a pony got adrift, they at once surrounded him, barking furiously, and the noise conveyed to the night watchman that the outside watchers had observed something wrong. I remember one night that Grisi got free and dashed out of the stables, followed by the whole party of pups, who rounded him up on the Green Park, and after a struggle Mackay secured the truant and brought him back, the dogs following with an air of pride as though conscious of having done their duty.

We had been able to obtain only nine dogs,* five bitches and four dogs, but so prolific were they that before midwinter we had a young family of nine pups, five of these being born on the *Nimrod*. There were many more births, but most of the puppies came to an untimely end, there being a marked difference between the mothers as regards maternal instincts. Gwendoline, known as the 'mad bitch', took no care at all of her pups, whilst Daisy not only mothered her own but also a surviving puppy belonging to Gwen, which was taken from her when the culpable carelessness she had exhibited in the rearing of her offspring had resulted in the death of the remainder. The younger pups born at winter quarters did not attain the same size when grown up as did Possum's pups, born on the *Nimrod*. This may be due either to the very cold world they were born into or to the fact that their mothers were much smaller than Possum. The old dogs that we brought were kept tied up except when out for exercise or training in a sledge, for not only did they chase and kill penguins when we had these birds with us, and hunt placid, stupid Weddell seals, but two of the best dogs had a violent antipathy toward each other, and more than once fierce fights took place in consequence. Tripp, one of our dogs, was pure white in colour, and was a fine upstanding beast of a very affectionate disposition. Adams looked after Tripp, taking him for his sledge-training, whilst Marshall fancied Scamp, who

* We were agreeably surprised with these dogs, for it must be remembered that their forebears had not lived under polar conditions since 1899, and that none of the animals had experienced Antarctic weather, nor had they been trained for the work they had to perform on the ice.

was an older dog, more set in his bones and with a black-and-white coat. It was between these two that the battles raged, and I think there was little to choose between them as far as strength and courage were concerned.

The presence of the dogs around winter quarters and on our walks was very cheerful, and gave a homelike feeling to the place, and our interest in the pups was always fresh, for as they gradually grew up each one developed characteristics and peculiarities of its own. Names were given to them regardless of their sex. Roland, for example, did not belong to the sterner sex, and was in her earlier days a very general favourite. She had a habit of watching for the door to be opened, and then launching herself, a white furry ball, into the midst of the party in the hut. Ambrose, a great big sleepy dog, was so named by Adams, perhaps owing to his portly proportions, which might bear resemblance to the well-favoured condition of a monk.

All the pups were white, or would have been white if some of them had not elected to sleep in the dustbin where the warm ashes were thrown at night time; indeed, the resting places these little creatures found were varied and remarkable. In cold weather they always gravitated to the light and heat of the stables, but if the temperature was not much below zero, they slept outside, three or four bundled together inside a cork bale, another squeezed into an empty tin, another in the dustbin, and so on. Most of them learned by sad experience the truth of the ancient words!

> Such are the perils that environ
> The man who meddles with cold iron,

for sometimes an agonising wail would proceed from a puppy and the poor little beast would be found with its tongue frozen fast to a tin in which it had been searching for some succulent remains. I have mentioned the puppies' usefulness in keeping watch on the ponies. They did the same service as regards the older dogs, which were tied up, for if by chance one of these dogs got adrift, he was immediately pursued by a howling mob of puppies; when the larger puppies were eventually chained up, the smaller ones watched them, too, with jealous eye. After enjoying some months of freedom, it seemed to be a terrible thing to the young dogs when first a collar was put on and their freedom was taken from them, and even less did they enjoy the experience of being taken to the sledge and there taught to pull.

Our experience on the *Discovery* expedition, specially during the long southern journey when we had so much trouble with our mixed crowd of dogs, rather prejudiced me against these animals as a means of traction, and we only took them as a standby in the event of the ponies breaking down. Since we were reduced to four ponies, it became necessary to consider the dogs as a possible factor in our work, and so their training was important. Peary's account of his expeditions shows that in the Arctic regions dogs have been able to traverse long distances very quickly. In one instance over ninety miles were accomplished in twenty-three hours, but this evidently had been done on smooth sea ice or on the smooth glaciated surface of the land: such a feat would be impossible on the Antarctic Barrier surface.

CHAPTER 9

The Conquest of Mount Erebus

March 5: Party starts from winter quarters to ascend Mount Erebus:
Camp 2750 ft. above sea level: March 6, altitude 5630 ft. and depot
made: March 7, Fierce blizzard, Brocklehurst badly frostbitten:
March 8, camp 11,400 ft.: March 9, highest point reached
13,370 ft.: Descent safely accomplished

The arrangement of all the details relating to settling in our winter quarters, the final touches to the hut, the building of the pony stables and the meteorological screen, and the collection of stores, engaged our attention up to March 3. Then we began to seek some outlet for our energies that would be useful in advancing the cause of science, and the work of the expedition. I was very anxious to make a depot to the south for the furtherance of our southern journey in the following summer, but the sheet of open water that intervened between us and Hut Point forbade all progress in that direction, neither was it possible for us to make a journey toward the western mountains, where the geology might have been studied with the probability of most interesting results.

There was one journey possible, a somewhat difficult undertaking certainly, yet gaining an interest and excitement from that very reason, and this was an attempt to reach the summit of Mount Erebus. For many reasons the accomplishment of this work seemed to be desirable. In the first place the observations of temperature and wind currents at the summit of this great mountain would have an important bearing on the movements of the upper air, a meteorological problem as yet but imperfectly understood. From a geological point of view the mountain ought to reveal some interesting facts, and apart from scientific considerations, the ascent of a mountain over 13,000 ft. in height, situated so far south, would be a matter of pleasurable excitement both to those who were selected as climbers and to the rest of us who wished for our companions' success. After consideration I decided that Professor David, Mawson, and Mackay should constitute the party that was to try to reach the summit, and they were to be provisioned for ten days. A supporting party, consisting of Adams, Marshall, and Brocklehurst, was to assist the main party as far as feasible. The whole expedition was to be under Adams's charge until he decided that it was time for his party to return, and the Professor was then to be in charge of the advance party. In my written instructions to Adams, he was given the option of going on to the summit if he thought it feasible for his party to push on; and he actually did so, though the supporting party was not so well equipped for the mountain work as the advance party, and was provisioned for six days only. Instructions were given that the supporting party was not to hamper the main party, especially as regarded the division of provisions, but, as a matter of fact, instead of hampering, the three men became of great assistance to the advance division, and lived entirely on their own stores and equipment during the whole trip. No sooner was it decided to make the ascent, which was arranged for, finally, on March 4, than the winter quarters became busy with the bustle of preparation. There were crampons to be made, food bags to be prepared and filled, sleeping bags to be overhauled, ice axes to be got out, and a hundred and one things to be seen to; yet such was the energy thrown into this work that the men were ready for the road and made a start at 8:30 a.m. on the 5th.

In a previous chapter I have described the nature and extent of equipment necessary for a sledging trip, so that it is not necessary now to go into details regarding the preparations for this particular journey, the only variation from the usual standard arrangement being in the matter of quantity of food. In the ascent of a mountain such as Erebus it was obvious that a limit would soon be reached beyond which it would be impossible to use a sledge. To meet these circumstances the advance party had made an arrangement of straps by which their single sleeping bags could be slung in the form of a knapsack upon their backs, and inside the bags the remainder of their equipment could be packed. The men of the supporting party, in case they should journey beyond ice over which they could drag the sledge, had made the same preparations for transferring their load to their shoulders. When they started I must confess that I saw but little prospect of the whole party reaching the top, yet when, from the hut, on the third day out, we saw through Armytage's powerful telescope six tiny black spots slowly crawling up the immense deep snowfield to the base of the rugged rocky spurs that descended to the edge of the field, and when I saw next day out on the skyline the same small figures, I realised that the supporting party were going the whole way. On the return of this expedition Adams and the Professor made a full report, with the help of which I will follow the progress of the party, the members of which were winning their spurs not only on their first Antarctic campaign, but in their first attempt at serious mountaineering.

Mount Erebus bears a name that has loomed large in the history of polar exploration both north and south. Sir James Clark Ross, on January 28, 1841, named the great volcano at whose base our winter quarters were placed after the leading ship of his expedition. The final fate of that ship is linked with the fate of Sir John Franklin and one of the most tragic stories of Arctic exploration, but though both the *Erebus* and *Terror* have sunk far from the scenes of their first exploration, that brilliant period of Antarctic discovery will ever be remembered by the mountains which took their names from those stout ships. Standing as a sentinel at the gate of the Great Ice Barrier, Erebus forms a magnificent picture. The great mountain rises from sea level to an altitude of over 13,000 ft., looking out across the Barrier, with its enormous snow-clad bulk towering above the white slopes that run up from the coast. At the top of the mountain an immense depression marks the site of the old crater, and from the side of this rises the active cone, generally marked by steam or smoke. The ascent of such a mountain would be a matter of difficulty in any part of the world, hardly to be attempted without experienced guides, but the difficulties were accentuated by the latitude of Erebus, and the party started off with the full expectation of encountering very low temperatures. The men all recognised, however, the scientific value of the achievement at which they were aiming, and they were determined to do their utmost to reach the crater itself. How they fared and what they found will be told best by extracts from the report which was made to me.

On March 5, after the busy day and night of preparation, the start was made. Breakfast was served at 6 a.m., and one of the eleven-foot sledges was packed and lashed, the total weight of the load and sledge being 560 lb. I took a photograph of the party as they started off. They got under way from the hut at a quarter to nine, all hands accompanying them across the rocky ridge at the back of the hut, lifting the sledge and load bodily over this, and then helping the party to pull along the slopes of Back Door Bay across Blue Lake up the eastern slope to the first level. There we said farewell to the mountain party. They first steered straight up a snow slope and skirted closely some rocky ridges and moraines in order to avoid crevassed glaciers. About a mile out and four hundred feet above sea level a glacial moraine barred their path, and they had to portage the sledge over it by slipping ice axes under the load between the runners and bearers of the sledge and lifting it over the obstruction. On the further side of the moraine was a sloping surface of ice and névé on which the sledge capsized for the first time. Light snow was falling, and there was a slight wind. The report supplied to me by Professor David and Adams depicts in a graphic manner these first experiences of this party in sledging.

Pulling the sledge proved fairly heavy work in places; at one spot, on the steep slope of a small glacier, the party had a hard struggle, mostly on their hands and knees, in their efforts to drag the sledge up the surface of smooth blue ice thinly coated with loose snow. This difficulty surmounted, they encountered some sastrugi, which impeded their progress somewhat. 'Sastrugi' means wind furrow, and is the name given to those annoying obstacles to sledging, due to the action of the wind on the snow. A blizzard has the effect of scooping out hollows in the snow, and this is especially the case when local currents are set up owing to some rock or point of land interrupting the free run of the wind. These sastrugi vary in depth from two or three inches to three or four feet, according to the position of any rock masses that may be near and to the force of the wind forming them. The raised masses of snow between the hollows are difficult to negotiate with a sledge, especially when they run more or less parallel to the course of the traveller. Though they have many disadvantages, still there are times when their presence is welcome; especially is this the case when the sky is overcast and the low stratus cloud obliterates all landmarks. At these times a dull grey light is over everything, and it is impossible to see the way to steer unless one takes the line of sastrugi and notes the angle it makes with the compass course, the compass for the moment being placed on the snow to obtain the direction. In this way one can steer a fairly accurate course, occasionally verifying it by calling a halt and laying off the course again with the compass, a precaution that is very necessary, for at times the sastrugi alter in direction.

The sledgers, at this particular juncture, had much trouble in keeping their feet, and the usual equanimity of some of the men was disturbed, their remarks upon the subject of sastrugi being audible above the soft pad of the finnesko, the scrunch of the ski boots, and the gentle sawing sound of the sledge runners on the soft snow. About 6 p.m. the party camped at a small nunatak of black rock, about 2750 ft. above sea level and a distance of seven miles from winter quarters. After a good hot dinner they turned in to their sleeping bags in the tents and were soon sound asleep. The following morning, when the men got up for breakfast, the temperature was 10° below zero Fahrenheit, whilst at our winter quarters at the same time it was zero. They found, on starting, that the gradient was becoming much steeper, being 1 in 5, and sastrugi, running obliquely to their course, caused the sledge to capsize frequently. The temperature was 8° below zero Fahrenheit, but the pulling was heavy work and kept the travellers warm. They camped that night, March 6, at an altitude of 5630 ft., having travelled only three miles during the whole day, but they had ascended over 2800 ft. above their previous camp. The temperature that night was 28° below zero Fahrenheit. The second camp was in a line with the oldest crater of Erebus, and from the nature of the volcanic fragments lying around, the Professor was of the opinion that Erebus had been producing a little lava within its crater quite recently.

On the following morning Adams decided that the supporting party should make the attempt with the forward party to reach the summit. I had left the decision in this matter to his discretion, but I myself had not considered there would be much chance of the three men of the supporting party gaining the summit, and had not arranged their equipment with that object in view. They were thus handicapped by having a three-man sleeping bag, which bulky article one man had to carry; they also were not so well equipped for carrying packs, bits of rope having to act as substitutes for the broad straps provided for the original advance party. The supporting party had no crampons, and so found it more difficult, in places, to get a grip with their feet on the slippery surface of the snow slopes. However, the Professor, who had put bars of leather on his ski boots, found that these answered as well as crampons, and lent the latter to Marshall. Both Adams and the Professor wore ski boots during the whole of the ascent. Skis could not be used for such rough climbing, and had not been taken. All the men were equipped with both finnesko and ski boots and with the necessaries for camping, and individual tastes had been given some latitude in the matter of the clothing worn and carried.

The six men made a depot of the sledge, some of the provisions and part of the cooking utensils at the second camp, and then resumed the climb again. They started off with tent poles amongst other equipment, but after going for half a mile they realised it would be impossible to climb the mountain with these articles, which were taken back to the depot. Each man carried a weight of about 40 lb., the party's gear consisting chiefly of sleeping bags, two tents, cooking apparatus, and provisions for three days. The snow slopes became steeper, and at one time Mackay, who was cutting steps on the hard snow with his ice axe, slipped and glissaded with his load for about a hundred feet, but his further downward career was checked by a projecting ledge of snow, and he was soon up again. On the third evening, March 7, the party camped about 8750 ft. above sea level, the temperature at that time being 20° below zero Fahrenheit.

Between 9 and 10 p.m. that night a strong wind sprang up, and when the men awoke the following morning they found a fierce blizzard blowing from the south-east. It increased in fury as the day wore on, and swept with terrific force down the rocky ravine where they were camped. The whirling snow was so dense and the roaring wind so loud that, although the two sections were only about ten yards apart, they could neither see nor hear each other. Being without tent poles, the tents were just doubled over the top ends of the sleeping bags so as to protect the openings from the drifting snow, but, in spite of this precaution, a great deal of snow found its way into the bags. In the afternoon Brocklehurst emerged from the three-man sleeping bag, and instantly a fierce gust whirled away one of his wolfskin mits; he dashed after it, and the force of the wind swept him some way down the ravine. Adams, who had left the bag at the same time as Brocklehurst, saw the latter vanish suddenly, and in endeavouring to return to the bag to fetch Marshall to assist in finding Brocklehurst he also was blown down by the wind. Meanwhile, Marshall, the only remaining occupant of the bag, had much ado to keep himself from being blown, sleeping bag and all, down the ravine. Adams had just succeeded in reaching the sleeping bag on his hands and knees when Brocklehurst appeared, also on his hands and knees, having, by desperate efforts, pulled himself back over the rocks. It was a close call for he was all but completely gone, so biting was the cold, before he reached the haven of the sleeping bag. He and Adams crawled in, and then, as the bag had been much twisted up and drifted with snow while Marshall had been holding it down, Adams and Marshall got out to try and straighten it out. The attempt was not very successful, as they were numb with cold and the bag, with only one person inside, blew about, so they got into it again. Shortly afterwards Adams made another attempt, and whilst he was working at it the wind got inside the bag, blowing it open right way up. Adams promptly got in again, and the adventure thus ended satisfactorily. The men could do nothing now but lie low whilst the blizzard lasted. At times they munched a plasmon biscuit or some chocolate. They had nothing to drink all that day, March 8, and during the following night, as it would have been impossible to have kept a lamp alight to thaw out the snow. They got some sleep during the night in spite of the storm. On awaking at 4 a.m. the following day, the travellers found that the blizzard was over, so, after breakfast, they started away again at about 5:30 a.m.

The angle of ascent was now steeper than ever, being thirty-four degrees, that is, a rise of 1 in 1½. As the hard snow slopes were much too steep to climb without cutting steps with an ice axe, they kept as much as possible to the bare rocks. Occasionally the arête would terminate upward in a large snow slope, and when this was the case they cut steps across the slope to any other bare rocks which seemed to persist for some distance in an upward direction. Brocklehurst, who was wearing ski boots, began to feel the cold attacking his feet, but did not think it was serious enough to change into finnesko. At noon they found a fair camping ground, and made some tea. They were, at this time, some 800 ft. below the rim of the old crater and were feeling the effects of the high altitude and the extreme cold. Below them was a magnificent panorama of clouds, coast and Barrier snow, but they could not afford to spend much time admiring it. After a hasty meal they tackled the ascent again. When they were a little distance from the top of the rim of the main crater, Mackay elected to work his way alone with his ice axe up a long and very steep névé slope instead of following the less difficult and safer route by the rocks where the rest of the party were proceeding. He passed out of sight, and then the others heard him call out that he was getting weak and did not think he could carry on much longer. They made haste to the top of the ridge, and Marshall and the Professor dropped to the point where he was likely to be found. Happily, they met him coming toward them, and Marshall took his load, for he looked much done up. It appeared that Mackay had found the work of cutting steps with his heavy load more difficult than he had anticipated, and he only just managed to reach safety when he fell and fainted. No doubt this was due, in part, to mountain sickness, which, under the severe conditions and at the high altitude the party had attained, also affected Brocklehurst.

Having found a camping place, they dropped their loads, and the members of the party were at leisure to observe the nature of their surroundings. They had imagined an even plain of névé or glacier ice filling the extinct crater to the brim and sloping up gradually to the active cone at its southern end, but instead of this they found themselves on the very brink of a precipice of black rock, forming the inner edge of the old crater. This wall of dark lava was mostly vertical, while, in some places, it overhung, and was from eighty to a hundred feet in height. The base of the cliff was separated from the snow plain beyond by a deep ditch like a huge dry moat, which was evidently due to the action of blizzards. These winds, striking fiercely from the south-east against the great inner wall of the old crater, had given rise to a powerful back eddy at the edge of the cliff, and it was this eddy which had scooped out the deep trench in the hard snow. The trench was from thirty to forty feet deep, and was bounded by more or less vertical sides. Around our winter quarters any isolated rock or cliff face that faced the south-east blizzard wind exhibited a similar phenomenon, though,

of course, on a much smaller scale. Beyond the wall and trench
was an extensive snow field with the active cone and crater at its
southern end, the latter emitting great volumes of steam, but what
surprised the travellers most were the extraordinary structures
which rose here and there above the surface of the snow field.
They were in the form of mounds and pinnacles of the most varied
and fantastic appearance. Some resembled beehives, others were
like huge ventilating cowls, others like isolated turrets, and others
again resembled various animals in shape. The men were unable at
first sight to understand the origin of these remarkable structures,
and as it was time for food, they left the closer investigation for
later in the day.

As they walked along the rampart of the old crater wall to find a
camping ground, their figures were thrown up against the skyline,
and down at our winter quarters they were seen by us, having been
sighted by Armytage with his telescope. He had followed the party
for the first two days with the glasses, but they were lost to view
when they began to work through the rocky ground, and it was just
on the crater edge that they were picked up again by the telescope.

The camp chosen for the meal was in a little rocky gully on the
north-west slope of the main cone, and about fifty feet below the
rim of the old crater. Whilst some cooked the meal, Marshall
examined Brocklehurst's feet, as the latter stated that for some time
past he had lost all feeling in them. When his ski boots and socks
had been taken off, it was found that both his big toes were black,
and that four more toes, though less severely affected, were also
frostbitten. From their appearance it was evident that some hours
must have elapsed since this had occurred. Marshall and Mackay set
at work at once to restore circulation in the feet by warming and
chafing them. Their efforts were, under the circumstances, fairly
successful, but it was clear that ultimate recovery from so severe
a frostbite would be both slow and tedious. Brocklehurst's feet,
having been thoroughly warmed, were put into dry socks and
finnesko stuffed with sennegrass, and then all hands went to lunch
at 3:30 p.m. It must have required great pluck and determination
on his part to have climbed almost continuously for nine hours up
the steep and difficult track they had followed with his feet so badly
frostbitten. After lunch Brocklehurst was left safely tucked up in
the three-man sleeping bag, and the remaining five members of the

party started off to explore the floor of the old crater. Ascending to the crater rim, they climbed along it until they came to a spot where there was a practicable breach in the crater wall and where a narrow tongue of snow bridged the névé trench at its base.

They all roped up directly they arrived on the hard snow in the crater and advanced cautiously over the snow plain, keeping a sharp lookout for crevasses. They steered for some of the remarkable mounds already mentioned, and when the nearest was reached and examined, they noticed some curious hollows, like partly roofed-in drains, running toward the mound. Pushing on slowly, they reached eventually a small parasitic cone, about 1000 ft. above the level of their camp, and over a mile distant from it. Sticking out from under the snow were lumps of lava, large feldspar crystals, from one to three inches in length, and fragments of pumice; both feldspar and pumice were in many cases coated with sulphur. Having made as complete an examination as time permitted, they started to return to camp, no longer roped together, as they had not met any definite crevasses on their way out. They directed their steps toward one of the ice mounds, which bore a whimsical resemblance to a lion couchant, and from which smoke appeared to be issuing. To the Professor the origin of these peculiar structures was now no longer a mystery, for he recognised that they were the outward and visible signs of fumaroles. In ordinary climates, a fumarole, or volcanic vapour well, may be detected by the thin cloud of steam above it, and usually one can at once feel the warmth by passing one's hand into the vapour column, but in the rigour of the Antarctic climate the fumaroles of Erebus have their vapour turned into ice as soon as it reaches the surface of the snow plain. Thus ice mounds, somewhat similar in shape to the sinter mounds formed by the geysers of New Zealand, of Iceland and of Yellowstone Park, are built up round the orifices of the fumaroles of Erebus. Whilst exploring one of these fumaroles, Mackay fell suddenly up to his thighs into one of its concealed conduits, and only saved himself from falling in deeper still by means of his ice axe. Marshall had a similar experience at about the same time.

The party arrived at camp shortly after 6 p.m., and found Brocklehurst progressing as well as could be expected. They sat on the rocks after tea admiring the glorious view to the west. Below them was a vast rolling sea of cumulus cloud, and far away the western mountains glowed in the setting sun. Next morning, when they got up at 4 a.m., they had a splendid view of the shadow of Erebus projected on the field of cumulus cloud below them by the rising sun. Every detail of the profile of the mountain as outlined on the clouds could readily be recognised. After breakfast, while Marshall was attending to Brocklehurst's feet, the hypsometer, which had become frozen on the way up, was thawed out and a determination of the boiling-point made. This, when reduced and combined with the mean of the aneroid levels, made the altitude of the old crater rim, just above the camp, 11,400 ft. At 6 a.m. the party left the camp and made all speed to reach the summit of the present crater. On their way across the old crater, Mawson photographed the fumarole that resembled the lion and also took a view of the active crater about one and a half miles distant, though there was considerable difficulty in taking photographs owing to the focal plane shutter having become jammed by frost. Near the furthest point reached by the travellers on the preceding afternoon they observed several patches of yellow ice and found on examination that the colour was due to sulphur. They next ascended several rather steep slopes formed of alternating beds of hard snow and vast quantities of large and perfect feldspar crystals, mixed with pumice. A little farther on they reached the base of the volcano's active cone. Their progress was now painfully slow, as the altitude and cold combined to make respiration difficult. The cone of Erebus is built up chiefly of blocks of pumice, from a few inches to a few feet in diameter. Externally these were grey or often yellow owing to incrustations of sulphur, but when broken they were of a resinous brown colour. At last, a little after 10 a.m., on March 10, the edge of the active crater was reached, and the little party stood on the summit of Erebus, the first men to conquer perhaps the most remarkable summit in the world. They had travelled about two and a half miles from the last camp, and had ascended just 2000 ft., and this journey had taken them over four hours, The report describes most vividly the magnificent and awe-inspiring scene before them.

'We stood on the verge of a vast abyss, and at first could see neither to the bottom nor across it on account of the huge mass of steam filling the crater and soaring aloft in a column 500 to

1000 ft. high. After a continuous loud hissing sound, lasting for some minutes, there would come from below a big dull boom, and immediately great globular masses of steam would rush upwards to swell the volume of the snow-white cloud which ever sways over the crater. This phenomenon recurred at intervals during the whole of our stay at the crater. Meanwhile, the air around us was extremely redolent of burning sulphur. Presently a pleasant northerly breeze fanned away the steam cloud, and at once the whole crater stood revealed to us in all its vast extent and depth. Mawson's angular measurement made the depth 900 ft. and the greatest width about half a mile. There were at least three well-defined openings at the bottom of the cauldron, and it was from these that the steam explosions proceeded. Near the south-west portion of the crater there was an immense rift in the rim, perhaps 300 to 400 ft. deep. The crater wall opposite the one at the top of which we were standing presented features of special interest. Beds of dark pumiceous lava or pumice alternated with white zones of snow. There was no direct evidence that the snow was bedded with the lava, though it was possible that such may have been the case. From the top of one of the thickest of the lava or pumice beds, just where it touched the belt of snow, there rose scores of small steam jets all in a row. They were too numerous and too close together to have been each an independent fumarole; the appearance was rather suggestive of the snow being converted into steam by the heat of the layer of rock immediately below it.'

While at the crater's edge the party made a boiling point determination by the hypsometer, but the result was not so satisfactory as that made earlier in the morning at the camp. As the result of averaging aneroid levels, together with the hypsometer determination at the top of the old crater, Erebus may be calculated to rise to a height of 13,370 ft. above sea level. As soon as the measurements had been made and some photographs had been taken by Mawson, the party returned to the camp, as it had been decided to descend to the base of the main cone that day, a drop of 8000 ft.

On the way back a traverse was made of the main crater and levels taken for constructing a geological section. Numerous specimens of the unique feldspar crystals and of the pumice and sulphur were collected. On arriving in camp the travellers made a hasty meal, packed up, shouldered their burdens once more and started down the steep mountain slope. Brocklehurst insisted on carrying his own heavy load in spite of his frostbitten feet. They followed a course a little to the west of the one they took when ascending. The rock was rubbly and kept slipping under their feet, so that falls were frequent. After descending a few hundred feet they found that the rubbly spur of rock down which they were floundering ended abruptly in a long and steep névé slope. Three courses were now open to them: they could retrace their steps to the point above them where the rocky spur had deviated from the main arête; cut steps across the névé slope; or glissade down some five or six hundred feet to a rocky ledge below. In their tired state preference was given to the path of least resistance, which was offered by the glissade, and they therefore rearranged their loads so that they would roll down easily. They were now very thirsty, but they found that if they gathered a little snow, squeezed it into a ball and placed it on the surface of a piece of rock, it melted at once almost on account of the heat of the sun and thus they obtained a makeshift drink. They launched their loads down the slope and watched them as they bumped and bounded over the wavy ridges of névé. Brocklehurst's load, which contained the cooking utensils, made the noisiest descent, and the aluminium cookers were much battered when they finally fetched up against the rocks below. Then the members of the party, grasping their ice axes firmly, followed their gear. As they gathered speed on the downward course and the chisel edge of the ice axe bit deeper into the hard névé, their necks and faces were sprayed with a shower of ice. All reached the bottom of the slope safely, and they repeated this glissade down each succeeding snow slope toward the foot of the main cone. Here and there they bumped heavily on hard sastrugi and both clothes and equipment suffered in the rapid descent; unfortunately also, one of the aneroids was lost and one of the hypsometer thermometers broken. At last the slope flattened out to the gently inclined terrace where the depot lay, and they reached it by walking. Altogether they had dropped down 5000 ft. between three in the afternoon and seven in the evening.

Adams and Marshall were the first to reach the depot, the rest of the party, with the exception of Brocklehurst, having made a detour to the left in consequence of having to pursue some lost luggage in that direction. At the depot they found that the blizzard of the 8th had played havoc with their gear, for the sledge had been overturned and some of the load scattered to a distance and partly covered with drift snow. After dumping their packs, Adams and Marshall went to meet Brocklehurst, for they noticed that a slight blizzard was springing up. Fortunately, the wind soon died down, the weather cleared, and the three were able to regain the camp. Tea was got ready, and the remainder of the party arrived about 10 p.m. They camped that night at the depot and at 3 a.m. next day got up to breakfast. After breakfast a hunt was made for some articles that were still missing, and then the sledge was packed and the march homeward commenced at 5:30 a.m. They now found that the sastrugi caused by the late blizzard were very troublesome, as the ridges were from four to five feet above the hollows and lay at an oblique angle to the course. Rope brakes were put on the sledge runners, and two men went in front to pull when necessary, while two steadied the sledge, and two were stationed behind to pull back when required. It was more than trying to carry on at this juncture, for the sledge either refused to move or suddenly it took charge and overran those who were dragging it, and capsizes occurred every few minutes. Owing to the slippery nature of the ground some members of the party who had not crampons or barred ski boots were badly shaken up, for they sustained numerous sudden falls. One has to experience a surface like this to realise how severe a jar a fall entails. The only civilised experience that is akin to it is when one steps unknowingly on a slide which some small street boy has made on the pavement. Marshall devised the best means of assisting the progress of the sledge. When it took charge he jumped on behind and steered it with his legs as it bumped and jolted over the sastrugi, but he found sometimes that his thirteen stone weight did not prevent him from being bucked right over the sledge and flung on the névé on the other side.

They reached the nunatak where they had made their first camp on the way up, six miles distant from Cape Royds, at about 7:30 a.m. By this time there was every symptom of the approach of a blizzard, and the snow was beginning to drift before a gusty south-easterly wind. This threatened soon to cut them off from all view of the winter quarters. They were beginning to feel very tired, one of the tents had a large hole burned in it, the oil supply was almost done, and one of the primus stoves had been put out of action as the result of the glissade; so, in the circumstances, they decided to make a dash for Cape Royds, leaving their sledge and equipment to be picked up later. In the grey uncertain light the sastrugi did not show up in relief, and every few feet some member of the party stumbled and fell, sprawling over the snow. At last their eyes were gladdened by the shining surface of the Blue Lake only half a mile distant from winter quarters. Now that the haven was at hand, and the stress and strain over, their legs grew heavy and leaden, and that last half mile seemed one of the hardest they had covered. It was fortunate that the weather did not become worse.

Meanwhile, at winter quarters, we had been very busy opening cases and getting things shipshape outside, with the result that the cubicles of the absentees were more or less filled with a general accumulation of stores. When Armytage reported that he saw the party on their way down the day before they arrived at the hut, we decided to make the cubicles tidy for the travellers. We had just begun on the Professor's cubicle when, about 11 a.m. I left the hut for a moment and was astonished to see within thirty yards of me, coming over the brow of the ridge by the hut, six slowly moving figures. I ran toward them shouting: 'Did you get to the top?' There was no answer, and I asked again. Adams pointed with his hand upward, but this did not satisfy me, so I repeated my question. Then Adams said: 'Yes', and I ran back to the hut and shouted to the others, who all came streaming out to cheer the successful venturers. We shook hands all around and opened some champagne, which tasted like nectar to the wayworn people. Marshall prescribed a dose to us stay-at-home ones, so that we might be able to listen quietly to the tale the party had to tell.

Except to Joyce, Wild, and myself, who had seen similar things on the former expedition, the eating and drinking capacity of the returned party was a matter of astonishment. In a few minutes Roberts had produced a great saucepan of Quaker oats and milk, the contents of which disappeared in a moment, to be followed by the greater part of a fresh cut ham and homemade bread, with New Zealand fresh butter. The six had evidently found on the slopes of Erebus six fully developed, polar sledging appetites. The meal at last ended, came more talk, smokes and then bed for the weary travellers.

After some days' delay on account of unfavourable weather, a party consisting of Adams, the Professor, Armytage, Joyce, Wild and Marshall, equipped with a seven-foot sledge, tent, and provisions, as a precaution against possible bad weather, started out to fetch in the eleven-foot sledge with the explorers' equipment. After a heavy pull over the soft, new-fallen snow, in cloudy weather, with the temperature at midday 29° below zero Fahrenheit, and with a stiff wind blowing from the south-east, they sighted the nunatak, recovered the abandoned sledge and placing the smaller one on top, pulled them both back as far as Blue Lake. I went out to meet the party, and we left the sledge at Blue Lake until the following day, when two of the Manchurian ponies were harnessed to the sledges and the gear was brought in to winter quarters.

Professor David gave me a short summary of the scientific results of the ascent, from which I have made the following extracts:

'Among the scientific results may be mentioned the calculation of the height of the mountain. Sir Jas. C. Ross in 1841 estimated the height to be 12,367 ft. The National Antarctic Expedition, 1901, determined its height at first to be 13,120 ft., but this was subsequently altered to 12,922 ft., the height now given on the Admiralty Chart of this region. Our observations for altitude were made partly with aneroids and partly with a hypsometer. All the aneroid levels and hypsometer observations have been calculated by means of simultaneous readings of the barometer taken at our winter quarters, Cape Royds. These observations show that the rim of the second or main crater of Erebus is about 11,350 ft. above sea level and that the summit of the active crater is about 13,350 ft. above sea level. The fact may be emphasised that in both the methods adopted by us for estimating the altitude of the mountain, atmospheric pressure was the sole factor on which we relied. The determination arrived at by the *Discovery* was based on measurements made with a theodolite from sea level. It is, of course, quite possible that Ross's original estimate may have been correct, as this native volcano may have increased in height by about a thousand feet during the sixty-seven years which have elapsed since his expedition.

'As regards the geological structure of Erebus, there is evidence of the existence of four superimposed craters. The oldest and lowest, and at the same time the largest, of these attained an altitude of between 6000 and 7000 ft. above sea level, and was fully six miles in diameter: the second rises to 11,350 ft. and has a diameter of over two miles: the third crater rises to a height of fully 12,200 ft.; and its former outline has now been almost obliterated by the material of the modern active cone and crater. The latter, which rises about 800 ft. above the former, is composed chiefly of fragments of pumice. These vary in size from an inch or so to a yard in diameter. Quantities of feldspar crystals are interspersed with them, and both are encrusted with sulphur.

'The active crater measures about half a mile by one-third of a mile in diameter, and is about 900 ft. in depth. The active crater of Erebus is about three times as deep as that of Vesuvius. The fresh volcanic bombs picked up by us at spots four miles distant from the crater and lying on the surface of comparatively new snow are evidences that Erebus has recently been projecting lava to great heights.

'Two features in the geology of Erebus which are specially distinctive are: the vast quantities of large and perfect feldspar crystals, and the ice fumaroles. The crystals are from two or three inches in length; many of them have had their angles and edges slightly rounded by attrition, but numbers of them are beautifully perfect.

'Its remarkable crystals, rare lavas and unique fumaroles are some of its most interesting geological features: it served as a gigantic tide gauge to record the flood level of the greatest recent glaciation of Antarctica, when the whole of Ross Island was but a nunatak in a gigantic field of ice.

'Its situation between the belt of polar calms and the South Pole; its isolation from the disturbing influence of large land masses; its great height, which enables it to penetrate the whole system of atmospheric circulation, and the constant steam cloud at its summit, swinging to and fro like a huge wind vane, combine to make Erebus one of the most interesting places on earth to the meteorologist.'

CHAPTER 10

Winter quarters during Polar night 1908
Notes on spring sledging journeys

Meteorological observations: The anemometer: Night watchman's duties: Fierce blizzard on March 13: Preliminary journey on the Barrier surface starts August 12: Hut Point reached August 14: Party starts for Hut Point on September 1, to leave there some gear and provisions in readiness for the Southern Journey

After the journey to the summit of Erebus we began to settle down and prepare for the long winter months that were rapidly approaching. Already the nights were lengthening and stars becoming familiar objects in the sky. Our main work was to secure the hut firmly against possible damage from the south-east blizzards. After everything had been made safe as far as it lay in our power, we felt that if anything untoward happened it would not be our fault, so we turned our attention to the scientific studies that lay to our hand. As we were only a small party, it was impossible for all of us to carry on scientific work and, at the same time, attend to what I might call the household duties. It was the most important for the geologists of the expedition to get as far afield as practicable before the winter night closed in on us, so every day both the Professor and Priestley were out early and late, with their collecting bags and geological hammers, finding on every successive trip they made within a radius of three or four miles of the winter quarters new and interesting geological specimens, the examination of which would give them plenty of work in the winter months. Scattered around Cape Royds were large numbers of granite boulders of every size and colour, deposited there by the great receding ice sheet that once filled McMurdo Sound and covered the lower slopes of Erebus. The geologists were full of delight that circumstances should have placed our winter quarters at a spot so fruitful for their labours. Murray was equally pleased at the prospect of the biological work which lay before him, for hardly a day passed without someone bringing in a report of the existence of another lake or tarn, and soon we realised that around us lay more than a dozen of these lakelets which might possibly prove a fruitful field for biological study. To Mawson the many varied forms of ice and snow, both in the lakes and on the surrounding hills, gave promise of encouraging results in that branch of physics in which he was particularly interested. The lengthening nights also gave us indications that the mysterious Aurora Australis would soon be waving its curtains and beams over our winter quarters, and as information on this phenomenon was greatly needed, Mawson made preparations for recording the displays.

The meteorological screen had been set up and observations begun before the Erebus party left. Now that all hands were back at the hut, a regular system of recording the observations was arranged. Adams, who was the meteorologist of the expedition, took all the observations from 8 a.m. to 8 p.m. The night watchman took them from 10 p.m. to 6 a.m. These observations were taken every two hours, and it may interest the reader to learn what was done in this way, though I do not wish to enter here into a lengthy dissertation on meteorology. The observations on air temperature, wind, and direction of cloud have an important bearing on similar observations taken in more temperate climes, and in a place like the Antarctic, where up till now our knowledge has been so meagre, it was most essential that every bit of information bearing on meteorological phenomena should be noted. We were in a peculiarly favourable position for observing not only the changes that took place in the lower atmosphere but also those which took place in the higher strata of the atmosphere. Erebus, with steam and smoke always hanging above it, indicated by the direction assumed by the cloud what the upper air currents were doing, and thus we were in touch with an excellent high-level observatory.

The instruments under Adams's care were as complete as financial considerations had permitted. The meteorological screen contained a maximum thermometer, that is, a thermometer which indicates the highest temperature reached during the period elapsing between two observations. It is so constructed that when the mercury rises in the tube it remains at its highest point, though the temperature might fall greatly shortly afterward. After reading the recorded height, the thermometer is shaken, and this operation causes the mercury to drop to the actual temperature obtaining at the moment of observation; the thermometer is then put back into the screen and is all ready for the next reading taken two hours later. A minimum thermometer registered the lowest temperature that occurred between the two hourly readings, but this thermometer was not a mercury one, as mercury freezes at a temperature of about 39° below zero, and we therefore used spirit thermometers. When the temperature drops the surface of the column of spirit draws down a little black indicator immersed in it, and if the temperature rises and the spirit advances in consequence, the spirit flows past the indicator, which remains at the lowest point, and on the observations being taken its position is read on the graduated scale. By these instruments we were always able to ascertain what the highest temperature and what the lowest temperature had been throughout the two hours during which the observation screen had not been visited. In addition to the maximum and minimum thermometers, there were the wet and dry bulb thermometers. The dry bulb records the actual temperature of the air at the moment, and we used a spirit thermometer for this purpose. The wet bulb consisted of an ordinary thermometer, around the bulb of which was tied a little piece of muslin that had been dipped in water and of course froze at once on exposure to the air. The effect of the evaporation from the ice which covered the bulb was to cause the temperature recorded to be lower than that recorded by the dry bulb therm-ometer in proportion to the amount of water present in the atmosphere at the time. To ensure accuracy the wet bulb therm-ometers were changed every two hours, the thermometer which was read being brought back to the hut and returned to the screen later freshly sheathed in ice. It was, of course, impossible to wet the exposed thermometer with a brush dipped in water, as is the practice in temperate climates, for water could not be carried from the hut to the screen without freezing into solid ice. To check the thermometers there was also kept in the screen a self-recording thermometer, or thermograph. This is a delicate instrument fitted with metal discs, which expand or contract readily with every fluctuation of the temperature. Attached to these discs is a delicately poised lever carrying a pen charged with ink, and the point of this pen rests against a graduated roll of paper fastened to a drum, which is revolved by clockwork once in every seven days. The pen thus draws a line on the paper, rising and falling in sympathy with the changes in the temperature of the air.

All these instruments were contained inside the meteorological screen, which was so constructed that while there was free access of air, the wind could not strike through it with any violence, neither could the sun throw its direct beams on the sensitive thermometers inside. On the flat top of the screen were nailed two pieces of wood in the form of a cross, the long axis of which lay in the true meridian, that is, one end pointing due south, the other end due north. On a small rod attached to the fore end of the screen was a vane that floated out in the opposite direction to that from which the wind was blowing, and by reference to the vane and the cross the direction of the wind was ascertained and noted when the other observations were taken. To record the force of the wind and the number of miles it travelled between each observation, there was an instrument called an anemometer, which rested on one of the uprights supporting the meteorological screen; the type of anemometer used by the expedition is known as the 'Robinson'. It consists of four cups or hemispheres revolving on a pivot which communicates by a series of cogs with a dial having two hands like the hands of a watch. The long hand makes one revolution and records five miles, and the smaller hand records up to five hundred miles. At a glance we could thus tell the number of miles the wind had blown during the time elapsing between successive observations. In ordinary climates the work of reading these instruments was a matter of little difficulty and only took a few minutes, but in the Antarctic, especially when a blizzard was blowing, the difficulty was much increased and the strong wind often blew out the hurricane lamp which was used to read the instruments in the darkness. On these occasions the unfortunate observer had to return to the hut, relight the lamp and again struggle up the windy ridge to the screen.

In addition to the meteorological screen, there was another erection built on the top of the highest ridge by Mawson, who placed there an anemometer of his own construction to register the strength of the heaviest gusts of wind during a blizzard. We found that the squalls frequently blew with a force of over a hundred miles an hour. There remained still one more outdoor instrument connected with weather observation, that was the snow gauge. The Professor, by utilising some spare lengths of stove chimney, erected a snow gauge into which was collected the falling snow whenever a blizzard blew. The snow was afterward taken into the hut in the vessel into which it had been deposited, and when it was melted down we were able to calculate fairly accurately the amount of the snowfall. This observation was an important one, for much depends on the amount of precipitation in the Antarctic regions. It is on the precipitation in the form of snow, and on the rate of evaporation, that calculations regarding the formation of the huge snow fields and glaciers depend. We secured our information regarding the rate of evaporation by suspending measured cubes of ice and snow from rods projecting at the side of the hut, where they were free from the influence of the interior warmth. Inside the hut was kept a standard mercurial barometer, which was also read every two hours, and in addition to this there was a barograph which registered the varying pressure of the atmosphere in a curve for a week at a time. Every Monday morning Adams changed the paper on both thermograph and barograph, and every day recorded the observations in the meteor-ological log. It will be seen that the meteorologist had plenty to occupy his time, and generally when the men came in from a walk they had some information to record.

As soon as the ice was strong enough to bear in the bay, Murray commenced his operations there. His object was the collection of the different marine creatures that rest on the bottom of the sea or creep about there, and he made extensive preparations for their capture. A hole was dug through the ice, and a trap let down to the bottom; this trap was baited with a piece of penguin or seal, and the shellfish, crustacea and other marine animals found their way in through the opening in the top, and the trap was usually left down for a couple of days. When it was hauled up, the contents were transferred to a tin containing water, and then taken to the hut and thawed out, for the contents always froze during the quarter of a mile walk homeward. As soon as the animals thawed out they were sorted into bottles and then killed by various chemicals, put into spirits and bottled up for examination when they reached England. Later on Murray found that the trap business was not fruitful enough, so whenever a crack opened in the bay ice, a line was let down, one end being made fast at one end of the crack, and the length of the line allowed to sink in the water horizontally for a distance of sixty yards. A hole was dug at each end of the line and a small dredge was let down and pulled along the bottom, being hauled up through the hole at the far end. By this means much richer collections were made, and rarely did the dredge come up without some interesting specimens. When the crack froze over again, the work could still be continued so long as the ice was broken at each end of the line, and Priestley for a long time acted as Murray's assistant, helping him to open the holes and pull the dredge.

When we took our walks abroad, everyone kept his eyes open for any interesting specimen of rock or any signs of plant life, and Murray was greatly pleased one day when we brought back some moss. This was found in a fairly sheltered spot beyond Back Door Bay and was the only specimen that we obtained in the neighborhood of the winter quarters before the departure of the sun. Occasionally we came across a small lichen and some curious algae growing in the volcanic earth, but these measured the extent of the terrestrial vegetation in this latitude. In the north polar regions, in a corresponding latitude, there are eighteen different kinds of flowering plants, and there even exists a small stunted tree, a species of willow.

Although terrestrial vegetation is so scanty in the Antarctic, the same cannot be said of the subaqueous plant life. When we first arrived and some of us walked across the north shore of Cape Royds, we saw a great deal of open water in the lakes, and a little later, when all these lakes were frozen over, we walked across them, and looking down through the clear ice, could see masses of brilliantly coloured algae and fungi. The investigation of the plant life in the lakes was one of the principal things undertaken by Murray, Priestley, and the Professor during the winter months.

After the Erebus party returned, a regular winter routine was arranged for the camp. Brocklehurst took no part in the duties at this time, for his frostbitten foot prevented his moving about, and shortly after his return Marshall saw that it would be necessary to amputate at least part of the big toe. The rest of the party all had a certain amount of work for the common weal, apart from their own scientific duties. From the time we arrived we always had a night watchman, and we now took turns to carry out this important duty. Roberts was exempt from night watchman's duties, as he was busy with the cooking all day, so for the greater part of the winter every thirteenth night each member took the night watch. The ten o'clock observations was the night watchman's first duty, and from that hour till nine o'clock next morning he was responsible for the wellbeing and care of the hut, ponies, and dogs. His most important duties were the two-hourly meteorological observations, the upkeep of the fire and the care of the acetylene gas plant. The fire was kept going all through the night, and hot water was ready for making the breakfast when Roberts was called at 7:30 in the morning. The night watch was by no means an unpleasant duty, and gave each of us an opportunity, when his turn came around, of washing clothes, darning socks, writing and doing little odd jobs which could not receive much attention during the day. The night watchman generally took his bath either once a fortnight or once a month, as his inclination prompted him.

Some individuals had a regular program which they adhered to strictly. For instance, one member, directly the rest of the staff had gone to bed, cleared the small table in front of the stove, spread a rug on it and settled down to a complicated game of patience, having first armed himself with a supply of coffee against the wiles of the drowsy god. After the regulation number of games had been played, the despatch box was opened, and letters, private papers and odds and ends were carefully inspected and replaced in their proper order, after which the journal was written up. These important matters over, a ponderous book on historical subjects received its share of attention.

Socks were the only articles of clothing that had constantly to be repaired, and various were the expedients used to replace the heels, which, owing to the hard footgear, were always showing gaping holes. These holes had to be constantly covered, for we were not possessed of an unlimited number of any sort of clothes, and many and varied were the patches. Some men used thin leather, others canvas, and others again a sort of coarse flannel to sew on instead of darning the heels of the socks. Toward the end of the winter, the wardrobes of the various members of the expedition were in a very patched condition.

During the earlier months the night watchman was kept pretty busy, for the ponies took a long time to get used to the stable and often tried to break loose and upset things out there generally. These sudden noises took the watchman out frequently during the night, and it was a comfort to us when the animals at last learned to keep fairly quiet in their stable. The individual was fortunate who obtained a good bag of coal for his night watch, with plenty of lumps in it, for there was then no difficulty in keeping the temperature of the hut up to 40° Fahrenheit, but a great deal of our coal was very fine and caused much trouble during the night. To meet this difficulty we had recourse to lumps of seal blubber, the watchman generally laying in a stock for himself before his turn came for night duty. When placed on top of the hot coal the blubber burned fiercely, and it was a comfort to know that with the large supply of seals that could easily be obtained in these latitudes, no expedition need fear the lack of emergency fuel. There was no perceptible smell from the blubber in burning, though fumes came from the bit of hairy hide generally attached to it. The thickness of the blubber varied from two to four inches. Some watchmen during the night felt disinclined to do anything but read and take the observations, and I was amongst this number, for though I often made plans and resolutions as to washing and other necessary jobs, when the time came, these plans fell through, with the exception of the bath.

Toward the middle of winter some of our party stayed up later than during the time when there was more work outside, and there gradually grew into existence an institution known as eleven o'clock tea. The Professor was greatly attached to his cup of tea and generally undertook the work of making it for men who were still out of bed. Some of us preferred a cup of hot fresh milk, which was easily made from the excellent dried milk of which we had a large quantity. By one o'clock in the morning, however, nearly all the occupants of the hut were wrapped in deep and more or less noisy slumber. Some had a habit of talking in their sleep, and their fitful phrases were carefully treasured up by the night watchman for retailing at the breakfast table next morning; sometimes also the dreams of the night before were told by the dreamer to his own great enjoyment, if not to that of his audience. About five o'clock in the morning came the most trying time for the watchman. Then one's eyes grew heavy and leaden, and it took a deal of effort to prevent oneself from falling fast asleep. Some of us went in for cooking more or less elaborate meals. Marshall, who had been to a school of cookery before we left England, turned out some quite respectable bread and cakes. Though people jeered at the latter when placed on the table, one noticed that next day there were never any left. At 7:30 a.m. Roberts was called, and the watchman's night was nearly over. At this hour also Armytage or Mackay was called to look after the feeding of the ponies, but before midwinter day Armytage had taken over the entire responsibility of the stables and ponies, and he was the only one to get up. At 8:30 a.m. all hands were called, special attention being paid to turning out the messman for the day, and after some minutes of luxurious half-wakefulness, people began to get up, expressing their opinions forcibly if the temperature of the hut was below freezing point, and informing the night watchman of his affinity to Jonah if his report was that it was a windy morning. Dressing was for some of the men a very simple affair, consisting merely in putting on their boots and giving themselves a shake; others, who undressed entirely, got out of their pajamas into their cold underclothing. At a quarter to nine the call came to let down the table from its position near the roof, and the messman then bundled the knives, forks and spoons on to the board, and at nine o'clock sharp everyone sat down to breakfast.

The night watchman's duties were over for a fortnight, and the messman took on his work. The duties of the messman were more onerous than those of the night watchman. He began, as I have stated, by laying the table – a simple operation owing to the primitive conditions under which we lived. He then garnished this with three or four sorts of hot sauces to tickle the tough palates of some of our party. At nine o'clock, when we sat down, the messman passed up the bowls of porridge and the big jug of hot milk, which was the standing dish every day. Little was heard in the way of conversation until this first course had been disposed of. Then came the order from the messman, 'Up bowls', and reserving our spoons for future use, the bowls were passed along. If it were a 'fruit day', that is, a day when the second course consisted of bottled fruit, the bowls were retained for this popular dish.

At twenty-five minutes to ten breakfast was over and we had had our smokes. All dishes were passed up, the table hoisted out of the way, and the messman started to wash up the breakfast things, assisted by his cubicle companion and by one or two volunteers who would help him to dry up. Another of the party swept out the hut; and this operation was performed three times a day, so as to keep the building in a tidy state. After finishing the breakfast things, the duty of the man in the house was to replenish the melting pots with ice, empty the ashes and tins into the dust box outside, and get in a bag of coal. By half past ten the morning work was accomplished and the messman was free until twenty minutes to one, when he put the water on for the midday tea. At one o'clock tea was served and we had a sort of counter lunch. This was a movable feast, for scientific and other duties often made some of our party late, and after it was over there was nothing for the messman to do in the afternoon except to have sufficient water ready to provide tea at four o'clock. At a quarter past six the table was brought down again and dinner, the longest meal of the day, was served sharp at 6:30. One often heard the messman anxiously inquiring what the dinner dishes were going to consist of, the most popular from his point of view being those which resulted in the least amount of grease on the plates. Dinner was over soon after seven o'clock and then tea was served. Tobacco and conversation kept us at table until 7:30, after which the same routine of washing up and sweeping out the hut was gone through. By 8:30 the messman had finished his duties for the day, and his turn did not come around again for another thirteen days. The state of the weather made the duties lighter or heavier, for if the day happened to be windy, the emptying of dishwater and ashes and the getting in of fresh ice was an unpleasant job. In a blizzard it was necessary to put on one's Burberries even to walk the few yards to the ice box and back.

In addition to the standing jobs of night watchman and messman there were also special duties for various members of the expedition who had particular departments to look after. Adams every morning, directly after breakfast, wound up the chronometers and the chronometer watches, and rated the instruments. He then attended to the meteorological work and took out his pony for exercise. If he were going far afield he delegated the readings to some members of the scientific staff who were generally in the vicinity of winter quarters. Marshall, as surgeon, attended to any wounds, and issued necessary pills, and then took out one of the ponies for exercise. Wild, who was storekeeper, was responsible for the issuing of all stores to Roberts, and had to open the cases of tinned food and dig out of the snowdrifts in which it was buried the meat required for the day, either penguin, seal, or mutton. Joyce fed the dogs after breakfast, the puppies getting a dish of scraps over from our meals after breakfast and after dinner. When daylight returned after our long night, he worked at training the dogs to pull a sledge every morning. The Professor generally went off to 'geologise', or Priestley and Murray worked on the floe dredging or else took the temperatures of the ice in shafts which the former had energetically sunk in the various lakes around us. Mawson was occupied with his physical work, which included auroral observations and the study of the structure of the ice, the determination of atmospheric electricity and many other things. In fact, we were all busy, and there was little cause for us to find the time hang heavy on our hands; the winter months sped by and this without our having to sleep through them, as has often been done before by polar expeditions. This was due to the fact that we were only a small party and that our household duties, added to our scientific work, fully occupied our time.

It would only be repetition to chronicle our doings from day to day during the months that elapsed from the disappearance of the sun until the time arrived when the welcome daylight come back to us. We lived under conditions of steady routine, affected only by short spells of bad weather, and found amply sufficient to occupy ourselves in our daily work, so that the spectre known as 'polar ennui' never made its appearance. Midwinter's Day and birthdays were the occasions of festivals, when our teetotal regime was broken through and a sort of mild spree indulged in. Before the sun finally went hockey and soccer were the outdoor games, while indoors at night some of us played bridge, poker, and dominoes. Joyce, Wild, Marston, and Day during the winter months spent much time in the production of the *Aurora Australis*, the first book ever written, printed, illustrated, and bound in the

Antarctic. Through the generosity of Messrs. Joseph Causton and Sons, Limited, we had been provided with a complete printing outfit and the necessary paper for the book, and Joyce and Wild had been given instruction in the art of typesetting and printing, Marston being taught etching and lithography. They had hardly become skilled craftsmen, but they had gained a good working knowledge of the branches of the business. When we had settled down in the winter quarters, Joyce and Wild set up the little hand press and sorted out the type, these preliminary operations taking up all their spare time for some days, and then they started to set and print the various contributions that were sent in by members of the expedition. The early days of the printing department were not exactly happy, for the two amateur typesetters found themselves making many mistakes, and when they had at last 'set up' a page, made all the necessary corrections, and printed off the required number of copies, they had to undertake the laborious work of 'dissing', that is, of distributing the type again. They plodded ahead steadily, however, and soon became more skilful, until at the end of a fortnight or three weeks they could print two pages in a day. A lamp had to be placed under the type rack to keep it warm, and a lighted candle was put under the inking plate, so that the ink would keep reasonably thin in consistency. The great trouble experienced by the printers at first was in securing the right pressure on the printing plate and even inking of the page, but experience showed them where they had been at fault. Day meanwhile prepared the binding by cleaning, planing, and polishing wood taken from the Venesta cases in which our provisions were packed. Marston reproduced the illustrations by algraphy, or printing from aluminium plates. He had not got a proper lithographic press, so had to use an ordinary etching press, and he was handicapped by the fact that all our water had a trace of salt in it. This mineral acted on the sensitive plates, but Marston managed to produce what we all regarded as creditable pictures. In its final form the book had about one hundred and twenty pages, and it had at least assisted materially to guard us from the danger of lack of occupation during the polar night.

On March 13 we experienced a very fierce blizzard. The hut shook and rocked in spite of our sheltered position, and articles that we had left lying loose outside were scattered far and wide.

Even cases weighing from fifty to eighty pounds were shifted from where they had been resting, showing the enormous velocity of the wind. When the gale was over we put everything that was likely to blow away into positions of greater safety. It was on this day also that Murray found living microscopical animals on some fungus that had been thawed out from a lump of ice taken from the bottom of one of the lakes. This was one of the most interesting biological discoveries that had been made in the Antarctic, for the study of these minute creatures occupied our biologist for a great part of his stay in the south, and threw a new light on the capability of life to exist under conditions of extreme cold and in the face of great variations of temperature. We all became vastly interested in the rotifers during our stay, and the work of the biologist in this respect was watched with keen attention. From our point of view there was an element of humour in the endeavours of Murray to slay the little animals he had found. He used to thaw them out from a block of ice, freeze them up again, and repeat this process several times without producing any result as far as the rotifers were concerned. Then he tested them in brine so strongly saline that it would not freeze at a temperature above minus 7°F, and still the animals lived. A good proportion of them survived a temperature of 200°F. It became a contest between rotifers and scientist, and generally the rotifers seemed to triumph.

At the end of March there was still open water in the bay and we observed a killer whale chasing a seal. About this time we commenced digging a trench in Clear Lake and obtained, when we came to water, samples of the bottom mud and fungus, which was simply swarming with living organisms. The sunsets at the beginning of April were wonderful; arches of prismatic colours, crimson- and golden-tinged clouds, hung in the heavens nearly all day, for time was going on and soon the sun would have deserted us. The days grew shorter and shorter, and the twilight longer. During these sunsets the western mountains stood out gloriously and the summit of Erebus was wrapped in crimson when the lower slopes had faded into grey. To Erebus and the western mountains our eyes turned when the end of the long night grew near in the month of August, for the mighty peaks are the first to catch up and tell the tale of the coming glory and the last to drop the crimson mantle from their high shoulders as night draws on.

Tongue and pencil would sadly fail in attempting to describe the magic of the colouring in the days when the sun was leaving us. The very clouds at this time were iridescent with rainbow hues. The sunsets were poems. The change from twilight into night, sometimes lit by a crescent moon, was extraordinarily beautiful, for the white cliffs gave no part of their colour away, and the rocks beside them did not part with their blackness, so the effect of deepening night over these contrasts was singularly weird. In my diary I noted that throughout April hardly a day passed without an auroral display. On more than one occasion the auroral showed distinct lines of colour, merging from a deep red at the base of the line of light into a greenish hue on top. About the beginning of April the temperature began to drop considerably, and for some days in calm, still weather the thermometer often registered 40° below zero.

On April 6, Marshall decided that it was necessary to amputate Brocklehurst's big toe, as there was no sign of it recovering like the other toes from the frostbite he had received on the Erebus journey. The patient was put under chloroform and the operation was witnessed by an interested and sympathetic audience. After the bone had been removed, the sufferer was shifted into my room, where he remained till just before Midwinter's Day, when he was able to get out and move about again. We had about April 8 one of the peculiar southerly blizzards so common during our last expedition, the temperature varying rapidly from minus 23° to plus 4°F. This blizzard continued till the evening of the 11th, and when it had abated we found the bay and sound clear of ice again. I began to feel rather worried about this and wished for it to freeze over, for across the ice lay our road to the south. We observed occasionally about this time that peculiar phenomenon of McMurdo Sound called 'earth shadows'. Long dark bars, projected up into the sky from the western mountains, made their appearance at sunrise. These lines are due to the shadow of the giant Erebus being cast across the western mountains. Our days were now getting very short and the amount of daylight was a negligible quantity. We boarded up the remainder of the windows, and depended entirely upon the artificial light in the winter quarters. The light given by the acetylene gas was brilliant, the four burners lighting the whole of the hut.

When daylight returned and sledging began about the middle of August, on one of our excursions on the Cape Royds peninsula, we found growing under volcanic earth a large quantity of fungus. This was of great interest to Murray, as plant life of any sort is extremely rare in the Antarctic. Shortly after this a strong blizzard cast up a quantity of seaweed on our ice foot; this was another piece of good fortune, for on the last expedition we obtained very little seaweed.

When Midwinter's Day had passed and the twilight that presaged the return of the sun began to be more marked day by day, I set on foot the arrangements for the sledging work in the forthcoming spring. It was desirable that, at as early a date as possible, we should place a depot of stores at a point to the south, in preparation for the departure of the southern party, which was to march toward the Pole. I hoped to make this depot at least one hundred miles from the winter quarters. Then it was desirable that we should secure some definite information regarding the condition of the snow surface on the Barrier, and I was also anxious to afford the various members of the expedition some practice in sledging before the serious work commenced. Some of us had been in the Antarctic before, but the majority of the men had not yet had any experience of marching and camping on snow and ice, in low temperatures.

The ponies had been kept in good training by means of regular exercise and constant attention during the winter, but although they were thoroughly fit, and, indeed, apparently anxious for an opportunity to work off some of their superfluous energy, I did not propose to take them on the preliminary sledging journeys. It seemed to be unwise to take any unnecessary risk of further loss now that we had only four ponies left, few enough for the southern journey later in the season. For this reason, manhauling was the order for the first journeys.

During the winter I had given a great deal of earnest consideration to the question of the date at which the party that was to march toward the Pole should start from the hut. The goal that we hoped to attain lay over 880 statute miles to the south, and the brief summer was all too short a time in which to march so far into the unknown and return to winter quarters. The ship would have to leave for the north about the end of February, for the ice would then be closing in, and, moreover, we could not hope to carry on our sledges much more than a three months' supply of provisions, on anything like full rations. I finally decided that the southern party should leave the winter quarters about October 28, for if we started earlier it was probable that the ponies would suffer from the severe cold at nights, and we would gain no advantage from getting away early in the season, if, as a result, the ponies were incapacitated before we had made much progress.

The date for the departure of the southern party having been fixed, it became necessary to arrange for the laying of the depot during the early spring, and I thought that the first step toward this should be a preliminary journey on the Barrier surface, in order to gain an idea of the conditions that would be met with, and to ascertain whether the motor car would be of service, at any rate for the early portion of the journey. The sun had not yet returned and the temperature was very low indeed, but we had proved in the course of the *Discovery* expedition that it is quite possible to travel under these conditions. I therefore started on this preliminary journey on August 12, taking with me Professor David, who was to lead the northern party toward the South Magnetic Pole, and Bertram Armytage, who was to take charge of the party that was to make a journey into the mountains of the west later in the year. The reader can imagine that it was not with feelings of unalloyed pleasure that we turned our backs on the warm, well-found hut and faced our little journey out into the semi-darkness and intense cold, but we did get a certain amount of satisfaction from the thought that at last we were actually beginning the work we had come south to undertake.

We were equipped for a fortnight with provisions and camp gear, packed on one sledge, and had three gallons of petroleum in case we should decide to stay out longer. A gallon of oil will last a party of three men for about ten days under ordinary conditions, and we could get more food at Hut Point if we required it. We took three one-man sleeping bags, believing that they would be sufficiently warm in spite of the low temperature. The larger bags, holding two or three men, certainly give greater warmth, for the occupants warm one another, but, on the other hand, one's rest is very likely to be disturbed by the movements of a companion. We were heavily clothed for this trip, because the sun would not rise above the horizon until another ten days had passed.

Our comrades turned out to see us off, and the pony Quan pulled the sledge with our camp gear over the sea ice until we got close to the glacier south of Cape Barne, about five miles from the winter quarters. Then he was sent back, for the weather was growing thick, and, as already explained, I did not want to run any risk of losing another pony from our sadly diminished team. We proceeded close in by the skuary, and a little further on pitched camp for lunch. Professor David, whose thirst for knowledge could not be quenched, immediately went off to investigate the geology of the neighbourhood. After lunch we started to pull our sledge around the coast toward Hut Point, but the weather became worse, making progress difficult, and at 6 p.m. we camped close to the tide crack at the south side of Turk's Head. We slept well and soundly, although the temperature was about forty degrees below zero, and the experience made me more than ever convinced of the superiority of one-man sleeping bags.

On the following morning, August 13, we marched across to Glacier Tongue, having to cross a wide crack that had been ridged up by ice pressure between Tent Island and the Tongue. As soon as we had crossed we saw the depot standing up clear against the skyline on the Tongue. This was the depot that had been made by the ship soon after our first arrival in the sound. We found no difficulty in getting on to the Tongue, for a fairly gentle slope led up from the sea ice to the glacier surface. The snow had blown over from the south during the winter and made a good way. We found the depot intact though the cases, lying on the ice, had been bleached to a light yellow colour by the wind and sun. We had lunch on the south side of the Tongue, and found there another good way down to the sea ice. There is a very awkward crack on the south side, but this can hardly be called a tide crack. I think it is due to the fact that the tide has more effect on the sea ice than on the heavy mass of the Tongue, though there is no doubt this also is afloat; the rise and fall of the two sections of ice are not coincident, and a crack is produced. The unaccustomed pulling made us tired, and we decided to pitch a camp about four miles off Hut Point, before reaching Castle Rock. Castle Rock is distant three miles and a half from Hut Point, and we had always noticed that after we got abeam of the rock the final march on to the hut seemed very long, for we were always weary by that time.

We reached the old *Discovery* winter quarters at Hut Point on the morning of August 14, and after a good breakfast I took the Professor and Armytage over all the familiar ground. It was very interesting to me to revisit the old scenes. There was the place where, years before, when the *Discovery* was lying fast in the ice close to the shore, we used to dig for the ice that was required for the supply of fresh water. The marks of the picks and shovels were still to be seen. I noticed an old case bedded in the ice, and remembered the day when it had been thrown away. Around the hut was collected a very large amount of debris. The only lake, or rather pool, that lay near these winter quarters was quite a tiny sheet of water in comparison with the large lakes at Cape Royds, and I realised more fully the special advantages we had at our winter quarters as far as biological and zoological work were concerned. Through the Gap we saw the Barrier stretched out before us – the long white road that we were shortly to tread. The fascination of the unknown was strong upon me, and I longed to be away toward the south on the journey that I hoped would lay bare the mysteries of the place of the pole.

We climbed to the top of Crater Hill with a collecting bag and the Professor's camera, and here we took some photographs and made an examination of the cone. Professor David expressed the opinion that the ice sheet had certainly passed over this hill, which is about 1100 ft. high, for there was distinct evidence of glaciation. We climbed along the ridge to Castle Rock, about four miles to the north, and made an examination of the formation there. Then we returned to the hut to have a square meal and get ready for our journey across the Barrier.

The old hut had never been a very cheerful place, even when we were camped alongside it in the *Discovery,* and it looked doubly inhospitable now, after having stood empty and neglected for six years. One side was filled with cases of biscuit and tinned meat, and the snow that had found its way in was lying in great piles around the walls. There was no stove, for this had been taken away with the *Discovery,* and coal was scattered about the floor with other debris and rubbish. Besides the biscuits and the tinned beef and mutton there was some tea and coffee stored in the hut. We cleared a spot on which to sleep, and decided that we would use the cases of biscuit and meat to build another hut inside the main one, so that the quarters would be a little more cozy. I proposed to use this hut as a stores depot in connection with the southern journey, for if the ice broke out in the Sound unexpectedly early, it would be difficult to convey provisions from Cape Royds to the Barrier, and, moreover, Hut Point was twenty miles further south than our winter quarters. We spent that night on the floor of the hut, and slept fairly comfortably, though not as well as on the previous night in the tent, because we were not so close to one another.

On the morning of the following day (August 15) we started away about 9 a.m., crossed the smooth ice to Winter Harbour, and passed close around Cape Armitage. We there found cracks and pressed up ice, showing that there had been Barrier movement, and about three miles further on we crossed the spot at which the sea ice joins the Barrier, ascending a slope about eight feet high. Directly we got on to the Barrier ice we noticed undulations on the surface. We pushed along and got to a distance of about twelve miles from Hut Point in eight hours. The surface generally was hard, but there were very marked sastrugi, and at times patches of soft snow. The conditions did not seem favourable for the use of the motor car because we had already found that the machine could not go through soft snow for more than a few yards, and I foresaw that if we brought it out on to the Barrier it would not be able to do much in the soft surface that would have to be traversed. The condition of the surface varied from mile to mile, and it would be impracticable to keep changing the wheels of the car in order to meet the requirements of each new surface.

The temperature was very low, although the weather was fine. At 6 p.m. the thermometer showed fifty-six degrees below zero, and the petroleum used for the lamp had become milky in colour and of a creamy consistency. That night the temperature fell lower still, and the moisture in our sleeping bags, from our breath and Burberries, made us very uncomfortable when the bags had thawed out with the warmth of our bodies. Everything we touched was appallingly cold, and we got no sleep at all. The next morning (August 16) the weather was threatening, and there were indications of the approach of a blizzard, and I therefore decided to march back to Hut Point, for there was no good purpose to be served by taking unnecessary risks at that stage of the expedition.

We had some warm food, of which we stood sorely in need after the severe night, and then started at 8 a.m. to return to Hut Point. By hard marching, which had the additional advantage of warming us up, we reached the old hut again at three o'clock that afternoon, and we were highly delighted to get into its shelter. The sun had not yet returned, and though there was a strong light in the sky during the day, the Barrier was not friendly under winter conditions.

We reached the hut none too soon, for a blizzard sprang up, and for some days we had to remain in shelter. We utilised the time by clearing up the portion of the hut that we proposed to use, even sweeping it with an old broom we found, and building a shelter of the packing cases, piling them right up to the roof around a space about twenty feet by ten; and thus we made comparatively cosy quarters. We rigged a table for the cooking gear, and put everything neatly in order. My two companions were, at this time, having their first experience of polar life under marching conditions as far as equipment was concerned, and they were gaining knowledge that proved very useful to them on the later journeys.

On the morning of August 22, the day on which the sun once more appeared above the horizon, we started back for the winter quarters, leaving Hut Point at 5 a.m. in the face of a bitterly cold wind from the north-east, with low drift. We marched without a stop for nine miles, until we reached Glacier Tongue and then had an early lunch. An afternoon march of fourteen miles took us to the winter quarters at Cape Royds, where we arrived at 5 p.m. We were not expected at the hut, for the weather was thick and windy, but our comrades were delighted to see us, and we had a hearty dinner and enjoyed the luxury of a good bath.

The chief result of this journey was to convince me that we could not place much reliance on the motor car for the southern journey. Professor David and Armytage had received a good baptism of frost, and as it was very desirable that all the members of the expedition should have personal experience of travelling over the ice and snow in low temperatures before the real work began, I arranged to despatch a small party every week to sledge stores and equipment south to Hut Point. These journeys were much alike in general character, though they all gave rise to incidents that were afterward related in the winter quarters.

On September 1, Wild, Day, and Priestley started for Hut Point via Glacier Tongue with 450 lb. of gear and provisions, their instructions being to leave 230 lb. of provisions at the *Discovery* hut in readiness for the southern journey. They made a start at 10:20 a.m., being accompanied by Brocklehurst with a pony for the first five miles. The weather was fine, but a very low barometer gave an indication that bad weather was coming. I did not hesitate to let these parties face bad weather, because the road they were to travel was well known, and a rough experience would be very useful to the men later in the expedition's work. The party camped in the snow close to the south side of Glacier Tongue.

Next morning (September 2) the weather was still bad, and they were not able to make a start until after noon. At 1:20 p.m. they ran out of the northerly wind into light southerly airs with intervals of calm, and they noticed that at the meeting of the two winds the clouds of drift were formed into whirling columns, some of them over forty feet high. They reached the *Discovery* hut at 4:30 p.m., and soon turned in, the temperature being forty degrees below zero. When they dressed at 5:30 a.m. (September 3) they found that a southerly wind with heavy drift rendered a start on the return journey inadvisable. After breakfast they walked over to Observation Hill, where they examined a set of stakes which Ferrar and Wild had placed in the Gap glacier in 1902. The stakes showed that the movement of the glacier during the six years since the stakes had been put into position had amounted to a few inches only. The middle stake had advanced eight inches and those next it on either side about six inches. At noon the wind dropped, and although the drift was still thick, the party started back, steering by the sastrugi till the Tongue was reached. They camped for the night in the lee of the glacier, with a blizzard blowing over them and the temperature rising, the result being that everything was uncomfortably wet. They managed to sleep, however, and when they awoke the next morning the weather was clear, and they had an easy march in, being met beyond Cape Barne by Joyce, Brocklehurst, and the dogs. They had been absent four days.

Each party came back with adventures to relate, experiences to compare, and its own views on various matters of detail connected with sledge travelling. Curiously enough, every one of the parties encountered bad weather, but there were no accidents, and all the men seemed to enjoy the work.

Early in September a party consisting of Adams, Marshall, and myself started for Hut Point, and we decided to make one march of the twenty-three miles, and not camp on the way. We started at 8 a.m., and when we were nearly at the end of the journey, and were struggling slowly through bad snow toward the hut, close to the end of Hut Point, a strong blizzard came up. Fortunately I knew the bearings of the hut, and how to get over the ice foot. We abandoned the extra weights we were pulling for the depot, and managed to get to the hut at 10 p.m. in a sorely frostbitten condition, almost too tired to move. We were able to get ourselves some hot food, however, and were soon all right again. I mention the incident merely to show how constantly one has to be on guard against the onslaughts of the elements in the inhospitable regions of the south.

CHAPTER II

The Southern Journey
*Preparation: Depot A laid: First days of the march from
winter quarters: Start from Hut Point, November 3*

By the middle of September a good supply of provisions, oil, and
gear had been stored at Hut Point. All the supplies required for the
southern journey had been taken there, in order that the start
might be made from the most southern base available. During this
period, while the men were gaining experience and getting into
training, the ponies were being exercised regularly along the sea
ice from winter quarters across to Cape Barne, and I was more
than satisfied with the way in which they did their work. I felt that
the little animals were going to justify the confidence I had
reposed in them when I had brought them all the way from
Manchuria to the bleak Antarctic. I tried the ponies with loads of
varying weights in order to ascertain as closely as possible how
much they could haul with maximum efficiency, and after watching the results of the experiments very carefully came to the
conclusion that a load of 650 lb. per pony should be the maximum.
It was obvious that if the animals were overloaded their speed
would be reduced, so that there would be no gain to us, and if we
were to accomplish a good journey to the south it was important
that they should not be tired out in the early stages of the march
over the Barrier surface. The weight I have mentioned was to
include that of the sledge itself, which was about 60 lb.

When the question of weight came to be considered I could
realise the seriousness of the loss of the four ponies, during the
winter. It was evident that we would be unable to take with us
toward the Pole as much food as I would have liked.

I decided to place a depot one hundred geographical miles south
of the *Discovery* winter quarters, the depot to consist of pony
maize. The party, consisting of Adams, Marshall, Wild, Marston,

Joyce and myself, left Cape Royds on September 22 with a load of about 170 lb. per man, and the motor car towed the sledges as far as Inaccessible Island, at the rate of about six miles an hour. We took two tents and two three-man sleeping bags, for we expected to meet very low temperatures. I had decided to take neither ponies nor dogs, so we took the sledges on ourselves, travelling over a fairly good surface as far as the *Discovery* hut, where we passed the first night. The journey was a severe one, for the temperature, at times, got down to 59° below zero F. We reached the main depot in latitude 79° 36' South, longitude 168° East, on October 6. This we called 'Depot A'. It was marked with an upturned sledge and a black flag on a bamboo rod. We deposited a gallon tin of oil and 167 lb. of pony maize so that our load would be considerably reduced for the first portion of the journey when we started south. The weather was very severe on the return journey and we did not reach the old *Discovery* winter quarters until October 13. We had been twenty-one days out, but had been able to march only on fourteen and a half days. The next day we started for Cape Royds and had the good fortune to meet the motor car a mile and a half south of Cape Barne. The sledges were soon hitched on, and we drove triumphantly to winter quarters — having travelled 320 statute miles since September 22.

During our absence the northern party consisting of Professor David, Mawson, and Mackay, had started on the journey that was to result in the attainment of the South Magnetic Pole. I had said goodbye to Professor David and his two companions on September 22 and we did not meet again until March 1, 1909. In chapter 22 the Professor tells the story of the northern journey.

The southern party was to leave winter quarters on October 29; so on the return of the party from Depot A we commenced final preparations for the attempt to reach the South Pole. I decided that four men should go south, I myself to be one of them, and that we should take provisions for ninety-one days: this amount of food with the other equipment would bring the load per pony up to the weight fixed as the maximum safe load. Early in 1907 I had proposed that one party should travel to the east across the Barrier surface toward King Edward VII Land but the accidents that had left us with only four ponies caused me to abandon this project. The ponies would have to go south, the motor car would not travel on the Barrier, and the dogs were required for the southern depot journey. I deemed it best to confine the efforts of the sledging parties to the two Poles, Geographical and Magnetic, and to send a third party into the western mountains with the object of studying geological conditions and, in particular, of searching for fossils.

The men selected to go with me were Adams, Marshall, and Wild. A supporting party was to accompany us for a certain distance in order that we might start fairly fresh from a point beyond the rough ice off Minna Bluff, and we would take the four ponies and four sledges.

Arrangements were made for sending out a party early in December to lay a depot for the northern party. When this had been done, the same party would proceed to the western mountains. On January 15, 1909, a depot party, under the command of Joyce, was to lay a depot near Minna Bluff containing sufficient stores for the return of the southern party from that point. This same party was to return to Hut Point, reload its sledge and march out to the depot a second time, there to await the arrival of the southern party until February 10, 1909. If the southern party had not arrived by that date Joyce and his companions were to go back to Hut Point and thence to the ship.

Before my departure from winter quarters on the southern journey, I left instructions which provided for the conclusion of the work of the Expedition in its various branches, and for the relief of the men left in the Antarctic, in the event of the non-return of the southern party. I gave Murray command of the Expedition in my absence and full instructions. The trials of the motor car in the neighbourhood of the winter quarters had proved that it could not travel over a soft snow surface, and the depot journey had shown me that the surface of the Barrier was covered with soft snow, much softer and heavier than it had been in 1902, at the time of the *Discovery* expedition. In fact I was satisfied that, with the Barrier in its then condition, no wheeled vehicle could travel over it. The wheels would simply sink in until the body of the car rested on the snowy surface. We had made alterations in the wheels and we had reduced the weight of the car to an absolute minimum by the removal of every unnecessary part, but still it could do little on a soft surface, and it would certainly be quite useless with any weight behind, for the driving wheels would simply scoop holes for themselves. The use of sledge runners under the front wheel, with broad, spiked driving wheels, might have enabled us to get the car over some of the soft surfaces, but this equipment would not have been satisfactory on hard, rough ice, and constant changes would occupy too much time. I had confidence in the ponies, and I thought it best not to attempt to take the car south from the winter quarters.

The provisioning of the southern party was a matter that received long and anxious consideration. Marshall went very carefully into the question of the relative food values of the various supplies, and we were able to derive much useful information from the experience of previous expeditions. We decided on a daily ration of 34 oz. per man; the total weight of food to be carried, on the basis of supplies for ninety-one days, would therefore be 773½ lb. The staple items were to be biscuits and pemmican. The biscuits, as I have stated, were of wheatmeal with 25 percent of plasmon added, and analysis showed that they did not contain more than 3 percent of water. The pemmican had been supplied by Beauvais, of Copenhagen, and consisted of the finest beef, dried and powdered, with 60 percent of beef fat added. It contained only a small percentage of water. The effort of the polar explorer is to get his foods as free from water as possible, for the moisture represents so much useless weight to be carried.

The daily allowance of food for each man on the journey, as long as full rations were given, was to be as follows:

	oz.
Pemmican	7.5
Emergency ration	1.5
Biscuit	16.0
Cheese or chocolate	2.0
Cocoa	.7
Plasmon	1.0
Sugar	4.3
Quaker Oats	1.0
	34.0

Tea, salt, and pepper were extras not weighed in with the daily allowance. We used about two ounces of tea per day for the four men. The salt and pepper were carried in small bags, each bag to last one week. Some of the biscuit had been broken up and 1 lb. per week for each man was intended to be used for thickening the hoosh, the amount so used to be deducted from the ordinary allowance of biscuit.

Everything was ready for the start on the journey toward the Pole as the end of October approached, and we looked forward with keen anticipation to the venture. The supporting party was to consist of Joyce, Marston, Priestley, Armytage, and Brocklehurst, and was to accompany us for ten days. Day was to have been a member of this party, but he damaged his foot while tobogganing down a slope at the winter quarters, and had to stay behind. The weather was not very good during our last days at the hut, but there were signs that summer was approaching. The ponies were in good condition. We spent the last few days overhauling the sledges and equipment, and making sure that everything was sound and in its right place. In the evenings we wrote letters for those at home, to be delivered in the event of our not returning from the unknown regions into which we hoped to penetrate.

Events of the southern journey were recorded day by day in the diary I wrote during the long march. I read this diary when we had got back to civilisation, and arrived at the conclusion that to rewrite it would be to take away the special flavour which it possesses. It was written under conditions of much difficulty, and often of great stress, and these conditions I believe it reflects. I am therefore publishing the diary with only such minor amendments in the phraseology as are necessary in order to make it easily understood. The reader will understand that when one is writing in a sleeping bag, with the temperature very low and food rather short, a good proportion of the 'ofs', 'ands' and 'thes' get left out. The story will probably seem bald, but it is at any rate a faithful record of what occurred. I will deal more fully with some aspects of the journey in a later chapter. The altitudes given in the diary were calculated at the time, and were not always accurate. The corrected altitudes are given on the map and in a table at the end of the book. The distances were calculated by means of a sledge meter, checked by observations of the sun, and are approximately accurate.

October 29, 1908. A glorious day for our start; brilliant sunshine and a cloudless sky, a fair wind from the north, in fact, everything that could conduce to an auspicious beginning. We had breakfast at 7 a.m., and at 8:30 the sledges that the motor was to haul to Glacier Tongue were taken down by the penguin rookery and over to the rough ice. At 9:30 a.m. the supporting party started and was soon out of sight, as the motor was running well. At 10 a.m. we four of the southern party followed. As we left the hut where we had spent so many months in comfort, we had a feeling of real regret that never again would we all be together there. It was dark inside, the acetylene was feeble in comparison with the sun outside, and it was small compared to an ordinary dwelling, yet we were sad at leaving it. Last night as we were sitting at dinner the evening sun entered through the ventilator and a circle of light shone on the picture of the Queen. Slowly it moved across and lit up the photograph of his Majesty the King. This seemed an omen of good luck, for only on that day and at that particular time could this have happened, and today we started to strive to plant the Queen's flag on the last spot of the world. At 10 a.m. we met Murray and Roberts, and said goodbye, then went on our way. Both of these, who were to be left, had done for me all that men could do in their own particular line of work to try and make our little expedition a success. A clasp of the hands means more than many words, and as we turned to acknowledge their cheer and saw them standing on the ice by the familiar cliffs, I felt that we must try to do well for the sake of everyone concerned in the expedition.

Hardly had we been going for an hour when Socks went dead lame. This was a bad shock, for Quan had for a full week been the same. We had thought that our troubles in this direction were over. Socks must have hurt himself on some of the sharp ice. We had to go on, and I trust that in a few days he will be all right. I shall not start from our depot at Hut Point until he is better or until I know actually what is going to happen. The lameness of a pony in our present situation is a serious thing. If we had eight, or even six, we could adjust matters more easily, but when we are working to the bare ounce it is very serious.

At 1 p.m. we halted and fed the ponies. As we sat close to them on the sledge Grisi suddenly lashed out, and striking the sledge with his hoof, struck Adams just below the knee. Three inches higher and the blow would have shattered his knee cap and ended his chance of going on. As it was the bone was almost exposed, and he was in great pain, but said little about it. We went on and at 2:30 p.m. arrived at the sledges which had gone on by motor yesterday, just as the car came along after having dragged the other sledges within a quarter of a mile of the Tongue. I took on one sledge, and Day started in rather soft snow with the other sledges, the car being helped by the supporting party in the worst places. Pressure ridges and drift just off the Tongue prevented the car going further, so I gave the sledge Quan was dragging to Adams, who was leading Chinaman, and went back for the other. We said goodbye to Day, and he went back, with Priestley and Brockle-hurst helping him, for his foot was still very weak.

We got to the south side of Glacier Tongue at 4 p.m., and after a cup of tea started to grind up the maize in the depot. It was hard work, but we each took turns at the crusher, and by 8 p.m. had ground sufficient maize for the journey. It is now 11 p.m., and a high warm sun is shining down, the day calm and clear. We had hoosh at 9 p.m. Adams' leg is very stiff and sore. The horses are fairly quiet, but Quan has begun his old tricks and is biting his tether. I must send for wire rope if this goes on.

At last we are out on the long trail, after four years' thought and work. I pray that we may be successful, for my heart has been so much in this.

There are numbers of seals lying close to our camp. They are nearly all females, and will soon have young. Erebus is emitting three distinct columns of steam today, and the fumaroles on the old crater can be seen plainly. It is a mercy that Adams is better tonight. I cannot imagine what he would have done if he had been knocked out for the southern journey, his interest in the expedition has been so intense. Temperatures plus 2°F, distance for the day, 14½ miles.

October 30. At Hut Point. Another gloriously fine day. We started away for Hut Point at 10:30 a.m., leaving the supporting party to finish grinding the maize. The ponies were in good fettle and went away well, Socks walking without a sledge, while Grisi had 500 lb., Quan 430 lb., and Chinaman 340 lb. Socks seems better today. It is a wonderful change to get up in the morning and put on ski boots without any difficulty, and to handle cooking vessels without 'burning' one's fingers on the frozen metal. I was glad to see all the ponies so well, for there had been both wind and drift during the night. Quan seems to take a delight in biting his tether when anyone is looking, for I put my head out of the tent occasionally during the night to see if they were all right, and directly I did so Quan started to bite his rope. At other times they were all quiet.

We crossed one crack that gave us a little trouble, and at 1:30 p.m. reached Castle Rock, travelling at one mile and three-quarters per hour. There I changed my sledge, taking on Marshall's sledge with Quan, for Grisi was making hard work of it, the surface being very soft in places. Quan pulled 500 lb. just as easily and at 3 p.m. we reached Hut Point, tethered the ponies, and had tea. There was a slight north wind. At 5 p.m. the supporting party came up. We have decided to sleep in the hut, but the supporting party are sleeping in the tent at the very spot where the *Discovery* wintered six years ago. Tomorrow I am going back to the Tongue for the rest of the fodder. The supporting party elected to sleep out because it is warmer, but we of the southern party will not have a solid roof over our heads for some months to come, so will make the most of it. We swept the debris out. Wild killed a seal for fresh meat and washed the liver at the seal hole, so tomorrow we will have a good feed. Half a tin of jam is a small thing for one man to eat when he has a sledging appetite, and we are doing our share, as when we start there will be no more of these luxuries. Adams's leg is better, but stiff. Our march was nine and a half miles today. It is now 10 p.m.

October 31. This day started with a dull snowy appearance, which soon developed into a snowstorm, but a mild one with little drift. I wanted to cross to Glacier Tongue with Quan, Grisi, and Chinaman.

During the morning we readjusted our provision weights and unpacked the bags. In the afternoon it cleared, and at 3:30 p.m. we got under way, Quan pulling our sleeping equipment. We covered the eight miles and a half to Glacier Tongue in three hours, and as I found no message from the hut, nor the gear I had asked to be sent down, I concluded it was blowing there also, and so decided to walk on after dinner. I covered the twelve miles in three hours, arriving at Cape Royds at 11:30, and had covered the twenty-three miles between Hut Point and Cape Royds in six hours, marching time. They were surprised to see me, and were glad to hear that Adams and Socks were better. I turned in at 2 a.m. for a few hours' sleep. It had been blowing hard with thick drift, so the motor had not been able to start for Glacier Tongue. On my way to Cape Royds I noticed several seals with young ones, evidently just born. Murray tells me that the temperature has been plus 22°F.

November 1. Had breakfast at 6 a.m., and Murray came on the car with me, Day driving. There was a fresh easterly wind. We left Cape Royds at 8 a.m., and arrived off Inaccessible Island at twenty minutes past eight, having covered a distance of eight miles. The car was running very well. Then off Tent Island we left the car, and hauled the sledge, with the wire rope, etc., around to our camp off Glacier Tongue. Got under way at 10 a.m., and reached Hut Point at 2 p.m., the ponies pulling 500 and 550 lb. each. Grisi bolted with his sledge, but soon stopped. The ponies pulled very well, with a bad light and a bad surface. We arranged the packing of the sledges in the afternoon, but we are held up because of Socks. His foot is seriously out of order, It is almost a disaster, for we want every pound of hauling power. This evening it is snowing hard, with no wind. Adams's leg is much better. Wild noticed a seal giving birth to a pup. The baby measured 3 ft. 10 in. in length, and weighed 50 lb. I turned in early tonight, for I had done thirty-nine miles in the last twenty-four hours.

November 2. Dull and snowy during the early hours of today. When we awoke we found that Quan had bitten through his tether and played havoc with the maize and other fodder. Directly he saw me coming down the ice foot, he started off, dashing from one sledge to another, tearing the bags to pieces and trampling the food out. It was ten minutes before we caught him. Luckily one sledge of fodder was untouched. He pranced around, kicked up his heels, and showed that it was a deliberate piece of destructiveness on his part, for he had eaten his fill. His distended appearance was obviously the result of many pounds of maize.

In the afternoon three of the ponies hauled the sledges with their full weights across the junction of the sea and the Barrier ice, and in spite of the soft snow they pulled splendidly. We are now all ready for a start the first thing tomorrow. Socks seems much better, and not at all lame. The sun is now (9 p.m.) shining gloriously, and the wind has dropped, all auguring for a fine day tomorrow. The performance of the ponies was most satisfactory, and if they will only continue so for a month, it will mean a lot to us. Adams's leg is nearly all right.

November 3. Started at 9:30 from Hut Point, Quan pulling 660 lb., Grisi 615 lb., Socks 600 lb., and Chinaman 600 lb. Five men hauled 660 lb., 153 lb. of this being pony feed for our party. It was a beautifully fine day, but we were not long under way when we found that the surface was terribly soft, the ponies at times sinking in up to their bellies and always over their hocks.

We picked up the other sledges at the Barrier junction, and Brocklehurst photographed us all, with our sledge flags flying and the Queen's Union Jack. At 10:50 we left the sea ice, and instead of finding the Barrier surface better, discovered that the snow was even softer than earlier in the day. The ponies pulled magnific-ently, and the supporting party toiled on painfully in their wake. Every hour the pony leaders changed places with the sledge haulers. At 1 p.m. the advance party with the ponies pitched camp and tethered out the ponies, and soon lunch was under way, consisting of tea with plasmon, plasmon biscuits, and cheese. At 2:30 we struck camp, the supporting party with the man sledge going on in advance, while the others with the ponies did the camp work. By 4 p.m. the surface had improved in places, so that the men did not break through the crust so often, but it was just as hard work as ever for the ponies. The weather kept beautifully fine, with a slight south-east wind. The weather sides of the ponies were quite dry, but their lee sides were frosted with congealed sweat. Whenever it came to our turn to pull, we perspired freely. As the supporting party are not travelling as fast as the ponies, we have decided to take them on only for two more days, and then we of the southern party will carry the remainder of the pony feed from their sledge on our backs. So tomorrow morning we will depot nearly 100 lb. of oil and provisions, which will lighten the load on the supporting party's sledge a good deal.

We camped at 6 p.m., and, after feeding the ponies, had our dinner, consisting of pemmican, emergency ration, plasmon bis-cuits and plasmon cocoa, followed by a smoke, the most ideal smoke a man could wish for after a day's sledging. As there is now plenty of biscuit to spare, we gave the gallant little ponies a good feed of them after dinner. They are now comfortably standing in the sun, with the temperature plus 14°F, and occasionally pawing the snow. Grisi has dug a large hole already in the soft surface. We have been steering a south-east course all day, keeping well to the north of White Island to avoid the crevasses. Our distance for the day is 12 miles (statute) 300 yards.

November 4. Started at 8:30 this morning; fine weather, but bad light. Temperature plus 9°F. We wore goggles, as already we are feeling the trying light. The supporting party started first, and with an improved surface during the morning they kept ahead of the ponies, who constantly broke through the crust. As soon as we passed the end of White Island, the surface became softer, and it was trying work for both men and ponies. However, we did 9 miles 500 yards (statute) up to 1 p.m., the supporting party going the whole time without being relieved. Their weights had been reduced by nearly 100 lb., as we depoted that amount of oil and provision last night. In the afternoon the surface was still softer, and when we came to camp at 6 p.m. the ponies were plainly tired. The march for the day was 16 miles, 500 yards (statute), over fourteen miles geographical, with a bad surface, so we have every reason to be pleased with the ponies. The supporting party pulled hard. The cloud rolled away from Erebus this evening, and it is now warm, clear, and bright to the north, but dark to the south. I am steering about east-south-east to avoid the crevasses off White Island, but tomorrow we go south-east. We fixed our position tonight from bearings, and find that we are thirty-four miles south of Cape Royds. Everyone is fit and well.

November 5. On turning out this morning, we found the weather overcast, with slight snow falling and only a few landmarks visible to the north, nothing to the south. We got under way at 8:15 a.m., steering by compass. The light was so bad that the sastrugi could not be seen, though of the latter there was not much, for there was a thick coating of fallen snow. The surface was very bad for ponies and men. The ponies struggled gamely on through the tiring morning, and we camped for lunch at 1 p.m., having done 8 miles 1200 yards. After lunch we started at 2:15 p.m. in driving snow, but our steering was very wild. We had been making a south-east course all the morning, but in the afternoon the course was a devious one. Suddenly Marshall, who was leading Grisi, got his legs into a crevasse, and Grisi also; they recovered themselves, and Marshall shouted out to me. I stopped my horse and went to his assistance in getting the sledge off the snow bridge covering the chasm. The crevasse was about 3 ft. wide, with the sides widening out below. No bottom could be seen. The line of direction was north-west by south-east. I at once altered the course to east, but in about a quarter of an hour Wild, Adams, and Marshall got into a narrow crevasse, so I stopped and pitched camp, to wait until the weather cleared and we could get some idea of our actual position. This was at 3 p.m., the sledge meter recording 9 miles 1200 yards (statute) for the day. At 4 p.m. it commenced to drift and blow, and it is blowing hard and gustily now. It is very unfortunate to be held up like this, but I trust that it will blow itself out tonight and be fine tomorrow. The ponies will be none the worse for the rest. We wore goggles today, as the light was so bad and some of us got a touch of snow blindness.

November 6. Lying in our sleeping bags all day except when out feeding the ponies, for it has been blowing a blizzard, with thick drift, from south by west. It is very hard to be held up like this, for each day means the consumption of 40 lb. of pony feed alone. We only had a couple of biscuits each for lunch, for I can see that we must retrench at every setback if we are going to have enough food to carry us through. We started with ninety-one days' food, but with careful management we can make it spin out to 110 days. If we have not done the job in that time it is God's will. Some of the supporting party did not turn out for any meal during the last twenty-four hours. Quan and Chinaman have taken their feeds constantly, but Socks and Grisi not so well. They all like Maujee ration and eat that up before touching the maize. They have been very quiet, standing tails to the blizzard, which has been so thick that at times we could not see them from the peepholes of our tents. There are great drifts all around the tents, and some of the sledges are buried. This evening about 5:30 the weather cleared a bit and the wind dropped. When getting out the feed boxes at 6 p.m. I could see White Island and the Bluff, so I hope that tomorrow will be fine. The barometer has been steady all day at 28.60 in., with the temperature up to 18°F, so it is quite warm, and in our one-man sleeping bags each of us has a little home, where he can read and write and look at the penates and lares brought with him. I read *Much Ado About Nothing* during the morning. The surface of the Barrier is better, for the wind has blown away a great deal of the soft snow, and we will, I trust, be able to see any crevasses before we are on to them. This is our fourth day out from Hut Point, and we are only twenty miles south. We must do better than this if we are to make much use of the ponies. I would not mind the blizzard so much if we had only to consider ourselves, for we can save on the food, whereas the ponies must be fed full.

November 7. Another disappointing day. We got up at 5 a.m. to breakfast, so as to be in time to start at 8 a.m. We cleared all the drift off our sledges, and, unstowing them, examined the runners, finding them to be in splendid condition. This work, with the assistance of the supporting party, took us till 8:30 a.m. Shortly afterward we got under way, saying goodbye to the supporting party, who are to return today. As we drew away, the ponies pulling hard, our comrades gave us three cheers. The weather was thick and overcast, with no wind. Part of White Island could be seen, and Observation Hill, astern, but before us lay a dead white wall, with nothing, even in the shape of a cloud, to guide our steering. Almost immediately after we left we crossed a crevasse, and before we had gone half a mile we found ourselves in a maze of them, only detecting their presence by the ponies breaking through the crust and saving themselves, or the man leading a pony putting his foot through. The first one Marshall crossed with Grisi was 6 ft. wide, and when I looked down there was nothing to be seen but a black yawning void. Just after this, I halted Quan on the side of one, as I thought in the uncertain light, but I found that we were standing on the crust in the centre, so I very gingerly unharnessed him from the sledge and got him across. Then the sledge, with our three months' provisions, was pulled out of danger. Following this, Adams crossed another crevasse, and China-man got his forefoot into the hole at the side. I, following with Quan, also got into difficulties, and so I decided that it was too risky to proceed, and we camped between two large crevasses. We picketed the ponies out and pitched one tent, to wait till the light became better, for we were courting disaster by proceeding in that weather. Thus ended our day's march of under a mile, for about 1 p.m. it commenced to snow, and the wind sprang up from the south-west with drift. We pitched our second tent and had lunch, consisting of a pot of tea, some chocolate and two biscuits each. The temperature was plus 12°F at noon.

It blew a little in the afternoon, and I hope to find it clear away this pall of dead white stratus that stops us. The ponies were in splendid trim for pulling this morning, but, alas! we had to stop. Grisi and Socks did not eat up their food well at lunch or dinner. The temperature this evening is plus 9°F, and the ponies feel chilly. Truly this work is one demanding the greatest exercise of patience, for it is more than trying to have to sit here and watch the time going by, knowing that each day lessens our stock of food. The supporting party got under way about 9:30 a.m., and we could see them dwindling to a speck in the north. They will, no doubt, be at Hut Point in a couple of days. We are now at last quite on our own resources, and as regards comfort in the tents are very well off, for with only two men in each tent, there is ample room. Adams is sharing one with me, whilst Marshall and Wild have the other. Wild is cook this week, so they keep the cooker and the primus lamp in their tent, and we go across to meals, after first feeding the ponies. Next week Adams will be cook, so the cooking will be done in the tent I am in. We will also shift about so that we will take turns with each other as tentmates. On the days on which we are held up by weather we read, and I can only trust that these days may not be many. I am just finishing reading *The Taming of the Shrew*. I have Shakespeare's *Comedies*, Marshall has Borrow's *The Bible in Spain*, Adams has Arthur Young's *Travels in France*, and Wild has *Sketches by Boz*. When we have finished we will change around. Our allowance of tobacco is very limited, and on days like these it disappears rapidly, for our anxious minds are relieved somewhat by a smoke. In order to economise my cigarettes, which are my luxury, I whittled out a holder from a bit of bamboo today, and so get a longer smoke, and also avoid the paper sticking to my lips, which have begun to crack already from the hot metal pot and the cold air.

NOTE. The difficulties of travelling over snow and ice in a bad light are very great. When the light is diffused by clouds or mist, it casts no shadows on the dead white surface, which consequently appears to the eye to be uniformly level. Often as we marched, the sledges would be brought up all standing by a sastrugus, or snow mound, caused by the wind, and we would be lucky if we were not tripped up ourselves. Small depressions would escape the eye altogether, and when we thought that we were marching along on a level surface, we would suddenly step down two or three feet. The strain on the eyes under these conditions is very great, and it is when the sun is covered and the weather is thickish that snow blindness is produced. Snow blindness, with which we all became acquainted during the southern journey, is a very painful complaint. The first sign of the approach of the trouble is running at the nose; then the sufferer begins to see double, and his vision gradually becomes blurred. The more painful symptoms appear very soon. The blood vessels of the eyes swell, making one feel as though sand had got in under the lids, and then the eyes begin to water freely and gradually close up. The best method of relief is to drop some cocaine into the eye, and then apply a powerful astringent, such as sulphate of zinc, in order to reduce the distended blood vessels. The only way to guard against an attack is to wear goggles the whole time, so that the eyes may not be exposed to the strain caused by the reflection of the light from all quarters. These goggles are made so that the violet rays are cut off, these rays being the most dangerous, but in warm weather, when one is perspiring on account of exertion with the sledges, the glasses fog, and it becomes necessary to take them off frequently in order to wipe them. The goggles we used combined red and green glasses, and so gave a yellow tint to everything and greatly subdued the light. When we removed them, the glare from the surrounding whiteness was intense, and the only relief was to get inside one of the tents which were made of green material, very restful to the eyes. We noticed that during the spring journey, when the temperature was very low and the sun was glaring on us, we did not suffer from snow blindness. The glare of the light reflected from the snow on bright days places a very severe strain on the eyes, and the rays of the sun are flashed back from millions of crystals. The worst days, as far as snow blindness was concerned, were when the sun was obscured, so that the light came equally from every direction, and the temperature was comparatively high.

November 8. Drawn blank again! In our bags all day while outside the snow is drifting hard and blowing freshly at times. The temperature was plus 8°F at noon. The wind has not been really strong; if it had been I believe that the weather would have been over sooner. It is a sore trial to one's hopes and patience to lie and watch the drift on the tent side and to know that our valuable pony food is going, and this without benefiting the animals themselves. Indeed, Socks and Grisi have not been eating well, and the hard maize does not agree with them. At lunch we had only a couple of biscuits and some chocolate, and used our oil to boil some Maujee ration for the horses, so that they had a hot hoosh. They all ate it readily which is a comfort. This standing for four days in drift with 24° of frost is not good for them, and we are anxiously looking for finer weather. Tonight it is clearer, and we could see the horizon and some of the crevasses. We seem to be in a regular nest of them. The occupants of the other tent have discovered that it is pitched on the edge of a previously unseen one. We had a hot hoosh tonight, consisting of pemmican, with emergency ration and the cocoa. This warmed us up, for to lie from breakfast time at 6 a.m. for twelve or thirteen hours without hot food in this temperature is chilly work. If only we could get under way and put some good marches in, we would feel more happy. It is 750 miles as the crow flies from our winter quarters to the Pole, and we have done only fifty-one miles as yet. But still the worst will turn to the best, I doubt not. That a polar explorer needs a large stock of patience in his equipment there was no denying. The sun is showing thin and pale through the drift this evening, and the wind is more gusty, so we may have it really fine tomorrow. I read some of Shakespeare's comedies today.

November 9. A different story today. When we woke up at 4:30 a.m. it was fine, calm, and clear, such a change from the last four days. We got breakfast at 5 a.m., and then dug the sledges out of the drift. After this we four walked out to find a track amongst the crevasses, but unfortunately they could only be detected by probing with our ice axes, and these disclosed all sorts, from narrow cracks to great ugly chasms with no bottom visible. A lump of snow thrown down one would make no noise, so the bottom must have been very far below. The general direction was southeast and north-west, but some curved around to the south and some to the east. There was nothing for it but to trust to Providence, for we had to cross them somewhere. At 8:30 a.m. we got under way, the ponies not pulling very well, for they have lost condition in the blizzard and were stiff. We got over the first few crevasses without difficulty, then all of a sudden Chinaman went down a crack which ran parallel to our course. Adams tried to pull him out and he struggled gamely, and when Wild and I, who were next, left our sledges and hauled along Chinaman's sledge, it gave him more scope, and he managed to get on to the firm ice, only just in time, for three feet more and it would have been all up with the southern journey. The three-foot crack opened out into a great fathomless chasm, and down that would have gone the horse, all our cooking gear and biscuits and half the oil, and probably Adams as well. But when things seem the worst they turn to the best, for that was the last crevasse we encountered, and with a gradually improving surface, though very soft at times, we made fair headway. We camped for lunch at 12:40 p.m., and the ponies ate fairly well. Quan is pulling 660 lb., and had over 700 lb. till lunch; Grisi has 590 lb., Chinaman 570 lb., and Socks 600 lb. In the afternoon the surface further improved, and at 6 p.m. we camped, having done 14 miles 600 yards, statute. The Bluff is showing clear, and also Castle Rock miraged up astern of us. White Island is also clear, but a stratus cloud overhangs Erebus, Terror, and Discovery. At 6:20 p.m. we suddenly heard a deep rumble, lasting about five seconds, that made the air and the ice vibrate. It seemed to come from the eastward, and resembled the sound and had the effect of heavy guns firing. We conjecture that it was due to some large mass of the Barrier breaking away, and the distance must be at least fifty miles from where we are. It was startling, to say the least of it. Tonight we boiled some Maujee ration for the ponies, and they took this feed well. It has a delicious smell, and we ourselves would have enjoyed it. Quan is now engaged in the pleasing occupation of gnawing his tether rope. I tethered him up by the hind leg to prevent him attacking this particular thong, but he has found out that by lifting his hind leg he can reach the rope, so I must get out and put a nose bag on him. The temperature is now plus 5°F, but it feels much warmer, for there is a dead calm and the sun is shining.

CHAPTER 12

Beyond all former footsteps
November 10 to December 4
Steady progress: The sighting of new land

November 10. Got up to breakfast at 6 a.m., and under way at 8:15 a.m. During the night we had to get out to the ponies. Quan had eaten away the straps on his rug, and Grisi and Socks were fighting over it. Quan had also chewed Chinaman's tether, and the latter was busy at one of the sledges, chewing rope. Happily he has not the same mischievous propensities as Quan, so the food bags were not torn about. All these things mean work for us when the day's march is over, repairing the damage done. The ponies started away well, with a good hard surface to travel on, but a bad light, so we, being in finnesko, had frequent falls over the sastrugi. I at last took my goggles off, and am paying the penalty tonight, having a touch of snow blindness. During the morning the land to the west became more distinct, and the going still better, so that when we camped for lunch, we had covered nine and a half statute miles. All the ponies, except Quan, showed the result of the Maujee ration, and are quite loose. Directly we started after lunch, we came across the track of an Adelie penguin. It was most surprising, and one wonders how the bird came out here. It had evidently only passed a short time before, as its tracks were quite fresh. It had been travelling on its stomach a good way, and its course was due east toward the sea, but where it had come from was a mystery, for the nearest water in the direction from which it came was over fifty miles away, and it had at least another fifty miles to do before it could reach food and water. The surface in the afternoon became appallingly soft, the ponies sinking in up to their hocks, but there was hard snow underneath. At 6 p.m. we camped, with a march for the day of 15 miles 1550 yards statute. The sun came out in the afternoon, so we turned our sleeping bags inside out and dried them. Today's temperature ranged from plus

3°F in the morning to plus 12°F. at noon. At 8 p.m. it was plus 5°F. There is now a light north wind, and I expect Erebus will be clear soon; bearings and angles put us sixty miles from our depot, where lies 167 lb. of pony food.

November 11. It was 8:40 before we got under way this morning, for during the night the temperature dropped well below zero, and it was minus 12° when we got up and found our finnesko and all our gear frozen hard, just like spring sledging times. We had to unpack the sledges and scrape the runners, for the sun had melted the snow on the upper surfaces, and the water had run down and frozen hard during the night on the under sides. The surface was again terribly soft, but there were patches of hard sastrugi beneath, and on one of these Quan must have stepped, for to our great anxiety he suddenly went lame about 11 a.m. I thought it was just the balling of the snow on his feet, but on scraping this off he still was lame. Fortunately, however, he improved greatly and was practically all right after lunch. During the night, the snow always balls on the ponies' feet, and it is one of our regular jobs to scrape it off, before we harness up in the morning. The snow was not so thick on the surface in the afternoon, only about 5 in., and we got on fairly well. The Bluff is now sixteen miles to the north-west of us, and all the well-known land is clear, Erebus sending out a huge volume of steam, that streams away to the south-west right past Mount Discovery, fifty miles from its crater. Again this afternoon we passed an Adelie penguin track. The bird was making the same course as the one we had passed before. At 6:30 p.m. we camped, having done fifteen statute miles. After dinner we got bearings which put us forty-seven miles from our depot. I do trust that the weather will hold up till we reach it. It is cold tonight writing, the temperature being minus 9°F. The land to the south-south-west is beautifully clear.

November 13. No diary yesterday, for I had a bad attack of snow blindness, and am only a bit better tonight. We did a good march yesterday of over fifteen miles over fair surface, and again today did fifteen miles, but the going was softer. The ponies have been a trouble again. I found Quan and Chinaman enjoying the former's rug. They have eaten all the lining. The weather has been beautifully fine, but the temperature down to 12° below zero. The others' eyes are all right. Wild, who has been suffering, has been better today. Snow blindness is a particularly unpleasant thing. One begins by seeing double, then the eyes feel full of grit; this makes them water and eventually one cannot see at all. All yesterday afternoon, though I was wearing goggles, the water kept running out of my eyes, and, owing to the low temperature, it froze on my beard. However, the weather is beautiful, and we are as happy as can be, with good appetites, too good in fact for the amount of food we are allowing ourselves. We are on short rations, but we will have horse meat in addition when the ponies go under. We have saved enough food to last us from our first depot into the Bluff, where, on the way back, we will pick up another depot that is to be laid out by Joyce during January next. I trust we will pick up the depot tomorrow night and it will be a relief, for it is a tiny speck in this snowy plain, and is nearly sixty miles from the nearest land. It is much the same as picking up a buoy in the North Sea with only distant mountains for bearings. We are now clear of the pressure round the Bluff, and the travelling should be good until we reach the depot. On the spring journey we got into the crevasses off the Bluff, these crevasses being due to the movement of the ice-sheet impinging against the long arm of the Bluff reaching out to the eastward. Close in the pressure is much more marked, the whole surface of the Barrier rising into hillocks and splitting into chasms. When the summer sun plays on these and the wind sweeps away the loose snow, a very slippery surface is presented, and the greatest care has to be exercised to prevent the sledges skidding into the pits, often over 100 ft. deep. As one gets further away from the area of disturbance the ridges flatten out, the pits disappear, and the crevasses become cracks. We are now on to level going, clear of any dangers.

November 14. Another beautiful day, but with a low temperature (minus 7°F at 6 p.m.). During the morning there was a wind from the west-south-west, bitterly cold on our faces and burst lips, but the sun was warm on our backs. The ponies pulled well, and in spite of somewhat deep snow they got on very well. We stopped at noon for bearings, and to get the sun's altitude for latitude, and at lunch worked out our position. We expected to see the depot tonight or tomorrow morning, but during the afternoon, when we halted for a spell, we found that our 'ready use' tin of kerosene had dropped off a sledge, so Adams ran back three miles and found it. This caused a delay, and we camped at 6 p.m. We were just putting the position on the chart after dinner when Wild, who was outside looking through the Goertz glasses, shouted out that he could see the depot, and we rushed out. There were the flag and sledge plainly to be seen through the glasses. It is an immense relief to us, for there is stored at the depot four days' pony feed and a gallon of oil. We will sleep happily tonight. The Barrier surface now is covered with huge sastrugi, rounded off and running west south-west and east-north-east, with soft snow between. We have never seen the surface alike for two consecutive days. The Barrier is as wayward and as changeful as the sea.

November 15. Another beautiful day. We broke camp at 8 a.m., and reached our depot at 9:20 a.m. We found everything intact, the flag waving merrily in the breeze, the direction of which was about west-south-west. We camped there and at once proceeded to redistribute weights and to parcel our provisions to be left there. We found that we had saved enough food to allow for three days' rations, which ought to take us into the Bluff on our return, so we made up a bag of provisions and added a little oil to the tin we had been using from, leaving half a gallon to take us the fifty-odd miles to the Bluff on the way back. We then depoted our spare gear and finnesko, and our tin of sardines and pot of black currant jam. We had intended these provisions for Christmas Day, but the weight is too much; every ounce is of importance. We took on the maize, and the ponies are now pulling 449 lb. each. Quan was pulling 469 lb. before the depot was reached, so he had nothing added to his load. All this arranging took time, and it was nearly noon before we had finished. We took an observation for latitude and variation, and found the latitude to be 79° 36' South, and the variation 155° East. Had lunch at noon and started due south at 1:15 p.m., the ponies pulling well. As the afternoon went on the surface of the Barrier altered to thick, crusty snow, with long rounded sastrugi about 4 ft. high, almost looking like small undulations, running south-west to north-west, with small sastrugi on top running west and east. Camped at 6 p.m., having done 12 miles 1500 yards (statute) today. There are some high, stratified, light clouds in the sky, the first clouds we have had for nearly a week. The sun now, at 9 p.m., is beautifully warm, though the air temperature is minus 2°F. It is dead calm. We are going to build a snow mound at each camp as a guide to our homeward track, and as our camps will only be seven miles apart, these marks ought to help us. The mystery of the Barrier grips us, and we long to know what lies in the unknown to the south. This we may do with good fortune in another fortnight.

NOTE. I wrote that the provisions left at the depot would suffice for three days, but as a matter of fact there was not more than a two days' supply. We felt that we ought to take on every ounce of food that we could, and that if we got back to the depot we would be able to manage as far as the Bluff all right. During the winter we had thought over the possibility of making the mounds as a guide for the return march, and had concluded that though they would entail extra work, we might be well repaid if we picked up only one or two of them at critical times. We had with us two shovels, and ten minutes' work was sufficient to raise a mound 6 or 7 ft. high. We wondered whether the mounds would disappear under the influence of wind and sun, and our tracks remain, whether the tracks would disappear and the mounds remain, whether both tracks and mounds would disappear, or whether both would remain. As we were not keeping in towards the land, but were making a bee-line for the south, it was advisable to neglect no precaution, and as events turned out, the mounds were most useful. They remained after the sledge tracks had disappeared, and they were a very great comfort to us during the journey back from our farthest south point.

November 16. We started again this morning in gloriously fine weather, the temperature minus 15°F (down to minus 25°F during the night). The ponies pulled splendidly. All the western mountains stood up, miraged into the forms of castles. Even the Bluff could be seen in the far distance, changed into the semblance of a giant keep. Before starting, which we did at 7:40 a.m., we made a mound of snow, 6 ft. high, as a guide to us on our homeward way, and as it was built on a large sastrugi, we saw it for two and a half statute miles after starting. At twenty minutes to twelve, we halted for latitude observations, and found that we had reached 78° 50' South. After lunch the surface changed somewhat, but the going was fairly good, in fact we covered 17 miles 200 yards (statute), a record day for us. This evening it is cloudy, high cumulus going from south-east to north-west. The temperature tonight is minus 5°F, but it being dead calm we feel quite warm. A hot sun during the day dried our reindeer skin sleeping bags, the water, or rather ice, all drying out of them, so we sleep in dry bags again. It has been a wonderful and successful week, so different to this time six years ago, when I was toiling along five miles a day over the same ground. Tonight one can see the huge mountain range to the south of Barne Inlet. In order to further economise food we are saving three lumps of sugar each every day, so in time we will have a fair stock. The great thing is to advance our food supply as far south as possible before the ponies give out. Everyone is in splendid health, eyes all right again, and only minor troubles, such as split lips, which do not allow us to laugh. Wild steered all day, and at every hourly halt I put the compass down to make the course we are going straight as a die to the south. Chinaman, or 'The Vampire', as Adams calls him, is not so fit; he is stiff in the knees and has to be hauled along. Quan, *alias* 'Blossom', is A1, but one cannot leave him for a moment, otherwise he would have his harness chewed up. Within the last week he has had the greater part of a horse cloth, about a fathom of rope, several pieces of leather, and odds and ends such as a nose-bag buckle, but his digestion is marvellous, and he seems to thrive on his strange diet. He would rather eat a yard of creosoted rope than his maize and Maujee, indeed he often, in sheer wantonness, throws his food all over the snow.

November 17. A dull day when we started at 9:50 a.m., but the mountains abeam were in sight till noon. The weather then became completely overcast, and the light most difficult to steer in; a dead white wall was what we seemed to be marching to, and there was no direct light to cast even the faintest shadow on the sastrugi. I steered from noon to 1 p.m., and from lunch till 6 p.m., but the course was most erratic, and we had to stop every now and then to put the compass down to verify our course and alter it if necessary. Our march for the day was 16 miles 200 yard (statute) through a bad surface, the ponies sinking in up to their hocks. This soft surface is similar to that we experienced last trip south, for the snow had a crust easily broken through and about 6 in. down an airspace, then similar crusts and airspaces in layers. It was trying work for the ponies, but they all did splendidly in their own particular way. Old 'Blossom' plods stolidly through it; Chinaman flounders rather painfully, for he is old and stiff nowadays; Grisi and Socks take the soft places with a rush; but all get through the day's work and feed up at night, though Quan evinces disgust at not having more Maujee ration and flings his maize out of his nose-bag. One wonders each night what trouble they will get into. This morning, on turning out, we found Grisi lying down unable to get up. He had got to the end of his tether, and could not draw back his leg. He was shivering with cold, though the temperature was only minus 5°. Today we had a plus temperature, for the first time since leaving – plus 9°F at noon, and plus 5°F at 6 p.m. The pall of cloud no doubt acts as a blanket, and so we were warm, too warm in fact for marching.

November 18. Started at 8 a.m. in clearer weather, and the sun remained visible all day, though during the morning it was snowing from the south, and made the steering very difficult. The surface has been simply awful. We seem to have arrived at a latitude where there is no wind and the snow remains where it falls, for we were sinking in well over our ankles, and the poor ponies are having a most trying time. They break through the crust on the surface and flounder up to their hocks, and at each step they have to pull their feet out through the brittle crust. It is telling more on Chinaman than on the others, and he is going slowly. The chafing of the snow crust on his fetlocks has galled them, so we will have to shoot him at the next depot in about three days' time. The ponies are curious animals. We give them full meals, and yet they prefer to gnaw at any odd bits of rope. Quan got my jacket in his teeth this morning as I was scraping the snow off his hind feet, and I had to get out last night to stop Socks biting and swallowing lumps out of Quan's tail. If we had thought that they would have been up to these games, we would have had a longer wire to tether them, so as to keep them apart. It is possible that we have reached the windless area around the Pole, for the Barrier is a dead, smooth, white plain, weird beyond description, and having no land in sight, we feel such tiny specks in the immensity around us. Overhead this afternoon, when the weather cleared, were wonderful lines of clouds, radiating from the south-west, travelling very fast to the north-east. It seems as though we were in some other world, and yet the things that concern us most for the moment are trivial, such as split lips and big appetites. Already the daily meals seem all too short, and we wonder what it will be like later on, when we are really hungry. I have had that experience once, and my companions will soon have it again with me. All the time we are moving south to our wished-for goal, and each day we feel that another gain has been made. We did 15 miles 500 yards today.

November 19. Started at 8:15 this morning with a fresh southerly breeze and drift. The temperature was plus 2°F, and this was the temperature all day, making it cold travelling, but good for the ponies, who, poor beasts, had to plough through a truly awful surface, sinking in 8 or 10 in. at every step. This does not seem very deep, but when one goes on hour after hour it is a strain on man and horse, for we have to hold the ponies up as they stumble along. In spite of the surface and the wind and drift, we cover 15 miles 200 yards (statute) by 6 p.m. and were glad to camp, for our beards and faces were coated in ice, and our helmets had frozen stiff on to our faces. We got sights for latitude at noon, and found that we were in latitude 80° 32' South. On the last journey I was not in that latitude till December 16, though we left Hut Point on November 2, a day earlier than we did this time. The ponies have truly done well. I wrote yesterday that we seemed to be in a windless area, but today alters that opinion. The sastrugi are all pointing clearly due south, and if we have the wind on our way back it will be a great help. The same radiant points in the clouds south-east to north-west were visible again today, and at times when it cleared somewhat a regular nimbus cloud, similar to the rain clouds in the 'doldrums', could be seen. At the base of the converging point of the south-east part of cloud there seemed to rise other clouds to meet the main body. The former trended directly from the horizon at an angle of 30° to meet the main body, and did not seem to be more than a few miles off. The drift on the Barrier surface was piled up into heaps of very fine snow, with the smallest grains, and on encountering these the sledges ran heavily. The crust that has formed, when broken through, discloses loose-grained snow, and the harder crust, about 8 in. down, is almost even. I suppose that the top 8 in. represents the year's snowfall.

November 20. Started at 8:55 a.m. in dull, overcast weather again, but the sun broke through during the morning, so we had something to steer by. The surface has been the worst we have encountered so far, terribly soft, but we did 15 miles 800 yards (statute) for the day. The latter part of the afternoon was better. It seems to savour of repetition to write each day of the heavy going and the soft surface, but these factors play a most important part in our daily work, and it causes us a great deal of speculation as to what we will eventually find as we get further south. The whole place and conditions seem so strange and so unlike anything else in the world in our experience, that one cannot describe them in fitting words. At one moment one thinks of Coleridge's *Ancient Mariner*: 'Alone, alone; all, all alone, alone on a wide, wide sea', and then when the mazy clouds spring silently from either hand and drift quickly across our zenith, not followed by any wind, it seems uncanny. There comes a puff of wind from the north, another from the south, and anon one from the east or west, seeming to obey no law, acting on erratic impulses. It is as though we were truly at the world's end, and were bursting in on the birthplace of the clouds and the nesting home of the four winds, and one has a feeling that we mortals are being watched with a jealous eye by the forces of nature. To add to these weird impressions that seem to grow on one in the apparently limitless waste, the sun tonight was surrounded by mock suns and in the zenith was a bow, turning away from the great vertical circle around the sun. These circles and bows were the colour of the rainbow. We are all fairly tired tonight, and Wild is not feeling very fit, but a night's rest will do him good. The ponies are all fit except poor old Chinaman, and he must go tomorrow. He cannot keep up with the others, and the bad surface has played him out. The temperature is zero F.

November 21. Started at 7:30 a.m. as we had to come to camp early tonight, and we wanted to get a good latitude observation at noon. Although we got away early, however, all morning we were steering through thick weather with driving ice crystals, and at noon there was no chance of getting the sun for latitude. We came to camp at 12:30 p.m., just as the weather cleared a little, and we could see land on our right hand, but only the base of the mountains, so could not identify them. Chinaman came up at last, struggling painfully along, so when we made our depot this evening he was shot. We will use the meat to keep us out longer, and will save on our dried stores. The temperature at noon was only plus 8°F, and the little wind that there was has been extremely cold. The wind veers round and round the compass, and the clouds move in every direction. The surface of the Barrier was better today, but still the ponies sank in 8 in. at least. The sastrugi point toward the south-east, this being the direction of the most usual wind here. This evening it cleared, and we could see land almost ahead, and the great mass of land abaft the beam to the north of Barne Inlet. Our day's march was 15 miles 450 yards. We are now south of the 81st parallel, and feel that we are well on the road to our wished-for goal. This is now our second depot, and we intend to leave about 80 lb. of pony meat, one tin of biscuits (27 lb.), some sugar, and one tin of oil, to see us back to Depot A. It is late now, for all arrangements for the depot took time. There was a lot of work in the arranging of the sledges for the remaining three ponies, packing stores, skinning Chinaman, and cutting him up, all in a low temperature.

NOTE. The killing of the ponies was not pleasant work, but we had the satisfaction of knowing that the animals had been well fed and well treated up to the last, and that they suffered no pain. When we had to kill a pony, we threw up a snow mound to leeward of the camp, so that no smell of blood could come down wind, and took the animal behind this, out of sight of the others. As a matter of fact, the survivors never displayed any interest at all in the proceedings, even the report of the revolver used in the killing failing to attract their attention. The sound did not travel far on the wide open plain. The revolver was held about 3 in. from the forehead of the victim and one shot was sufficient to cause instant death. The throat of the animal was cut immediately and the blood allowed to run away. Then Marshall and Wild would skin the carcass, and we took the meat off the legs, shoulders, and back. In the case of Chinaman the carcass was opened and the liver and undercut secured, but the job was such a lengthy one that we did not repeat it in the case of the other animals. Within a very short time after killing the carcass would be frozen solid, and we always tried to cut the meat up into as small pieces as possible before this occurred, for the cutting became very much more difficult after the process of freezing was complete. On the following days, whenever there was time to spare, we would proceed with the cutting until we had got all the meat ready for cooking. It was some time before we found out that it was better merely to warm the meat through when we wanted to eat it, and not attempt to cook it properly. It was fairly tender when only warmed, but if it were boiled it became very tough, and we would not spare enough oil to stew it in order to soften it thoroughly. Our supply of oil had been cut down very fine in order to save weight. The only meat that we cooked thoroughly was that from Grisi, because we found, at a later stage of the journey, that this meat was not good, and we thought that cooking might make it less liable to cause attacks of dysentery. We used the harness from the dead pony to make stays for the sledge which would be left at the depot. The sledge was reared on to its end, about 3 ft. being sunk into the snow, and a bamboo with a black flag stuck on the top, so that we might be able to find the little 'cache' of food on the return journey. Stays were required lest a blizzard should blow down the whole erection.

November 22. A beautiful morning. We left our depot with its black flag flying on the bamboo lashed to a discarded sledge, stuck upright in the snow, at 8:20 a.m. We have now three ponies dragging 500 lb. each, and they did splendidly through the soft snow. The going, I am thankful to say, is getting better, and here and there patches of harder surface are to be met with. The outstanding feature of today's march is that we have seen new land to the south — land never seen by human eyes before. The land consists of great snow-clad heights rising beyond Mount Longstaff, and also far inland to the north of Mounts Markham. These heights we did not see on our journey south on the last expedition, for we were too close to the land or, rather, foothills, but now at the great distance we are out they can be seen plainly. It has been a beautifully clear day, and all the well-known mountains are clearly visible. The coast trends about south by east, so that we are safe for a good long way south. We camped at noon and got a good meridian altitude and azimuth. We found our latitude to be 81° 8' South. In the afternoon we steered a little to the east of south, and camped at 6 p.m. with 15 miles 250 yards (statute) to the credit of the day. This is good, for the ponies have a heavy load, but they are well fed. We were rather long at lunch camp, for we tried to pull out Adams's tooth, which has given him great pain, so much that he has not slept at night at all. But the tooth broke, and he has a bad time now. We were not equipped on this trip for tooth-pulling. Wild is better today, but fatty food is not to his taste just now, so he had a good feed of horse flesh. We all liked it, for it filled us well, in spite of being somewhat tough. The flavour was good and it means a great saving of our other food. The temperature has risen to plus 7°F, and the surface of the Barrier is good for sledge-hauling.

November 23. Our record march today, the distance being 17 miles 1650 yards statute. It has been a splendid day for marching, with a cool breeze from the south and the sun slightly hidden. The horses did very well indeed, and the surface has improved, there being fairly hard sastrugi from the south. We are gradually rising the splendid peaks of Longstaff and Markham. The former, from our present bearing, has several sharp peaks, and the land fades away in the far distance to the south, with numbers of peaks showing, quite new to human eyes. All the old familiar mountains, toward which I toiled so painfully last time I was here, are visible, and what a difference it is now! Tonight there is a fresh wind from what appears at this distance to be a strait between Longstaff and Markham, and a low drift is flying along. Wild is better tonight, but he was tired after the long march. We made him a cup of our emergency Oxo for lunch, and that bucked him up for the afternoon. He has not eaten much lately, but says that he feels decidedly better tonight. Marshall has just succeeded in pulling out Adams's tooth so now the latter will be able to enjoy horse meat. This evening we had it fried, and so saved all our other food except biscuits and cocoa. It is my week as cook now, and Wild is my tent companion.

November 24. Started this morning at 7:55, and made a good march of 10 miles 600 yards (statute) up to 1 p.m., when we camped for lunch. We marched from 2:30 to 6 p.m., and camped then for the night. When we started there was a searching breeze in our faces, which gradually increased during the day with low drift, and it was blowing a summer blizzard when we camped this evening, the temperature up to plus 17°F, and the drift melting in the tent and on all our gear. The ponies did splendidly again, in spite of soft surface, our day's run being 17 miles 680 yards statute.

The Barrier surface is still as level as a billiard table, with no sign of any undulation or rise; but if the Barrier shows no sign of change it is otherwise with the mountains. Each mile shows us new land, and most of it consists of lofty mountains, whose heights at present we cannot estimate. They are well over 10,000 ft. The great advantage of being out from the coast is now obvious, for we can see a long range of sharp peaked mountains running to the westward from Mounts Markham, and forming the south side of Shackleton Inlet on the east side of Mounts Markham, and other peaks and one table-topped mountain standing away to the south between Longstaff and Markham. There appears to be a wide strait or inlet between Longstaff and the new land east of Markham. Then trending about south-east from Longstaff is a lofty range of mountains which we will see more closely as we move south. I trust that the blizzard will blow itself out tonight, so that we may have easy going tomorrow. Wild is much better today, and took his ordinary food. We had fried pony for dinner tonight, and raw pony frozen on the march. The going is very good, but we can only afford a little oil to cook up the meat for meals.

November 25. Started at 8 a.m. this morning in fairly good weather. The wind has gone during the night, leaving our tents drifted up with fine snow. The land was obscured nearly all day, but toward the evening it cleared and we could see the details of the coast. There appears to be a series of inlets and capes opening at all angles, and with no fixed coastline, though the lofty range of mountains continues to the south with a very slight trend to the eastward. The surface of the Barrier was very trying today, for the snow had no consistency and slipped away as one trod on it. It was not so trying for the ponies, and they did 17 miles 1600 yards. We had frozen raw pony meat to eat on the march, and a good hoosh of pony meat and pemmican for dinner. Wild is practically all right, and Adams finds a wisdom tooth growing in place of the one he lost. Our eyes are not too comfortable just now. It is a wonderful place we are in, all new to the world, and yet I feel that I cannot describe it. There is an impression of limitless solitude about it all that makes us feel so small as we trudge along, a few dark specks on the snowy plain, and watch the new land appear.

November 26. A day to remember, for we have passed the 'farthest South' previously reached by man. Tonight we are in

latitude 82° 18½' South, longitude 168° East, and this latitude we
have been able to reach in much less time than on the last long
march with Captain Scott, when we made latitude 82° 16½' our
'farthest South'. We started in lovely weather this morning, with
the temperature plus 19°F, and it has been up to plus 20°F during
the day, giving us a chance to dry our sleeping bags. We were
rather anxious at starting about Quan, who had a sharp attack of
colic, the result no doubt of his morbid craving for bits of rope and
other odds and ends in preference to his proper food. He soon got
well enough to pull, and we got away at 7:40 a.m., the surface still
very soft. There are abundant signs that the wind blows strongly
from the south-south-east during the winter, for the sastrugi are
very marked in that direction. There are extremely large circular
crystals of snow on the Barrier surface, and they seem hard and
brittle. They catch the light from the sun, each one forming a
reflector that dazzles the eyes as one glances at the million points of
light. As each hour went on today, we found new interest to the
west, where the land lies, for we opened out Shackleton Inlet, and
up the inlet lies a great chain of mountains, and far into the west
appear more peaks; to the west of Cape Wilson appears another
chain of sharp peaks about 10,000 ft. high, stretching away to the
north beyond the Snow Cape, and continuing the land on which
Mount A. Markham lies. To the south-south-east ever appear new
mountains. I trust that no land will block our path. We celebrated
the breaking of the 'farthest South' record with a four-ounce
bottle of Curaçao, sent us by a friend at home. After this had been
shared out into two tablespoonfuls each, we had a smoke and a talk
before turning in. One wonders what the next month will bring
forth. We ought by that time to be near our goal, all being well.

NOTE. It falls to the lot of few men to view land not previously
seen by human eyes, and it was with feelings of keen curiosity, not
unmingled with awe, that we watched the new mountains rise
from the great unknown that lay ahead of us. Mighty peaks they
were, the eternal snows at their bases, and their rough-hewn forms
rising high toward the sky. No man of us could tell what we would
discover in our march south, what wonders might not be revealed
to us, and our imaginations would take wings until a stumble in
the snow, the sharp pangs of hunger, or the dull ache of physical

weariness brought back our attention to the needs of the immediate present. As the days wore on, and mountain after mountain came into view, grimly majestic, the consciousness of our insignificance seemed to grow upon us. We were but tiny black specks crawling slowly and painfully across the white plain, and bending our puny strength to the task of wresting from nature secrets preserved inviolate through all the ages. Our anxiety to learn what lay beyond was none the less keen, however, and the long days of marching over the Barrier surface were saved from monotony by the continued appearance of new land to the south-east.

November 27. Started at 8 a.m., the ponies pulling well over a bad surface of very soft snow. The weather is fine and clear save for a strong mirage, which throws all the land up much higher than it really is. All day we have seen new mountains arise, and it is causing us some anxiety to note that they trend more and more to the eastward, for that means an alteration of our course from nearly due south. Still they are a long way off, and when we get up to them we may find some strait that will enable us to go right through them and on south. One speculates greatly as we march along, but patience is what is needed. I think that the ponies are feeling the day-in, day-out drudgery of pulling on this plain. Poor beasts, they cannot understand, of course, what it is all for, and the wonder of the great mountains is naught to them, though one notices them at times looking at the distant land. At lunch time I took a photograph of our camp, with Mount Longstaff in the background. We had our sledge flags up to celebrate the breaking of the southern record. The long snow cape marked on the chart as being attached to Mount Longstaff is not really so. It is attached to a lower bluff mountain to the north of Mount Longstaff. The most northerly peak of Mount Longstaff goes sheer down into the Barrier, and all along this range of mountains are very steep glaciers, greatly crevassed. As we pass along the mountains the capes disappear, but there are several well-marked ones of which we have taken angles. Still more mountains appeared above the horizon during the afternoon, and when we camped tonight some were quite clearly defined, many, many miles away. The temperature has been up to plus 22°F today, and we took the opportunity of drying our sleeping bags, which we turned inside out and laid on the sledges. Tonight the temperature is plus 13°F. We find that raw frozen pony meat cools one on the march, and during the ten minutes' spell after an hour's march we all cut up meat for lunch or dinner; in the hot sun it thaws well. This fresh meat ought to keep away scurvy from us. Quan seems much better today, but Grisi does not appear fit at all. He seems to be snow blind. Our distance today was 16 miles 1200 yards.

November 28. Started at 7:50 a.m. in beautiful weather, but with a truly awful surface, the ponies sinking in very deeply. The sledges ran easily, as the temperature was high, plus 17° to plus 20°F, the hot sun making the snow surface almost melt. We halted at noon for a latitude observation, and found our latitude to be 82° 38' South. The land now appears more to the east, bearing south-east by south, and some very high mountains a long way off with lower foothills, can be seen in front, quite different to the land abeam of us, which consists of huge sharp pointed mountains with crevassed glaciers moving down gullies in their sides. Marshall is making a careful survey of all the principal heights. All day we have been travelling up and down long undulations, the width from crest to crest being about one and a half miles, and the rise about 1 in 100. We can easily see the line by our tracks sometimes being cut off sharp when we are on the down gradient and appearing again a long way astern as we rise. The first indication of the undulation was the fact of the mound we had made in the morning disappearing before we had travelled a quarter of a mile. During the afternoon the weather was very hot. A cool breeze had helped us in the forenoon, but it died away later. Marshall has a touch of snow blindness, and both Grisi and Socks were also affected during the day. When we camped tonight Grisi was shot. He had fallen off during the last few days, and the snow blindness was bad for him, putting him off his feed. He was the one chosen to go at the depot we made this evening. This is Depot C, and we are leaving one week's provisions and oil, with horse meat, to carry us back to Depot B. We will go on tomorrow with 1200 lb. weight (nine weeks' provisions), and we four will pull with the ponies, two on each sledge. It is late now, 11 p.m., and we have just turned in. We get up at 5:30 every morning. Our march for the day was 15 miles 1500 yards statute.

November 29. Started at 8:45 a.m. with adjusted loads of 630 lb. on each sledge. We harnessed up ourselves, but found that the ponies would not pull when we did, and as the loads came away lightly, we untoggled our harness. The surface was very soft, but during the morning there were occasional patches of hard sastrugi, all pointing south-south-east. This is the course we are now steering, as the land is trending about south-east by east. During the day still more great mountains appeared to the south-east, and to the west we opened up several huge peaks, 10,000 to 15,000 ft. in height. The whole country seems to be made up of range after range of mountains, one behind the other. The worst feature of today's march was the terribly soft snow in the hollows of the great undulations we were passing. During the afternoon one place was so bad that the ponies sank in right up to their bellies, and we had to pull with might and main to get the sledges along at all. When we began to ascend the rise on the southern side of the undulation it got better. The ponies were played out by 5:45 p.m., especially old Quan, who nearly collapsed, not from the weight of the sledge, but from the effort of lifting his feet and limbs through the soft snow. The weather is calm and clear, but very hot, and it is trying to man and beast. We are on a short allowance of food, for we must save all we can, so as to help the advance as far as possible. Marshall has taken the angles of the new land today. He does this regularly. The hypsometer readings at 1 p.m. are very high now if there is no correction, and it is not due to weather. We must be at about sea level. The undulations run about cast by south, and west by west, and are at the moment a puzzle to us. I cannot think that the feeding of the glaciers from the adjacent mountains has anything to do with their existence. There are several glaciers, but their size is inconsiderable compared to the vast extent of Barrier affected. The glaciers are greatly crevassed. There are enormous granite cliffs at the foot of the range we are passing, and they stand vertically about 4000 to 5000 ft. without a vestige of snow upon them. The main bare rocks appear to be like the schists of the western mountains opposite our winter quarters, but we are too far away, of course, to be able to tell with any certainty. Down to the south are mountains entirely clear of snow, for their sides are vertical, and they must be not less than 8000 to 9000 ft. in height. Altogether it is a weird and wonderful country. The only familiar thing is the broad expanse of Barrier to the east, where as yet no land appears. We did 14 miles 900 yards (statute) today, and are tired. The snow came well above our ankles, and each step became a labour. Still we are making our way south, and each mile gained reduces the unknown. We have now done over 300 miles due south in less than a month.

November 30. We started at 8 a.m. this morning. Quan very shaky and seemingly on his last legs, poor beast. Both he and Socks are snow blind, so we have improvised shades for their eyes, which we trust will help them a little. We took turns of an hour each hauling at Quan's sledge, one at each side, to help him. Socks, being faster, always gets ahead and then has a short spell, which eases him considerably. We advanced very slowly today, for the surface was as bad as ever till the afternoon, and the total distance covered was 12 miles 150 yards. Quan was quite played out, so we camped at 5:45 p.m. We give the ponies ample food, but they do not eat it all, though Quan whinnies for his every meal time. He is particularly fond of the Maujee ration, and neglects his maize for it. Again today we saw new land to the south, and unfortunately for our quick progress in that direction, we find the trend of the coast more to the eastward. A time is coming, I can see, when we will have to ascend the mountains, for the land runs round more and more in an easterly direction. Still after all we must not expect to find things cut and dried and all suited to us in such a place. We will be thankful if we can keep the ponies as far as our next depot which will be in latitude 84° South. They are at the present moment lying down in the warm sun. It is a beautifully calm clear evening; indeed as regards weather we have been wonderfully fortunate, and it has given Marshall the chance to take all the necessary angles for the survey of these new mountains and coastline. Wild is cook this week, and my week is over so I am now living in the other tent. We are all fit and well, but our appetites are increasing at an alarming rate. We noticed this tonight after the heavy pulling today. A great deal of the land we are passing seems to consist of granite in huge masses, and here and there are much-crevassed glaciers pouring down between the mountains, perhaps from some inland ice sheet similar to that in the north of Victoria Land. The mountains show great similarity in outline, and there is no sign of any volcanic action at all so far. The temperature for the day has ranged between plus 16° and plus 12°F, but the hot sun has made things appear much warmer.

December 1. Started at 8 a.m. today. Quan has been growing weaker each hour, and we practically pulled the sledge. We passed over three undulations, and camped at 1 p.m. In the afternoon we only did four miles, Quan being led by Wild. He also led Socks with one sledge, whilst Adams, Marshall, and I hauled 200 lb. each on the other sledge, over a terribly soft surface. Poor old Quan was quite finished when we came to camp at 6 p.m., having done 12 miles 200 yards, so he was shot. We all felt losing him, I particularly, for he was my special horse ever since he was ill last March. I had looked after him, and in spite of all his annoying tricks he was a general favourite. He seemed so intelligent. Still it was best for him to go, and like the others he was well fed to the last. We have now only one pony left, and are in latitude 83° 16′ South. Ahead of us we can see the land stretching away to the east, with a long white line in front of it that looks like a giant Barrier, and nearer a very crusted-up appearance, as though there were great pressure ridges in front of us. It seems as though the Barrier end had come, and that there is now going to be a change in some gigantic way in keeping with the vastness of the whole place. We fervently trust that we will not be delayed in our march south. We are living mainly on horsemeat now, and on the march, to cool our throats when pulling in the hot sun, we chew some raw frozen meat. There was a slight breeze for a time today, and we felt chilly, as we were pulling stripped to our shirts. We wear our goggles all the time, for the glare from the snow surface is intense and the sky is cloudless. A few wisps of fleecy cloud settle on the tops of the loftiest mountains, but that is all. The surface of the Barrier still sparkles with the million frozen crystals which stand apart from the ordinary surface snow. One or two new peaks came in sight today, so we are ever adding to the chain of wonderful mountains that we have found. At one moment our thoughts are on the grandeur of the scene, the next of what we would have to eat if only we were let loose in a good restaurant. We are very hungry these days, and we know that we are likely to be for another three months. One of the granite cliffs we are nearing is over 6000 ft. sheer, and much bare rock is showing, which must have running water on it as the hot sun plays down. The moon was visible in the sky all day and it was something familiar, yet far removed from these days of hot sunshine and wide white pathways. The temperature is now plus 16°F, and it is quite warm in the tent.

December 2. Started at 8 a.m., all four of us hauling one sledge, and Socks following behind with the other. He soon got into our regular pace, and did very well indeed. The surface during the morning was extremely bad and it was heavy work for us. The sun beat down on our heads and we perspired freely, though we were working only in shirts and pajama trousers, whilst our feet were cold in the snow. We halted for lunch at 1 p.m., and had some of Quan cooked, but he was very tough meat, poor old beast. Socks, the only pony left now, is lonely. He whinnied all night for his lost companion. At 1 p.m. today we had got close enough to the disturbance ahead of us to see that it consisted of enormous pressure ridges, heavily crevassed and running a long way east, with not the slightest chance of our being able to get southing that way any longer on the Barrier. So after lunch we struck due south in toward the land, which is now running in a south-east direction, and at 6 p.m. we were close to the ridges off the coast. There is a red hill about 3000 ft. in height, which we hope to ascend tomorrow, so as to gain view of the surrounding country. Then we will make our way, if possible with the pony, up a glacier ahead of us on to the huge ice, and on to the Pole if all goes well. It is an anxious time for us, for time is precious and food more so; we will be greatly relieved if we find a good route through the mountains. Now that we are close to the land we can see more clearly the nature of the mountains. From Mount Longstaff in a south-east direction, the land appears to be far more glaciated than further north, and since the valleys are very steep, the glaciers that they contain are heavily crevassed. These glaciers bear out in a north-east direction into the Barrier. Immediately opposite our camp the snow seems to have been blown off the steep mountain sides. The mountain ahead of us, which we are going to climb tomorrow, is undoubtedly granite, but very mildly weathered. In the distance it looked like volcanic rock, but now there can be no doubt that it consists of granite. Evidently the great ice sheet has passed over this part of the land, for the rounded forms could not have been caused by ordinary weathering. Enormous pressure ridges that run out from the south of the mountain ahead must be due to a glacier far greater in extent than any we have yet met. The glacier that comes out of Shackleton Inlet makes a disturbance in the Barrier ice, but not nearly as great as the disturbance in our immediate neighbourhood at the present time. The glacier at Shackleton Inlet is quite a short one. We have now closed in to the land, but before we did so we could see the rounded tops of great mountains extending in a south-easterly direction. If we are fortunate enough to reach the summit of the mountain tomorrow, we should be able to see more clearly the line of these mountains to the south-east. It would be very interesting to follow along the Barrier to the south-east, and see the trend of the mountains but that does not enter into our program. Our way lies to the south. How one wishes for time and unlimited provisions. Then indeed we could penetrate the secrets of this great lonely continent. Regrets are vain, however, and we wonder what is in store for us beyond the mountains if we are able to get there. The closer observation of these mountains ought to give geological results of importance. We may have the good fortune to discover fossils, or at any rate to bring back specimens that will determine the geological history of the country and prove a connection between the granite boulders lying on the slopes of Erebus and Terror and the land lying to the far south. Our position tonight is latitude 83° 28' South, longitude 171° 30' East. If we can get on the mountain tomorrow, it will be the pioneer landing in the far south. We travelled 11 miles 1450 yards (statute) today, which was not bad, seeing that we were pulling 180 lb. per man on a bad surface. We got a photograph of the wonderful red granite peaks close to us, for now we are only eight miles or so off the land. The temperature is plus 20°, with a high barometer. The same fine weather continues, but the wind is cold in the early morning, when we turn out at 5:30 a.m. for breakfast.

December 4. Unable to write yesterday owing to bad attack of snow blindness, and not much better tonight, but I must record the events of the two most remarkable days that we have experienced since leaving the winter quarters. After breakfast at 5:30 a.m. yesterday, we started off from camp, leaving all camp gear standing and a good feed by Socks to last him the whole day. We got under way at 9 a.m., taking four biscuits, four lumps of sugar, and two ounces of chocolate each for lunch. We hoped to get water at the first of the rocks when we landed. Hardly had we gone one hundred yards when we came to a crevasse, which we did not see very distinctly, for the light was bad, and the sun obscured by clouds. We roped up and went on in single file, each with his ice-pick handy. I found it very difficult to see clearly with my goggles, and so took them off, and the present attack of snow blindness is the result, for the sun came out gloriously later on. We crossed several crevasses filled with snow except at the sides, the gaps being about 2 ft. wide, and the whole crevasses from 10 to 20 ft. across. Then we were brought up all standing by an enormous chasm of about 80 ft. wide and 300 ft. deep which lay right across our route. This chasm was similar to, only larger than, the one we encountered in latitude 80° 30' South when on the southern journey with Captain Scott during the *Discovery* expedition. By making a detour to the right we found that it gradually pinched out and became filled with snow, and so we were able to cross and resume our line to the land, which very deceptively appeared quite close but was really some miles away.

Crossing several ridges of ice pressure and many more crevasses, we eventually at 12:30 p.m. reached an area of smooth blue ice in which were embedded several granite boulders, and here we obtained a drink of delicious water formed by the sun playing on the rock face and heating the ice at the base. After travelling for half a mile, we reached the base of the mountain which we hoped to climb in order to gain a view of the surrounding country. This hill is composed of granite, the red appearance being no doubt due to iron. At 1 p.m. we had a couple of biscuits and some water, and then started to make our way up the precipitous rock face. This was the most difficult part of the whole climb, for the granite was weathered and split in every direction, and some of the larger pieces seemed to be just nicely balanced on smaller pieces, so that one could almost push them over by a touch. With great difficulty we clambered up this rock face, and then ascended a gentle snow slope to another rocky bit, but not so difficult to climb. From the top of this ridge there burst upon our view an open road to the south, for there stretched before us a great glacier running almost south and north between two huge mountain ranges. As far as we could see, except toward the mouth, the glacier appeared to be smooth, yet this was not a certainty, for the distance was so great. Eagerly we clambered up the remaining ridges and over a snow slope, and found ourselves at the top of the mountain, the height being 3350 ft. according to aneroid and hypsometer. From the summit we could see the glacier stretching away south inland till at last it seemed to merge in high inland ice. Where the glacier fell into the Barrier about north-east bearing, the pressure waves were enormous, and for miles the surface of the Barrier was broken up. This was what we had seen ahead of us the last few days, and we now understood the reason of the commotion on the Barrier surface. To the south-east we could see the lofty range of mountains we had been following still stretching away in the same direction, and we can safely say that the Barrier is bounded by a chain of mountains extending in a south-easterly direction as far as the 86th parallel South. The mountains to the west appear to be more heavily glaciated than the ones to the eastward. There are some huge granite faces on the southern sides of the mountains, and these faces are joined up by cliffs of a very dark hue. To the south-south-east, toward what is apparently the head of the glacier, there are several sharp cones of very black rock, eight or nine in all. Beyond these are red granite faces, with sharp, needlelike spurs, similar in appearance to the 'cathedral' rocks described by Armitage in connection with the *Discovery* expedition to the western mountains. Further on to the south the mountains have a bluff appearance, with long lines of stratification running almost horizontally. This bluff mountain range seems to break about sixty miles away, and beyond can be seen dimly other mountains. Turning to the west, the mountains on that side appeared to be rounded and covered with huge masses of ice, and glaciers showing the lines of crevasses. In the far distance there is what looked like an active volcano. There is a big mountain with a cloud on the top, bearing all the appearance of steam from an active cone. It would be very interesting to find an active volcano so far south. After taking bearings of the trend of the mountains, Barrier and glacier, we ate our frugal lunch and wished for more, and then descended. Adams had boiled the hypsometer and taken the temperature on the top, whilst Marshall, who had carried the camera on his back all the way up, took a couple of photographs. How we wished we had more plates to spare to get a record of the wonderful country we were passing through. At 4 p.m. we began to descend, and at 5 p.m. we were on the Barrier again. We were rather tired and very hungry when, at 7 p.m., we reached our camp. After a good dinner, and a cupful of Maujee ration in the hoosh as an extra, we turned in.

Today, *December 4*, we got under way at 8 a.m. and steered into the land, for we could see that there was no question as to the way we should go now. Though on the glacier we might encounter crevasses and difficulties not to be met with on the Barrier, yet on the latter we could get no further than 86° South, and then would have to turn in toward the land and get over the mountains to reach the Pole. We felt that our main difficulty on the glacier route would be with the pony Socks, and we could not expect to drag the full load ourselves as yet without relay work. Adams, Marshall, and I pulled one sledge with 680 lb. weight, and Wild followed with Socks directly in our wake, so that if we came to a crevasse he would have warning. Everything went on well except that when we were close in to land, Marshall went through the snow covering of a crevasse. He managed to hold himself up by his arms. We could see no bottom to this crevasse. At 1 p.m. we were close to the snow slope up which we hoped to reach the interior of the land and thence get on to the glacier. We had lunch and then proceeded, finding, instead of a steep, short slope, a long, fairly steep gradient. All the afternoon we toiled at the sledge, Socks pulling his load easily enough, and eventually, at 5 p.m., reached the head of the pass, 2000 ft. above sea level. From that point there was a gentle descent toward the glacier, and at 6 p.m. we camped close to some blue ice with granite boulders embedded in it, around which were pools of water. This water saves a certain amount of our oil, for we have not to melt snow or ice. We turned in at 8 p.m., well satisfied with the day's work. The weather now is wonderfully fine, with not a breath of wind, and a warm sun beating down on us. The temperature was up to plus 22°F at noon, and is now plus 18°F. The pass through which we have come is flanked by great granite pillars at least 2000 ft. in height and making a magnificent entrance to the 'Highway to the South'. It is all so interesting and everything is on such a vast scale that one cannot describe it well. We four are seeing these great designs and the play of nature in her grandest moods for the first time, and possibly they may never be seen by man again. Poor Marshall had another four miles' walk this evening, for he found that he had lost his Jaeger jacket off the sledge. He had therefore to tramp back uphill for it, and found it two miles away on the trail. Socks is not feeding well. He seems lonely without his companions. We gave him a drink of thaw water this evening, but he did not seem to appreciate it, preferring the snow at his feet.

CHAPTER 13

On the Great Glacier
December 5 to 17
Appearance of a bird in 83° 40' South latitude: Our last pony engulfed, December 7: Dangerous travelling in a maze of crevasses: Discovery of coal at an altitude of 6100 ft.

December 5. Broke camp sharp at 8 a.m. and proceeded south down an icy slope to the main glacier. The ice was too slippery for the pony, so Wild took him by a circuitous route to the bottom on snow. At the end of our ice slope, down which the sledge skidded rapidly, though we had put on rope brakes and hung on to it as well as we could, there was a patch of soft snow running parallel with the glacier, which here trended about south-west by south. Close ahead of us were the massed up, fantastically shaped and split masses of pressure across which it would have been impossible for us to have gone, but, fortunately, it was not necessary even to try, for close in to the land was a snow slope free from all crevasses, and along this gentle rise we made our way. After a time this snow slope gave place to blue ice, with numberless cracks and small crevasses across which it was quite impossible for the pony to drag the sledge without a serious risk of a broken leg in one of the many holes, the depth of which we could not ascertain. We therefore unharnessed Socks, and Wild took him over this bit of ground very carefully, whilst we others first hauled our sledge and then the pony sledge across to a patch of snow under some gigantic granite pillars over 2000 ft. in height, and here, close to some thaw water, we made our lunch camp. I was still badly snow blind, so stayed in camp whilst Marshall and Adams went on to spy out a good route to follow after lunch was over. When they returned they informed me that there was more cracked-up blue ice ahead, and that the main pressure of the glacier came in very close to the pillar of granite that stood before us, but that beyond that there appeared to be a snow slope and good going. The most remarkable thing they reported was that as they were walking along a bird, brown in colour with a white line under each wing, flew just over their heads and disappeared to the south. It is, indeed, strange to hear of such an incident in latitude 83° 40' South. They were sure it was not a skua gull, which is the only bird I could think of that would venture down here, and the gull might have been attracted by the last dead pony, for when in latitude 80° 30' South, on my last southern trip, a skua gull arrived shortly after we had killed a dog.

After lunch we started again, and by dint of great exertions managed, at 6 p.m., to camp after getting both sledges and then the pony over another couple of miles of crevassed blue ice. We then went on and had a look ahead, and saw that we are going to have a tough time tomorrow to get along at all. I can see that it will, at least, mean relaying three or four times across nearly half a mile of terribly crevassed ice, covered in places with treacherous snow, and razor-edged in other places, all of it sloping down toward the rock debris-strewn shore on the cliff side. We are camped under a wonderful pillar of granite that has been arounded by the winds into a perfectly symmetrical shape, and is banded by lines of gneiss. There is just one little patch of snow for our tents, and even that bridges some crevasses. Providence will look over us tonight, for we can do nothing more. One feels that at any moment some great piece of rock may come hurtling down, for all around us are pieces of granite, ranging from the size of a hazelnut to great boulders twenty to forty tons in weight, and on one snow slope is the fresh track of a fallen rock. Still we can do no better, for it is impossible to spread a tent on the blue ice, and we cannot get any further tonight. We are leaving a depot here. My eyes are my only trouble, for their condition makes it impossible for me to pick out the route or do much more than pull. The distance covered today was 9 miles with 4 miles relay.

December 6. Started at 8 a.m. today in fine weather to get our loads over the half mile of crevassed ice that lay between us and the snow slope to the south-south-west. We divided up the load and managed to get the whole lot over in three journeys, but it was an awful job, for every step was a venture, and I, with one eye entirely blocked up because of snow blindness, felt it particularly uncomfortable work. However, by 1 p.m. all our gear was safely over, and the other three went back for Socks. Wild led him, and by 2 p.m. we were all camped on the snow again. Providence has indeed looked after us. At 3 p.m. we started south-south-west up a long slope to the right of the main glacier pressure. It was very heavy going, and we camped at 5 p.m. close to a huge crevasse, the snow bridge of which we crossed. There is a wonderful view of the mountains, with new peaks and ranges to the south-east, south and south-west. There is a dark rock running in conjunction with the granite on several of the mountains. We are now over 1700 ft. up on the glacier, and can see down on to the Barrier. The cloud still hangs on the mountain ahead of us; it certainly looks as though it were a volcano cloud, but it may be due to condensation. The lower current clouds are travelling very fast from south-south-east to north-north-west. The weather is fine and clear, and the temperature plus 17°F.

December 7. Started at 8 a.m., Adams, Marshall and self pulling one sledge. Wild leading Socks behind. We travelled up and down slopes with very deep snow, into which Socks sank up to his belly, and we plunged in and out continuously, making it very trying work. Passed several crevasses on our right hand and could see more to the left. The light became bad at 1 p.m., when we camped for lunch, and it was hard to see the crevasses, as most were more or less snow-covered. After lunch the light was better, and as we marched along we were congratulating ourselves upon it when suddenly we heard a shout of 'help' from Wild. We stopped at once and rushed to his assistance, and saw the pony sledge with the forward end down a crevasse and Wild reaching out from the side of the gulf grasping the sledge. No sign of the pony. We soon got up to Wild, and he scrambled out of the dangerous position, but poor Socks had gone. Wild had a miraculous escape. He was following up our tracks, and we had passed over a crevasse which was entirely covered with snow, but the weight of the pony broke through the snow crust and in a second all was over. Wild says he just felt a sort of rushing wind, the leading rope was snatched from his hand, and he put out his arms and just caught the further edge of the chasm. Fortunately for Wild and us, Socks' weight snapped the swingle-tree of the sledge, so it was saved, though the upper bearer is broken. We lay down on our stomachs and looked over into the gulf, but no sound or sign came to us; a black bottomless pit it seemed to be. We hitched the pony sledge to ourselves and started off again, now with a weight of 1000 lb. for the four of us. Camped at 6:20 p.m., very tired, having to retreat from a maze of crevasses and rotten ice on to a patch where we could pitch our tents. We are indeed thankful for Wild's escape. When I think over the events of the day I realise what the loss of the sledge would have meant to us. We would have had left only two sleeping bags for the four of us, and I doubt whether we could have got back to winter quarters with the short equipment. Our chance of reaching the Pole would have been gone. We take on the maize to eat ourselves. There is one ray of light in this bad day, and that is that, anyhow we could not have taken Socks on much further. We would have had to shoot him tonight, so that although his loss is a serious matter to us, for we had counted on the meat, still we know that for traction purposes he would have been of little further use. When we tried to camp tonight we stuck our ice axes into the snow to see whether there were any more hidden crevasses, and everywhere the axes went through. It would have been folly to have pitched our camp in that place, as we might easily have dropped through during the night. We had to retreat a quarter of a mile to pitch the tent. It was very unpleasant to turn back, even for this short distance, but on this job one must expect reverses.

December 8. Started at 8 a.m. and immediately began dodging crevasses and pits of unknown depth. Wild and I were leading, for, thank heaven, my eyes are fit and well again. We slowly toiled up a long crevassed slope, and by lunch time were about 1900 ft. up the glacier. We had covered 6 miles 150 yards of an uphill drag, with about 250 lb. per man to haul. After lunch we still travelled up, but came on to blue glacier ice almost free from crevasses, so did much better, the sledges running easily. We camped at 6 p.m., the day's journey having been 12 miles 150 yards. The slope we went up in the morning, was not as bad as we had anticipated, but quite bad enough for us to be thankful that we are out, at any rate for a time, from the region of hidden crevasses. The hypsometer tonight gave our height as 2300 ft. above sea level. It is beautifully fine still. We have been wonderfully fortunate in this, especially in view of the situation we are in.

December 9. Another splendid day as far as the weather is concerned, and much we needed it, for we have had one of our hardest day's work and certainly the most dangerous so far. We started at 7:45 a.m. over the blue ice, and in less than an hour were in a perfect maze of crevasses, some thinly bridged with snow and others with a thicker and therefore more deceptive covering. Marshall went through one and was only saved by his harness. He had quite disappeared down below the level of the ice, and it was one of those crevasses that open out from the top, with no bottom to be seen, and I dare say there was a drop of at least 1000 ft. Soon after, Adams went through, then I did. The situation became momentarily more dangerous and uncertain. The sledges, skidding about, came up against the sheer, knife-like edges of some of the crevasses, and thus the bow of the second sledge, which had been strained when Socks fell, gave way. We decided to relay our gear over this portion of a glacier until we got on to safer ground, and it was well past eleven o'clock before we had got both sledges on to better ice. We camped at 11:45 a.m. to get the sun's meridian altitude, and, to save time while watching the sun's rise and fall, decided to lunch at noon. The latitude we found to be 84° 2' South, which is not so bad considering that we have been hauling our heavy load of 250 lb. per man uphill for the last two days. At noon we were nearly 2500 ft. above sea level. In the afternoon we had another heavy pull, and now are camped between two huge crevasses, but on a patch of hard snow. We pitched camp at 6 p.m., very tired and extremely hungry after dragging uphill all the afternoon for over five hours. It is 8 p.m. now, and we are nearly 3000 ft. above sea level. Low cumulus clouds are hanging to the south of us, as they have done for many days past, obscuring any view in that direction. We are anxiously hoping to find soon a level and inland ice sheet so that we can put on more speed. The distance today was 11 miles 1450 yards plus two miles relay. The talk now is mainly about food and the things we would like to eat, and at meal times our hoosh disappears with far too great speed. We are all looking forward to Christmas Day, for then, come what may, we are going to be full of food.

December 10. Falls, bruises, cut shins, crevasses, razor-edged ice, and a heavy upward pull have made up the sum of the day's trials, but there has been a measure of compensation in the wonderful scenery, the marvellous rocks and the covering of a distance of 11 miles 860 yards toward our goal. We started at 7:30 a.m. amongst crevasses, but soon got out of them and pulled up a long slope of snow. Our altitude at noon was 3250 ft. above sea level. Then we slid down a blue ice slope, after crossing crevasses. Marshall and I each went down one. We lunched at 1 p.m. and started at 2 p.m. up a long ridge by the side moraine of the glacier. It was heavy work, as the ice was split and presented knife-like edges between the cracks, and there were also some crevasses. Adams got into one. The going was terribly heavy, as the sledges brought up against the ice edges every now and then, and then there was a struggle to get them started again. We changed our foot gear, substituting ski boots for the finnesko, but nevertheless had many painful falls on the treacherous blue ice, cutting our hands and shins. We are all much bruised. We camped on a patch of snow by the land at 6 p.m. The rocks of the moraine are remarkable, being of every hue and description. I cannot describe them, but we will carry specimens back for the geologists to deal with. The main rocks of the 'Cloudmaker', the mountain under which we are camped, appear to be slates, reef quartz and a very hard, dark brown rock, the name of which I do not know. The erratics of marble, conglomerate, and breccia are beautiful, showing a great mass of wonderful colours, but these rocks we cannot take away. We can only take with us small specimens of the main rocks, as weight is of importance to us, and from these small specimens the geologists must determine the character of the land. This mountain is the one we thought might be an active volcano when we saw it from the mountain at the foot of the glacier, but the cloud has blown away from its head today, and we can see definitely that it is not a volcano. It is a remarkable sight as it towers above us with the snow clinging to its sides. Tonight there is a cold north wind. I climbed about 600 ft. up the mountain and got specimens of the main rocks in situ. The glacier is evidently moving very slowly, and not filling as much of the valley as it did at some previous date, for the old moraines lie higher up in terraces. Low cumulus clouds to the south are hiding some of the new land in that direction. We are all very hungry and tired tonight after the day's fight with glacier. Whilst I went up the mountain to spy out the land the others ground up the balance of the maize, brought for pony feed, between flat stones, in order that we may use it ourselves to eke out our supply of food. The method of preparation was primitive, but it represented the only way of getting it fit to cook without the necessity of using more oil than we can spare for lengthy boiling. The temperature was plus 12°F at noon today, and is plus 14° now at 8 p.m. We are getting south, and we hope to reach the inland ice in a couple of days; then our marching will be faster. The weather is still fine.

December 11. A heavy day. We started away at 7:40 a.m. and tried to keep alongside the land, but the ice of the glacier sloped so much that we had to go on to the ridge, where the sledges could run without side slipping. This slipping cuts the runners very badly. We crossed the medial moraine, and found rock there with what looked like plant impressions. We collected some specimens.

In the afternoon we found the surface better, as the cracks were nearly all filled up with water turned to ice. We camped for lunch on rubbly ice. After lunch we rounded some pressure ridges fairly easily, and then pulled up a long ice slope with many sharp points. All the afternoon we were passing over ice in which the cracks had been closed up, and we began to have great hopes that the end of the glacier was in sight, and that we would soon be able to put in some good marches on the plateau. At 5 p.m. we found more cracks and a mass of pressure ice ahead and land appeared as the clouds ahead lifted. I cannot tell what it means, but the position makes us anxious. The sledges will not stand much more of this ice work, and we are still 340 geographical miles away from the Pole. Thank God the weather is fine still. We camped at 6 p.m. on hard ice between two crevasses. There was no snow to pack round the tents, so we had to put the sledges and the provision bags on the snow cloths. We made the floor level inside by chipping away the points of ice with our ice axes. We were very hungry after hoosh tonight. Awkward features about the glacier are the little pits filled with mud, of which I collected a small sample.* It seems to be ground down rock material, but what the action has been I cannot tell. The hot sun, beating down on this mud, makes it gradually sink into the body of the glacier, leaving a rotten ice covering through which we often break. It is like walking over a cucumber frame, and sometimes the boulders that have sunk down through the ice can be seen 3 to 4 ft. below the surface. The ice that has formed above the sunken rocks is more clear than the ordinary

* These pits are known as cryoconite holes.

glacier ice. We are 3700 ft. up, and made 8 miles 900 yards to the good today. We have the satisfaction of feeling that we are getting south, and perhaps tomorrow may see the end of all our difficulties. Difficulties are just things to overcome after all. Everyone is very fit.

December 12. Our distance – three miles for the day – expresses more readily than I can write it the nature of the day's work. We started at 7:40 a.m. on the worst surface possible, sharp edged blue ice full of chasms and crevasses, rising to hills and descending into gullies; in fact, a surface that could not be equalled in any polar work for difficulty in travelling. Our sledges are suffering greatly, and it is a constant strain on us both to save the sledges from breaking or going down crevasses, and to save ourselves as well. We are a mass of bruises where we have fallen on the sharp ice, but, thank God, no-one has even a sprain. It has been relay work today, for we could only take on one sledge at a time, two of us taking turns at pulling the sledge whilst the others steadied and held the sledge to keep it straight. Thus we would advance one mile, and then return over the crevasses and haul up the other sledge. By repeating this today for three miles we marched nine miles over a surface where many times a slip meant death. Still we have advanced three miles to the south, and tonight we are camped on a patch of névé. By using our ice axes we made a place for the tent. The weather is still splendidly fine, though low clouds obscure our horizon to the south. We are anxiously hoping to cross the main pressure tomorrow, and trust that we will then have better travelling. Given good travelling, we will not be long in reaching our goal. Marshall is putting in the bearings and angles of the new mountains. They still keep appearing to the west and east. Distance 3 miles 500 yards, with relays 9 miles 1500 yards.

December 13. We made a start at 8 a.m. and once again went up hill and down dale, over crevasses and blue, ribbed ice, relaying the sledges. We had covered about a mile when we came to a place where it seemed almost impossible to proceed. However, to our right, bearing about south-west by south, there seemed to be better surface and we decided to make a detour in that direction in order, if possible, to get round the pressure. While returning for one of the sledges I fell on the ice and hurt my left knee, which was a serious matter, or rather might have been. I have had a bandage on all the afternoon while pulling, and the knee feels better now, but one realises what it would mean if any member of our party were to be damaged under these conditions and in this place. This afternoon we came on to a better surface, and were able to pull both sledges instead of relaying. We are still gradually rising, and tonight our hypsometer gives 203.7, or 4370 ft. up. There is a cool southerly wind; indeed, more than we have had before, and as we have only a patch of névé on the glacier for our tents, we had to take the provision bags and gear off the sledges to keep the tent cloths down. The temperature is plus 19°F. New mountains are still appearing to the west-south-west as we rise. We seem now to be going up a long yellow track, for the ice is not so blue, and we are evidently travelling over an old moraine, where the stones have sunk through the ice when its onward movement has been retarded. I am sure that the bulk of the glacier is growing less, but the onward movement still continues, though at a much slower pace than at some previous period. The gain for the day was five miles, and in addition we did four miles relay work.

December 14. This has been one of our hardest day's work so far. We have been steering all day about south-south-west up the glacier, mainly in the bed of an ancient moraine, which is full of holes through which the stones and boulders have melted down long years ago. It has been snowing all day with a high temperature, and this has made everything very wet. We have ascended over 1000 ft. today, our altitude at 6 p.m. being 5600 ft. above sea level, so the mountains to the west must be from 10,000 to 15,000 ft. in height, judging from their comparative elevation. My knee is better today. We have had a heavy pull and many falls on the slippery ice. Just before camping, Adams went through some snow, but held up over an awful chasm. Our sledges are much the worse for wear, and the one with the broken bow constantly strikes against the hard, sharp ice, pulling us up with a jerk and often flinging us down. At this high altitude the heavy pulling is very trying, especially as we slip on the snow covering the blue ice. There has evidently been an enormous glaciation here, and now it is dwindling away. Even the mountains show signs of this. Tonight our hopes are high that we are nearly at the end of the rise and that soon we will reach our longed-for plateau. Then southward indeed! Food is the determining factor with us. We did 7½ miles today.

December 15. Started at 7:40 a.m. in clear weather. It was heavy going uphill on the blue ice, but gradually we rose the land ahead, and it seemed as though at last we were going to have a change, and that we would see something new. At lunchtime we were on a better surface, with patches of snow, and we could see stretching out in front of us what was apparently a long, wide plain. It looked as though now really we were coming to the level ground for which we have longed, especially as the hypsometer gave us an altitude of 7230 ft., but this altitude at night came down to 5830 ft., so the apparent height may be due to barometric pressure and change of weather, for in the afternoon a stiff breeze from the south-west sprang up. The temperature was plus 18°F at noon, and when the wind came up it felt cold, as we were pulling in our pajama trousers, with nothing underneath. We have been going steadily uphill all the afternoon, but on a vastly improved surface, consisting of hard névé instead of blue ice and no cracks, only covered in crevasses, which are easily seen. Ahead of us really lies the plateau. We can also see ahead of us detached mountains, piercing through the inland ice, which is the road to the south for us. Huge mountains stretch out to the east and west. After last week's toil and anxiety the change is delightful. The distance covered today was 13 miles 200 yards.

December 16. We started at 7 a.m., having had breakfast at 5:30 a.m. It was snowing slightly for the first few hours, and then the weather cleared. The surface was hard and the going good. We camped at noon and took sights for latitude, and ascertained that our position was 84° 50' South. Ahead of us we could see a long slope, icy and crevassed, but we did 13 miles 1650 yards for the day. We camped at 5:30 p.m., and got ready our depot gear. We have decided to travel as lightly as possible, taking only the clothes we are wearing, and we will leave four days' food, which I calculate should get us back to the last depot on short ration. We have now traversed nearly one hundred miles of crevassed ice, and risen 6000 ft. on the largest glacier in the world. One more crevassed slope, and we will be on the plateau, please God. We are all fit and well. The temperature tonight is plus 15°F, and the wind is blowing freshly from the south-west. There are splendid ranges of mountains to the west-south-west, and we have an extended view of glacier and mountains. Ahead of us lie three sharp peaks, connected up and forming an island in what is apparently inland ice or the head of the glacier. The peaks lie due south of us. To the eastward and westward of this island the ice bears down from the inland ice sheet, and joins the head of the glacier proper. To the westward the mountains along the side of the glacier are all of the bluff type, and the lines of stratification can be seen plainly. Still further to the westward, behind the frontal range, lie sharper peaks, some of them almost perfect cones. The trend of the land from the 'Cloudmaker' is about south-south-west. We are travelling up the west side of the glacier. On the other side, to the east, there is a break in the bluff mountains, and the land beyond runs away more to the south-east. The valley is filled with pressure ice, which seems to have come from the inland ice sheet. The mountains to the south-east also show lines of stratification. I hope that the photographs will be clear enough to give an idea of the character of this land. These mountains are not beautiful in the ordinary acceptance of the term, but they are magnificent in their stern and rugged grandeur. No foot has ever trod on their mighty sides, and until we reached this frozen land no human eyes had seen their forms.

December 17. We made a start at 7:20 a.m. and had an uphill pull all the morning over blue ice with patches of snow, which impeded our progress until we learned that the best way was to rush the sledges over them, for it was very difficult to keep one's footing on the smooth ice, and haul the sledges astern over the snow. By 1 p.m. we had done eight miles of this uphill work, and in the afternoon we did four more. We had worked from 7:23 a.m. until 6:40 p.m. with one hour's rest for lunch only and it seems as though twelve miles was not much, but the last two hours' going was very stiff. We had to take on one sledge at a time up the icy slope, and even then we had to cut steps with our ice axes as we went along. The work was made more difficult by the fact that a strong southerly wind was dead in our faces. The second sledge we hauled up the rise by means of the alpine rope. We made it fast to the sledge, went on with the first sledge till the rope was stretched out to its full length, then cut a place to stand on, and by our united efforts hauled the sledge up to where we stood. We repeated this until we had managed to reach a fairly level spot with both the sledges, and we pitched our tents on a small patch of snow. There was not enough of the snow to make fast the snow cloths of the tents, and we had to take the gear off the sledges and pile that round to supplement the snow. We have burned our boats behind us now as regards warm clothing, for this afternoon we made a depot in by the rocks of the island we are passing, and there left everything except the barest necessaries. After dinner tonight Wild went up the hillside in order to have a look at the plateau. He came down with the news that the plateau is in sight at last, and that tomorrow should see us at the end of our difficulties. He also brought down with him some very interesting geological specimens, some of which certainly look like coal. The quality may be poor, but I have little doubt that the stuff is coal. If that proves to be the case, the discovery will be most interesting to the scientific world. Wild tells me that there are about six seams of this dark stuff, mingled with sandstone, and that the seams are from 4 in. to 7 or 8 ft. in thickness. There are vast quantities of it lying on the hillside. We took a photograph of the sandstone, and I wish very much that we could spare time to examine the rocks more thoroughly. We may be able to do this on the way back. We have but little time for geological work, for our way is south and time is short, but we found that the main rock is sandstone and on our way back we will collect some. I expect that this will be the most southerly rock that we shall obtain, for we ought to reach the plateau tomorrow, and then there will be no more land close to us. It is gusty tonight, but beautifully clear. The altitude, according to the hypsometer, is 6100 ft.

NOTE. When I showed the specimens to Professor David after our return to the *Nimrod,* he stated definitely that some of them were coal and others 'mother of coal'.

CHAPTER 14

On the plateau to the farthest south
December 18, 1908 to January 8, 1909
December 21, Midsummer Day, with 28° of frost: Christmas Day
at an altitude of 9500 ft. in latitude 85° 55' South: Christmas fare:
Last depot on January 4: Blinding blizzard for two days,
January 7, 8: Altitude 11,600 ft.

December 18. Almost up: The altitude tonight is 7400 ft. above sea level. This has been one of our hardest days, but worth it, for we are just on the plateau at last. We started at 7:30 a.m., relaying the sledges, and did 6 miles 600 yards, which means nearly 19 miles for the day of actual travelling. All the morning we worked up loose, slippery ice, hauling the sledges up one at a time by means of the alpine rope, then pulling in harness on the less stiff rises. We camped for lunch at 12:45 p.m. on the crest of a rise close to the pressure and in the midst of crevasses, into one of which I managed to fall, also Adams. Whilst lunch was preparing I got some rock from the land, quite different to the sandstone of yesterday. The mountains are all different just here. The land on our left shows beautifully clear stratified lines, and on the west side sandstone stands out, greatly weathered. All the afternoon we relayed up a long snow slope, and we were hungry and tired when we reached camp. We have been saving food to make it spin out, and that increases our hunger; each night we all dream of foods. We save two biscuits per man per day, also pemmican and sugar, eking out our food with pony maize, which we soak in water to make it less hard. All this means that we have now five weeks' food, while we are about 300 geographical miles from the Pole, with the same distance back to the last depot we left yesterday, so we must march on short food to reach our goal. The temperature is plus 16°F tonight, but a cold wind all the morning cut our faces and broken lips. We keep crevasses with us still, but I think that tomorrow will see the end of this. When we passed the main slope today, more mountains appeared to the west of south, some with sheer cliffs and others rounded off, ending in long snow slopes. I judge the southern limit of the mountains to the west to be about latitude 86° South.

December 19. Not on the plateau level yet, though we are tonight 7888 ft. up, and still there is another rise ahead of us. We got breakfast at 5 a.m. and started at 7 a.m. sharp, taking on one sledge. Soon we got to the top of a ridge, and went back for the second sledge, then hauled both together all the rest of the day. The weight was about 200 lb. per man, and we kept going until 6 p.m., with a stop of one hour for lunch. We got a meridian altitude at noon, and found that our latitude was 85° 5' South. We seem unable to get rid of the crevasses, and we have been falling into them and steering through them all day in the face of a cold southerly wind, with a temperature varying from plus 15° to plus 9°F. The work was very heavy, for we were going uphill all day, and our sledge runners, which have been suffering from the sharp ice and rough travelling, are in a bad way. Soft snow in places greatly retarded our progress, but we have covered our ten miles, and now are camped on good snow between two crevasses. I really think that tomorrow will see us on the plateau proper. This glacier must be one of the largest, if not the largest, in the world. The sastrugi seem to point mainly to the south, so we may expect head winds all the way to the Pole. Marshall has a cold job tonight, taking the angles of the new mountains to the west, some of which appeared today. After dinner we examined the sledge runners and turned one sledge end for end, for it had been badly torn while we were coming up the glacier, and in the soft snow it clogged greatly. We are still favoured with splendid weather, and that is a great comfort to us, for it would be almost impossible under other conditions to travel amongst these crevasses, which are caused by the congestion of the ice between the headlands when it was flowing from the plateau down between the mountains. Now there is comparatively little movement, and many of the crevasses have become snow-filled. Tonight we are 290 geographical miles from the Pole. We are thinking of our Christmas dinner. We will be full that day, anyhow.

December 20. Not yet up, but nearly so. We got away from camp at 7 a.m., with a strong head wind from the south, and this wind continued all day, with a temperature ranging from plus 7° to plus 5°. Our beards coated with ice. It was an uphill pull all day around pressure ice, and we reached an altitude of over 8000 ft. above sea level. The weather was clear, but there were various clouds, which were noted by Adams. Marshall took bearings and angles at noon, and we got the sun's meridian altitude, showing that we were in latitude 85° 17′ South. We hope all the time that each ridge we come to will be the last, but each time another rises ahead, split up by pressure, and we begin the same toil again. It is trying work and as we have now reduced our food at breakfast to one pannikin of hoosh and one biscuit, by the time the lunch hour has arrived, after five hours' hauling in the cold wind up the slope, we are very hungry. At lunch we have a little chocolate, tea with plasmon, a pannikin of cocoa, and three biscuits. Today we did 11 miles, 950 yards (statute), having to relay the sledges over the last bit, for the ridge we were on was so steep that we could not get the two sledges up together. Still, we are getting on; we have only 279 more miles to go, and then we will have reached the Pole. The land appears to run away to the south-east now, and soon we will be just a speck on this great inland waste of snow and ice. It is cold tonight. I am cook for the week, and started tonight. Everyone is fit and well.

December 21. Midsummer Day, with 28° of frost! We have frostbitten fingers and ears, and a strong blizzard wind has been blowing from the south all day, all due to the fact that we have climbed to an altitude of over 8000 ft. above sea level. From early morning we have been striving to the south, but six miles is the total distance gained, for from noon, or rather from lunch at 1 p.m., we have been hauling the sledges up, one after the other, by standing pulls across crevasses and over great pressure ridges. When we had advanced one sledge some distance, we put up a flag on a bamboo to mark its position, and then roped up and returned for the other. The wind, no doubt, has a great deal to do with the low temperature, and we feel the cold, as we are going on short commons. The altitude adds to the difficulties, but we are getting south all the time. We started away from camp at 6:45 a.m. today, and except for an hour's halt at lunch, worked on until 6 p.m. Now we are camped in a filled-up crevasse, the only place where snow to put around the tents can be obtained, for all the rest of the ground we are on is either névé or hard ice. We little thought that this particular pressure ridge was going to be such an obstacle; it looked quite ordinary, even a short way off, but we have now decided to trust nothing to eyesight, for the distances are so deceptive up here. It is a wonderful sight to look down over the glacier from the great altitude we are at, and to see the mountains stretching away east and west, some of them over 15,000 ft. in height. We are very hungry now, and it seems as cold almost as the spring sledging. Our beards are masses of ice all day long. Thank God we are fit and well and have had no accident, which is a mercy, seeing that we have covered over 130 miles of crevassed ice.

December 22. As I write of today's events, I can easily imagine I am on a spring sledging journey, for the temperature is minus 5°F and a chilly south-easterly wind is blowing and finds its way through the walls of our tent, which are getting worn. All day long, from 7 a.m., except for the hour when we stopped for lunch, we have been relaying the sledges over the pressure mounds and across crevasses. Our total distance to the good for the whole day was only four miles southward, but this evening our prospects look brighter, for we must now have come to the end of the great glacier. It is flattening out, and except for crevasses there will not be much trouble in hauling the sledges tomorrow. One sledge today, when coming down with a run over a pressure ridge, turned a complete somersault, but nothing was damaged, in spite of the total weight being over 400 lb. We are now dragging 400 lb. at a time up the steep slopes and across the ridges, working with the alpine rope all day, and roping ourselves together when we go back for the second sledge, for the ground is so treacherous that many times during the day we are saved only by the rope from falling into fathomless pits. Wild describes the sensation of walking over this surface, half ice and half snow, as like walking over the glass roof of a station. The usual query when one of us falls into a crevasse is! 'Have you found it?' One gets somewhat callous as regards the immediate danger, though we are always glad to meet crevasses with their coats off, that is, not hidden by the snow covering. Tonight we are camped in a filled-in crevasse. Away to the north down the glacier a thick cumulus cloud is lying, but some of the largest mountains are standing out clearly.

Immediately behind us lies a broken sea of pressure ice. Please God, ahead of us there is a clear road to the Pole.

December 23. Eight thousand eight hundred and twenty feet up, and still steering upward amid great waves of pressure and ice falls, for our plateau, after a good morning's march, began to rise in higher ridges, so that it really was not the plateau after all. Today's crevasses have been far more dangerous than any others we have crossed, as the soft snow hides all trace of them until we fall through. Constantly today one or another of the party has had to be hauled out from a chasm by means of his harness, which had alone saved him from death in the icy vault below. We started at 6:40 a.m. and worked on steadily until 6 p.m., with the usual lunch hour in the middle of the day. The pony maize does not swell in the water now, as the temperature is very low and the water freezes. The result is that it swells inside after we have eaten it. We are very hungry indeed, and talk a great deal of what we would like to eat. In spite of the crevasses, we have done thirteen miles today to the south, and we are now in latitude 85° 41' South. The temperature at noon was plus 6°F and at 6 p.m. it was minus 1°F, but it is much lower at night. There was a strong south-east to south-south-east wind blowing all day, and it was cutting to our noses and burst lips. Wild was frostbitten. I do trust that tomorrow will see the end of this bad travelling, so that we can stretch out our legs for the Pole.

December 24. A much better day for us; indeed, the brightest we have had since entering our Southern Gateway. We started off at 7 a.m. across waves and undulations of ice, with some one or other of our little party falling through the thin crust of snow every now and then. At 10:30 a.m. I decided to steer more to the west, and we soon got on to a better surface, and covered 5 miles 250 yards in the forenoon. After lunch, as the surface was distinctly improving, we discarded the second sledge, and started our afternoon's march with one sledge. It has been blowing freshly from the south and drifting all day, and this, with over 40° of frost, has coated our faces with ice. We get superficial frostbites every now and then. During the afternoon the surface improved greatly, and the cracks and crevasses disappeared, but we are still going uphill, and from the summit of one ridge saw some new land, which runs south-south-east down to latitude 86° South. We camped at

6 p.m., very tired and with cold feet. We have only the clothes we stand up in now, as we depoted everything else, and this continued rise means lower temperatures than I had anticipated. Tonight we are 9095 ft. above sea level, and the way before us is still rising. I trust that it will soon level out, for it is hard work pulling at this altitude. So far there is no sign of the very hard surface that Captain Scott speaks of in connection with his journey on the Northern Plateau. There seem to be just here regular layers of snow, not much windswept, but we will see better the surface conditions in a few days. Tomorrow will be Christmas Day, and our thoughts turn to home and all the attendant joys of the time. One longs to hear 'the hansoms slurring through the London mud'. Instead of that, we are lying in a little tent, isolated high on the roof of the end of the world, far, indeed, from the ways trodden of men. Still, our thoughts can fly across the wastes of ice and snow and across the oceans to those whom we are striving for and who are thinking of us now. And, thank God, we are nearing our goal. The distance covered today was 11 miles 250 yards.

December 25. Christmas Day. There has been from 45° to 48° of frost, drifting snow and a strong biting south wind, and such has been the order of the day's march from 7 a.m. to 6 p.m. up one of the steepest rises we have yet done, crevassed in places. Now, as I write, we are 9500 ft. above sea level, and our latitude at 6 p.m. was 85° 55' South. We started away after a good breakfast, and soon came to soft snow, through which our worn and torn sledge-runners dragged heavily. All morning we hauled along, and at noon had done 5 miles 250 yards. Sights gave us latitude 85° 51' South. We had lunch then, and I took a photograph of the camp with the Queen's flag flying and also our tent flags, my companions being in the picture. It was very cold, the temperature being minus 16°F, and the wind went through us. All the afternoon we worked steadily uphill, and we could see at 6 p.m. the new land plainly trending to the south-east. This land is very much glaciated. It is comparatively bare of snow, and there are well-defined glaciers on the side of the range, which seems to end up in the south-east with a large mountain like a keep. We have called it 'The Castle'. Behind these the mountains have more gentle slopes and are more rounded. They seem to fall away to the south-east, so that, as we are going south, the angle opens and we will soon miss them. When we camped at 6 p.m. the wind was decreasing. It is hard to understand this soft snow with such a persistent wind, and I can only suppose that we have not yet reached the actual plateau level, and that the snow we are travelling over just now is on the slopes, blown down by the south and south-east wind. We had a splendid dinner. First came hoosh, consisting of pony ration boiled up with pemmican and some of our emergency Oxo and biscuit. Then in the cocoa water I boiled our little plum pudding, which a friend of Wild's had given him. This, with a drop of medical brandy, was a luxury which Lucullus himself might have envied; then came cocoa, and lastly cigars and a spoonful of *creme de menthe* sent us by a friend in Scotland. We are full tonight, and this is the last time we will be for many a long day. After dinner we discussed the situation, and we have decided to still further reduce our food. We have now nearly 500 miles, geographical, to do if we are to get to the Pole and back to the spot where we are at the present moment. We have one month's food, but only three weeks' biscuit, so we are going to make each week's food last ten days. We will have one biscuit in the morning, three at midday, and two at night. It is the only thing to do. Tomorrow we will throw away everything except the most absolute necessities. Already we are, as regards clothes, down to the limit, but we must trust to the old sledge runners and dump the spare ones. One must risk this. We are very far away from all the world, and home thoughts have been much with us today, thoughts interrupted by pitching forward into a hidden crevasse more than once. Ah, well, we shall see all our own people when the work here is done. Marshall took our temperatures tonight. We are all two degrees subnormal, but as fit as can be. It is a fine open-air life and we are getting south.

December 26. Got away at 7 a.m sharp, after dumping a lot of gear. We marched steadily all day except for lunch, and we have done 14 miles 480 yards on an uphill march, with soft snow at times and a bad wind. Ridge after ridge we met, and though the surface is better and harder in places, we feel very tired at the end of ten hours' pulling. Our height tonight is 9590 ft. above sea level according to the hypsometer. The ridges we meet with are almost similar in appearance. We see the sun shining on them in the distance, and then the rise begins very gradually. The snow gets soft, and the weight of the sledge becomes more marked. As we near the top the soft snow gives place to a hard surface, and on the summit of the ridge we find small crevasses. Every time we reach the top of a ridge we say to ourselves: 'Perhaps this is the last', but it never is the last; always there appears away ahead of us another ridge. I do not think that the land lies very far below the ice sheet, for the crevasses on the summits of the ridges suggest that the sheet is moving over land at no great depth. It would seem that the descent toward the glacier proper from the plateau is by a series of terraces. We lost sight of the land today, having left it all behind us, and now we have the waste of snow all around. Two more days and our maize will be finished. Then our hooshes will be more woefully thin than ever. This shortness of food is unpleasant, but if we allow ourselves what, under ordinary circumstances, would be a reasonable amount, we would have to abandon all idea of getting far south.

December 27. If a great snow plain, rising every seven miles in a steep ridge, can be called a plateau, then we are on it at last, with an altitude above the sea of 9820 ft. We started at 7 a.m. and marched till noon, encountering at 11 a.m. a steep snow ridge which pretty well cooked us, but we got the sledge up by noon and camped. We are pulling 150 lb. per man. In the afternoon we had good going till 5 p.m. and then another ridge as difficult as the previous one, so that our backs and legs were in a bad way when we reached the top at 6 p.m., having done 14 miles 930 yards for the day. Thank heaven it has been a fine day, with little wind. The temperature is minus 9°F. This surface is most peculiar, showing layers of snow with little sastrugi all pointing south-south-east. Short food make us think of plum puddings, and hard half-cooked maize gives us indigestion, but we are getting south. The latitude is 86° 19' South tonight. Our thoughts are with the people at home a great deal.

December 28. If the Barrier is a changing sea, the plateau is a changing sky. During the morning march we continued to go up hill steadily, but the surface was constantly changing. First there was soft snow in layers, then soft snow so deep that we were well over our ankles, and the temperature being well below zero, our feet were cold through sinking in. No one can say what we are going to find next, but we can go steadily ahead. We started at 6:55

a.m., and had done 7 miles 200 yards by noon, the pulling being very hard. Some of the snow is blown into hard sastrugi, some that look perfectly smooth and hard have only a thin crust through which we break when pulling; all of it is a trouble. Yesterday we passed our last crevasse, though there are a few cracks or ridges fringed with crystals shining like diamonds, warning us that the cracks are open. We are now 10,199 ft. above sea level, and the plateau is gradually flattening out, but it was heavy work pulling this afternoon. The high altitude and a temperature of 48° of frost made breathing and work difficult. We are getting south – latitude 86° 31' South tonight. The last sixty miles we hope to rush, leaving everything possible, taking one tent only and using the poles of the other as marks every ten miles, for we will leave all our food sixty miles off the Pole except enough to carry us there and back. I hope with good weather to reach the Pole on January 12, and then we will try and rush it to get to Hut Point by February 28. We are so tired after each hour's pulling that we throw ourselves on our backs for a three-minute spell. It took us over ten hours to do 14 miles 450 yards today, but we did it all right. It is a wonderful thing to be over 10,000 ft. up, almost at the end of the world. The short food is trying, but when we have done the work we will be happy. Adams had a bad headache all yesterday, and today I had the same trouble, but it is better now. Otherwise we are all fit and well. I think the country is flattening out more and more, and hope tomorrow to make fifteen miles, at least.

December 29. Yesterday I wrote that we hoped to do fifteen miles today, but such is the variable character of this surface that one cannot prophesy with any certainty an hour ahead. A strong southerly wind, with from 44° to 49° of frost, combined with the effect of short rations, made our distance 12 miles 600 yards instead. We have reached an altitude of 10,310 ft., and an uphill gradient gave us one of the most severe pulls for ten hours that would be possible. It looks serious, for we must increase the food if we are to get on at all, and we must risk a depot at seventy miles off the Pole and dash for it then. Our sledge is badly strained, and on the abominably bad surface of soft snow is dreadfully hard to move. I have been suffering from a bad headache all day, and Adams also was worried by the cold. I think that these headaches are a form of mountain sickness, due to our high altitude. The others have bled from the nose, and that must relieve them. Physical effort is always trying at a high altitude, and we are straining at the harness all day, sometimes slipping in the soft snow that overlies the hard sastrugi. My head is very bad. The sensation is as though the nerves were being twisted up with a corkscrew and then pulled out. Marshall took our temperatures tonight, and we are all at about 94°, but in spite of this we are getting south. We are only 198 miles off our goal now. If the rise would stop the cold would not matter, but it is hard to know what is man's limit. We have only 150 lb. per man to pull, but it is more severe work than the 250 lb. per man up the glacier was. The Pole is hard to get.

December 30. We only did 4 miles 100 yards today. We started at 7 a.m., but had to camp at 11 a.m., a blizzard springing up from the south. It is more than annoying. I cannot express my feelings. We were pulling at last on a level surface, but very soft snow, when at about 10 a.m. the south wind and drift commenced to increase, and at 11 a.m. it was so bad that we had to camp. And here all day we have been lying in our sleeping bags trying to keep warm and listening to the threshing drift on the tent side. I am in the cooking tent, and the wind comes through, it is so thin. Our precious food is going and the time also, and it is so important to us to get on. We lie here and think of how to make things better, but we cannot reduce food now, and the only thing will be to rush all possible at the end. We will do and are doing all humanly possible. It is with Providence to help us.

December 31. The last day of the old year, and the hardest day we have had almost, pushing through soft snow uphill with a strong head wind and drift all day. The temperature is minus 7°F, and our altitude is 10,477 ft. above sea level. The altitude is trying. My head has been very bad all day, and we are all feeling the short food, but still we are getting south. We are in latitude 86° 54' South tonight, but we have only three weeks' food and two weeks' biscuit to do nearly 500 geographical miles. We can only do our best. Too tired to write more tonight. We all get iced up about our faces, and are on the verge of frostbite all the time. Please God the weather will be fine during the next fourteen days. Then all will be well. The distance today was eleven miles.

Note. If we had only known that we were going to get such cold weather as we were at this time experiencing, we would have kept a pair of scissors to trim our beards. The moisture from the condensation of one's breath accumulated on the beard and trickled down on to the Burberry blouse. Then it froze into a sheet of ice inside, and it became very painful to pull the Burberry off in camp. Little troubles of this sort would have seemed less serious to us if we had been able to get a decent feed at the end of the day's work, but we were very hungry. We thought of food most of the time. The chocolate certainly seemed better than the cheese, because the two spoonfuls of cheese per man allowed under our scale of diet would not last as long as the two sticks of chocolate. We did not have both at the same meal. We had the bad luck at this time to strike a tin in which the biscuits were thin and overbaked. Under ordinary circumstances they would probably have tasted rather better than the other biscuits, but we wanted bulk. We soaked them in our tea so that they would swell up and appear larger, but if one soaked a biscuit too much, the sensation of biting something was lost, and the food seemed to disappear much too easily.

January 1, 1909. Head too bad to write much. We did 11 miles 900 yards (statute) today, and the latitude at 6 p.m. was 87° 6½' South, so we have beaten North and South records. Struggling uphill all day in very soft snow. Everyone done up and weak from want of food. When we camped at 6 p.m. fine warm weather, thank God. Only 172½ miles from the Pole. The height above sea level, now 10,755 ft., makes all work difficult. Surface seems to be better ahead. I do trust it will be so tomorrow.

January 2. Terribly hard work today. We started at 6:45 a.m. with a fairly good surface, which soon became very soft. We were sinking in over our ankles, and our broken sledge, by running sideways, added to the drag. We have been going uphill all day, and tonight are 11,034 ft. above sea level. It has taken us all day to do 10 miles 450 yards, though the weights are fairly light. A cold wind, with a temperature of minus 14°F, goes right through us now, as we are weakening from want of food, and the high altitude makes every movement an effort, especially if we stumble on the march. My head is giving me trouble all the time. Wild seems the most fit of us. God knows we are doing all we can, but the outlook is serious if this surface continues and the plateau gets higher, for we are not travelling fast enough to make our food spin out and get back to our depot in time. I cannot think of failure yet. I must look at the matter sensibly and consider the lives of those who are with me. I feel that if we go on too far it will be impossible to get back over this surface, and then all the results will be lost to the world. We can now definitely locate the South Pole on the highest plateau in the world, and our geological work and meteorology will be of the greatest use to science; but all this is not the Pole. Man can only do his best, and we have arrayed against us the strongest forces of nature. This cutting south wind with drift plays the mischief with us, and after ten hours of struggling against it one pannikin of food with two biscuits and a cup of cocoa does not warm one up much. I must think over the situation carefully tomorrow, for time is going on and food is going also.

January 3. Started at 6:55 a.m., cloudy but fairly warm. The temperature was minus 8°F at noon. We had a terrible surface all the morning, and did only 5 miles 100 yards. A meridian altitude gave us latitude 87° 22' South at noon. The surface was better in the afternoon, and we did six geographical miles. The temperature at 6 p.m. was minus 11°F. It was an uphill pull toward the evening, and we camped at 6:20 p.m., the altitude being 11,220 ft. above the sea. Tomorrow we must risk making a depot on the plateau, and make a dash for it, but even then, if this surface continues, we will be two weeks in carrying it through.

January 4. The end is in sight. We can only go for three more days at the most, for we are weakening rapidly. Short food and a blizzard wind from the south, with driving drift, at a temperature of 47° of frost, have plainly told us today that we are reaching our limit, for we were so done up at noon with cold that the clinical thermometer failed to register the temperature of three of us at 94°. We started at 7:40 a.m., leaving a depot on this great wide plateau, a risk that only this case justified, and one that my comrades agreed to, as they have to every one so far, with the same cheerfulness and regardlessness of self that have been the means of our getting as far as we have done so far. Pathetically small looked the bamboo, one of the tent poles, with a bit of bag sewn on as a flag, to mark our stock of provisions, which has to take us back to our depot, one hundred and fifty miles north. We lost sight of it in half an hour, and are now trusting to our footprints in the snow to guide us back to each bamboo until we pick up the depot again. I trust that the weather will keep clear. Today we have done 12½ geographical miles, and with only 70 lb. per man to pull it is as hard, even harder, work than the 100 odd lb. was yesterday, and far harder than the 250 lb. were three weeks ago, when we were climbing the glacier. This, I consider, is a clear indication of our failing strength. The main thing against us is the altitude of 11,200 ft. and the biting wind. Our faces are cut, and our feet and hands are always on the verge of frostbite. Our fingers, indeed, often go, but we get them around more or less. I have great trouble with two fingers on my left hand. They had been badly jammed when we were getting the motor up over the ice face at winter quarters, and the circulation is not good. Our boots now are pretty well worn out, and we have to halt at times to pick the snow out of the soles. Our stock of sennegrass is nearly exhausted, so we have to use the same frozen stuff day after day. Another trouble is that the lamp wick with which we tie the finnesko is chafed through, and we have to tie knots in it. These knots catch the snow under our feet, making a lump that has to be cleared every now and then. I am of the opinion that to sledge even in the height of summer on this plateau, we should have at least forty ounces of food a day per man, and we are on short rations of the ordinary allowance of thirty-two ounces. We depoted our extra underclothing to save weight about three weeks ago, and are now in the same clothes night and day. One suit of underclothing, shirt and guernsey, and our thin Burberries, now all patched. When we get up in the morning, out of the wet bag, our Burberries become like a coat of mail at once, and our heads and beards get iced-up with the moisture when breathing on the march. There is half a gale blowing dead in our teeth all the time. We hope to reach within 100 geographical miles of the Pole; I am confident that the Pole lies on the great plateau we have discovered, miles and miles from any outstanding land. The temperature tonight is minus 24°F.

January 5. Today headwind and drift again, with 50° of frost, and a terrible surface. We have been marching through 8 in. of snow, covering sharp sastrugi, which plays havoc with our feet, but we have done 13⅓ geographical miles, for we increased our food, seeing that it was absolutely necessary to do this to enable us to accomplish anything. I realise that the food we have been having has not been sufficient to keep up our strength, let alone supply the wastage caused by exertion, and now we must try to keep warmth in us, though our strength is being used up. Our temperatures at 5 a.m. were 94°F. We got away at 7 a.m. sharp and marched till noon, then from 1 p.m. sharp till 6 p.m. All being in one tent makes our camp work slower, for we are so cramped for room, and we get up at 4:40 a.m. so as to get away by 7 a.m. Two of us have to stand outside the tent at night until things are squared up inside, and we find it cold work. Hunger grips us hard, and the food supply is very small. My head still gives me great trouble. I began by wishing that my worst enemy had it instead of myself, but now I don't wish even my worst enemy to have such a headache; still, it is no use talking about it. Self is a subject that most of us are fluent on. We find the utmost difficulty in carrying through the day, and we can only go for two or three more days. Never once has the temperature been above zero since we got on to the plateau, though this is the height of summer. We have done our best, and we thank God for having allowed us to get so far.

January 6. This must be our last outward march with the sledge and camp equipment. Tomorrow we must leave camp with some food, and push as far south as possible, and then plant the flag. Today's story is 57° of frost, with a strong blizzard and high drift; yet we marched 13¼ geographical miles through soft snow, being helped by extra food. This does not mean full rations, but a bigger ration than we have been having lately. The pony maize is all finished. The most trying day we have yet spent, our fingers and faces being frostbitten continually. Tomorrow we will rush south with the flag. We are at 88° 7' South tonight. It is our last outward march. Blowing hard tonight. I would fail to explain my feelings if I tried to write them down, now that the end has come. There is only one thing that lightens the disappointment, and that is the feeling that we have done all we could. It is the forces of nature that have prevented us from going right through. I cannot write more.

January 7. A blinding, shrieking blizzard all day, with the temperature ranging from 60° to 70° of frost. It has been impossible to leave the tent, which is snowed up on the lee side. We have been lying in our bags all day, only warm at food time, with fine snow making through the walls of the worn tent and covering our bags.

We are greatly cramped. Adams is suffering from cramp every now and then. We are eating our valuable food without marching. The wind has been blowing eighty to ninety miles an hour. We can hardly sleep. Tomorrow I trust this will be over. Directly the wind drops we march as far south as possible, then plant the flag, and turn homeward. Our chief anxiety is lest our tracks may drift up, for to them we must trust mainly to find our depot; we have no land bearings in this great plain of snow. It is a serious risk that we have taken, but we had to play the game to the utmost, and Providence will look after us.

January 8. Again all day in our bags, suffering considerably physically from cold hands and feet, and from hunger, but more mentally, for we cannot get on south, and we simply lie here shivering. Every now and then one of our party's feet go, and the unfortunate beggar has to take his leg out of the sleeping bag and have his frozen foot nursed into life again by placing it inside the shirt, against the skin of his almost equally unfortunate neighbour. We must do something more to the south, even though the food is going, and we weaken lying in the cold, for with 72° of frost the wind cuts through our thin tent, and even the drift is finding its way in and on to our bags, which are wet enough as it is. Cramp is not uncommon every now and then, and the drift all round the tent has made it so small that there is hardly room for us at all. The wind has been blowing hard all day; some of the gusts must be over seventy or eighty miles an hour. This evening it seems as though it were going to ease down, and directly it does we shall be up and away south for a rush. I feel that this march must be our limit. We are so short of food, and at this high altitude, 11,600 ft., it is hard to keep any warmth in our bodies between the scanty meals. We have nothing to read now, having depoted our little books to save weight, and it is dreary work lying in the tent with nothing to read, and too cold to write much in the diary.

CHAPTER 15

Farthest South
January 9, 1909
The Union Jack planted in 88° 23' South, longitude 162° East

January 9. Our last day outwards. We have shot our bolt, and the tale is latitude 88° 23' South, longitude 162° East. The wind eased down at 1 a.m., and at 2 a.m. we were up and had breakfast. At 4 a.m. started south, with the Queen's Union Jack, a brass cylinder containing stamps and documents to place at the furthest south point, camera, glasses, and compass. At 9 a.m. we were in 88° 23' South, half running and half walking over a surface much hardened by the recent blizzard. It was strange for us to go along without the nightmare of a sledge dragging behind us. We hoisted Her Majesty's flag and the other Union Jack afterwards, and took possession of the plateau in the name of His Majesty. While the Union Jack blew out stiffly in the icy gale that cut us to the bone, we looked south with our powerful glasses, but could see nothing but the dead white snow plain. There was no break in the plateau as it extended toward the Pole, and we feel sure that the goal we have failed to reach lies on this plain. We stayed only a few minutes, and then, taking the Queen's flag and eating our scanty meal as we went, we hurried back and reached our camp about 3 p.m. We were so dead tired that we only did two hours' march in the afternoon and camped at 5:30 p.m. The temperature was minus 19°F. Fortunately for us, our tracks were not obliterated by the blizzard; indeed, they stood up, making a trail easily followed. Homeward bound at last. Whatever regrets may be, we have done our best.

CHAPTER 16

The return march
January 10 to February 22

*First homeward marches: Back on the Barrier: Attacks of
dysentery: Chinaman depot reached February 13: Depot
A reached February 20: Nearing Bluff Depot*

January 10. We started at 7:30 a.m. with a fair wind, and marched
all day, with a stop of one hour for lunch, doing over 18½
geographical miles to the north. It has, indeed, been fortunate for
us that we have been able to follow our outward track for the force
of the gale had torn the flags from the staffs. We will be all right
when we pick up our depot. It has been a big risk leaving our food
on the great white plain, with only our sledge tracks to guide us
back. Tonight we are all tired out, but we have put a good march
behind us. The temperature is minus 9°F.

January 11. A good day. We have done nearly 17 geographical
miles. We have picked up our depot and now are following
the sledge tracks to the north. The temperature has been minus
15°F. There has been tremendous wind here and the sastrugi are
enormous.

January 12. We did 14 miles 100 yards today with little wind to
help us. The surface was very heavy and we found enormous
sastrugi. The wind is getting up tonight. I hope for a good breeze
behind us tomorrow.

January 13. It was heavy pulling all day, but we did a good distance in spite of it, getting 15 miles 1650 yards to the north. We
have the sail up continually, but I cannot say that it has been very
much help today. The temperature, minus 18°F nearly all the
time, makes things very cold, and we ourselves slept badly last
night. I did not sleep at all, for both my heels are frostbitten and
have cracked open, and I also have cracks under some of my toes;
but we can march all right, and are moving over the ground very

fast. We must continue to do so, for we have only about 20 lb. of biscuit to last us over 140 miles, and I expect there will be little in the locker by the time we strike our glacier head depot. The surface has been very severe today.

January 14. A strong following blizzard all day gave us our best day's run of the whole trip, 20 miles 1600 yards in ten hours. We decided to cut down the rations by another biscuit, as we have only six days' biscuit left on short ration, and 120 miles to go before we reach the depot, so we feel very hungry, and with the temperature minus 18°F to minus 21°F, all day in the wind, one easily gets frostbitten.

January 15. Started in a strong blizzard at 7:30 a.m. with a temperature of minus 23°F, and march steadily till noon, doing 9½ miles; then marched from 1:30 p.m. till 6 p.m., making a total distance for the day of 20 miles, statute. It has been thick, with a pale sun only shining through, but we are still able to follow our old sledge tracks, though at times they are very faint. Unfortunately, when we halted at 3:30 p.m. for a spell, we found that the sledge meter had disappeared, and discovered that it had broken off short at the brass fitting. This is a serious loss to us, for all our Barrier distances between depots are calculated on it, and although we have another depoted at the foot of the glacier we do not know the slip. We must now judge distance till we get a sight of land.

January 16. With a strong following blizzard, we did 18½ miles to the north today. My burst heels gave me great pain all day. Marshall dressed them tonight. We saw land again today after being out of sight of it for nearly three weeks.

January 17. Started sharp at 7 a.m., in a fresh blizzard wind, with a temperature of minus 23°F, we did our best march, for it was mainly downhill and we covered 22' miles. At 10 a.m. we came up to our Christmas camp, and there took on a bamboo we had left, and which now comes in useful for our sail. This sail is now our great help. We dropped over 500 ft. today, and in three days ought to reach our depot at this rate.

January 18. Our best day, 26' miles downhill, with a strong following wind. We have nearly got to the end of the main icefall. The temperature has risen sensibly, it being minus 14°F tonight, and the hypsometer, 196.5°, shows a good rise. With luck we may reach our depot tomorrow night. With food now in hand, we had a decent feed tonight. I have been very unlucky today, falling into many crevasses and hurting my shoulder badly. I have also had many falls, besides the trouble with the bad heels on the hard stuff.

January 19. Another record day, for we have done about twenty-nine miles to the north, rushing under sail down ice falls and through crevasses, till, at 6 p.m., we picked up our sledge tracks of December 18 outwards. We camped, dead beat, at 6:30 p.m., and had a good hoosh. We have descended to 7500 ft., and the temperature tonight is minus 14°F. We are now only 8½ miles from our depot, which we will reach tomorrow morning, all being well. This strong blizzard wind has been an immense help this way, though not outwards for us.

January 20. Although we have not covered so much ground today, we have had an infinitely harder time. We started at 7 a.m. on our tracks of December 19, and at 7:30 passed the camp of the evening of the 18th. For two hours we were descending a snow slope, with heavy sastrugi, and then struck a patch of badly crevassed névé, about half a mile across. After that we got on to blue slippery ice, where our finnesko had no hold. A gale was blowing, and often fierce gusts came along, sweeping the sledge sideways, and knocking us off our feet. We all had many falls, and I had two specially heavy ones which shook me up severely. When we reached the steep slopes where we had roped the sledges up on our outward journey, we lowered the sledge down by means of the alpine rope, using an ice axe as a bollard to lower by. On several occasions one or more of us lost our footing, and were swept by the wind down the ice slope, with great difficulty getting back to our sledge and companions. We arrived at our depot at 12:30 p.m. with sore and aching bodies. The afternoon was rather better, as, after the first hour, we got off the blue ice on to snow. However, bad as the day has been, we have said farewell to that awful plateau, and are well on our way down the glacier.

January 21. Started at 7:45 a.m. with a fresh southerly breeze, so we still have valuable assistance from our sail. The heavy falls I had yesterday have so shaken me that I have been very ill today. I harnessed up for a while, but soon had to give up pulling and walk by the sledge; but, as the course has been downhill nearly all day and a fair wind has been assisting, the others have had no difficulty in getting along at a good pace, and we have covered seventeen miles. The weather is much warmer, the temperature tonight being about minus 1°F.

January 22. Started at 7:30 a.m. on a good surface that changed to crevassed ice slopes in the afternoon, down which we made fair progress. Am still too ill to harness up, but as the pull was not much it did not matter. Indeed, we had another man out of harness guiding the sledge. The distance today was 15½ miles.

January 23. Similar weather, surface and work. Fine and warm; temperature plus 8°F.

January 24. One of our hardest day's work, and certainly the longest, for we started at 6:45 a.m., went on till 12:50 p.m., had lunch, started at 2 p.m., went on till 6 p.m., had a cup of tea, and went on till 9 p.m. Then we had our single pot of hoosh and one biscuit, for we have only two days' food left and one day's biscuit on much reduced ration, and we have to cover forty miles of crevasses to reach our depot before we can get any more food. I am now all right again, though rather weak. We had a terribly hard time in the crevassed ice this morning, and now our sledge has not much more than half a runner on one side, and is in a very shaky state. However, I believe we are safe now. The distance today was sixteen miles, statute.

January 25. We started away from camp at 6:45 a.m., marched till noon, when we had a cup of tea, and then marched till 3 p.m., when we had lunch, consisting of a cup of tea, two biscuits, two spoonsful of cheese. Then we marched till 9 p.m., when we had one pot of hoosh and one biscuit. We did twenty-six miles; fine weather. The food is all finished but one meal. No biscuit, only cocoa, tea, salt, and pepper left, very little of these also. Must reach depot tomorrow. It was fairly good going today till the last two hours, and then we were falling into most dangerous crevasses and were saved only by our harness. Very tired indeed. Thank God warm and fine weather. We can see our depot rock in the distance, so hope to reach it tomorrow. Turning in now, 11 p.m.; breakfast as usual 5 a.m. The temperature is plus 12°F.

January 26 and 27. Two days written up as one, and they have been the hardest and most trying we have ever spent in our lives, and will ever stand in our memories. Tonight (the 27th) we have had our first solid food since the morning of the 26th. We came to the end of all our provisions except a little cocoa and tea, and from

7 a.m. on the 26th till 2 p.m. on the 27th we did sixteen miles over the worst surfaces and most dangerous crevasses we have ever encountered, only stopping for tea or cocoa till they were finished, and marching twenty hours at a stretch, through snow 10 to 18 in. thick as a rule, with sometimes 2½ ft. of it. We fell into hidden crevasses time after time, and were saved by each other and by our harness. In fact, only an all-merciful Providence has guided our steps to tonight's safety at our depot. I cannot describe adequately the mental and physical strain of the last forty-eight hours. When we started at 7 a.m. yesterday, we immediately got into soft snow, an uphill pull with hidden crevasses. The biscuit was all finished, and with only one pannikin of hoosh, mostly pony maize, and one of tea, we marched till noon. Then we had one pannikin of tea and one ounce of chocolate, and marched till 4:45 p.m. We had one pannikin of tea. There was no more food. We marched till 10 p.m., then one small pannikin of cocoa. Marched till 2 a.m., when we were played out. We had one pannikin of cocoa, and slept till 8 a.m. Then a pannikin of cocoa, and we marched till 1 p.m. and camped, about half a mile from the depot. Marshall went on for food, and we got a meal at 2 p.m. We turned in and slept. Adams fell exhausted in his harness, but recovered and went on again. Wild did the same the night before.

January 28. Thank God we are on the Barrier again at last. We got up at 1 a.m. this morning, had breakfast, consisting of tea and one biscuit, and got under way at 3 a.m. We reached the depot in half an hour without any difficulty. The snow here was deep enough to carry us over the crevasses that had impeded our progress so much on the outward march. We had proper breakfast at 5 a.m. then dug out our depot. The alternate falls of snow and thaws had frozen solidly in a great deal of our gear, and our spare sledge meter was deeply buried. We marched along till we were close to the Gap, then had lunch. At 1 p.m. we were through the Gap and on to the crevassed and ridged Barrier surface. We are now safe, with six days' food and only fifty miles to the depot, but Wild has developed dysentery. We are at a loss to know what is the cause of it. It may possibly be due to the horse meat. The weather has been fairly fine all day, though clouding up from the south towards noon, and we were assisted by a fresh southerly breeze up the slope to the head of the Gap. Indeed, we needed it, for the heavy surface and our dilapidated sledge made the hauling extremely hard. Just before we left the glacier I broke through the soft snow, plunging into a hidden crevasse. My harness jerked up under my heart, and gave me rather a shakeup. It seemed as though the glacier were saying: 'There is the last touch of you; don't you come up here again.' It was with a feeling of intense relief that we left this great glacier, for the strain had been hard, and now we know that except for blizzards and thick weather, which two factors can alone prevent us from finding our depots in good time, we will be all right. The light became bad this evening when we were on the last hour before camping, and we cannot say for certain whether we are clear of the main chasm by the land or not, so must give its line of direction a wide berth. The temperature is well up, plus 26°F, and it is warm indeed after the minus temperatures which have been our lot for the last month or so.

January 29. We are having a most unfriendly greeting from the Barrier. We got up as usual and had breakfast at 5:30 a.m. the weather thick and overcast, but the land showing enough for us to steer by. We got away at 7:20 a.m., and soon after it began to snow, which in a temperature of plus 30°F melted on the sledge and all our gear, making everything into a miserably wet state. We had to put the compass down every now and then, for it became too thick to see any landmarks, and at 9:30 the wind suddenly sprang up from the east, cold and strong, freezing solid all our wet clothes, and the various things on the sledge. It was blowing a blizzard with snow and heavy drift in less than five minutes from the time the wind started, and with difficulty we managed to get up one tent and crawl into it, where we waited in the hope that the weather would clear. As there was no sign of an improvement at noon we pitched the other tent, had food, and lay in our bags patching our worn-out clothes. All day the blizzard has continued to blow hard, with extra violent gusts at times. Our tents get snowed up, and we have to clear them by kicking at the snow every now and then.

January 30. We made a start at 8:15 a.m., after spending three-quarters of an hour digging out our sledges and tents from the drift of the blizzard, which stopped at 1 a.m. It was clear over part of the land as we started, but soon snow began to fall again and the weather became very thick; yet, steering on a course, we came through the crevasses and drift without even touching one, though before, in good light, we have had to turn and twist to avoid them. The surface was heavy for pulling on, owing to the fine snow from the blizzard, but we did thirteen miles for the day, working a full ten hours till 7:50 p.m. The weather cleared right up in the afternoon, and we made a good course. Wild is seedy today, but we hope that as soon as he reaches Grisi depot he will be better. We have no variety of food, and only have four miserably thin biscuits a day to eke out the horse meat. The plasmon is all finished and so are we ourselves by the end of the day's march. The sledge also is in a terribly bad state, but as soon as we reach the depot all will be well. The surface in the afternoon improved, and is much better than we had hoped for. The temperature is plus 24°F, fine and warm. A heavy day's pull, but we were assisted by the wind in the afternoon. Wild is still seedy, just walking in harness. The surface is good, and we are rapidly nearing the depot. Short of food, down to twenty ounces a day. Very tired. Good weather.

January 31. Started at 7 a.m., Wild bad with dysentery. Picked up mound 4 p.m., and camped at 6 p.m. Very bad surface. Did 13½ miles.

February 1. Started 7 a.m.; awful surface at times. Wild very bad. Picked up mound. Camped 6 p.m., having done nearly fourteen miles.

February 2. Started at 6:40 a.m. and camped 7 p.m. at depot. Wild and self dysentery; dead tired, bad surface, with undulations. Did 13' miles. Ray's birthday, celebrated with two lumps of sugar, making five each in cocoa.

February 3. Started with new sledge and 150 lb. more weight at 8:40 a.m.; camped at 5:30 p.m. Only five miles; awfully soft snow surface. All acute dysentery due to meat. Trust that sleep will put us right. Could go no farther tonight. Wild very bad, self weaker, others assailed also. Bad light, short food, surface worse than ever. Snow one foot deep. Got up 4:30 a.m. after going to bed 11 p.m. No more tonight. Temperature plus 5°F. Dull.

February 4. Cannot write more. All down with acute dysentery; terrible day. No march possible; outlook serious . . . Fine weather.

February 5. Eight miles today; dead tired. Dysentery better, but Adams not too right. Camped at 5:30 p.m. We are picking up the mounds well. Too weak on half rations to write much. Still hanging on to geological specimens. Please God we will get through all right. Great anxiety.

February 6. Did ten miles today. All better and a better surface. Terribly hungry. Six biscuits per day and one pannikin horse meat each meal. Picked up November 28 mound and made camp. I do trust this hunger will not weaken us too much. It has been great anxiety. Thank God the dysentery stopped and the surface better. We may do more tomorrow, as there are signs of wind from the south-east. Temperature plus 9°F.

February 7. Blowing hard blizzard. Kept going till 6 p.m. Adams and Marshall renewed dysentery. Dead tired. Short food; very weak.

February 8. Did twelve miles. We had fine weather after 10 a.m. Started from camp in blizzard. Adams and Marshall still dysentery; Wild and I all right. Feel starving for food. Talk of it all day. Anyhow, getting north, thank God. Sixty-nine miles to Chinaman depot.

February 9. Strong following blizzard, and did 14½ miles to north. Adams not fit yet. All thinking and talking of food.

February 10. Strong following wind. Did 20 miles 300 yards. Temperature plus 22°F. All thinking and talking of food.

February 11. We did 16½ miles today, and continued to pick up the mounds, which is a great comfort. The temperature is plus 20°F tonight. All our thoughts are of food. We ought to reach the depot in two days. Now we are down to half a pannikin of meat and five biscuits a day. Adams not all right yet, and Wild shaky tonight. Good surface and following wind. We were up at 4:45 a.m. and camped at 6 p.m.

February 12. Fine day, with no wind. We were up at 4:30 a.m., and marched till 6 p.m., doing 14½ miles. Adams sighted the depot flag at 6 p.m. The temperature has ranged from plus 5° to plus 20°F. Passed sastrugi running south-south-east in the afternoon. Slight westerly wind. Very tired.

February 13. Breakfast at 4:40 a.m. We packed up, with a cold wind blowing, and reached the depot, with all our food finished, at 11:30 a.m. There we got Chinaman's liver, which we have had tonight. It tasted splendid. We looked round for any spare bits of meat, and while I was digging in the snow I came across some hard red stuff, Chinaman's blood frozen into a solid core. We dug it up, and found it a welcome addition to our food. It was like beef tea when boiled up. The distance today was twelve miles, with a light wind.

February 14. A good surface today, but no wind. The pulling was hard, and the temperature plus 10° to plus 18°F. We did 11½ miles. We are still weak, but better, the horse blood helps. Burst lips are our greatest trouble.

February 15. My birthday today. I was given a present of a cigarette made out of pipe tobacco and some coarse paper we had with us. It was delicious. A hard pull today, and my head is very bad again. The distance was 12½ miles, with a fairly good surface and fine weather. We are picking up our mounds with great regularity. The land can be seen faintly through the haze in the distance. We have found undulations even out here, but not very marked, running in the usual direction. Temperature minus 3°F, at noon.

February 16. A fair surface today, but no wind. The sastrugi are disappearing. We are appallingly hungry. We are down to about half a pannikin of half-cooked horsemeat a meal and four biscuits a day. We covered thirteen miles today, with the temperature from zero to minus 7°F. There are appearances of wind from the south, long windy streamers of torn stratus. We are so weak now that even to lift our depleted provision bag is an effort. When we break camp in the morning we pull the tent off the poles and take it down before we move the things inside, for the effort of lifting the sleeping bags, etc., through the doorway is too great. At night when we have come to camp we sometimes have to lift our legs one at a time with both hands in getting into the tent. It seems a severe strain to lift one's feet without aid after we have stiffened from the day's march. Our fingers are extremely painful. Some of us have big blisters that burst occasionally.

February 17. I thought we were in for it and was not wrong. Today we have been marching in a blinding blizzard, with 42° of frost, but, thank heaven, the wind was behind us and we have done nineteen miles, the sledge with the sail up often overrunning us, and then at other times getting into a patch of soft snow and bringing us up with a jerk. The harness round our weakened stomachs gives us a good deal of pain when we are brought up suddenly. We started at 6:40 a.m. and marched till 6 p.m., and today we had three pannikins of semi-cooked horse meat and six biscuits on the strength of the good march. We all have tragic dreams of getting food to eat, but rarely have the satisfaction of dreaming that we are actually eating. Last night I did taste bread and butter. We look at each other as we eat our scanty meals and feel a distinct grievance if one man manages to make his hoosh last longer than the rest of us. Sometimes we do our best to save a bit of biscuit for the next meal, but it is a much debated question whether it is best to eat all the food at once or to save. I eat all my lunch biscuit, but keep a bit from dinner to eat in the bag so as to induce sleep. The smaller the quantity of biscuits grows the more delicious they taste.

February 18. The wind dropped during the night, and at 4:40 a.m. we got up, picked our buried sledge out of the drift, and were under way at 7 a.m. There was little wind, and the temperature was minus 20°F at noon. This afternoon we sighted old Discovery. What a homelike appearance it has. Its big bluff form showed out in the north-west, and we felt that the same mountain might at that very moment be drawing the eyes of our own people at winter quarters. It seemed to be a connecting link. Perhaps they will be wondering whether we are in sight of it.

February 19. A very cold south wind today, but we turned out at 4:40 a.m., with a temperature of minus 20° F. We have been hungry and cold all day, but did 14½ miles on a good surface. We sighted Mount Erebus in the morning. The old landmarks are so pleasant. Camped at 6 p.m., temperature minus 10° F. We ought to reach Depot A tomorrow. We have picked up the last mound except one. If we had food all would be well, but we are now at the end of our supplies again, except for some scraps of meat scraped off the bones of Grisi after they had been lying on the snow in the sun for all these months. We dare not risk it until the worst comes. Still in five days more we ought to be in the land of plenty.

February 20. Started to get up at 4:40 a.m. It is almost a farce to talk of getting up to 'breakfast' now, and there is no call of 'Come on, boys; good hoosh.' No good hoosh is to be had. In less time than it has taken me to write this the food is finished, and then our hopes and thoughts lie wholly in the direction of the next feed, so called from force of habit. It was dull and overcast today, and we could see only a little way. Still we made progress, and at 4 p.m.

we reached Depot A. The distance for the day was fourteen miles, with 52° of frost. We sighted the depot at 2:30 p.m., and now we have enough food to carry us to the Bluff Depot. We had run out of food when we reached the depot today, and we have had a good hoosh tonight. The unaccustomed pemmican fat made me feel quite queer, but I enjoyed the pudding we made out of biscuits and the tin of jam which we originally intended to have for Christmas Day, but which we left behind when on the way south in order to save weight. Our depoted tobacco and cigarettes were here, and it is difficult to describe the enjoyment and luxury of a good smoke. I am sure that the tobacco will make up for the shortage of food. I do not doubt but that the Bluff Depot will have been laid all right by Joyce. Anyhow we must stake on it, for we have not enough food to carry us to the ship. Joyce knows his work well and we talk now of nothing but the feeds that we will have when we reach the Bluff. That depot has been the bright beacon ahead through these dark days of hunger. Each time we took in another hole in our belts we have said that it will be all right when we get to the Bluff Depot, and now we are getting toward it.

February 21. We got up at 4:40 a.m., just as it commenced to blow, and the wind continued all day, a blizzard with as low as 67° of frost. We could not get warm, but we did twenty miles. In ordinary polar work one would not think of travelling in such a severe blizzard, but our need is extreme, and we must keep going. It is neck or nothing with us now. Our food lies ahead, and death stalks us from behind. This is just the time of the year when the most bad weather may be expected. The sun now departs at night, and the darkness is palpable by the time we turn in, generally about 9:30 p.m. We are so thin that our bones ache as we lie on the hard snow in our sleeping bags, from which a great deal of the hair has gone. Tonight we stewed some of the scraps of Grisi meat, and the dish tasted delicious. Too cold to write more. Thank God, we are nearing the Bluff.

February 22. A splendid day. We did 20½ miles, and on the strength of the distance had a good feed. About 11 a.m. we suddenly came across the tracks of a party of four men, with dogs. Evidently the weather has been fine and they have been moving at a good pace toward the south. We could tell that the weather has been fine, for they were wearing ski boots instead of finnesko, and occasionally we saw the stump of a cigarette. The length of the steps showed that they were going fast. We are now camped on the tracks, which are fairly recent, and we will try to follow them to the Bluff, for they must have come from the depot. This assures us that the depot was laid all right. I cannot imagine who the fourth man can be, unless it was Buckley, who might be there now that the ship is in. We passed their noon camp, and I am certain that the ship is in, for there were tins lying around bearing brands different from those of the original stores. We found three small bits of chocolate and a little bit of biscuit at the camp after carefully searching the ground for such unconsidered trifles, and we 'turned backs' for them. I was unlucky enough to get the bit of biscuit, and a curious unreasoning anger took possession of me for a moment at my bad luck. It shows how primitive we have become, and how much the question of even a morsel of food affects our judgment. We are near the end of our food, but as we have staked everything on the Bluff Depot, we had a good feed tonight. If we do not pick up the depot, there will be absolutely no hope for us.

CHAPTER 17

The final stage
February 23 to March 4
Bluff Depot reached: Marshall's condition worse on February 25:
Marshall and Adams remain in camp while Shackleton and Wild
make a forced march to Hut Point: On board Nimrod: *Relief*
party start to bring in Marshall and Adams: All safe
on board ship March 4, 1909

February 23. Started at 6:45 a.m. in splendid weather, and at 11 a.m., while halting for a spell, Wild saw the Bluff Depot miraged up. It seemed to be quite close, and the flags were waving and dancing as though to say, 'Come, here I am, come and feed.' It was the most cheerful sight our eyes have ever seen, for we had only a few biscuits left. These we at once devoured. The Grisi meat had given Wild renewed dysentery. After a short camp we pushed on. A flashing light appeared to be on the depot, and when we reached it at 4 p.m., this turned out to be a biscuit tin, which had been placed in the snow so as to catch the light of the sun. It was like a great cheerful eye twinkling at us. The depot had appeared much closer than it really was, because we were accustomed to judging from the height of an ordinary depot, whereas this one was built on a snow mound over 10 ft. high, with two bamboos lashed together on top, and three flags. It was a splendid mark. Joyce and his party have done their work well. Now we are safe as regards food, and it only remains for us to reach the ship. I climbed up on top of the depot, and shouted to those below of the glorious feeds that awaited us. First I rolled down three tins of biscuits, then cases containing luxuries of every description, many of them sent by friends. There were Carlsbad plums, eggs, cakes, plum puddings, gingerbread and crystallised fruit, even fresh boiled mutton from the ship. After months of want and hunger, we suddenly found ourselves able to have meals fit for the gods, and with appetites that the gods might have envied. Apart from the luxuries there was an ample supply of ordinary sledging rations. Tonight we improvised a second cooking stand out of a biscuit tin, and used our second primus to cook some of the courses. Our dream of food has come true, and yet after we had eaten biscuits and had two pannikins of pemmican, followed by cocoa, our contracted bodies would not stand the strain of more food, and reluctantly we had to stop. I cannot tell what a relief it has been to us. There is nothing much in the way of news from the ship, only just a letter saying that she had arrived on January 5, and that all was well. This letter, dated January 20, is signed by Evans, who evidently is the Evans who towed us down in the *Koonya*. We now only have to catch the ship, and I hope we will do that. Wild is better tonight. The temperature is plus 10°F, fine and warm. I am writing in my bag with biscuits beside me, and chocolate and jam.

February 24. We got up at 5 a.m., and at 7 a.m. had breakfast, consisting of eggs, dried milk, porridge, and pemmican, with plenty of biscuits. We marched until 1 p.m., had lunch and then marched until 8 p.m., covering a distance of fifteen miles for the day. The weather was fine. Though we have plenty of weight to haul now we do not feel it so much as we did the smaller weights when we were hungry. We have good food inside us, and every now and then on the march we eat a bit of chocolate or biscuit. Warned by the experience of Scott and Wilson on the previous southern journey, I have taken care not to overeat. Adams has a wonderful digestion, and can go on without any difficulty. Wild's dysentery is a bit better today. He is careful of his feeding and has only taken things that are suitable. It is a comfort to be able to pick and choose. I cannot understand a letter I received from Murray about Mackintosh getting adrift on the ice, but no doubt this will be cleared up on our return. Anyhow, everyone seems to be all right. There was no news of the northern party or of the western party. We turned in full of food tonight.

February 25. We turned out at 4 a.m. for an early start, as we are in danger of being left if we do not push ahead rapidly and reach the ship. On going into the tent for breakfast I found Marshall suffering from paralysis of the stomach and renewed dysentery, and while we were eating a blizzard came up. We secured everything as the Bluff showed masses of ragged cloud, and I was of opinion that it was going to blow hard. I did not think Marshall fit to travel through the blizzard. During the afternoon, as we were lying in the bags, the weather cleared somewhat, though it still blew hard. If Marshall is not better tonight, I must leave him with Adams and push on, for time is going on, and the ship may leave on March 1, according to orders, if the Sound is not clear of ice. I went over through the blizzard to Marshall's tent. He is in a bad way still, but thinks that he could travel tomorrow.

February 27 (1 a.m.). The blizzard was over at midnight, and we got up at 1 a.m., had breakfast at 2, and made a start at 4. At 9:30 a.m. we had lunch, at 3 p.m. tea, at 7 p.m. hoosh, and then marched till 11 p.m. Had another hoosh, and turned in at 1 a.m. We did twenty-four miles. Marshall suffered greatly, but stuck to the march. He never complains.

March 5. Although we did not turn in until 1 a.m. on Feb. 27th, we were up again at 4 a.m. and after a good hoosh, we got under way at 6 a.m. and marched until 1 p.m. Marshall was unable to haul, his dysentery increasing, and he got worse in the afternoon, after lunch. At 4 p.m. I decided to pitch camp, leave Marshall under Adams's charge, and push ahead with Wild, taking one day's provisions and leaving the balance for the two men at the camp. I hoped to pick up a relief party at the ship. We dumped everything off the sledge except a prismatic compass, our sleeping bags and food for one day, and at 4:30 p.m. Wild and I started, and marched till 9 p.m. Then we had a hoosh, and marched until 2 a.m. of the 28th, over a very hard surface. We stopped for one hour and a half off the north-east end of White Island, getting no sleep, and marched till 11 a.m., by which time our food was finished. We kept flashing the heliograph in the hope of attracting attention from Observation Hill, where I thought that a party would be on the lookout, but there was no return flash. The only thing to do was to push ahead, although we were by this time very tired. At 2:30 p.m. we sighted open water ahead, the ice having evidently broken out four miles south of Cape Armitage, and an hour and a half later a blizzard wind started to blow, and the weather got very thick. We thought once that we saw a party coming over to meet us, and our sledge seemed to grow lighter for a few minutes, but the 'party' turned out to be a group of penguins at the ice edge. The weather was so thick that we could not see any distance ahead, and we arrived at the ice edge suddenly. The ice was swaying up and down, and there was grave risk of our being carried out. I decided to abandon the sledge, as I felt sure that we would get assistance at once when we reached the hut, and time was becoming important. It was necessary that we should get food and shelter speedily. Wild's feet were giving him a great deal of trouble. In the thick weather we could not risk making Pram Point, and I decided to follow another route seven miles round by the other side of Castle Rock. We clambered over crevasses and snow slopes, and after what seemed an almost interminable struggle reached Castle Rock, from whence I could see that there was open water all around the north. It was indeed a different homecoming from what we had expected. Out on the Barrier and up on the plateau our thoughts had often turned to the day when we would get back to the comfort and plenty of the winter quarters, but we had never imagined fighting our way to the back door, so to speak, in such a cheerless fashion. We reached the top of Ski Slope at 7:45 p.m., and from there we could see the hut and the bay. There was no sign of the ship, and no smoke or other evidence of life at the hut. We hurried on to the hut, our minds busy with gloomy possibilities, and found not a man there. There was a letter stating that the northern party had reached the Magnetic Pole, and that all the parties had been picked up except ours. The letter added that the ship would be sheltering under Glacier Tongue until February 26. It was now February 28, and it was with very keen anxiety in our minds that we proceeded to search for food. If the ship was gone, our plight, and that of the two men left out on the Barrier, was a very serious one.

We improvised a cooking vessel, found oil and a Primus lamp, and had a good feed of biscuit, onions, and plum pudding, which were amongst the stores left at the hut. We were utterly weary but we had no sleeping gear, our bags having been left with the sledge, and the temperature was very low. We found a piece of roofing felt, which we wrapped around us, and then we sat up all night, the darkness being relieved only when we occasionally lighted the lamp in order to secure a little warmth. We tried to burn the magnetic hut in the hope of attracting attention from the ship, but we were not able to get it alight. We tried, too, to tie the Union Jack to Vince's cross, on the hill, but we were so played out that our cold fingers could not manage the knots. It was a bad night for us, and we were glad indeed when the light came again. Then we managed to get a little warmer, and at 9 a.m. we got the magnetic hut alight, and put up the flag. All our fears vanished when in the distance we saw the ship, miraged up. We signalled with the heliograph, and at 11 a.m. on March 1 we were on board the *Nimrod* and once more safe amongst friends. I will not attempt to describe our feelings. Everyone was glad to see us, and keen to know what we had done. They had given us up for lost, and a search party had been going to start that day in the hope of finding some trace of us. I found that every member of the expedition was well, that the plans had worked out satisfactorily, and that the work laid down had been carried out. The ship had brought nothing but good news from the outside world. It seemed as though a great load had been lifted from my shoulders.

The first thing was to bring in Adams and Marshall, and I ordered out a relief party at once. I had a good feed of bacon and fried bread, and started at 2:30 p.m. from the Barrier edge with Mackay, Mawson, and McGillan, leaving Wild on the *Nimrod*. We marched until 10 p.m., had dinner and turned in for a short sleep. We were up again at 2 a.m. the next morning (March 2), and travelled until 1 p.m., when we reached the camp where I had left the two men. Marshall was better, the rest having done him a lot of good, and he was able to march and pull. After lunch we started back again, and marched until 8 p.m. in fine weather. We were under way again at 4 a.m. the next morning, had lunch at noon, and reached the ice edge at 3 p.m. There was no sign of the ship, and the sea was freezing over. We waited until 5 p.m., and then found that it was possible to strike land at Pram Point. The weather was coming on bad, clouding up from the south-east, and Marshall was suffering from renewed dysentery, the result of the heavy marching. We therefore abandoned one tent and one sledge at the ice edge, taking on only the sleeping bags and the specimens. We climbed up by Crater Hill, leaving everything but the sleeping bags, for the weather was getting worse, and at 9:35 p.m. commenced to slide down toward Hut Point. We reached the winter quarters at 9:50, and Marshall was put to bed. Mackay and I lighted a carbide flare on the hill by Vince's cross, and after dinner all hands turned in except Mackay and myself. A short time after

Mackay saw the ship appear. It was now blowing a hard blizzard, but Mackintosh had seen our flare from a distance of nine miles. Adams and I went on board the *Nimrod,* and Adams, after surviving all the dangers of the interior of the Antarctic continent, was nearly lost within sight of safety. He slipped at the ice edge, owing to the fact that he was wearing new finnesko, and he only just saved himself from going over. He managed to hang on until he was rescued by a party from the ship.

A boat went back for Marshall and the others, and we were all safe on board at 1 a.m. on March 4.

CHAPTER 18

Some notes on the Southern Journey

'Turning backs': Pony soup: The 'Wild roll': Frostbite: Glacier surfaces: Painful falls: Particular duties assigned to each member of the southern party

We brought back with us from the journey toward the Pole vivid memories of how it feels to be intensely, fiercely hungry. During the period from November 15, 1908, to February 23, 1909, we had but one full meal, and that was on Christmas Day. Even then we did not keep the sense of repletion for very long for within an hour or two it seemed to us that we were as hungry as ever. Our daily allowance of food would have been a small one for a city worker in a temperate climate, and in our case hunger was increased by the fact that we were performing vigorous physical labour in a very low temperature. We looked forward to each meal with keen anticipation, but when the food was in our hands it seemed to disappear without making us any the less ravenous. The evening meal at the end of ten hours' sledging used to take us a long time to prepare. The sledges had to be unpacked and the camp pitched. Then the cooker was filled with snow and the primus lamp lit, often no easy matter with our cold, frostbitten fingers. The materials for the thin hoosh would be placed in the boiling pot, with the addition, perhaps, of some pony maize, and the allowance of tea was placed in the outer boiler. The tea was always put in a strainer, consisting of a small tin in which we had punched a lot of holes, and it was removed directly the water had come to the boil. We used to sit around the cooker waiting for our food, and at last the hoosh would be ready and would be ladled into the pannikins by the cook of the week. The scanty allowance of biscuit would be distributed and we would commence the meal. In a couple of minutes the hot food would be gone, and we would gnaw carefully around the sides of our biscuits, making them last as long as possible. Marshall used sometimes to stand his pannikin of hoosh in the snow for a little while, because it got thicker as it cooled, but it was a debatable point whether this paid. One seemed to be getting more solid food, but there was a loss of warmth and in the minus temperatures on the plateau we found it advisable to take our hoosh very hot. We would make the biscuits last as long as possible, and sometimes we tried to save a bit to eat in the sleeping bag later on, but it was hard to do this. If one of us dropped a crumb, the others would point it out, and the owner would wet his finger in his mouth and pick up the morsel. Not the smallest fragment was allowed to escape.

We used to 'turn backs' in order to ensure equitable division of the food. The cook would pour the hoosh into the pannikins and arrange the biscuits in four heaps. Perhaps someone would suggest that one pannikin had rather less in it than another, and if this view was endorsed by the others there would be a readjustment. Then when we were all satisfied that the food had been divided as fairly as possible, one man would turn his back, and another, pointing at one pannikin or group of biscuits would say, 'Whose?' The man who had his back turned, and therefore could not see the food, would give a name, and so the distribution would proceed, each of us always feeling sure that the smallest share had fallen to his lot. At lunch time there would be chocolate or cheese to distribute on alternate days, and we much preferred the chocolate days to the cheese days. The chocolate seemed more satisfying, and it was more easily divided. The cheese broke up into very small fragments on the march, and the allowance, which amounted to two spoonfuls per man, had to be divided up as nearly as possible into four equal heaps. The chocolate could be easily separated into sticks of equal size. It can be imagined that the cook for the week had no easy task. His work became more difficult still when we were using pony meat, for the meat and blood, when boiled up, made a delightful broth, while the fragments of meat sunk to the bottom of the pot. The liquor was much the better part of the dish, and no-one had much relish for the little dice of tough and stringy meat, so the cook had to be very careful indeed. Poor old Chinaman was a particularly tough and stringy horse.

We found that the meat from the neck and rump was the best, the most stringy portions coming from the ribs and legs. We took all the meat we could, tough or tender, and as we went south in the days when the horse meat was fairly plentiful, we used to suck frozen, raw fragments as we marched along. Later we could not afford to use the meat except on a definite allowance. The meat to be used during the day was generally cut up when we took a spell in the morning, and the bag containing the fragments was hung on the back of the sledge in order that the meat might be softened by the sun. It cut more easily when frozen than when partially thawed, but our knives gradually got blunt, and on the glacier we secured a rock on which to sharpen them. During the journey back, when every ounce of weight was of great importance, we used one of our geological specimens, a piece of sandstone, as a knife-sharpener. The meat used to bulk large in the pot, but as fresh meat contains about 60 percent of moisture, it used to shrink considerably in the process of cooking, and we did not have to use very much snow in the pot.

We used the meat immediately we had started to kill the ponies in order to save the other food, for we knew that the meat contained a very large percentage of water, so that we would be carrying useless weight with it. The pemmican and biscuits, on the other hand, contained very little moisture, and it was more profitable to keep them for the march further south, when we were likely to want to reduce the loads as far as possible. We left meat at each depot, to provide for the march back to the coast, but always took on as much as possible of the prepared foods. The reader will understand that the loss of Socks, which represented so many pounds of meat, was a very severe blow to us, for we had after that to use sledging stores at the depots to make up for the lost meat. If we had been able to use Socks for food, I have no doubt that we would have been able to get further south, perhaps even to the Pole itself, though in that case we could hardly have got back in time to catch the ship before she was forced to leave by the approach of winter.

When we were living on meat our desire for cereals and farinaceous foods became stronger; indeed any particular sort of food of which we were deprived seemed to us to be the food for which nature craved. When we were short of sugar we would dream of sweet stuffs, and when biscuits were in short supply our thoughts were concerned with crisp loaves and all the other good things displayed in the windows of the bakers' shops. During the last weeks of the journey outwards, and the long march back, when our allowance of food had been reduced to twenty ounces per man a day, we really thought of little but food. The glory of the great mountains that towered high on either side, the majesty of the enormous glacier up which we travelled so painfully, did not appeal to our emotions to any great extent. Man becomes very primitive when he is hungry and short of food, and we learned to know what it is to be desperately hungry. I used to wonder sometimes whether the people who suffer from hunger in the big cities of civilisation felt as we were feeling, and I arrived at the conclusion that they did not, for no barrier of law and order would have been allowed to stand between us and any food that had been available. The man who starves in a city is weakened, hopeless, spiritless, and we were vigorous and keen. Until January 9 the desire for food was made the more intense by our knowledge of the fact that we were steadily marching away from the stores of plenty.

We could not joke about food, in the way that is possible for the man who is hungry in the ordinary sense. We thought about it most of the time, and on the way back we used to talk about it, but always in the most serious manner possible. We used to plan out the enormous meals that we proposed to have when we got back to the ship and, later, to civilisation. On the outward march we did not experience really severe hunger until we got on the great glacier, and then we were too much occupied with the heavy and dangerous climbing over the rough ice and crevasses to be able to talk much. We had to keep some distance apart in case one man fell into a crevasse. Then on the plateau our faces were generally coated with ice, and the blizzard wind blowing from the south made unnecessary conversation out of the question. Those were silent days, and our remarks to one another were brief and infrequent. It was on the march back that we talked freely of food, after we had got down the glacier and were marching over the Barrier surface. The wind was behind us, so that the pulling was not very heavy, and as there were no crevasses to fear we were able to keep close together. We would get up at 5 a.m. in order to make a start at 7 a.m., and after we had eaten our scanty breakfast, that seemed only to accentuate hunger, and had begun the day's march, we could take turns in describing the things we would eat in the good days to come. We were each going to give a dinner to the others in turn, and there was to be an anniversary dinner every year, at which we would be able to eat and eat and eat. No French chef ever devoted more thought to the invention of new dishes than we did.

It is with strange feelings that I look back over our notes, and see the wonderful meals that we were going to have. We used to tell each other, with perfect seriousness, about the new dishes that we had thought of, and if the dish met with general approval there would be a chorus of, 'Ah! That's good.' Sometimes there would be an argument as to whether a suggested dish was really an original invention, or whether it did not too nearly resemble something that we had already tasted in happier days. The 'Wild roll' was admitted to be the high-water mark of gastronomic luxury. Wild proposed that the cook should take a supply of well-seasoned minced meat, wrap it in rashers of fat bacon, and place around the whole an outer covering of rich pastry so that it would take the form of a big sausage-roll. Then this roll would be fried with plenty of fat. My best dish, which I must admit I put forward with a good deal of pride as we marched over the snow, was a sardine pastry, made by placing well fried sardines inside pastry. At least ten tins of sardines were to be emptied on to a bed of pastry, and the whole then rolled up and cooked, preparatory to its division into four equal portions. I remember one day Marshall came forward with a proposal for a thick roll of suet pudding with plenty of jam all over it, and there arose quite a heated argument as to whether he could fairly claim this dish to be an invention, or whether it was not the jam roll already known to the housewives of civilisation. There was one point on which we were all agreed, and that was that we did not want any jellies or things of that sort at our future meals. The idea of eating such elusive stuff as jelly had no appeal to us at all.

On a typical day during this backward march we would leave camp at about 6:40 a.m., and half an hour later would have recovered our frostbitten fingers, while the moisture on our clothes, melted in the sleeping bags, would have begun to ablate, after having first frozen hard. We would be beginning to march with some degree of comfort, and one of us would remark,

'Well, boys, what are we going to have for breakfast today?' We had just finished our breakfast as a matter of fact, consisting of half a pannikin of tea, but the meal had not taken the keenness from our appetites. We used to try to persuade ourselves that our half biscuit was not quite a half, and sometimes we managed to get a little bit more that way. The question would receive our most serious and careful consideration at once, and we would proceed to weave from our hungry imaginations a tale of a day spent in eating. 'Now we are on board ship,' one man would say. 'We wake up in a bunk, and the first thing we do is to stretch out our hands to the side of the bunk and get some chocolate, some Garibaldi biscuits and some apples. We eat those in the bunk, and then we get up for breakfast. Breakfast will be at eight o'clock, and we will have porridge, fish, bacon and eggs, cold ham, plum pudding, sweets, fresh roll and butter, marmalade and coffee. At eleven o'clock we will have hot cocoa, open jam tarts, fried cod's roe and slices of heavy plum cake. That will be all until lunch at one o'clock. For lunch we will have Wild roll, shepherd's pie, fresh soda bread, hot milk, treacle pudding, nuts, raisins, and cake. After that we will turn in for a sleep, and we will be called at 3:45, when we will reach out again from the bunks and have doughnuts and sweets. We will get up then and have big cups of hot tea and fresh cake and chocolate creams. Dinner will be at six, and we will have thick soup, roast beef and Yorkshire pudding, cauliflower, peas, asparagus, plum pudding, fruit, apple pie with thick cream, scones and butter, port wine, nuts, and almonds and raisins. Then at midnight we will have a really big meal, just before we go to bed. There will be melon, grilled trout and butter sauce, roast chicken with plenty of livers, a proper salad with eggs and very thick dressing, green peas and new potatoes, a saddle of mutton, fried suet pudding, peach Melba, egg curry, plum pudding and sauce, Welsh rarebit, Queen's pudding, angels on horseback, cream cheese and celery, fruit, nuts, port wine, milk, and cocoa. Then we will go to bed and sleep till breakfast time. We will have chocolate and biscuits under our pillows, and if we want anything to eat in the night we will just have to get it.' Three of us would listen to this program and perhaps suggest amendments and improvements generally in the direction of additional dishes, and then another one of us would take up the running and sketch another glorious day of feeding and sleeping.

I dare say that all this sounds very greedy and uncivilised to the reader who has never been on the verge of starvation, but as I have said before, hunger makes a man primitive. We did not smile at ourselves or at each other as we planned wonderful feats of overeating. We were perfectly serious about the matter, and we noted down in the back pages of our diaries details of the meals that we had decided to have as soon as we got back to the places where food was plentiful. All the morning we would allow our imaginations to run riot in this fashion. Then would come one o'clock, and I would look at my watch and say 'Camp!' We would drop the harness from our tired bodies and pitch the tent on the smoothest place available, and three of us would get inside to wait for the thin and scanty meal, while the other man filled the cooker with snow and fragments of frozen meat. An hour later we would be on the march again, once more thinking and talking of food, and this would go on until the camp in the evening. We would have another scanty meal, and turn into the sleeping bags, to dream wildly of food that somehow we could never manage to eat.

The dysentery from which we suffered during the latter part of the journey back to the coast was certainly due to the meat from the pony Grisi. This animal was shot one night when in a greatly exhausted condition, and I believe that his flesh was made poisonous by the presence of the toxin of exhaustion, as is the case with animals that have been hunted. Wild was the first to suffer, at the time when we started to use Grisi meat with the other meat, and he must have been unfortunate enough to get the greater part of the bad meat on that occasion. The other meat we were using then came from Chinaman, and seemed to be quite wholesome. A few days later we were all eating Grisi meat, and we all got dysentery. The meat could not have become affected in any way after the death of the pony, because it froze hard within a very short time. The manner in which we managed to keep on marching when suffering, and the speed with which we recovered when we got proper food, were rather remarkable, and the reason, no doubt, was that the dysentery was simply the result of the poison, and was not produced by organic trouble of any sort.

We had a strong wind behind us day after day during this period, and this contributed in a very large measure to our safety, for in the weakened condition we had then reached we could not have made long marches against a head wind, and without long marches we would have starved between the depots. We had a sail on the sledge, formed of the floorcloth of a tent, and often the sledge would overrun us, though at other times it would catch in a drift and throw us heavily.

When we were travelling along during the early part of the journey over the level Barrier surface, we felt the heat of the sun severely, though as a matter of fact the temperature was generally very low, sometimes as low as zero F though the season was the height of summer. It was quite usual to feel one side of the face getting frozen while the other side was being sunburned. The ponies would have frozen perspiration on their coats on the sheltered side, while the sun would keep the other side hot and dry, and as the day wore on and the sun moved round the sky the frosted area on the animals would change its position in sympathy. I remember that on December 4 we were marching stripped to our shirts, and we got very much sunburned, though at noon that day the air temperature showed ten degrees of frost. When we started to climb the glacier and marched close to the rocks, we felt the heat much more, for the rocks acted as radiators, and this experience weighed with me in deciding to leave all the spare clothing and equipment at the Upper Glacier Depot, about seven thousand feet up. We did not expect to have to climb much higher, but, as the reader knows, we did not reach the plateau until we had climbed over ten thousand feet above sea level, and so we felt the cold extremely. Our windproof Burberry clothing had become thin by this time, and had been patched in many places in consequence of having been torn on the sharp ice. The wind got in through a tear in my Burberry trousers one day and I was frostbitten on the under part of the knee. This frostbite developed into an open wound, into which the wool from my underclothing worked, and I had finally to perform a rather painful operation with a knife before the wound would heal. We were continually being frostbitten up on the plateau, and when our boots had begun to give out and we were practically marching on the sennegrass inside the finnesko, our heels got frostbitten. My heels burst when we got on to hard stuff, and for some time my socks were caked with blood at the end of every day's march. Finally Marshall put some 'New-skin' on a pad, and that stuck on well until the cracks had healed. The scars are likely to remain with me. In the very cold days, when our strength had begun to decrease, we found great difficulty in hoisting the sail on our sledge, for when we lifted our arms above our heads in order to adjust the sail, the blood ran from our fingers and they promptly froze. Ten minutes or a quarter of an hour sometime elapsed before we could get the sledge properly rigged. Our troubles with frostbite were no doubt due in a measure to the lightness of our clothing, but there was compensation in the speed with which we were able to travel. I have no doubt at all that men engaged in polar exploration should be clothed as lightly as is possible, even if there is a danger of frostbite when they halt on the march.

The surface over which we travelled during the southern journey changed continually. During the first few days we found a layer of soft snow on top of a hard crust, with more soft snow underneath that again. Our weight was sufficient to break through the soft snow on top, and if we were pulling the increased pressure would cause the crust to break also, letting us through into the second layer of soft snow. This surface made the travelling very heavy. Until we had got beyond Minna Bluff we often passed over high, sharp sastrugi, and beyond that we met with ridges four to six feet high. The snow generally was dry and powdery, but some of the crystals were large, and showed in reflected light all the million colours of diamonds. After we had passed latitude 80° South the snow got softer day by day, and the ponies would often break through the upper crust and sink in right up to their bellies. When the sun was hot the travelling would be much better, for the surface snow got near the melting point and formed a slippery layer not easily broken. Then again a fall in the temperature would produce a thin crust, through which one broke very easily. Between latitude 80° South and 83° South there were hard sastrugi under the soft snow, and the hoofs of the horses suffered in consequence. The surface near the land was broken up by pressure from the glaciers, but right alongside the mountains there was a smooth plain of glassy ice, caused by the freezing of water that had run off the rocky slopes when they were warm under the rays of the sun. This process had been proceeding on the snow slopes that we had to climb in order to reach the glacier. Here at the foot of the glacier there were pools of clear water around the rocks, and we were able to drink as much as we wanted, though the contact of the cold water with our cracked lips was painful.

The glacier itself presented every variety of surface, from soft snow to cracked and riven blue ice, by-and-by the only constant feature were the crevasses, from which we were never free. Some were entirely covered with a crust of soft snow, and we discovered them only when one of us broke through, and hung by his harness from the sledge. Others occurred in mazes of rotten ice, and were even more difficult to negotiate than the other sort. The least unpleasant of the crevasses were those that were wide open and easily seen, with firm ice on either side. If these crevasses were not too wide, we would pull the sledges up to the side, then jump over, and pull them after us. This was more difficult than it sounds from the fact that the ice gave only a very uncertain footing, but we always had the harness as a safeguard in case of a fall. If the crevasses were wide we had to made a detour. The sledges, owing to their length, were not liable to slip down a crevasse, and we felt fairly safe when we were securely attached to them by the harness. When the surface was so bad that relay work became necessary we used to miss the support of a sledge on the back journeys. We would advance one sledge half a mile or a mile, put up a bamboo pole to mark the spot, and then go back for the other. We were roped together for the walk back to the second sledge, but even then we felt a great deal less secure than when harnessed to one of the long, heavy sledges. On some days we had to travel up steep slopes of smooth ice, and often it became necessary to cut steps with our ice axes, and haul the sledges after us with the alpine rope. When we had gone up about sixty feet, the length of the rope, we would haul up the sledge to which we had attached the lower end, and jamb it so that it could not slide back. Then one of us would slide down in order to fix the rope to the other sledge.

One of the curious features of the glacier was a yellow line, evidently an old moraine, extending for thirty or forty miles. The rocks of the moraine had gradually sunk in out of sight, the radiation of the sun's heat from them causing the ice to melt and let them through, and there had remained enough silt and dust to give the ice a dirty yellow appearance. The travelling along this old moraine was not so bad, but on either side of it there was a mass of pressure ice, caused by the constriction of the glacier between the mountains to the east and west. Unfortunately we brought back no photographs of this portion of the glacier. The number of plates at our disposal was limited, and on the outward march we decided not to take many photographs in case we found interesting land or mountains in the far south nearer the Pole. We thought that we would be able to secure as many photographs of the glacier as we wanted on the way back if we had the plates to spare, but as a matter of fact when we did get on to the glacier a second time we were so short of food that we could not afford the time to unpack the camera, which had to be stowed away carefully on the sledge in order to avoid damage to it.

Many nights on the glacier there was no snow on which to pitch the tents, and we had to spend perhaps an hour smoothing out a space on a rippled, sharp-pointed sea of ice. The provision bags and sledges had to be packed on the snow cloths around the tents, and it was indeed fortunate for us that we did not meet with any bad weather while we were marching up the glacier. Had a blizzard come on while we were asleep, it would have scattered our goods far and wide, and we would have been faced with a very serious position. All the time that we were climbing the glacier we had a northerly wind behind us, although the direction of the sastrugi showed clearly that the prevailing wind was from the south; when we were coming back later in the season the wind was behind us all the time. We encountered a strong wind on the outward journey when near the top of the glacier, and as the ice slopes were covered with snow it was difficult to pull the sledges up them. When we reached the same slopes on the way back, the summer sun had cleared the snow from them, leaving clear ice, and we simply glissaded down all but the steepest slopes, although one of the sledge runners was very badly torn. We had to travel carefully on the steep slopes, for if we had let the sledge get out of hand it would have run away altogether, and would probably have been smashed up hundreds of feet below.

The Upper Glacier Depot was overhung by great cliffs of rock, shattered by the frosts and storms of countless centuries, and many fragments were poised in such a fashion that scarcely more than a touch seemed needed to bring them hurtling down. All around us on the ice lay rocks that had recently fallen from the heights, and we wondered whether some boulder would come down upon us while we were in camp. We had no choice of a camping ground, as all around was rough ice. The cliffs were composed largely of weathered sandstone, and it was on the same mountains, higher up the glacier, that the coal was found, at a point where the slope was comparatively gentle. Looking down from this height, we could see the glacier stretching away to the point of junction with the Barrier, the mountains rising to east and west. Many of the mountains to the west of the glacier were more or less dome-shaped, but there were some sharp conical peaks to the westward of the particular mountain under which the Upper Glacier Depot had been placed. There were three distinct peaks, and the plateau ice sweeping down made a long moraine on the west side of the glacier. To the eastward there was a long ridge of high mountains, fairly uniform in shape and without any sharp peaks, but with ridges, apparently of granite, projecting toward the west and so constricting the glacier. The mountains were distant about twenty-five miles, but well-defined stratification lines could plainly be seen. Below us, as we looked from the depot, could be seen the cumulus clouds that always hung above 'The Cloudmaker'.

When we looked to the south from this depot we saw no clouds; there was nothing but hard clear sky. The sky gave no indication of the blizzard winds that were to assail us when we reached the plateau, and after we had gone as far south as we could and retraced our footsteps to the depot, we looked back and saw the same clear sky, with a few wisps of fleecy cloud in it. We had no doubt that below those clouds the pitiless gale was still raging across the great frozen plain, and that the wind which followed us during our march back to the coast was coming from the vicinity of the Pole. As we advanced from the Upper Glacier Depot we came upon great ice falls. The surface looked smooth from a distance, and we thought that we were actually on the plateau, but as we advanced we saw that before us lay enormous ridges rising abruptly. We had to relay our gear over these ridges, and often at the tops there would be a great crevasse, from which would radiate smaller crevasses fringed with crystals and showing ghastly depths below. We would creep forward to see what lay on the other side, and perhaps would find a fall of fifty feet, with a grade of about 1 in 3. Many times we risked our sledge on very severe slopes, allowing it to glissade down, but other times the danger of a smash was too great, and we had to lower the sledge slowly and carefully with the rope. The ice was safe enough to walk upon at this time except at the ridges, where the crevasses were severe, for the smaller crevasses in the hollows and slopes could be passed without difficulty.

The ice falls delayed us a good deal, and then we got into soft snow, over which the sledge dragged heavily. We thought that we were finally on the plateau level, but within a few days we came to fresh ridges and waves of pressure ice. The ice between the waves was very rotten, and many times we fell through when we put our weight on it. We fastened the alpine rope to the sledge harness, and the first man pulled at a distance of about eighteen feet from the sledge, while the whole party was so scattered that no two men could fall into a crevasse together. We got on to better ground by steering to the westward, but this step was rather dangerous, for by taking this course we travelled parallel with the crevasses and were not able to meet them at right angles. Many times we nearly lost the sledge and ourselves when the ice started to break away into an unseen crevasse running parallel with our course. We felt very grateful to Providence that the weather remained clear, for we could not have moved a yard over this rotten ice in thick weather without courting disaster. I do not know whether the good weather we experienced in that neighbourhood was normal. We generally had about seven miles of easy going after we had passed one ridge in this area, and then another ridge would rise up ahead of us, and we would start to climb again. There were always crevasses at the top of the ridges, suggesting that the ice was moving over land at no great depth.

We passed the last ridge at last, and reached the actual plateau, but instead of hard névé, such as the *Discovery* expedition had encountered in the journey to the plateau beyond the mountains west of McMurdo Sound, we found soft snow and hard sastrugi. All the sastrugi pointed to the south, and the wind blew strongly nearly all the time from the south or south-east, with an occasional change to the south-west. Sometimes we marched on hard sastrugi, and at other times we had soft snow under our feet, but could feel the sastrugi on which the snow was lying. I formed the opinion that during the winter on the plateau the wind must blow with terrible violence from the south, and that the hard sastrugi are produced then. Still further south we kept breaking through a hard crust that underlay the soft surface snow, and we then sank in about eight inches. This surface, which made the marching heavy, continued to the point at which we planted the flag. After the long blizzard, from the night of January 6 until the morning of January 9, we had a better surface over which to make our final march southwards, for the wind had swept the soft snow away and produced a fairly hard surface, over which, unencumbered with a sledge as we were, we could advance easily.

We found the surface generally to be improved on the march back. The blizzard winds had removed the soft surface snow, and incidentally uncovered many of the crevasses. We were following our outward tracks, and often I noticed the tracks led us to the edge of a crevasse which had been covered previously and over which we had passed in ignorance of our danger on the march southwards. When we got to the head of the glacier we tried to take a short cut to the point where we had left the Upper Glacier Depot, but we got enmeshed in a maze of crevasses and pressure ridges to the eastward, and so had to steer in a westerly direction again in order to get clear. The dangers that we did know were preferable to those that we did not know. On the way down the glacier we found all the snow stripped away by the wind and sun for nearly one hundred miles, and we travelled over slippery blue ice, with innumerable cracks and sharp edges. We had many painful falls during this part of the journey. Then, when about forty miles from the foot of the glacier, we got into deep soft snow again, over which rapid progress was impossible. There had evidently been a heavy snowfall in this area while we were further south, and for days, while our food was running short, we could see ahead of us the rocks under which the depot had been placed. We toiled with painful slowness toward the rocks, and as the reader has already learned we were without any food at all for the last thirty hours of that march. We found the Barrier surface to be very soft when we got off the Glacier, but after we had passed Grisi Depot there was an improvement. The surface remained fairly good until we reached the winter quarters, and in view of our weakened condition it was fortunate for us that it did so.

In reviewing the experience gained on the southern journey, I do not think that I could suggest any improvement in equipment for any future expedition. The Barrier surface evidently varies in a remarkable fashion, and its condition cannot be anticipated with any degree of certainty. The traveller must be prepared for either a hard surface or a very soft one, and he may get both surfaces in the course of one day's march. The eleven-foot sledge is thoroughly suitable for the work, and our method of packing the stores and hauling the sledges did not develop any weak points. We would have been glad to have had crampons for use on the glacier; what would be better still would be heavy alpine boots with nails all around, for very often the surface would give little grip to crampons, which would only touch the rough ice at one or two points. The temperature is too cold to permit of the explorer wearing ordinary leather boots, and some boot would have to be designed capable of keeping the feet warm and carrying the nails all around. A mast consisting of a bamboo lashed to the forward oil box proved as efficient as could be required for use in connection with a sail on the sledges. It was easily rigged and had no elaborate stays. I would suggest no change in the clothing, for the light woollen underclothing, with thin windproof material outside, proved most satisfactory in every way. We could certainly not have travelled so fast had we been wearing the regulation pilot cloth garment generally used in polar exploration. Our experience made it obvious that a party which hopes to reach the Pole must take more food per man than we did, but how the additional weight is to be provided for is a matter for individual consideration. I would not take cheese again; for although it is a good food, we did not find it as palatable as chocolate, which is practically as sustaining. Our other foods were all entirely satisfactory.

Each member of the southern party had his own particular duties to perform. Adams had charge of the meteorology, and his work involved the taking of temperatures at regular intervals, and the boiling of the hypsometer, sometimes several times in a day. He took notes during the day, and wrote up the observations at night in the sleeping bag. Marshall was the cartographer and took the angles and bearings of all the new land; he also took the meridian altitudes and the compass variation as we went south. When a meridian altitude was taken, I generally had it checked by each member of the party, so that the mean could be taken.

Marshall's work was about the most uncomfortable possible, for at the end of a day's march, and often at lunch time, he would have to stand in the biting wind handling the screws of the theodolite. The map of the journey was prepared by Marshall, who also took most of the photographs. Wild attended to the repair of the sledges and equipment, and also assisted me in the geological observations and the collection of specimens. It was he who found the coal close to the Upper Glacier Depot. I kept the courses and distances, worked out observations and laid down our directions. We all kept diaries. I had two, one my observation book, and the other the narrative diary.

CHAPTER 19

Return of the *Nimrod*
The ship blocked by ice off Beaufort Island: Mails landed twenty-eight miles from Cape Royds on January 3: Mackintosh and McGillan travel over ice to winter quarters: Narrow escapes: They reach hut January 12

After leaving us on February 22, the *Nimrod* had an uneventful voyage back to New Zealand. Fair winds were encountered all the way, and the ice gave no difficulty, the coast of New Zealand being sighted twelve days after the departure from Cape Royds. During the winter the *Nimrod* had been laid up in Port Lyttelton waiting till the time arrived to bring us back to civilisation. The little ship had been docked and thoroughly overhauled, so that all effects of the severe treatment she received during the first voyage down to the ice had been removed, and she was once more ready to battle with the floes. Toward the end of the year stores were taken on board, for there was a possibility that a party might have to spend a second winter at Cape Royds, if the men comprising one of the sledging expeditions had not returned, and, of course, there was always the possibility of the *Nimrod* herself being caught in the ice and frozen in for the winter. Sufficient stores were taken on board to provide for any such eventualities, and as much coal as could be stowed away was also carried. Captain P. F. Evans, who had commanded the *Koonya* at the time she towed the *Nimrod* down the Antarctic Circle, was appointed master of the *Nimrod* under my power of attorney, Captain England having resigned on account of ill health after reaching New Zealand earlier in the year.

The *Nimrod* left Lyttelton on December 1, 1908, and encountered fine weather for the voyage southwards. On the evening of the 3rd, the wind being favourable, the propeller was disconnected, and the vessel proceeded under sail alone until the 20th, when she was in latitude 66° 30' South, longitude 178° 28' West. The 'blink' of ice was seen ahead and the ship was hove to until steam had been raised and the propeller connected. Then Captain Evans set sail again, and proceeded toward the pack. The vessel was soon in brash ice, and after pushing through this for a couple of hours reached the pack, and made her way slowly through the lanes. Numerous seals were basking on the floes, regarding the ship with their usual air of mild astonishment. On the following day the pack was more congested, and the progress southward was slow, so much so that the crew found time to kill and skin several crabeater seals. Open water was reached again that evening, and at noon on the 22nd the *Nimrod* was in latitude 68° 20' South, longitude 175° 23' East, and proceeding under sail through the open water of Ross Sea. The belt of pack ice had been about sixty miles wide.

On December 26 the *Nimrod* reached latitude 70° 42' South, longitude 173° 4' West, the position in which, in 1843, Sir James Ross sighted 'compact, hummocky ice', but found only drift ice, with plenty of open water. A sounding gave no bottom with 1575 fathoms of wire, so that the theory that the ice seen by Ross was resting on land was completely disproved. At noon on the 27th the *Nimrod* which was proceeding in a south-east direction, was brought up by thick floes in latitude 72° 8' South, longitude 173° 1' West. Progress became possible again later in the day, and at four o'clock on the following morning the *Nimrod* was in open water, with the blink of pack to the eastward. Captain Evans had kept east with the hope of sighting King Edward VII Land, but the pack seemed to be continuous in that direction, and on the 30th he therefore shaped a course for Cape Bird, and on January 1, 1909, Mount Erebus was sighted. The experience of Captain Evans on this voyage confirms my own impression that, under normal conditions, the pack that stretches out from the Barrier to the eastward of the Ross Sea is not penetrable, and that the *Discovery* was able to push to within sight of King Edward VII Land in 1902 for the reason that the ice was unusually open that season.

The progress of the *Nimrod* toward the winter quarters was blocked by ice off Beaufort Island, and after manoeuvring about for three hours Captain Evans made the vessel fast to a floe with ice anchors. The next morning he cast off from the floe, and with the help of the current, which seems to set constantly to the west between Cape Bird and Beaufort Island, and by taking advantage of lanes of open water, gradually proceeded in two days to a point only twenty-eight miles from Cape Royds. Some heavy bumps against the floes tested the strength of the vessel, and finally what appeared to be fast ice was encountered, so that no further progress toward the south was possible for the time.

There seemed to be no immediate possibility of the *Nimrod* reaching Cape Royds, and Captain Evans therefore decided to send Mackintosh with three men to convey a mailbag and the news of the ship's arrival to the winter quarters. The party was to travel over the sea ice with a sledge, and it did not seem that there would be any great difficulties to be encountered. A start was made at 10:15 a.m. on January 3, the party consisting of Mackintosh, McGillan, Riches, and Paton, with one sledge, a tent, sleeping bags, cooking equipment and a supply of provisions. The distance to be covered was about twenty-five miles. In the afternoon Mackintosh sent Riches and Paton back to the ship, and he reduced the load on the sledge by leaving fifty pounds of provisions in a depot. The travelling became very rough, the two men encountering both bad ice and soft snow. They camped at 7:50 p.m. and started for Cape Royds again at 1:55 a.m. on the following day. They soon got on to a better surface, and made good progress until 5:30 a.m., when they met with open water, with pressure ice floating past. This blocked the way. They walked for two hours in a westerly direction to see how far the open water extended, but did not reach the end of it. The whole of the ice to the southward seemed to be moving, and the stream at the spot at which they were then standing was travelling at the rate of about three miles an hour. They breakfasted at 7:30 a.m., and then started back for the ship, as there seemed to be no chance of reaching Cape Royds in consequence of the open water.

Presently Mackintosh found that there was open water ahead, blocking the way to the ship, and a survey of the position from a hummock revealed the unpleasant fact that the floe ice was breaking up altogether, and that they were in most serious danger of drifting out into the sound. Safety lay in a hurried dash for the shore to the east, and they proceeded to drag their sledge across rough ice and deep snow with all possible speed. At places they had to lift the sledge bodily over the ice faces, and when, after an hour's very heavy work, they arrived off the first point of land, they found an open lane of water barring their way. 'We dragged on to the next point, which appeared to be safe,' wrote Mackintosh in his diary. 'The floes were small and square in shape. Every two hundred yards we had to drag our sledge to the edge of a floe, jump over a lane of water, and then with a big effort pull the sledge after us. After an hour of this kind of work our hands were cut and bleeding, and our clothes, which, of course, froze as stiff as boards, were wet through to the waist, for we had frequently slipped and fallen when crossing from floe to floe. At 2:30 p.m. we were near to the land, and came to a piece of glacier ice that formed a bridge. The floe that we were on was moving rapidly, so we had to make a great effort and drag our sledge over a six-foot breach. Our luck was in, and we pulled our sledge a little way up the face of the fast ice, and unpacked it. We were in a safe position again, and none too soon, for fifteen minutes later there was open water where we had gained the land.'

Mackintosh decided to go into camp near the spot where they had landed, as a journey across the rocks and the glaciers of the coast was not a thing to be undertaken lightly, and would probably be impossible unless the mailbag was left behind. McGillan, moreover, had developed snow blindness, and both men were very tired. I will quote from Mackintosh's report on the subsequent experience of this little party.

'Early the next morning I found McGillan in great pain,' wrote Mackintosh. 'His eyes were closed up completely, and his face was terribly swollen. The only remedy I could apply was to bathe them, and this seemed to give him some relief. From an elevated position I had a good look around for the ship, and could not see a trace of her. As the day wore on my own eyes became painful. I fervently hoped I was not going to be as bad as my companion, for we would then be in a very difficult position. The morning of January 6 found us both blind. McGillan's face was frightfully swollen, and his eyes completely and tightly shut, so that he did not know that I was attacked too. At first I refrained from telling him, but the pain was very severe, and I had to tell him. By the painful process of forcing my eyelids apart with my fingers I could see a little, but I was not able to do this for long. I continued to bathe McGillan's eyes, and then suffered six hours' agony, ending in a good long sleep, from which I awoke refreshed and much better. I was able to see without effort. McGillan was also much better, and our relief, after the anxiety we had felt, was very great. By midnight we had improved so much that we walked to the penguin rookery, where we had great fun with the birds and found several eggs.'

The men stayed in camp for several days, seeing no sign of the ship, and after their eyes were better spent a good deal of time studying the neighbourhood and especially the bird life. They cut down their food to two meals a day, as their supply of food was not large. Finally, Mackintosh decided that he would leave the mail-bag in the tent, it being too heavy to carry for any distance, and march in to Cape Royds. They made a start on the morning of January 11, carrying forty pounds each, including food for three meals, and expected to be able to reach the winter quarters within twenty-four hours. The first portion of the journey lay over hills of basaltic rock, at the base of Mount Bird, and they thought it best to get as high as possible in order to avoid the valleys and glaciers. They went up about five thousand feet, and had fairly easy travelling over slopes until they got well on to the glaciers. Then their troubles commenced. They were wearing ski boots without spikes, and had many heavy falls on the slippery ice. 'We were walking along, each picking his own tracks, and were about fifty yards apart, foolishly not roped, when I happened to look around to speak to my companion, and found that he had disappeared,' wrote Mackintosh. 'Suddenly I heard my name called faintly from the bowels of the glacier, and immediately rushed toward the place from which the sound proceeded. I found McGillan in a yawning chasm, many feet beneath me, and held up on a projection of ice. I took off my straps from my pack and to them tied my waist lashing, and lowered this extemporised rope down to him. It just reached his hand, and with much pulling on my part and knee climbing on his, he got safely to the surface of the glacier again. The primus stove and our supply of food had gone further down the crevasse. We tried to hook them up, and in doing so I lost my straps and line which I had attached to a ski stick, so we were left almost without equipment. As soon as McGillan had recovered from the shock he had received we started off again, with the spare strap tying the two of us together. We crossed over many snow bridges that covered the dangers underneath, but soon we were in a perfect hotbed of crevasses. They were impassable and lay right across our path, so that we could look down into awful depths. We turned and climbed higher in order to get a clear passage around the top. We were roped together and I was in the lead, with McGillan behind, so that when I fell, as I often did, up to my waist in a crevasse, he could pull me out again. We found a better surface higher up, but when we began to descend we again got into crevassed regions. At first the crevasses were ice-covered gaps, but later we came to huge open ones, whose yawning depths made us shudder. It was not possible to cross them. We started to ascend again, and soon came to a bridge of ice across a huge crevasse about twenty feet wide. We lashed up tighter, and I went off in the lead, straddle-legged across the narrow bridge. We both reached the other side in safety, but one slip, or the breaking of the bridge, would have precipitated us into those black depths below.'

The two men found their way blocked by crevasses in whichever direction they turned, and at last reached a point from which ascent was out of the question, while below lay a steep slope running down for about three thousand feet. They could not tell what lay at the bottom of the slope, but their case was desperate, and they decided to glissade down. Their knives, which they attempted to use as brakes, were torn from their grasp, but they managed to keep their heels in the snow, and although they passed crevasses, none lay directly in their path. They reached the bottom in safety at 4 p.m. on the 11th. They were very hungry and had practically no food, but they could get forward now, and at 6 p.m. they could see Cape Royds and were travelling over a smooth surface. They ate a few biscuit crumbs and half a tin of condensed milk, the only other food they had being a little chocolate. Soon snow commenced to fall, and the weather became thick, obscuring their view of the Cape. They could not see two yards ahead, and for two hours they stumbled along in blinding snow. They rested for a few minutes, but their clothes were covered with ice, icicles hung from their faces, and the temperature was very low. In a temporary clearing of the blizzard Mackintosh thought that he could make out the Cape and they dashed off, but at lunch time on the 12th they were still wandering over the rocks and snow, heavy snow cutting off all view of the surrounding country. Soon after this the snow ceased to fall, though the drift snow, borne along by the blizzard wind, still made the weather thick. Several times they thought that they saw Cape Royds, but found that they had been mistaken. As a matter of fact they were quite close to the winter quarters when, at about 7 p.m., they were found by Day. They were in a state of complete exhaustion, and were just managing to stagger along because they knew that to stop meant death. Within a few minutes they were in the hut, where warm food, dry clothes, and a good rest soon restored them. They had a narrow escape from death, and would probably have never reached the hut had not Day happened to be outside watching for the return of the ship.

Mackintosh and McGillan reached the hut on January 12, but in the meantime the *Nimrod* had arrived at Cape Royds, and had gone north again in search of the missing men. Murray had sailed in the *Nimrod,* and as events turned out, he was not able to get back to the hut for about ten days. 'We were having tea on the afternoon of January 5, and Marston happened to open the door, there was the *Nimrod* already moored to the edge of the fast ice, not more than a mile away,' wrote Murray in a report on the summer work. 'We ran toward the ship, over the rotten sea ice, in boots or slippers as chanced, with the one idea that is uppermost in these circumstances – to get "letters from home". We were doomed to disappointment. Before we had finished greeting our old friends, the officers asked us, "Has Mackintosh arrived?" and we learned to our horror that he and a companion had left the ship two days before and thirty miles north of Cape Royds, to try to bring the letters sooner to us over the sea ice, over the bay where only a few days ago we saw a broad sheet of open water to the horizon, and which was even now only filled with loose pack! So we got no home letters, and had good reason to believe that our friends had lost their lives in the endeavour to bring them. We knew that they must have embarked on a large floe, and little expected to see them again. On January 7 the *Nimrod* left Cape Royds to seek for the lost men on the chance that they might have got ashore near Cape Bird. Within a few hours she was caught by the pack which was drifting rapidly southward along the shore of Ross Island. Driven almost on shore near Horseshoe Bay, the ship, by dint of hard steaming, got a little way off the land, and was there beset by the ice and so remained from the 7th to the 15th, with only a few hours' ineffectual steaming during the first day or two. At length she was rigidly jammed and was carried helplessly by a great eddy of the pack away toward the western side of the sound, and gradually northward.

'On January 12 she was as tight as though frozen in for the winter. In the afternoon sudden pressure affected all the ice from the *Nimrod* as far as we could see. Great blocks of ice, six or eight feet in thickness, were tossed and piled on the surface of the floes. These pressure heaps were formed on each side of the ship's bow, but she took no harm, and in about an hour the pressure ceased. On the morning of January 15 there was not the slightest sign of slacking of the pack, but in the early afternoon, Harbourd, from the crow's nest, saw lanes of water at no great distance to the east. Steam was got up and in a few hours we had left our prison and got into a broad lane, with only thin ice which the ship could charge, and the open water was in sight. Shortly after midnight we got clear of the ice. When released we were not very far from the Nordenskjold Ice Barrier.

'The deceptive appearance of loose pack was impressed upon us. For many hours there was blue water apparently only a mile or two ahead, but it never appeared to get any nearer for hours, and we could not be sure it was really near till we were within a few hundred yards of the edge. All this time in the pack we were in doubt as to the fate of Mackintosh, or rather, we had not much doubt about it, for we had given him up for lost, but we were helpless to do anything. On the afternoon of the 16th, on which day we cleared the ice, we had passed Beaufort Island and were approaching through very loose pack the only piece of shore on which there was any chance of finding the lost men. Near the end of this stretch of beach, where it is succeeded by hopeless cliffs, a small patch of greenish colour was seen, and the telescope showed the details of a deserted camp, a tent torn to ribbons and all the camp gear lying around. A boat was sent ashore in charge of Davis, who found the bag of letters, and a note from Mackintosh pinned to the tent, telling of his risky attempt to cross the mountains nearly a week before. Knowing the frightfully crevassed character of the valley between Mount Bird and Mount Erebus, there seemed to us little hope that they would get through. The crevassed slope extends right to the top of Mount Bird, and is very steep toward the Erebus side. When we reached Cape Royds about midnight, only two men came out to meet the ship. One of the men was Mackintosh's comrade in all his adventures, and we soon learned that all had ended well.'

In the meantime the Bluff Depot party had started off to place a supply of provisions off Minna Bluff in readiness for the return of the southern party. The crew of the *Nimrod* proceeded to take on board the geological and zoological specimens collected by the expedition and stored at the hut, so that all might be in readiness for the final departure when the parties had been picked up. Then followed weeks of uncertainty as to the fate of the men who were away.

CHAPTER 20

Bluff Depot journey
January 15 to February 16, 1909
Dog team with load of 500 lb: A Discovery *depot: southern party*
overdue: Sledge marks of outward march of southern party found:
Good work by dogs

A party, under Joyce, left Cape Royds on January 15 to place, at a point about fourteen miles off Minna Bluff, a depot of stores for the use of the southern party on its return journey. This work was very important as the four members of the southern party would be depending on this depot to supply them with the provisions necessary for the last 100 miles or so of the journey back to winter quarters.

Joyce was accompanied by Mackintosh, Day, and Marston. They took one sledge (with 500 lb. of provisions) drawn by eight dogs. They camped for the night at Glacier Tongue, and had to remain there until the 18th owing to a blizzard. A seven-foot sledge was loaded with 300 lb. of stores from the depot at the Tongue, and the four men took on the two sledges with a total weight of 800 lb. The dogs pulled very well, and the party reached Hut Point at midnight on the 18th.

Rapid progress was made over the Barrier surface, although they had unpleasant experiences with crevasses, and at midnight on January 25 the party reached their destination. During the spring journey* of 1908 I had fixed the site of this depot, and arranged all details with Joyce.

The total height of the mound of snow, on the top of which two bamboos lashed together carried three black flags, was twenty-two feet. The depot could be seen at a distance of eight miles.

The party started north again on the 27th. After they had travelled a short way, Day sighted a pole about 8 ft. high (with a

* See p. 152.

tattered flag attached) projecting from the snow, some distance to the west of their course. Joyce was able to identify this pole as marking the site of the depot laid out for the return of the *Discovery's* southern party in 1902.

Rapid progress was made toward Cape Armitage until the area of crevasses was reached again, when for thirty-seven miles the party twisted and turned in order to make a course past these obstacles. Joyce reported that he had counted 127 ranging from two to thirty feet in width. On the 30th the men were held up by another blizzard, which completely buried the dogs and sledge; but they reached Hut Point at 11 p.m. on January 31.

Having secured a second load of stores from the depot (including some luxuries, such as apples and fresh mutton, brought by a party from the *Nimrod*), Joyce started again for Bluff Depot on February 2. He kept a course toward Cape Crozier for two days and then marched south. The party reached the Bluff Depot for the second time on February 8.

They found, to their surprise, that the southern party had not arrived. It came on to blow from the south, and the wind turned into a howling blizzard which did not cease until the 11th. The men climbed to the top of the snow mound and searched the horizon with glasses, expecting to see the southern party loom up out of the whiteness. As this party was now eleven days overdue, their non-arrival caused great anxiety.

After a consultation, it was decided (1) to lay depot flags in toward the Bluff, so that there would be no chance of the southern party missing the food depot; and (2) to march due south to look for the southern party.

After the flags had been laid three and a half miles apart, with directions where to find the depot, the march due south commenced. At every halt the horizon was examined, through glasses, from the top of the sledge.

On the 13th, Day found the hoof prints of the ponies made on the outward march of the southern party three months before; the tracks of the four sledges showed distinctly. These tracks were followed for seven hours when they were lost.

Joyce then decided to return to the Bluff Depot, and the party arrived there at noon on the 16th. They found everything just as they had left it.

After examining the flags to the eastward, the party started on the march back to the coast, filled with gloomy thoughts as to the fate of the southern party, then eighteen days overdue.

CHAPTER 21

Notes on the Western Journey

Christmas Day at Knob Head Mountain: In search of fossils:
Adrift on a floe: Party picked up by the Nimrod, *January 26*

Meanwhile the western party, which had left the winter quarters for the second time on December 9, had been working in the western mountains. The three men (Armytage, Priestley, and Brocklehurst) reached the stranded moraines on December 13, and on this occasion succeeded in securing a large supply of skuas' eggs. The anticipated feast was not enjoyed, however, for only about a dozen of the eggs were 'good enough for eating', to quote the words of a member of the party. The other eggs were thrown on to the snow near the tent, and the result was an invasion of skuas. They not only ate the eggs, but also made themselves a general nuisance by pulling about the sledge harness and stores. At this time the men were troubled with patches of thin ice, about an eighth to a quarter of an inch thick, forming a lenticle, the top of the middle being sometimes as much as five or six inches from the actual surface. When these patches of ice were trodden on they broke down, and not infrequently disclosed a puddle of salt water an inch or two deep. Priestley thought that they were the final product of the thawing of snowdrifts, and owed their character to the fact that the salt water worked faster from below than did the sun from above.

On December 15 the party started to ascend the Ferrar Glacier, Priestley examining the rocks carefully on the way with a view to securing fossils if any were to be found. The surface was hard for the most part, soft snow being encountered where ice had been expected. On December 19 they were held up by a blizzard, and then they got on to very slippery crevassed ice. On December 20 they camped near the Solitary Rocks, at the spot where Captain Scott had camped after leaving Dry Valley. The idea of getting to

Depot Nunatak had to be abandoned, for a heavy snowfall made the travelling difficult, and the time at the disposal of the expedition was short. Priestley worked under the Bluff between Dry Valley and the east fork of the glacier without success and then they moved over to Obelisk Mount. An examination of the Solitary Rocks proved that the map was incorrect at this point. The previous expedition had thought that the rocks formed an island, with the glacier flowing down on either side, but a close examination showed that the rocks were in reality a peninsula, joined to the main north wall by an isthmus of granite at least one thousand feet high. Priestley proceeded with geological and survey work in the neighbourhood. On December 24 a new camp was pitched at the foot of Knob Head Mountain.

Christmas Day was spent at this camp, and, as was the case with the other sledging expeditions that were out at the time, a special feast was provided. For breakfast they had hoosh, sardines in tomato sauce and raisins; for lunch, Garibaldi biscuits and jelly; and for dinner, potted boneless chicken and a small plum pudding. Armytage picked up a piece of sandstone with fernlike markings, but Priestley was not hopeful of finding fossils in the greatly altered sandstone. The day was spent in geological work. 'We lose the sun here about 9:30 p.m.,' noted Priestley in his diary, 'and it is curious to observe the sudden change from bright light to darkness in the tent, while outside the thin surface of ice covering the thaw water round the rocks immediately contracts with reports like a succession of pistol shots, and sometimes breaks up and flies about in all directions, making a noise like broken glass. This is the effect of the quick cooling of the ice by the cold plateau wind immediately the sun's influence is withdrawn. The plum pudding was "top-hole". Must remember to give one of the potholed sandstones to Wild for the New Zealand girl who gave him the plum pudding.'

On December 27 the men proceeded down the glacier again in order to see whether the northern party had arrived at Butter Point. Priestley studied the moraines on the way down, and made an extensive collection of specimens, and on January 1 they arrived at the depot. They had constant trouble with crevasses and 'potholes' on the way down the glacier, but met with no serious accident. The snow bridges many times let them through up to their knees or waists, but never broke away entirely. The weather was unpleasantly warm for the sort of work they were undertaking, since the snow was thawing, and they were constantly wet.

They found no sign of the northern party at Butter Point, and after waiting there until the 6th they proceeded to the 'stranded moraines,' a day's trek to the south, in order that geological specimens might be secured. The moraines, which were found by the *Discovery* expedition, and are relics of the days of more extensive glaciation, present a most varied collection of rocks, representative of the geological conditions to be found in the mountains to the west, and are of very great interest on that account. After spending two days at this spot, the party went back to Butter Point with about 250 lb. of specimens, and camped again till the 11th. Still there was no sign of the northern party, and on the 12th they went north to Dry Valley. There Priestley found a raised beach, about sixty feet above sea level, and Brocklehurst climbed the mountain known as the Harbour Heights.

They went back to the depot on the 14th, and pitched camp in order to wait for the northern party until the 25th, when they were to make their way back to winter quarters, or signal for the ship by means of the heliograph. On January 24–25 this party had a very narrow escape from disaster. They were camped on the sea ice at the foot of Butter Point, intending to move off on the return journey early on the morning of the 25th. Their position was apparently one of safety. Armytage had examined the tide crack along the shore, and had found no sign of more than ordinary movement, and the ice in the neighbourhood seemed to be quite fast. At 7 a.m. on the 24th Priestley was first out of the tent, and a few minutes later he came running back to his companions to tell them that the ice they were on had broken away and was drifting away north to open sea. The other two men turned out promptly, and found that his statement was only too true. There were two miles of open water between the floe and the shore, and they were apparently moving steadily out to sea. 'When we found that the ice had gone out,' wrote Armytage in his report to me, 'we struck camp, loaded up the sledge, and started away with the object of seeing whether we could get off the floe to the north. The position seemed to be rather serious, for we could not hope to cross any stretch of open water, there was no reasonable expectation of assistance from the ship, and most of our food was at Butter Point.

We had not gone very far to the north before we came to an impassable lane of open water, and we decided to return to our original position. We went into camp and had breakfast at 11 a.m. Then we held a consultation and agreed that it would be best to stop where we then were for a time, at any rate, on the off chance of the ship coming along one of the lanes to pick us up on the following day, or of the current changing and the ice once more touching the shore. We waited till three o'clock in the afternoon, but there did not seem to be any improvement in the position. The killer whales were spouting in the channels, and occasionally bumping the ice under us. Then we marched north again, but met with open water in every direction, and after we had marched right round the floe we got into camp at the old position at 10 p.m. We had a small meal of hoosh and biscuit. We had only four days' provisions on the floe with us, and I decided that we would have to go on short rations. We were encouraged by the fact that we had apparently ceased to move north, and were perhaps getting nearer the fast ice again. We got into our sleeping bags in order to keep warm. At 11:30 p.m. Brocklehurst turned out to see whether the position had changed, and reported that we seemed to be within a few hundred yards of the fast ice, and still moving toward the land. I got out of my bag and put on my finnesko, and at midnight saw that we were very close to the fast ice, probably not more than two hundred yards away. I ran back as fast as I could, deciding that there was a prospect of an attempt to get ashore proving successful, and gave the other two men a shout. They struck the camp and loaded up within a very few minutes, while I went back to the edge of the floe at the spot toward which chance had first directed my steps. Just as the sledge got up to me, I felt the floe bump the fast ice. Not more than six feet of the edge touched, but we were just at that spot, and we rushed over the bridge thus formed. We had only just got over when the floe moved away again, and this time it went north to the open sea. The only place at which it touched the fast ice was that to which I had gone when I left the tent, and had I happened to go to any other spot we would not have escaped. We made our way to Butter Point, and at about three o'clock in the morning camped and had a good meal. Then we turned in and slept. When we got up for breakfast, there was open water where we had been drifting on the floe, and I sighted the *Nimrod* under sail, ten or twelve miles out. We laid the heliograph on to the vessel, and after flashing for about an hour got a reply. The *Nimrod* came alongside the fast ice at three o'clock in the afternoon of January 26, and we went on board with our equipment and specimens. We left a depot of provisions and oil at Butter Point in case the northern party should reach that point after our departure.'

On January 22 and 23 a fresh wind blew from the south and commenced to break up the ice sheet in the neighbourhood of Cape Royds, compelling the ship to refasten further to the southward. From this point Davis took a sledge party to Hut Point with despatches that the supporting party was to convey to me at the Bluff Depot. On the 25th the ice had broken up to such an extent that Captain Evans thought there would be a chance of getting far enough across McMurdo Sound to search the western coastline for the party that had been exploring the western mountains, and also for the northern party, which might by that time have returned from the journey to the Magnetic Pole and reached Butter Point. The *Nimrod* stood out into the sound, and from a distance of ten or twelve miles a heliograph was seen twinkling near Butter Point. The ship was able to get right alongside the fast ice, and picked up Armytage, Priestley, and Brocklehurst.

After this date fine weather was experienced only at short intervals, the season being advanced, and as a consequence the fast ice that remained in the sound commenced to break up rapidly, and took the form of pack trending northwards. When blizzards blew, as they did frequently, the *Nimrod* moored on the lee side of a stranded iceberg in the neighbourhood of Cape Barne, with the object of preserving her position without the consumption of more coal than was absolutely necessary. After the ice had broken up sufficiently, shelter was found under Glacier Tongue.

The waiting was rather unpleasant for the remaining members of the shore party and for those on board the ship, for the time was approaching when it would be necessary to leave for the north unless the *Nimrod* was to be frozen in for the winter, and two of the parties were still out. I had left instructions that if the northern party had not returned by February 1 a search was to be made along the western coast in a northerly direction. The party was three weeks overdue, and on February 1, therefore, the *Nimrod* went north, and Captain Evans proceeded to make a close examination of the coast. The ship did not get back to the hut until February 11. During this time Murray and Priestley found work of scientific interest. Priestley tramped the country, and now that the snow had in great measure disappeared, was enabled to see various interesting geological deposits previously covered up. Beds of sponge spicules, enclosing various other fossils, were evidence of recent elevation of the sea bottom. A thick deposit of salts was found on a mound between two lakes, and some curious volcanic formations were discovered. The smaller ponds were entirely melted, and gave a chance to find some forms of life not evident in winter. The penguins continued to afford Murray material for study.

The *Nimrod*'s search for the northern party was both difficult and dangerous. Captain Evans had to keep close to the coast, in order to guard against the possibility of overlooking a signal, which might consist only of a small flag, and the sea was obstructed by pack ice. He was to go north as far as a sandy beach on the northern side of the Drygalski Barrier, and he performed his duty most thoroughly in the face of what he afterwards modestly described as 'small navigational difficulties'. The beach, which had been marked on the chart, was found to have no existence in fact, but the *Nimrod* reached the neighbourhood indicated, and then proceeded south again, still searching every yard of the coast. On the 4th a tent was sighted on the edge of the Barrier, and when a double detonator was fired the three men who had been to the Magnetic Pole came tumbling out and ran down toward the edge of the ice. Mawson was in such a hurry that he fell down a crevasse, and did not get out again until a party from the ship went to his assistance. 'They were the happiest men I have ever seen,' said Davis in describing the finding of the party. Their sledge, equipment, and specimens were taken on the *Nimrod*, which was able to moor right alongside the fast ice, and then Captain Evans proceeded back to the winter quarters. In the chapters that follow Professor David tells the story of the Northern Party's journey.

CHAPTER 22

Extracts from the narrative of Professor David

Final instructions: Loss of a cooker: Camp at Butter Point: Travelling over sea ice heavy relay work: Cooking with blubber: Seal bouillon: Drygalski Glacier: Depot laid: Preparations for trek inland: Depot at Mount Larsen: New Year's Day in Latitude 74° 18': Arrival at Magnetic Pole (mean position of) January 16, 1909, 72° 25' S., 155° 16' E.: Union Jack hoisted at 3:30 p.m.

The final instructions for the journey of the northern party were read over to me in the presence of Mawson and Dr Mackay, at Cape Royds on September 19, 1908. They were as follows:

British Antarctic Expedition, 1907
Cape Royds, September 19, 1908

*Instructions for Northern Sledge-party
under Command of Professor E. David*

DEAR SIR, The sledge party which you have charge of consists of yourself, Douglas Mawson, and Alistair Mackay.

You will leave winter quarters on or about October 1, 1908. The main objects of your journey are to be as follows:

(1) To take magnetic observations at every suitable point with a view of determining the dip and the position of the Magnetic Pole. If time permits, and your equipment and supplies are sufficient, you will try and reach the Magnetic Pole.

(2) To make a general geological survey of the coast of Victoria Land. In connection with this work you will not sacrifice the time that might be used to carry out the work noted in paragraph (1). It is unnecessary for me to describe or instruct you as to details *re* this work, as you know so much better than I do what is requisite.

(3) I particularly wish you to be able to work at the geology of the western mountains, and for Mawson to spend at least

one fortnight at Dry Valley to prospect for minerals of economic value on your return from the north, and for this work to be carried out satisfactorily you should return to Dry Valley not later than the first week of January. I do not wish to limit you to an exact date for return to Dry Valley if you think that by lengthening your stay up north you can reach the Magnetic Pole, but you must not delay, if time is short, on your way south again to do geological work. I consider that the *thorough* investigation of Dry Valley is of supreme importance.

(4) The *Nimrod* is expected in the sound about January 15, 1909. It is quite possible you may see her from the west. If so, you should try to attract attention by heliograph to winter quarters. You should choose the hours noon to 1 p.m. to flash your signal, and if seen at winter quarters the return signal will be flashed to you, and the *Nimrod* will steam across as far as possible to meet you and wait at the ice edge. If the ship is not in, and if she is and your signals are not seen, you will take into account your supply of provisions and proceed either to Glacier Tongue or Hut Point to replenish if there is not a sufficient amount of provision at Butter Point for you.

(5) *Re* Butter Point. I will have a depot of at least fourteen days' food and oil cached there for you. If there is not enough in that supply you ought to return as mentioned in paragraph (4).

(6) I shall leave instructions for the master of the *Nimrod* to proceed to the most accessible point at the west coast and there ship all your specimens. But before doing this, he must ship all the stores that are lying at winter quarters, and also keep in touch with the fast ice to the south on the lookout for the southern sledge party. The southern party will not be expected before February 1, so if the ship arrives in good time you may have all your work done before our arrival from the south.

(7) If by February 1, after the arrival of the *Nimrod,* there is no evidence that your party has returned, the *Nimrod* will proceed north along the coast, keeping as close to the land as possible, on the lookout for a signal from you flashed by

heliograph. The vessel will proceed very slowly. The ship will not go north of Cape Washington. This is a safeguard in event of any accident occurring to your party.

(8) I have acquainted both Mawson and Mackay with the main facts of the proposed journey. In the event of any accident happening to you, Mawson is to be in charge of the party.

(9) Trusting that you will have a successful journey and a safe return.

> I am, yours faithfully,
>> (Sgd.) ERNEST H. SHACKLETON
>> *Commander*

Professor David
Cape Royds
Antarctic

> Cape Royds
> British Antarctic Expedition, *September 20,* 1907

Professor David

DEAR SIR, – If you reach the Magnetic Pole, you will hoist the Union Jack on the spot, and take possession of it on behalf of the above expedition for the British nation.

When you are in the western mountains, please do the same at one place, taking possession of Victoria Land as part of the British Empire.

If economic minerals are found, take possession of the area in the same way on my behalf as Commander of this expedition.

> Yours faithfully,
>> (Sgd.) ERNEST H. SHACKLETON
>> *Commander*

We had a farewell dinner that night.

The following day, September 20, a strong south-easterly blizzard was blowing. In the afternoon the wind somewhat moderated, and there was less drift. Mackay had been making a sail for our journey to the Magnetic Pole, and we now tried the sail on two sledges lashed together on the ice at Backdoor Bay. We used the tent poles of one of the sledging tents as a mast. The wind was blowing very strongly and carried off the two sledges with a weight on them of 300 lb., in addition to the weights of Mackay and myself. We considered this a successful experiment.

The weather continued bad till the night of the 24th.

On September 25 we were up at 5:30 a.m., and found that the blizzard had subsided. Priestley, Day, and I started in the motorcar, dragging behind us two sledges over the sea ice. One sledge, with its load, weighed 606 lb.; the other weighed 250 lb. At first Day travelled on his first gear; he then found that the engine became heated, and we had to stop for it to cool down. He discovered while we were waiting that one of the cylinders was not firing. This he soon fixed up all right. He then remounted the car and he put her on to the second gear. With the increased power given by the repaired cylinder we now sped over the floe ice at fourteen miles an hour, much to the admiration of the seals and penguins. When, however, we had travelled about ten miles from winter quarters, and were some five miles westerly from Tent Island, we encountered numerous sastrugi of softish snow, the car continually sticking fast in the ridges. A little low drift was flying over the ice surface, brought up by a gentle blizzard. We left the heavy sledge ten miles out, and then with only the light sledge to draw behind us, Day found that he was able to travel on his third gear at eighteen miles an hour. At this speed the sledge, whenever it took one of the snow sastrugi at right angles, leapt into the air like a flying fish and came down with a bump on the surface of the ice. We had just reached Flagstaff Point, and were taking a turn in toward the shore opposite the Penguin Rookery when the blizzard wind caught the side of the sledge nearly broadside on, and capsized it heavily. So violent was the shock that the aluminium cooking apparatus was knocked out of its straps, and the blizzard wind immediately started trundling this metal cylinder over the smooth ice. Day stopped his car as soon as possible, Priestley and I jumped off, and immediately gave chase to the runaway cooker. Meanwhile, the cooker had fallen to pieces, so to speak; the tray part came away from the big circular cover; the melter and the supports for the cooking pot and for the main outer covering also came adrift as well as the cooking pot itself. The lid of the last mentioned fell off, and immediately dumped on to the ice the three pannikins and our three spoons. These articles raced one after another over the smooth ice surface in the direction of the open water of Ross Sea. The spoons were easily captured, as also were the pannikins, but the large snow melter, the main outer casing, and the tray kept revolving in front of us at a speed which was just sufficient to outclass our own most desperate efforts. Finally, when we were nearly upon them, they took a joyous leap over the low cliff of floe ice and disappeared one after another most exasperatingly in the black waters of Ross Sea.

This was a shrewd loss, as aluminium cookers were, of course, very scarce.

The following day we had intended laying out our second depot, but as some of the piston rings of the motorcar needed repair, we decided to postpone the departure until the day after. That afternoon, after the repairs had been completed, Day and Armytage went out for a little tobogganning before dinner. Late in the evening Armytage returned dragging slowly and painfully a sledge bearing the recumbent, though not inanimate, form of Day. We crowded round to inquire what was the matter, and found that just when Armytage and Day were urging their wild career down to steep snow slope Day's foot had struck an unyielding block of kenyte lava, and the consequence had been very awkward for the foot. As no-one but Day could be trusted to drive the motorcar, this accident necessitated a further postponement of the laying of our second depot.

On October 3, the weather having cleared, Day, Priestley, Mackay, and I started with two sledges to lay our second depot. All went well for about eight miles out, then the carburetor played up. Possibly there was some dirt in the nozzle. Day took it all to pieces in the cold wind, and spent three-quarters of an hour fixing it up. We then started off again gaily in good style. We crossed a large crack in the sea ice where there were numbers of seals and Emperor penguins. On the other side of this crack our wheels stuck fast in snow sastrugi. All hands got on to the spokes and started swinging the car backwards and forwards; when we got a good swing on, Day would suddenly snatch on the power and over we would go – that is, over one of the sastrugi – only to find, often, that we had just floundered into another one ahead. In performing one of these evolutions Priestley, who, as usual, was working like a Trojan, got his hand rather badly damaged through its being jammed between the spokes of the car wheel and the framework. Almost immediately afterwards one of my fingers was nearly broken, through the same cause, the flesh being torn off one of my knuckles; and then Mackay seriously damaged his wrist in manipulating what Joyce called the 'thumb-breaking' starter. Still we went floundering along over the sastrugi and ice cracks, Day every now and then getting out to lighten the car and limping alongside. At last we succeeded in reaching a spot amongst the snow sastrugi on the sea ice, fifteen miles distant from our winter quarters. Here we dumped the load intended for the northern party, and then Day had a hard struggle to extricate the car from the tangle of sastrugi and ice cracks. At last, after two capsizes of the sledges, we got back into camp at 10 p.m., all thoroughly exhausted, all wounded and bandaged. Brocklehurst carried Day on his back for about a quarter of a mile from where we left the car up to our winter quarters.

October 4 was a Sunday, and after the morning service we took the ponies out for exercise. In the evening the gramophone discoursed appropriate music, concluding with the universal favourite, 'Lead, Kindly Light'.

Meanwhile, Mackay had his damaged wrist attended to, and I put the question to him as to whether or not he was prepared to undertake the long journey to the Magnetic Pole under the circumstances. He said that he was quite ready, provided Mawson and I did not object to his going with his wrist damaged and in a sling. We raised no objection, and so the matter was settled. All that night Mawson and I were occupied in writing final letters and packing little odds and ends.

The following morning, October 5, after an early breakfast, we prepared for the final start. Brocklehurst took a photograph of us just before we started, then Day, Priestley, Roberts, Mackay, Mawson and I got aboard, some on the motorcar, some on the sledges. Those remaining behind gave us three cheers, Day turned on the power, and away we went. A light wind was blowing from the south-east at the time of our start, bringing a little snow with it and another blizzard seemed impending.

After travelling a little over two miles, just beyond Cape Barne, the snow had become so thick that the coastline was almost entirely hidden from our view. Under these circumstances I did not think it prudent to take the motorcar further, so Mackay,

Mawson, and I bid adieu to our good friends. Strapping on our harness, we toggled on to the sledge rope, and with a 'One, two, three and away', started on our long journey over the sea ice.

We reached our ten-mile depot at 7 p.m. and got up our tent. We slept that night on the floe ice, with about three hundred fathoms of water under our pillow.

The following morning, October 6, we started our relay work. We dragged the Christmas Tree sledge on first, as we were specially liable to lose parcels off it, for a distance of from one-third to half a mile. Then we returned and fetched up what we called the Plum Duff sledge, chiefly laden with our provisions. The weather may be described as thick, with snow falling at intervals. We camped that night amongst screw pack ice within less than a mile of our fifteen-mile depot.

The following day, October 7, was beautifully fine and calm. We started about 9 a.m. and sledged over pressure ice ridges and snow sastrugi, reaching our fifteen-mile depot in three-quarters of an hour. Here we camped and repacked our sledges. We took the wholemeal plasmon biscuits out of two of the biscuit tins and packed them into canvas bags. This saved us a weight of about 8 lb.

We started again in the afternoon, relaying with the two sledges. The sledging again was heavy on account of the fresh, soft snow, and small sastrugi. We had a glorious view of the western mountains, crimsoned in the light of the setting sun. We camped that night close to a seal hole which belonged to a fine specimen of Weddell seal. We were somewhat disturbed that night by the snorting and whistling of the seals as they came up for their blows . . .

On October 10, we were awakened by the chatter of some Emperor penguins who had marched down on our tent during the night to investigate us. The sounds may be described as something between the cackle of a goose and the chortle of a kookaburra. On peeping out of the Burberry spout of our tent I saw four standing by the sledges. They were much interested at the sight of me, and the conversation between them became lively. They evidently took us for penguins of an inferior type, and the tent for our nest. They watched, and took careful note of all our doings, and gave us a good sendoff when we started about 8:30 a.m. The sky was overcast, and light snow began to fall in the afternoon. A little later a mild blizzard sprang up from the south-east; we thought this a favourable opportunity for testing the sailing qualities of our sledges, and so made sail on the Plum Duff sledge. As Mackay put it, we 'brought her to try with main course'. As the strength of the blizzard increased, we found that we could draw both sledges simultaneously, which was, of course, a great saving in labour. We were tempted to carry on in the increasing strength of the blizzard rather longer than was wise, and consequently, when at last we decided that we must camp, had great difficulty in getting the tent up. We slipped the tent over the poles placed close to the ground in the lee of a sledge. While two of us raised the poles, the third shovelled snow on to the skirt of the tent, which we pulled out little by little, until it was finally spread to its full dimensions. We were glad to turn in and escape from the biting blast and drifting snow.

Sunday, October 11. A violent blizzard was still blowing, and we lay in our sleeping bag until past noon, by which time the snow had drifted high upon the door side of our tent. As this drift was pressing heavily on our feet and cramping us, I got up and dug it away. The cooker and primus were then brought in and we all got up and had some hoosh and tea. The temperature, as usually happens in a blizzard, had now risen considerably, being 8.5° F at 1:30 p.m. The copper wire on our sledges was polished and burnished by the prolonged blast against it of tiny ice crystals, and the surface of the sea ice was also brightly polished in places. As it was still blowing we remained in our sleeping bag for the rest of that day as well as the succeeding night.

When we rose at about 2 a.m. on Monday, October 12, the blizzard was over. We found very heavy snowdrifts on the lee side of our sledges, and it took us a considerable time to dig these away and get the hard snow raked out of all the chinks and crannies among the packages on the sledges. We made a start about 4 a.m., and all that day meandered amongst broken pack ice. It was evident that the south-east blizzards drive large belts of broken floe ice in this direction across McMurdo Sound to the western shore. The fractured masses of sea ice, inclined at all angles to the horizontal, are frozen in later, as the cold of winter becomes more intense, and, of course, constitute a very difficult surface for sledging.

October 13. We camped at the foot of a low ice cliff, about 600 yards south-south-east of Butter Point. Butter Point is merely an angle in this low ice cliff near the junction of the Ferrar Glacier valley with the main shore of Victoria Land. This cliff was from fifteen to twenty feet in height, and formed of crevassed glacier ice.

During part of this day Mawson and Mackay were busy making a mast and boom for the second sledge, it being our intention to use the tent floorcloth as a sail. Meanwhile I sorted out the material to be left at the depot at Butter Point.

The following day, Wednesday, October 14, we spent the morning in re-sorting the loads on our sledges. We depoted two tins of wholemeal plasmon biscuits, each weighing about 27 lb., also Mackay's mountaineering nail boots, and my spare headgear material and mitts. Altogether we lightened the load by about 70 lb. We sunk the two full tins of biscuits and a tin containing boots, etc., a short distance in the glacier ice to prevent the blizzards blowing them away. We then lashed to the tins a short bamboo flagpole, carrying one of our black depot flags, and securely fastened to its base one of our empty airtight milk tins, in which we placed our letters. In these letters for Lieutenant Shackleton and R. E. Priestley respectively, I stated that in consequence of our late start from Cape Royds, and also on account of the comparative slowness of our progress thence to Butter Point, it was obvious that we could not return to Butter Point until January 12, at the earliest, instead of the first week of January, as was originally anticipated. We ascertained months later that this little depot survived the blizzards, and that Armytage, Priestley, and Brocklehurst had no difficulty in finding it, and that they had read our letters.

October 14. Leaving the depot about 9 a.m., we started sledging across New Harbour in the direction of Cape Bernacchi. In the afternoon a light southerly wind sprang up bringing a little snow with it, the fall lasting from about 12:30 to 2:30 p.m. We steered in the direction of what appeared to us to be an uncharted island. On arriving at it, however, we discovered that it was a true iceberg, formed of hard blue glacier ice with a conspicuous black band near its summit formed of fine dark gravel. The iceberg was about a quarter of a mile in length, and thirty to forty feet high.

October 15. We had a glorious view up the valley of the Ferrar Glacier. The cold was now less severe; at 8 p.m. the temperature was 9.5° F.

October 16. We were up at 3:30 a.m., and got under way at 5:30. A cold wind was blowing from the south, and after some trouble we set sail on both sledges, using the green floorcloth on the Christmas Tree sledge, and Mackay's sail on the Plum Duff sledge. A short time after we set sail it fell nearly calm; thick cloud gathered; a light wind sprang up from the south-east, veering to east-north-east, then back again to south-east in the afternoon. Fine snow fell for about three hours, forming a layer nearly a quarter of an inch in thickness. Toward evening we reached one of the bergs that had been miraged up the night before. It was four hundred yards long, and eighty yards wide, and was a true iceberg formed of glacier ice; Mackay, Mawson, and I explored this. Like the previous iceberg, its surface was pitted with numerous deep dust wells.

As the shore was high and rocky, and seemed not more than half a mile distant, I went over toward it after our evening meal. On the way, for the first time, I met with a structure in the sea ice known as pancake ice. The surface of the ice showed a rounded polygonal structure something like the tops of a number of large weathered basaltic columns. The edges of these polygons were slightly raised, but sufficiently rounded off by thawing or ablation to afford an easy surface for the runners of our sledge. Close in shore the pancake ice was traversed by deep tidal cracks.

October 17. Mawson, Mackay, and I landed at Cape Bernacchi, a little over a mile north of our previous camp. Here we hoisted the Union Jack just before 10 a.m. and took possession of Victoria Land for the British Empire. Cape Bernacchi is a low rocky promontory, the geology of which is extremely interesting. The dominant type of rock is a pure white coarsely crystalline marble; this has been broken through by granite rocks, the latter in places containing small red garnets. After taking possession we resumed our sledging, finding the surface of pancake ice very good.

October 18. We reached an interesting headland today about one and a quarter miles from our preceding camp. The rocks bore a general resemblance to those at Cape Bernacchi. Mawson thought that some of the quartz veins traversing this headland would prove to be auriferous. After leaving this Point the wind freshened considerably. We had previously hoisted sail, and the wind was sufficiently strong to admit of our pulling both sledges together. The total distance travelled was seven statute miles. This was the most favourable wind we experienced during the whole of our journey to and from the Magnetic Pole.

That night I experienced a rather bad attack of snow blindness through neglecting to wear my snow goggles regularly. Finding that my eyes were no better next morning, and my sight being dim I asked Mawson to take my place at the end of the long rope, the foremost position in the team. Mawson proved himself on this occasion and afterward so remarkably efficient at picking out the best track for our sledges, and steering a good course, that at my request he occupied this position throughout the rest of the journey.

The next two days were uneventful, except for the fact that we occasionally had extremely heavy sledging over screw pack ice and high and long sastrugi.

On the night of October 20, we camped on the sea ice about three-quarters of a mile off shore. To the north-east of us was an outward curve of the shoreline, shown as a promontory on the existing chart. Early the next morning I walked over to the shore to geologise, and found the rocky headland composed of curious gneissic granite veined with quartz. On ascending this headland I noticed to my surprise that what had been previously supposed to be a promontory was really an island separated by a narrow strait from the mainland.

While Mawson determined the position of this island by taking a round of angles with the theodolite, Mackay and I crossed the strait and explored the island, pacing and taking levels. The rocks of which the erratics and boulder-bearing gravels were formed were almost without exception of igneous origin. One very interesting exception was a block of weathered clayey limestone. This was soft and yellowish grey externally, but hard and blue on the freshly fractured surfaces inside. It contained traces of small fossils which appeared to be seeds of plants. Two chips of this rock were fortunately preserved, sufficient for chemical analysis and microscopic examination. There could be little doubt that this clayey limestone has been derived from the great sedimentary formation, named by H. T. Ferrar, the Beacon sandstone. The island which we had been exploring we named provisionally Terrace Island. It was approximately triangular in shape, and the side facing the strait, down which we travelled, measured one mile 1200 yards in length.

October 23. Today we held a serious council as to the future of our journey toward the Magnetic Pole. It was quite obvious that at our present rate of travelling, about four statute miles daily by the relay method, we could not get to the Pole and return to Butter Point early in January. I suggested that the most likely means of getting to the Pole and back in the time specified by Lieutenant Shackleton would be to travel on half-rations depoting the remainder of our provisions at an early opportunity. Mawson and Mackay agreed, after some discussion, to try this expedient, and we decided to think the matter over for a few days and then make our depot.

October 24. We reached in the evening a long rocky point of gneissic granite, which we called Gneiss Point. After our evening hoosh we walked across to the point and collected a number of interesting geological specimens, including blocks of kenyte lava.

October 25 proved a very heavy day for sledging, as we had to drag the sledges over new snow from three to four inches deep. In places it had a tough top crust which we would break through up to our ankles. We met also several obstacles in the way of wide cracks in the sea ice, from six to ten feet in width, and several miles in length. The seawater between the walls of the cracks had only recently been frozen over, so that the ice was only just thick enough to bear the sledges.

In pursuing our north-westerly course we were now crossing a magnificent bay, which trended westward some five or six miles away from the course we were steering. On either side of this bay were majestic ranges of rocky mountains parted from one another at the head of the bay by an immense glacier with steep ice falls. On examining these mountains with a field glass it was evident that in their lower portions they were formed of granite and gneiss, producing reddish brown soils. At the higher levels, further inland, there were distinct traces of rocks showing horizontal stratification. The highest rock of all was black in colour, and evidently very hard, apparently some three hundred feet in thickness. Below this was some softer stratified formation, approximately one thousand

feet in thickness. We concluded that the hard top layer was composed of igneous rock, possibly a lava, while the horizontal stratified
formation belonged in all probability to the Beacon sandstone
formation. Some fine nunataks of dark rock rose from the south-
east side of the great glacier. On either side of this glacier were high
terraces of rock reaching back for several miles from a modern
valley edge to the foot of still higher ranges. It was obvious that
these terraces marked the position of the floor of the old valley at a
time when the glacier ice was several thousand feet higher than it is
now, and some ten miles wider than at present. The glacier trended
inland in a general south-westerly direction.

We longed to turn our sledges shoreward and explore these
inland rocks, but this would have involved a delay of several days –
probably a week at least – and we could not afford the time.
Mawson took a series of horizontal and vertical angles with the
theodolite to all the upper peaks in these ranges. We were much
puzzled to determine on what part of the charted coast this wide
bay and great glacier valley was situated. We found out much later
that the point opposite which we had now arrived was in reality
Granite Harbour, and that its position was not shown correctly on
the chart.

October 27. The weather was beautifully clear and sunshiny, and
we had a glorious view of the great mountain ranges on either side
of Granite Harbour. The rich colouring of warm sepia brown and
terra cotta in these rocky hills was quite a relief to the eye. Wind
springing up in the south-east, we made sail on both sledges, and
this helped us a good deal over the soft snow and occasional
patches of sharp-edged brash ice.

Toward evening we fetched up against some high ice pressure
cracks with the ice ridged up six to eight feet high in huge tumbled
blocks. We seemed to have got into a labyrinth of these pressure
ridges from which there was no outlet. At last, after several capsizes
of the sledges and some chopping through the ice ridges by
Mackay, we got the sledges through, and camped on a level piece
of ice. Mawson and I at this time were still wearing finnesko, while
Mackay had taken to ski boots.

October 28. The sledging was again very heavy over sticky, soft
snow alternating with hard sastrugi and patches of consolidated
brash ice. After our evening hoosh, Mawson and I went over to

the shore, rather more than half a mile distant, in order to study the rocks. These we found were composed of coarse red granite; the top of the granite was much smoothed by glacier ice, and strewn with large erratic blocks. In places the granite was intersected by black dykes of basic rocks. One could see that the glacier ice, about a quarter of a mile inland from the rocky shore, had only recently retreated and laid bare the glaciated rocky surface. We found a little moss here amongst the crevices in the granite rock.

October 29 was beautifully fine, though a keen and fresh wind, rather unpleasantly cold, was blowing from off the high mountain plateau to our west. We were all thoroughly done up at night after completing our four miles of relay work. That evening we discussed the important question of whether it would be possible to eke out our food supplies with seal meat so as to avoid putting ourselves on half rations, and we all agreed that this should be done. We made up our minds that at the first convenient spot we would make a depot of any articles of equipment, geological specimens, etc., in order to lighten our sledges, and would at the same time, if the spot was suitable, make some experiments with seal meat. The chief problem in connection with the latter was how to cook it without the aid of paraffin oil, as we could not afford paraffin for this purpose.

October 30 was full of interest for us, as well as hard work. In the early morning, between 2:30 a.m. and 6:30 a.m., a mild blizzard was blowing. We got under way a little later and camped at about 10:30 a.m. for lunch alongside a very interesting rocky point. Mawson got a good set of theodolite angles from the top of this point

We tried, on that day, the experiment of strengthening the brew of the tea by using the old tea leaves of a previous meal mixed with the next ones. This was Mackay's idea, and Mawson and I at the time did not appreciate the experiment. Later on, however, we were very glad to adopt it.

The weather was now daily becoming warmer and the saline snow on the sea ice became sticky in consequence. It gripped the runners of the sledges like glue, and we were only able with our greatest efforts to drag the sledges over this at a snail's pace. We were all thoroughly exhausted that evening when we camped at the base of a rocky promontory about 180 ft. high. This cliff was formed of coarse gneiss, with numerous dark streaks, and enclosures of huge masses of greenish-grey quartzite. After our evening hoosh we walked over to a very interesting small island about three-quarters of a mile distant. It was truly a most wonderful place geologically, and was a perfect elysium for the mineralogist. The island, which we afterwards called Depot Island, was accessible on the shoreward side, but rose perpendicularly to a height of 200 ft. above sea level on the other three sides. There was very little snow or ice upon it, the surface being almost entirely formed of gneissic granite. This granite was full of dark enclosures of basic rocks, rich in black mica and huge crystals of hornblende. It was in these enclosures that Mawson discovered a translucent brown mineral, which he believed to be monazite, but which has since proved to be titanium mineral.

October 31. We packed up and made for the island at 9:30 a.m. The sledging was extremely heavy, and we fell into a tide crack on the way, but the sledge was got over safely. Mackay sighted a seal about six hundred yards distant from the site of our new camp near the island, and just then, we noticed that another seal had bobbed up in the tide crack close to our old camp. Mackay and Mawson at once started off in the direction where the first seal had been sighted. It proved to be a bull seal in very good condition, and they killed it by knocking it on the head with an ice axe. Meanwhile, I unpacked the Duff sledge and took it out to them. Returning to the site of our camp I put up the tent, and on going back to Mawson and Mackay found that they had finished fletching the seal. We loaded up the empty sledge with seal blubber, resembling bars of soap in its now frozen condition, steak and liver, and returned to camp for lunch.

After lunch we took some blubber and seal meat on to the island, intending to try the experiment of making a blubber fire in order to cook the meat. We worked our way a short distance up a steep, rocky gully, and there built a fireplace out of magnificent specimens of hornblende rock. It seemed a base use for such magnificent mineralogical specimens, but necessity knows no laws. We had brought with us our primus lamp in order to start the fire. We put blubber on our iron shovel, warmed this underneath by means of the heat of the primus lamp so as to render down the oil from it, and then lit the oil. The experiment was not altogether successful. Mawson cooked for about three hours, closely and anxiously watched by Mackay and myself. Occasionally he allowed us to taste small snacks of the partly cooked seal meat, which were pronounced to be delicious.

While the experiment was at its most critical stage, at about 6 p.m., we observed sudden swirls of snowdrift high up on the western mountains, coming rapidly to lower levels. For a few minutes we did not think seriously of the phenomenon, but as the drift came nearer we saw that something serious was in the air. Mackay and I rushed down to our tent, the skirt of which was only temporarily secured with light blocks of snow. We reached it just as it was struck by the sudden blizzard which had descended from the western mountains. There was no time to dig further blocks of snow, all we could do was to seize the heavy food bags on our sledges, weighing sixty pounds each, and rush them on to the skirt of the tent. The blizzard struck our kitchen on the island simultaneously with our tent, and temporarily Mawson lost his mitts and most of the tidbits of seal meat, but these were quickly recovered, and he came rushing down to join us in securing the tent. While Mawson in frantic haste chopped out blocks of snow and dumped them on to the skirt of the tent, Mackay, no less frantically, struggled with our sleeping bag, which had been turned inside out to air, and which by this time was covered with drift snow. He quickly had it turned right side in again, and dashed it inside the tent. At last everything was secured, and we found ourselves safe and sound inside the tent.

On November 1 we breakfasted off a mixture of our ordinary hoosh and seal meat. After some discussion we decided that our only hope of reaching the Magnetic Pole lay in our travelling on half rations from our present camp to the point on the coast at the Drygalski Glacier, where we might for the first time hope to be able to turn inland with reasonable prospect of reaching the Magnetic Pole. Mawson was emphatic that we must conserve six weeks of full rations for our inland journey to and from the Pole. This necessitated our going on half rations from this island to the far side of the Drygalski Glacier, a distance of about one hundred statute miles. In order to supplement the regular half rations we intended to take seal meat.

While I was busy in calculating the times and distances for the remainder of our journey, and proportioning the food rations to suit our new program, Mawson and Mackay conducted further experiments on the cooking of seal meat with blubber. While at our winter quarters, Mackay had made some experiments on the use of blubber as a fuel. He had constructed a blubber lamp, the wick of which kept alight for several hours at a time, feeding itself on the seal oil. He had tried the experiment of heating up water over this blubber lamp, and was partly successful at the time when we left winter quarters for our present sledging journey. But his experiments at the time were not taken very seriously, and the blubber lamp was left behind, a fact which we now much regretted. An effective cooking stove was, however, evolved, as the result of a series of experiments this day, out of one of our large empty biscuit tins. The lid of this was perforated with a number of circular holes for the reception of wicks. Its edges were bent down, so as to form supports to keep the wick holder about half an inch above the bottom of the biscuit tin. The wick holder was put in place; wicks were made of pieces of old calico food bags rolled in seal blubber, or with thin slices of seal blubber enfolded in them, the calico being done up in little rolls for the purpose of making wicks, as one rolls a cigarette, the seal blubber taking the place of the tobacco in this case. Lumps of blubber were laid around the wick holder. Then, after some difficulty, the wicks were lighted. They burned feebly at first, as seal blubber has a good deal of water in it. After some minutes of fitful spluttering, the wicks got fairly alight, and as soon as the lower part of the biscuit tin was raised to a high temperature, the big lumps of blubber at the side commenced to have the water boiled out of them and the oil rendered down. This oil ran under the wick holder and supplied the wicks at their base. The wicks, now fed with warm, pure seal oil, started to burn brightly, and even fiercely, so that it became necessary occasionally to damp them down with chips of fresh blubber. We tried the experiment of using lumps of salt as wicks, and found this fairly successful, but we decided to rely for wicks chiefly on our empty food bags, and thought possibly that if these ran out we might have recourse to moss. But the empty food bags supplied sufficient wick for our need.

That day, by means of galvanised iron wires, we slung the inner pot from our aluminium cooker over the lighted wicks of our blubber cooker, thawed down snow in it, added chips of seal meat and made a delicious bouillon. This had a rich red colour and seemed very nutritious, but to me was indigestible. While Mawson was still engaged on further cooking experiments, Mackay and I ascended to the highest point of the island, selected a spot for a cairn to mark our depot, and Mackay commenced building the cairn. Meanwhile, I returned to camp.

It had, of course, become clear to us, in view of our experience of the already cracking sea ice near Granite Harbour, as well as in view of our comparatively slow progress by relay, that our retreat back to camp from the direction of the Magnetic Pole would in all probability be entirely cut off through the breaking up of the sea ice. Under these circumstances we determined to take the risk of the *Nimrod* arriving safely on her return voyage at Cape Royds, where she would receive the instructions to search for us along the western coast, and also the risk of her not being able to find our depot and ourselves. We knew that there was a certain amount of danger in adopting this course, but we felt that we had got on so far with the work entrusted to us by our Commander that we could not honourably now turn back. Under these circumstances we each wrote farewell letters to those who were nearest and dearest, and the following morning, November 2, we were up at 4:30 a.m. After putting all the letters into one of our empty dried milk tins, and fitting on the airtight lid, I walked with it to the island and climbed up to the cairn. Here, after carefully depoting several bags of geological specimens at the base of the flagstaff, I lashed the little post office by means of cord and copper wire securely to the flagstaff, and then carried some large slabs of exfoliated granite to the cairn, and built them up on the leeward side of it in order to strengthen it against the southerly blizzards. A keen wind was blowing, as was usual in the early morning, off the high plateau, and one's hands got frequently frostbitten in the work of securing the tin to the flagstaff. The cairn was at the seaward end of a sheer cliff two hundred feet high.

It was later than usual when we started our sledges, and the pulling proved extremely heavy. The sun's heat was thawing the snow surface and making it extremely sticky. Our progress was so painfully slow that we decided, after with great efforts doing two miles, to camp, have our hoosh, and then turn in for six hours, having meanwhile started the blubber lamp. At the expiration of that time we intended to get out of our sleeping bag, breakfast, and start sledging about midnight. We hoped that by adopting nocturnal habits of travelling, we would avoid the sticky ice surface which by daytime formed such an obstacle to our progress. We carried out this program on the evening of November 2, and the morning of November 3. We found the experiment fairly successful, as at midnight and for a few hours afterward the temperature remained sufficiently low to keep the surface of the snow on the sea ice moderately crisp.

On November 3 and 4 the weather was fine, and we made fair progress.

On the following day, November 5, we were opposite a very interesting coastal panorama, some twenty miles north of Granite Harbour. Magnificent ranges of mountains, steep slopes free from snow and ice, stretched far to the north and far to the south of us, and finished away inland, toward the heads of long glacier-cut valleys, in a vast upland snow plateau. The rocks which were exposed to view in the lower part of these ranges were mostly of warm sepia brown to terra cotta tint, and were evidently built up of a continuation of the gneissic rocks and red granites which we had previously seen. Above these crystalline rocks came a belt of greenish-grey rock, apparently belonging to some stratified form-ation and possibly many hundreds of feet in thickness; the latter was capped with a black rock that seemed to be either a basic plateau lava or a huge sill. In the direction of the glacier valleys, the plateau was broken up into a vast number of conical hills of various shapes and heights, all showing evidence of intense glacial action in the past. The hills were here separated from the coastline by a continuous belt of piedmont glacier ice. This last terminated where it joined the sea ice in a steep slope, or low cliff, and in places was very much crevassed. Mawson, at our noon halt for lunch, continued taking the angles of all these ranges and valleys with our theodolite.

The temperature was now rising, being as high as 22° F at noon on November 5. We had a very heavy sledging surface that day, there being much consolidated brash ice, sastrugi, pie crust snow, and numerous cracks in the sea ice. As an offset to these troubles we had that night, for the first time, the use of our new frying pan, constructed by Mawson out of one of our empty paraffin tins. This tin had been cut in half down the middle parallel to its broad surfaces, and loops of iron wire being added, it was possible to suspend it inside the empty biscuit tin above the wicks of our blubber lamp. We found that in this frying pan we could rapidly render down the seal blubber into oil, and as soon as the oil boiled we dropped into the pan small slices of seal liver or seal meat. The liver took about ten minutes to cook in the boiling oil, the seal meat about twenty minutes. These facts were ascertained by the empirical method. Mawson discovered by the same method that the nicely browned and crisp residue from the seal blubber, after the oil in it had become rendered down, was good eating, and had a fine nutty flavour. We also found, as the result of later experiments, that dropping a little seal's blood into the boiling oil produced eventually a gravy of very fine flavour. If the seal's blood was poured in rapidly into the boiling oil, it made a kind of gravy pancake, which we also considered very good as a variety.

We had a magnificent view this day of fresh ranges of mountains to the north of Depot Island. At the foot of these was an extensive terrace of glacier ice, a curious type of piedmont glacier. Its surface was strongly convex near where it terminated seaward in a steep slope or low cliff. In places this ice was heavily crevassed. At a distance of several miles inland, it reached the spurs of an immense coastal range, while in the wide gaps in this range the ice trended inland as far as the eye could see until it blended in the far distance with the skyline high up on the great inland plateau.

A little before 9 p.m. on November 5 we left our sleeping bag, and found snow falling, with a fresh and chilly breeze from the south. The blubber lamp, which we had lighted before we had turned in, had got blown out. We built a chubby house for it of snow blocks to keep off the wind, and relighted it, and then turned into the sleeping bag again while we waited for the snow and chips of seal meat in our cooking pot to become converted into a hot bouillon; the latter was ready after an interval of about one hour and a half. Just before midnight we brought the cooker alight into the tent in order to protect it from the blizzard which was now blowing and bringing much falling snow with it. Mawson's cooking experiments continued to be highly successful and entirely satisfactory to the party.

We waited for the falling snow to clear sufficiently to enable us to see a short distance ahead, and then started again, the blizzard still blowing with a little low drift. After doing a stage of pulling on both sledges to keep ourselves warm in the blizzard we set sail – always a chilly business – and the wind was a distinct assistance to us. We encountered a good deal of brash ice that day, and noticed that this type of ice surface was most common in the vicinity of icebergs, which just here were very numerous. The brash ice is probably formed by the icebergs surging to and fro in heavy weather like a lot of gigantic Yermaks, and crunching up the sea ice in their vicinity. The latter, of course, refreezes, producing a surface covered with jagged edges and points.

We were now reduced to one plasmon biscuit each for breakfast and one for evening meal, and we were unanimous in the opinion that we had never before fully realised how very nice these plasmon biscuits were. We became exceedingly careful even over the crumbs. As some biscuits were thicker than others, the cook for the week would select three biscuits, place them on the outer cover of our aluminium cooker, and get one of his mates to look in an opposite direction while the messman pointed to a biscuit and said, 'Whose?' The mate with averted face, or shut eyes, would then state the owner, and the biscuit was earmarked for him, and so with the other two biscuits. Grievous was the disappointment of the man to whose lot the thinnest of the three biscuits had fallen. Originally, on this sledge journey, when biscuits were more plentiful, we used to eat them regardless of the loss of crumbs, munching them boldly, with the result that occasional crumbs fell on the floorcloth. Not so now. Each man broke his biscuit over his own pannikin of hoosh, so that any crumbs produced in the process of fracture fell into the pannikin. Then, in order to make sure that there were no loose fragments adhering to the morsel we were about to transfer to our mouths, we tapped the broken chip, as well as the biscuit from which it had been broken, on the sides of the pannikin, so as to shake into it any loose crumbs. Then, and then only, was it safe to devour the previous morsel. Mackay, who adopted this practice in common with the rest of us, said it reminded him of the old days when the sailors tapped each piece of broken biscuit before eating it in order to shake out the weevils.

Mawson and I now wore our ski boots instead of finnesko, the weather being warmer, and the ski boot giving one a better grip on the snow surface of the sea ice. The rough leather took the skin off my right heel, but Mackay fixed it up later in the evening, that is, my heel, with some 'Newskin'.

We sledged on uneventfully for the remainder of November 6, and during the 7th, and on November 8 it came on to blow again with fresh falling snow. The blizzard was still blowing when the time came for us to pitch our tent. We had a severe struggle to get the tent up in the high wind and thick falling snow. At last the work was accomplished, and we were all able to turn into our sleeping bag, pretty tired, at about 12:30 p.m.

The weather was still bad the following day, November 9. After breakfast of seal's liver, and digging out the sledges from the snowdrift, we started in the blizzard, the snow still falling. After a little while we made sail on both sledges. The light was very bad on account of the thick falling snow, and we were constantly falling up to our knees in the cracks in the sea ice. It seemed miraculous that in spite of these very numerous accidents we never sprained an ankle.

That day we saw a snow petrel, and three skua gulls visited our camp. At last the snow stopped falling and the wind fell light, and we were much cheered by the fine, though distant, view of the Nordenskjold Ice Barrier to the north of us. We were all extremely anxious to ascertain what sort of a surface for sledging we should meet with on this great glacier. According to the Admiralty chart, prepared from observations by the *Discovery* expedition, this glacier was between twenty-four and thirty miles wide, and projected over twenty miles from the rocky shore into the sea. We hoped that we might be able to cross it without following a circuitous route along its seaward margins.

We started off on November 10, amongst very heavy sastrugi and ridges of broken pack ice. Cracks in the sea ice were extremely numerous. The temperature was up to plus 3° F at 8 a.m. That day when we pitched camp we were within half a mile of the southern edge of the Nordenskjold Ice Barrier.

The following day, November 11, as Mawson wished to get an accurate magnetic determination with the Lloyd-Creak dip circle, we decided to camp, Mackay and I exploring the glacier surface to select a suitable track for our sledges while Mawson took his observations. After breakfast we removed everything containing iron several hundred yards away from the tent, leaving Mawson alone inside it in company with the dip circle. We found that the ascent from the sea ice to the Nordenskjold Ice Barrier was a comparatively easy one. The surface was formed chiefly of hard snow glazed in places, partly through thawing and refreezing, partly through the polishing of this windward surface by particles of fresh snow driven over it by the blizzards. The surface ascended gradually to a little over one hundred feet above the level of the sea ice, passing into a wide undulating plain which stretched away to the north as far as the eye could see.

We returned to Mawson with the good news that the Nordenskjold Ice Barrier was quite practicable for sledging, and would probably afford us a much more easy surface than the sea ice over which we had previously been passing. Mawson informed us, as the result of his observations with the dip circle, that the Magnetic Pole was probably about forty miles further inland than the theoretical mean position calculated for it from the magnetic observations of the *Discovery* expedition seven years ago.

Early on the morning of November 12 we packed up, and started to cross the Nordenskjold Ice Barrier. We noticed here that there were two well-marked sets of sastrugi, one set, nearly due north and south, formed by the strong southerly blizzards, the other set, crossing nearly at right angles, coming from the west and formed by the cold land winds blowing off the high plateau at night on to the sea.

November 12 was an important one in the history of Mawson's triangulation of the coast, for he was able in the morning to sight simultaneously Mount Erebus and Mount Melbourne, as well as Mount Lister. We were fortunate in having a very bright and clear day on this occasion, and the round of angles obtained by Mawson with the theodolite were in every way satisfactory.

November 13. We were still on the Nordenskjold Ice Barrier. The temperature in the early morning, about 3 a.m., was minus 13° F. Mawson had provided an excellent dish for breakfast consisting of crumbed seal meat and seal's blood, which proved delicious. We got under way about 2 a.m. It was a beautiful sunshiny day with a gentle cold breeze off the western plateau. When we had sledged for about one thousand yards Mawson suddenly exclaimed that he could see the end of the barrier where it terminated in a white cliff only about six hundred yards ahead. We halted the sledge, and while Mawson took some more theodolite angles Mackay and I reconnoitred ahead but could find no way down the cliff. We returned to the sledge and all pulled on for another quarter of a mile. Once more we reconnoitred, and this time both Mawson and I found some steep slopes formed by drifted snow which were just practicable for a light sledge lowered by an alpine rope. We chose what seemed to be the best of these; Mackay tied the alpine rope around his body, and taking his ice axe, descended the slope cautiously, Mawson and I holding on to the rope meanwhile. The snow slope proved fairly soft, giving good foothold, and he was soon at the bottom without having needed any support from the alpine rope. He then returned to the top of the slope, and we all set to work unpacking the sledges. We made fast one of the sledges to the alpine rope, and after loading it lightly lowered it little by little down the slope, one of us guiding the sledge while the other two slacked out the alpine rope above. The man who went with the sledge to the bottom would unload it there on the sea ice and then climb up the slope, the other two meanwhile pulling up the empty sledge. This manoeuvre was repeated a number of times until eventually the whole of our food and equipment, including two sledges, were safely down on the sea ice below.

We were all much elated at having got across the Nordenskjold Ice Barrier so easily and so quickly. We were also fortunate in securing a seal; Mackay went off and killed this, bringing back seal steak, liver, and a considerable quantity of seal blood. From the last Mackay said he intended to manufacture a black pudding.

While Mackay had been in pursuit of the seal meat Mawson had taken a meridian attitude while I kept the time for him. After our hoosh we packed the sledges, and Mawson took a photograph showing the cliff forming the northern boundary of the Nordenskjold Ice Barrier. This cliff was about forty feet in height. There can be little doubt, I think, that the greater part of this Nordenskjold Ice Barrier is afloat.

The sun was so warm this day that I was tempted before turning in to the sleeping bag to take off my ski boots and socks and give my feet a snow bath, which was very refreshing.

The following day, November 14, we were naturally anxious to be sure of our exact position on the chart, in view of the fact that we had come to the end of the ice barrier some eighteen miles quicker than the chart led us to anticipate. Mawson accordingly worked up his meridian altitude, and I plotted out the angular distances he had found respectively, for Mount Erebus, Mount Lister, and Mount Melbourne. As the result of the application of our calculations to the chart it became evident that we had actually crossed the Nordenskjold Ice Barrier of Captain Scott's survey, and were now opposite what on this chart was termed Charcot Bay. This was good news and cheered us up very much, as it meant that we were nearly twenty miles further north than we previously thought we were. The day was calm and fine, and the surface of the sea ice was covered with patches of soft snow with nearly bare ice between, and the sledging was not quite as heavy as usual. In the evening two skua gulls went for our seal meat during the interval that we were returning for the second sledge after pulling on the first one.

We had a magnificent view of the rocky coastline, which is here most impressive. The sea ice stretched away to the west of us for several miles up to a low cliff and slope of piedmont glacier ice, with occasional black masses of rock showing at its edge. Several miles further inland the piedmont glacier ice terminated abruptly against a magnificent range of mountains, tabular for the most part but deeply intersected. In the wide gaps between this coast range were vast glaciers fairly heavily crevassed, descending by steep slopes from an inland plateau to the sea.

We were still doing our travelling by night and sleeping during the afternoon. When we arose from our sleeping bags at 8 p.m. on the night of November 15, there was a beautifully perfect 'Noah's Ark' in the sky; the belts of cirrus stratus composing the ark stretched from south-south-west to north-north-east, converging toward the horizon in each of these directions. Fleecy sheets of frost smoke arose from over the open water on Ross Sea, and formed dense cumulus clouds. This, of course, was a certain indication to us that open water was not far distant, and impressed upon us the necessity of making every possible speed if we hoped to reach our projected point of departure on the coast for the Magnetic Pole before the sea ice entirely broke up.

The following day, November 17, after a very heavy sledging over loose powdery snow six inches deep, we reached a low glacier and ice cliff. We were able to get some really fresh snow from this barrier or glacier, the cliffs of which were from thirty to forty feet high. It was a great treat to get fresh water at last, as since we had left the Nordenskjold Ice Barrier the only snow available for cooking purposes had been brackish.

November 18 was bright and sunny, but the sledging was terribly heavy. The sun had thawed the surface of the saline snow and our sledge runners had become saturated with soft water. We were so wearied with the great effort necessary to keep the sledges moving that at the end of each halt we fell sound asleep for five minutes or so at a time across the sledges. On such occasions one of the party would wake the others up, and we would continue our journey. We were even more utterly exhausted than usual at the end of this day.

By this time, however, we were in sight of a rocky headland which we took to be Cape Irizar, and we knew that this cape was not very far to the south of the Drygalski Glacier. Indeed, already a long line was showing on the horizon which could be no other than the eastward extension of this famous and, as it afterward proved, formidable glacier.

November 19. We had another heavy day's sledging, ankle deep in the soft snow. We only did two miles of relay work this day, and yet were quite exhausted at the end of it.

November 20. Being short of meat, we killed a seal calf and cow, and so replenished our larder. At the end of the day's sledging I walked over about two miles to a cliff face, about six miles south of Cape Irizar. The rocks all along this part of the shore were formed of coarse gneissic granite, of which I was able to collect some specimens. The cliff was about one hundred feet high where it was formed of the gneiss, and above this rose a capping of from seventy to eighty feet in thickness of heavily crevassed blue glacier ice. There were here wide tide cracks between the sea ice and the foot of the sea cliff. These were so wide that it was difficult to cross them.

November 21. The sledging was painfully heavy over thawing saline snow surface and sticky sea ice. We were only able to do two and two-third miles.

November 22. On rounding the point of the low ice barrier, thirty to forty feet high, we obtained a good view of Cape Irizar, and also of the Drygalski Ice Barrier.

November 23. We found that a mild blizzard was blowing, but we travelled on through it as we could not afford to lose any time. The blizzard died down altogether about 3 a.m., and was succeeded by a gentle westerly wind off the plateau. That evening, after our tent had been put up and we had finished the day's meal, I walked over a mile to the shore. The prevailing rock was still gneissic granite with large whitish veins of aplitic granite. A little bright green moss was growing on tiny patches of sand and gravel, and in some of the cracks in the granite. The top of the cliff was capped by the blue glacier ice. With the help of steps cut by my ice axe I climbed some distance up this in order to try and get some fresh ice for cooking purposes, but close to the top of the slope I accidentally slipped and glissaded most unwillingly some distance down before I was able to check myself by means of the chisel edge of the ice axe. My hands were somewhat cut and bruised, but otherwise no damage was done.

November 24. A strong keen wind was blowing off the plateau from the west-south-west. We were all suffering from want of sleep, and although the snow surface was better than it had been for some little time we still found the work of sledging very fatiguing. A three-man sleeping bag, where you are wedged in more or less tightly against your mates, where all snore and shin one another and each feels on waking that he is more shinned against than shinning, is not conducive to real rest; and we rued the day that we chose the three-man bag in preference to the one-man bags.

On the following day, November 26, we saw on looking back that the rocky headland, where I had collected the specimens of granite and moss, was not part of the mainland but a small island.

We had some good sledging here over pancake ice nearly free from snow and travelled fast. While Mackay secured some seal meat Mawson and I ascended the rocky promontory, climbing at first over rock, then over glacier ice, to a height of about six hundred feet above the sea. The rock was a pretty red granite traversed by large dykes of black rocks. From the top of the headland to the north we had a magnificent view across the level surface of sea ice far below us. We saw that at a few miles from the shore an enormous iceberg, frozen into the floe, lay right across the path which we had intended to travel in our northerly course on the morrow. To the north-west of us was Gelkie Inlet, and beyond that stretching as far as the eye could follow was the great Drygalski Glacier. Beyond the Drygalski Glacier were a series of rocky hills. One of these was identified as probably being Mount Neumayer. Several mountains could be seen further to the north of this, but the far distance was obscured from view by cloud and mist so that we were unable to make out the outline of Mount Nansen. It was evident that the Drygalski Glacier was bounded landward on the north by a steep cliff of dark, highly jointed rock, and we were not a little concerned to observe with our field glasses that the surface of the Drygalski Glacier was wholly different to that of the Nordenskjold Ice Barrier. It was clear that the surface of the Drygalski Glacier was formed of jagged surfaces of ice very heavily crevassed, and projecting in the form of immense séracs separated from one another by deep undulations or chasms; but we could see that, at the extreme eastern extension, some thirty miles from where we were standing, the surface appeared fairly smooth. It was obvious from what we had seen looking out to sea to the east of our camp that there were large bodies of open water trending shorewards in the form of long lanes at no great distance. The lanes of water were only partly frozen over, and some of these were interposed between us and the Drygalski Glacier. Clearly not a moment was to be lost if we were to reach the glacier before the sea ice broke up. A single strong blizzard would now have converted the whole of the sea ice between us and the glacier into a mass of drifting pack.

The following day, November 27, we decided to run our sledges to the east of the large berg which we had observed on the previous day, and this course apparently would enable us to avoid a wide and ugly looking tide crack extending northward from the rocky point at our previous camp. The temperature was now as high as from plus 26° to plus 28° F at midday, consequently the saline snow and ice were all day more or less sticky and slushy. We camped near the large berg.

On the morning of November 28 we packed up and started our sledges, and pulled them over a treacherous slushy tide crack, and then headed them around an open lead of water in the sea ice. At 3 a.m. we had lunch near the east end of the big berg. Near here Mackay and Mawson succeeded in catching and killing an Emperor penguin, and took the breast and liver. This bird was caught close to a lane of open water in the sea ice. We found that in the direction of the berg this was thinly frozen over, and for some time it seemed as though our progress further north was completely blocked. Eventually we found a place where the ice might just bear our sledges. We strengthened this spot by laying down on it slabs of sea ice and shovelfuls of snow, and when the causeway was completed – not without Mackay breaking through the ice in one place and very nearly getting a ducking – we rushed our sledges over safely, although the ice was so thin that it bent under their weight. We were thankful to get them both safely to the other side.

We now found ourselves amongst some very high sastrugi of hard tough snow. We had to drag the sledges over a great number of these, which were nearly at right angles to our course. This work proved extremely fatiguing. The sastrugi were from five to six feet in height. As we were having dinner at the end of our day's sledging we heard a loud report which we considered to be due to the opening of a new crack in the sea ice. We thought it was possible that this crack was caused by some movement of the great active Drygalski Glacier, now only about four miles ahead of us to the north.

We got out of our sleeping bag soon after 8 p.m. on the evening of the 28th, and started just before midnight. The ice surface over which we were sledging this day had a curious appearance resembling rippling stalagmites, or what may be termed ice marble. This opacity appeared to be due to a surface enamel of partly thawed snow. This surface kept continually cracking as we passed over it with a noise like that of a whip being cracked. It was evidently in a state of tension, being contracted by the cold which attained its maximum soon after midnight, for, although of course we had for many weeks past been having the midnight sun, it was still so low in the heavens toward midnight that there was an appreciable difference in the temperature between midnight and the afternoon.

We were now getting very short of biscuits, and as a consequence were seized with food obsessions, being unable to talk about anything but cereal foods, chiefly cakes of various kinds and fruits. Whenever we halted for a short rest we could discuss nothing but the different dishes with which we had been regaled in our former lifetime at various famous restaurants and hotels.

The plateau wind blew keenly and strongly all day on November 29. As we advanced further to the north the ice surface became more and more undulatory, rising against us in great waves like waves of the sea. Evidently these waves were due to the forward movement, and consequent pressure of the Drygalski Glacier. We had a fine view from the top of one of these ridges over the surface of the Drygalski Glacier, to the edge of the inland plateau. Far inland, perhaps forty or fifty miles away, we could see the great névé fields, which fed the Drygalski Glacier, descending in conspicuous ice falls, and beyond these loomed dim mountains. At the end of this day we hardly knew whether we were on the edge of the sea ice or on the thin edge of the Drygalski Glacier. Probably, I think, we were on very old sea ice, perhaps representing the accumulations of several successive seasons.

It fell calm at about 9 p.m., but just before midnight, November 29–30, the plateau wind returned, blowing stronger than ever. As the sun during the afternoon had now considerable heating power, we tried the experiment of putting snow into our aluminium cooking pot, the exterior of which by this time was permanently coated with greasy lamp black from the blubber lamp, and leaving the pot exposed in the evening to the direct rays of the sun. The lamp black, of course, formed an excellent absorbent of the sun's heat rays. On getting out of the sleeping bag at 9 p.m. on November 29 I found that about half the snow I had put into the cooking pot had been thawed down by the sun's heat. This, of course, saved both paraffin and blubber. It takes, of course, as much energy to thaw ice or snow at a temperature of 32° F to form a given volume of water as it does to raise that water from 32° F up to boiling point. As our snow and ice used for domestic purposes frequently had a temperature of many degrees below zero, the heat energy necessary to thaw it was greater than that required to raise the water from freezing point to boiling point.

As we advanced with our sledge on the early morning of November 30, the ice ridges fronting us became higher and steeper, and we had much ado straining with all our might on the steep ice slopes to get the sledges to move, and they skidded a good deal as we dragged them obliquely up the slopes. The plateau wind, too, had freshened, and was now blowing on our port bow at from fifteen to twenty miles an hour, bringing with it a good deal of low drift. At last, about 10 a.m., the plateau wind dropped and with it the drift, and the weather became warm and sunny.

The glacier now spread before us as a great billowy sea of pale green ice, with here and there high embankments of marble-like névé resembling railway embankments. Unfortunately for our progress, the trend of the latter was nearly at right angles to our course. As we advanced still further north the undulations became more and more pronounced, the embankments higher and steeper. These embankments were now bounded by cliffs from forty to fifty feet in height, with overhanging cornices of tough snow. The cliffs faced northward. The deep chasms which they produced formed a very serious obstacle to our advance, and we had to make some long detours in order to head them off. On studying one of these chasms it seemed to me that their mode of origin was somewhat as follows: in the first place the surface of the ice had become strongly ridged through forward movement of the glacier, with perhaps differential frictional resistance, the latter causing a series of undulations; the top of each ice undulation would then be further raised by an accumulation of snow partly carried by the west-north-west plateau wind, partly by the southerly blizzard wind. These two force components produced these overhanging cliffs facing the north. For some reason the snow would not lie at the bottoms of the troughs between the undulations. Probably they were swept bare by the plateau wind. It was hardly to be wondered at that we were unable to advance our sledges more than about one mile and a half that day.

The next day, December 1, the hauling of our sledges became much more laborious. For half a day we struggled over high sastrugi, hummocky ice ridges, steep undulations of bare blue ice with frequent chasms impassable for a sledge, unless it was unloaded and lowered by alpine rope. After struggling on for a little over half a mile we decided to camp, and while Mawson took magnetic observations and theodolite angles, Mackay and I reconnoitred ahead for between two and three miles to see if there was any way at all practicable for the sledge out of these mazes of chasms, undulations, and séracs. Mackay and I were roped together for this exploratory work, and fell into about a score of crevasses before we returned to camp, though in this case we never actually fell with our head and shoulders below the lids of the crevasses, as they were mostly filled at the surface with tough snow. We had left a black signal flag on top of a conspicuous ice mound as a guide to us as to the whereabouts of the camp, and we found this a welcome beacon when we started to return, as it was by no means an easy task finding one's way across this storm-tossed ice sea, even when one was only a mile or two from the camp. On our return we found that Mawson was just completing his observations. He found that the dip of the needle here was 2½° off the vertical. We brought the tent down from where he had been taking magnetic observations, and treading warily, because of crevasses, set it up again close to our sledge, and had lunch.

That afternoon we discussed the situation at some length. It appeared that the Drygalski Glacier must be at least twenty miles in width. If we were to cross it along the course which we were now following at the rate of half a mile every half day it would obviously take at least twenty days to get to the other side, and this estimate did not allow for those unforeseen delays which experience by this time had taught us were sure to occur. The view which Mackay and I had obtained of the glacier ice ahead of us showed that our difficulties, for a considerable distance, would materially increase. Under these circumstances we were reluctantly forced to the conclusion that our only hope of ultimate success lay in retreat. We accordingly determined to drag the sledges back off the glacier on to the sea ice by the way along which we had come.

Early on the morning of December 2 the retreat began. Owing to the fog, there was some difficulty in picking up our old sledge tracks.

December 3. We were still travelling eastward parallel to southern edge of the glacier.

December 4. Reconnoitring expedition.

December 5. Mackay brought back to camp a most welcome addition to our larder – over 30 lb. of seal meat. To secure this he had made a long journey over the sea ice.

December 6. We left our camp on the south side of glacier, and struck across high ridges of blue ice into the small valley which we had prospected on December 4.

December 7 and 8. We were still struggling across this glacier.

December 9. The glacier ice kept cracking from time to time with sharp reports. Possibly this may have been due to the expansion of the ice under the influence of the hot sun (the temperature at midnight being as high as plus 19° F). At one spot the sledges had to be dragged up a grade of 1 in 3 over smooth blue glacier ice. Just before camping time Mackay sighted open water on the northern edge of the Drygalski Ice Barrier, from three to four miles away. It was now clear that we could not hope for sea ice over which to sledge westward to that part of the shore where we proposed to make our final depot before attempting the ascent of the great inland plateau in order to reach the Magnetic Pole.

December 10. We were much rejoiced at the end of the day's sledging to find ourselves at last off the true glacier type of surface, and on to a surface of the undulating barrier type. This improvement in the surface enabled us to steer westward. At first we had to incline to north-west to skirt some high ice ridges, and then we were able to go nearly due west.

December 11. We had a fine view of 'Terra Nova' Bay, and as far as could be judged the edge of the Drygalski Ice Barrier on the north was now scarcely a mile distant. We were much surprised at the general appearance of the outline of the ice. It did not agree, as far as we could judge, with the shape of this region as shown on the Admiralty chart, and we could see no certain indication whatever of what was called, on the chart, 'the low, sloping shore'. Accordingly we halted a little earlier than usual in order to reconnoitre. There was a conspicuous ice mound about half a mile to the north-west of this camp. Mackay started off with the field glasses for a general look round from this point of vantage. Mawson started changing his plates in the sleeping bag, while I prepared to go out with my sketch book and get an outline panoramic view of the grand coast ranges now in sight. Crevasses of late had been so few and far between that I thought it was an unnecessary precaution to take my ice axe with me, but I had scarcely gone more than six yards from the tent when the lid of a crevasse suddenly collapsed under me at a point where there was absolutely no outward or visible sign of its existence, and let me down suddenly nearly up to my shoulders. I only saved myself from going right down by throwing my arms out and staying myself on the snow lid on either side. The lid was so rotten that I dared not make any move to extricate myself, or I might have been precipitated into the abyss. Fortunately Mawson was close at hand, and on my calling to him, he came out of our sleeping bag, and bringing an ice axe, chipped a hole in the firm ice on the edge of the crevasse nearest to me. He then inserted the chisel edge of the ice axe in the hole and, holding on to the pick point, swung the handle toward me: grasping this, I was able to extricate myself and climbed out on to the solid ice.

It was a beautiful day, the coastline showing up very finely, and I was able to get from the ice mound a sketch of the mountains. Mawson also took three photographs, making a panoramic view of this part of the coast. He was able, also, to get a valuable series of angles with the theodolite, which showed that the shape of the coastline here necessitated serious modification of the existing chart.

Far beyond the golden mountains to the north and west lay our goal, but as yet we knew not whether we were destined to fail or succeed. Meanwhile no time was to be lost in hurrying on and preparing for a dash on to the plateau, if we were to deserve success.

The following day, December 12, we sledged on for half a mile until we were a little to the west of the conspicuous ice mound previously described. We concluded that as this ice mound commanded such a general view of the surrounding country, it must itself be a conspicuous object to anyone approaching the Drygalski Glacier by sea from the north; and so we decided that as there was still no trace of the 'low, sloping shore' of the chart, and that as the spot at which we had now arrived was very near to the area so named on the chart, we would make our depot. We intended to leave at this depot one of our sledges with any spare equipment, a little food, and all our geological specimens, and proceed thence shoreward and inland with one sledge only. We estimated that we still had fully 220 miles to travel from this depot on the Drygalski Glacier to the Magnetic Pole. It was, therefore, necessary now to make preparations for a journey there and back of at least 440 miles. We thought that with detours the journey might possibly amount to 500 miles.

We could see, even from our distance of from twenty to thirty miles from the shoreline, that we had no light task before us in order to win a way on to the high inland plateau.

Our first business was to lay in a stock of provisions sufficient to last us for our 500 miles for further journeying. Mackay started for a small inlet about a mile and a half distant from our camp, where he found a number of seals and Emperor and Adelie penguins. He killed some seals and Emperor penguins, and loaded a good supply of seal steak, blubber, liver, and penguin steak and liver on to the sledge. In the course of his hunting, he fell through an ice bridge, at a tide crack, up to his waist in the water. Mawson and I went out to meet him when the sledge was loaded, and helped to drag it back to camp. We found it very hot in the tent, the weather being fine and sunny. It was delightful to be able at last to rest our weary limbs after the many weeks of painful toil over the sea ice and the Drygalski Glacier.

We started cooking our meat for the sledging trip on the following day, December 13, our intention being to take with us provisions for seven weeks, in addition to equipment, including scientific instruments, etc. We estimated that the total weight would amount to about 670 lb. We were doubtful, in our then stale and weakened condition, whether we should be able to pull such a load over the deep loose snow ahead of us, and then drag it up the steep ice slopes of the great glaciers which guarded the route to the plateau.

The sun was so hot that it started melting the fat out of our pemmican bags, so that the fat actually oozed through not only the canvas of the bags themselves, but also through the thick brown canvas of the large fortnightly foodbags, which formed a sort of tank for containing the pemmican bags, and we found it necessary at once to shade the foodbags from the sun by piling our Burberry garments over them. Leather straps, tar rope, tins, sledge harness, lamp black off the blubber cooker, warmed by the rays of the sun, all commenced to sink themselves more or less rapidly into the névé.

We unpacked and examined both sledges, and found that of the two, the runners of the Duff Sledge were the less damaged. As the result of the rough treatment to which it had recently been subjected, one of the iron brackets of this sledge was broken, but we replaced it with a sound one from the discarded Christmas Tree Sledge.

The following day, December 14, we were still busy preparing for the great trek inland. Mackay was busy cooking Emperor penguin and seal meat for the plateau journey; Mawson was employed in transferring the scientific instrument boxes and the Venesta boxes in which our primus lamp and other light gear were packed from the Christmas Tree sledge on to the Duff sledge. He also scraped the runners of the sledge with pieces of broken glass in order to make their surfaces as smooth as possible. I was busy fixing up depot flags, writing letters to the Commander of the *Nimrod,* Lieutenant Shackleton, and my family, and fixing up a milk tin to serve as a post office on to the depot flagpole. When all our preparations were completed we drew the Christmas Tree sledge with some of our spare clothing, our blubber cooker, a biscuit tin with a few broken biscuits, and all our geological specimens to the top of the ice mound, about a quarter of a mile distant. On reaching the top of the mound we cut trenches with our ice axes in which to embed the runners of the sledge, fixed the runners in these grooves, piled the chipped ice on top, then lashed to the sledge, very carefully, the flagpole about six feet high, with the black flag displayed on the top of it. The wind blew keenly off the plateau before our labours were completed. We all felt quite sorry and downcast at parting with this sledge, which by this time seemed to us like a bit of home. We then returned to camp. Just previous to depoting this sledge, Mackay fixed another small depot flag close to the open sea a few yards back from the edge of the ice cliff.

Soon after we had turned into our sleeping bags, a gentle blizzard started to blow from west by south. This continued all night, increasing in intensity in the morning. We were able to see great whale-backed clouds, very much like those with which we had been familiar over Mount Erebus, forming over Mount Nansen. As this blizzard wind was blowing partly against us, we decided that we would wait until it had either slackened off or decreased in force.

The blizzard continued till midnight of December 15–16, when its force markedly decreased. We breakfasted accordingly just after midnight. I dug out the sledge from the snow which had drifted over it, and Mackay cached some seal meat in an adjoining ice mound. At last, about 7 a.m., we made a start, and we were delighted to find that, chiefly as the result of the three days' rest in camp, we were able to pull our sledge – weighing about 670 lb. – with comparative ease. The snow, though soft, had become crusted over the surface through the thaw brought on by the blizzard, followed by freezing during the succeeding cold night. The sledging was certainly heavy, but not nearly so distressing as that which we had recently experienced in crossing the Drygalski Glacier. We steered toward the great black nunatak midway between Mount Nansen and Mount Larsen, as Mawson and Mackay both considered that in this direction lay our chief hope of finding a practical route to the high plateau.

On December 17 we had a very interesting day. The sledging was rather heavy, being chiefly over soft snow and pie crust snow. It was difficult to decide sometimes whether we were on fresh-water ice or on sea ice. Here and there we crossed ice ridges, evidently pressure ridges of some kind. These would be traversed by crevasses which showed the ice in such places to be at least thirty to forty feet in thickness. Close to our final camping ground for the day was a long shallow valley or barranca; it was from one hundred and twenty to one hundred and thirty yards in width. The near side was steep, though not too steep for us to have let our sledge down; but the far side was precipitous, being bounded by an overhanging cliff from twenty to thirty feet high. The floor of this valley was deeply and heavily crevassed. This sunken valley, therefore, formed a serious obstacle to our advance.

While Mackay was preparing the hoosh Mawson travelled to the right, and I to the left along this valley seeking for a possible crossing place. At last Mawson found a narrow spot where there had been an ice bridge over the valley, but this had become cracked through at the centre. It was nevertheless strong enough to bear our sledge. Near this ice bridge Mawson stated that he noticed muddy material containing what appeared to be foraminifera, squeezed up from below. The day had been calm and clear, and we were able to get detailed sketches of this part of the coast range.

The following day we made for the ice bridge with our sledge, and found that the crack crossing it had opened to a width of eighteen inches during the night. The far side had become, too, somewhat higher than the near side. We had little difficulty in getting the sledge over, and after crossing several other cracks in the ice and névé without mishap, reached once more a fairly level surface.

At lunch time, soon after midnight, we reached some very interesting glacial moraines in the form of large to small blocks, mostly of eruptive rock, embedded in the ice. It was probable, from their general distribution, that they formed part of an old moraine of Mount Nansen, though now about fifteen miles in advance of the present glacier front. We collected a number of specimens from this moraine.

Fine rolls of cumulus clouds were gathering to our north-east. The day was calm with occasional gleams of sunshine. After the plateau wind had died down about 2 p.m. it commenced to snow a little, the snow coming from between south-west and west-south-west.

At midnight on December 19 we started sledging in the falling snow, guided partly by the direction of the wind, partly by that of the pressure ridges and crevasses, occasionally taking compass bearings. Before we had gone far we reached a tide crack with open water three to four feet wide. There was also a width of about eighteen feet of recently formed thin ice at this tide crack. We tasted the water in this crack and found that it was distinctly salt. It was clear then that at this part of our journey we were travelling over sea ice. About half a mile further on we reached another open tide crack, and had to make a considerable detour in order to get over it. The surface of the ice was now thawing, and we trudged through a good deal of slushy snow, with here and there shallow pools of water as blue as the Blue Grotto of Capri. On the far side of this second tide crack, and beyond the blue pools, we reached a large pressure ridge forming a high and steep scarped slope barring our progress. Its height was about eighty feet. There was nothing for it, if we were to go forward, but to drag our heavy sledge up this steep slope. It was extremely exhausting work, and we were forced to halt a few times, and had to take the sledge occasionally somewhat obliquely up the slope where it was very steep. In such cases the sledge frequently skidded. Our troubles were increased by the fact that this ice slope was traversed by numerous crevasses, which became longer and wider the further we advanced in this direction.

At last we got to the slope, only to see in the dim light that there were a succession of similar slopes ahead of us, becoming continually higher and steeper. The ice, too, became a perfect network of crevasses, some of which were partly open, but most of them covered over with snow lids. Suddenly, when crossing one of these snow lids, just as he was about to reach the firm ice on the other side, there was a slight crash and Mawson instantly disappeared from sight. Fortunately the toggle at the end of his sledge rope held, and he was left swinging in the empty space between the walls of the crevasse, being suspended by his harness attached to the sledge rope. Mackay and I hung on to the rope in case it should part at the toggle, where it was somewhat worn. Meanwhile, Mawson called out from below to pass him down the alpine rope. Leaving Mackay to keep hold of the toggle end of Mawson's harness rope, I hurried back to the sledge, which was about ten feet behind, and just as I was trying to disengage a coil of rope Mawson called out that he felt he was going. I ran back and helped Mackay to keep a strain on Mawson's harness rope. Mawson then said that he was all right. Probably at the time he felt he was going the rope had suddenly cut back through the lid of the crevasse and let him down for a distance of about a couple of feet. Altogether he was about eight feet down below the level of the snow lid. While I now held on to Mawson's harness rope Mackay hurried back to the sledge, and with his Swedish knife, cut the lashing around the alpine rope, and started uncoiling it, making a bowline at the end in which Mawson could put his foot. Meanwhile Mawson secured some ice crystals from the side of the crevasse, and threw them up for examination. The alpine rope having been lowered, Mawson put his foot in the bowline and got Mackay to haul his leg up as high as his bent knee would allow it to go, then, calling to him to hold tight the rope, Mawson, throwing the whole weight of his body on to it, raised himself about eighteen inches by means of his arms so as to be able to straighten his right leg. Meanwhile, I took in the slack of his harness rope. He then called to me to hold tight the harness rope, as he was going to rest his whole weight on that, so as to take the strain off the alpine rope. Mackay then was able to pull the alpine rope up about eighteen inches, which had the effect of bending up Mawson's right leg as before. Mackay then held fast the alpine rope, and

Mawson again straightened himself up on it, resting his whole weight on that rope. Thus little by little he was hoisted up to the under surface of the snow lid, but as his harness rope had cut back a narrow groove in this snow lid several feet from where the snow gave way under him, Mawson now found his head and shoulders pressing against the under side of the snow lid, and had some difficulty in breaking through this in order to get his head out. At last the top of his head emerged, a sight for which Mackay and I were truly thankful, and presently he was able to get his arms up, and soon his body followed, and he got safely out on the near side of the crevasse. After this episode we were extra cautious in crossing the crevasses, but the ice was simply seamed with them. Twice when our sledge was being dragged up ice pressure ridges it rolled over sideways with one runner in a crevasse, and once the whole sledge all but disappeared into a crevasse, the snow lid of which had partly collapsed under its weight. Had it gone down completely it would certainly have dragged the three of us down with it, as it weighed nearly one-third of a ton. It was clear that these high pressure ridges and numerous crevasses were caused now, not by the Drygalski, but by the Nansen Glacier.

It was just commencing to snow, and wind was freshening from the south-west. We were now in a perfect labyrinth of crevasses and pressure ridges. Snow continued falling heavily accompanied by a blizzard wind, for the rest of that day and the whole of the succeeding night. Inside the tent we experienced some discomfort through the dripping of water caused by the thawing snow. As usual during a blizzard the temperature rose, and although the sun's heat rays were partly intercepted by the falling snow, quite sufficient warmth reached the side of the tent nearest the sun to produce this thaw. Pools of water lodged on the foot of our sleeping bag, but we were able to keep the head of it fairly dry by fixing up our Burberry blouses and trousers across the poles on the inside of the tent so as to make a temporary waterproof lining just above our heads. We were all thoroughly exhausted, and slept until about 7 a.m. the following day, December 20. By that time the snow had cleared, after about six inches had fallen.

December 20. After morning hoosh we held a council of war. The question was whether we should continue pulling on in the direction of the nunatak rising from the Mount Nansen Glacier, or whether we should retreat and try some other way which might lead us to the plateau. Mackay was in favour of hauling ahead over the Mount Nansen Glacier, while Mawson and I favoured retreat, and trying a passage in some other direction.

At last we decided to retreat. Our fortunes now, so far as the possibility of reaching the Magnetic Pole were concerned, seemed at a low ebb. It was already December 20, and we knew that we had to be back at our depot on the Drygalski Glacier not later than February 1 or 2, if there was to be a reasonable chance of our being picked up by the *Nimrod*. We had not yet climbed more than 100 ft. or so above sea level, and even this little altitude was due to our having climbed ice pressure ridges, which from time to time dipped down again to sea level. We knew that we had to travel at least 480 to 500 miles before we could hope to get to the Magnetic Pole and back to our depot, and there remained only six weeks in which to accomplish this journey, and at the same time we would have to pioneer a road up to the high plateau. Now that everything was buried under soft snow it was clear that sledging would be far slower and more laborious than ever.

We started off to reconnoitre in a south-westerly direction with the intention of seeing whether the Mount Bellingshausen Glacier slope would be more practicable for our sledges than the Mount Nansen Glacier. We trudged through soft thawing snow with here and there shallow pools of water on the surface of the ice. This, of course, saturated our socks, which froze as the temperature fell during the night. After proceeding about two and a half miles we observed with the field glasses that the foot of the Mount Bellingshausen Glacier was not only steep but broken and rugged. We decided to examine what appeared to be a narrow stretch of snow mantling around the base of a granite mountain, one of the offshoots from the Mount Larsen massif. After crossing much pressure ice and many crevasses, and floundering amongst the boulders of old moraines, we reached some shallow lakes of thawed snow near the junction between the sea ice and the foot of the snow slope for which we had been steering.

After paddling, unwillingly, in the shallow lakes, we reached the foot of what proved now to be not a snow slope but a small branch glacier. This was covered with a considerable depth of soft newly drifted snow, and we found the ascent in consequence very tiring as we sunk at each step in the soft snow over our knees. At last we attained an altitude of 1200 ft. above sea level, and were then high enough to see that the upper part of this branch glacier joined the Mount Bellingshausen Glacier at about 800 ft. higher and some half-mile further on. We were well pleased with this discovery, but as the glacier front ascended about 1500 ft. in less than a mile we did not look forward to the task of getting our heavy sledge up this steep slope, encumbered as it was with soft deep thawing snow.

On our return to the shoreline down the glacier slope we discovered that it was slightly crevassed in places, though not heavily so. At the foot of the glacier, and a short distance toward our camp, we found a moraine gravel. This was intermixed with a dark marine clay containing numerous remains of serpulae, pecten shells, bryozoa, foraminifera, etc., Mackay also found a perfect specimen of a solitary coral, allied to Deltocyathus, and also a Waldheimia. All these specimens were carefully preserved and brought into camp. While we were collecting these specimens we could hear the roar of many mountain torrents descending the steep granite slopes of the great mountain mass to the south of our branch glacier. Occasionally, too, we heard the boom and crash of an avalanche descending from the high mountain top. Such sounds were strange to our ears, accustomed so long to the almost perfect solitude and silence of the Antarctic, hitherto broken only by the bleating of baby seals and the call of the penguins.

Mawson discovered in another part of the moraine, nearer to our camp, a bright green mineral forming thin crusts on a very pretty quartz and felspar porphyry. These we decided to examine more carefully on the morrow. We were all thoroughly exhausted after the day's work, and Mackay had a rather bad attack of snow blindness. For some time after we got into the sleeping bag, and before we dozed off, we could still hear the intermittent roar of avalanches like the booming of distant artillery.

The following day, December 22, we picked our way with our sledge cautiously amongst the crevasses and over the pressure mounds, the traversing of which gave us some trouble in places, and eventually reached a fairly good track along the ice parallel to the moraine from which we had been collecting the day previous.

As we skirted the foot of the small branch glacier we noticed several small puffs of snow near the top angle of the snow slope which we proposed to escalade. Just as we were pulling our sledge to the foot of this slope the puff of wind with drift snow developed suddenly into a strong blizzard. We pulled in against this with great difficulty for half an hour, then camped at the foot of the slope.

We were able now to economise fuel, as we could bale the water out of these rock pools and streams for making our hoosh, tea, and cocoa. All that night the blizzard raged, and we thought any moment that the tent would be ripped up from top to bottom. It was getting very thin by this time and had already been frequently repaired by Mackay and Mawson.

December 24. About 7 a.m I got up and dug away the drift snow from the lee side of the tent, which was cramping our feet and legs, and found that it was still snowing heavily outside, and blowing hard as well. In the afternoon the blizzard slacked off somewhat, and the drift nearly ceased. We got up accordingly and had a meal. We halved our sledge load, repacked the sledge, and by dint of great exertions dragged it up the steep snow and ice slope to a height of 800 ft. above the sea. This was done in the teeth of a mild but freshening blizzard. The blizzard at last got too strong for us, so that we left the load at the altitude mentioned and returned back to our tent with the empty sledge.

Mackay's eyes, still suffering from the effects of snow blindness, were treated with a solution of thin tabloids (laminae) of sulphate of zinc and cocaine, with the result that his eyes were much better the following day, December 25. We started shortly before noon and commenced dragging up the second part of our load to the accompaniment of the music of murmuring streams. During our interval for lunch, Mawson was able to get some theodolite angles. We had the great satisfaction, when we turned in at 10 p.m. on Christmas Eve, to find that we were above the uncomfortable zone of thaw, and everything around us was once more crisp and dry, though cold. Our spirits, too, mounted with the altitude. We were now over 1200 ft. above sea level.

The following day, December 25, was Christmas Day. When I awoke, I noticed a pile of snow on top of the sleeping bag close to my head. At first, before I was fully awake, I imagined that it was the moisture condensed from Mawson's breath. Then I heard the gentle patter of snowflakes, and, on turning my head in the direction in which the rustling proceeded, saw that the wind had undermined the skirt of our tent, and was blowing the snow in through a small opening it had made. Accordingly, I slipped out and snowed up the skirt again, trampling the snow down firmly. A plateau wind was now blowing with almost blizzard force.

About two hours later we got up, and after some trouble with the primus lamp on account of the wind, had our breakfast, but as the wind was blowing dead against us, we turned into the sleeping bag for a short time. It was nearly noon before the wind died down, and we started off with our sledge, still relaying with half loads, the day being now beautifully clear and sunny. At the 1300 ft. level we started our sledge meter again, having lifted it off the ice while we were going up the steep slope. A little further on we were able to put the whole of our load again on to the sledge and so dispense with further relay work. This, too, was a great blessing.

When we arrived at our spot for camping that night we had the satisfaction of finding that we were over 2000 ft. above sea level, and that we had, in addition to the climbing, travelled that day about four miles. The plateau wind had almost gone, and once more we revelled in being not only high, but dry. Having no other kind of Christmas gift to offer, Mawson and I presented Mackay with some sennegrass for his pipe, his tobacco having long ago given out. We slept soundly that Christmas night.

On December 26 we observed dense dark snow clouds to the north-east, and a little light snow commenced to fall, but fortunately the weather cleared toward the afternoon. Mawson lost one of his blue sweaters off the sledge, but he and Mackay went back some distance and recovered it. Toward the afternoon we found it necessary to cross a number of fairly large crevasses. These were completely snowed over, and although we frequently fell through up to our knees, we had no serious trouble from them on this occasion. Some of them were from twenty to thirty feet in width, and it was fortunate for us that the snow lids were strong enough to carry safely the sledge and ourselves. Mackay suggested, for greater security, fastening the alpine rope around Mawson, who was in the lead, and securing the other end of it to the sledge. The rope was left just slack enough to admit of the strain of hauling being taken by the harness rope, hence Mawson had two strings to his bow in case of being suddenly precipitated into a crevasse. This was a good system, which we always adopted afterward in crossing heavily crevassed ice.

The following day, December 27, we decided to make a small depot of our ski boots (as by this time it appeared we were getting off the glacier ice on to hard snow and névé where we should not require them) and also of all our geological specimens, and about one day's food supply, together with a small quantity of oil – a supply for about two days in one of our oil cans. The following is a list of the provisions: Powdered cheese (enough for two meals), tea (for four meals), twenty-five lumps of sugar, hoosh for one meal, chocolate (for one and a half meals), twelve biscuits.

We also left an empty biscuit tin into which we crammed our ski boots, and our three ice axes, using one of them stuck upright as a staff for a small blue flag to mark the depot. Mawson took some good bearings with the prismatic compass, and we then proceeded on our way. This depot we called the Larsen Depot, as it was close to one of the southern spurs of Mount Larsen.

All eyes were now strained, as we advanced with our sledge, to see whether there was still any formidable range of mountains ahead of us barring our path to the plateau. At one time it seemed as though there was a high range in the dim distance, but a careful examination with the field glasses showed that this appearance was due only to clouds. Our joy and thankfulness were unbounded when we at last realised that apparently there was now a fairly easy ascent of hard névé and snow on to the plateau. That day we sledged a little over ten miles. During the night there was a very strong radiant in the sky from about south-west to north-east, with a movement of altro stratus cloud from north-west to south-east. Therefore, probably, this radiant was due to formation of great rolls of cloud curled over by the antitrade wind as it pressed forward in a south-easterly direction. The rolls of clouds were distinctly curved convexly toward the south-east.

The following day, December 28, we travelled on northwest-ward in thick cloudy weather, at first quite calm. At about 10 a.m. a breeze set in from the sea, spreading westward over the top of Mount Nansen over 8000 ft. above sea level. Above Nansen it met the upper current wind and was obviously deflected by it in a south-easterly direction. Meanwhile, in the direction of the coast the sky was very dark and lowering, and probably snow was falling there. Remarkable pillars of cloud formed over the Mount Larsen group. These were photographed by Mawson. We passed over occasional patches of nearly bare glacier ice, alternating with stretches of hard névé. When we camped that evening we had sledged a little over ten miles, and a keen, cold wind was blowing gently off the high plateau to our west.

The following day, December 28, was clear, calm, and cold, and on December 30 Mounts Larsen and Bellingshausen were disappearing below the horizon, and several mountains were showing up clearly and sharply to the north of us, the principal peaks of which were at first identified by us as Mount New Zealand and Mount Queensland of Captain Scott's chart. Later Mawson concluded that the western of the two at any rate was new and unnamed.

There was still a strong plateau wind. We were now at an altitude of about 4500 ft. Once more, as in winter time, our breath froze into lumps of ice, cementing our Burberry helmets to our beards and mustaches. Our distance travelled was eleven miles, and we were still travelling on an upgrade, being now nearly 5000 ft. above sea level.

December 31. Mawson took a fresh set of magnetic observations. We camped for this purpose at the bottom of a wide undulation in the névé surface. We were disappointed at his announcement that he made out that the Magnetic Pole was further inland than had been originally estimated. What with the observations with the Lloyd-Creak dip circle, and the time occupied in repairing the rents in the tent, we ran ourselves somewhat short of time for our sledging that day, and did not camp until a little before midnight We were still dragging the sledge on an upgrade; the surface was softer and more powdery than before, and the sastrugi heavier. Also we had been obliged to put ourselves on somewhat shorter rations than before, as we had to take one-eighth of our rations out in order to form an emergency food supply in the event of our journey to and from the Magnetic Pole proving longer than we originally anticipated.

That night, about a mile before reaching camp, we sighted to the west of us, much to our surprise, some distinct ice falls. This showed us that the snow desert over which we were travelling had still some kind of creeping movement in it. A skua gull came to visit us this New Year's Eve. He had been following us up for some time in the distance, mistaking us, perhaps, for seals crawling inland to die, as is not infrequently the habit of these animals. We were now about eighty miles inland from the nearest open water. The run for the day was about ten miles. We felt very much exhausted when we turned into our sleeping bag that night.

January 1, 1909 (New Year's Day), was a beautiful calm day with a very light gentle plateau wind, with fairly high temperature. The sky was festooned in the direction of Mount Nansen with delicate wispy cirrus clouds converging in a north-east direction. Mawson took observations for latitude and for magnetic deviation at noon. He made our latitude at noon to be 74° 18'. That night Mawson gave us a grand hoosh and a rich pot of cocoa in celebration of New Year's Day. We all thoroughly enjoyed this meal after our exhausting march.

On January 2 we noticed that the sastrugi were gradually swinging around into a direction a little north of west. The snow was frequently soft in large patches, which made sledging very heavy. We ascended altogether about 290 ft., but we crossed a large number of broad undulations, the troughs of which were from thirty to forty feet below their crests. These undulations considerably increased the work of sledging. We were much exhausted when the time came for camping. We were beginning to suffer, too, from hunger, and would have liked more to drink if we could have afforded it. We talked of what we would have drunk if we had had the chance. Mackay said he would have liked to drink a gallon of buttermilk straight off; Mawson would have preferred a big basin of cream; while I would have chosen several pots of the best coffee with plenty of hot milk.

We were still climbing on January 3, having ascended another 500 ft. It proved the heaviest day's sledging since we reached the plateau. The snow was still softer than on the previous day, and the surface was more undulating than ever, the troughs of the undulations being about fifty feet below the crests. The sastrugi themselves were from two to three feet in height. The crests of the large undulations were usually formed of hard snow, the strong winds having blown any loose material off them. This loose material had accumulated to some depth in the troughs, and hence made the wide patches of soft snow which made our sledge drag so heavily as we crossed them. By dint of great efforts we managed to finish our ten miles for that day.

The next day, January 4, we were pleased to find that there was less upgrade than on the prévious day. We were now at an altitude of over 6000 ft., and found respiration in the cold, rarefied air distinctly trying. It was not that we suffered definitely from mountain sickness, but we felt weaker than usual as the result, no doubt, of the altitude combined with the cold. On the whole the sledging was a little easier today than the preceding day, and again we managed to do our ten miles.

On the morning of January 5 we found the sky thickly overcast, except to the south and the south-east where clear strips of blue were showing. We thought that snow was coming. The weather was perfectly calm, comparatively warm, but the light dull. We could still see the new inland mountain and Mount New Zealand distinctly. The sun was so oppressively hot when it peeped out from behind the clouds that one could feel it burning the skin on one's hands. We sledged ten miles.

January 6. Today the weather was gloriously fine. Bright, warm sunshine with a crisp, cold air in the early morning and the weather almost calm. The pulling was rather heavy during the afternoon; possibly the hot sun may have somewhat softened the surface of the snow. This morning I left off my crampons and put on a new pair of finnesko. These later proved somewhat slippery, and in falling heavily this afternoon over one of the sastrugi I slightly strained some muscles on the inner side of my left leg, just below the knee. This gave me a considerable amount of pain for the rest of the journey. Mackay lost all his stockings and socks off the bamboo pole of the sledge, but was fortunate enough to recover them after walking back over a mile on our tracks.

January 7. We were up at 5 a.m., when the temperature was minus 13°F. We were anxious to arrive at the end of our first five miles in good time for Mawson to get a meridian attitude, and take theodolite angles to the new mountain and Mount New Zealand, which were now almost disappearing from view below the horizon. Mawson made our latitude today 73° 43'. This was one of the coldest days we had as yet experienced on the plateau, the wind blowing from west by north. We all felt the pulling very much today, possibly because it was still slightly uphill, and probably partly on account of mountain lassitude. The distance travelled was ten miles.

Friday, January 8. Today, also, was bitterly cold. The wind blew very fresh for some little time before noon from a direction about west by north, raising much low drift. Our hands were frostbitten several times when packing up the sledge. The cold blizzard continued for the whole day. Mawson's right cheek was frostbitten, and also the top of my nose. The wind was blowing all the time at an angle of about 45° on the port bow of our sledge. We just managed to do our ten miles and were very thankful when the time came for camping.

The following day, January 9, a very cold plateau wind was still blowing, the horizon being hazy with low drift. We were now completely out of sight of any mountain ranges, and were toiling up and down amongst the huge billows of a snow sea. The silence and solitude were most impressive. About 10:30 a.m. a well-marked parhelion, or mock sun, due to floating ice crystals in the air, made its appearance. It had the form of a wide halo with two mock suns at either extremity of the equator of the halo parallel to the horizon and passing through the real sun. Mawson was able to make his magnetic deviation observation with more comfort, as toward noon the wind slackened and the day became gloriously bright and clear. In the afternoon it fell calm.

We were feeling the pinch of hunger somewhat, and as usual our talk under these circumstances turned chiefly on restaurants, and the wonderfully elaborate dinners we would have when we returned to civilisation. Again we accomplished our ten miles, and were now at an altitude of over 7000 ft.

January 10 was also a lovely day, warm and clear; the snow surface was good and we travelled quickly.

January 11. We were up about 7 a.m., the temperature at that time being minus 12°F. It was a cold day, and we had a light wind nearly southerly. Mawson had a touch of snow blindness in his right eye. Both he and Mackay suffered much through the skin of their lips peeling off, leaving the raw flesh exposed. Mawson, particularly, experienced great difficulty every morning in getting his mouth opened, as his lips were firmly glued together by congealed blood.

That day we did eleven miles, the surface being fairly firm, and there being no appreciable general upgrade now, but only long ridged undulations, with sastrugi. We noticed that these sastrugi had now changed direction, and instead of trending from nearly west, or north of west, eastward, now came more from the southeast directed toward the north-west. This warned us that we might anticipate possibly strong head winds on our return journey, as our course at the time was being directed almost north-west, following from time to time the exact bearing of the horizontal magnetic compass. The compass was now very sluggish, in fact the theodolite compass would scarcely work at all. This pleased us a good deal, and at first we all wished more power to it: then amended the sentiment and wished less power to it. The sky was clear, and Mawson got good magnetic meridian observations by means of his very delicately balanced horizontal moving needle in his Brunton transit instrument.

January 12. The sky today was overcast, the night having been calm and cloudy. A few snowflakes and fine ice crystals were falling. We sledged today ten and three-quarter miles.

That evening, after hoosh, Mawson, on carefully analyzing the results set forth in the advance copy of the Discovery Expedition Magnetic Report, decided that although the matter was not expressly so stated, the Magnetic Pole, instead of moving easterly, as it had done in the interval between Sabine's observations in 1841 and the time of the *Discovery* expedition, in 1902, was likely now to be travelling somewhat to the north-west. The results of dip readings taken at intervals earlier in the journey also agreed with this decision. It would be necessary, therefore, to travel farther in that direction than we had anticipated in order to reach our goal. This was extremely disquieting news, for all of us, as we had come almost to the limit of our provisions, after making allowance for enough to take us back on short rations to the coast. In spite of the anxiety of the situation, extreme weariness after sledging enabled us to catch some sleep.

The following morning, January 13, we were up about 6 a.m. A light snow was falling, and fine ice crystals made the sky hazy. There was a light wind blowing from about south-south-east. About 8 a.m. the sun peeped through with promise of a fine day. We had had much discussion during and after breakfast as to our future movements. The change in the position of the Pole necessitated, of course, a change in our plans. Mawson carefully reviewed his observations as to the position of the Magnetic Pole, and decided that in order to reach it we would need to travel for another four days. The horizontally moving needle had now almost ceased to work. We decided to go on for another four days and started our sledging. It was a cold day with a light wind, the temperature at about 10:30 a.m. being minus 6°F. At noon Mawson took a magnetic reading with the Lloyd-Creak dip circle, which was now fifty minutes off the vertical, that is, 89° 10'. At noon the latitude was just about 73° South. That day we sledged thirteen miles.

January 14. The day was gloriously clear and bright with a warm sun. A gentle wind was blowing from about south-south-east, and there was a little cumulus cloud far ahead of us over the horizon. The surface of the snow over which we were sledging was sparkling with large reconstructed ice crystals, about half an inch in width and one-sixteenth of an inch in thickness. These crystals form on this plateau during warm days when the sun's heat leads to a gentle upward streaming of the cold air with a small amount of moisture in it from beneath. Under these influences, combined with the thawing of the surface snow, these large and beautiful ice crystals form rapidly in a single day. The heavy runners of our sledge rustled gently as they crushed the crystals by the thousand. It seemed a sacrilege. Our run today was twelve miles one hundred and fifty yards.

January 15. We were up today at 6 a.m. and found a cold southerly breeze blowing, the temperature being minus 19°F at 6:30 a.m. Mawson got a good latitude determination today, 72° 42'.

At about twenty minutes before true noon Mawson took magnetic observations with the dip circle, and found the angle now only fifteen minutes off the vertical, the dip being 89° 45'. We were very much rejoiced to find that we were now so close to the Magnetic Pole. The observations made by Bernacchi, during the two years of the *Discovery* expedition's sojourn at their winter quarters on Ross Island, showed that the amplitude of daily swing of the magnet was sometimes considerable. The compass, at a distance from the Pole, pointing in a slightly varying direction at different times of the day, indicates that the polar centre executes a daily round of wanderings about its mean position. Mawson considered that we were now practically at the Magnetic Pole, and that if we were to wait for twenty-four hours taking constant observations at this spot the Pole would, probably, during that time, come vertically beneath us. We decided, however, to go on to the spot where he concluded the approximate mean position of the Magnetic Pole would lie. That evening the dip was 89° 48'. The run for the day was fourteen miles.

From the rapid rate at which the dip had been increasing recently, as well as from a comparison of Bernacchi's magnetic observations, Mawson estimated that we were now about thirteen miles distant from the probable mean position of the South Magnetic Pole. He stated that in order to accurately locate the mean position possibly a month of continuous observation would be needed, but that the position he indicated was now as close as we could locate it. We decided accordingly, after discussing the matter fully that night, to make a forced march of thirteen miles to the approximate mean position of the Pole on the following day, put up the flag there, and return eleven miles back on our tracks the same day. Our method of procedure on this journey of twenty-four miles is described in the journal of the following day.

Saturday, January 16. We were up at about 6 a.m., and after breakfast we pulled on our sledge for two miles. We then depoted all our heavy gear and equipment with the exception of the tent, sleeping bag, primus stove, and cooker, and a small quantity of food, all of which we placed on the sledge together with the legs of the dip circle and those of the theodolite to serve as marks. We pulled on for two miles and fixed up the legs of the dip circle to guide us back on our track, the compass moving in the horizontal plane being now useless for keeping us on our course. At two miles further we fixed up the legs of the theodolite, and two miles further put up our tent, and had a light lunch. We then walked five miles in the direction of the Magnetic Pole so as to place us in the mean position calculated for it by Mawson, 72° 25' South latitude, 155° 16' East longitude. Mawson placed his camera so as to focus the whole group, and arranged a trigger which could be released by means of a string held in our hands so as to make the exposure by means of the focal plane shutter. Meanwhile, Mackay and I fixed up the flagpole. We then bared our heads and hoisted the Union Jack at 3:30 p.m. with the words uttered by myself, in conformity with Lieutenant Shackleton's instructions, 'I hereby take possession of this area now containing the Magnetic Pole for the British Empire.' At the same time I fired the trigger of the camera by pulling the string. Thus the group were photographed in the manner shown on the plate. The blurred line connected with my right hand represents the part of the string in focus blown from side to side by the wind. Then we gave three cheers for his Majesty the King.

There was a pretty sky at the time to the north of us with low cumulus clouds, and we speculated at the time as to whether it was possible that an arm of the sea, such as would produce the moisture to form the cumulus, might not be very far distant. In view of our subsequent discovery of a deep indent in the coastline in a southerly direction beyond Cape North, it is possible that the sea at this point is at no very considerable distance.

The temperature at the time we hoisted the flag was exactly 0° F. It was an intense satisfaction and relief to all of us to feel that at last, after so many days of toil, hardship, and danger, we had been able to carry out our leader's instructions, and to fulfil the wish of Sir James Clarke Ross that the South Magnetic Pole should be actually reached, as he had already in 1831 reached the North Magnetic Pole. At the same time we were too utterly weary to be capable of any great amount of exultation. I am sure the feeling that was uppermost in all of us was one of devout and heartfelt thankfulness to the kind Providence which had so far guided our footsteps in safety to that goal. With a fervent 'Thank God' we all did a right about turn, and as quick a march as tired limbs would allow back in the direction of our little green tent in the wilderness of snow.

It was a weary tramp back over the hard and high sastrugi, and we were very thankful when at last we saw a small dark cone, which we knew was our tent, rising from above the distant snow ridges. On reaching the tent we each had a little cocoa, a biscuit and a small lump of chocolate. We then sledged slowly and wearily back, picking up first the legs of the theodolite, then those of the dip circle. We finally reached our depot a little before 10 p.m.

In honour of the event we treated ourselves that night to a hoosh which though modest was larger in volume than usual, and was immensely enjoyed. Mawson repacked the sledge after hoosh time, and we turned into the sleeping bag faint and weary, but happy with the great load of apprehension of possible failure, that had been hanging over us for so many weeks, at last removed from our minds. We all slept soundly after twenty-four miles of travel.

CHAPTER 23

The return march
January 17 to February 5

March of 250 miles back to our depot on Drygalski Glacier: Sugar in the hoosh: A question of route: Ice dongas: Nearing the coast: A barranca: Severe climbing: Our unhappy lot: A double detonator: Mawson in a crevasse: Afternoon tea on board the Nimrod

I called the camp a little before 10 a.m. the following morning. We now discussed the situation and our chances of catching the *Nimrod,* if she came in search of us along the coast in the direction of our depot on the Drygalski Glacier. We had agreed, before we decided to do the extra four days' march to the shifted position of the Magnetic Pole, that on our return journey we would do not less than thirteen miles a day. At the Magnetic Pole we were fully 260 statute miles distant, as the skua flies, from our depot on the Drygalski Glacier. As we had returned eleven of these miles on the day previous, we still had 249 miles to cover. We accordingly decided to try and get back to our Drygalski depot by February 1. This gave us fifteen days. Consequently we would have to average sixteen and two-third miles a day in order to reach the coast in the time specified. This, of course, did not allow for any delay on account of blizzards, and we had seen from the evidence of the large sastrugi that blizzards of great violence must occasionally blow in these quarters, and from the direction of the sastrugi during our last few days' march it was clear that the dominant direction of the blizzard would be exactly in our teeth. The prospect, therefore, of reaching our depot in the specified time did not appear bright. Providentially we had most beautiful and glorious weather for our start on January 17. It remained fine for the whole day, and we were greatly favoured by a light wind which now blew from between north-west and west-north-west – a perfectly fair wind for our journey. In fact the wind changed direction with us. It had helped us by blowing from the south-east, just before we reached the Magnetic Pole, and now it was blowing in the opposite direction, helping us home. That day, in spite of the late start, we sledged sixteen miles.

On January 18 the weather again was fine, and we had a hard day's sledging. Unfortunately Mawson's left leg became very lame and pained him a good deal. Our run for the day was sixteen miles two hundred yards. This was the end of my week's cooking, and we were able to indulge that night in a fairly abundant hoosh, also in very milky and sweet cocoa, and Mackay admitted that he actually felt moderately full after it for the first time since we had left the Drygalski Depot.

The following day, January 19, we boiled the hypsometer at our camp, and found the level to be about 7350 ft. above the sea. The boiling point was 196.75° F. That morning we had quite an unusual diversion. Mawson, who is a bold culinary experimenter, being messman for the week, tried the experiment of surreptitiously introducing a lump of sugar into the pemmican. Mackay detected an unusual flavour in the hoosh, and cross-questioned Mawson severely on the subject. Mawson admitted a lump of sugar. Mackay was thereupon roused to a high pitch of indignation, and stated that this awful state of affairs was the result of going out sledging with 'two foreigners'. We had a great struggle that day to make our sixteen miles, but we just managed it.

Owing to some miscalculation, for which I was responsible, we discovered that we had no tea for this week, our sixth week out, unless we took it out of the tea bag for the seventh week. Accordingly we halved the tea in the seventh week bag, and determined to collect our old tea bags at each of our old camps as we passed them, and boil these bags together with the small pittance of fresh tea. And here I may mention the tastes of the party in the matter of tea somewhat differed. Mackay liked his tea thoroughly well and long boiled, whereas Mawson and I liked it made by just bringing the water to the boil; as soon as we smelt the aroma of tea coming from underneath the outer lid of the cooker we used to shut off the primus lamp immediately and decant the tea into the pannikins. Mackay had always objected to this procedure when we were sledging along the sea ice where water boils at about 212° F; now, however, he had a strong scientific argument in his favour for keeping the pot boiling for a few minutes after the tea had been put in. He pointed out that at our present altitude water boiled at just over 196° F, a temperature which he maintained was insufficient to extract the proper juices and flavour from the tea, unless the boiling was very much prolonged. Mawson, however, averred – on chemical and physical grounds – that with the diminished atmospheric pressure certain virtuous constituents of the tea could be extracted at a lower temperature. The discussion was highly scientific and exhilarating, though not very finite. It was agreed as a compromise to allow the boiling to continue for three or four minutes after the water had come to the boil before the tea was poured out. As in our progress coastward we were continually coming upon more old tea bags at our old camps, and always collected these and did not throw away any that had been used before we soon had quite an imposing collection of muslin bags with old tea leaves, and with the thorough boiling that they now got there was a strong flavour of muslin super added to that of old tea. Nevertheless the drink was nectar.

January 20. We were still able today to follow our sledge tracks, which was a great blessing, the magnetic needle being of so little use to us. We had the wind slightly against us, bringing up a little low drift. Again we made our sixteen mile run, though with great difficulty, for the wind had been blowing freshly all day on our starboard bow.

In view of the good progress that we had made, and after carefully calculating out the provisions left over, Mawson, who was at this time messman, proposed that we should return to nearly full rations, as we were becoming coming much exhausted through insufficient food. This proposal was, of course, hailed with delight.

On January 21 there was a light wind with low temperature, clear sky and hot sun, which combined to consolidate the surface over which we were sledging. By this time Mackay and Mawson's raw lips, which had been cracked and bleeding for about a fortnight previously, were now much better. Mawson's lame leg had also improved. Again we did our sixteen-mile run.

January 22. We were up soon after 7 a.m. It was a clear day with bright sunshine. The wind started soon after 5 a.m., constantly freshening, as it usually did in this part of the plateau, till about 3 p.m. Then it gradually died down by about 10 p.m. The temperature at 7:15 a.m. was minus 20° F, and at this altitude we found the wind very trying. Today we had to sledge over a great deal of pie crust snow, which was very fatiguing. We had since the day before yesterday lost our old sledge tracks. Today we sledged fifteen miles.

January 23. The weather was bright and cold with a light southerly wind. This day was very fatiguing, the sledging being over patches of soft snow and pie crust snow. At the same time we were conscious that although we were sledging up and down wide undulations we were on the whole going downhill, and the new mountain (first seen by Mackay on January 21) was already showing up as an impressive massif. The air was cold and piercing. Mawson's right leg was still painful. That night we were all very much exhausted, and were obliged to allow ourselves fully eight hours' sleep. Our run was sixteen miles.

January 24. Today we had more heavy sledging over a lot of pie crust snow and soft snow. The wind was blowing somewhat against us at about twelve miles an hour, the temperature being minus 4° F in the afternoon. A low drift was sweeping in waves over the snow desert; it was a desolate scene. Later in the day we were cheered by the sight of Mount Baxter.

Toward evening we had some discussion as to whether we were following approximately our old outgoing tracks. Mackay thought we were nearer to the new mountain than before, I thought we were farther south-west, Mawson, who was leading, contended that we were pretty well on our old course. Just then I discovered that we were actually on our old sledge tracks, which showed up plainly for a short distance between the newly formed sastrugi. This spoke volumes for Mawson's skill as a navigator. Distance sledged sixteen miles.

January 25. It was blowing a mild blizzard. We estimated at lunch time that we were about eighty and a half miles distant now from our Mount Larsen Depot. The temperature during the afternoon was minus 3° F. We all felt, as usual, much fatigued after the day's sledging. For the past four or five days we each took an Easton syrup tablet for the last stage but one before reaching camp, and this certainly helped to keep us going. This evening the blizzard died down about 8 p.m., and Mount Nansen was sighted just before we camped.

January 26. We lost our old sledge tracks again today. The weather turned cloudy in the afternoon, and the light was very bad. We now reached a surface of hard marble-like névé, which descended by short steep slopes. We did not at first realise that we were about to descend what we had termed the Ice Falls on the outward journey. Every now and then the sledge would take charge and rush down this marble staircase, bumping very heavily over the steps. Mawson and I frequently came heavy croppers. Mawson put on crampons outside his finnesko to enable him to get a grip of the slippery surface, but my crampons were frozen so hard and so out of shape that I was unable to get them on, so I followed behind and steadied the sledge as it continued bumping its way down the marble steps. At last we reached once more a flattened surface and camped. Our run for the day was fourteen and a half miles.

January 27. This morning we all felt very slack after the night spent in the closely covered sleeping bag, the sky at the time being cloudy. During the morning fine snow fell and the weather was quite thick to the south and east of us. Mawson steered us by the trend of the sastrugi. As the day wore on, the weather cleared up and we had a good view of the new mountain, Mount New Zealand, and Mount Baxter. The pulling at first was very hard, being uphill, but later we had a good run downhill to the spot where we camped for lunch. After lunch we sledged down a still steeper slope, the sledge occasionally taking charge. At this spot Mackay partially fell into a crevasse. Today we were much cheered by the sight at last of Mount Larsen. By the time we reached the spot where we camped that night we had a good clear view of Larsen. The distance travelled was sixteen miles. We were now only about forty miles from our Mount Larsen Depot.

January 28. We turned out of the sleeping bag today at about 6:30 a.m. A blizzard was blowing, and after breakfast we had much difficulty in the cold wind in getting up the mast and sail. Mackay, who usually did the greater part of this work, got his hands rather badly frostbitten before our preparations were completed. We used the thick green canvas floor cloth as a sail; the tent poles served us for a mast, and a piece of bamboo did duty as a yard.

The wind was blowing at, perhaps, about twenty-five miles an hour, and as soon as we started the sledge, it began to travel at such a hot pace that Mackay and Mawson, with their long legs, were kept walking at the top of their speed, while I, with my shorter ones, was kept on a jog trot. Occasionally, in an extra strong puff of wind, the sledge took charge. On one of these occasions it suddenly charged into me from behind, knocked my legs from under me, and nearly juggernauted me. I was quickly rescued from this undignified position under the sledge runners by Mawson and Mackay. We had now arrived at a part of the plateau where the monotonous level or gently undulating surface gave place to sharp descents. It was necessary in these cases for one of us to untoggle from the front of the sledge and to toggle on behind, so as to steer and steady it. About noon, when we were in full career, the bow of the sledge struck one of the high sastrugi obliquely and the sledge was capsized heavily, but fortunately nothing was broken. After righting the sledge, we camped for lunch.

At lunch, with a faint hope of softening the stern heart of our messman for the week – Mackay – and inducing him to give us an extra ration of food, I mildly informed him that it was my birthday. He took the hint and we all fared sumptuously at lunch and dinner that day. The day's run was twenty miles. It had been one of the most fatiguing days that we had as yet experienced, and we were all utterly exhausted when we turned into our sleeping bag at 8:30 p.m.

January 29. We were up at about 8 a.m., and found that the plateau wind was still blowing at a speed of about fifteen miles an hour. After our experience of the preceding day we decided that we would not make sail on the sledge, and as a matter of fact, found that pulling the sledge in the ordinary way was far less wearying than the sailing had proved the preceding day. We pulled on steadily hour after hour, and Mounts Nansen and Larsen grew every moment clearer and larger, and we began to hope that we might be able to reach our depot at Mount Larsen that night. But later in the day, Mawson's sprained leg caused him a good deal of pain, and we had almost decided to camp at a point nearly twenty miles from our preceding camp, when Mackay's sharp eyes sighted, at a distance of about a mile, our little blue flag, tied to the ice axe at our depot. We soon reached the depot, fixed up the tent, had a good hoosh, and turned into the sleeping bag past midnight.

We were up at 9 a.m. on January 30. The day was sunny, but ominous clouds were gathering overhead as well as to the south. After breakfast we collected the material at our depot, chiefly ski boots, ice axes, oil, a little food, and geological specimens, and loaded these on to our sledge. We found that, owing to the alternate thawing and freezing of the snow at our depot, our ski boots were almost filled with solid ice. The work of chipping out this ice proved a slow and tedious job, and we did not get started until about 11 a.m. Soon after we got going we found ourselves for a time in a meshwork of crevasses. These were from a foot up to about twenty feet in width.

After crossing a number of crevasses, we discovered that the wheel of our sledge meter had disappeared. Probably it had got into one of the crevasses, and gone to the bottom. As we were now so close to the end of our journey, the loss of this, which earlier in our travels would have been a serious disaster, was not of much importance. We had run about eight miles before we discovered the loss of our sledge meter wheel. At lunch time Mawson compounded a wonderful new hoosh made out of seal liver, pounded up with a geological hammer, and mixed with crushed biscuit.

We had some discussion as to whether it would be better to descend on to the sea ice by the old track up which we had come, which we termed Backstairs Passage, or make down the main Larsen Glacier to the point where it junctioned with the Drygalski Glacier. Mackay was in favour of the former, Mawson and I of the latter. Had we descended by our old route, we should have had to retrace our steps and become involved in a very arduous uphill piece of sledging necessitating an ascent of at least 1000 to 1500 ft. in a distance of a little over a mile. As subsequent events proved, Mackay was right and we were wrong.

We held on down the main glacier with the imposing cliffs and slopes of dark-red granite and blackish eruptive rock intermixed with it close on our left. Mawson's leg was now so bad that it was only with considerable pain and difficulty that he could proceed, and both Mackay's and my eyes were affected a good deal by snow blindness and were painful. We found as we advanced that at about six miles easterly from our lunch camp, the surface of the Mount Larsen Glacier descended at a very steep angle. Somewhat ahead to the right it was clear that, where it junctioned with the Drygalski Glacier, it was seamed by enormous crevasses and traversed by strong pressure ridges. We held on with our sledge on a course which took us close to the north side of the glacier. At last the descent became so steep that it was with the utmost difficulty that we could hold the sledge back and prevent its charging down the slope. We halted here and Mackay went ahead to reconnoitre. Presently he came back and said that the narrow strip of snow covering the glacier ice, near its contact with the rocky cliffs on our left, was continuous right down to the bottom of the slope, and he thought it was practicable, if we made rope brakes for the runners on our sledge, to lower it down this steep slope in safety. He fixed on some brakes of brown tarred rope by just twisting the rope spirally around the sledge runners. We then cautiously started the sledge down the steepest bit of the slope, all of us ready to let go in case the sledge took charge. The rope brake worked wonders, and it was even necessary to put a slight pull on the sledge in places in order to get it down the steep snow surface. We had left the great crevasses and ice falls near the junction of the Mount Larsen and Drygalski Glaciers a little to our right.

We now found ourselves on an ice surface quite unlike anything which we had hitherto experienced. In the foreground were some small frozen lakes close to the foot of the granite hills; on the far side of the lakes were beautiful glacial moraines. All around the lakes, and for a considerable distance up the ice slopes descending toward them, the surface of the ice was formed of a series of large thin anastomosing curved plates of ice.

After sledging for a short distance over surfaces of this kind, sloping somewhat steeply to the small lakes, we decided to camp on the pale green ice of one of these lakes. Mawson tested this ice and found that it was strong enough to hold, though evidently of no great thickness. We sledged along this lake for a few hundred yards to its north-east end. There was a little snow here which would do for loading the skirt of our tent. By this time the sky was thickly overcast. We fixed up the tent, chopping little holes in the surface of the smooth ice, in which to socket the ends of the tent poles, and while Mackay cooked, Mawson and I snowed the skirt.

This was subsequent to a little reconnoitring which we each did. It was 2 a.m. before we camped on the lake ice, and 4 a.m. before we turned in to our sleeping bag.

January 31. We were up about 11 a.m., having slept soundly after the very exhausting work of our previous day's sledging. During the night it had snowed heavily, there being fully from three to four inches of newly fallen snow covering everything around us, and it was still snowing while we were having breakfast. After breakfast the snow nearly ceased, and we took half the load off our sledge and started with the remainder to try and work a passage out of the ice pressure ridges of the combined Drygalski and Larsen Glaciers on to the smoother sea ice, and eventually on to the Drygalski Ice Barrier. While Mawson and Mackay pulled, I steadied the sledge on the lower side in rounding the steep sidelings. We were still sledging over the leafy or tile ice, which mostly crunched underfoot with a sharp tinkling sound. We skirted the lateral moraine for a distance of over half a mile, following a depression in the ice surface apparently produced by a stream, the outlet of the waters of the small lakes. At one spot Mawson crashed right through into the water beneath, and got wet up to his thighs. In spite of my efforts to keep it on even keel, the sledge frequently capsizes on these steep sidelings. At last, after struggling up and down heavy slopes, and over low-lying areas of rotten ice, which every here and there let us through into the water beneath, we arrived at the foot of an immense ice pressure ridge. It was a romantic looking spot, though at the time we did not exactly appreciate its beauties. To our left was a huge cliff of massive granite rising up steeply to heights of about 2000 ft. The combined pressure of the Drygalski and Mount Larsen Glaciers had forced the glacier ice up into great ridges, trending somewhat obliquely to the coast cliff.

We went back to the tent where we got some hot tea, of which Mawson, particularly, was very glad, as he was somewhat cooled down as the result of his wetting. Then we packed up the remainder of our belongings on the sledge and dragged it down to where we had dumped the half load on the near side of the pressure ridge. Mackay reconnoitred ahead, and found that the large pressure ridge, which appeared to bar our progress toward our depot, gradually came nearer and nearer in to the granite cliff, until it pressed hard against the cliff face. Obviously, then, we were impounded by this huge pressure ridge, and would have to devise some means of getting over it. Taking our ice axes we smoothed a passage across part of the ridge. This proved a very tough piece of work. We then unloaded the sledge and passed each one of our packages over by hand. Finally we dragged the sledge up and hoisted it over and and lowered it down safely on the other side. After this we reloaded the sledge and dragged it for some considerable distance over more of the leafy ice surface alternating with flattish depressions of rotten ice and snow, with water just beneath. We were now troubled, not only by the tile ice surface, but also by small channels with steep banks, apparently eroded by glacial streams which had been flowing, as the result of the thaw, while we were on the Magnetic Pole plateau. We were also worried from time to time as to how to get over the vast number of intersecting crevasses which lay in our path.

Little by little the surface improved as we sledged toward our depot. After lunch, the sledging surface, though still heavy, owing to the newly fallen snow, improved a little, but we soon found our progress barred by what may be termed an ice donga, apparently an old channel formed by a river of thaw water. We encountered three such dongas that afternoon. They were from a few feet up to fifty or a hundred feet or more in width, and from ten to twenty feet deep, and bounded by precipitous or overhanging sides.

After a considerable amount of reconnoitring by Mackay and Mawson, and often making considerable detours with our sledge, we managed to cross them. Our difficulties were increased by the innumerable crevasses and steep ice ridges. Some of these crevasses were open, while others were roofed over with tough snow. We fell into these crevasses from time to time, and on one occasion, Mackay and I fell into the same crevasse simultaneously, he up to his shoulders and I up to my waist. Fortunately we were able, by throwing out our arms, to prevent ourselves from falling right through the snow lid. While we were sledging on through the night amongst this network of crevasses, the sky became heavily overcast, and it commenced to snow. At last we succeeded in getting within less than a mile of the moraine containing the boulders of remarkable sphenediorite, specimens of which we had collected at that spot on our outward journey.

Here we camped and turned into our sleeping bag at 7 a.m. on February 1.

It continued snowing heavily during the day, the fall being about six inches in depth. Mawson's sprained leg pained him a great deal. We estimated that we were now only about sixteen miles, as the skua flies, from our depot on the Drygalski Glacier, but as we had only two days' food left, it became imperative to push on without delay. We started sledging in the thick driving snow on the evening of February 1. The surface was covered with a layer of soft snow, nine inches in thickness, but in the drifts it was, of course, deeper. The work of sledging under these circumstances was excessively laborious and exhausting, and besides it was impossible to keep our proper course while the blizzard lasted. Accordingly, we camped at 8 p.m., and after our evening meal we rolled into our sleeping bag and slid into the dreamless sleep that comes to the worn and weary wanderer.

At 8 a.m. on February 2 we were rejoiced to find the sun shining in a clear sky. We intended making a desperate attempt this day to reach our depot, as we knew that the *Nimrod* would be due – perhaps overdue – by the night. We saw as we looked back that our track of yesterday was about as straight as a corkscrew. Once more we pulled out over the soft snow, and although refreshed somewhat by our good sleep we found the work extremely trying and toilsome. We crossed an ice donga, and about four miles out reached the edge of a second donga. Here we decided to leave everything but our sledge, tent, sleeping bag, cooking apparatus, oil and food, and make a forced march right on to the Drygalski Depot. Accordingly we camped, had tea and two biscuits each, and fixed up our depot, including the Lloyd Creak dip circle, theodolite and legs, geological collection, etc., and marked the spot with a little blue flag tied on to an ice axe.

We now found the sledge, thus lightened, distinctly easier to pull, and after making a slight detour, crossed the donga by a snow bridge. Soon we reached another donga, and successfully crossed it. At three and a half miles further at 8 p.m. we camped again and had a little cheese and biscuit. After this short halt we pulled on again, steering north 8° east magnetic. Mawson occasionally swept the horizon with our excellent field glasses in hopes of sighting our depot. Suddenly he exclaimed that he saw the depot flag distinctly on its ice mound, apparently about seven miles distant, but it was well around on the starboard bow of our sledge on a bearing of south 38° west magnetic. Mackay and I were much excited at Mawson's discovery. Mackay seized the field glasses as soon as Mawson put them down and directed them to the spot indicated, but could see no trace of the flag; then I looked through the glasses with equally negative results. Mawson opined that we must both be snow blind. Then he looked through them again, and at once exclaimed that he could see no trace of the flag now. The horizon seemed to be walloping up and down, just as though it was boiling, evidently the result of a mirage. Mawson, however, was so confident that he had seen the flag when he first looked, that we altered course to south 38° west magnetic, and after we had gone a little over a mile, and reached the top of a slight eminence in the ice surface, we were rejoiced to hear the announcement that he could now see the depot flag distinctly. We kept on sledging for several miles further. At midnight, when the temperature had fallen to zero, I felt that the big toe of my right foot was getting frostbitten. My ski boots had all day been filled with the soft snow and the warmth of my foot had thawed the snow, so that my socks were wet through; and now, since the springing up of the wind and the sudden fall in temperature, the water in the socks had turned to ice. So we halted, got up the tent, started the primus and prepared for a midnight meal, while, with Mawson's assistance, I got off my frozen ski boots and socks and restored the circulation in my toe, and put on some socks less icy than those I had just taken off.

We were much refreshed by our supper, and then started off again, thinking that at last we should reach our depot, or at all events, the small inlet a little over a mile distant from it, but 'the best laid schemes of mice and men gang aft agley.' There was an ominous white streak ahead of us with a dark streak just behind it, and we soon saw that this was due to a ravine or barranca in the snow and ice surface interposing itself between ourselves and our depot. We soon reached the near cliff of the barranca.

The barranca was about two hundred yards in width, and from thirty to forty feet deep. It was bound by a vertical cliff or very steeply inclined slope on the near side, the north-west side, and by an overhanging cliff festooned with stalactites on the south-east side. To the north-east a strip of dark sea-water was visible between the walls of the barranca, which evidently communicated by a long narrow channel with the ocean outside, some three miles distant. Inland, the barranca extended for many miles as far as the eye could reach. The bottom of the barranca immediately beneath us was floored with sea ice covered with a few inches of snow. This ice was traversed by large tide cracks, and we were much excited to see that there were a number of seals and Emperor penguins dotted over the ice floor. We determined to try and cross the barranca. We looked up and down the near cliff for a practicable spot where we could let down our sledge, and soon found a suitable slope, a little to the north-east of us, formed by a steep snow drift. We sledged on to this spot, and making fast the alpine rope to the bow of the sledge, lowered it cautiously, stern first, to the bottom. The oil cans in the rear of the sledge were rattled up somewhat when it struck bottom, but no harm was done. At the bottom we had some trouble in getting the sledge over the gaping tide cracks, some ten to fifteen feet deep and three to five feet wide.

Arrived at the middle of the floor of the barranca, Mackay killed two Emperor penguins, and took their breasts and livers to replenish our exhausted larder. Meanwhile, Mawson crossed to the far side of the floor of the barranca on the lookout for a possible spot where we might swarm up. I joined him a few minutes later, and as I was feeling much exhausted after the continuous forced marches back from the Magnetic Pole, asked him to take over the leadership of the expedition. I considered that under the circumstances I was justified in taking this step. We had accomplished the work assigned to us by our leader, having reached the Magnetic Pole. We were within two or three miles of our Drygalski Depot, and although the only food left there was two days' supply of broken biscuits with a little cheese, we had a good prospect of meat supply, as the barranca abounded in seals and penguins, so that for the present we had no reason to apprehend the danger of starvation. On the other hand, as regards our ultimate personal safety, our position was somewhat critical. We were not even certain that the *Nimrod* had arrived at all in Ross Sea that season, though we thought it, of course, very probable that she had. In the next case, on the assumption that she had arrived, it was very possible that in view of the great difficulties of making a thorough search along the two hundred miles of coast, at any part of which we might have been camped – difficulties arising from heavy belts of pack ice and icebergs, as well as from the deeply indented character of that bold and rugged coast – it was quite possible that the *Nimrod* would miss sighting our depot flags altogether. In the event of the *Nimrod* not appearing within a few days, it would be necessary to take immediate and strenuous action with a view either to wintering at the spot, or with a view to an attempt to sledge back around the great mountain massifs and over the many steeply crevassed glaciers for over two hundred miles to our winter quarters at Cape Royds. Even now, in the event of some immediate strenuous action being necessary, if the *Nimrod* were to suddenly appear at some point along the coast, I thought it would be best for Mawson, who was less physically exhausted than myself, to be in charge. He had, throughout the whole journey, shown excellent capacity for leadership, fully justi-fying the opinion held of him by Lieutenant Shackleton when providing in my instructions that in event of anything happening to myself Mawson was to assume the leadership. When I spoke to him on the subject, he at first demurred, but finally said that he would act for a time, and would think the matter over at his leisure before definitely deciding to become permanently the leader. I offered to give him authority in writing as leader, but this he declined to receive.

Meanwhile, the examination of the cliff face on the south-east side of the barranca showed that there was one very difficult but apparently possible means of ascent. We returned to where we had left Mackay, and then we three dragged the sledge around to the edge of a rather formidable tide crack, behind which lay the mound of snow up which we hoped to climb; our idea being to unpack our sledge, drag it to the top of this steep mound, and, rearing it on end at the top of the mound, use it as a ladder for scaling the overhanging cliff above. Mackay managed to cross the tide crack, using the bamboo poles of our tent as a bridge, and after some difficulty, reached the top of the snow mound under the overhanging cliff. Much to our disappointment, however, he discovered that the mound was formed of very soft snow, his ice axe sinking in to the whole depth of the handle directly he placed it on top of the mound. It was obvious that as our sledge would sink in to at least an equal depth, the top of it would then be too short to enable any of us to scale the overhanging cliff by its means. We were, therefore, reluctantly compelled to drag our sledge back again over the tide cracks to the north-west side of the barranca down which we had previously lowered our sledge. We then discovered that, as in classical times, while the descent to Avernus was easy, it was difficult and toilsome to retrace one's steps. With Mawson ahead with the ice axe and towing rope, and Mackay and I on either side of the sledge in the rear, we managed by pulling and pushing together to force the sledge up a few inches at a time. At each short halt, Mawson would stick in the ice axe, take a turn of the leading rope around it, and support the sledge in this way for a brief interval while we all got our breath. At last the forty feet of steep slope was successfully negotiated, and we found ourselves once more on the level plain at the top of the barranca, but, of course, on the wrong side in reference to our depot. As we were within three miles of the open sea we thought it would be safe to camp here, as had the *Nimrod* sighted our depot flag and stood in to the coast, we could easily have hurried down to the entrance of the inlet and made signals to her.

We had now been up since 8 a.m. on the previous day, and were very thankful to be able to enter our tent, and have a meal off a stew of minced penguin liver. We then turned into the sleeping bag at about 7 a.m. Just about a quarter of an hour after we had turned in, as we learned later, the *Nimrod* must have passed, bound north toward Mount Melbourne, within three miles of the ice cliff on which our tent was now situated. Owing, however, to a light wind with snow drift, she was unable to sight either our depot flag or tent.

February 3. After sleeping in the bag from 7 a.m. until 11 a.m. we got up and had breakfast, packed our sledge, and started along the north bank of the snow canyon. The snow and ice at the bottom were dotted with basking seals and moulting Emperor penguins. Fully a hundred seals could be counted in places in a distance of as many yards along the canyon. At about one mile from the camp we reached a small branch canyon, which we had to head off by turning to our right. We now proceeded about one and a half miles further along the edge of the main canyon, and in our then tired and weak state were much dispirited to find that it still trended inland for a considerable distance. We now halted by the sledge while Mackay went ahead to try and find a crossing, and presently Mawson and I were rejoiced to hear him shout that he had discovered a snow bridge across the canyon. Presently he rejoined us, and together we pulled the sledge to the head of the snow bridge. It was a romantic spot. A large slice of the snow or névé cliff had fallen obliquely across the canyon, and its surface had then been raised and partially levelled up with soft drift snow. There was a crevasse at both the near and far ends of the bridge, and the middle was sunk a good deal below the abutments. Stepping over the crevasse at the near end, we launched the sledge with a run down to the centre of the bridge, then struggled up the steep slope facing us, Mackay steadying the sledge from falling off the narrow causeway, while we all three pulled for all we were worth. In another minute or two we were safely across with our sledge, thankful that we had now surmounted the last obstacle that intervened between us and our depot.

While heading for the depot we sighted an Emperor penguin close to our track. Mackay quickly slew him, and took his flesh and liver for our cooking pot. Two miles further on we camped. Mawson minced the Emperor's flesh and liver, and after adding a little snow, I boiled it over our primus so as to make one and a half pots of soupy mincemeat for each of us. This was the most satisfying meal we had had for many a long day. After lunch we sledged on for over one and a half miles further toward the depot, and at about 10:30 p.m. reached an ice mound on the south side of the inlet in which the snow canyon terminated seawards. This camping spot was a little over a mile distant from our depot. We were now all thoroughly exhausted and decided to camp. The spot we had selected seemed specially suitable, as from the adjacent ice mound we could get a good view of the ocean beyond the Drygalski Barrier. While Mawson and I got up the tent, Mackay went to kill a seal at the shore of the inlet. He soon returned with plenty of seal meat and liver. He said that he had found two young seals, and had killed one of them; that they had both behaved in a most unusual manner, scuttling away quickly and actively at his approach, instead of waiting without moving, as did most of the Weddell seals, of which we had hitherto had experience. We discovered later that these two seals belonged to the comparatively rare variety known as Ross seal. After a delicious meal of seal blubber, blood, and oil, with fried meal and liver, cooked by Mawson, Mawson and I turned into the sleeping bag, leaving Mackay to take the first of our four-hour watches on the lookout for the *Nimrod*. During his watch he walked up to our depot and dug out our biscuit tin, which had served us as a blubber lamp and cooker, together with the cut-down paraffin tin which we had used as a frying pan. Both these he carried down to our tent. There he lit the blubber lamp just outside the tent and cooked some penguin meat, regaling himself at intervals, during his four hours' watch, with dainty morsels from the savoury dish. When he called me up at 4 a.m. I found that he had thoughtfully put into the frying pan a junk of Emperor's breast, weighing about two pounds, for me to toy with during my watch. A chilly wind was blowing off the plateau and I was truly thankful for an occasional nibble at the hot penguin meat. After cooking some more penguin meat I called up Mawson soon after 8 a.m. on February 4, and immediately afterward turned into the bag, and at once dropped off sound asleep.

Mawson did not call Mackay and myself until after 2 p.m. We at once rolled up the sleeping bag, and Mawson cooked a generous meal of seal and penguin meat and blubber, while Mackay made a thin soupy broth on the primus. Meanwhile, I went on to the ice mound with the field glasses, but could see nothing in the way of a ship to seaward and returned to the tent. We all thoroughly enjoyed our liberal repast, and particularly relished the seal's blood, gravy, and seal oil.

After the meal we discussed our future plans. We decided that we had better move the tent that afternoon up to our old depot, where it would be a conspicuous object from the sea, and where, too, we could command a more extensive view of the ocean. We also talked over what we had best do in the event of the *Nimrod* not turning up, and decided that we ought to attempt to sledge overland to Hut Point, keeping ourselves alive on the way, as best we might, with seal meat. It must be admitted that the prospect of tackling two hundred miles of coast, formed largely of steep rocky foreshores, alternating with heavily crevassed glacier ice, was not a very bright one. We also discussed the date at which we ought to start trekking southward. Mackay thought we ought to commence making our preparations at once, and that unless the *Nimrod* arrived within a few days we ought to start down the coast with our sledge, tent, sleeping bag, cooker, and seal meat, leaving a note at the depot for the *Nimrod*, in case she should arrive later, asking her to look out for us along the coast, and if she couldn't sight us, to lay depots of food and oil for us at certain specified spots. He considered that by this method we could make sure of beginning the long journey in a sound state of health and, if fortunate, might reach Hut Point before the beginning of the equinoctial gales in March. Mawson and I, on the other hand, thought that we ought to wait on at our present camp until late in February.

From whatever point of view we looked at it, our present lot was not a happy one. The possibility of a long wait in the gloomy region of the Drygalski Glacier, with its frequent heavy snows at this season of the year, and leaden sky vaulted over the dark sea, was not pleasing to contemplate. Still less cheerful was the prospect of a long, tedious, and dangerous sledge journey toward Hut Point. Even the diet of seal and penguin, just for the moment so nice, largely because novel, would soon savour of *toujours perdrix*.

Dispirited by forebodings of much toil and trouble, we were just preparing to set our weary limbs in motion to pack up our belongings for the short trek up to the depot, when Bang! went something, seemingly close to the door of our tent; the sound thrilled us; in another instant the air reverberated with a big boom! much louder than the first sound. Mawson gave tongue first, roaring out, 'A gun from the ship!' and dived for the tent door. As the latter was narrow and funnel shaped there was for the moment some congestion of traffic. I dashed my head forward to where I saw a small opening, only in time to receive a few kicks from the departing Mawson. Just as I was recovering my equilibrium, Mackay made a wild charge, rode me down, and trampled over my prostrate body. When at length I struggled to my feet, Mawson had got a lead of a hundred yards and Mackay of about fifty. 'Bring something to wave,' shouted Mawson, and I rushed back to the tent and seized Mackay's rucksack. As I ran forward this time, what a sight met my gaze. There was the dear old *Nimrod*, not a quarter of a mile away, steaming straight toward us up the inlet, her bows just rounding the entrance. At the sight of the three of us running frantically to meet the ship, hearty ringing cheers burst forth from all on board. How those cheers stirred every fibre of one's being! It would be hard, indeed, for anyone, not situated as we had been, to realise the sudden revulsion of our feelings. In a moment, as dramatic as it was heavenly, we seemed to have passed from death into life. My first feelings were of intense relief and joy; then of fervent gratitude to the kind Providence which had so mercifully led our friends to our deliverance.

A sudden shout from Mackay called me back to earth, 'Mawson's fallen into a deep crevasse. Look out, it's just in front of you!' I then saw that Mackay was kneeling on the snow near the edge of a small oblong sapphire blue hole in the névé. 'Are you all right, Mawson?' he sang out, and from the depth came up the welcome word, 'Yes'. Mackay then told me that Mawson was about twenty feet down the crevasse. We decided to try and pull him up with the sledge harness, and hurried back to the sledge, untoggled the harness, ran back with it to the crevasse, and let one end down to Mawson. We found, however, that our combined strength was insufficient to pull him up, and that there was a risk, too, of the snow lid at the surface falling in on Mawson, if weight was put upon it, unless it was strengthened with some planking. Accordingly, we gave up the attempt to haul Mawson up, and while I remained at the crevasse holding one end of the sledge harness Mackay hurried off for help to the Nimrod, which was now berthing alongside the south wall of the inlet, about two hundred yards distant. Mackay shouted to those on board, 'Mawson has fallen down a crevasse, and we got to the Magnetic Pole.' The accident had taken place so suddenly that those on board had not realised in the least what had happened. A clear, firm, cheery voice, that was strange to me, was now heard issuing prompt orders for a rescue party. Almost in less time than it takes to write it, officers and sailors were swarming over the bows of the Nimrod, and dropping on to the ice barrier beneath. I called down to Mawson that help was at hand. He said that he was quite comfortable at present; that there was sea water at the bottom of the crevasse, but that he had been able to sustain himself a couple of feet above it on the small ledge that had arrested his fall. Meanwhile, the rescue party, headed by the first officer of the *Nimrod*, J. K. Davis, had arrived on the scene. The crevasse was bridged with a suitable piece of sawn timber, and Davis, with that spirit of thoroughness which characterises all his work, promptly had himself lowered down the crevasse. On reaching the bottom he transferred the rope by which he had been lowered to Mawson, and with a long pull and a strong pull and a pull altogether, the company of the *Nimrod* soon had Mawson safe on top, none the worse for the accident with an exception that his back was slightly bruised. As soon as the rope was cast free from Mawson, it was let down again for Davis, and presently he, too, was safely on top.

And now we had a moment of leisure to see who constituted the rescue party. There were the dear old faces so well known on our voyage together the previous year, and interspersed with them were a few new faces. Here were our old comrades, Armytage and Brocklehurst, Dr Michell, Harbourd (the officer who – as we learned later – had sighted our depot flag), our good stewards Ansell and Ellis, the genial boatswain Cheetham, Paton, and a number of others. What a joyous grasping of hands and hearty all-around welcoming followed. Foremost among them all to welcome us was Captain Evans, who had commanded the S.S. *Koonya,* which towed the *Nimrod* from Lyttleton to beyond the Antarctic Circle, and it goes without saying that the fact that the *Nimrod* was now in the command of a master of such experience, so well and favourably known in the shipping world of New Zealand and Australia, gave us the greatest satisfaction. He hastened to assure me of the safety and good health of my wife and family. While willing hands packed up our sledge, tent, and other belongings, Captain Evans walked with us to the rope ladder hanging over the bows of the *Nimrod*.

Quickly as all this had taken place, Mackay had already found time to secure a pipe and some tobacco from one of our crew, and was now puffing away to his heart's content. We were soon all on the deck of the *Nimrod* once more, and were immediately stood up in a row to be photographed. As soon as the cameras had worked their wicked will upon us, for we were a sorry sight, our friends hurried us off for afternoon tea. After our one hundred and twenty-two days of hard toil over the sea ice of the coast and the great snow desert of the hinterland, the little ship seemed to us as luxurious as an ocean liner. To find oneself seated once more in a comfortable chair, and to be served with new-made bread, fresh butter, cake, and tea, was Elysium.

We heard of the narrow escape of Armytage, Priestley, and Brocklehurst, when they were being carried out to sea, with only two days' provisions, on a small ice floe surrounded by killer whales; and how, just after the momentary grounding of the floe, they were all just able to leap ashore at a spot where they were picked up later by the *Nimrod*. We also heard the extra-ordinary adventures and escape of Mackintosh and MacGillan in their forced march overland, without tent or sleeping bag, from Mount Bird to Cape Royds; of the departure of the supporting party to meet the southern party; and, in short, of all the doings at Cape Royds and on the *Nimrod* since we had last heard any news. Pleasantly the buzz of our friends' voices blended itself with the gentle fizzing of steam from the *Nimrod*'s boiler, and surely since the days of John Gilpin 'were never folk so glad' as were we three.

After afternoon tea came the joy of reading the home letters, and finding that the news was good. Later we three had a novel experience, the first real wash for over four months. After much diligent work with hot water, soap, and towel, some of the outer casing of dirt was removed, and bits of our real selves began to show through the covering of seal oil and soot. Dinner followed at 6 p.m., and it is scarcely necessary to add that, with our raging appetites and all the new types of dainty food around us, we overate ourselves. This did not prevent us from partaking liberally of hot cocoa and gingerbread biscuits before turning in at 10 p.m. None but those whose bed for months has been on snow and ice can realise the luxury of a real bunk, blankets, and pillow, in a snug little cabin. A few minutes' happy reverie preceded sound sleep. At last our toilsome march was over, the work that had been given us to do was done, and done just in the nick of time; the safety of those nearest and dearest to us was assured, and we could now lay down our weary limbs to rest.

Under Providence one felt one owed one's life to the patient and thorough search, sound judgment, and fine seamanship of Captain Evans, and the devotion to duty of his officers and crew:

and no pen can describe how that night one's heart overflowed with thankfulness for all the blessings of that day. One's last thought in the twilight that comes between wakefulness and sleep is expressed in the words of our favourite record on the gramophone, the hymn so grandly sung by Evan Williams:

> So long Thy power hath blest me, sure
> it still will lead me on.'

CHAPTER 24

A brief retrospect
Total distance travelled: Travelling over sea ice: The Drygalski
Glacier: Backstairs passage: Results of journey: How to spend
a week at the Magnetic Pole

If one may be permitted to take a brief retrospect of our journey, the following considerations present themselves: the total distance travelled from Cape Royds to the Magnetic Pole and back to our depot on the Drygalski Glacier was about 1260 miles. Of this, 740 miles was relay work, and we dragged a weight of, at first, a little over half a ton, and finally somewhat under half a ton for the whole of this distance. For the remaining 520 miles from the Drygalski Depot to the Magnetic Pole and back we dragged a weight, at first, of 670 lb., but this finally became reduced to about 450 lb., owing to consumption of food and oil, by the time that we returned to our depot.

We were absent on our sledge journey for one hundred and twenty-two days, of which five days were spent in our tent during heavy blizzards, and five days partly in experimenting in cooking with blubber and partly in preparing supplies of seal meat for the journey from the sea ice over the high plateau, and three days in addition were taken up in reconnoitring, taking magnetic observations, etc. We therefore covered this distance of 1260 miles in 109 travelling days, an average of about eleven and a half miles a day.

We had laid two depots before our final start, but as these were distant only ten miles and fifteen miles respectively from our winter quarters, they did not materially help us. We had no supporting party, and with the exception of help from the motor-car in laying out these short depots, we pulled the sledges for the whole distance without assistance except, on rare occasions, from the wind.

The travelling over the sea ice was at first pretty good, but from Cape Bernacchi to the Nordenskjold Ice Barrier we were much hampered by screwed pack ice with accompanying high and hard snow ridges. Toward the latter part of October and during November and part of December the thawing surface of saline snow, clogging and otherwise impeding our runners, made the work of sledging extremely laborious. Moreover, on the sea ice – especially toward the last part of our journey over it – we had ever present the risk of a blizzard breaking the ice up suddenly all around us, and drifting us out to sea. There can be no doubt, in view of the wide lanes of open water in the sea ice on the south side of the Drygalski Glacier, when we reached it on November 30, that we got to *glacies firma* only in the nick of time.

Then there was the formidable obstacle of the Drygalski Glacier, with its wide and deep chasms, its steep ridges and crevasses, the passage of this glacier proving so difficult that, although only a little over twenty miles in width, it took us a fortnight to get across. On the far side of the Drygalski was the open sea forcing us to travel shoreward over the glacier surface. Then had come the difficult task of pioneering a way up to the high plateau – the attempt to force a passage up the Mount Nansen Glacier – our narrow escapes from having our sledge engulfed in crevasses – the heavy blizzard with deep new fallen snow and then our retreat from that region of high pressure ridges and crevasse entanglements – our abandonment of the proposed route up the snout of the Bellingshausen Glacier, and finally our successful ascent up the small tributary glacier, the 'backstairs passage', to the south of Mount Larsen.

On the high plateau were: the difficulty of respiration, biting winds with low temperatures, difficult sledging – sometimes against blizzards – over broad undulations and high sastrugi, the cracking of our lips, fingers, and feet, exhaustion from insufficient rations, disappointment at finding that the Magnetic Pole had shifted further inland than the position previously assigned to it. Then, after we had just succeeded by dint of great efforts in reaching the Pole of verticity, came the necessity for forced marches, with our sledge, of from sixteen to twenty miles a day in order to reach the coast with any reasonable prospect of our being picked up by the *Nimrod*.

Then came our choice of the difficult route down the snout of the Bellingshausen Glacier, and our consequent difficulties in surmounting the ice pressure ridges; then the difficulty of sledging over the 'tile ice' surface, the opposing ice barrancas formed by the thaw water while we were on the high plateau; the final heavy snow blizzard; our loss of direction when sledging in bad light and falling snow, and finally our arrest by the deep barranca of what afterward was known as Relief Inlet.

But ours were not the only, nor the greatest, difficulties connected with our journey. There were many disappointments, dangers, and hardships for the captain, officers, and crew of the *Nimrod* in their search for us along that two hundred miles of desolate and, for the great part, inaccessible coastline. How often black spots ashore, proving on nearer view to be seals or penguins, had been mistaken for depot flags; how often the glint of sunlight off brightly reflecting facets of ice had been thought to be 'helios', only the disappointed ones can tell; how often, too, the ship was all but aground, at other times all but beset in the ice pack in the efforts to get a clearer view of the shoreline in order to discover our depot! This is a tale that the brave men who risked their lives to save ours will scorn to tell, but it is nevertheless true.

As the result of our journey to the Magnetic Pole and back, Mawson was able to join up in his continuous triangulation survey, Mount Erebus with Mount Melbourne, and to show with approximate accuracy the outline of the coastline, and the position and height of several new mountains. He and I obtained geological collections, sketches, and notes – especially on glacial geology – along the coastline, and he also took a series of photographs; while Mackay determined our altitudes on the plateau by means of the hypsometer. Mawson also made magnetic determinations, and I was able to gather some meteorological information.

Unfortunately the time available during our journey was too short for detailed magnetic, geological, or meteorological observations. Nevertheless, we trust that the information obtained has justified the journey. At all events we have pioneered a route to the Magnetic Pole, and we hope that the path thus found will prove of use to future observers.

It is easy, of course, to be wise after the event, but there is no doubt that had we known that there was going to be an abundance of seals all along the coast, and had we had an efficient team of dogs, we could have accomplished our journey in probably half the time that it actually occupied. Future expeditions to the South Magnetic Pole would probably do well to land a strong and well-equipped party, either at Relief Inlet or, better, as near to Backstairs Passage as the ship can be taken, and as early in December as the state of the sea ice makes navigation possible. A party of three, with a supporting party also of three, with good dog teams and plenty of fresh seal meat, could travel together for about seventy miles inland; then the supporting party might diverge and ascend Mount Nansen from its inland extremity. The other party, meanwhile, might proceed to the Magnetic Pole at not less than fifteen miles a day. This should admit of their spending from a week to a fortnight at the Pole, and they should then be able to return to the coast early in February. Meanwhile, there would be plenty of scope for a third party to explore the foothills of Mount Larsen and Mount Nansen, search and map their wonderful moraines, and examine the deeply indented rocky coastline from Nansen to the – as yet untrodden – volcano Mount Melbourne.

CHAPTER 25

All aboard: the return to New Zealand

*An oar breaks: Disaster averted: Last view of winter quarters: Supplies
left at Cape Royds: New coastline: Anchored at mouth of Lord's River,
Stewart Island, March 22: Arrived Lyttelton, March 25, 1909*

The *Nimrod*, with the members of the northern party aboard, got
back to the winter quarters on February 11 and landed Mawson.
The hut party at this period consisted of Murray, Priestley,
Mawson, Day, and Roberts. No news had been heard of the
southern party, and the depot party, commanded by Joyce, was
still out. The ship lay under Glacier Tongue most of the time,
making occasional visits to Hut Point in case some of the men
should have returned. On February 20 it was found that the depot
party had reached Hut Point, and had not seen the southern party.
The temperature was becoming lower, and the blizzards were
more frequent.

The instructions left by me had provided that if we had not
returned by February 25, a party was to be landed at Hut Point,
with a team of dogs, and on March 1 a search party was to go
south. In connection with the landing party, Murray showed
Captain Evans my full instructions that the party was to be landed
on the 25th, and on this being understood the *Nimrod* left Cape
Royds on the 21st with the party, whilst Murray remained in
charge at Cape Royds, which was now cut off by sea from Hut
Point. Murray was in no way responsible for the failure of that
party to be landed, and this is a point I did not make clear in the
first edition of my book; it is therefore due to Murray to make this
explanation. All arrangements being completed, most of the members of the expedition then on board went ashore at Cape Royds to
get the last of their property packed ready for departure. The ship
was lying under Glacier Tongue when I arrived at Hut Point with
Wild on February 28 and after I had been landed with the relief

party in order to bring in Adams and Marshall, it proceeded to Cape Royds in order to take on board the remaining members of the shore party and some specimens and stores.

The *Nimrod* anchored a short distance from the shore, and two boats were launched. The only spot convenient for embarkation near the ship's anchorage was at a low ice cliff in Backdoor Bay. Everything had to be lowered by ropes over the cliff into the boats. Some hours were spent in taking on board the last of the collections, the private property, and various stores.

A stiff breeze was blowing, making work with the boats difficult, but by 6 a.m. on March 2 there remained to be taken on board only the men and dogs. The operation of lowering the dogs one by one into the boats was necessarily slow, and while it was in progress the wind freshened to blizzard force, and the sea began to run dangerously. The waves had deeply undercut the ice cliff, leaving a projecting shelf. One boat, in charge of Davis, succeeded in reaching the ship, but a second boat, commanded by Harbourd, was less fortunate. It was heavily loaded with twelve men and a number of dogs, and before it had proceeded many yards from the shore an oar broke. The *Nimrod* was forced to slip her moorings and steam out of the bay, as the storm had become so severe that she was in danger of dragging her anchors and going on the rocks. An attempt to float a buoy to the boat was not successful, and for some time Harbourd and the men with him were in danger. They could not get out of the bay owing to the force of the sea, and the projecting shelf of ice threatened disaster if they approached the shore. The flying spray had encased the men in ice, and their hands were numb and half frozen. At the end of an hour they managed to make fast to a line stretched from an anchor a few yards from the cliff, the men who had remained on shore pulling this line taut. The position was still dangerous, but all the men and dogs were hauled up the slippery ice face into safety before the boat sank. Hot drinks were soon ready in the hut, and the men dried their clothes as best they could before the fire. Nearly all the bedding had been sent on board, and the temperature was low, but they were thankful to have escaped with their lives.

The weather was bitter on the following morning (March 3), and the *Nimrod,* which had been sheltering under Glacier Tongue, came back to Cape Royds. A heavy sea was still running, but a new landing place was selected in the shelter of the cape, and all the men and dogs were got aboard. The ship went back to the Glacier Tongue anchorage to wait for the relief party.

About ten o'clock that night Mackintosh was walking the deck engaged in conversation with some other members of the expedition. Suddenly he became excited and said, 'I feel that Shackleton has arrived at Hut Point.' He was very anxious that the ship should go up to the Point, but nobody gave much attention to him. Then Dunlop advised him to go up to the crow's nest if he was sure about it, and look for a signal. Mackintosh went aloft, and immediately saw our flare at Hut Point. The ship at once left for Hut Point, reaching it at midnight, and by 2 a.m. on March 4 the entire expedition was safe on board.

There was now no time to be lost if we were to attempt to complete our work. The season was far advanced, and the condition of the ice was a matter for anxiety, but I was most anxious to undertake exploration with the ship to the westward, toward Adelie Land, with the idea of mapping the coastline in that direc-tion. As soon as all the members of the expedition were on board the *Nimrod,* therefore, I gave orders to steam north, and in a very short time we were under way. It was evident that the sea in our neighbourhood would be frozen over before many hours had passed, and although I had foreseen the possibility of having to spend a second winter in the Antarctic when making my arrangements, we were all very much disinclined to face the long wait if it could be avoided. I wished first to round Cape Armitage and pick up the geological specimens and gear that had been left at Pram Point, but there was heavy ice coming out from the south, and this meant imminent risk of the ship being caught and perhaps 'nipped'. I decided to go into shelter under Glacier Tongue in the little inlet on the north side for a few hours, in the hope that the southern wind, that was bringing out the ice, would cease and that we would then be able to return and secure the specimens and gear. This was about two o'clock on the morning of March 4, and we members of the southern party turned in for a much-needed rest.

At eight o'clock on the morning of the 4th we again went down the sound. Young ice was forming over the sea, which was now calm, the wind having entirely dropped, and it was evident that we must be very quick if we were to escape that year. We brought the *Nimrod* right alongside the pressure ice at Pram Point, and I pointed out the little depot on the hillside. Mackintosh at once went off with a party of men to bring the gear and specimens down, while another party went out to the seal rookery to see if they could find a peculiar seal that we had noticed on our way to the hut on the previous night. The seal was either a new species or the female of the Ross seal. It was a small animal, about four feet six inches long, with a broad white band from its throat right down to its tail on the underside. If we had been equipped with knives on the previous night we would have dispatched it, but we had no knives and were, moreover, very tired, and we therefore left it. The search for the seal proved fruitless, and as the sea was freezing over behind us I ordered all the men on board directly the stuff from the depot had been got on to the deck, and the *Nimrod* once more steamed north. The breeze soon began to freshen, and it was blowing hard from the south when we passed the winter quarters at Cape Royds. We all turned out to give three cheers and to take a last look at the place where we had spent so many happy days. The hut was not exactly a palatial residence, and during our period of residence in it we had suffered many discomforts, not to say hardships, but, on the other hand, it had been our home for a year that would always live in our memories. We had been a very happy little party within its walls, and often when we were far away from even its measure of civilisation it had been the Mecca of all our hopes and dreams. We watched the little hut fade away in the distance with feelings almost of sadness, and there were few men aboard who did not cherish a hope that some day they would once more live strenuous days under the shadow of mighty Erebus.

I left at the winter quarters on Cape Royds a supply of stores sufficient to last fifteen men for one year. The vicissitudes of life in the Antarctic are such that such a supply might prove of the greatest value to some future expedition. The hut was locked up and the key hung up outside where it would be easily found, and we readjusted the lashing of the hut so that it might be able to withstand the attacks of the blizzards during the years to come. Inside the hut I left a letter stating what had been accomplished by the expedition, and giving some other information that might be useful to a future party of explorers. The stores left in the hut included oil, flour, jams, dried vegetables, biscuits, pemmican, plasmon, matches, and various tinned meats, as well as tea, cocoa, and necessary articles of equipment. If any party has to make use of our hut in the future, it will find there everything required to sustain life.

The wind was still freshening as we went north under steam and sail on March 4, and it was fortunate for us that this was so, for the ice that had formed on the sea water in the sound was thickening rapidly, assisted by the old pack, of which a large amount lay across our course. I was anxious to pick up a depot of geological specimens on Depot Island, left there by the northern party, and with this end in view the *Nimrod* was taken on a more westerly course than would otherwise have been the case. The wind, however, was freshening to a gale, and we were passing through streams of ice, which seemed to thicken as we neared the shore. I decided that it would be too risky to send a party off for the specimens, as there was no proper lee to this small island, and the consequences of even a short delay might be serious. I therefore gave instructions that the course should be altered to due north. The following wind helped us, and on the morning of March 6 we were off Cape Adare. I wanted to push between the Balleny Islands and the mainland, and make an attempt to follow the coastline from Cape North westward, so as to link it up with Adelie Land. No ship had ever succeeded in penetrating to the westward of Cape North, heavy pack having been encountered on the occasion of each attempt. The *Discovery* had passed through the Balleny Islands and sailed over part of the so-called Wilkes Land of the maps, but the question of the existence of this land in any other position had been left open.

We steamed along the pack ice, which was beginning to thicken, and although we did not manage to do all that I had hoped, we had the satisfaction of pushing our little vessel along that coast to longitude 166° 14' East, latitude 69° 47' South, a point further west than had been reached by any previous expedition. On the morning of March 8 we saw, beyond Cape North, a new coastline extending first to the southward and then to the west for a distance of over forty-five miles. We took angles and bearings, and Marston sketched the main outlines. We were too far away to take any photographs that would have been of value, but the sketches show very clearly the type of the land. Professor David was of the opinion that it was the northern edge of the polar plateau. The coast seemed to consist of cliffs, with a few bays in the distance. We would all have been glad of an opportunity to explore the coast thoroughly, but that was out of the question; the ice was getting thicker all the time, and it was becoming imperative that we should escape to clear water without further delay. There was no chance of getting farther west at that point, and as the new ice was forming between the old pack of the previous year and the land, we were in serious danger of being frozen in for the winter at a place where we could not have done any geological work of importance. We therefore moved north along the edge of the pack, making as much westing as possible, in the direction of the Balleny Islands. I still hoped that it might be possible to skirt them and find Wilkes Land. It was awkward work, and at times the ship could hardly move at all.

Finally, about midnight on March 9, I saw that we must go north, and the course was set in that direction. We were almost too late, for the ice was closing in and before long we were held up, the ship being unable to move at all. The situation looked black, but we discovered a lane through which progress could be made, and in the afternoon of the 10th we were in fairly open water, passing through occasional lines of pack. Our troubles were over, for we had a good voyage up to New Zealand, and on March 22 dropped anchor at the mouth of Lord's River, on the south side of Stewart Island. I did not go to a port because I wished to get the news of the expedition's work through to London before we faced the energetic newspapermen.

That was a wonderful day to all of us. For over a year we had seen nothing but rocks, ice, snow, and sea. There had been no colour and no softness in the scenery of the Antarctic; no green growth had gladdened our eyes, no musical notes of birds had come to our ears. We had had our work, but we had been cut off from most of the lesser things that go to make life worthwhile. No person who has not spent a period of his life in those 'stark and sullen solitudes that sentinel the Pole' will understand fully what trees and flowers, sun-flecked turf and running streams mean to the soul of a man. We landed on the stretch of beach that separated the sea from the luxuriant growth of the forest, and scampered about like children in the sheer joy of being alive. I did not wish to dispatch my cablegrams from Half Moon Bay until an hour previously arranged, and in the meantime we revelled in the warm sand on the beach, bathed in the sea, and climbed amongst the trees. We lit a fire and made tea on the beach, and while we were having our meal the wekas, the remarkable flightless birds found only in New Zealand, came out from the bush for their share of the good things. These quaint birds, with their long bills, brown plumage and quick, inquisitive eyes, have no fear of men, and their friendliness seemed to us like a welcome from that sunny land that had always treated us with such openhearted kindliness. The clear, musical notes of other birds came to us from the trees, and we felt that we needed only good news from home to make our happiness and contentment absolutely complete. One of the scientific men found a cave showing signs of native occupation in some period of the past, and was fortunate enough to discover a stone adze made of the rare pounamu, or greenstone.

Early next morning we hove up the anchor, and at 10 a.m. we entered Half Moon Bay. I went ashore to dispatch my cablegrams, and it was strange to see new faces on the wharf after fifteen months during which we had met no-one outside the circle of our little party. There were girls on the wharf, too, and everyone was glad to see us in the hearty New Zealand way. I dispatched my cablegrams from the little office, and then went on board again and ordered the course to be set for Lyttelton, the port from which we had sailed on the first day of the previous year. We arrived there on March 25 late in the afternoon.

The people of New Zealand would have welcomed us, I think, whatever had been the result of our efforts, for their keen interest in Antarctic exploration has never faltered since the early days of the *Discovery* expedition, and their attitude toward us was always that of warm personal friendship. But the news of the measure of success we had achieved had been published in London and flashed back to the southern countries, and we were met out in the harbour and on the wharves by cheering crowds. Enthusiastic friends boarded the *Nimrod* almost as soon as she entered the heads, and when our little vessel came alongside the quay, the crowd on deck became so great that movement was almost impossible. Then I was handed great bundles of letters and cablegrams. The loved ones at home were well, the world was pleased with our work, and it seemed as though nothing but happiness could ever enter life again.

Penguins

Some notes by James Murray, biologist to the expedition

Though so much has been written about them, the penguins always excite fresh interest in everyone who sees them for the first time. There is endless interest in watching them, the dignified Emperor, dignified notwithstanding his clumsy waddle, going along with his wife (or wives) by his side, the very picture of a successful, self-satisfied, happy, unsuspicious countryman, gravely bowing like a Chinaman before a yelping dog; and the little undignified matter-of-fact Adelie, minding his own business in a way worthy of emulation. They are perfectly adapted to a narrow round of life, and when compelled to face matters outside of their experience they often behave with apparent stupidity, but sometimes show a good deal of intelligence.

Their resemblance to human beings is always noticed. This is party due to the habit of walking erect, but there are truly a great many human traits about them. They are the civilised nations of these regions, and their civilisation, if much simpler than ours, is in some respects higher and more worthy of the name. But there is a good deal of human nature in them too. As in the human race, their gathering in colonies does not show any true social instinct. They are merely gregarious; each penguin is in the rookery for his own ends, there is no thought of the general good. You might exterminate an Adelie rookery with the exception of one bird, and he would be in no way concerned so long as you left him alone.

Some little suggestion of altruism will appear in dealing with the nesting habits of the Adelie. Thieving is known, among the Adelies at least. One very pleasing trait is shown, which they have in common with man. Eating is not with them the prime business in life, as it is with the common fowl and most animals. Both Emperors and Adelies, when the serious business of nesting is off their minds, show a legitimate curiosity. Having fed and got into good condition they leave the sea and go off in parties, apparently to see the country, and travel for days and weeks.

The Emperor

We saw the Emperor only as a summer visitor. Having finished nesting, fed up and become glossy and beautiful, they came up out of the sea in large or small parties, apparently to have a good time before moulting. While the Adelies were nesting they began to come in numbers to inspect the camp. Passing among the Adelies, the two kinds usually paid no attention to one another, but sometimes an Adelie would think an Emperor came too close to her nest, and a curious unequal quarrel would ensue, the little impudence pecking and scolding, and the Emperor scolding back, with some loss of dignity. Though more than able to hold her own with the tongue, the Adelie knew the value of discretion whenever the Emperor raised his flipper.

They were curious about any unusual object and would come a long way to see a motorcar or a man. When out on these excursions the leader of a party keeps them together by a long shrill squawk. Distant parties salute in this way and continue calling till they get pretty close. A party could be made to approach by imitating this call. The first party to arrive inspected the boat, then crossed the lake to the camp. Soon they discovered the dogs, and thereafter all other interests were swallowed up in the interest excited by them. After the first discovery crowds came every day for a long time, and from the manner in which they went straight to the kennels one was tempted to believe that the fame of them had been noised abroad.

Ceremonies of meeting

Emperors are very ceremonious in meeting other Emperors or men or dogs. They come up to a party of strangers in a straggling procession, some big important aldermanic fellow leading. At a respectful distance from the man or dog they halt, the old male waddles close up and bows gravely till his beak is almost touching his breast. Keeping his head bowed he makes a long speech, in a muttering manner, short sounds following in groups of four or five. Having finished the speech, the head is still kept bowed a few seconds for politeness' sake, then it is raised and he describes with his bill as large a circle as the joints of his neck will allow, looking in your face at last to see if you have understood. If you have not comprehended, as is usually the case, he tries again. He is very patient with your stupidity, and feels sure that he will get it into your dull brain if he keeps at it long enough. By this time his followers are getting impatient. They are sure he is making a mess of it. Another male will waddle forward with dignity, elbow the first aside as if to say, 'I'll show you how it ought to be done', and goes through the whole business again. Their most solemn ceremonies were used toward the dogs, and three old fellows have been seen calmly bowing and speaking simultaneously to a dog, which for its part was yelping and straining at its chain in the effort to get at them.

Left to themselves the Emperor penguins seem perfectly peaceable, and no sign of quarrelling was ever noticed. When a party of them was driven into a narrow space they resented the jostling, and flippers were freely used, making resounding whacks, which apparently are not felt through the dense feathery fur. The flipper strikes with equal facility forward or backward.

They seem to regard men as penguins like themselves. They are quite unsuspicious and slow to take alarm, so long as you stay still or move very slowly. If you walk too fast among them, or if you touch them, they get frightened and run away, only fighting when closely pressed. As one slowly retreats, fighting, he has a ludicrous resemblance to a small boy being bullied by a big one, his flipper toward the foe elevated in defense, and making quick blows at the bully. It is well to keep clear of that flipper when he strikes, for it is very powerful, and might break an arm.

Emperors were killed by the dogs, but it is likely that the animals hunted in couples to do this. A long fight was witnessed between an Emperor and the dog Ambrose, the largest of our dogs native to the Antarctic. The penguin was quick enough in movement to keep always facing the dog, and the flipper and long sharp bill were efficient weapons, as Ambrose seemed to appreciate. Only the bill was used, and it appeared to be due to short sight that the blow always fell short. Many of the apparently stupid acts of both kinds of penguins are doubtless to be traced to their very defective sight in air.

The Emperor can hardly be said to migrate since he remains to breed during the winter darkness, and spends the summer among the ice or on shore in the same region. Yet he travels a good deal, and the meaning of some of his journeyings remains a mystery. The visits of touring parties to the camp have been described. At the same season (early summer), when the motorcar was making frequent journeys southward to Glacier Tongue with stores for depot laying, we crossed on the way a great many penguin tracks. Many of these were beaten roads, where large parties had passed, some walking, some tobogganning. They all trended roughly to the south-east, and the wing marks and footmarks showed that they were all outward bound from the open sea toward the shore of Ross Island. Some of the roads were twelve miles or more from the open sea. There were no return tracks.

We expected to find that they had gone in to seek sheltered moulting places, but on a motor trip to the Turk's Head we skirted a long stretch of the coast and found no Emperors.

On journeys they often travel many miles walking erect, when they get along at a very slow shuffle, making only a few inches at each step. In walking thus they keep their balance by the assistance of the tail, which forms a tripod with the legs. When on a suitable snow surface they progress rapidly by tobogganning, a very graceful motion, when they make sledges of their breasts and propel themselves by the powerful legs, balancing and perhaps improving their speed by means of the wings.

Eight of them visited the motorcar one day, near Tent Island, sledging swiftly toward us. Two of them were very determined fighters and refused to be driven away. One obstinate, phlegmatic old fellow, who wasn't going to be hurried by anybody, did learn to hustle as the car bore down upon him.

The Adelie
The Adelie is always comical. He pops out of the water with startling suddenness, like a jack in the box, alights on his feet, gives his tail a shake, and toddles off about his business. He always knows where he wants to go, and what he wants to do, and isn't easily turned aside from his purpose.

In the water the Adelie penguins move rapidly and circle in the same way as a porpoise or a dolphin, for which they are easily mistaken at a little distance. On level ice or snow they can run pretty fast, getting along about as fast as a man at a smart walk. They find even a small crack a serious obstruction, and pause and measure with the eye one of a few inches before very cautiously hopping it. They flop down and toboggan over any opening more than a few inches wide. They can climb hills of a very steep angle, but on uneven ground they use their flippers as balancers. They toboggan with great speed on snow or ice, or even on the bare rocks when scared, but in that case their flippers are soon bleeding. Very rarely they swim in the water like ducks. They lie much lower in the water than the duck. The neck is below the surface and the head is just showing.

The Adelie is very brave in the breeding season. His is true courage, not the courage of ignorance, for after he has learned to know man, and fear him, he remains to defend the nest against any odds. When walking among the nests one is assailed on all sides by powerful bills. Most of the birds sit still on the nests, but the more pugnacious ones run at you from a distance and often take you unawares. We wore for protection long felt boots reaching well above the knee. Some of the clever ones knew that they were wasting their efforts on the felt boots, and would come up behind, hop up and seize the skin above the boot, and hang on tight, beating with their wings. One of these little furies, hanging to your flesh and flapping his strong flippers so fast that you can hardly see them move, is no joke. A man once stumbled and fell into a colony of Adelies, and before he could recover himself and scramble out they were upon him, and he bore the marks of their fury for some time.

Some birds became greatly interested in the camp, and wanted to nest there. One bird (we believe it was always the same one) couldn't be kept away, and came daily, sometimes bringing some friends. As he passed among the dogs, which were barking and trying to get at him, he stood and defied them all, and when we turned out to try to drive him away, he offered to take us all on too, and was finally saved against his will, and carried away by Brocklehurst, a wildly struggling, unconquerable being.

The old birds enjoy play, while the young ones have no leisure for play, being engrossed in satisfying the enormous appetites they have when growing. Four or five Adelies were playing on the ice floe. One acted as leader, advanced to the edge of the floe, waited for the others to line up, raised his flipper, when they all dived in. In a few seconds they all popped out again, and repeated the performance, always apparently directed by the one. And so they went on for hours. While the *Nimrod* was frozen in the pack, some dozens of them were disporting themselves in a sea pool alongside. They swam together in the duck fashion, then at a squawk from one they all dived and came up at the other side of the pool.

Early in October they began to arrive at the rookery, singly or in pairs. The first to come were males, and they at once began to scrape up the frozen ground to make hollows for their nests, and to collect stones for the walls with which they surround them. The digging is hard work and is done by the feet, the bird lying prone and kicking out backward. As soon as any apology for a nest is ready the males begin displaying. He points his bill vertically upward, flaps his wings slowly, inflates his chest, and makes a series of low booming sounds, which increase in loudness, then die away again, the throat vibrating strongly. Then he slowly subsides into the usual attitude. We supposed this to be a part of his courtship, or as some phrased it 'advertising for a wife', but there is good reason to suppose that the pairing is done before the birds leave the sea. Generally the male's displaying passes entirely disregarded. He continues it all through the nesting season, till the chicks are nearly fledged and the moulting time is near. An epidemic of displaying often took the whole rookery at once, when the hens were mostly away disporting themselves in the sea.

When the rookery is pretty well filled, and the nest building is in full swing, the birds have a busy and anxious time. To get enough of suitable small stones is a matter of difficulty, and may involve long journeys for each single stone. The temptation is too strong for some of them, and they become habitual thieves. The majority remain stupidly honest. Amusing complications result. The bearing of the thief clearly shows that he knows he is doing wrong. He has a conscience, at least a human conscience, i.e. the fear of being found out. Very different is the furtive look of the thief, long after he is out of danger of pursuit, from the expression of the honest penguin coming home with a hard-earned stone.

An honest one was bringing stones from a long distance. Each stone was removed by a thief as soon as the owner's back was turned. The honest one looked greatly troubled as he found that his heap didn't grow, but he seemed incapable of suspecting the cause.

A thief, sitting on its own nest, was stealing from an adjacent nest, whose honest owner was also at home, but looking unsuspectingly in another direction. Casually he turned his head and caught the thief in the act. The thief dropped the stone and pretended to be busy picking up an infinitesimal crumb from the neutral ground.

The stone-gathering is a very strong part of the nesting instinct. It was kept up while sitting on the eggs, and if at a late stage they lost their eggs or young, they reverted to the heaping of stones, which they did in a halfhearted way. Unmated birds occupied the fringe of the rookery, and amused themselves piling and stealing till the chicks began to hatch out.

After the two eggs were laid the males appeared to do most of the work. At any hour the males predominated, a very few pairs were at the nests, and relieving guard was rarely noticed. The females were never seen in the majority. Those which had been recently down to feed could be recognised by the fresh crustacea around the nests. Judging by this sign, it would seem that some birds never leave the nest to feed during the whole period of incubation. Many birds lost their mates through the occasional breaking loose of a dog. These birds couldn't leave the nests.

Rearing the chicks

The rookery is most interesting after the chicks arrive. Many curious things happen as they grow. The young chicks are silvery or slatey grey, with darker heads, which are for the first day or so heavy and hang down helplessly. As soon as they are hatched the mothers take equal share in tending them, whatever they may have been doing before that. For some weeks the nest cannot be left untended or the chicks would perish of cold or fall victims to the skuas. The parents keep regular watches, going down in turn to feed, and relieving guard is an interesting ceremony. The bird just arrived from the sea hurries to the nest. It is anxious to see the chick, and to feed it; the other is unwilling to resign, but at last reluctantly gets off the nest, evidently very stiff, stretches itself, and hangs about for a while before going down to the sea.

When the young ones can hold up their heads the feeding begins. At first the parent tries to induce its offspring to feed by tickling its bill and throat. The old bird opens its mouth and the chick puts its head right in and picks the food out of the throat. The bird can be seen bringing it up into the throat by an effort. If the young is unwilling to feed some food is thrown right up on to the ground and a little of it picked up again and placed on the chick's bill. After learning the way there is no need for such inducement, and the parents are taxed to satisfy the clamouring for more.

For some weeks after the young are hatched life in the rookery goes smoothly along. One parent is always on the nest and the young birds do not wander. Then the trouble begins. The young begin to move about and if anything disturbs the colony they run about in panic. As they don't know nest or parent they cannot return home. They meet the case by adopting parents, and run under any bird they come to. The old birds resent this and a chick is often pecked away from nest after nest till exhausted. The skuas get some at this time, but it is surprising how few. Most of the chicks take some old one unawares and get in the nest. She may have a chick already, or chicks, but as she doesn't know which is her own she cannot drive the intruder away. A sorely puzzled bird may be seen trying to cover four gigantic chicks. Some of the less precocious youngsters stay at home long enough to get to know the nest, and can find their way home after wandering a few yards. Such homes keep together a little longer.

The time comes when both parents must be absent together to get enough food for the growing chicks. Then the social order of the rookery breaks down and chaos begins. The social condition which is evolved out of the chaos is one of the most remarkable in nature, yet it serves its purpose and saves the race. A kind of communism is established, but the old birds have no part in it. They cherish the fiction that they have nests and children, and when they come up from the sea after feeding it is their intention to find the nest and feed their own young only. The young ones, for their part, establish a community of parents, and yet it isn't exactly that either, though it works out as if it were. It is each bird for itself. The chick assumes the first old one that comes within its reach to be its parent. Perhaps it really thinks so, as they are all alike.

An old bird, coming up full of shrimps, is met by clamorous youngsters before it has time to begin the search for its hypothetical home. They order it to stand and deliver. It objects and scolds, and runs off. It may be by the irony of fate that it is its own young which accost it, but it can't know that. The chickens are both imperative and wheedling. Then begins one of those parent hunts which were so familiar at the end of the season. The end is never in doubt from the first. Every now and again the old one stops and expostulates. This shows weakness. There is no indecision on the part of the young one. It never seems anxious as to the result, but in the most matter of fact and persistent manner hunts the old one down. The hunts àre often long and exhausting. One chase was witnessed at Pony Lake beside the camp. Nine times they circled the lake, and the hunt was not over when the watcher had to leave. On that occasion they must have travelled miles. At the end the old one stops, and still spluttering and protesting, delivers up. One would think that in these circumstances the weaker chicks would go to the wall, but it does not appear to be so. There are no ill-nourished young ones to be seen. Perhaps the hunts take so long that all get a chance.

A few days after the eggs began to hatch there was a severe blizzard, which lasted several days. Snow was banked up around most of the birds. A snowdrift crossed the densest part of the rookery, partly burying many birds. In the deepest part nests and birds were covered out of sight, and the only indication of the whereabouts of a bird was a little funnel in the snow, at the bottom of which an anxious eye could be seen. Many less deeply buried birds had freed one wing or both, which became stiff with cold, as they could not be got back again. The snow, melting by the heat of their bodies, and refreezing, made walls of ice around the birds. Many got alarmed and left the nests, when the snow fell in and buried them. In the warm sunny weather that followed the melting snow filled many nests with pools of water. Some birds showed ingenuity in dealing with these floods. They moved their nests, stone by stone (always keeping a hollow for the eggs or chicks), as much as their own width till they reached dry ground. While the snowdrift remained some birds whose nests were buried scraped hollows in the snow and collected a few stones. On a moderate estimate about half the young perished in this blizzard.

The old Adelies do not mind the cold. Their thick blubber and dense fur sufficiently protect them. In a blizzard they will lie still and let the snow cover them. Going to the rookery once after a blizzard I could see no penguins; they had entirely disappeared. Suddenly at some movement or noise I was surrounded by them; they had sprung up out of the snow.

Domestic entanglements

While the Adelie appears to be entirely moral in his domestic arrangements, his stupidity (or his shortsightedness, which causes him to seem stupid) gives rise to many domestic complications. No doubt the presence of our camp upset the social economy, and probably when undisturbed nothing of the kind would occur. He has little sense of locality, and one little heap of stones is very like another, yet pairs seem to have no means of recognising one another but by the rendezvous of the nest. Husbands and wives, parents and children, do not know one another, but if found at the nest are accepted as bona fide.

All the birds go to their nests without hesitation when they come from the sea by the familiar route, but if taken from their nests to some other part of the rookery some find their way back without difficulty, others are quite lost. They are most puzzled when moved only a little away from home, and they will fight to keep another bird's nest while their own is only a couple of feet away. A bird will defend an egg or chick in the nest, but if it is removed just outside it will peck at it and destroy it.

Considering these facts it will be evident that if the rookery be disturbed confusion follows. A mere walk among the nests caused innumerable entanglements. One bird would leave the nest in fright, flop down a yard away beside a nest already occupied, or on a nest left exposed by another scared bird. Then one-sided fights would begin, one bird attacking another under the impression that it had usurped its nest, the rightful owner troubling little about the vicious pecking he was receiving, sitting calmly in conscious rectitude. A fight of this kind has been watched for an hour at a time, three neighbouring nests having been disturbed. One bird had got into another's nest, a second was trying to establish a claim to the occupied nest of a third, and meanwhile the chicks of number one were neglected in the cold. A bird which had no family came and covered the chicks, but looked conscious of wrongdoing and kept ready to bolt on a second's notice. All these birds but the last wanted their own nests and were within a yard of them without knowing it.

In all such cases, even when a bird got established on the wrong nest, there was always an adjustment afterward. When they calmed down they became uneasy, probably observing the landmarks more critically, and would even leave a nest with chicks for their own empty nest. A chick removed from the nest and put alongside was not recognised, and the old bird never seemed to connect the facts of the empty nest and the chick beside it. If a chick were taken from the nest under the old bird's very eyes and held in front of it, it was always the chick that was viciously attacked, not the aggressor.

Some experiments were tried on them in order to trace the workings of the penguin mind. If a man stood between a bird and its nest so as to prevent it from getting on to it, the bird would make many attempts to reach home, rushing furiously at the man. After a time it would appear to meditate, and then walk off rather disconsolately, make a tour of the colony to which it belonged, and approach the nest from another side. It appeared greatly astonished that the intruder was still there. This curious trait was often seen. It is like the ostrich burying its head in the sand and imagining it is safe, or like a man refusing to believe his own eyes. It appears to think that if it takes a turn around, or comes to its nest from the other side, the horrible vision will disappear.

A bird was taken from a nest which had a chick in it and put down at a little distance. Meantime the chick was put in a neighbour's nest. Presently the bird came running up. It started back on seeing the empty nest, not in alarm or fear, but exactly as if thinking, 'I've come to the wrong house!' and trotted off to a distant part of the rookery. Her reasoning seemed to be this: 'There was a chick in my nest, therefore this empty nest cannot be mine.' She couldn't imagine the chick leaving the nest, and so never searched for it. It was only a yard from the nest all the time. After half an hour's searching in vain for any place like home she returned to the nest, and accepted the restored chick as a matter of course.

A lost chick was never sought for. There would be no use; it couldn't be recognised. On account of this peculiarity we were able to make many readjustments of the family arrangements.

When the blizzard destroyed so many chicks we distributed the young from nests where there were two to nests where there were none. They were usually adopted eagerly and the plan was quite successful.

When both birds are at a nest that is disturbed, or when the mate comes up from feeding to relieve guard, there is an interchange of civilities in the form of a loud squawking in unison, accompanied by a curious movement. The birds' necks are crossed, and at each squawk they are changed from side to side, first right then left. The harsh complaining clamour which they make was for long mistaken for quarrelling.

A bird returning from the sea came to the wrong nest and tried to enter into conversation with the occupant, who would have nothing to do with him. She knew her mate had just gone off for the day, and wouldn't be such a fool as to come back too early, so she sat still, indifferent to the squawking of the other. A look of distress came into his face as he failed to get any response, and he was slow to realise that he had made a mistake.

A small colony was found with about two dozen large chicks, unattended by any old birds. They were driven across the lake to a larger colony. Halfway over a few old birds were squatted, enjoying a rest. When the chicks saw them they ran up to them joyfully, saying: 'Here's pa and ma, hooray!' To their surprise they got the reverse of a cordial welcome, being driven away with vicious peckings. They were driven on to the larger colony and were swallowed up in it.

The Adelies are not demonstrative of their affections. It is difficult to discover if they have any beyond the instinctive affection for the young. The pairing appears to be a purely business matter, and the mates don't even show any power to recognise one another. A penguin was injured by the dogs, but it seemed possible that it might recover, so we did not at once put it out of pain. In a couple of days it died. Shortly after we noticed a live penguin standing by it. We removed the dead bird to a distance, and after a while found the other standing beside it as before. It was the general opinion that it was the dead bird's mate which had found it out. Such an action is entirely opposed to what we expect after a long study of their habits. There are always plenty of dead birds about a rookery, and the living go about entirely indifferent to them. It is puzzling in any point of view, but it is less difficult to believe that the bird found its dead mate than that it took an interest in a dead stranger.

Altruism

When the young birds are well grown, if there is an alarm they flock together, and any old birds present in the colony form a wall of defence between the young and the enemy. This habit has given rise to the belief that they are somewhat communistic in their social order, and that the defence of the colony is a concerted action. It is not so. Each bird is defending its own young one only, and will often fight with another of the defending birds, or peck at any young one which comes in its way.

There are real instances of altruism or kindness to strangers. Our passage through the rookery frightened away the parents of a very young chick. A bird passing at the distance of a few yards noticed it and came over to it. He cocked his head on one side and looked at it, as if saying: 'Hullo! this little beggar's deserted; must do something for him.' He tickled its bill, as the parents do when coaxing the very young chicks to feed, but it was too much frightened to feed. After coaxing it in this way for some time he turned away and put some food upon the ground, and, lifting a little in his bill, he put some on each side of the chick's bill. Just then the rightful parent returned and the helper ran off. This was not an isolated case, but was observed on several occasions.

One incident seemed to reveal true social instincts. From a small colony of about two dozen nests all the eggs but one were taken in order to find out if the birds would lay again. As it turned out they did not. The birds sat on their empty nests for some time, then they disappeared. When the time came for the solitary egg to hatch, about a dozen of the nests were reoccupied and the birds took their share in defending the one chick.

Departure of the young

When they have shed most of their down the young birds congregate at the edge of the sea. They cease from hunting the old ones for food, and appear to be waiting for something. When the right time comes, which they seem to know perfectly, they dive into the sea, sometimes in small parties, sometimes singly, disappear for a time, and may be seen popping up far out to sea. They dive and come up very awkwardly, but swim well.

It is marvellous how fully instinct makes these birds independent. The parents do not take them to the water and teach them to swim. They haven't even the example of the old birds, which stay behind to moult. At an early age they become independent of their own parents, and earn their living by hunting any old bird they find. Though they have spent their lives on land, and only know that food is something found in an old bird's throat, when the time comes they leave the land and plunge boldly into the sea, untaught, to get their living by straining crustacea out of the water in the same way as the whale does.

Some of our party reported that they saw penguins teaching the young to swim, but if this ever happens it is not general. Time and again the young have been watched leaving as described, entirely on their own. At that season nearly all the old birds are in the moult and never venture into the water.

Like the Emperor, the Adelie is fond of travelling when family cares are off his mind. The great blizzard which wiped our half the rookery left hundreds of old birds free. They began to explore the adjacent country in bands. The round of the lakes was a favourite trip and broad beaten roads marked this route. Tracks also led to the summits of some of the hills, though the shortsighted Adelie could hardly go there for the view.

There was no general trek southward, such as the Emperors made, yet the southern party found tracks of two at a distance of some eighty miles from the sea.

Nebuchadnezzar and Nicodemus

These names dignified two penguin chicks. While chaos reigned in the rookery I found them exhausted and covered with mire, having been hunted and pecked through the rookery. They were taken to the house, put in a large cage in the porch, and fed by hand with sardines and fish cakes. The feeding was disagreeable. They didn't like the food and shook it out of their bills in disgust. So it was necessary to force it down their throats till it was beyond their reach.

In a few days they became quite tame and recognised those who fed them. Familiar only with our peculiar method of feeding them, one of them indicated when he was hungry by taking my finger into his bill. We shortened their names to Nebby and Nicky, and they answered to them, but they answered equally readily to the common name of Bill. The sounds of the rookery reached them and sometimes greatly excited them and they made desperate efforts to get through the netting of their cage. At these times we would take them out for a walk. They made no attempt to go to the rookery, and were rather frightened.

Nebuchadnezzar was a very friendly little fellow, and would follow me about outside, and come running when called. The feeding was unnatural, and for this reason, doubtless, in a few weeks they died.

The ringed penguin

A single ringed penguin appeared at Cape Royds at the end of the breeding season, just as the Adelies were beginning to moult. No ringed penguin had been seen in this part of the Antarctic before. It was evidently a stray one which had come ashore to moult. It is about the same size as the Adelie, but is more agile. It was at the season when the young Adelies go off to sea. At a little distance the ringed penguin, among a crowd of old Adelies, looked somewhat like a young Adelie with the white throat. I picked him up by the legs to investigate. To my surprise he curled round and bit me on the hand. An Adelie could not do so. A closer examination showed what he was.

Southern Journey distances
by the commander of the expedition

The following table gives detailed information regarding the distances travelled day by day on the southern journey.

The number of geographical miles given in the first column covers the period from November 15, 1908, to January 9, 1909. The distances have been taken from the chart after all corrections have been made, and represent a direct line from camp to camp.

In the second column will be found the noon latitudes, calculated from observations taken as opportunity offered.

The last column shows the distances travelled day by day according to the sledge meter, and these figures take into account all deviations and detours so often rendered necessary by the condition of the surface. The reliability of the sledge meter is proved by the fact that on the homeward journey we were able to determine our positions without taking latitude observations. Only one observation was taken on the return journey (January 31, 1909), and on that occasion the theodolite confirmed the record of the sledge meter.

The latitude observations noted in this table were taken with a three-inch theodolite, which was carefully adjusted before the start for the southern journey. An observation taken on the return journey, in February, when the position was known from bearings, showed that the instrument was correct. The observations were only taken with the theodolite 'face left', but as the instrument was in good adjustment this was sufficient.

On the outward journey the last latitude observation was taken in latitude 87° 22' South. The remainder of the distance marched toward the south was calculated by sledge meter and dead reckoning. The accuracy of the sledge meters used was proved by the fact that on the return journey we were able to pick up the depots without taking observations. The 'slip' was ascertained by careful tests before the start of the journey.

The chronometer watches taken were rated before leaving and on the return, and the error was only eight seconds. All bearings, angles, and azimuths were taken with the theodolite. Variation was ascertained by means of a compass attached to the theodolite, and the steering compasses were checked accordingly. At noon each day the prismatic compasses were placed in the true meridian, and checked against the theodolite compass and the steering compasses.

The total distance marched, from October 29 to March 4, as recorded on the sledge meters, was 1755 miles 209 yards statute, this including relay work and back marches.

Date	Geog. miles	Noon latitude	Statute miles	Yards	Relay
[1908]					
Oct 29	—	—	14	880	—
Oct 30 [Hut Point]	—	—	9	880	—
Oct 31 [back to Royds]	—	—	23	—	—
Nov 1 [to Hut Point]	—	—	23	—	—
Nov 2 [blizzard]	—	—	no march	—	—
Nov 3	—	—	12	300	—
Nov 4	—	—	16	500	—
Nov 5	—	—	9	1200	—
Nov 6 [blizzard]	—	—	no march	—	—
Nov 7	—	—	1	—	—
Nov 8 [blizzard]	—	—	no march	—	—
Nov 9	—	—	14	600	—
Nov 10	—	—	15	1550	—
Nov 11	—	—	15	—	—
Nov 12	—	—	15	1650	—
Nov 13	—	—	15	1550	—
Nov 14	—	—	15	100	—
Nov 15	7,39 [from noon]	79° 36' S	12	1500	—
Nov 16	14.91	—	17	200	—
Nov 17	13.3	—	16	200	—
Nov 18	13	—	15	500	—
Nov 19	13.7	—	15	200	—
Nov 20	13.6	—	15	800	—
Nov 21	13.3	—	15	500	—
Nov 22	16	—	15	250	—
Nov 23	14	—	14	1650	—
Nov 24	15.4	—	14	680	—
Nov 25	14.6	—	14	1600	—
Nov 26	13.2	82° 12' S	14	1700	—
Nov 27	15.5	—	14	1200	—
Nov 28	13.6	82° 39' S	14	1500	—
Nov 29	11.7	—	14	900	—
Nov 30	11	—	12	150	—
Dec 1	10,5	—	12	200	—
Dec 2	10,3	—	11	1450	—
Dec 3 [Mount Hope]	—	—	20	—	—
Dec 4	10.5	83° 33' S	10	—	—

Date	Geog. miles	Noon latitude	Statute miles	Yards	Relay
[1908]					
Dec 5	3.1	—	5	—	4
Dec 6	4.1	—	4	—	3
Dec 7	9.1	—	10	570	—
Dec 8	7.7	—	12	150	—
Dec 9	9.8	84° 2' S	11	1450	2
Dec 10	9.8	—	11	860	—
Dec 11	7.2	—	8	900	—
Dec 12	3.1	—	3	500	6 1000
Dec 13	4.5	—	5	—	6
Dec 14	8	—	7	880	2
Dec 15	11.5	—	13	200	—
Dec 16	12	84° 53' S	13	1650	—
Dec 17	9.1	—	12	250	1
Dec 18	3	—	6	600	12
Dec 19	7.4	—	10	—	1 880
Dec 20	10	85° 19' S	11	950	1
Dec 21	7	—	6	—	3
Dec 22	7	—	4	—	6
Dec 23	6.2	—	13	—	—
Dec 24	9.2	—	11	250	—
Dec 25	9.2	—	10	650	—
Dec 26	11.4	—	14	480	—
Dec 27	12	—	14	930	—
Dec 28	11.7	—	14	450	—
Dec 29	10.1	—	12	600	—
Dec 30	3.7	—	4	100	—
Dec 31	8.5	—	11	—	—
[1909]					
Jan 1	9.7	86° 59' S	11	900	—
Jan 2	9.1	—	10	450	—
Jan 3	12.6	87° 22' S	11	1680	—
Jan 4	12.2	—	14	660	—
Jan 5	13.4	—	15	480	—
Jan 6	13.2	[88° 7' camp]	15	313	—
Jan 7 [blizzard]	—	—	no march	—	—
Jan 8 [blizzard]	—	—	no march	—	—
Jan 9	16.5	88° 23' S [farthest south]	18	704 [from camp]	—
			18	704 [back]	
			4	40 [to camp]	
Jan 10	—	—	21	308	—
Jan 11	—	—	19	1500	—
Jan 12	—	—	14	100	—
Jan 13	—	—	15	1500	—
Jan 14	—	—	20	1600	—
Jan 15	—	—	20	—	—
Jan 16	—	—	8	800	—
Jan 17	—	—	22	850	—
Jan 18	—	—	26	900	—
Jan 19	—	—	29	—	—
Jan 20	—	—	15	800	—
Jan 21	—	—	17	—	—
Jan 22	—	—	15	900	—
Jan 23	—	—	14	100	—
Jan 24	—	—	16	—	—
Jan 25	—	—	26	—	—
Jan 26	—	—}	16	{—	—
Jan 27	—	—}		{—	—
Jan 28	—	—	14	890	—
Jan 29 [blizzard]	—	—	2	—	—

Date	Geog. miles	Noon latitude	Statute miles	Yards	Relay
[1909]					
Jan 30	—	—	13	—	—
Jan 31	—	82° 58'	13	850	—
Feb 1	—	—	13	1400	—
Feb 2	—	—	13	900	—
Feb 3	—	—	5	900	—
Feb 4 [dysentery]	—	—	no march	—	—
Feb 5	—	—	8	—	—
Feb 6	—	—	10	—	—
Feb 7	—	—	12	—	—
Feb 8	—	—	12	—	—
Feb 9	—	—	14	900	—
Feb 10	—	—	20	300	—
Feb 11	—	—	16	1320	—
Feb 12	—	—	14	450	—
Feb 13	—	—	12	—	—
Feb 14	—	—	11	1400	—
Feb 15	—	—	12	440	—
Feb 16	—	—	13	—	—
Feb 17	—	—	19	200	—
Feb 18	—	—	15	400	—
Feb 19	—	—	14	440	—
Feb 20	—	—	14	—	—
Feb 21	—	—	20	—	—
Feb 22	—	—	20	800	—
Feb 23	—	—	15	300	—
Feb 24	—	—	14	—	—
Feb 25 [blizzard]	—	—	no march	—	—
Feb 26 [left A and M]	—	—	24	—	—
Feb 27	—	— }	39	{ —	—
Feb 28	—	— }		{ —	—
Mar 1	—	— }		{ —	—
Mar 2	—	— }	63	{ —	—
Mar 3	—	— }	[30 out, 33 back]	{ —	—
Mar 4	—	— }		{ —	—

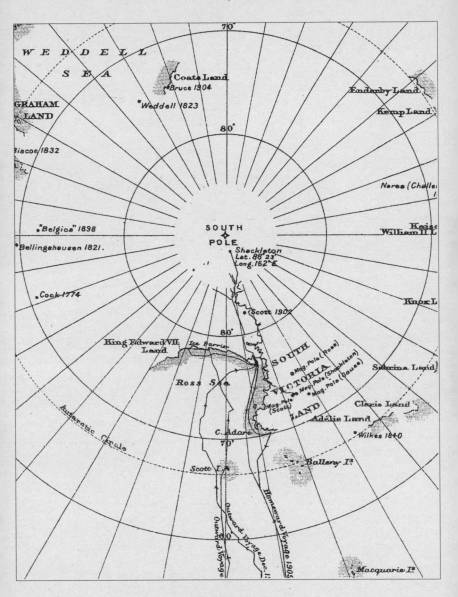

Detail of Shackleton's map showing
his approach to the South Pole

SOUTH
The Endurance expedition

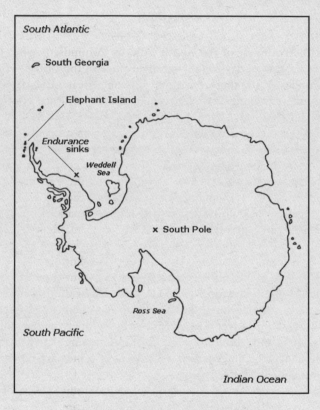

Map showing South Georgia, Elephant Island,
and the final position of the *Endurance*

PREFACE

After the conquest of the South Pole by Amundsen, who, by a narrow margin of days only, was in advance of the British Expedition under Scott, there remained but one great main object of Antarctic journeyings – the crossing of the South Polar continent from sea to sea.

When I returned from the Nimrod Expedition on which we had to turn back from our attempt to plant the British flag on the South Pole, being beaten by stress of circumstances within ninety-seven miles of our goal, my mind turned to the crossing of the continent, for I was morally certain that either Amundsen or Scott would reach the Pole on our own route or a parallel one. After hearing of the Norwegian success I began to make preparations to start a last great journey – so that the first crossing of the last continent should be achieved by a British Expedition.

We failed in this object, but the story of our attempt is the subject for the following pages, and I think that though failure in the actual accomplishment must be recorded, there are chapters in this book of high adventure, strenuous days, lonely nights, unique experiences, and, above all, records of unflinching determination, supreme loyalty, and generous self-sacrifice on the part of my men which, even in these days that have witnessed the sacrifices of nations and regardlessness of self on the part of individuals, still will be of interest to readers who now turn gladly from the red horror of war and the strain of the last five years to read, perhaps with more understanding minds, the tale of the White Warfare of the South. The struggles, the disappointments, and the endurance of this small party of Britishers, hidden away for nearly two years in the fastnesses of the Polar ice, striving to carry out the ordained task and ignorant of the crises through which the world was passing, make a story which is unique in the history of Antarctic exploration.

Owing to the loss of the *Endurance* and the disaster to the *Aurora*, certain documents relating mainly to the organisation and preparation of the Expedition have been lost; but, anyhow, I had no intention of presenting a detailed account of the scheme of preparation, storing, and other necessary but, to the general reader, unimportant affairs, as since the beginning of this century every book on Antarctic exploration has dealt fully with this matter. I therefore briefly place before you the inception and organisation of the Expedition, and insert here the copy of the programme which I prepared in order to arouse the interest of the general public in the Expedition.

The Trans-continental Party

The first crossing of the Antarctic continent, from sea to sea via the Pole, apart from its historic value, will be a journey of great scientific importance.

The distance will be roughly 1800 miles, and the first half of this, from the Weddell Sea to the Pole, will be over unknown ground. Every step will be an advance in geographical science. It will be learned whether the great Victoria chain of mountains, which has been traced from the Ross Sea to the Pole, extends across the continent and thus links up (except for the ocean break) with the Andes of South America, and whether the great plateau around the Pole dips gradually towards the Weddell Sea.

Continuous magnetic observations will be taken on the journey. The route will lead towards the Magnetic Pole, and the determination of the dip of the magnetic needle will be of importance in practical magnetism. The meteorological conditions will be carefully noted, and this should help to solve many of our weather problems.

The glaciologist and geologist will study ice-formations and the nature of the mountains, and this report will prove of great scientific interest.

Scientific Work by Other Parties

While the Transcontinental party is carrying out, for the British Flag, the greatest Polar journey ever attempted, the other parties will be engaged in important scientific work.

Two sledging-parties will operate from the base on the Weddell Sea. One will travel westwards towards Graham Land, making observations, collecting geological specimens, and proving whether there are mountains in that region linked up with those found on the other side of the Pole.

Another party will travel eastward toward Enderby Land, carrying out a similar programme, and a third, remaining at the base, will study the fauna of the land and sea, and the meteorological conditions.

From the Ross Sea base, on the other side of the Pole; another party will push southward and will probably await the arrival of the Transcontinental party at the top of the Beardmore Glacier, near Mount Buckley, where the first seams of coal were discovered in the Antarctic. This region is of great importance to the geologist, who will be enabled to read much of the history of the Antarctic in the rocks.

Both the ships of the Expedition will be equipped for dredging, sounding, and every variety of hydrographical work. The Weddell Sea ship will endeavour to trace the unknown coast-line of Graham Land, and from both the vessels, with their scientific staffs, important results may be expected.

The several shore parties and the two ships will thus carry out geographical and scientific work on a scale and over an area never before attempted by any one Polar expedition.

This will be the first use of the Weddell Sea as a base for exploration, and all the parties will open up vast stretches of unknown land. It is appropriate that this work should be carried out under the British Flag, since the whole of the area southward to the Pole is British territory. In July 1908, Letters Patent were issued under the Great Seal declaring that the Governor of the Falkland Islands should be the Governor of Graham Land (which forms the western side of the Weddell Sea), and another section of the same proclamation defines the area of British territory as 'situated in the South Atlantic Ocean to the south of the 50th parallel of south latitude, and lying between 20 degrees and 80 degrees west longitude.' Reference to a map will show that this includes the area in which the present Expedition will work.

How the Continent will be crossed

The Weddell Sea ship, with all the members of the Expedition operating from that base, will leave Buenos Ayres in October 1914, and endeavour to land in November in latitude 78 degrees south.

Should this be done, the Transcontinental party will set out on their 1800-mile journey at once, in the hope of accomplishing the march across the Pole and reaching the Ross Sea base in five months. Should the landing be made too late in the season, the party will go into winter quarters, lay out depots during the autumn and the following spring, and as early as possible in 1915 set out on the journey.

The Transcontinental party will be led by Sir Ernest Shackleton, and will consist of six men. It will take 100 dogs with sledges, and two motor-sledges with aerial propellers. The equipment will embody everything that the experience of the leader and his expert advisers can suggest. When this party has reached the area of the Pole, after covering 800 miles of unknown ground, it will strike due north towards the head of the Beardmore Glacier, and there it is hoped to meet the outcoming party from the Ross Sea. Both will join up and make for the Ross Sea base, where the previous Expedition had its winter quarters.

In all, fourteen men will be landed by the *Endurance* on the Weddell Sea. Six will set out on the Transcontinental journey, three will go westward, three eastward, and two remain at the base carrying on the work already outlined.

The *Aurora* will land six men at the Ross Sea base. They will lay down depots on the route of the Transcontinental party, and make a march south to assist that party, and to make geological and other observations as already described.

Should the Transcontinental party succeed, as is hoped, in crossing during the first season, its return to civilisation may be expected about April 1915. The other sections in April 1916.

The Ships of the Expedition

The two ships for the Expedition have now been selected.

The *Endurance*, the ship which will take the Transcontinental party to the Weddell Sea, and will afterwards explore

along an unknown coast-line, is a new vessel, specially constructed for Polar work under the supervision of a committee
of Polar explorers. She was built by Christensen, the famous
Norwegian constructor of sealing vessels, at Sandefjord. She is
barquentine rigged, and has triple-expansion engines giving
her a speed under steam of nine to ten knots. To enable her to
stay longer at sea, she will carry oil fuel as well as coal. She is of
about 350 tons, and built of selected pine, oak, and greenheart.
This fine vessel, equipped, has cost the Expedition £14,000.

The *Aurora*, the ship which will take out the Ross Sea party,
has been bought from Dr Mawson. She is similar in all respects
to the *Terra Nova*, of Captain Scott's last Expedition. She had
extensive alterations made by the Government authorities in
Australia to fit her for Dr Mawson's Expedition, and is now at
Hobart, Tasmania, where the Ross Sea party will join her in
October next.

* * *

I started the preparations in the middle of 1913, but no public
announcement was made until January 13, 1914. For the last six
months of 1913 I was engaged in the necessary preliminaries, solid
mule work, showing nothing particular to interest the public, but
essential for an Expedition that had to have a ship on each side of
the Continent, with a land journey of eighteen hundred miles to
be made, the first nine hundred miles to be across an absolutely
unknown land mass.

On January 1, 1914, having received a promised financial support
sufficient to warrant the announcement of the Expedition, I made
it public.

The first result of this was a flood of applications from all classes
of the community to join the adventure. I received nearly five
thousand applications, and out of these were picked fifty-six men.

In March, to my great disappointment and anxiety, the promised financial help did not materialise, and I was now faced with
the fact that I had contracted for a ship and stores, and had
engaged the staff, and I was not in possession of funds to meet
these liabilities. I immediately set about appealing for help, and
met with generous response from all sides. I cannot here give the
names of all who supported my application, but whilst taking this

opportunity of thanking everyone for their support, which came from parts as far apart as the interior of China, Japan, New Zealand, and Australia, I must particularly refer to the munificent donation of £24,000 from the late Sir James Caird, and to one of £10,000 from the British Government. I must also thank Mr Dudley Docker, who enabled me to complete the purchase of the *Endurance*, and Miss Elizabeth Dawson Lambton, who since 1901 has always been a firm friend to Antarctic exploration, and who again, on this occasion, assisted largely. The Royal Geographical Society made a grant of £1000; and last, but by no means least, I take this opportunity of tendering my grateful thanks to Dame Janet Stancomb Wills, whose generosity enabled me to equip the *Endurance* efficiently, especially as regards boats (which boats were the means of our ultimate safety), and who not only, at the inception of the Expedition, gave financial help, but also continued it through the dark days when we were overdue, and funds were required to meet the need of the dependents of the Expedition.

The only return and privilege an explorer has in the way of acknowledgment for the help accorded him is to record on the discovered lands the names of those to whom the Expedition owes its being.

Owing to the exigencies of the war the publication of this book has been long delayed, and the detailed maps must come with the scientific monographs. I have the honour to place on the new land the names of the above and other generous donors to the Expedition. The two hundred miles of new coast-line I have called Caird Coast. Also, as a more personal note, I named the three ship's boats, in which we ultimately escaped from the grip of the ice, after the three principal donors to the Expedition – the *James Caird*, the *Stancomb Wills* and the *Dudley Docker*. The two last-named are still on the desolate sandy spit of Elephant Island, where, under their shelter, twenty-two of my comrades eked out a bare existence for four and a half months.

The *James Caird* is now in Liverpool, having been brought home from South Georgia after her adventurous voyage across the sub-Antarctic ocean.

Most of the Public Schools of England and Scotland helped the Expedition to purchase the dog teams, and I named a dog after each school that helped. But apart from these particular donations I again thank the many people who assisted us.

So the equipment and organisation went on. I purchased the *Aurora* from Sir Douglas Mawson, and arranged for Mackintosh to go to Australia and take charge of her, there sending sledges, equipment and most of the stores from this side, but depending somewhat on the sympathy and help of Australia and New Zealand for coal and certain other necessities, knowing that previously these two countries had always generously supported the exploration of what one might call their hinterland.

Towards the end of July all was ready, when suddenly the war clouds darkened over Europe.

It had been arranged for the *Endurance* to proceed to Cowes, to be inspected by His Majesty on the Monday of Cowes week. But on Friday I received a message to say that the King would not be able to go to Cowes. My readers will remember how suddenly came the menace of war. Naturally, both my comrades and I were greatly exercised as to the probable outcome of the danger threatening the peace of the world.

We sailed from London on Friday, August 1, 1914, and anchored off Southend all Saturday. On Sunday afternoon I took the ship off Margate, growing hourly more anxious as the ever-increasing rumours spread; and on Monday morning I went ashore and read in the morning paper the order for general mobilisation.

I immediately went on board and mustered all hands and told them that I proposed to send a telegram to the Admiralty offering the ships, stores, and, if they agreed, our own services to the country in the event of war breaking out. All hands immediately agreed, and I sent off a telegram in which everything was placed at the disposal of the Admiralty. We only asked that, in the event of the declaration of war, the Expedition might be considered as a single unit, so as to preserve its homogeneity. There were enough trained and experienced men amongst us to man a destroyer. Within an hour I received a laconic wire from the Admiralty saying 'Proceed'. Within two hours a longer wire came from Mr Winston Churchill, in which we were thanked for our offer, and saying that the authorities desired that the Expedition, which had the full sanction and support of the Scientific and Geographical Societies, should go on.

So, according to these definite instructions, the *Endurance* sailed to Plymouth. On Tuesday the King sent for me and handed me the Union Jack to carry on the Expedition. That night, at midnight, war broke out. On the following Saturday, August 8, the *Endurance* sailed from Plymouth, obeying the direct order of the Admiralty. I make particular reference to this phase of the Expedition as I am aware that there was a certain amount of criticism of the Expedition having left the country, and regarding this I wish further to add that the preparation of the Expedition had been proceeding for over a year, and large sums of money had been spent. We offered to give the Expedition up without even consulting the donors of this money, and but few thought that the war would last through these five years and involve the whole world. The Expedition was not going an a peaceful cruise to the South Sea Islands, but to a most dangerous, difficult, and strenuous work that has nearly always involved a certain percentage of loss of life. Finally, when the Expedition did return, practically the whole of those members who had come unscathed through the dangers of the Antarctic took their places in the wider field of battle, and the percentage of casualties amongst the members of this Expedition is high.

The voyage out to Buenos Ayres was uneventful, and on October 26 we sailed from that port for South Georgia, the most southerly outpost of the British Empire. Here, for a month, we were engaged in final preparation. The last we heard of the war was when we left Buenos Ayres. Then the Russian Steam-Roller was advancing. According to many the war would be over within six months. And so we left, not without regret that we could not take our place there, but secure in the knowledge that we were taking part in a strenuous campaign for the credit of our country.

Apart from private individuals and societies I here acknowledge most gratefully the assistance rendered by the Dominion Government of New Zealand and the Commonwealth Government of Australia at the start of the Ross Sea section of the Expedition; and to the people of New Zealand and the Dominion Government I tender my most grateful thanks for their continued help, which was invaluable during the dark days before the relief of the Ross Sea Party.

Mr James Allen (acting Premier), the late Mr McNab (Minister of Marine), Mr Leonard Tripp, Mr Mabin, and Mr Toogood, and many others have laid me under a debt of gratitude that can never be repaid.

This is also the opportunity for me to thank the Uruguayan Government for their generous assistance in placing the government trawler, *Instituto de Pesca*, for the second attempt at the relief of my men on Elephant Island.

Finally, it was the Chilean Government that was directly responsible for the rescue of my comrades. This southern Republic was unwearied in its efforts to make a successful rescue, and the gratitude of our whole party is due to them. I especially mention the sympathetic attitude of Admiral Munoz Hurtado, head of the Chilean Navy, and Captain Luis Pardo, who commanded the *Yelcho* on our last and successful venture.

Sir Daniel Gooch came with us as far as South Georgia. I owe him my special thanks for his help with the dogs, and we all regretted losing his cheery presence, when we sailed for the South.

CHAPTER I

Into the Weddell Sea

I decided to leave South Georgia about December 5, and in the intervals of final preparation scanned again the plans for the voyage to winter quarters. What welcome was the Weddell Sea preparing for us? The whaling captains at South Georgia were generously ready to share with me their knowledge of the waters in which they pursued their trade, and, while confirming earlier information as to the extreme severity of the ice conditions in this sector of the Antarctic, they were able to give advice that was worth attention.

It will be convenient to state here briefly some of the considerations that weighed with me at that time and in the weeks that followed. I knew that the ice had come far north that season and, after listening to the suggestions of the whaling captains, had decided to steer to the South Sandwich Group, round Ultima Thule, and work as far to the eastward as the fifteenth meridian west longitude before pushing south. The whalers emphasised the difficulty of getting through the ice in the neighbourhood of the South Sandwich Group. They told me they had often seen the floes come right up to the group in the summer-time, and they thought the Expedition would have to push through heavy pack in order to reach the Weddell Sea. Probably the best time to get into the Weddell Sea would be the end of February or the beginning of March. The whalers had gone right round the South Sandwich Group and they were familiar with the conditions. The predictions they made induced me to take the deck-load of coal, for if we had to fight our way through to Coats' Land we would need every ton of fuel the ship could carry.

I hoped that by first moving to the east as far as the fifteenth meridian west we would be able to go south through looser ice, pick up Coats' Land and finally reach Vahsel Bay, where Filchner

made his attempt at landing in 1912. Two considerations were
occupying my mind at this juncture. I was anxious for certain
reasons to winter the *Endurance* in the Weddell Sea, but the
difficulty of finding a safe harbour might be very great. If no safe
harbour could be found, the ship must winter at South Georgia. It
seemed to me hopeless now to think of making the journey across
the continent in the first summer, as the season was far advanced
and the ice conditions were likely to prove unfavourable. In view
of the possibility of wintering the ship in the ice, we took extra
clothing from the stores at the various stations in South Georgia.

The other question that was giving me anxious thought was the
size of the shore party. If the ship had to go out during the winter,
or if she broke away from winter quarters, it would be preferable
to have only a small, carefully selected party of men ashore after
the hut had been built and the stores landed. These men could
proceed to lay out depots by man-haulage and make short journeys
with the dogs, training them for the long early march in the
following spring. The majority of the scientific men would live
aboard the ship, where they could do their work under good
conditions. They would be able to make short journeys if required,
using the *Endurance* as a base. All these plans were based on an
expectation that the finding of winter quarters was likely to be
difficult. If a really safe base could be established on the continent, I
would adhere to the original programme of sending one party to the
south, one to the west round the head of the Weddell Sea towards
Graham Land, and one to the east towards Enderby Land.

We had worked out details of distances, courses, stores required,
and so forth. Our sledging ration, the result of experience as well as
close study, was perfect. The dogs gave promise, after training, of
being able to cover fifteen to twenty miles a day with loaded
sledges. The transcontinental journey, at this rate, should be completed in 120 days unless some unforeseen obstacle intervened. We
longed keenly for the day when we could begin this march, the last
great adventure in the history of South Polar exploration, but a
knowledge of the obstacles that lay between us and our starting-
point served as a curb on impatience. Everything depended upon
the landing. If we could land at Filchner's base there was no reason
why a band of experienced men should not winter there in safety.
But the Weddell Sea was notoriously inhospitable and already we

knew that its sternest face was turned toward us. All the conditions in the Weddell Sea are unfavourable from the navigator's point of view. The winds are comparatively light, and consequently new ice can form even in the summer-time. The absence of strong winds has the additional effect of allowing the ice to accumulate in masses, undisturbed. Then great quantities of ice sweep along the coast from the east under the influence of the prevailing current, and fill up the bight of the Weddell Sea as they move north in a great semicircle. Some of this ice doubtless describes almost a complete circle, and is held up eventually, in bad seasons, against the South Sandwich Islands. The strong currents, pressing the ice masses against the coasts, create heavier pressure than is found in any other part of the Antarctic. This pressure must be at least as severe as the pressure experienced in the congested North Polar basin, and I am inclined to think that a comparison would be to the advantage of the Arctic. All these considerations naturally had a bearing upon our immediate problem, the penetration of the pack and the finding of a safe harbour on the continental coast.

The day of departure arrived. I gave the order to heave anchor at 8.45 a.m. on December 5, 1914, and the clanking of the windlass broke for us the last link with civilisation. The morning was dull and overcast, with occasional gusts of snow and sleet, but hearts were light aboard the *Endurance*. The long days of preparation were over and the adventure lay ahead.

We had hoped that some steamer from the north would bring news of war and perhaps letters from home before our departure. A ship did arrive on the evening of the 4th, but she carried no letters, and nothing useful in the way of information could be gleaned from her. The captain and crew were all stoutly pro-German, and the 'news' they had to give took the unsatisfying form of accounts of British and French reverses. We would have been glad to have had the latest tidings from a friendlier source. A year and a half later we were to learn that the *Harpoon*, the steamer which tends the Grytviken station, had arrived with mail for us not more than two hours after the *Endurance* had proceeded down the coast.

The bows of the *Endurance* were turned to the south, and the good ship dipped to the south-westerly swell. Misty rain fell during the forenoon, but the weather cleared later in the day, and we had a good view of the coast of South Georgia as we moved

under steam and sail to the south-east. The course was laid to carry
us clear of the island and then south of South Thule, Sandwich
Group. The wind freshened during the day, and all square sail was
set, with the foresail reefed in order to give the look-out a clear
view ahead; for we did not wish to risk contact with a 'growler',
one of those treacherous fragments of ice that float with surface
awash. The ship was very steady in the quarterly sea, but certainly
did not look as neat and trim as she had done when leaving the
shores of England four months earlier. We had filled up with coal
at Grytviken, and this extra fuel was stored on deck, where it
impeded movement considerably. The carpenter had built a false
deck, extending from the poop-deck to the chart-room. We had
also taken aboard a ton of whale-meat for the dogs. The big
chunks of meat were hung up in the rigging, out of reach but not
out of sight of the dogs, and as the *Endurance* rolled and pitched,
they watched with wolfish eyes for a windfall.

I was greatly pleased with the dogs, which were tethered about
the ship in the most comfortable positions we could find for them.
They were in excellent condition, and I felt that the Expedition
had the right tractive-power. They were big, sturdy animals, chosen
for endurance and strength, and if they were as keen to pull our
sledges as they were now to fight one another, all would be well.
The men in charge of the dogs were doing their work enthus-
iastically, and the eagerness they showed to study the natures and
habits of their charges gave promise of efficient handling and good
work later on.

During December 6 the *Endurance* made good progress on a
south-easterly course. The northerly breeze had freshened during
the night and had brought up a high following sea. The weather
was hazy, and we passed two bergs, several growlers, and numerous lumps of ice. Staff and crew were settling down to the routine.
Bird life was plentiful, and we noticed Cape pigeons, whale-birds,
terns, mollymauks, nellies, sooty and wandering albatrosses in the
neighbourhood of the ship. The course was laid for the passage
between Sanders Island and Candlemas Volcano. December 7
brought the first check. At six o'clock that morning the sea, which
had been green in colour all the previous day, changed suddenly to
a deep indigo. The ship was behaving well in a rough sea, and
some members of the scientific staff were transferring to the

bunkers the coal we had stowed on deck. Sanders Island and Candlemas were sighted early in the afternoon, and the *Endurance* passed between them at 6 p.m. Worsley's observations indicated that Sanders Island was, roughly, three miles east and five miles north of the charted position. Large numbers of bergs, mostly tabular in form, lay to the west of the islands, and we noticed that many of them were yellow with diatoms. One berg had large patches of red-brown soil down its sides. The presence of so many bergs was ominous, and immediately after passing between the islands we encountered stream-ice. All sail was taken in and we proceeded slowly under steam. Two hours later, fifteen miles north-east of Sanders Island, the *Endurance* was confronted by a belt of heavy pack-ice, half a mile broad and extending north and south. There was clear water beyond, but the heavy south-westerly swell made the pack impenetrable in our neighbourhood. This was disconcerting. The noon latitude had been 57 degrees 26 minutes S., and I had not expected to find pack-ice nearly so far north, though the whalers had reported pack-ice right up to South Thule.

The situation became dangerous that night. We pushed into the pack in the hope of reaching open water beyond, and found ourselves after dark in a pool which was growing smaller and smaller. The ice was grinding around the ship in the heavy swell, and I watched with some anxiety for any indication of a change of wind to the east, since a breeze from that quarter would have driven us towards the land. Worsley and I were on deck all night, dodging the pack. At 3 a.m. we ran south, taking advantage of some openings that had appeared, but met heavy rafted pack-ice, evidently old; some of it had been subjected to severe pressure. Then we steamed north-west and saw open water to the north-east. I put the *Endurance*s' head for the opening, and, steaming at full speed, we got clear. Then we went east in the hope of getting better ice, and five hours later, after some dodging, we rounded the pack and were able to set sail once more. This initial tussle with the pack had been exciting at times. Pieces of ice and bergs of all sizes were heaving and jostling against each other in the heavy south-westerly swell. In spite of all our care the *Endurance* struck large lumps stem on, but the engines were stopped in time and no harm was done. The scene and sounds throughout the day were very fine. The swell was dashing against the sides of huge bergs and leaping right to the top of their icy cliffs. Sanders Island lay to the south, with a few rocky faces peering through the misty swirling clouds that swathed it most of the time, the booming of the sea running into ice-caverns, the swishing break of the swell on the loose pack, and the graceful bowing and undulating of the inner pack to the steeply rolling swell, which here was robbed of its break by the masses of ice to windward.

We skirted the northern edge of the pack in clear weather with a light south-westerly breeze and an overcast sky. The bergs were numerous. During the morning of December 9 an easterly breeze brought hazy weather with snow, and at 4.30 p.m. we encountered the edge of pack-ice in lat. 58 degrees 27 minutes S., long. 22 degrees 08 minutes W. It was one-year-old ice interspersed with older pack, all heavily snow-covered and lying west-south-west to east-north-east. We entered the pack at 5 p.m., but could not make progress, and cleared it again at 7.40 p.m. Then we steered east-north-east and spent the rest of the night rounding the pack. During the day we had seen adelie and ringed penguins, also several humpback and finner whales. An ice-blink to the westward indicated the presence of pack in that direction. After rounding the pack we steered S. 40 degrees E., and at noon on the 10th had reached lat. 58 degrees 28 minutes S., long. 20 degrees 28 minutes W. Observations showed the compass variation to be 1½ degrees less than the chart recorded. I kept the *Endurance* on the course till midnight, when we entered loose open ice about ninety miles south-east of our noon position. This ice proved to fringe the pack, and progress became slow. There was a long easterly swell with a light northerly breeze, and the weather was clear and fine. Numerous bergs lay outside the pack.

The *Endurance* steamed through loose open ice till 8 a.m. on the 11th, when we entered the pack in lat. 59 degrees 46 minutes S., long. 18 degrees 22 minutes W. We could have gone farther east, but the pack extended far in that direction, and an effort to circle it might have involved a lot of northing. I did not wish to lose the benefit of the original southing. The extra miles would not have mattered to a ship with larger coal capacity than the *Endurance* possessed, but we could not afford to sacrifice miles unnecessarily. The pack was loose and did not present great difficulties at this stage. The foresail was set, in order to take advantage of the northerly breeze. The ship was in contact with the ice occasionally and received some heavy blows. Once or twice she was brought up all standing against solid pieces, but no harm was done. The chief concern was to protect the propeller and rudder. If a collision seemed to be inevitable the officer in charge would order 'slow' or 'half speed' with the engines, and put the helm over so as to strike the floe a glancing blow. Then the helm would be put over towards the ice with the object of throwing the propeller clear of it, and the ship would forge ahead again. Worsley, Wild, and I, with three officers, kept three watches while we were working through the pack, so that we had two officers on deck all the time. The carpenter had rigged a six-foot wooden semaphore on the bridge to enable the navigating officer to give the seamen or scientists at the wheel the direction and the exact amount of helm required. This device saved time, as well as the effort of shouting. We were pushing through this loose pack all day, and the view from the crow's-nest gave no promise of improved conditions ahead. A Weddell seal and a crab-eater seal were noticed on the floes, but we did not pause to secure fresh meat. It was important that we should make progress towards our goal as rapidly as possible, and there was reason to fear that we should have plenty of time to spare later on if the ice conditions continued to increase in severity.

On the morning of December 12 we were working through loose pack which later became thick in places. The sky was overcast and light snow was falling. I had all square sail set at 7 a.m. in order to take advantage of the northerly breeze, but it had to come in again five hours later when the wind hauled round to the west. The noon position was lat. 60 degrees 26 minutes S., long. 17 degrees 58 minutes W., and the run for the twenty-four hours had been only 33 miles. The ice was still badly congested, and we were pushing through narrow leads and occasional openings with the floes often close abeam on either side. Antarctic, snow and stormy petrels, fulmars, white-rumped terns, and adelies were around us. The quaint little penguins found the ship a cause of much apparent excitement and provided a lot of amusement aboard. One of the standing jokes was that all the adelies on the floe seemed to know Clark, and when he was at the wheel rushed along as fast as their legs could carry them, yelling out 'Clark!

Clark!' and apparently very indignant and perturbed that he never waited for them or even answered them.

We found several good leads to the south in the evening, and continued to work southward throughout the night and the following day. The pack extended in all directions as far as the eye could reach. The noon observation showed the run for the twenty-four hours to be 54 miles, a satisfactory result under the conditions. Wild shot a young Ross seal on the floe, and we manoeuvred the ship alongside. Hudson jumped down, bent a line on to the seal, and the pair of them were hauled up. The seal was 4 ft. 9 in. long and weighed about ninety pounds. He was a young male and proved very good eating, but when dressed and minus the blubber made little more than a square meal for our twenty-eight men, with a few scraps for our breakfast and tea. The stomach contained only amphipods about an inch long, allied to those found in the whales at Grytviken.

The conditions became harder on December 14. There was a misty haze, and occasional falls of snow. A few bergs were in sight. The pack was denser than it had been on the previous days. Older ice was intermingled with the young ice, and our progress became slower. The propeller received several blows in the early morning, but no damage was done. A platform was rigged under the jib-boom in order that Hurley might secure some kinematograph pictures of the ship breaking through the ice. The young ice did not present difficulties to the *Endurance*, which was able to smash a way through, but the lumps of older ice were more formidable obstacles, and conning the ship was a task requiring close attention. The most careful navigation could not prevent an occasional bump against ice too thick to be broken or pushed aside. The southerly breeze strengthened to a moderate south-westerly gale during the afternoon, and at 8 p.m. we hove to, stem against a floe, it being impossible to proceed without serious risk of damage to rudder or propeller. I was interested to notice that, although we had been steaming through the pack for three days, the north-westerly swell still held with us. It added to the difficulties of navigation in the lanes, since the ice was constantly in movement.

The *Endurance* remained against the floe for the next twenty-four hours, when the gale moderated. The pack extended to the horizon in all directions and was broken by innumerable narrow lanes. Many bergs were in sight, and they appeared to be travelling through the pack in a south-westerly direction under the current influence. Probably the pack itself was moving north-east with the gale. Clark put down a net in search of specimens, and at two fathoms it was carried southwest by the current and fouled the propeller. He lost the net, two leads, and a line. Ten bergs drove to the south through the pack during the twenty-four hours. The noon position was 61 degrees 31 minutes S., long. 18 degrees 12 minutes W. The gale had moderated at 8 p.m., and we made five miles to the south before midnight and then we stopped at the end of a long lead, waiting till the weather cleared. It was during this short run that the captain, with semaphore hard-a-port, shouted to the scientist at the wheel: 'Why in Paradise don't you port!' The answer came in indignant tones: 'I am blowing my nose.'

The *Endurance* made some progress on the following day. Long leads of open water ran towards the south-west, and the ship smashed at full speed through occasional areas of young ice till brought up with a heavy thud against a section of older floe. Worsley was out on the jib-boom end for a few minutes while Wild was conning the ship, and he came back with a glowing account of a novel sensation. The boom was swinging high and low and from side to side, while the massive bows of the ship smashed through the ice, splitting it across, piling it mass on mass and then shouldering it aside. The air temperature was 37 degrees Fahr., pleasantly warm, and the water temperature 29 degrees Fahr. We continued to advance through fine long leads till 4 a.m. on December 17, when the ice became difficult again. Very large floes of six-months-old ice lay close together. Some of these floes presented a square mile of unbroken surface; and among them were patches of thin ice and several floes of heavy old ice. Many bergs were in sight, and the course became devious. The ship was blocked at one point by a wedge-shaped piece of floe, but we put the ice-anchor through it, towed it astern, and proceeded through the gap. Steering under these conditions required muscle as well as nerve. There was a clatter aft during the afternoon, and Hussey, who was at the wheel, explained that 'the wheel spun round and threw me over the top of it!' The noon position was lat. 62 degrees 13 minutes S., long. 18 degrees 53 minutes W., and the

run for the preceding twenty-four hours had been 32 miles in a
south-westerly direction. We saw three blue whales during the
day and one emperor penguin, a 58-lb. bird, which was added to
the larder.

The morning of December 18 found the *Endurance* proceeding
amongst large floes with thin ice between them. The leads were
few. There was a northerly breeze with occasional snow-flurries.
We secured three crab-eater seals – two cows and a bull. The bull
was a fine specimen, nearly white all over and 9 ft. 3 in. long; he
weighed 600 lb. Shortly before noon further progress was barred
by heavy pack, and we put an ice-anchor on the floe and banked
the fires. I had been prepared for evil conditions in the Weddell
Sea, but had hoped that in December and January, at any rate, the
pack would be loose, even if no open water was to be found.
What we were actually encountering was fairly dense pack of a
very obstinate character. Pack-ice might be described as a gigantic
and interminable jigsaw-puzzle devised by nature. The parts of
the puzzle in loose pack have floated slightly apart and become
disarranged; at numerous places they have pressed together again;
as the pack gets closer the congested areas grow larger and the
parts are jammed harder till finally it becomes 'close pack', when
the whole of the jigsaw-puzzle becomes jammed to such an
extent that with care and labour it can be traversed in every
direction on foot. Where the parts do not fit closely there is, of
course, open water, which freezes over, in a few hours after
giving off volumes of 'frost-smoke'. In obedience to renewed
pressure this young ice 'rafts', so forming double thicknesses of a
toffee-like consistency. Again the opposing edges of heavy floes
rear up in slow and almost silent conflict, till high 'hedgerows' are
formed round each part of the puzzle. At the junction of several
floes chaotic areas of piled-up blocks and masses of ice are formed.
Sometimes 5-ft. to 6-ft. piles of evenly shaped blocks of ice are
seen so neatly laid that it seems impossible for them to be Nature's
work. Again, a winding canyon may be traversed between icy
walls 6 ft. to 10 ft. high, or a dome may be formed that under
renewed pressure bursts upward like a volcano. All the winter
the drifting pack changes – grows by freezing, thickens by rafting,
and corrugates by pressure. If, finally, in its drift it impinges on
a coast, such as the western shore of the Weddell Sea, terrific

pressure is set up and an inferno of ice-blocks, ridges, and hedge-rows results, extending possibly for 150 or 200 miles offshore. Sections of pressure ice may drift away subsequently and become embedded in new ice.

I have given this brief explanation here in order that the reader may understand the nature of the ice through which we pushed our way for many hundreds of miles. Another point that may require to be explained was the delay caused by wind while we were in the pack. When a strong breeze or moderate gale was blowing the ship could not safely work through any except young ice, up to about two feet in thickness. As ice of that nature never extended for more than a mile or so, it followed that in a gale in the pack we had always to lie to. The ship was 3 ft. 3 in. down by the stern, and while this saved the propeller and rudder a good deal, it made the *Endurance* practically unmanageable in close pack when the wind attained a force of six miles an hour from ahead, since the air currents had such a big surface forward to act upon. The pressure of wind on bows and the yards of the foremast would cause the bows to fall away, and in these conditions the ship could not be steered into the narrow lanes and leads through which we had to thread our way. The falling away of the bows, more-over, would tend to bring the stern against the ice, compelling us to stop the engines in order to save the propeller. Then the ship would become unmanageable and drift away, with the possi-bility of getting excessive sternway on her and so damaging rudder or propeller, the Achilles heel of a ship in pack-ice.

While we were waiting for the weather to moderate and the ice to open, I had the Lucas sounding-machine rigged over the rudder-trunk and found the depth to be 2810 fathoms. The bot-tom sample was lost owing to the line parting 60 fathoms from the end. During the afternoon three adelie penguins approached the ship across the floe while Hussey was discoursing sweet music on the banjo. The solemn-looking little birds appeared to appreciate 'It's a Long Way to Tipperary', but they fled in horror when Hussey treated them to a little of the music that comes from Scot-land. The shouts of laughter from the ship added to their dismay, and they made off as fast as their short legs would carry them. The pack opened slightly at 6.15 p.m., and we proceeded through lanes for three hours before being forced to anchor to a floe for the night. We fired a Hjort mark harpoon, No. 171, into a blue whale on this day. The conditions did not improve during December 19. A fresh to strong northerly breeze brought haze and snow, and after proceeding for two hours the *Endurance* was stopped again by heavy floes. It was impossible to manoeuvre the ship in the ice owing to the strong wind, which kept the floes in movement and caused lanes to open and close with dangerous rapidity. The noon observation showed that we had made six miles to the south-east in the previous twenty-four hours. All hands were engaged during the day in rubbing shoots off our potatoes, which were found to be sprouting freely. We remained moored to a floe over the following day, the wind not having moderated; indeed, it freshened to a gale in the afternoon, and the members of the staff and crew took advantage of the pause to enjoy a vigorously contested game of football on the level surface of the floe alongside the ship. Twelve bergs were in sight at this time. The noon position was lat. 62 degrees 42 minutes S., long. 17 degrees 54 minutes W., showing that we had drifted about six miles in a north-easterly direction.

Monday, December 21, was beautifully fine, with a gentle west-north-westerly breeze. We made a start at 3 a.m. and proceeded through the pack in a south-westerly direction. At noon we had gained seven miles almost due east, the northerly drift of the pack having continued while the ship was apparently moving to the south. Petrels of several species, penguins, and seals were plentiful, and we saw four small blue whales. At noon we entered a long lead to the southward and passed around and between nine splendid bergs. One mighty specimen was shaped like the Rock of Gibraltar but with steeper cliffs, and another had a natural dock that would have contained the Aquitania. A spur of ice closed the entrance to the huge blue pool. Hurley brought out his kinematograph-camera, in order to make a record of these bergs. Fine long leads running east and south-east among bergs were found during the afternoon, but at midnight the ship was stopped by small, heavy ice-floes, tightly packed against an unbroken plain of ice. The outlook from the mast-head was not encouraging. The big floe was at least 15 miles long and 10 miles wide. The edge could not be seen at the widest part, and the area of the floe must have been not less than 150 square miles. It appeared to be formed of year-old ice, not very thick and with very few hummocks or ridges in it. We thought it must have been formed at sea in very calm weather and drifted up from the south-east. I had never seen such a large area of unbroken ice in the Ross Sea.

We waited with banked fires for the strong easterly breeze to moderate or the pack to open. At 6.30 p.m. on December 22 some lanes opened and we were able to move towards the south again. The following morning found us working slowly through the pack, and the noon observation gave us a gain of 19 miles S. 41 degrees W. for the seventeen and a half hours under steam. Many year-old adelies, three crab-eaters, six sea-leopards, one Weddell and two blue whales were seen. The air temperature, which had been down to 25 degrees Fahr. on December 21, had risen to 34 degrees Fahr. While we were working along leads to the southward in the afternoon, we counted fifteen bergs. Three of these were table-topped, and one was about 70 ft high and 5 miles long. Evidently it had come from a barrier-edge. The ice became heavier but slightly more open, and we had a calm night with fine long leads of open water. The water was so still that new ice was forming on the leads. We had a run of 70 miles to our credit at noon on December 24, the position being lat. 64 degrees 32 minutes S., long. 17 degrees 17 degrees W. All the dogs except eight had been named. I do not know who had been responsible for some of the names, which seemed to represent a variety of tastes. They were as follows: Rugby, Upton, Bristol, Millhill, Songster, Sandy, Mack, Mercury, Wolf, Amundsen, Hercules, Hackenschmidt, Samson, Sammy, Skipper, Caruso, Sub, Ulysses, Spotty, Bosun, Slobbers, Sadie, Sue, Sally, Jasper, Tim, Sweep, Martin, Splitlip, Luke, Saint, Satan, Chips, Stumps, Snapper, Painful, Bob, Snowball, Jerry, Judge, Sooty, Rufus, Sidelights, Simeon, Swanker, Chirgwin, Steamer, Peter, Fluffy, Steward, Slippery, Elliott, Roy, Noel, Shakespeare, Jamie, Bummer, Smuts, Lupoid, Spider, and Sailor. Some of the names, it will be noticed, had a descriptive flavour.

Heavy floes held up the ship from midnight till 6 a.m. on December 25, Christmas Day. Then they opened a little and we made progress till 11.30 a.m., when the leads closed again. We had encountered good leads and workable ice during the early part of the night, and the noon observation showed that our run for the twenty-four hours was the best since we entered the pack a fortnight earlier. We had made 71 miles S. 4 degrees W. The ice held us up till the evening, and then we were able to follow some leads for a couple of hours before the tightly packed floes and the increasing wind compelled a stop. The celebration of Christmas was not forgotten. Grog was served at midnight to all on deck. There was grog again at breakfast, for the benefit of those who had been in their bunks at midnight. Lees had decorated the wardroom with flags and had a little Christmas present for each of us. Some of us had presents from home to open. Later there was a really splendid dinner, consisting of turtle soup, whitebait, jugged hare, Christmas pudding, mince-pies, dates, figs and crystallised fruits, with rum and stout as drinks. In the evening everybody joined in a 'sing-song.' Hussey had made a one-stringed violin, on which, in the words of Worsley, he 'discoursed quite painlessly'. The wind was increasing to a moderate south-easterly gale and no advance could be made; so we were able to settle down to the enjoyments of the evening.

The weather was still bad on December 26 and 27, and the *Endurance* remained anchored to a floe. The noon position on the 26th was lat. 65 degrees 43 minutes S., long. 17 degrees 36 minutes W. We made another sounding on this day with the Lucas machine and found bottom at 2819 fathoms. The specimen brought up was a terrigenous blue mud (glacial deposit) with some radiolaria. Everyone took turns at the work of heaving in, two men working together in ten-minute spells.

Sunday, December 27, was a quiet day aboard. The southerly gale was blowing the snow in clouds off the floe and the temperature had fallen to 23 degrees Fahr. The dogs were having an uncomfortable time in their deck quarters. The wind had moderated by the following morning, but it was squally with snow-flurries, and I did not order a start till 11 p.m. The pack was still close, but the ice was softer and more easily broken. During the pause the carpenter had rigged a small stage over the stern. A man was stationed there to watch the propeller and prevent it striking heavy ice, and the arrangement proved very valuable. It saved the rudder as well as the propeller from many blows.

The high winds that had prevailed for four and a half days gave way to a gentle southerly breeze in the evening of December 29.

Owing to the drift we were actually eleven miles farther north than we had been on December 25. But we made fairly good progress on the 30th in fine, clear weather. The ship followed a long lead to the south-east during the afternoon and evening, and at 11 p.m. we crossed the Antarctic Circle. An examination of the horizon disclosed considerable breaks in the vast circle of pack-ice, interspersed with bergs of different sizes. Leads could be traced in various directions, but I looked in vain for an indication of open water. The sun did not set that night, and as it was concealed behind a bank of clouds we had a glow of crimson and gold to the southward, with delicate pale green reflections in the water of the lanes to the south-east.

The ship had a serious encounter with the ice on the morning of December 31. We were stopped first by floes closing around us, and then about noon the *Endurance* got jammed between two floes heading east-north-east. The pressure heeled the ship over six degrees while we were getting an ice-anchor on to the floe in order to heave astern and thus assist the engines, which were running at full speed. The effort was successful. Immediately afterwards, at the spot where the *Endurance* had been held, slabs of ice 50 ft. by 15 ft. and 4 ft. thick were forced ten or twelve feet up on the lee floe at an angle of 45 degrees. The pressure was severe, and we were not sorry to have the ship out of its reach. The noon position was lat. 66 degrees 47 minutes S., long. 15 degrees 52 minutes W., and the run for the preceding twenty-four hours was 51 miles S. 29 minutes E.

'Since noon the character of the pack has improved,' wrote Worsley on this day. 'Though the leads are short, the floes are rotten and easily broken through if a good place is selected with care and judgment. In many cases we find large sheets of young ice through which the ship cuts for a mile or two miles at a stretch. I have been conning and working the ship from the crow's-nest and find it much the best place, as from there one can see ahead and work out the course beforehand, and can also guard the rudder and propeller, the most vulnerable pars of a ship in the ice. At midnight, as I was sitting in the "tub" I heard a clamorous noise down on the deck, with ringing of bells, and realised that it was the New Year.' Worsley came down from his lofty seat and met Wild, Hudson, and myself on the bridge, where we shook hands and wished one another a happy and successful New Year. Since entering the pack on December 11 we had come 480 miles, through loose and close pack-ice. We had pushed and fought the little ship through, and she had stood the test well, though the propeller had received some shrewd blows against hard ice and the vessel had been driven against the floe until she had fairly mounted up on it and slid back rolling heavily from side to side. The rolling had been more frequently caused by the operation of cracking through thickish young ice, where the crack had taken a sinuous course. The ship, in attempting to follow it, struck first one bilge and then the other, causing her to roll six or seven degrees. Our advance through the pack had been in a S.10 degrees E. direction, and I estimated that the total steaming distance had exceeded 700 miles. The first 100 miles had been through loose pack, but the greatest hindrances had been three moderate south-westerly gales, two lasting for three days each and one for four and a half days. The last 250 miles had been through close pack alternating with fine long, leads and stretches of open water.

During the weeks we spent manoeuvring to the south through the tortuous mazes of the pack it was necessary often to split floes by driving the ship against them. This form of attack was effective against ice up to three feet in thickness, and the process is interesting enough to be worth describing briefly. When the way was barred by a floe of moderate thickness we would drive the ship at half speed against it, stopping the engines just before the impact. At the first blow the *Endurance* would cut a V-shaped nick in the face of the floe, the slope of her cutwater often causing her bows to rise till nearly clear of the water, when she would slide backwards, rolling slightly. Watching carefully that loose lumps of ice did not damage the propeller, we would reverse the engines and back the ship off 200 to 300 yds. She would then be driven full speed into the V, taking care to hit the centre accurately. The operation would be repeated until a short dock was cut, into which the ship, acting as a large wedge, was driven. At about the fourth attempt, if it was to succeed at all, the floe would yield. A black, sinuous line, as though pen-drawn on white paper, would appear ahead, broadening as the eye traced it back to the ship. Presently it would be broad enough to receive her, and we would forge ahead. Under the bows and alongside, great slabs of ice were being turned over and slid back on the floe, or driven down and under the ice or ship. In thus way the *Endurance* would split a 2-ft. to 3-ft. floe a square mile in extent. Occasionally the floe, although cracked across, would be so held by other floes that it would refuse to open wide, and so gradually would bring the ship to a standstill. We would then go astern for some distance and again drive her full speed into the crack, till finally the floe would yield to the repeated onslaughts.

CHAPTER 2

New land

The first day of the New Year (January 1, 1915) was cloudy, with
a gentle northerly breeze and occasional snow-squalls. The condition of the pack improved in the evening, and after 8 p.m. we
forged ahead rapidly through brittle young ice, easily broken by
the ship. A few hours later a moderate gale came up from the
east, with continuous snow. After 4 a.m. on the 2nd we got into
thick old pack-ice, showing signs of heavy pressure. It was much
hummocked, but large areas of open water and long leads to the
south-west continued until noon. The position then was lat. 69
degrees 49 minutes S., long. 15 degrees 42 minutes W., and the
run for the twenty-four hours had been 124 miles S. 3 degrees W.
This was cheering.

The heavy pack blocked the way south after midday. It would
have been almost impossible to have pushed the ship into the ice,
and in any case the gale would have made such a proceeding
highly dangerous. So we dodged along to the west and north,
looking for a suitable opening towards the south. The good run
had given me hope of sighting the land on the following day, and
the delay was annoying. I was growing anxious to reach land on
account of the dogs, which had not been able to get exercise for
four weeks, and were becoming run down. We passed at least two
hundred bergs during the day, and we noticed also large masses of
hummocky bay-ice and ice-foot. One floe of bay-ice had black
earth upon it, apparently basaltic in origin, and there was a large
berg with a broad band of yellowish brown right through it. The
stain may have been volcanic dust. Many of the bergs had quaint
shapes. There was one that exactly resembled a large two-funnel
liner, complete in silhouette except for smoke. Later in the day we
found an opening in the pack and made 9 miles to the south-west,
but at 2 a.m. on January 3 the lead ended in hummocky ice,

impossible to penetrate. A moderate easterly gale had come up with snow-squalls, and we could not get a clear view in any direction. The hummocky ice did not offer a suitable anchorage for the ship, and we were compelled to dodge up and down for ten hours before we were able to make fast to a small floe under the lee of a berg 120 ft. high. The berg broke the wind and saved us drifting fast to leeward. The position was lat. 69 degrees 59 minutes S., long. 17 degrees 31 minutes W. We made a move again at 7 p.m., when we took in the ice-anchor and proceeded south, and at 10 p.m. we passed a small berg that the ship had nearly touched twelve hours previously. Obviously we were not making much headway. Several of the bergs passed during this day were of solid blue ice, indicating true glacier origin.

By midnight of the 3rd we had made 11 miles to the south; and then came to a full stop in weather so thick with snow that we could not learn if the leads and lanes were worth entering. The ice was hummocky, but, fortunately, the gale was decreasing, and after we had scanned all the leads and pools within our reach we turned back to the north-east. Two sperm and two large blue whales were sighted, the first we had seen for 260 miles. We saw also petrels, numerous adelies, emperors, crab-eaters, and sea-leopards. The clearer weather of the morning showed us that the pack was solid and impassable from the south-east to the south-west, and at 10 a.m. on the 4th we again passed within five yards of the small berg that we had passed twice on the previous day. We had been steaming and dodging about over an area of twenty square miles for fifty hours, trying to find an opening to the south, south-east, or south-west, but all the leads ran north, north-east, or northwest. It was as though the spirits of the Antarctic were pointing us to the backward track – the track we were determined not to follow. Our desire was to make easting as well as southing so as to reach the land, if possible, east of Ross's farthest south and well east of Coats' Land. This was more important as the prevailing winds appeared to be to easterly, and every mile of easting would count. In the afternoon we went west in some open water, and by 4 p.m. we were making west-south-west with more water opening up ahead. The sun was shining brightly, over three degrees high at midnight, and we were able to maintain this direction in fine weather till the following noon. The position

then was lat. 70 degrees 28 minutes S., long. 20 degrees 16 minutes
W., and the run had been 62 miles S. 62 degrees W. At 8 a.m.
there had been open water from north round by west to south-
west, but impenetrable pack to the south and east. At 3 p.m. the
way to the south-west and west-north-west was absolutely blocked,
and as we experienced a set to the west, I did not feel justified in
burning more of the reduced stock of coal to go west or north. I
took the ship back over our course for four miles, to a point where
some looser pack gave faint promise of a way through; but, after
battling for three hours with very heavy hummocked ice and
making four miles to the south, we were brought up by huge
blocks and floes of very old pack. Further effort seemed useless at
that time, and I gave the order to bank fires after we had moored
the *Endurance* to a solid floe. The weather was clear, and some
enthusiastic football-players had a game on the floe until, about
midnight, Worsley dropped through a hole in rotten ice while
retrieving the ball. He had to be retrieved himself.

Solid pack still barred the way to the south on the following
morning (January 6). There was some open water north of the
floe, but as the day was calm and I did not wish to use coal in a
possibly vain search for an opening to the southward, I kept the
ship moored to the floe. This pause in good weather gave an
opportunity to exercise the dogs, which were taken on to the floe
by the men in charge of them. The excitement of the animals was
intense. Several managed to get into the water, and the muzzles
they were wearing did not prevent some hot fights. Two dogs
which had contrived to slip their muzzles fought themselves into
an icy pool and were hauled out still locked in a grapple. However, men and dogs enjoyed the exercise. A sounding gave a depth
of 2400 fathoms, with a blue mud bottom. The wind freshened
from the west early the next morning, and we started to skirt the
northern edge of the solid pack in an easterly direction under sail.
We had cleared the close pack by noon, but the outlook to the
south gave small promise of useful progress, and I was anxious now
to make easting. We went north-east under sail, and after making
thirty-nine miles passed a peculiar berg that we had been abreast
of sixty hours earlier. Killer-whales were becoming active around
us, and I had to exercise caution in allowing anyone to leave
the ship. These beasts have a habit of locating a resting seal by

looking over the edge of a floe and then striking through the ice from below in search of a meal; they would not distinguish between seal and man.

The noon position on January 8 was lat. 70 degrees 0 minutes S., long. 19 degrees 09 minutes W. We had made 66 miles in a north-easterly direction during the preceding twenty-four hours. The course during the afternoon was east-south-east through loose pack and open water, with deep hummocky floes to the south. Several leads to the south came in view, but we held on the easterly course. The floes were becoming looser, and there were indications of open water ahead. The ship passed not fewer than five hundred bergs that day, some of them very large. A dark water-sky extended from east to south-south-east on the following morning, and the *Endurance*, working through loose pack at half speed, reached open water just before noon. A rampart berg 150 ft. high and a quarter of a mile long lay at the edge of the loose pack, and we sailed over a projecting foot of this berg into rolling ocean, stretching to the horizon. The sea extended from a little to the west of south, round by east to north-north-east, and its welcome promise was supported by a deep water-sky to the south. I laid a course south by east in an endeavour to get south and east of Ross's farthest south (lat. 71 degrees 30 minutes S.).

We kept the open water for a hundred miles, passing many bergs but encountering no pack. Two very large whales, probably blue whales, came up close to the ship, and we saw spouts in all directions. Open water inside the pack in that latitude might have the appeal of sanctuary to the whales, which are harried by man farther north. The run southward in blue water, with a path clear ahead and the miles falling away behind us, was a joyful experience after the long struggle through the ice-lanes. But, like other good things, our spell of free movement had to end. The *Endurance* encountered the ice again at 1 a.m. on the 10th. Loose pack stretched to east and south, with open water to the west and a good water-sky. It consisted partly of heavy hummocky ice showing evidence of great pressure, but contained also many thick, flat floes evidently formed in some sheltered bay and never subjected to pressure or to much motion. The swirl of the ship's wash brought diatomaceous scum from the sides of this ice. The water became thick with diatoms at 9 a.m., and I ordered a cast to be made. No bottom was found at 210 fathoms. The *Endurance* continued to advance southward through loose pack that morning. We saw the spouts of numerous whales and noticed some hundreds of crab-eaters lying on the floes. White-rumped terns, Antarctic petrels and snow-petrels were numerous, and there was a colony of adelies on a low berg. A few killer-whales, with their characteristic high dorsal fin, also came in view. The noon position was lat. 72 degrees 02 minutes S., long. 16 degrees 07 minutes W., and the run for the twenty-four hours had been 136 miles S. 6 degrees E.

We were now in the vicinity of the land discovered by Dr W. S. Bruce, leader of the *Scotia* Expedition, in 1904, and named by him Coats' Land. Dr Bruce encountered an ice-barrier in lat. 72 degrees 18 minutes S., long. 10 degrees W., stretching from north-east to south-west. He followed the barrier-edge to the south-west for 150 miles and reached lat. 74 degrees 1 minute S., long. 22 degrees W. He saw no naked rock, but his description of rising slopes of snow and ice, with shoaling water off the barrier-wall, indicated clearly the presence of land. It was up those slopes, at a point as far south as possible, that I planned to begin our march across the Antarctic continent. All hands were watching now for the coast described by Dr Bruce, and at 5 p.m. the look-out reported an appearance of land to the south-south-east. We could see a gentle snow-slope rising to a height of about one thousand feet. It seemed to be an island or a peninsula with a sound on its south side, and the position of its most northerly point was about 72 degrees 34 minutes S., 16 degrees 40 minutes W. The *Endurance* was passing through heavy loose pack, and shortly before midnight she broke into a lead of open sea along a barrier-edge. A sounding within one cable's length of the barrier-edge gave no bottom with 210 fathoms of line. The barrier was 70 ft. high, with cliffs of about 40 ft. The *Scotia* must have passed this point when pushing to Bruce's farthest south on March 6, 1904, and I knew from the narrative of that voyage, as well as from our own observation, that the coast trended away to the south-west. The lead of open water continued along the barrier-edge, and we pushed forward without delay.

An easterly breeze brought cloud and falls of snow during the morning of January 11. The barrier trended south-west by south, and we skirted it for fifty miles until 11 am. The cliffs in the morning were 20 ft. high, and by noon they had increased to 110 and 115 ft. The brow apparently rose 20 to 30 ft. higher. We were forced away from the barrier once for three hours by a line of very heavy pack-ice. Otherwise there was open water along the edge, with high loose pack to the west and north-west. We noticed a seal bobbing up and down in an apparent effort to swallow a long silvery fish that projected at least eighteen inches from its mouth. The noon position was lat. 73 degrees 13 minutes S., long. 20 degrees 43 minutes W., and a sounding then gave 155 fathoms at a distance of a mile from the barrier. The bottom consisted of large igneous pebbles. The weather then became thick, and I held away to the westward, where the sky had given indications of open water, until 7 p.m., when we laid the ship alongside a floe in loose pack. Heavy snow was falling, and I was anxious lest the westerly wind should bring the pack hard against the coast and jam the ship. The *Nimrod* had a narrow escape from a misadventure of this kind in the Ross Sea early in 1908.

We made a start again at 5 a.m. the next morning (January 12) in overcast weather with mist and snow-showers, and four hours later broke through loose pack-ice into open water. The view was obscured, but we proceeded to the south-east and had gained 24 miles by noon, when three soundings in lat. 74 degrees 4 minutes S., long. 22 degrees 48 minutes W. gave 95, 128, and 103 fathoms, with a bottom of sand, pebbles, and mud. Clark got a good haul of biological specimens in the dredge. The *Endurance* was now close to what appeared to be the barrier, with a heavy pack-ice foot containing numerous bergs frozen in and possibly aground. The solid ice turned away towards the north-west, and we followed the edge for 48 miles N. 60 degrees W. to clear it.

Now we were beyond the point reached by the *Scotia*, and the land underlying the ice-sheet we were skirting was new. The northerly trend was unexpected, and I began to suspect that we were really rounding a huge ice-tongue attached to the true barrier-edge and extending northward. Events confirmed this suspicion. We skirted the pack all night, steering north-west; then went west by north till 4 a.m. and round to south-west. The course at 8 a.m. on the 13th was south-south-west. The barrier at midnight was low and distant, and at 8 a.m. there was merely a narrow ice-foot about two hundred yards across separating it from the open water. By noon there was only an occasional shelf

of ice-foot. The barrier in one place came with an easy sweep to
the sea. We could have landed stores there without difficulty. We
made a sounding 400 ft. off the barrier but got no bottom at 676
fathoms. At 4 p.m., still following the barrier to the southwest, we
reached a corner and found it receding abruptly to the south-east.
Our way was blocked by very heavy pack, and after spending two
hours in a vain search for an opening, we moored the *Endurance* to
a floe and banked fires. During that day we passed two schools of
seals, swimming fast to the north-west and north-north-east. The
animals swam in close order, rising and blowing like porpoises, and
we wondered if there was any significance in their journey northward at that time of the year. Several young emperor penguins had
been captured and brought aboard on the previous day. Two of
them were still alive when the *Endurance* was brought alongside the
floe. They promptly hopped on to the ice, turned round, bowed
gracefully three times, and retired to the far side of the floe. There
is something curiously human about the manners and movements
of these birds. I was concerned about the dogs. They were losing
condition and some of them appeared to be ailing. One dog had
to be shot on the 12th. We did not move the ship on the 14th. A
breeze came from the east in the evening, and under its influence
the pack began to work off shore. Before midnight the close ice
that had barred our way had opened and left a lane along the foot
of the barrier. I decided to wait for the morning, not wishing to
risk getting caught between the barrier and the pack in the event
of the wind changing. A sounding gave 1357 fathoms, with a
bottom of glacial mud. The noon observation showed the position
to be lat. 74 degrees 09 minutes S., long. 27 degrees 16 minutes W.
We cast off at 6 a.m. on the 15th in hazy weather with a north-
easterly breeze, and proceeded along the barrier in open water.
The course was south-east for sixteen miles, then south-south-
east. We now had solid pack to windward, and at 3 p.m. we passed
a bight probably ten miles deep and running to the north-east. A
similar bight appeared at 6 p.m. These deep cuts strengthened the
impression we had already formed that for several days we had
been rounding a great mass of ice, at least fifty miles across,
stretching out from the coast and possibly destined to float away at
some time in the future. The soundings – roughly, 200 fathoms at
the landward side and 1300 fathoms at the seaward side – suggested

that this mighty projection was afloat. Seals were plentiful. We saw large numbers on the pack and several on low parts of the barrier, where the slope was easy. The ship passed through large schools of seals swimming from the barrier to the pack off shore. The animals were splashing and blowing around the *Endurance*, and Hurley made a record of this unusual sight with the kinematograph-camera.

The barrier now stretched to the south-west again. Sail was set to a fresh easterly breeze, but at 7 p.m. it had to be furled, the *Endurance* being held up by pack-ice against the barrier for an hour. We took advantage of the pause to sound and got 268 fathoms with glacial mud and pebbles. Then a small lane appeared ahead. We pushed through at full speed, and by 8.30 p.m. the *Endurance* was moving southward with sails set in a fine expanse of open water. We continued to skirt the barrier in clear weather. I was watching for possible landing-places, though as a matter of fact I had no intention of landing north of Vahsel Bay, in Luitpold Land, except under pressure of necessity. Every mile gained towards the south meant a mile less sledging when the time came for the overland journey.

Shortly before midnight on the 15th we came abreast of the northern edge of a great glacier or overflow from the inland ice, projecting beyond the barrier into the sea. It was 400 or 500 ft. high, and at its edge was a large mass of thick bay-ice. The bay formed by the northern edge of this glacier would have made an excellent landing-place. A flat ice-foot nearly three feet above sea-level looked like a natural quay. From this ice-foot a snow-slope rose to the top of the barrier. The bay was protected from the south-easterly wind and was open only to the northerly wind, which is rare in those latitudes. A sounding gave 80 fathoms, indicating that the glacier was aground. I named the place Glacier Bay, and had reason later to remember it with regret.

The *Endurance* steamed along the front of this ice-flow for about seventeen miles. The glacier showed huge crevasses and high pressure ridges, and appeared to run back to ice-covered slopes or hills 1000 or 2000 ft. high. Some bays in its front were filled with smooth ice, dotted with seals and penguins. At 4 a.m. on the 16th we reached the edge of another huge glacial overflow from the ice-sheet. The ice appeared to be coming over low hills and was heavily broken. The cliff-face was 250 to 350 ft. high, and the ice surface two miles inland was probably 2000 ft. high. The cliff-front showed a tide-mark of about 6 ft., proving that it was not afloat. We steamed along the front of this tremendous glacier for 40 miles and then, at 8.30 a.m., we were held up by solid pack-ice, which appeared to be held by stranded bergs. The depth, two cables off the barrier-cliff, was 134 fathoms. No further advance was possible that day, but the noon observation, which gave the position as lat. 76 degrees 27 minutes S. long. 28 degrees 51 minutes W., showed that we had gained 124 miles to the south-west during the preceding twenty-four hours. The afternoon was not without incident. The bergs in the neighbourhood were very large, several being over 200 ft. high, and some of them were firmly aground, showing tidemarks. A barrier-berg bearing north-west appeared to be about 25 miles long. We pushed the ship against a small banded berg, from which Wordie secured several large lumps of biotite granite. While the *Endurance* was being held slow ahead against the berg a loud crack was heard, and the geologist had to scramble aboard at once. The bands on this berg were particularly well defined; they were due to morainic action in the parent glacier. Later in the day the easterly wind increased to a gale. Fragments of floe drifted past at about two knots, and the pack to leeward began to break up fast. A low berg of shallow draught drove down into the grinding pack and, smashing against two larger stranded bergs, pushed them off the bank. The three went away together pell-mell. We took shelter under the lee of a large stranded berg.

A blizzard from the east-north-east prevented us leaving the shelter of the berg on the following day (Sunday, January 17). The weather was clear, but the gale drove dense clouds of snow off the land and obscured the coast-line most of the time. 'The land, seen when the air is clear, appears higher than we thought it yesterday; probably it rises to 3000 ft. above the head of the glacier. Caird Coast, as I have named it, connects Coats' Land, discovered by Bruce in 1904, with Luitpold Land, discovered by Filchner in 1912. The northern part is similar in character to Coats' Land. It is fronted by an undulating barrier, the van of a mighty ice-sheet that is being forced outward from the high interior of the Ant-arctic Continent and apparently is sweeping over low hills, plains, and shallow seas as the great Arctic ice-sheet once pressed over

Northern Europe. The barrier surface, seen from the sea, is of a faint golden brown colour. It terminates usually in cliffs ranging from 10 to 300 ft. in height, but in a very few places sweeps down level with the sea. The cliffs are of dazzling whiteness, with wonderful blue shadows. Far inland higher slopes can be seen, appearing like dim blue or faint golden fleecy clouds. These distant slopes have increased in nearness and clearness as we have come to the south-west, while the barrier cliffs here are higher and apparently firmer. We are now close to the junction with Luitpold Land. At this southern end of the Caird Coast the ice-sheet, undulating over the hidden and imprisoned land, is bursting down a steep slope in tremendous glaciers, bristling with ridges and spikes of ice and seamed by thousands of crevasses. Along the whole length of the coast we have seen no bare land or rock. Not as much as a solitary nunatak has appeared to relieve the surface of ice and snow. But the upward sweep of the ice-slopes towards the horizon and the ridges, terraces, and crevasses that appear as the ice approaches the sea tell of the hills and valleys that lie below.'

The *Endurance* lay under the lee of the stranded berg until 7 a.m. on January 18. The gale had moderated by that time, and we proceeded under sail to the south-west through a lane that had opened along the glacier-front. We skirted the glacier till 9.30 a.m., when it ended in two bays, open to the northwest but sheltered by stranded bergs to the west. The coast beyond trended south-south-west with a gentle land-slope.

'The pack now forces us to go west 14 miles, when we break through a long line of heavy brash mixed with large lumps and "growlers". We do this under the foretopsail only, the engines being stopped to protect the propeller. This takes us into open water, where we make S. 50 degrees W. for 24 miles. Then we again encounter pack which forces us to the north-west for 10 miles, when we are brought up by heavy snow-lumps, brash, and large, loose floes. The character of the pack slows change. The floes are very thick and are covered by deep snow. The brash between the floes is so thick and heavy that we cannot push through without a great expenditure of power, and then for a short distance only. We therefore lie to for a while to see if the pack opens at all when this north-east wind ceases.'

Our position on the morning of the 19th was lat. 76 degrees 34 minutes S., long. 31 degrees 30 minutes W. The weather was good, but no advance could be made. The ice had closed around the ship during the night, and no water could be seen in any direction from the deck. A few lanes were in sight from the mast-head. We sounded in 312 fathoms, finding mud, sand, and pebbles. The land showed faintly to the east. We waited for the conditions to improve, and the scientists took the opportunity to dredge for biological and geological specimens. During the night a moderate north-easterly gale sprang up, and a survey of the position on the 20th showed that the ship was firmly beset. The ice was packed heavily and firmly all round the *Endurance* in every direction as far as the eye could reach from the masthead. There was nothing to be done till the conditions changed, and we waited through that day and the succeeding days with increasing anxiety. The east-north-easterly gale that had forced us to take shelter behind the stranded berg on the 16th had veered later to the north-east, and it continued with varying intensity until the 22nd. Apparently this wind had crowded the ice into the bight of the Weddell Sea, and the ship was now drifting south-west with the floes which had enclosed it. A slight movement of the ice round the ship caused the rudder to become dangerously jammed on the 21st, and we had to cut away the ice with ice-chisels, heavy pieces of iron with 6-ft. wooden hafts. We kept steam up in readiness for a move if the opportunity offered, and the engines running full speed ahead helped to clear the rudder. Land was in sight to the east and south about sixteen miles distant on the 22nd. The land-ice seemed to be faced with ice-cliffs at most points, but here and there slopes ran down to sea-level. Large crevassed areas in terraces parallel with the coast showed where the ice was moving down over foot-hills. The inland ice app-eared for the most part to be undulating, smooth, and easy to march over, but many crevasses might have been concealed from us by the surface snow or by the absence of shadows. I thought that the land probably rose to a height of 5000 ft. forty or fifty miles inland. The accurate estimation of heights and distances in the Antarctic is always difficult, owing to the clear air, the confusing monotony of colouring, and the deceptive effect of mirage and refraction. The land appeared to increase in height to the southward, where we saw a line of land or barrier that must have been seventy miles, and possibly was even more distant.

Sunday, January 24, was a clear sunny day, with gentle easterly and southerly breezes. No open water could be seen from the mast-head, but there was a slight water-sky to the west and north-west. 'This is the first time for ten days that the wind has varied from north-east and east, and on five of these days it has risen to a gale. Evidently the ice has become firmly packed in this quarter, and we must wait patiently till a southerly gale occurs or currents open the ice. We are drifting slowly. The position today was 76 degrees 49 minutes S., 33 degrees 51 minutes W. Worsley and James, working on the floe with a Kew magnetometer, found the variation to be six degrees west.' Just before midnight a crack developed in the ice five yards wide and a mile long, fifty yards ahead of the ship. The crack had widened to a quarter of a mile by 10 a.m. on the 25th, and for three hours we tried to force the ship into this opening with engines at full speed ahead and all sails set. The sole effect was to wash some ice away astern and clear the rudder, and after convincing myself that the ship was firmly held I abandoned the attempt. Later in the day Crean and two other men were over the side on a stage chipping at a large piece of ice that had got under the ship and appeared to be impeding her movement. The ice broke away suddenly, shot upward and overturned, pinning Crean between the stage and the haft of the heavy 11-ft. iron pincher. He was in danger for a few moments, but we got him clear, suffering merely from a few bad bruises. The thick iron bar had been bent against him to an angle of 45 degrees.

The days that followed were uneventful. Moderate breezes from the east and south-west had no apparent effect upon the ice, and the ship remained firmly held. On the 27th, the tenth day of inactivity, I decided to let the fires out. We had been burning half a ton of coal a day to keep steam in the boilers, and as the bunkers now contained only 67 tons, representing thirty-three days' steaming, we could not afford to continue this expenditure of fuel. Land still showed to the east and south when the horizon was clear. The biologist was securing some interesting specimens with the hand-dredge at various depths. A sounding on the 26th gave 360 fathoms, and another on the 29th 449 fathoms. The drift was to the west, and an observation on the 31st (Sunday) showed that the ship had made eight miles during the week. James and Hudson rigged the wireless in the hope of hearing the monthly message from the Falkland Islands. This message would be due about 3.20 a.m. on the following morning, but James was doubtful about hearing anything with our small apparatus at a distance of 1630 miles from the dispatching station. We heard nothing, as a matter of fact, and later efforts were similarly unsuccessful. The conditions would have been difficult even for a station of high power.

We were accumulating gradually a stock of seal meat during these days of waiting. Fresh meat for the dogs was needed, and seal-steaks and liver made a very welcome change from the ship's rations aboard the *Endurance*. Four crab-eaters and three Weddells, over a ton of meat for dog and man, fell to our guns on February 2, and all hands were occupied most of the day getting the carcasses back to the ship over the rough ice. We rigged three sledges for man-haulage and brought the seals about two miles, the sledging parties being guided among the ridges and pools by semaphore from the crow's-nest. Two more seals were sighted on the far side of a big pool, but I did not allow them to be pursued. Some of the ice was in a treacherous condition, with thin films hiding cracks and pools, and I did not wish to risk an accident.

A crack about four miles long opened in the floe to the stern of the ship on the 3rd. The narrow lane in front was still open, but the prevailing light breezes did not seem likely to produce any useful movement in the ice. Early on the morning of the 5th a north-easterly gale sprang up, bringing overcast skies and thick snow. Soon the pack was opening and closing without much loosening effect. At noon the ship gave a sudden start and heeled over three degrees. Immediately afterwards a crack ran from the bows to the lead ahead and another to the lead astern. I thought it might be possible to reeve the ship through one of these leads towards open water, but we could see no water through the thick snow; and before steam was raised, and while the view was still obscured, the pack closed again. The northerly gale had given place to light westerly breezes on the 6th. The pack seemed to be more solid than ever. It stretched almost unbroken to the horizon in every direction, and the situation was made worse by very low temperatures in succeeding days. The temperature was down to zero on the night of the 7th and was two degrees below zero on the 8th. This cold spell in midsummer was most unfortunate from our point of view, since it cemented the pack and tightened the grip of the ice upon the ship. The slow drift to the southwest continued, and we caught occasional glimpses of distant uplands on the eastern horizon. The position on the 7th was lat. 76 degrees 57 minutes S., long. 35 degrees 7 minutes W. Soundings on the 6th and 8th found glacial mud at 630 and 529 fathoms.

The *Endurance* was lying in a pool covered by young ice on the 9th. The solid floes had loosened their grip on the ship itself, but they were packed tightly all around. The weather was foggy. We felt a slight northerly swell coming through the pack, and the movement gave rise to hope that there was open water near to us. At 11 a.m. a long crack developed in the pack, running east and west as far as we could see through the fog, and I ordered steam to be raised in the hope of being able to break away into this lead. The effort failed. We could break the young ice in the pool, but the pack defied us. The attempt was renewed on the 11th, a fine clear day with blue sky. The temperature was still low, −2 degrees Fahr. at midnight. After breaking through some young ice the *Endurance* became jammed against soft floe. The engines running full speed astern produced no effect until all hands joined in 'sallying' ship. The dog-kennels amidships made it necessary for the people to gather aft, where they rushed from side to side in a mass in the confined space around the wheel. This was a ludicrous affair, the men falling over one another amid shouts of laughter without producing much effect on the ship. She remained fast while all hands jumped at the word of command, but finally slid off when the men were stamping hard at the double. We were now in a position to take advantage of any opening that might appear. The ice was firm around us, and as there seemed small chance of making a move that day, I had the motor crawler and warper put out on the floe for a trial run. The motor worked most successfully, running at about six miles an hour over slabs and ridges of ice hidden by a foot or two of soft snow. The surface was worse than we would expect to face on land or barrier-ice. The motor warped itself back on a 600-fathom steel wire and was taken aboard again. 'From the mast-head the mirage is continually giving us false alarms. Everything wears an aspect of unreality.

Icebergs hang upside down in the sky; the land appears as layers of silvery or golden cloud. Cloud-banks look like land, icebergs masquerade as islands or nunataks, and the distant barrier to the south is thrown into view, although it really is outside our range of vision. Worst of all is the deceptive appearance of open water, caused by the refraction of distant water, or by the sun shining at an angle on a field of smooth snow or the face of ice-cliffs below the horizon.'

Endurance
[*Scott Polar Research Institute*]

The second half of February produced no important change in our situation. Early in the morning of the 14th I ordered a good head of steam on the engines and sent all hands on to the floe with ice-chisels, prickers, saws, and picks. We worked all day and throughout most of the next day in a strenuous effort to get the ship into the lead ahead. The men cut away the young ice before the bows and pulled it aside with great energy. After twenty-four hours' labour we had got the ship a third of the way to the lead. But about 400 yds. of heavy ice, including old rafted pack, still separated the *Endurance* from the water, and reluctantly I had to admit that further effort was useless. Every opening we made froze up again quickly owing to the unseasonably low temperature. The young ice was elastic and prevented the ship delivering a strong, splitting blow to the floe, while at the same time it held the older ice against any movement. The abandonment of the attack was a great disappointment to all hands. The men had worked long hours without thought of rest, and they deserved success. But the task was beyond our powers. I had not abandoned hope of getting clear, but was counting now on the possibility of having to spend a winter in the inhospitable arms of the pack. The sun, which had been above the horizon for two months, set at midnight on the 17th, and, although it would not disappear until April, its slanting rays warned us of the approach of winter. Pools and leads appeared occasionally, but they froze over very quickly.

We continued to accumulate a supply of seal meat and blubber, and the excursions across the floes to shoot and bring in the seals provided welcome exercise for all hands. Three crab-eater cows shot on the 21st were not accompanied by a bull, and blood was to be seen about the hole from which they had crawled. We surmised that the bull had become the prey of one of the killer-whales. These aggressive creatures were to be seen often in the lanes and pools, and we were always distrustful of their ability or willingness to discriminate between seal and man. A lizard-like head would show while the killer gazed along the floe with wicked eyes. Then the brute would dive, to come up a few moments later, perhaps, under some unfortunate seal reposing on the ice. Worsley examined a spot where a killer had smashed a hole 8 ft. by 12 ft. in 122 in. of hard ice, covered by 22 in. of snow. Big blocks of ice had been tossed on to the floe surface. Wordie, engaged in measuring the thickness of young ice, went through to his waist one day just as a killer rose to blow in the adjacent lead. His companions pulled him out hurriedly.

On the 22nd the *Endurance* reached the farthest south point of her drift, touching the 77th parallel of latitude in long. 35 degrees W. The summer had gone; indeed the summer had scarcely been with us at all. The temperatures were low day and night, and the pack was freezing solidly around the ship. The thermometer recorded 10 degrees below zero Fahr. at 2 a.m. on the 22nd. Some hours earlier we had watched a wonderful golden mist to the southward, where the rays of the declining sun shone through vapour rising from the ice. All normal standards of perspective vanish under such conditions, and the low ridges of the pack, with mist lying between them, gave the illusion of a wilderness of mountain-peaks like the Bernese Oberland. I could not doubt now that the *Endurance* was confined for the winter. Gentle breezes from the east, south, and south-west did not disturb the hardening floes. The seals were disappearing and the birds were leaving us. The land showed still in fair weather on the distant horizon, but it was beyond our reach now, and regrets for havens that lay behind us were vain. 'We must wait for the spring, which may bring us better fortune. If I had guessed a month ago that the ice would grip us here, I would have established our base at one of the landing-places at the great glacier. But there seemed no reason to anticipate then that the fates would prove unkind. This calm weather with intense cold in a summer month is surely exceptional. My chief anxiety is the drift. Where will the vagrant winds and currents carry the ship during the long winter months that are ahead of us? We will go west, no doubt, but how far? And will it be possible to break out of the pack early in the spring and reach Vahsel Bay or some other suitable landing-place? These are momentous questions for us.'

On February 24 we ceased to observe ship routine, and the *Endurance* became a winter station. All hands were on duty during the day and slept at night, except a watchman who looked after the dogs and watched for any sign of movement in the ice. We cleared a space of 10 ft. by 20 ft. round the rudder and propeller, sawing through ice 2 ft. thick, and lifting the blocks with a pair of tongs made by the carpenter. Crean used the blocks to make an ice-house for the dog Sally, which had added a little litter of pups to the strength of the expedition. Seals appeared occasionally, and we killed all that came within our reach. They represented fuel as well as food for men and dogs. Orders were given for the after-hold to be cleared and the stores checked, so that we might know exactly how we stood for a siege by an Antarctic winter. The dogs went off the ship on the following day. Their kennels were placed on the floe along the length of a wire rope to which the leashes were fastened. The dogs seemed heartily glad to leave the ship, and yelped loudly and joyously as they were moved to their new quarters. We had begun the training of teams, and already there was keen rivalry between the drivers. The flat floes and frozen leads in the neighbourhood of the ship made excellent training grounds. Hockey and football on the floe were our chief recreations, and all hands joined in many a strenuous game. Worsley took a party to the floe on the 26th and started building a line of igloos and 'dogloos' round the ship. These little buildings were constructed, Esquimaux fashion, of big blocks of ice, with thin sheets for the roofs. Boards or frozen sealskins were placed over all, snow was piled on top and pressed into the joints, and then water was thrown over the structures to make everything firm. The ice was packed down flat inside and covered with snow for the dogs, which preferred, however, to sleep outside except when the weather was extraordinarily severe. The tethering of the dogs was a simple matter. The end of a chain was buried about eight inches in the snow, some fragments of ice were pressed around it, and a little water poured over all. The icy breath of the Antarctic cemented it in a few moments. Four dogs which had been ailing were shot. Some of the dogs were suffering badly from worms, and the remedies at our disposal, unfortunately, were not effective. All the fit dogs were being exercised in the sledges, and they took to the work with enthusiasm. Sometimes their eagerness to be off and away produced laughable results, but the drivers learned to be alert. The wireless apparatus was still rigged, but we listened in vain for the Saturday-night time-signals from New Year Island, ordered for our benefit by the Argentine Government. On Sunday the 28th, Hudson waited at 2 a.m. for the Port Stanley monthly signals, but could hear nothing. Evidently the distances were too great for our small plant.

CHAPTER 3

Winter months

The month of March opened with a severe north-easterly gale. Five Weddells and two crab-eaters were shot on the floe during the morning of March 1, and the wind, with fine drifting snow, sprang up while the carcasses were being brought in by sledging parties. The men were compelled to abandon some of the blubber and meat, and they had a struggle to get back to the ship over the rough ice in the teeth of the storm. This gale continued until the 3rd, and all hands were employed clearing out the 'tween-decks, which was to be converted into a living- and dining-room for officers and scientists. The carpenter erected in this room the stove that had been intended for use in the shore hut, and the quarters were made very snug. The dogs appeared indifferent to the blizzard. They emerged occasionally from the drift to shake themselves and bark, but were content most of the time to lie, curled into tight balls, under the snow. One of the old dogs, Saint, died on the night of the 2nd, and the doctors reported that the cause of death was appendicitis.

When the gale cleared we found that the pack had been driven in from the north-east and was now more firmly consolidated than before. A new berg, probably fifteen miles in length, had appeared on the northern horizon. The bergs within our circle of vision had all become familiar objects, and we had names for some of them. Apparently they were all drifting with the pack. The sighting of a new berg was of more than passing interest, since in that comparatively shallow sea it would be possible for a big berg to become stranded. Then the island of ice would be a centre of tremendous pressure and disturbance amid the drifting pack. We had seen something already of the smashing effect of a contest between berg and floe, and had no wish to have the helpless *Endurance* involved in such a battle of giants. During the 3rd the seal meat and blubber was re-stowed on hummocks around the ship. The frozen masses had been sinking into the floe. Ice, though hard and solid to the touch, is never firm against heavy weights. An article left on the floe for any length of time is likely to sink into the surface-ice. Then the salt water will percolate through and the article will become frozen into the body of the floe.

Clear weather followed the gale, and we had a series of mock suns and parhelia. Minus temperatures were the rule, 21 degrees below zero Fahr. being recorded on the 6th. We made mattresses for the dogs by stuffing sacks with straw and rubbish, and most of the animals were glad to receive this furnishing in their kennels. Some of them had suffered through the snow melting with the heat of their bodies and then freezing solid. The scientific members of the expedition were all busy by this time. The meteorologist had got his recording station, containing anemometer, barograph, and thermograph, rigged over the stern. The geologist was making the best of what to him was an unhappy situation; but was not altogether without material. The pebbles found in the penguins were often of considerable interest, and some fragments of rock were brought up from the sea floor with the sounding-lead and the drag-net. On the 7th Wordie and Worsley found some small pebbles, a piece of moss, a perfect bivalve shell, and some dust on a berg fragment, and brought their treasure-trove proudly to the ship. Clark was using the drag-net frequently in the leads and secured good hauls of plankton, with occasional specimens of greater scientific interest. Seals were not plentiful, but our store of meat and blubber grew gradually. All hands ate seal meat with relish and would not have cared to become dependent on the ship's tinned meat. We preferred the crab-eater to the Weddell, which is a very sluggish beast. The crab-eater seemed cleaner and healthier. The killer-whales were still with us. On the 8th we examined a spot where the floe-ice had been smashed up by a blow from beneath, delivered presumably, by a large whale in search of a breathing-place. The force that had been exercised was astonishing. Slabs of ice 3 ft. thick, and weighing tons, had been tented upwards over a circular area with a diameter of about 25 ft., and cracks radiated outwards for more than 20 ft.

The quarters in the 'tween-decks were completed by the 10th, and the men took possession of the cubicles that had been built.

The largest cubicle contained Macklin, McIlroy, Hurley, and Hussey and it was named 'The Billabong'. Clark and Wordie lived opposite in a room called 'Auld Reekie'. Next came the abode of 'The Nuts' or engineers, followed by 'The Sailors' Rest', inhabited by Cheetham and McNeish. 'The Anchorage' and 'The Fumarole' were on the other side. The new quarters became known as 'The Ritz', and meals were served there instead of in the ward room. Breakfast was at 9 a.m., lunch at 1 p.m., tea at 4 p.m., and dinner at 6 p.m. Wild, Marston, Crean, and Worsley established themselves in cubicles in the wardroom, and by the middle of the month all hands had settled down to the winter routine. I lived alone aft.

Worsley, Hurley, and Wordie made a journey to a big berg, called by us the Rampart Berg, on the 11th. The distance out was 7½ miles, and the party covered a total distance of about 17 miles. Hurley took some photographs and Wordie came back rejoicing with a little dust and some moss.

'Within a radius of one mile round the berg there is thin young ice, strong enough to march over with care,' wrote Worsley. 'The area of dangerous pressure, as regards a ship, does not seem to extend for more than a quarter of a mile from the berg. Here there are cracks and constant slight movement, which becomes exciting to the traveller when he feels a piece of ice gradually upending beneath his feet. Close to the berg the pressure makes all sorts of quaint noises. We heard tapping as from a hammer, grunts, groans and squeaks, electric trams running, birds singing, kettles boiling noisily, and an occasional swish as a large piece of ice, released from pressure, suddenly jumped or turned over. We noticed all sorts of quaint effects, such as huge bubbles or domes of ice, 40 ft. across and 4 or 5 ft. high. Large sinuous pancake-sheets were spread over the floe in places, and in one spot we counted five such sheets, each about 2½ in. thick, imbricated under one another. They look as though made of barley-sugar and are very slippery.'

The noon position on the 14th was lat. 76 degrees 54 minutes S., long. 36 degrees 10 minutes W. The land was visible faintly to the south-east, distant about 36 miles. A few small leads could be seen from the ship, but the ice was firm in our neighbourhood. The drift of the *Endurance* was still towards the north-west.

I had the boilers blown down on the 15th, and the consumption of 2 cwt. of coal per day to keep the boilers from freezing then ceased. The bunkers still contained 52 tons of coal, and the daily consumption in the stoves was about 21 cwt. There would not be much coal left for steaming purposes in the spring, but I anticipated eking out the supply with blubber. A moderate gale from the north-east on the 17th brought fine, penetrating snow. The weather cleared in the evening, and a beautiful crimson sunset held our eyes. At the same time the ice-cliffs of the land were thrown up in the sky by mirage, with an apparent reflection in open water, though the land itself could not be seen definitely. The effect was repeated in an exaggerated form on the following day, when the ice-cliffs were thrown up above the horizon in double and treble parallel lines, some inverted. The mirage was due probably to lanes of open water near the land. The water would be about 30 degrees warmer than the air and would cause warmed strata to ascend. A sounding gave 606 fathoms, with a bottom of glacial mud. Six days later, on the 24th, the depth was 419 fathoms. We were drifting steadily, and the constant movement, coupled with the appearance of lanes near the land, convinced me that we must stay by the ship till she got clear. I had considered the possibility of making a landing across the ice in the spring, but the hazards of such an undertaking would be too great.

The training of the dogs in sledge teams was making progress. The orders used by the drivers were 'Mush' (Go on), 'Gee' (Right), 'Haw' (Left), and 'Whoa' (Stop). These are the words that the Canadian drivers long ago adopted, borrowing them originally from England. There were many fights at first, until the dogs learned their positions and their duties, but as days passed drivers and teams became efficient. Each team had its leader, and efficiency depended largely on the willingness and ability of this dog to punish skulking and disobedience. We learned not to interfere unless the disciplinary measures threatened to have a fatal termination. The drivers could sit on the sledge and jog along at ease if they chose. But the prevailing minus temperatures made riding unpopular, and the men preferred usually to run or walk alongside the teams. We were still losing dogs through sickness, due to stomach and intestinal worms.

Dredging for specimens at various depths was one of the duties during these days. The dredge and several hundred fathoms of wire line made a heavy load, far beyond the unaided strength

of the scientists. On the 23rd, for example, we put down a 2 ft.
dredge and 650 fathoms of wire. The dredge was hove in four
hours later and brought much glacial mud, several pebbles and
rock fragments, three sponges, some worms, *brachiopods*, and *fora-
miniferae*. The mud was troublesome. It was heavy to lift, and as it
froze rapidly when brought to the surface, the recovery of the
specimens embedded in it was difficult. A haul made on the 26th
brought a prize for the geologist in the form of a lump of sandstone
weighing 75 lb., a piece of fossiliferous limestone, a fragment of
striated shale, sandstone-grit, and some pebbles. Hauling in the
dredge by hand was severe work, and on the 24th we used the
Girling tractor-motor, which brought in 500 fathoms of line in
thirty minutes, including stops. One stop was due to water having
run over the friction gear and frozen. It was a day or two later that
we heard a great yell from the floe and found Clark dancing about
and shouting Scottish war-cries. He had secured his first complete
specimen of an Antarctic fish, apparently a new species.

Mirages were frequent. Barrier-cliffs appeared all around us on
the 29th, even in places where we knew there was deep water.
'Bergs and pack are thrown up in the sky and distorted into the
most fantastic shapes. They climb, trembling, upwards, spreading
out into long lines at different levels, then contract and fall down,
leaving nothing but an uncertain, wavering smudge which comes
and goes. Presently the smudge swells and grows, taking shape
until it presents the perfect inverted reflection of a berg on the
horizon, the shadow hovering over the substance. More smudges
appear at different points on the horizon. These spread out into
long lines till they meet, and we are girdled by lines of shining
snow-cliffs, laved at their bases by waters of illusion in which they
appear to be faithfully reflected. So the shadows come and go
silently, melting away finally as the sun declines to the west. We
seem to be drifting helplessly in a strange world of unreality. It is
reassuring to feel the ship beneath one's feet and to look down at
the familiar line of kennels and igloos on the solid floe.'

The floe was not so solid as it appeared. We had reminders
occasionally that the greedy sea was very close, and that the floe
was but a treacherous friend, which might open suddenly beneath
us. Towards the end of the month I had our store of seal meat and
blubber brought aboard. The depth as recorded by a sounding on

the last day of March was 256 fathoms. The continuous shoaling from 606 fathoms in a drift of 39 miles N. 26 degrees W. in thirty days was interesting. The sea shoaled as we went north, either to east or to west, and the fact suggested that the contour-lines ran east and west, roughly. Our total drift between January 19, when the ship was frozen in, and March 31, a period of seventy-one days, had been 95 miles in a N. 80 degrees W. direction. The icebergs around us had not changed their relative positions.

The sun sank lower in the sky, the temperatures became lower, and the *Endurance* felt the grip of the icy hand of winter. Two north-easterly gales in the early part of April assisted to consolidate the pack. The young ice was thickening rapidly, and though leads were visible occasionally from the ship, no opening of a consid- erable size appeared in our neighbourhood. In the early morning of April 1 we listened again for the wireless signals from Port Stanley. The crew had lashed three 20-ft. rickers to the mast-heads in order to increase the spread of our aerials, but still we failed to hear anything. The rickers had to come down subsequently, since we found that the gear could not carry the accumulating weight of rime. Soundings proved that the sea continued to shoal as the *Endurance* drifted to the north-west. The depth on April 2 was 262 fathoms, with a bottom of glacial mud. Four weeks later a sounding gave 172 fathoms. The presence of grit in the bottom samples towards the end of the month suggested that we were approaching land again.

The month was not uneventful. During the night of the 3rd we heard the ice grinding to the eastward, and in the morning we saw that young ice was rafted 8 to 10 ft. high in places. This was the first murmur of the danger that was to reach menacing proportions in later months. The ice was heard grinding and creaking during the 4th and the ship vibrated slightly. The movement of the floe was sufficiently pronounced to interfere with the magnetic work. I gave orders that accumulations of snow, ice, and rubbish alongside the *Endurance* should be shovelled away, so that in case of pressure there would be no weight against the topsides to check the ship rising above the ice. All hands were busy with pick and shovel during the day, and moved many tons of material. Again, on the 9th, there were signs of pressure. Young ice was piled up to a height of 11 ft. astern of the ship, and the old floe was cracked in places. The movement was not serious, but I realised that it might be the beginning of trouble for the Expedition. We brought certain stores aboard and provided space on deck for the dogs in case they had to be removed from the floe at short notice. We had run a 500-fathom steel wire round the ship, snow-huts, and kennels, with a loop out to the lead ahead, where the dredge was used. This wire was supported on ice-pillars, and it served as a guide in bad weather when the view was obscured by driving snow and a man might have lost himself altogether. I had this wire cut in five places, since otherwise it might have been dragged across our section of the floe with damaging effect in the event of the ice splitting suddenly.

Exercising dogs on the floe during a temporary hold up
[*Scott Polar Research Institute*]

The dogs had been divided into six teams of nine dogs each. Wild, Crean, Macklin, McIlroy, Marston, and Hurley each had charge of a team, and were fully responsible for the exercising, training, and feeding of their own dogs. They called in one of the surgeons when an animal was sick. We were still losing some dogs through worms, and it was unfortunate that the doctors had not the proper remedies. Worm-powders were to have been provided by the expert Canadian dog-driver I had engaged before sailing for the south, and when this man did not join the Expedition the matter was overlooked. We had fifty-four dogs and eight pups early in April, but several were ailing, and the number of mature dogs was reduced to fifty by the end of the month. Our store of seal meat amounted now to about 5000 lb., and I calculated that we had enough meat and blubber to feed the dogs for ninety days without trenching upon the sledging rations. The teams were working well, often with heavy loads. The biggest dog was Hercules, who tipped the beam at 86 lb. Samson was 11 lb. lighter, but he justified his name one day by starting off at a smart pace with a sledge carrying 200 lb. of blubber and a driver.

A new berg that was going to give us some cause for anxiety made its appearance on the 14th. It was a big berg, and we noticed as it lay on the north-west horizon that it had a hummocky, crevassed appearance at the east end. During the day this berg increased its apparent altitude and changed its bearing slightly. Evidently it was aground and was holding its position against the drifting pack. A sounding at 11 a.m. gave 197 fathoms, with a hard stony or rocky bottom. During the next twenty-four hours the *Endurance* moved steadily towards the crevassed berg, which doubled its altitude in that time. We could see from the mast-head that the pack was piling and rafting against the mass of ice, and it was easy to imagine what would be the fate of the ship if she entered the area of disturbance. She would be crushed like an egg-shell amid the shattering masses.

Worsley was in the crow's-nest on the evening of the 15th, watching for signs of land to the westward, and he reported an interesting phenomenon. The sun set amid a glow of prismatic colours on a line of clouds just above the horizon. A minute later Worsley saw a golden glow, which expanded as he watched it, and presently the sun appeared again and rose a semi-diameter clear above the western horizon. He hailed Crean, who from a position on the floe 90 ft. below the crow's-nest also saw the re-born sun. A quarter of an hour later from the deck Worsley saw the sun set a second time. This strange phenomenon was due to mirage or refraction. We attributed it to an ice-crack to the westward, where the band of open water had heated a stratum of air.

The drift of the pack was not constant, and during the succeeding days the crevassed berg alternately advanced and receded as the *Endurance* moved with the floe. On Sunday, April 18, it was only seven miles distant from the ship.

'It is a large berg, about three-quarters of a mile long on the side presented to us and probably well over 200 ft. high. It is heavily crevassed, as though it once formed the serac portion of a glacier.

Two specially wide and deep chasms across it from south-east to north-west give it the appearance of having broken its back on the shoal-ground. Huge masses of pressure-ice are piled against its cliffs to a height of about 60 ft., showing the stupendous force that is being brought to bear upon it by the drifting pack. The berg must be very firmly aground. We swing the arrow on the current-meter frequently and watch with keen attention to see where it will come to rest. Will it point straight for the berg, showing that our drift is in that direction? It swings slowly round. It points to the north-east end of the berg, then shifts slowly to the centre and seems to stop; but it moves again and swings 20 degrees clear of our enemy, to the south-west. . . . We notice that two familiar bergs, the Rampart Berg and the Peak Berg, have moved away from the ship. Probably they also have grounded or dragged on the shoal.'

A strong drift to the westward during the night of the 18th relieved our anxiety by carrying the *Endurance* to the lee of the crevassed berg, which passed out of our range of vision before the end of the month.

We said goodbye to the sun on May 1 and entered the period of twilight that would be followed by the darkness of midwinter. The sun by the aid of refraction just cleared the horizon at noon and set shortly before 2 p.m. A fine aurora in the evening was dimmed by the full moon, which had risen on April 27 and would not set again until May 6. The disappearance of the sun is apt to be a depressing event in the polar regions, where the long months of darkness involve mental as well as physical strain. But the *Endurance*'s company refused to abandon their customary cheerfulness, and a concert in the evening made the Ritz a scene of noisy merriment, in strange contrast with the cold, silent world that lay outside. 'One feels our helplessness as the long winter night closes upon us. By this time, if fortune had smiled upon the Expedition, we would have been comfortably and securely established in a shore base, with depots laid to the south and plans made for the long march in the spring and summer. Where will we make a landing now? It is not easy to forecast the future. The ice may open in the spring, but by that time we will be far to the north-west. I do not think we shall be able to work back to Vahsel Bay. There are possible landing-places on the western coast of the Weddell Sea, but can we reach any suitable spot early enough to attempt the overland journey next year? Time alone will tell. I do not think any member of the Expedition is disheartened by our disappointment. All hands are cheery and busy, and will do their best when the time for action comes. In the meantime we must wait.'

The ship's position on Sunday, May 2, was lat. 75 degrees 23 minutes S., long. 42 degrees 14 minutes W. The temperature at noon was 5 degrees below zero Fahr., and the sky was overcast. A seal was sighted from the mast-head at lunch-time, and five men, with two dog teams, set off after the prize. They had an uncomfortable journey outward in the dim, diffused light, which cast no shadows and so gave no warning of irregularities in the white surface. It is a strange sensation to be running along on apparently smooth snow and to fall suddenly into an unseen hollow, or bump against a ridge.

'After going out three miles to the eastward,' wrote Worsley in describing this seal-hunt, 'we range up and down but find nothing, until from a hummock I fancy I see something apparently a mile away, but probably little more than half that distance. I ran for it, found the seal, and with a shout brought up the others at the double. The seal was a big Weddell, over 10 ft. long and weighing more than 800 lb. But Soldier, one of the team leaders, went for its throat without a moment's hesitation, and we had to beat off the dogs before we could shoot the seal. We caught five or six gallons of blood in a tin for the dogs, and let the teams have a drink of fresh blood from the seal. The light was worse than ever on our return, and we arrived back in the dark. Sir Ernest met us with a lantern and guided us into the lead astern and thence to the ship.'

This was the first seal we had secured since March 19, and the meat and blubber made a welcome addition to the stores.

Three emperor penguins made their appearance in a lead west of the ship on May 3. They pushed their heads through the young ice while two of the men were standing by the lead. The men imitated the emperor's call and walked slowly, penguin fashion, away from the lead. The birds in succession made a magnificent leap 3 ft. clear from the water on to the young ice. Thence they tobogganed to the bank and followed the men away from the lead. Their retreat was soon cut off by a line of men.

'We walk up to them, talking loudly and assuming a threatening aspect. Notwithstanding our bad manners, the three birds turn towards us, bowing ceremoniously. Then, after a closer inspection, they conclude that we are undesirable acquaintances and make off across the floe. We head them off and finally shepherd them close to the ship, where the frenzied barking of the dogs so frightens them that they make a determined effort to break through the line. We seize them. One bird of philosophic mien goes quietly, led by one flipper. The others show fight, but all are imprisoned in an igloo for the night. . . . In the afternoon we see five emperors in the western lead and capture one. Kerr and Cheetham fight a valiant action with two large birds. Kerr rushes at one, seizes it, and is promptly knocked down by the angered penguin, which jumps on his chest before retiring. Cheetham comes to Kerr's assistance; and between them they seize another penguin, bind his bill and lead him, muttering muffled protests, to the ship like an inebriated old man between two policemen. He weighs 85lb., or 5 lb. less than the heaviest emperor captured previously. Keir and Cheetham insist that he is nothing to the big fellow who escaped them.'

This penguin's stomach proved to be filled with freshly caught fish up to 10 in. long. Some of the fish were of a coastal or littoral variety. Two more emperors were captured on the following day, and, while Wordie was leading one of them towards the ship, Wild came along with his team. The dogs, uncontrollable in a moment, made a frantic rush for the bird, and were almost upon him when their harness caught upon an ice-pylon, which they had tried to pass on both sides at once. The result was a seething tangle of dogs, traces, and men, and an overturned sled, while the penguin, three yards away, nonchalantly and indifferently surveyed the disturbance. He had never seen anything of the kind before and had no idea at all that the strange disorder might concern him. Several cracks had opened in the neighbourhood of the ship, and the emperor penguins, fat and glossy of plumage, were appearing in considerable numbers. We secured nine of them on May 6, an important addition our supply of fresh food.

The sun, which had made 'positively his last appearance' seven days earlier, surprised us by lifting more than half its disk above the horizon on May 8. A glow on the northern horizon resolved itself into the sun at 11 a.m. that day. A quarter of an hour later the unseasonable visitor disappeared again, only to rise again at 11.40

a.m., set at 1 p.m., rise at 1.10 p.m., and set lingeringly at 1.20 p.m. These curious phenomena were due to refraction, which amounted to 2 degrees 37 minutes at 1.20 p.m. The temperature was 15 degrees below zero Fahr. and we calculated that the refraction was 2 degrees above normal. In other words, the sun was visible 120 miles farther south than the refraction tables gave it any right to be. The navigating officer naturally was aggrieved. He had informed all hands on May 1 that they would not see the sun again for seventy days, and now had to endure the jeers of friends who affected to believe that his observations were inaccurate by a few degrees.

The *Endurance* was drifting north-north-east under the influence of a succession of westerly and south-westerly breezes. The ship's head, at the same time, swung gradually to the left, indicating that the floe in which she was held was turning. During the night of the 14th a very pronounced swing occurred, and when daylight came at noon on the 15th we observed a large lead running from the north-west horizon towards the ship till it struck the western lead, circling ahead of the ship, then continuing to the south-south-east. A lead astern connected with this new lead on either side of the *Endurance*, thus separating our floe completely from the main body of the pack. A blizzard from the south-east swept down during the 16th. At 1 p.m. the blizzard lulled for five minutes; then the wind jumped round to the opposite quarter and the barometer rose suddenly. The centre of a cyclonic movement had passed over us, and the compass recorded an extraordinarily rapid swing of the floe. I could see nothing through the mist and snow, and I thought it possible that a magnetic storm or a patch of local magnetic attraction had caused the compass, and not the floe, to swing. Our floe was now about 2½ miles long north and south and 3 miles wide east and west.

The month of May passed with few incidents of importance. Hurley, our handyman, installed our small electric-lighting plant and placed lights for occasional use in the observatory, the meteorological station, and various other points. We could not afford to use the electric lamps freely. Hurley also rigged two powerful lights on poles projecting from the ship to port and starboard. These lamps would illuminate the 'dogloos' brilliantly on the darkest winter's day and would be invaluable in the event of the floe breaking during the dark days of winter. We could imagine what it would mean to get fifty dogs aboard without lights while the floe was breaking and rafting under our feet. May 24, Empire Day, was celebrated with the singing of patriotic songs in the Ritz, where all hands joined in wishing a speedy victory for the British arms. We could not know how the war was progressing, but we hoped that the Germans had already been driven from France and that the Russian armies had put the seal on the Allies' success. The war was a constant subject of discussion aboard the *Endurance*, and many campaigns were fought on the map during the long months of drifting. The moon in the latter part of May was sweeping continuously through our starlit sky in great high circles. The weather generally was good, with constant minus temperatures. The log on May 27 recorded:

Brilliantly fine clear weather with bright moonlight throughout. The moon's rays are wonderfully strong, making midnight seem as light as an ordinary overcast midday in temperate climes. The great clearness of the atmosphere probably accounts for our having eight hours of twilight with a beautiful soft golden glow, to the northward. A little rime and glazed frost are found aloft. The temperature is −20 degrees Fahr. A few wisps of cirrus-cloud are seen and a little frost-smoke shows in one or two directions, but the cracks and leads near the ship appear to have frozen over again.

Crean had started to take the pups out for runs, and it was very amusing to see them with their rolling canter just managing to keep abreast by the sledge and occasionally cocking an eye with an appealing look in the hope of being taken aboard for a ride. As an addition to their foster-father, Crean, the pups had adopted Amundsen. They tyrannised over him most unmercifully. It was a common sight to see him, the biggest dog in the pack, sitting out in the cold with an air of philosophic resignation while a corpulent pup occupied the entrance to his 'dogloo'. The intruder was generally the pup Nelson, who just showed his forepaws and face, and one was fairly sure to find Nelly, Roger, and Toby coiled up comfortably behind him. At hoosh-time Crean had to stand by Amundsen's food, since otherwise the pups would eat the big dog's ration while he stood back to give them fair play. Sometimes their consciences would smite them and they would drag round a seal's head, half a penguin, or a large lump of frozen meat or blubber to Amundsen's kennel for rent. It was interesting to watch the big dog play with them, seizing them by throat or neck in what appeared to be a fierce fashion, while really quite gentle with them, and all the time teaching them how to hold their own in the world and putting them up to all the tricks of dog life.

The drift of the *Endurance* in the grip of the pack continued without incident of importance through June. Pressure was reported occasionally, but the ice in the immediate vicinity of the ship remained firm. The light was now very bad except in the period when the friendly moon was above the horizon. A faint twilight round about noon of each day reminded us of the sun; and assisted us in the important work of exercising the dogs. The care of the teams was our heaviest responsibility in those days. The movement of the floes was beyond all human control, and there was nothing to be gained by allowing one's mind to struggle with the problems of the future, though it was hard to avoid anxiety at times. The conditioning and training of the dogs seemed essential, whatever fate might be in store for us, and the teams were taken out by their drivers whenever the weather permitted. Rivalries arose, as might have been expected, and on the 15th of the month a great race, the 'Antarctic Derby', took place. It was a notable event. The betting had been heavy, and every man aboard the ship stood to win or lose on the result of the contest. Some money had been staked, but the wagers that thrilled were those involving stores of chocolate and cigarettes. The course had been laid off from Khyber Pass, at the eastern end of the old lead ahead of the ship, to a point clear of the jib-boom, a distance of about 700 yds. Five teams went out in the dim noon twilight, with a zero temperature and an aurora flickering faintly to the southward. The starting signal was to be given by the flashing of a light on the meteorological station. I was appointed starter, Worsley was judge, and James was timekeeper. The bos'n, with a straw hat added to his usual Antarctic attire, stood on a box near the winning-post, and was assisted by a couple of shady characters to shout the odds, which were displayed on a board hung around his neck – 6 to 4 on Wild, 'evens' on Crean, 2 to 1 against Hurley, 6 to 1 against Macklin, and 8 to 1 against McIlroy.

Canvas handkerchiefs fluttered from an improvised grandstand, and the pups, which had never seen such strange happenings before, sat round and howled with excitement. The spectators could not see far in the dim light, but they heard the shouts of the drivers as the teams approached and greeted the victory of the favourite with a roar of cheering that must have sounded strange indeed to any seals or penguins that happened to be in our neighbourhood. Wild's time was 2 min. 16 sec., or at the rate of 10½ miles per hour for the course.

We celebrated Midwinter's Day on the 22nd. The twilight extended over a period of about six hours that day, and there was a good light at noon from the moon, and also a northern glow with wisps of beautiful pink cloud along the horizon. A sounding gave 262 fathoms with a mud bottom. No land was in sight from the mast-head, although our range of vision extended probably a full degree to the westward. The day was observed as a holiday, necessary work only being undertaken, and, after the best dinner the cook could provide, all hands gathered in the Ritz, where speeches, songs, and toasts occupied the evening. After supper at midnight we sang 'God Save the King' and wished each other all success in the days of sunshine and effort that lay ahead. At this time the *Endurance* was making an unusually rapid drift to the north under the influence of a fresh southerly to south-westerly breeze. We travelled 39 miles to the north in five days before a breeze that only once attained the force of a gale and then for no more than an hour. The absence of strong winds, in comparison with the almost unceasing winter blizzards of the Ross Sea, was a feature of the Weddell Sea that impressed itself upon me during the winter months.

Another race took place a few days after the 'Derby'. The two crack teams, driven by Hurley and Wild, met in a race from Khyber Pass. Wild's team, pulling 910 lb., or 130 lb. per dog, covered the 700 yds. in 2 min. 9 sec., or at the rate of 11.1 miles per hour. Hurley's team, with the same load, did the run in 2 min. 16 sec. The race was awarded by the judge to Hurley owing to Wild failing to 'weigh in' correctly. I happened to be a part of the load on his sledge, and a skid over some new drift within fifty yards of the winning post resulted in my being left on the snow. It should be said in justice to the dogs that this accident, while justifying the disqualification, could not have made any material difference in the time.

The approach of the returning sun was indicated by beautiful sunrise glows on the horizon in the early days of July. We had nine hours' twilight on the 10th, and the northern sky, low to the horizon, was tinted with gold for about seven hours. Numerous cracks and leads extended in all directions to within 300 yds. of the ship. Thin wavering black lines close to the northern horizon were probably distant leads refracted into the sky. Sounds of moderate pressure came to our ears occasionally, but the ship was not involved. At midnight on the 11th a crack in the lead ahead of the *Endurance* opened out rapidly, and by 2 a.m. was over 200 yds. wide in places with an area of open water to the south-west. Sounds of pressure were heard along this lead, which soon closed to a width of about 30 yds. and then froze over. The temperature at that time was −23 degrees Fahr.

The most severe blizzard we had experienced in the Weddell Sea swept down upon the *Endurance* on the evening of the 13th, and by breakfast-time on the following morning the kennels to the windward, or southern side of the ship were buried under 5 ft. of drift. I gave orders that no man should venture beyond the kennels. The ship was invisible at a distance of fifty yards, and it was impossible to preserve one's sense of direction in the raging wind and suffocating drift. To walk against the gale was out of the question. Face and eyes became snowed up within two minutes, and serious frostbites would have been the penalty of persever-ance. The dogs stayed in their kennels for the most part, the 'old stagers' putting out a paw occasionally in order to keep open a breathing-hole. By evening the gale had attained a force of 60 or 70 miles an hour, and the ship was trembling under the attack. But we were snug enough in our quarters aboard until the morning of the 14th, when all hands turned out to shovel the snow from deck and kennels. The wind was still keen and searching, with a temperature of something like -30 degrees Fahr., and it was necessary for us to be on guard against frostbite. At least 100 tons of snow were piled against the bows and port side, where the weight of the drift had forced the floe downward. The lead ahead had opened out during the night, cracked the pack from north to south and frozen over again, adding 300 yds. to the distance between the ship and 'Khyber Pass'. The breakdown gang had completed its work by lunch-time. The gale was then decreasing and the three-days-old moon showed as a red crescent on the northern horizon. The temperature during the blizzard had ranged from −21 degrees to −33.5 degrees Fahr. It is usual for the temperature to rise during a blizzard, and the failure to produce any Föhn effect of this nature suggested an absence of high land for at least 200 miles to the south and south-west. The weather did not clear until the 16th. We saw then that the appearance of the surrounding pack had been altered completely by the blizzard. The 'island' floe containing the *Endurance* still stood fast, but cracks and masses of ice thrown up by pressure could be seen in all directions. An area of open water was visible on the horizon to the north, with a water indication in the northern sky.

The ice-pressure, which was indicated by distant rumblings and the appearance of formidable ridges, was increasingly a cause of anxiety. The areas of disturbance were gradually approaching the ship. During July 21 we could hear the grinding and crashing of the working floes to the south-west and west and could see cracks opening, working, and closing ahead. 'The ice is rafting up to a height of 10 or 15 ft. in places, the opposing floes are moving against one another at the rate of about 200 yds. per hour. The noise resembles the roar of heavy, distant surf. Standing on the stirring ice one can imagine it is disturbed by the breathing and tossing of a mighty giant below.' Early on the afternoon of the 22nd a 2-ft. crack, running south-west and north-east for a distance of about two miles, approached to within 35 yds. of the port quarter. I had all the sledges brought aboard and set a special watch in case it became necessary to get the dogs off the floe in a hurry. This crack was the result of heavy pressure 300 yds. away on the port bow, where huge blocks of ice were piled up in wild and threatening confusion. The pressure at that point was enormous. Blocks weighing many tons were raised 15 ft. above the level of the floe. I arranged to divide the night watches with Worsley and Wild, and none of us had much rest. The ship was shaken by heavy bumps, and we were on the alert to see that no dogs had fallen into cracks. The morning light showed that our island had been reduced considerably during the night. Our long months of rest and safety seemed to be at an end, and a period of stress had begun.

During the following day I had a store of sledging provisions, oil, matches, and other essentials placed on the upper deck handy to the starboard quarter boat, so as to be in readiness for a sudden emergency. The ice was grinding and working steadily to the southward, and in the evening some large cracks appeared on the port quarter, while a crack alongside opened out to 15 yds. The blizzard seemed to have set the ice in strong movement towards the north, and the south-westerly and west-south-westerly winds that prevailed two days out of three maintained the drift. I hoped that this would continue unchecked, since our chance of getting clear of the pack early in the spring appeared to depend upon our making a good northing. Soundings at this time gave depths of from 186 to 190 fathoms, with a glacial mud bottom. No land was in sight. The light was improving. A great deal of ice-pressure was heard and observed in all directions during the 25th, much of it close to the port quarter of the ship. On the starboard bow huge blocks of ice, weighing many tons and 5 ft. in thickness, were pushed up on the old floe to a height of 15 to 20 ft. The floe that held the *Endurance* was swung to and fro by the pressure during the day, but came back to the old bearing before midnight. 'The ice for miles around is much looser. There are numerous cracks and short leads to the north-east and south-east. Ridges are being forced up in all directions, and there is a water-sky to the south-east. It would be a relief to be able to make some effort on our own behalf; but we can do nothing until the ice releases our ship. If the floes continue to loosen, we may break out within the next few weeks and resume the fight. In the meantime the pressure continues, and it is hard to foresee the outcome. Just before noon today (July 26) the top of the sun appeared by refraction for one minute, seventy-nine days after our last sunset. A few minutes earlier a small patch of the sun had been thrown up on one of the black streaks above the horizon. All hands are cheered by the indication that the end of the winter darkness is near. . . Clark finds that with returning daylight the diatoms are again appearing. His nets and line are stained a pale yellow, and much of the newly formed ice has also a faint brown or yellow tinge. The diatoms cannot multiply without light, and the ice formed since February can be distinguished in the pressure-ridges by its clear blue colour. The older masses of ice are of a dark earthy brown, dull yellow, or reddish brown.'

The break-up of our floe came suddenly on Sunday, August 1, just one year after the *Endurance* left the South-West India Docks on the voyage to the Far South. The position was lat. 72 degrees 26 minutes S., long. 48 degrees 10 minutes W. The morning brought a moderate south-westerly gale with heavy snow, and at 8 a.m., after some warning movements of the ice, the floe cracked 40 yds. off the starboard bow. Two hours later the floe began to break up all round us under pressure and the ship listed over 10 degrees to starboard. I had the dogs and sledges brought aboard at once and the gangway hoisted. The animals behaved well. They came aboard eagerly as though realising their danger, and were placed in their quarters on deck without a single fight occurring. The pressure was cracking the floe rapidly, rafting it close to the ship and forcing masses of ice beneath the keel. Presently the *Endurance* listed heavily to port against the gale, and at the same time was forced ahead, astern, and sideways several times by the grinding floes. She received one or two hard nips, but resisted them without as much as a creak. It looked at one stage as if the ship was to be made the plaything of successive floes, and I was relieved when she came to a standstill with a large piece of our old 'dock' under the starboard bilge. I had the boats cleared away ready for lowering, got up some additional stores, and set a double watch. All hands were warned to stand by, get what sleep they could, and have their warmest clothing at hand. Around us lay the ruins of 'Dog Town' amid the debris of pressure-ridges. Some of the little dwellings had been crushed flat beneath blocks of ice; others had been swallowed and pulverised when the ice opened beneath them and closed again. It was a sad sight, but my chief concern just then was the safety of the rudder, which was being attacked viciously by the ice. We managed to pole away a large lump that had become jammed between the rudder and the stern-post, but I could see that damage had been done, though a close examination was not possible that day.

After the ship had come to a standstill in her new position very heavy pressure was set up. Some of the trenails were started and beams buckled slightly under the terrific stresses. But the *Endurance* had been built to withstand the attacks of the ice, and she lifted bravely as the floes drove beneath her. The effects of the pressure around us were awe-inspiring. Mighty blocks of ice, gripped between meeting floes, rose slowly till they jumped like cherry-stones squeezed between thumb and finger. The pressure of millions of tons of moving ice was crushing and smashing inexorably. If the ship was once gripped firmly her fate would be sealed.

The gale from the south-west blew all night and moderated during the afternoon of the 2nd to a stiff breeze. The pressure had almost ceased. Apparently the gale had driven the southern pack down upon us, causing congestion in our area; the pressure had stopped when the whole of the pack got into motion. The gale had given us some northing, but it had dealt the *Endurance* what might prove to be a severe blow. The rudder had been driven hard over to starboard and the blade partially torn away from the rudder-head. Heavy masses of ice were still jammed against the stern, and it was impossible to ascertain the extent of the damage at that time. I felt that it would be impossible in any case to effect repairs in the moving pack. The ship lay steady all night, and the sole sign of continuing pressure was an occasional slight rumbling shock. We rigged shelters and kennels for the dogs inboard.

The weather on August 3 was overcast and misty. We had nine hours of twilight, with good light at noon. There was no land in sight for ten miles from the mast-head. The pack as far as the eye could reach was in a condition of chaos, much rafted and consolidated, with very large pressure-ridges in all directions. At 9 p.m. a rough altitude of Canopus gave the latitude as 71 degrees 55 minutes 17 seconds S. The drift, therefore, had been about 37 miles to the north in three days. Four of the poorest dogs were shot this day. They were suffering severely from worms, and we could not afford to keep sick dogs under the changed conditions. The sun showed through the clouds on the northern horizon for an hour on the 4th. There was no open water to be seen from aloft in any direction. We saw from the masthead to west-south-west an appearance of barrier, land, or a very long iceberg, about 20-odd miles away, but the horizon clouded over before we could determine its nature. We tried twice to make a sounding that day, but failed on each occasion. The Kelvin machine gave no bottom at the full length of the line, 370 fathoms. After much labour we made a hole in the ice near the stern-post large enough for the Lucas machine with a 32-lb. lead; but this appeared to be too light.

The machine stopped at 452 fathoms, leaving us in doubt as to whether bottom had been reached. Then in heaving up we lost the lead, the thin wire cutting its way into the ice and snapping. All hands and the carpenter were busy this day making and placing kennels on the upper deck, and by nightfall all the dogs were comfortably housed, ready for any weather. The sun showed through the clouds above the northern horizon for nearly an hour.

The remaining days of August were comparatively uneventful. The ice around the ship froze firm again and little movement occurred in our neighbourhood. The training of the dogs, including the puppies, proceeded actively, and provided exercise as well as occupation. The drift to the north-west continued steadily. We had bad luck with soundings, the weather interfering at times and the gear breaking on several occasions, but a big increase in the depth showed that we had passed over the edge of the Weddell Sea plateau. A sounding of about 1700 fathoms on August 10 agreed fairly well with Filchner's 1924 fathoms, 130 miles east of our then position. An observation at noon of the 8th had given us lat. 71 degrees 23 minutes S., long. 49 degrees 13 minutes W. Minus temperatures prevailed still, but the daylight was increasing. We captured a few emperor penguins which were making their way to the south-west. Ten penguins taken on the 19th were all in poor condition, and their stomachs contained nothing but stones and a few cuttle-fish beaks. A sounding on the 17th gave 1676 fathoms, 10 miles west of the charted position of Morell Land. No land could be seen from the mast-head, and I decided that Morell Land must be added to the long list of Antarctic islands and continental coasts that on close investigation have resolved themselves into icebergs. On clear days we could get an extended view in all directions from the mast-head, and the line of the pack was broken only by familiar bergs. About one hundred bergs were in view on a fine day, and they seemed practically the same as when they started their drift with us nearly seven months earlier. The scientists wished to inspect some of the neighbouring bergs at close quarters, but sledge travelling outside the well-trodden area immediately around the ship proved difficult and occasionally dangerous. On August 20, for example, Worsley, Hurley, and Greenstreet started off for the Rampart Berg and got on to a lead of young ice that undulated perilously beneath their feet. A quick turn saved them.

A wonderful mirage of the *fata Morgana* type was visible on August 20. The day was clear and bright, with a blue sky overhead and some rime aloft.

'The distant pack is thrown up into towering barrier-like cliffs, which are reflected in blue lakes and lanes of water at their base. Great white and golden cities of Oriental appearance at close intervals along these clifftops indicate distant bergs, some not previously known to us. Floating above these are wavering violet and creamy lines of still more remote bergs and pack. The lines rise and fall, tremble, dissipate, and reappear in an endless transformation scene. The southern pack and bergs, catching the sun's rays, are golden, but to the north the ice-masses are purple. Here the bergs assume changing forms, first a castle, then a balloon just clear of the horizon, that changes swiftly into an immense mushroom, a mosque, or a cathedral. The principal characteristic is the vertical lengthening of the object, a small pressure-ridge being given the appearance of a line of battlements or towering cliffs. The mirage is produced by refraction and is intensified by the columns of comparatively warm air rising from several cracks and leads that have opened eight to twenty miles away north and south.'

We noticed this day that a considerable change had taken place in our position relative to the Rampart Berg. It appeared that a big lead had opened and that there had been some differential movement of the pack. The opening movement might presage renewed pressure. A few hours later the dog teams, returning from exercise, crossed a narrow crack that had appeared ahead of the ship. This crack opened quickly to 60 ft. and would have given us trouble if the dogs had been left on the wrong side. It closed on the 25th and pressure followed in its neighbourhood.

On August 24 we were two miles north of the latitude of Morell's farthest south, and over 10 degrees of longitude, or more than 200 miles, west of his position. From the mast-head no land could be seen within twenty miles, and no land of over 500 ft. altitude could have escaped observation on our side of long. 52 degrees W. A sounding of 1900 fathoms on August 25 was further evidence of the non-existence of New South Greenland. There was some movement of the ice near the ship during the concluding days of the month. All hands were called out in the night of August 26, sounds of pressure having been followed by the cracking of the ice alongside the ship, but the trouble did not develop immediately. Late on the night of the 31st the ice began to work ahead of the ship and along the port side. Creaking and groaning of timbers, accompanied by loud snapping sounds fore and aft, told their story of strain. The pressure continued during the following day, beams and deck planks occasionally buckling to the strain. The ponderous floes were grinding against each other under the influence of wind and current, and our ship seemed to occupy for the time being an undesirable position near the centre of the disturbance; but she resisted staunchly and showed no sign of water in the bilges, although she had not been pumped out for six months. The pack extended to the horizon in every direction. I calculated that we were 250 miles from the nearest known land to the westward, and more than 500 miles from the nearest outpost of civilisation, Wilhelmina Bay. I hoped we would not have to undertake a march across the moving ice-fields. The *Endurance* we knew to be stout and true; but no ship ever built by man could live if taken fairly in the grip of the floes and prevented from rising to the surface of the grinding ice. These were anxious days. In the early morning of September 2 the ship jumped and shook to the accompaniment of cracks and groans, and some of the men who had been in the berths hurried on deck. The pressure eased a little later in the day, when the ice on the port side broke away from the ship to just abaft the main rigging. The *Endurance* was still held aft and at the rudder, and a large mass of ice could be seen adhering to the port bow, rising to within three feet of the surface. I wondered if this ice had got its grip by piercing the sheathing.

CHAPTER 4

Loss of the *Endurance*

The ice did not trouble us again seriously until the end of September, though during the whole month the floes were seldom entirely without movement. The roar of pressure would come to us across the otherwise silent ice-fields, and bring with it a threat and a warning. Watching from the crow's-nest, we could see sometimes the formation of pressure-ridges. The sunshine glittered on newly riven ice-surfaces as the masses of shattered floe rose and fell away from the line of pressure. The area of disturbance would advance towards us, recede, and advance again. The routine of work and play on the *Endurance* proceeded steadily. Our plans and preparations for any contingency that might arise during the approaching summer had been made, but there seemed always plenty to do in and about our prisoned ship. Runs with the dogs and vigorous games of hockey and football on the rough snow-covered floe kept all hands in good fettle. The record of one or two of these September days will indicate the nature of our life and our surroundings.

September 4. – Temperature −14.1 degrees Fahr. Light easterly breeze, blue sky, and stratus clouds. During forenoon notice a distinct terra-cotta or biscuit colour in the stratus clouds to the north. This travelled from east to west and could conceivably have come from some of the Graham Land volcanoes, now about 300 miles distant to the north-west. The upper current of air probably would come from that direction. Heavy rime. Pack unbroken and unchanged as far as visible. No land for 22 miles. No animal life observed.'

September 7. – Temperature −10.8 degrees Fahr. Moderate easterly to southerly winds, overcast and misty, with light snow till midnight, when weather cleared. Blue sky and fine clear weather to noon. Much rime aloft. Thick fresh snow on ship and floe that glistens brilliantly in the morning sunlight. Little clouds of faint violet-coloured mist rise from the lower and brinier portions of the pack, which stretches unbroken to the horizon. Very great refraction all round. A tabular berg about fifty feet high ten miles west is a good index of the amount of refraction. On ordinary days it shows from the mast-head, clear-cut against the sky; with much refraction, the pack beyond at the back of it lifts up into view; today a broad expanse of miles of pack is seen above it. Numerous other bergs generally seen in silhouette are, at first sight, lost, but after a closer scrutiny they appear as large lumps or dark masses well below the horizon. Refraction generally results in too big an altitude when observing the sun for position, but today, the horizon is thrown up so much that the altitude is about 12' too small. No land visible for twenty miles. No animal life observed. Lower Clark's tow-net with 566 fathoms wire, and hoist it up at two and a half miles an hour by walking across the floe with the wire. Result rather meagre – jelly-fish and some fish larvae. Exercise dogs in sledge teams. The young dogs, under Crean's care, pull as well, though not so strongly, as the best team in the pack. Hercules for the last fortnight or more has constituted himself leader of the orchestra. Two or three times in the twenty-four hours he starts a howl – a deep, melodious howl – and in about thirty seconds he has the whole pack in full song, the great deep, booming, harmonious song of the half-wolf pack.'

By the middle of September we were running short of fresh meat for the dogs. The seals and penguins seemed to have abandoned our neighbourhood altogether. Nearly five months had passed since we killed a seal, and penguins had been seen seldom. Clark, who was using his trawl as often as possible, reported that there was a marked absence of plankton in the sea, and we assumed that the seals and the penguins had gone in search of their accustomed food. The men got an emperor on the 23rd. The dogs, which were having their sledging exercise, became wildly excited when the penguin, which had risen in a crack, was driven ashore, and the best efforts of the drivers failed to save it alive. On the following day Wild, Hurley, Macklin, and McIlroy took their teams to the Stained Berg, about seven miles west of the ship, and on their way back got a female crab-eater, which they killed, skinned, and left to be picked up later. They ascended to the top of the berg, which lay in about lat. 69 degrees 30' S., long. 51 degrees W., and from an elevation of 110 ft. could see no land. Samples of the discoloured ice from the berg proved to contain dust with black gritty particles or sand-grains. Another seal, a bull Weddell, was secured on the 26th. The return of seal-life was opportune, since we had nearly finished the winter supply of dog-biscuit and wished to be able to feed the dogs on meat. The seals meant a supply of blubber, moreover, to supplement our small remaining stock of coal when the time came to get up steam again. We initiated a daylight-saving system on this day by putting forward the clock one hour. 'This is really pandering to the base but universal passion that men, and especially seafarers, have for getting up late, otherwise we would be honest and make our routine earlier instead of flogging the clock.'

During the concluding days of September the roar of the pressure grew louder, and I could see that the area of disturbance was rapidly approaching the ship. Stupendous forces were at work and the fields of firm ice around the *Endurance* were being diminished steadily. September 30 was a bad day. It began well, for we got two penguins and five seals during the morning. Three other seals were seen. But at 3 p.m. cracks that had opened during the night alongside the ship commenced to work in a lateral direction. The ship sustained terrific pressure on the port side forward, the heaviest shocks being under the forerigging. It was the worst squeeze we had experienced. The decks shuddered and jumped, beams arched, and stanchions buckled and shook. I ordered all hands to stand by in readiness for whatever emergency might arise. Even the dogs seemed to feel the tense anxiety of the moment. But the ship resisted valiantly, and just when it appeared that the limit of her strength was being reached the huge floe that was pressing down upon us cracked across and so gave relief.

'The behaviour of our ship in the ice has been magnificent,' wrote Worsley. 'Since we have been beset her staunchness and endurance have been almost past belief again and again. She has been nipped with a million-ton pressure and risen nobly, falling clear of the water out on the ice. She has been thrown to and fro like a shuttlecock a dozen times. She has been strained, her beams arched upwards, by the fearful pressure; her very sides opened and closed again as she was actually bent and curved along her length, groaning like a living thing. It will be sad if such a brave little craft should be finally crushed in the remorseless, slowly strangling grip of the Weddell pack after ten months of the bravest and most gallant fight ever put up by a ship.'

The *Endurance* deserved all that could be said in praise of her. Shipwrights had never done sounder or better work; but how long could she continue the fight under such conditions? We were drifting into the congested area of the western Weddell Sea, the worst portion of the worst sea in the world, where the pack, forced on irresistibly by wind and current, impinges on the western shore and is driven up in huge corrugated ridges and chaotic fields of pressure. The vital question for us was whether or not the ice would open sufficiently to release us, or at least give us a chance of release, before the drift carried us into the most dangerous area. There was no answer to be got from the silent bergs and the grinding floes, and we faced the month of October with anxious hearts.

The leads in the pack appeared to have opened out a little on October 1, but not sufficiently to be workable even if we had been able to release the *Endurance* from the floe. The day was calm, cloudy and misty in the forenoon and clearer in the afternoon, when we observed well-defined parhelia. The ship was subjected to slight pressure at intervals. Two bull crab-eaters climbed on to the floe close to the ship and were shot by Wild. They were both big animals in prime condition, and I felt that there was no more need for anxiety as to the supply of fresh meat for the dogs. Seal-liver made a welcome change in our own menu. The two bulls were marked, like many of their kind, with long parallel scars about three inches apart, evidently the work of the killers. A bull we killed on the following day had four parallel scars, sixteen inches long, on each side of its body; they were fairly deep and one flipper had been nearly torn away. The creature must have escaped from the jaws of a killer by a very small margin. Evidently life beneath the pack is not always monotonous. We noticed that several of the bergs in the neighbourhood of the ship were changing their relative positions more than they had done for months past. The floes were moving.

Our position on Sunday, October 3, was lat. 69 degrees 14' S., long. 51 degrees 8' W. During the night the floe holding the ship aft cracked in several places, and this appeared to have eased the strain on the rudder. The forenoon was misty, with falls of snow, but the weather cleared later in the day and we could see that the pack was breaking. New leads had appeared, while several old leads had closed. Pressure-ridges had risen along some of the cracks. The thickness of the season's ice, now about 230 days old, was 4 ft. 5 in. under 7 or 8 in. of snow. This ice had been slightly thicker in the early part of September, and I assumed that some melting had begun below. Clark had recorded plus temperatures at depths of 150 and 200 fathoms in the concluding days of September. The ice obviously had attained its maximum thickness by direct freezing, and the heavier older floes had been created by the consolidation of pressure-ice and the overlapping of floes under strain. The air temperatures were still low, −24.5 Fahr. being recorded on October 4.

The movement of the ice was increasing. Frost-smoke from opening cracks was showing in all directions during October 6. It had the appearance in one place of a great prairie fire, rising from the surface and getting higher as it drifted off before the wind in heavy, dark, rolling masses. At another point there was the appearance of a train running before the wind, the smoke rising from the locomotive straight upwards; and the smoke columns elsewhere gave the effect of warships steaming in line ahead. During the following day the leads and cracks opened to such an extent that if the *Endurance* could have been forced forward for thirty yards we could have proceeded for two or three miles; but the effort did not promise any really useful result. The conditions did not change materially during the rest of that week. The position on Sunday, October 10, was lat. 69 degrees 21' S., long. 50 degrees 34' W. A thaw made things uncomfortable for us that day. The temperature had risen from − 10 degrees Fahr. to +29.8 degrees Fahr., the highest we had experienced since January, and the ship got dripping wet between decks. The upper deck was clear of ice and snow and the cabins became unpleasantly messy. The dogs, who hated wet, had a most unhappy air. Undoubtedly one grows to like familiar conditions. We had lived long in temperatures that would have seemed distressingly low in civilised life, and now we were made uncomfortable by a degree of warmth that would have left the unaccustomed human being still shivering. The thaw was an indication that winter was over, and we began preparations for reoccupying the cabins on the main deck. I had the shelter-house round the stern pulled down on the 11th and made other preparations for working the ship as soon as she got clear. The carpenter had built a wheel-house over the wheel aft as shelter in cold and heavy weather. The ice was still loosening and no land was visible for twenty miles.

The temperature remained relatively high for several days. All hands moved to their summer quarters in the upper cabins on the 12th, to the accompaniment of much noise and laughter. Spring was in the air, and if there were no green growing things to gladden our eyes, there were at least many seals, penguins, and even whales disporting themselves in the leads. The time for renewed action was coming, and though our situation was grave enough, we were facing the future hopefully. The dogs were kept in a state of uproar by the sight of so much game. They became almost frenzied when a solemn-looking emperor penguin inspected them gravely from some point of vantage on the floe and gave utterance to an apparently derisive 'Knark!' At 7 p.m. on the 13th the ship broke free of the floe on which she had rested to starboard sufficiently to come upright. The rudder freed itself, but the propeller was found to be athwartship, having been forced into that position by the floe some time after August 1. The water was very clear and we could see the rudder, which appeared to have suffered only a slight twist to port at the water-line. It moved quite freely. The propeller, as far as we could see, was intact, but it could not be moved by the hand-gear, probably owing to a film of ice in the stern gland and sleeve. I did not think it advisable to attempt to deal with it at that stage. The ship had not been pumped for eight months, but there was no water and not much ice in the bilges. Meals were served again in the wardroom that day.

The south-westerly breeze freshened to a gale on the 14th, and the temperature fell from +31 degrees Fahr. to −1 degree Fahr. At midnight the ship came free from the floe and drifted rapidly astern. Her head fell off before the wind until she lay nearly at right-angles across the narrow lead. This was a dangerous position for rudder and propeller. The spanker was set, but the weight of the wind on the ship gradually forced the floes open until the *Endurance* swung right round and drove 100 yds. along the lead. Then the ice closed and at 3 a.m. we were fast again. The wind died down during the day and the pack opened for five or six miles to the north. It was still loose on the following morning, and I had the boiler pumped up with the intention of attempting to clear the propeller; but one of the manholes developed a leak, the packing being perished by cold or loosened by contraction, and the boiler had to be emptied out again.

The pack was rather closer on Sunday the 17th. Top-sails and head-sails were set in the afternoon, and with a moderate north-easterly breeze we tried to force the ship ahead out of the lead; but she was held fast. Later that day heavy pressure developed. The two floes between which the *Endurance* was lying began to close and the ship was subjected to a series of tremendously heavy strains. In the engine-room, the weakest point, loud groans, crashes, and hammering sounds were heard. The iron plates on the floor buckled up and overrode with loud clangs. Meanwhile the floes were grinding off each other's projecting points and throwing up pressure-ridges. The ship stood the strain well for nearly an hour and then, to my great relief, began to rise with heavy jerks and jars. She lifted ten inches forward and three feet four inches aft, at the same time heeling six degrees to port. The ice was getting below us and the immediate danger had passed. The position was lat. 69 degrees 19' S., long. 50 degrees 40' W.

The next attack of the ice came on the afternoon of October 18th. The two floes began to move laterally, exerting great pressure on the ship. Suddenly the floe on the port side cracked and huge pieces of ice shot up from under the port bilge. Within a few seconds the ship heeled over until she had a list of thirty degrees to port, being held under the starboard bilge by the opposing floe. The lee boats were now almost resting on the floe. The midship dog-kennels broke away and crashed down on to the lee kennels, and the howls and barks of the frightened dogs assisted to create a perfect pandemonium. Everything mov-able on deck and below fell to the lee side, and for a few minutes it looked as if the *Endurance* would be thrown upon her beam ends. Order was soon restored. I had all fires put out and battens nailed on the deck to give the dogs a foothold and enable people to get about. Then the crew lashed all the mov-able gear. If the ship had heeled any farther it would have been necessary to release the lee boats and pull them clear, and Worsley was watching to give the alarm. Hurley meanwhile descended to the floe and took some photographs of the ship in her unusual position. Dinner in the wardroom that evening was a curious affair. Most of the diners had to sit on the deck, their feet against battens and their plates on their knees. At 8 p.m. the floes opened, and within a few minutes the *Endurance* was nearly upright again. Orders were given for the ice to be chipped clear of the rudder. The men poled the blocks out of the way when they had been detached from the floe with the long ice-chisels, and we were able to haul the ship's stern into a clear berth. Then the boiler was pumped up. This work was completed early in the morning of October 19, and dur-ing that day the engineer lit fires and got up steam very slowly, in order to economise fuel and avoid any strain on the chilled boilers by unequal heating. The crew cut up all loose lumber, boxes, etc., and put them in the bunkers for fuel. The day was overcast, with occasional snowfalls, the temperature +12 degrees Fahr. The ice in our neighbourhood was quiet, but in the distance pressure was at work. The wind freshened in the evening, and we ran a wire mooring astern. The barometer at 11 p.m. stood at 28.96, the lowest since the gales of July. An uproar among the dogs attracted attention late in the afternoon, and we found a 25-ft. whale cruising up and down in our pool. It pushed its head up once in characteristic killer fashion, but we judged from its small curved dorsal fin that it was a specimen of *Balaenoptera acutorostrata*, not *Orca gladiator*.

A strong south-westerly wind was blowing on October 20 and the pack was working. The *Endurance* was imprisoned securely in the pool, but our chance might come at any time. Watches were set so as to be ready for working ship. Wild and Hudson, Greenstreet and Cheetham, Worsley and Crean, took the deck watches, and the Chief Engineer and Second Engineer kept watch and watch with three of the A.B.s for stokers. The staff and the forward hands, with the exception of the cook, the carpenter and his mate, were on 'watch and watch' — that is, four hours on deck and four hours below, or off duty. The carpenter was busy making a light punt, which might prove useful in the navigation of lanes and channels. At 11 a.m. we gave the engines a gentle trial turn astern. Everything worked well after eight months of frozen inactivity, except that the bilge-pump and the discharge proved to be frozen up; they were cleared with some little difficulty. The engineer reported that to get steam he had used one ton of coal, with wood-ashes and blubber. The fires required to keep the boiler warm consumed one and a quarter to one and a half hundred-weight of coal per day. We had about fifty tons of coal remaining in the bunkers.

October 21 and 22 were days of low temperature, which caused the open leads to freeze over. The pack was working, and ever and anon the roar of pressure came to our ears. We waited for the next move of the gigantic forces arrayed against us. The 23rd brought a strong north-westerly wind, and the movement of the floes and pressure-ridges became more formidable. Then on Sunday, October 24, there came what for the *Endurance* was the beginning of the end. The position was lat. 69 degrees 11' S., long. 510 degrees 5' W. We had now twenty-two and a half hours of daylight, and throughout the day we watched the threatening advance of the floes. At 6.45 p.m. the ship sustained heavy pressure in a dangerous position. The attack of the ice is illustrated roughly in the appended diagram.

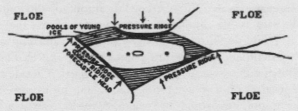

The shaded portions represent the pool, covered with new ice that afforded no support to the ship, and the arrows indicate the direction of the pressure exercised by the thick floes and pressure-ridges. The onslaught was all but irresistible. The *Endurance* groaned and quivered as her starboard quarter was forced against the floe, twisting the sternpost and starting the heads and ends of planking. The ice had lateral as well as forward movement, and the ship was twisted and actually bent by the stresses. She began to leak dangerously at once.

I had the pumps rigged, got up steam, and started the bilge-pumps at 8 p.m. The pressure by that time had relaxed. The ship was making water rapidly aft, and the carpenter set to work to make a coffer-dam astern of the engines. All hands worked, watch and watch, throughout the night, pumping ship and helping the carpenter. By morning the leak was being kept in check. The carpenter and his assistants caulked the coffer-dam with strips of blankets and nailed strips over the seams wherever possible. The main or hand pump was frozen up and could not be used at once. After it had been knocked out Worsley, Greenstreet, and Hudson went down in the bunkers and cleared the ice from the bilges. 'This is not a pleasant job,' wrote Worsley. 'We have to dig a hole down through the coal while the beams and timbers groan and crack all around us like pistol-shots. The darkness is almost complete, and we mess about in the wet with half-frozen hands and try to keep the coal from slipping back into the bilges. The men on deck pour buckets of boiling water from the galley down the pipe as we prod and hammer from below, and at last we get the pump clear, cover up the bilges to keep the coal out, and rush on deck, very thankful to find ourselves safe again in the open air.'

Monday, October 25, dawned cloudy and misty, with a minus temperature and a strong south-easterly breeze. All hands were pumping at intervals and assisting the carpenter with the cofferdam. The leak was being kept under fairly easily, but the outlook was bad. Heavy pressure-ridges were forming in all directions, and though the immediate pressure upon the ship was not severe, I realised that the respite would not be prolonged. The pack within our range of vision was being subjected to enormous compression, such as might be caused by cyclonic winds, opposing ocean currents, or constriction in a channel of some description. The pressure-ridges, massive and threatening, testified to the overwhelming nature of the forces that were at work. Huge blocks of ice, weighing many tons, were lifted into the air and tossed aside as other masses rose beneath them. We were helpless intruders in a strange world, our lives dependent upon the play of grim elementary forces that made a mock of our puny efforts. I scarcely dared hope now that the *Endurance* would live, and throughout that anxious day I reviewed again the plans made long before for the sledging journey that we must make in the event of our having to take to the ice. We were ready, as far as forethought could make us, for every contingency. Stores, dogs, sledges, and equipment were ready to be moved from the ship at a moment's notice.

The *Endurance* forced out of the floe by heavy pressure, 19 October
[*Scott Polar Research Institute*]

The following day brought bright clear weather, with a blue sky. The sunshine was inspiriting. The roar of pressure could be heard all around us. New ridges were rising, and I could see as the day wore on that the lines of major disturbance were drawing nearer to the ship. The *Endurance* suffered some strains at intervals. Listening below, I could hear the creaking and groaning of her timbers, the pistol-like cracks that told of the starting of a trenail or plank, and the faint, indefinable whispers of our ship's distress. Overhead the sun shone serenely; occasional fleecy clouds drifted before the southerly breeze, and the light glinted and sparkled on the million facets of the new pressure-ridges. The day passed slowly. At 7 p.m. very heavy pressure developed, with twisting strains that racked the ship fore and aft. The butts of planking were opened four and five inches on the starboard side, and at the same time we could see from the bridge that the ship was bending like a bow under titanic pressure. Almost like a living creature, she resisted the forces that would crush her; but it was a one-sided battle. Millions of tons of ice pressed inexorably upon the little ship that had dared the challenge of the Antarctic. The *Endurance* was now leaking badly, and at 9 p.m. I gave the order to lower boats, gear, provisions, and sledges to the floe, and move them to the flat ice a little way from the ship. The working of the ice closed the leaks slightly at mid-night, but all hands were pumping all night. A strange occurrence was the sudden appearance of eight emperor penguins from a crack 100 yds. away at the moment when the pressure upon the ship was at its climax. They walked a little way towards us, halted, and after a few ordinary calls proceeded to utter weird cries that sounded like a dirge for the ship. None of us had ever before heard the emperors utter any other than the most simple calls or cries, and the effect of this concerted effort was almost startling.

Then came a fateful day – Wednesday, October 27. The position was lat. 69 degrees 5' S., long. 51 degrees 30' W. The temperature was −8.5 degrees Fahr., a gentle southerly breeze was blowing and the sun shone in a clear sky. 'After long months of ceaseless anxiety and strain, after times when hope beat high and times when the outlook was black indeed, the end of the *Endurance* has come. But though we have been compelled to abandon the ship, which is crushed beyond all hope of ever being righted, we are alive and well, and we have stores and equipment for the task that lies before us. The task is to reach land with all the members of the Expedition. It is hard to write what I feel. To a sailor his ship is more than a floating home, and in the *Endurance* I had centred ambitions, hopes, and desires. Now, straining and groaning, her timbers cracking and her wounds gaping, she is slowly giving up her sentient life at the very outset of her career. She is crushed and abandoned after drifting more than 570 miles in a north-westerly direction during the 281 days since she became locked in the ice. The distance from the point where she became beset to the place where she now rests mortally hurt in the grip of the floes is 573 miles, but the total drift through all observed positions has been 1186 miles, and probably we actually covered more than 1500 miles. We are now 346 miles from Paulet Island, the nearest point where there is any possibility of finding food and shelter. A small hut built there by the Swedish expedition in 1902 is filled with stores left by the Argentine relief ship. I know all about those stores, for I purchased them in London on behalf of the Argentine Government when they asked me to equip the relief expedition. The distance to the nearest barrier west of us is about 180 miles, but a party going there would still be about 360 miles from Paulet Island and there would be no means of sustaining life on the barrier. We could not take from here food enough for the whole journey; the weight would be too great.

'This morning, our last on the ship, the weather was clear, with a gentle south-south-easterly to south-south-westerly breeze. From the crow's-nest there was no sign of land of any sort. The pressure was increasing steadily, and the passing hours brought no relief or respite for the ship. The attack of the ice reached its climax at 4 p.m. The ship was hove stern up by the pressure, and the driving floe, moving laterally across the stern, split the rudder and tore out the rudder-post and stern-post. Then, while we watched, the ice loosened and the *Endurance* sank a little. The decks were breaking upwards and the water was pouring in below. Again the pressure began, and at 5 p.m. I ordered all hands on to the ice. The twisting, grinding floes were working their will at last on the ship. It was a sickening sensation to feel the decks breaking up under one's feet, the great beams bending and then snapping with a noise like heavy gun-fire. The water was overmastering the pumps, and to avoid an explosion when it reached the boilers I had to give orders for the fires to be drawn and the steam let down. The plans for abandoning the ship in case of emergency had been made well in advance, and men and dogs descended to the floe and made their way to the comparative safety of an unbroken portion of the floe without a hitch. Just before leaving, I looked down the engine-room skylight as I stood on the quivering deck, and saw the engines dropping sideways as the stays and bed-plates gave way. I cannot describe the impression of relentless destruction that was forced upon me as I looked down and around. The floes, with the force of millions of tons of moving ice behind them, were simply annihilating the ship.'

Essential supplies had been placed on the floe about 100 yds. from the ship, and there we set about making a camp for the night. But about 7 p.m., after the tents were up, the ice we were occupying became involved in the pressure and started to split and

smash beneath our feet. I had the camp moved to a bigger floe
about 200 yds. away, just beyond the bow of the ship. Boats,
stores, and camp equipment had to be conveyed across a working
pressure-ridge. The movement of the ice was so slow that it did
not interfere much with our short trek, but the weight of the ridge
had caused the floes to sink on either side and there were pools of
water there. A pioneer party with picks and shovels had to build a
snow-causeway before we could get all our possessions across. By
8 p.m. the camp had been pitched again. We had two pole-tents
and three hoop-tents. I took charge of the small pole-tent, No. 1,
with Hudson, Hurley, and James as companions; Wild had the
small hoop-tent, No. 2, with Wordie, McNeish, and McIlroy.
These hoop-tents are very easily shifted and set up. The eight
forward hands had the large hoop-tent, No. 3; Crean had charge
of No. 4 hoop-tent with Hussey, Marston, and Cheetham; and
Worsley had the other pole-tent, No. 5, with Greenstreet, Lees,
Clark, Kerr, Rickenson, Macklin, and Blackborrow, the last
named being the youngest of the forward hands.

'Tonight the temperature has dropped to −16 degrees Fahr., and
most of the men are cold and uncomfortable. After the tents had
been pitched I mustered all hands and explained the position to
them briefly and, I hope, clearly. I have told them the distance to
the Barrier and the distance to Paulet Island, and have stated that I
propose to try to march with equipment across the ice in the
direction of Paulet Island. I thanked the men for the steadiness and
good morale they have shown in these trying circumstances, and
told them I had no doubt that, provided they continued to work
their utmost and to trust me, we will all reach safety in the end.
Then we had supper, which the cook had prepared at the big
blubber stove, and after a watch had been set all hands except the
watch turned in. For myself, I could not sleep. The destruction
and abandonment of the ship was no sudden shock. The disaster
had been looming ahead for many months, and I had studied my
plans for all contingencies a hundred times. But the thoughts that
came to me as I walked up and down in the darkness were not
particularly cheerful. The task now was to secure the safety of the
party, and to that I must bend my energies and mental power and
apply every bit of knowledge that experience of the Antarctic had
given me. The task was likely to be long and strenuous, and an

ordered mind and a clear programme were essential if we were to come through without loss of life. A man must shape himself to a new mark directly the old one goes to ground.

At midnight I was pacing the ice, listening to the grinding floe and to the groans and crashes that told of the death-agony of the *Endurance*, when I noticed suddenly a crack running across our floe right through the camp. The alarm-whistle brought all hands tumbling out, and we moved the tents and stores lying on what was now the smaller portion of the floe to the larger portion. Nothing more could be done at that moment, and the men turned in again; but there was little sleep. Each time I came to the end of my beat on the floe I could just see in the darkness the uprearing piles of pressure-ice, which toppled over and narrowed still further the little floating island we occupied. I did not notice at the time that my tent, which had been on the wrong side of the crack, had not been erected again. Hudson and James had managed to squeeze themselves into other tents, and Hurley had wrapped himself in the canvas of No. 1 tent. I discovered this about 5 a.m. All night long the electric light gleamed from the stern of the dying *Endurance*. Hussey had left this light switched on when he took a last observation, and, like a lamp in a cottage window, it braved the night until in the early morning the *Endurance* received a particularly violent squeeze. There was a sound of rending beams and the light disappeared. The connexion had been cut.

Morning came in chill and cheerless. All hands were stiff and weary after their first disturbed night on the floe. Just at daybreak I went over to the *Endurance* with Wild and Hurley, in order to retrieve some tins of petrol that could be used to boil up milk for the rest of the men. The ship presented a painful spectacle of chaos and wreck. The jib-boom and bowsprit had snapped off during the night and now lay at right angles to the ship, with the chains, martingale, and bob-stay dragging them as the vessel quivered and moved in the grinding pack. The ice had driven over the forecastle and she was well down by the head. We secured two tins of petrol with some difficulty, and postponed the further examination of the ship until after breakfast. Jumping across cracks with the tins, we soon reached camp, and built a fireplace out of the triangular watertight tanks we had ripped from the lifeboat. This we had done in order to make more room. Then we pierced a petrol-tin in half a dozen places with an ice-axe and set fire to it. The petrol blazed fiercely under the five-gallon drum we used as a cooker, and the hot milk was ready in quick time. Then we three ministering angels went round the tents with the life-giving drink, and were surprised and a trifle chagrined at the matter-of-fact manner in which some of the men accepted this contribution to their comfort. They did not quite understand what work we had done for them in the early dawn, and I heard Wild say, 'If any of you gentlemen would like your boots cleaned just put them outside.' This was his gentle way of reminding them that a little thanks will go a long way on such occasions.

The cook prepared breakfast, which consisted of biscuit and hoosh, at 8 a.m., and I then went over to the *Endurance* again and made a fuller examination of the wreck. Only six of the cabins had not been pierced by floes and blocks of ice. Every one of the starboard cabins had been crushed. The whole of the after part of the ship had been crushed concertina fashion. The forecastle and the Ritz were submerged, and the wardroom was three-quarters full of ice. The starboard side of the wardroom had come away. The motor-engine forward had been driven through the galley. Petrol-cases that had been stacked on the fore-deck had been driven by the floe through the wall into the wardroom and had carried before them a large picture. Curiously enough, the glass of this picture had not been cracked, whereas in the immediate neighbourhood I saw heavy iron davits that had been twisted and bent like the ironwork of a wrecked train. The ship was being crushed remorselessly.

Under a dull, overcast sky I returned to camp and examined our situation. The floe occupied by the camp was still subject to pressure, and I thought it wise to move to a larger and apparently stronger floe about 200 yds. away, off the starboard bow of the ship. This camp was to become known as Dump Camp, owing to the amount of stuff that was thrown away there. We could not afford to carry unnecessary gear, and a drastic sorting of equipment took place. I decided to issue a complete new set of Burberrys and underclothing to each man, and also a supply of new socks. The camp was transferred to the larger floe quickly, and I began there to direct the preparations for the long journey across the floes to Paulet Island or Snow Hill.

Hurley meanwhile had rigged his kinematograph-camera and

was getting pictures of the *Endurance* in her death-throes. While he was engaged thus, the ice, driving against the standing rigging and the fore-, main- and mizzen-masts, snapped the shrouds. The foretop and topgallant-mast came down with a run and hung in wreckage on the fore-mast, with the foreyard vertical. The main-mast followed immediately, snapping off about 10 ft. above the main deck. The crow's-nest fell within 10 ft. of where Hurley stood turning the handle of his camera, but he did not stop the machine, and so secured a unique, though sad, picture.

The issue of clothing was quickly accomplished. Sleeping-bags were required also. We had eighteen fur bags, and it was necessary, therefore, to issue ten of the Jaeger woollen bags in order to provide for the twenty-eight men of the party. The woollen bags were lighter and less warm than the reindeer bags, and so each man who received one of them was allowed also a reindeer-skin to lie upon. It seemed fair to distribute the fur bags by lot, but some of us older hands did not join in the lottery. We thought we could do quite as well with the Jaegers as with the furs. With quick dispatch the clothing was apportioned, and then we turned one of the boats on its side and supported it with two broken oars to make a lee for the galley. The cook got the blubber-stove going, and a little later, when I was sitting round the corner of the stove, I heard one man say, 'Cook, I like my tea strong.' Another joined in, 'Cook, I like mine weak.' It was pleasant to know that their minds were untroubled, but I thought the time opportune to mention that the tea would be the same for all hands and that we would be fortunate if two months later we had any tea at all. It occurred to me at the time that the incident had psychological interest. Here were men, their home crushed, the camp pitched on the unstable floes, and their chance of reaching safety apparently remote, calmly attend-ing to the details of existence and giving their attention to such trifles as the strength of a brew of tea.

During the afternoon the work continued. Every now and then we heard a noise like heavy guns or distant thunder, caused by the floes grinding together. 'The pressure caused by the congestion in this area of the pack is producing a scene of absolute chaos. The floes grind stupendously, throw up great ridges, and shatter one another mercilessly. The ridges, or hedgerows, marking the pressure-lines that border the fast-diminishing pieces of smooth floe-ice, are enormous. The ice moves majestically, irresistibly. Human effort is not futile, but man fights against the giant forces of Nature in a spirit of humility. One has a sense of dependence on the higher Power. Today two seals, a Weddell and a crab-eater, came close to the camp and were shot. Four others were chased back into the water, for their presence disturbed the dog teams, and this meant floggings and trouble with the harness. The arrangement of the tents has been completed and their internal management settled. Each tent has a mess orderly, the duty being taken in turn on an alphabetical rota. The orderly takes the hoosh-pots of his tent to the galley, gets all the hoosh he is allowed, and, after the meal, cleans the vessels with snow and stores them in sledge or boat ready for a possible move.'

'*October 29.* – We passed a quiet night, although the pressure was grinding around us. Our floe is a heavy one and it withstood the blows it received. There is a light wind from the north-west to north-north-west, and the weather is fine. We are twenty-eight men with forty-nine dogs, including Sue's and Sallie's five grown-up pups. All hands this morning were busy preparing gear, fitting boats on sledges, and building up and strengthening the sledges to carry the boats . . . The main motor-sledge, with a little fitting from the carpenter, carried our largest boat admirably. For the next boat four ordinary sledges were lashed together, but we were dubious as to the strength of this contrivance, and as a matter of fact it broke down quickly under strain . . . The ship is still afloat, with the spurs of the pack driven through her and holding her up. The forecastle-head is under water, the decks are burst up by the pressure, the wreckage lies around in dismal confusion, but over all the blue ensign flies still.

'This afternoon Sallie's three youngest pups, Sue's Sirius, and Mrs Chippy, the carpenter's cat, have to be shot. We could not undertake the maintenance of weaklings under the new conditions. Macklin, Crean, and the carpenter seemed to feel the loss of their friends rather badly. We propose making a short trial journey tomorrow, starting with two of the boats and the ten sledges. The number of dog teams has been increased to seven, Greenstreet taking charge of the new additional team, consisting of Snapper and Sallie's four oldest pups. We have ten working sledges to relay with five teams. Wild's and Hurley's teams will haul the cutter with the assistance of four men. The whaler and the other boats will follow, and the men who are hauling them will be able to help with the cutter at the rough places. We cannot hope to make rapid progress, but each mile counts. Crean this afternoon has a bad attack of snow-blindness.'

The weather on the morning of October 30 was overcast and misty, with occasional falls of snow. A moderate north-easterly breeze was blowing. We were still living on extra food, brought from the ship when we abandoned her, and the sledging and boating rations were intact. These rations would provide for twenty-eight men for fifty-six days on full rations, but we could count on getting enough seal and penguin meat to at least double this time. We could even, if progress proved too difficult and too injurious to the boats, which we must guard as our ultimate means of salvation, camp on the nearest heavy floe, scour the neighbouring pack for penguins and seals, and await the outward drift of the pack, to open and navigable water. 'This plan would avoid the grave dangers we are now incurring of getting entangled in impassable pressure-ridges and possibly irretrievably damaging the boats, which are bound to suffer in rough ice; it would also minimise the peril of the ice splitting under us, as it did twice during the night at our first camp. Yet I feel sure that it is the right thing to attempt a march, since if we can make five or seven miles a day to the north-west our chance of reaching safety in the months to come will be increased greatly. There is a psychological aspect to the question also. It will be much better for the men in general, to feel that, even though progress is slow, they are on their way to land than it will be simply to sit down and wait for the tardy north-westerly drift to take us out of this cruel waste of ice. We will make an attempt to move. The issue is beyond my power either to predict or to control.'

That afternoon Wild and I went out in the mist and snow to find a road to the north-east. After many devious turnings to avoid the heavier pressure-ridges, we pioneered a way for at least a mile and a half. and then returned by a rather better route to the camp. The pressure now was rapid in movement and our floe was suffering from the shakes and jerks of the ice. At 3 p.m., after lunch, we got under way, leaving Dump Camp a mass of debris. The order was that personal gear must not exceed two pounds per man, and this

meant that nothing but bare necessaries was to be taken on the
march. We could not afford to cumber ourselves with unnecessary
weight. Holes had been dug in the snow for the reception of private
letters and little personal trifles, the Lares and Penates of the members of the Expedition, and into the privacy of these white graves
were consigned much of sentimental value and not a little of
intrinsic worth. I rather grudged the two pounds allowance per
man, owing to my keen anxiety to keep weights at a minimum, but
some personal belongings could fairly be regarded as indispensable.
The journey might be a long one, and there was a possibility of a
winter in improvised quarters on an inhospitable coast at the other
end. A man under such conditions needs something to occupy his
thoughts, some tangible memento of his home and people beyond
the seas. So sovereigns were thrown away and photographs were
kept. I tore the fly-leaf out of the Bible that Queen Alexandra had
given to the ship, with her own writing in it, and also the wonderful
page of Job [38:29-30] containing the verse:

> Out of whose womb came the ice? And the hoary frost of
> Heaven, who hath gendered it?
> The waters are hid as with a stone, And the face of the deep is
> frozen.

The other Bible, which Queen Alexandra had given for the use
of the shore party, was down below in the lower hold in one of
the cases when the ship received her death-blow. Suitcases were
thrown away; these were retrieved later as material for making
boots, and some of them, marked 'solid leather', proved, to our
disappointment, to contain a large percentage of cardboard. The
manufacturer would have had difficulty in convincing us at the
time that the deception was anything short of criminal.

The pioneer sledge party, consisting of Wordie, Hussey, Hudson,
and myself, carrying picks and shovels, started to break a road
through the pressure-ridges for the sledges carrying the boats. The
boats, with their gear and the sledges beneath them, weighed each
more than a ton. The cutter was smaller than the whaler, but
weighed more and was a much more strongly built boat. The
whaler was mounted on the sledge part of the Girling tractor
forward and two sledges amidships and aft. These sledges were
strengthened with cross-timbers and shortened oars fore and aft.

The cutter was mounted on the aero-sledge. The sledges were the point of weakness. It appeared almost hopeless to prevent them smashing under their heavy loads when travelling over rough pressure-ice which stretched ahead of us for probably 300 miles. After the pioneer sledge had started the seven dog teams got off. They took their sledges forward for half a mile, then went back for the other sledges. Worsley took charge of the two boats, with fifteen men hauling, and these also had to be relayed. It was heavy work for dogs and men, but there were intervals of comparative rest on the backward journey, after the first portion of the load had been taken forward. We passed over two opening cracks, through which killers were pushing their ugly snouts, and by 5 p.m. had covered a mile in a north-north-westerly direction. The condition of the ice ahead was chaotic, for since the morning increased pressure had developed and the pack was moving and crushing in all directions. So I gave the order to pitch camp for the night on flat ice, which, unfortunately, proved to be young and salty. The older pack was too rough and too deeply laden with snow to offer a suitable camping-ground. Although we had gained only one mile in a direct line, the necessary deviations made the distance travelled at least two miles, and the relays brought the distance marched up to six miles. Some of the dog teams had covered at least ten miles. I set the watch from 6 p.m. to 7 a.m., one hour for each man in each tent in rotation.

During the night snow fell heavily, and the floor-cloths of the tents got wet through, as the temperature had risen to +25 degrees Fahr. One of the things we hoped for in those days was a temperature in the neighbourhood of zero, for then the snow surface would be hard, we would not be troubled by damp, and our gear would not become covered in soft snow. The killers were blowing all night, and a crack appeared about 20 ft. from the camp at 2 a.m. The ice below us was quite thin enough for the killers to break through if they took a fancy to do so, but there was no other camping-ground within our reach and we had to take the risk. When morning came the snow was falling so heavily that we could not see more than a few score yards ahead, and I decided not to strike camp. A path over the shattered floes would be hard to find, and to get the boats into a position of peril might be disastrous. Rickenson and Worsley started back for Dump Camp at 7 a.m. to get some wood and blubber for the fire, and an hour later we had hoosh, with one biscuit each. At 10 a.m. Hurley and Hudson left for the old camp in order to bring some additional dog-pemmican, since there were no seals to be found near us. Then, as the weather cleared, Worsley and I made a prospect to the west and tried to find a practicable road. A large floe offered a fairly good road for at least another mile to the northwest, and we went back prepared for another move. The weather cleared a little, and after lunch we struck camp. I took Rickenson, Kerr, Wordie, and Hudson as a breakdown gang to pioneer a path among the pressure-ridges. Five dog teams followed. Wild's and Hurley's teams were hitched on to the cutter and they started off in splendid style. They needed to be helped only once; indeed fourteen dogs did as well or even better than eighteen men. The ice was moving beneath and around us as we worked towards the big floe, and where this floe met the smaller ones there was a mass of pressed-up ice, still in motion, with water between the ridges. But it is wonderful what a dozen men can do with picks and shovels. We could cut a road through a pressure-ridge about 14 ft. high in ten minutes and leave a smooth, or comparatively smooth, path for the sledges and teams.

CHAPTER 5

Ocean Camp

In spite of the wet, deep snow and the halts occasioned by thus having to cut our road through the pressure-ridges, we managed to march the best part of a mile towards our goal, though the relays and the deviations again made the actual distance travelled nearer six miles. As I could see that the men were all exhausted I gave the order to pitch the tents under the lee of the two boats, which afforded some slight protection from the wet snow now threatening to cover everything. While so engaged one of the sailors discovered a small pool of water, caused by the snow having thawed, on a sail which was lying in one of the boats. There was not much – just a sip each; but, as one man wrote in his diary, 'One has seen and tasted cleaner, but seldom more opportunely found water.'

Next day broke cold and still with the same wet snow, and in the clearing light I could see that with the present loose surface, and considering how little result we had to show for all our strenuous efforts of the past four days, it would be impossible to proceed for any great distance. Taking into account also the possibility of leads opening close to us, and so of our being able to row north-west to where we might find land, I decided to find a more solid floe and there camp until conditions were more favourable for us to make a second attempt to escape from our icy prison. To this end we moved our tents and all our gear to a thick, heavy old floe about one and a half miles from the wreck and there made our camp. We called this 'Ocean Camp'. It was with the utmost difficulty that we shifted our two boats. The surface was terrible – like nothing that any of us had ever seen around us before. We were sinking at times up to our hips, and everywhere the snow was two feet deep.

I decided to conserve our valuable sledging rations, which would be so necessary for the inevitable boat journey, as much as possible, and to subsist almost entirely on seals and penguins.

A party was sent back to Dump Camp, near the ship, to collect as much clothing, tobacco, etc., as they could find. The heavy snow which had fallen in the last few days, combined with the thawing and consequent sinking of the surface, resulted in the total disappearance of a good many of the things left behind at this dump. The remainder of the men made themselves as comfortable as possible under the circumstances at Ocean Camp. This floating lump of ice, about a mile square at first but later splitting into smaller and smaller fragments, was to be our home for nearly two months. During these two months we made frequent visits to the vicinity of the ship and retrieved much valuable clothing and food and some few articles of personal value which in our light-hearted optimism we had thought to leave miles behind us on our dash across the moving ice to safety.

The collection of food was now the all-important consideration. As we were to subsist almost entirely on seals and penguins, which were to provide fuel as well as food, some form of blubber-stove was a necessity. This was eventually very ingeniously contrived from the ship's steel ash-chute, as our first attempt with a large iron oil-drum did not prove eminently successful. We could only cook seal or penguin hooshes or stews on this stove, and so uncertain was its action that the food was either burnt or only partially cooked; and, hungry though we were, half-raw seal meat was not very appetising. On one occasion a wonderful stew made from seal meat, with two or three tins of Irish stew that had been salved from the ship, fell into the fire through the bottom of the oil-drum that we used as a saucepan becoming burnt out on account of the sudden intense heat of the fire below. We lunched that day on one biscuit and a quarter of a tin of bully-beef each, frozen hard.

This new stove, which was to last us during our stay at Ocean Camp, was a great success. Two large holes were punched, with much labour and few tools, opposite one another at the wider or top end of the chute. Into one of these an oil-drum was fixed, to be used as the fireplace, the other hole serving to hold our saucepan. Alongside this another hole was punched to enable two saucepans to be boiled at a time; and farther along still a chimney made from biscuit-tins completed a very efficient, if not a very elegant, stove. Later on the cook found that he could bake a sort of flat bannock or scone on this stove, but he was seriously hampered for want of yeast or baking-powder.

An attempt was next made to erect some sort of a galley to protect the cook against the inclemencies of the weather. The party which I had sent back under Wild to the ship returned with, amongst other things, the wheel-house practically complete. This, with the addition of some sails and tarpaulins stretched on spars, made a very comfortable storehouse and galley. Pieces of planking from the deck were lashed across some spars stuck upright into the snow, and this, with the ship's binnacle, formed an excellent look-out from which to look for seals and penguins. On this platform, too, a mast was erected from which flew the King's flag and the Royal Clyde Yacht Club burgee.

I made a strict inventory of all the food in our possession, weights being roughly determined with a simple balance made from a piece of wood and some string, the counterweight being a 60-lb. box of provisions.

The dog teams went off to the wreck early each morning under Wild, and the men made every effort to rescue as much as possible from the ship. This was an extremely difficult task as the whole of the deck forward was under a foot of water on the port side, and nearly three feet on the starboard side. However, they managed to collect large quantities of wood and ropes and some few cases of provisions. Although the galley was under water, Bakewell managed to secure three or four saucepans, which later proved invaluable acquisitions. Quite a number of boxes of flour, etc., had been stowed in a cabin in the hold, and these we had been unable to get out before we left the ship. Having, therefore, determined as nearly as possible that portion of the deck immediately above these cases, we proceeded to cut a hole with large ice-chisels through the 3-in. planking of which it was formed. As the ship at this spot was under 5 ft. of water and ice, it was not an easy job. However, we succeeded in making the hole sufficiently large to allow of some few cases to come floating up. These were greeted with great satisfaction, and later on, as we warmed to our work, other cases, whose upward progress was assisted with a boat-hook, were greeted with either cheers or groans according to whether they contained farinaceous food or merely luxuries such as jellies. For each man by now had a good idea of the calorific value and nutritive and sustaining qualities of the various foods. It had a personal interest for us all. In this way we added to our scanty stock between two and three tons of provisions, about half of which was farinaceous food, such as flour and peas, of which we were so short. This sounds a great deal, but at one pound per day it would only last twenty-eight men for three months. Previous to this I had reduced the food allowance to nine and a half ounces per man per day. Now, however, it could be increased, and 'this afternoon, for the first time for ten days, we knew what it was to be really satisfied.'

I had the sledges packed in readiness with the special sledging rations in case of a sudden move, and with the other food, allowing also for prospective seals and penguins, I calculated a dietary to give the utmost possible variety and yet to use our precious stock of flour in the most economical manner. All seals and penguins that appeared anywhere within the vicinity of the camp were killed to provide food and fuel. The dog-pemmican we also added to our own larder, feeding the dogs on the seals which we caught, after removing such portions as were necessary for our own needs. We were rather short of crockery, but small pieces of venesta-wood served admirably as plates for seal steaks; stews and liquids of all sorts were served in the aluminium sledging-mugs, of which each man had one. Later on, jelly-tins and biscuit-tin lids were pressed into service.

Monotony in the meals, even considering the circumstances in which we found ourselves, was what I was striving to avoid, so our little stock of luxuries, such as fish-paste, tinned herrings, etc., was carefully husbanded and so distributed as to last as long as possible. My efforts were not in vain, as one man states in his diary: 'It must be admitted that we are feeding very well indeed, considering our position. Each meal consists of one course and a beverage. The dried vegetables, if any, all go into the same pot as the meat, and every dish is a sort of hash or stew, be it ham or seal meat or half and half. The fact that we only have two pots available places restrictions upon the number of things that can be cooked at one time, but in spite of, the limitation of facilities, we always seem to manage to get just enough. The milk-powder and sugar are necessarily boiled with the tea or cocoa.

'We are, of course, very short of the farinaceous element in our diet, and consequently have a mild craving for more of it. Bread is out of the question, and as we are husbanding the remaining cases of our biscuits for our prospective boat journey, we are eking out the supply of flour by making bannocks, of which we have from three to four each day. These bannocks are made from flour, fat, water, salt, and a little baking-powder, the dough being rolled out into flat rounds and baked in about ten minutes on a hot sheet of iron over the fire. Each bannock weighs about one and a half to two ounces, and we are indeed lucky to be able to produce them.'

A few boxes of army biscuits soaked with sea-water were distributed at one meal. They were in such a state that they would not have been looked at a second time under ordinary circumstances, but to us on a floating lump of ice, over three hundred miles from land, and that quite hypothetical, and with the unplumbed sea beneath us, they were luxuries indeed. Wild's tent made a pudding of theirs with some dripping.

Although keeping in mind the necessity for strict economy with our scanty store of food, I knew how important it was to keep the men cheerful, and that the depression occasioned by our surroundings and our precarious position could to some extent be alleviated by increasing the rations, at least until we were more accustomed to our new mode of life. That this was successful is shown in their diaries. 'Day by day goes by much the same as one another. We work; we talk; we eat. Ah, how we eat! No longer on short rations, we are a trifle more exacting than we were when we first commenced our "simple life", but by comparison with home standards we are positive barbarians, and our gastronomic rapacity knows no bounds.

'All is eaten that comes to each tent, and everything is most carefully and accurately divided into as many equal portions as there are men in the tent. One member then closes his eyes or turns his head away and calls out the names at random, as the cook for the day points to each portion, saying at the same time, "Whose?"

'Partiality, however unintentional it may be, is thus entirely obviated and everyone feels satisfied that all is fair, even though one may look a little enviously at the next man's helping, which differs in some especially appreciated detail from one's own. We break the Tenth Commandment energetically, but as we are all in the same boat in this respect, no one says a word. We understand each other's feelings quite sympathetically.

'It is just like school-days over again, and very jolly it is too, for the time being!'

Later on, as the prospect of wintering in the pack became more apparent, the rations had to be considerably reduced. By that time, however, everybody had become more accustomed to the idea and took it quite as a matter of course.

Our meals now consisted in the main of a fairly generous helping of seal or penguin, either boiled or fried. As one man wrote: 'We are now having enough to eat, but not by any means too much; and everyone is always hungry enough to eat every scrap he can get. Meals are invariably taken very seriously, and little talking is done till the hoosh is finished.'

Our tents made somewhat cramped quarters, especially during meal-times. 'Living in a tent without any furniture requires a little getting used to. For our meals we have to sit on the floor, and it is surprising how awkward it is to eat in such a position; it is better by far to kneel and sit back on one's heels, as do the Japanese.'

Each man took it in turn to be the tent 'cook' for one day, and one writes: 'The word "cook" is at present rather a misnomer, for whilst we have a permanent galley no cooking need be done in the tent.

'Really, all that the tent cook has to do is to take his two hoosh-pots over to the galley and convey the hoosh and the beverage to the tent, clearing up after each meal and washing up the two pots and the mugs. There are no spoons, etc., to wash, for we each keep our own spoon and pocket-knife in our pockets. We just lick them as clean as possible and replace them in our pockets after each meal.

'Our spoons are one of our indispensable possessions here. To lose one's spoon would be almost as serious as it is for an edentate person to lose his set of false teeth.'

During all this time the supply of seals and penguins, if not inexhaustible, was always sufficient for our needs.

Seal- and penguin-hunting was our daily occupation, and parties were sent out in different directions to search among the hum-mocks and the pressure-ridges for them. When one was found a signal was hoisted, usually in the form of a scarf or a sock on a pole, and an answering signal was hoisted at the camp.

Then Wild went out with a dog team to shoot and bring in the game. To feed ourselves and the dogs at least one seal a day was required. The seals were mostly crab-eaters, and emperor penguins were the general rule. On November 5, however, an adelie was caught, and this was the cause of much discussion, as the following extract shows: 'The man on watch from 3 a.m. to 4 a.m. caught an adelie penguin. This is the first of its kind that we have seen since January last, and it may mean a lot. It may signify that there is land somewhere near us, or else that great leads are opening up, but it is impossible to form more than a mere conjecture at present.'

No skuas, Antarctic petrels, or sea-leopards were seen during our two months' stay at Ocean Camp.

In addition to the daily hunt for food, our time was passed in reading the few books that we had managed to save from the ship. The greatest treasure in the library was a portion of the *Encyclopaedia Britannica*. This was being continually used to settle the inevitable arguments that would arise. The sailors were discovered one day engaged in a very heated discussion on the subject of Money and Exchange. They finally carne to the conclusion that the Encyclopaedia, since it did not coincide with their views, must be wrong.

'For descriptions of every American town that ever has been, is, or ever will be, and for full and complete biographies of every American statesman since the time of George Washington and long before, the Encyclopaedia would be hard to beat. Owing to our shortage of matches we have been driven to use it for purposes other than the purely literary ones though; and one genius having discovered that the paper used for its pages had been impregnated with saltpetre, we can now thoroughly recommend it as a very efficient pipe-lighter.'

We also possessed a few books on Antarctic exploration, a copy of Browning and one of *The Ancient Mariner*. On reading the latter, we sympathised with him and wondered what he had done with the albatross; it would have made a very welcome addition to our larder.

The two subjects of most interest to us were our rate of drift and the weather. Worsley took observations of the sun whenever possible, and his results showed conclusively that the drift of our floe was almost entirely dependent upon the winds and not much affected by currents. Our hope, of course, was to drift northwards to the edge of the pack and then, when the ice was loose enough, to take to the boats and row to the nearest land. We started off in fine style, drifting north about twenty miles in two or three days in a howling south-westerly blizzard. Gradually, however, we slowed up, as successive observations showed, until we began to drift back to the south. An increasing north-easterly wind, which commenced on November 7 and lasted for twelve days, damped our spirits for a time, until we found that we had only drifted back to the south three miles, so that we were now seventeen miles to the good. This tended to reassure us in our theories that the ice of the Weddell Sea was drifting round in a clockwise direction, and that if we could stay on our piece long enough we must eventually be taken up to the north, where lay the open sea and the path to comparative safety.

The ice was not moving fast enough to be noticeable. In fact, the only way in which we could prove that we were moving at all was by noting the change of relative positions of the bergs around us, and, more definitely, by fixing our absolute latitude and longitude by observations of the sun. Otherwise, as far as actual visible drift was concerned, we might have been on dry land.

For the next few days we made good progress, drifting seven miles to the north on November 24 and another seven miles in the next forty-eight hours. We were all very pleased to know that although the wind was mainly south-west all this time, yet we had made very little easting. The land lay to the west; so had we drifted to the east we should have been taken right away to the centre of the entrance to the Weddell Sea, and our chances of finally reaching land would have been considerably lessened.

Our average rate of drift was slow, and many and varied were the calculations as to when we should reach the pack-edge. On December 12, 1915, one man wrote: 'Once across the Antarctic Circle, it will seem as if we are practically halfway home again; and it is just possible that with favourable winds we may cross the circle before the New Year. A drift of only three miles a day would do it, and we have often done that and more for periods of three or four weeks.

'We are now only 250 miles from Paulet Island, but too much to the east of it. We are approaching the latitudes in which we were at this time last year, on our way down. The ship left South Georgia just a year and a week ago, and reached this latitude four or five miles to the eastward of our present position on January 3, 1915, crossing the circle on New Year's Eve.'

Thus, after a year's incessant battle with the ice, we had returned, by many strange turns of fortune's wheel, to almost identically the same latitude that we had left with such high hopes and aspirations twelve months previously; but under what different conditions now! Our ship crushed and lost, and we ourselves drifting on a piece of ice at the mercy of the winds. However, in spite of occasional setbacks due to unfavourable winds, our drift was in the main very satisfactory, and this went a long way towards keeping the men cheerful.

As the drift was mostly affected by the winds, the weather was closely watched by all, and Hussey, the meteorologist, was called upon to make forecasts every four hours, and sometimes more frequently than that. A meteorological screen, containing thermo-meters and a barograph, had been erected on a post frozen into the ice, and observations were taken every four hours. When we first left the ship the weather was cold and miserable, and altogether as unpropitious as it could possibly have been for our attempted march. Our first few days at Ocean Camp were passed under much the same conditions. At nights the temperature dropped to zero, with blinding snow and drift. One-hour watches were instituted, all hands taking their turn, and in such weather this job was no sinecure. The watchman had to be continually on the alert for cracks in the ice, or any sudden changes in the ice conditions, and also had to keep his eye on the dogs, who often became restless, fretful, and quarrelsome in the early hours of the morning. At the end of his hour he was very glad to crawl back into the com-parative warmth of his frozen sleeping-bag.

On November 6 a dull, overcast day developed into a howling blizzard from the south-west, with snow and low drift. Only those who were compelled left the shelter of their tent. Deep drifts formed everywhere, burying sledges and provisions to a depth of two feet, and the snow piling up round the tents threatened to burst the thin fabric. The fine drift found its way in through the ventilator of the tent, which was accordingly plugged up with a spare sock.

This lasted for two days, when one man wrote: 'The blizzard continued through the morning, but cleared towards noon, and it was a beautiful evening; but we would far rather have the screeching blizzard with its searching drift and cold damp wind, for we drifted about eleven miles to the north during the night.'

For four days the fine weather continued, with gloriously warm, bright sun, but cold when standing still or in the shade. The temperature usually dropped below zero, but every opportunity was taken during these fine, sunny days to partially dry our sleeping-bags and other gear, which had become sodden through our body-heat having thawed the snow which had drifted in on to them during the blizzard. The bright sun seemed to put new heart into all.

The next day brought a north-easterly wind with the very high temperature of 27 degrees Fahr. – only 5 degrees below freezing. 'These high temperatures do not always represent the warmth which might be assumed from the thermometrical readings. They usually bring dull, overcast skies, with a raw, muggy, moisture-laden wind. The winds from the south, though colder, are nearly always coincident with sunny days and clear blue skies.'

The temperature still continued to rise, reaching 33 degrees Fahr. on November 14. The thaw consequent upon these high temperatures was having a disastrous effect upon the surface of our camp. 'The surface is awful! – not slushy, but elusive. You step out gingerly. All is well for a few paces, then your foot suddenly sinks a couple of feet until it comes to a hard layer. You wade along in this way step by step, like a mudlark at Portsmouth Hard, hoping gradually to regain the surface. Soon you do, only to repeat the exasperating performance ad lib., to the accompaniment of all the expletives that you can bring to bear on the subject. What actually happens is that the warm air melts the surface sufficiently to cause drops of water to trickle down slightly, where, on meeting colder layers of snow, they freeze again, forming a honeycomb of icy nodules instead of the soft, powdery, granular snow that we are accustomed to.'

These high temperatures persisted for some days, and when, as occasionally happened, the sky was clear and the sun was shining it was unbearably hot. Five men who were sent to fetch some gear from the vicinity of the ship with a sledge marched in nothing but trousers and singlet, and even then were very hot; in fact they were afraid of getting sunstroke, so let down flaps from their caps to cover their necks. Their sleeves were rolled up over their elbows, and their arms were red and sunburnt in consequence. The temperature on this occasion was 26 degrees Fahr., or 6 degrees below freezing. For five or six days more the sun continued, and most of our clothes and sleeping-bags were now comparatively dry. A wretched day with rainy sleet set in on November 21, but one could put up with this discomfort as the wind was now from the south.

The wind veered later to the west, and the sun came out at 9 p.m. For at this time, near the end of November, we had the midnight sun. 'A thrice-blessed southerly wind' soon arrived to cheer us all, occasioning the following remarks in one of the diaries: 'Today is the most beautiful day we have had in the Antarctic – a clear sky, a gentle, warm breeze from the south, and the most brilliant sunshine. We all took advantage of it to strike tents, clean out, and generally dry and air ground-sheets and sleeping-bags.'

I was up early – 4 a.m. – to keep watch, and the sight was indeed magnificent. Spread out before one was an extensive panorama of ice-fields, intersected here and there by small broken leads, and dotted with numerous noble bergs, partly bathed in sunshine and partly tinged with the grey shadows of an overcast sky.

As one watched one observed a distinct line of demarcation between the sunshine and the shade, and this line gradually approached nearer and nearer, lighting up the hummocky relief of the ice-field bit by bit, until at last it reached us, and threw the whole camp into a blaze of glorious sunshine which lasted nearly all day.

'This afternoon we were treated to one or two showers of hail-like snow. Yesterday we also had a rare form of snow, or, rather, precipitation of ice-spicules, exactly like little hairs, about a third of an inch long.

'The warmth in the tents at lunch-time was so great that we had all the side-flaps up for ventilation, but it is a treat to get warm occasionally, and one can put up with a little stuffy atmosphere now and again for the sake of it. The wind has gone to the best quarter this evening, the south-east, and is freshening.'

On these fine, clear, sunny days wonderful mirage effects could be observed, just as occur over the desert. Huge bergs were apparently resting on nothing, with a distinct gap between their bases and the horizon; others were curiously distorted into all sorts of weird and fantastic shapes, appearing to be many times their proper height. Added to this, the pure glistening white of the snow and ice made a picture which it is impossible adequately to describe.

Later on, the freshening south-westerly wind brought mild, overcast weather, probably due to the opening up of the pack in that direction.

I had already made arrangements for a quick move in case of a sudden break-up of the ice. Emergency orders were issued; each man had his post allotted and his duty detailed; and the whole was so organised that in less than five minutes from the sounding of the alarm on my whistle, tents were struck, gear and provisions packed, and the whole party was ready to move off. I now took a final survey of the men to note their condition, both mental and physical. For our time at Ocean Camp had not been one of unalloyed bliss. The loss of the ship meant more to us than we could ever put into words. After we had settled at Ocean Camp she still remained nipped by the ice, only her stern showing and her bows overridden and buried by the relentless pack. The tangled mass of ropes, rigging, and spars made the scene even more desolate and depressing.

It was with a feeling almost of relief that the end came.

'November 21, 1915. – This evening, as we were lying in our tents we heard the Boss call out, "She's going, boys!" We were out in a second and up on the look-out station and other points of vantage, and, sure enough, there was our poor ship a mile and a half away struggling in her death-agony. She went down bows first, her stern raised in the air. She then gave one quick dive and the ice closed over her for ever. It gave one a sickening sensation to see it, for, mastless and useless as she was, she seemed to be a link with the outer world. Without her our destitution seems more emphasised, our desolation more complete. The loss of the ship sent a slight wave of depression over the camp. No one said much, but we cannot be blamed for feeling it in a sentimental way. It seemed as if the moment of severance from many cherished associations, many happy moments, even stirring incidents, had come as she silently up-ended to find a last resting-place beneath the ice on which we now stand. When one knows every little nook and corner of one's ship as we did, and has helped her time and again in the fight that she made so well, the actual parting was not without its pathos, quite apart from one's own desolation, and I doubt if there was one amongst us who did not feel some personal emotion when Sir Ernest, standing on the top of the look-out, said somewhat sadly and quietly, "She's gone, boys."

'It must, however, be said that we did not give way to depression for long, for soon everyone was as cheery as usual. Laughter rang out from the tents, and even the Boss had a passage-at-arms with the storekeeper over the inadequacy of the sausage ration, insisting that there should be two each "because they were such little ones", instead of the one and a half that the latter proposed.'

The psychological effect of a slight increase in the rations soon neutralised any tendency to downheartedness, but with the high temperatures surface-thaw set in, and our bags and clothes were soaked and sodden. Our boots squelched as we walked, and we lived in a state of perpetual wet feet. At nights, before the temperature had fallen, clouds of steam could be seen rising from our soaking bags and boots. During the night, as it grew colder, this all condensed as rime on the inside of the tent, and showered down upon us if one happened to touch the side inadvertently. One had to be careful how one walked, too, as often only a thin crust of ice and snow covered a hole in the floe, through which many an unwary member went in up to his waist. These perpetual soakings, however, seemed to have had little lasting effect, or perhaps it was not apparent owing to the excitement of the prospect of an early release.

A north-westerly wind on December 7 and 8 retarded our progress somewhat, but I had reason to believe that it would help to open the ice and form leads through which we might escape to open water. So I ordered a practice launching of the boats and stowage of food and stores in them. This was very satisfactory. We cut a slipway from our floe into a lead which ran alongside, and the boats took the water 'like a bird', as one sailor remarked. Our hopes were high in anticipation of an early release. A blizzard sprang up, increasing the next day and burying tents and packing-cases in the drift. On December 12 it had moderated somewhat and veered to the south-east, and the next day the blizzard had ceased, but a good steady wind from south and south-west continued to blow us north.

'December 15, 1915. – The continuance of southerly winds is exceeding our best hopes, and raising our spirits in proportion. Prospects could not be brighter than they are just now. The environs of our floe are continually changing. Some days we are almost surrounded by small open leads, preventing us from crossing over to the adjacent floes.'

After two more days our fortune changed, and a strong north-easterly wind brought 'a beastly cold, windy day' and drove us back three and a quarter miles. Soon, however, the wind once more veered to the south and south-west. These high temperatures, combined with the strong changeable winds that we had had of late, led me to conclude that the ice all around us was rotting and breaking up and that the moment of our deliverance from the icy maw of the Antarctic was at hand.

On December 20, after discussing the question with Wild, I informed all hands that I intended to try and make a march to the west to reduce the distance between us and Paulet Island. A buzz of pleasurable anticipation went round the camp, and everyone was anxious to get on the move. So the next day I set off with Wild, Crean, and Hurley, with dog teams, to the westward to survey the route. After travelling about seven miles we mounted a small berg, and there as far as we could see stretched a series of immense flat floes from half a mile to a mile across, separated from each other by pressure-ridges which seemed easily negotiable with pick and shovel. The only place that appeared likely to be formidable was a very much cracked-up area between the old floe that we were on and the first of the series of young flat floes about half a mile away.

December 22 was therefore kept as Christmas Day, and most of our small remaining stock of luxuries was consumed at the Christmas feast. We could not carry it all with us, so for the last time for eight months we had a really good meal – as much as we could eat. Anchovies in oil, baked beans, and jugged hare made a glorious mixture such as we have not dreamed of since our school-days. Everybody was working at high pressure, packing and repacking sledges and stowing what provisions we were going to take with us in the various sacks and boxes. As I looked round at the eager faces of the men I could not but hope that this time the fates would be kinder to us than in our last attempt to march across the ice to safety.

CHAPTER 6

The march between

With the exception of the night-watchman we turned in at 11 p.m., and at 3 a.m. on December 23 all hands were roused for the purpose of sledging the two boats, the *James Caird* and the *Dudley Docker*, over the dangerously cracked portion to the first of the young floes, whilst the surface still held its night crust. A thick sea-fog came up from the west, so we started off finally at 4.30 a.m., after a drink of hot coffee.

Practically all hands had to be harnessed to each boat in succession, and by dint of much careful manipulation and tortuous courses amongst the broken ice we got both safely over the danger-zone.

We then returned to Ocean Camp for the tents and the rest of the sledges, and pitched camp by the boats about one and a quarter miles off. On the way back a big seal was caught which provided fresh food for ourselves and for the dogs. On arrival at the camp a supper of cold tinned mutton and tea was served, and everybody turned in at 2 p.m. It was my intention to sleep by day and march by night, so as to take advantage of the slightly lower temperatures and consequent harder surfaces.

At 8 p.m. the men were roused, and after a meal of cold mutton and tea, the march was resumed. A large open lead brought us to a halt at 11 p.m., whereupon we camped and turned in without a meal. Fortunately just at this time the weather was fine and warm. Several men slept out in the open at the beginning of the march. One night, however, a slight snow-shower came on, succeeded immediately by a lowering of the temperature. Worsley, who had hung up his trousers and socks on a boat, found them iced-up and stiff; and it was quite a painful process for him to dress quickly that morning. I was anxious, now that we had started, that we should make every effort to extricate ourselves, and this temporary check so early was rather annoying. So that afternoon Wild and I ski-ed out to the crack and found that it had closed up again. We marked out the track with small flags as we returned. Each day, after all hands had turned in, Wild and I would go ahead for two miles or so to reconnoitre the next day's route, marking it with pieces of wood, tins, and small flags. We had to pick the road which though it might be somewhat devious, was flattest and had least hummocks. Pressure-ridges had to be skirted, and where this was not possible the best place to make a bridge of ice-blocks across the lead or over the ridge had to be found and marked. It was the duty of the dog-drivers to thus prepare the track for those who were toiling behind with the heavy boats. These boats were hauled in relays; about sixty yards at a time. I did not wish them to be separated by too great a distance in case the ice should crack between them, and we should be unable to reach the one that was in rear. Every twenty yards or so they had to stop for a rest and to take breath, and it was a welcome sight to them to see the canvas screen go up on some oars, which denoted the fact that the cook had started preparing a meal, and that a temporary halt, at any rate, was going to be made. Thus the ground had to be traversed three times by the boat-hauling party. The dog-sledges all made two, and some of them three, relays. The dogs were wonderful. Without them we could never have transported half the food and gear that we did.

We turned in at 7 p.m. that night, and at 1 a.m. next day, the 25th, and the third day of our march, a breakfast of sledging ration was served. By 2 a.m. we were on the march again. We wished one another a merry Christmas, and our thoughts went back to those at home. We wondered, too, that day, as we sat down to our 'lunch' of stale, thin bannock and a mug of thin cocoa, what they were having at home.

All hands were very cheerful. The prospect of a relief from the monotony of life on the floe raised all our spirits. One man wrote in his diary: 'It's a hard, rough, jolly life, this marching and camping; no washing of self or dishes, no undressing, no changing of clothes. We have our food anyhow, and always impregnated with blubber-smoke; sleeping almost on the bare snow and working as hard as the human physique is capable of doing on a minimum of food.'

We marched on, with one halt at 6 a.m., till half-past eleven. After a supper of seal steaks and tea we turned in. The surface now was pretty bad. High temperatures during the day made the upper layers of snow very soft, and the thin crust which formed at night was not sufficient to support a man. Consequently, at each step we went in over our knees in the soft wet snow. Sometimes a man would step into a hole in the ice which was hidden by the covering of snow, and be pulled up with a jerk by his harness. The sun was very hot and many were suffering from cracked lips.

Hauling the *James Caird*
[*Scott Polar Research Institute*]

Two seals were killed today. Wild and McIlroy, who went out to secure them, had rather an exciting time on some very loose, rotten ice, three killer-whales in a lead a few yards away poking up their ugly heads as if in anticipation of a feast.

Next day, December 26, we started off again at 1 a.m. 'The surface was much better than it has been for the last few days, and this is the principal thing that matters. The route, however, lay over very hummocky floes, and required much work with pick and shovel to make it passable for the boat-sledges. These are handled in relays by eighteen men under Worsley. It is killing work on soft surfaces.'

At 5 a.m. we were brought up by a wide open lead after an unsatisfactorily short march. While we waited, a meal of tea and two small bannocks was served, but as 10 a.m. came and there were no signs of the lead closing we all turned in.

It snowed a little during the day and those who were sleeping outside got their sleeping-bags pretty wet.

At 9.30 p.m. that night we were off again. I was, as usual, pioneering in front, followed by the cook and his mate pulling a small sledge with the stove and all the cooking gear on. These two, black as two Mohawk Minstrels with the blubber-soot, were dubbed 'Potash and Perlmutter'. Next come the dog teams, who soon overtake the cook, and the two boats bring up the rear. Were it not for these cumbrous boats we should get along at a great rate, but we dare not abandon them on any account. As it is we left one boat, the *Stancomb Wills*, behind at Ocean Camp, and the remaining two will barely accommodate the whole party when we leave the floe.

We did a good march of one and a half miles that night before we halted for 'lunch' at 1 a.m., and then on for another mile, when at 5 a.m. we camped by a little sloping berg.

Blackie, one of Wild's dogs, fell lame and could neither pull nor keep up with the party even when relieved of his harness, so had to be shot.

Nine p.m. that night, the 27th, saw us on the march again. The first 200 yds. took us about five hours to cross, owing to the amount of breaking down of pressure-ridges and filling in of leads that was required. The surface, too, was now very soft, so our progress was slow and tiring. We managed to get another three-quarters of a mile before lunch, and a further mile due west over a very hummocky floe before we camped at 5.30 a.m. Green-street and Macklin killed and brought in a huge Weddell seal weighing about 800 lb., and two emperor penguins made a welcome addition to our larder.

I climbed a small tilted berg nearby. The country immediately ahead was much broken up. Great open leads intersected the floes at all angles, and it all looked very unpromising. Wild and I went out prospecting as usual, but it seemed too broken to travel over.

'*December 29.* – After a further reconnaissance the ice ahead proved quite unnegotiable, so at 8.30 p.m. last night, to the intense disappointment of all, instead of forging ahead, we had to retire half a mile so as to get on a stronger floe, and by 10 p.m. we had camped and all hands turned in again. The extra sleep was much needed, however disheartening the check may be.'

During the night a crack formed right across the floe, so we hurriedly shifted to a strong old floe about a mile and a half to the east of our present position. The ice all around was now too broken and soft to sledge over, and yet there was not sufficient open water to allow us to launch the boats with any degree of safety. We had been on the march for seven days; rations were short and the men were weak. They were worn out with the hard pulling over soft surfaces, and our stock of sledging food was very small. We had marched seven and a half miles in a direct line and at this rate it would take us over three hundred days to reach the land away to the west. As we only had food for forty-two days there was no alternative, therefore, but to camp once more on the floe and to possess our souls with what patience we could till conditions should appear more favourable for a renewal of the attempt to escape. To this end, we stacked our surplus provisions, the reserve sledging rations being kept lashed on the sledges, and brought what gear we could from our but lately deserted Ocean Camp.

Our new home, which we were to occupy for nearly three and a half months, we called 'Patience Camp'.

CHAPTER 7

Patience Camp

The apathy which seemed to take possession of some of the men at the frustration of their hopes was soon dispelled. Parties were sent out daily in different directions to look for seals and penguins. We had left, other than reserve sledging rations, about 110 lb. of pemmican, including the dog-pemmican, and 300 lb. of flour. In addition there was a little tea, sugar, dried vegetables, and suet. I sent Hurley and Macklin to Ocean Camp to bring back the food that we had had to leave there. They returned with quite a good load, including 130 lb. of dry milk, about 50 lb. each of dog-pemmican and jam, and a few tins of potted meats. When they were about a mile and a half away their voices were quite audible to us at Ocean Camp, so still was the air.

We were, of course, very short of the farinaceous element in our diet. The flour would last ten weeks. After that our sledging rations would last us less than three months. Our meals had to consist mainly of seal and penguin; and though this was valuable as an anti-scorbutic, so much so that not a single case of scurvy occurred amongst the party, yet it was a badly adjusted diet, and we felt rather weak and enervated in consequence.

'The cook deserves much praise for the way he has stuck to his job through all this severe blizzard. His galley consists of nothing but a few boxes arranged as a table, with a canvas screen erected around them on four oars and the two blubber-stoves within. The protection afforded by the screen is only partial, and the eddies drive the pungent blubber-smoke in all directions.'

After a few days we were able to build him an igloo of ice-blocks, with a tarpaulin over the top as a roof.

'Our rations are just sufficient to keep us alive, but we all feel that we could eat twice as much as we get. An average day's food at present consists of ½ lb. of seal with ¼ pint of tea for breakfast, a

4-oz. bannock with milk for lunch, and ¼ pint of seal stew for supper. That is barely enough, even doing very little work as we are, for of course we are completely destitute of bread or potatoes or anything of that sort. Some seem to feel it more than others and are continually talking of food; but most of us find that the continual conversation about food only whets an appetite that cannot be satisfied. Our craving for bread and butter is very real, not because we cannot get it, but because the system feels the need of it.'

Owing to this shortage of food and the fact that we needed all that we could get for ourselves, I had to order all the dogs except two teams to be shot. It was the worst job that we had had throughout the Expedition, and we felt their loss keenly.

I had to be continually rearranging the weekly menu. The possible number of permutations of seal meat were decidedly limited. The fact that the men did not know what was coming gave them a sort of mental speculation, and the slightest variation was of great value.

'We caught an adelie today (January 26) and another whale was seen at close quarters, but no seals.

'We are now very short of blubber, and in consequence one stove has to be shut down. We only get one hot beverage a day, the tea at breakfast. For the rest we have iced water. Sometimes we are short even of this, so we take a few chips of ice in a tobacco-tin to bed with us. In the morning there is about a spoonful of water in the tin, and one has to lie very still all night so as not to spill it.'

To provide some variety in the food, I commenced to use the sledging ration at half strength twice a week.

The ice between us and Ocean Camp, now only about five miles away and actually to the south-west of us, was very broken, but I decided to send Macklin and Hurley back with their dogs to see if there was any more food that could be added to our scanty stock. I gave them written instructions to take no undue risk or cross any wide-open leads, and said that they were to return by midday the next day. Although they both fell through the thin ice up to their waists more than once, they managed to reach the camp. They found the surface soft and sunk about two feet. Ocean Camp, they said, 'looked like a village that had been razed to the ground and deserted by its inhabitants.' The floor-boards forming the old tent-bottoms had prevented the sun from thawing the snow directly underneath them, and were in consequence raised about two feet above the level of the surrounding floe.

The storehouse next the galley had taken on a list of several degrees to starboard, and pools of water had formed everywhere. They collected what food they could find and packed a few books in a venesta sledging-case, returning to Patience Camp by about 8 p.m. I was pleased at their quick return, and as their report seemed to show that the road was favourable, on February 2 I sent back eighteen men under Wild to bring all the remainder of the food and the third boat, the Stancomb Wills. They started off at 1 a.m., towing the empty boatsledge on which the *James Caird* had rested, and reached Ocean Camp about 3.30 a.m.

The camp
[*Scott Polar Research Institute*]

'We stayed about three hours at the Camp, mounting the boat on the sledge, collecting eatables, clothing, and books. We left at 6 a.m., arriving back at Patience Camp with the boat at 12.30 p.m., taking exactly three times as long to return with the boat as it did to pull in the empty sledge to fetch it. On the return journey we had numerous halts while the pioneer party of four were busy breaking down pressure-ridges and filling in open cracks with ice-blocks, as the leads were opening up. The sun had softened the surface a good deal, and in places it was terribly hard pulling.

Everyone was a bit exhausted by the time we got back, as we are not now in good training and are on short rations. Every now and then the heavy sledge broke through the ice altogether and was practically afloat. We had an awful job to extricate it, exhausted as we were. The longest distance which we managed to make without stopping for leads or pressure-ridges was about three quarters of a mile.

'About a mile from Patience Camp we had a welcome surprise. Sir Ernest and Hussey sledged out to meet us with dixies of hot tea, well wrapped up to keep them warm.

'One or two of the men left behind had cut a moderately good track for us into the camp, and they harnessed themselves up with us, and we got in in fine style.

'One excellent result of our trip was the recovery of two cases of lentils weighing 42 lb. each.'

The next day I sent Macklin and Crean back to make a further selection of the gear, but they found that several leads had opened up during the night, and they had to return when within a mile and a half of their destination. We were never able to reach Ocean Camp again. Still, there was very little left there that would have been of use to us.

By the middle of February the blubber question was a serious one. I had all the discarded seals' heads and flippers dug up and stripped of every vestige of blubber. Meat was very short too. We still had our three months' supply of sledging food practically untouched; we were only to use this as a last resort. We had a small supply of dog-pemmican, the dogs that were left being fed on those parts of the seals that we could not use. This dog-pemmican we fried in suet with a little flour and made excellent bannocks.

Our meat supply was now very low indeed; we were reduced to just a few scraps. Fortunately, however, we caught two seals and four emperor penguins, and next day forty adelies. We had now only forty days' food left, and the lack of blubber was being keenly felt. All our suet was used up, so we used seal-blubber to fry the meat in. Once we were used to its fishy taste we enjoyed it; in fact, like Oliver Twist, we wanted more.

On Leap Year day, February 29, we held a special celebration, more to cheer the men up than for anything else. Some of the cynics of the party held that it was to celebrate their escape from woman's wiles for another four years. The last of our cocoa was used today. Henceforth water, with an occasional drink of weak milk, is to be our only beverage. Three lumps of sugar were now issued to each man daily.

One night one of the dogs broke loose and played havoc with our precious stock of bannocks. He ate four and half of a fifth before he could be stopped. The remaining half, with the marks of the dog's teeth on it, I gave to Worsley, who divided it up amongst his seven tent-mates; they each received about half a square inch.

Lees, who was in charge of the food and responsible for its safe keeping, wrote in his diary: 'The shorter the provisions the more there is to do in the commissariat department, contriving to eke out our slender stores as the weeks pass by. No housewife ever had more to do than we have in making a little go a long way.

'Writing about the bannock that Peter bit makes one wish now that one could have many a meal that one has given to the dog at home. When one is hungry, fastidiousness goes to the winds and one is only too glad to eat up any scraps regardless of their antecedents. One is almost ashamed to write of all the titbits one has picked up here, but it is enough to say that when the cook upset some pemmican on to an old sooty cloth and threw it outside his galley, one man subsequently made a point of acquiring it and scraping off the palatable but dirty compound.'

Another man searched for over an hour in the snow where he had dropped a piece of cheese some days before, in the hopes of finding a few crumbs. He was rewarded by coming across a piece as big as his thumb-nail, and considered it well worth the trouble.

By this time blubber was a regular article of our diet either raw, boiled, or fried. 'It is remarkable how our appetites have changed in this respect. Until quite recently almost the thought of it was nauseating. Now, however, we positively demand it. The thick black oil which is rendered down from it, rather like train-oil in appearance and cod-liver oil in taste, we drink with avidity.'

We had now about enough farinaceous food for two meals all round, and sufficient seal to last for a month. Our forty days' reserve sledging rations, packed on the sledges, we wished to keep till the last.

But, as one man philosophically remarked in his diary: 'It will do us all good to be hungry like this, for we will appreciate so much more the good things when we get home.'

Seals and penguins now seemed to studiously avoid us, and on taking stock of our provisions on March 21 I found that we had only sufficient meat to last us for ten days, and the blubber would not last that time even, so one biscuit had to be our midday meal.

Our meals were now practically all seal meat, with one biscuit at midday; and I calculated that at this rate, allowing for a certain number of seals and penguins being caught, we could last for nearly six months. We were all very weak though, and as soon as it appeared likely that we should leave our floe and take to the boats I should have to considerably increase the ration. One day a huge sea-leopard climbed on to the floe and attacked one of the men. Wild, hearing the shouting, ran out and shot it. When it was cut up we found in its stomach several undigested fish. These we fried in some of its blubber, and so had our only 'fresh' fish meal during the whole of our drift on the ice.

'As fuel is so scarce we have had to resort to melting ice for drinking-water in tins against our bodies, and we treat the tins of dog-pemmican for breakfast similarly by keeping them in our sleeping-bags all night.

'The last two teams of dogs were shot today (April 2), the carcases being dressed for food. We had some of the dog-meat cooked, and it was not at all bad – just like beef, but, of course, very tough.'

On April 5 we killed two seals, and this, with the sea-leopard of a few days before, enabled us to slightly increase our ration. Everybody now felt much happier; such is the psychological effect of hunger appeased.

On cold days a few strips of raw blubber were served out to all hands, and it is wonderful how it fortified us against the cold.

Our stock of forty days' sledging rations remained practically untouched, but once in the boats they were used at full strength.

When we first settled down at Patience Camp the weather was very mild. New Year's Eve, however, was foggy and overcast, with some snow, and next day, though the temperature rose to 38 degrees Fahr., it was 'abominably cold and wet underfoot'. As a rule, during the first half of January the weather was comparatively warm, so much so that we could dispense with our mitts and work outside for quite long periods with bare hands. Up till the 13th it was exasperatingly warm and calm. This meant that our drift northwards, which was almost entirely dependent on the wind, was checked. A light southerly breeze on the 16th raised all our hopes, and as the temperature was dropping we were looking forward to a period of favourable winds and a long drift north.

On the 18th it had developed into a howling south-westerly gale, rising next day to a regular blizzard with much drift. No one left the shelter of his tent except to feed the dogs, fetch the meals from the galley for his tent, or when his turn as watchman came round. For six days this lasted, when the drift subsided somewhat, though the southerly wind continued, and we were able to get a glimpse of the sun. This showed us to have drifted 84 miles north in six days, the longest drift we had made. For weeks we had remained on the 67th parallel, and it seemed as though some obstruction was preventing us from passing it. By this amazing leap, however, we had crossed the Antarctic Circle, and were now 146 miles from the nearest land to the west of us – Snow Hill – and 357 miles from the South Orkneys, the first land directly to the north of us.

As if to make up for this, an equally strong north-easterly wind sprang up next day, and not only stopped our northward drift but set us back three miles to the south. As usual, high temperatures and wet fog accompanied these northerly winds, though the fog disappeared on the afternoon of January 25, and we had the unusual spectacle of bright hot sun with a north-easterly wind. It was as hot a day as we had ever had. The temperature was 36 degrees Fahr. in the shade and nearly 80 degrees Fahr. inside the tents. This had an awful effect on the surface, covering it with pools and making it very treacherous to walk upon. Ten days of northerly winds rather damped our spirits, but a strong southerly wind on February 4, backing later to south-east, carried us north again. High temperatures and northerly winds soon succeeded this, so that our average rate of northerly drift was about a mile a day in February. Throughout the month the diaries record alternately 'a wet day, overcast and mild', and 'bright and cold with light southerly winds'. The wind was now the vital factor with us and the one topic of any real interest.

The beginning of March brought cold, damp, calm weather, with much wet snow and overcast skies. The effect of the weather on our mental state was very marked. All hands felt much more cheerful on a bright sunny day, and looked forward with much more hope to the future, than when it was dull and overcast. This had a much greater effect than an increase in rations.

A south-easterly gale on the 13th lasting for five days sent us twenty miles north, and from now our good fortune, as far as the wind was concerned, never left us for any length of time. On the 20th we experienced the worst blizzard we had had up to that time, though worse were to come after landing on Elephant Island. Thick snow fell, making it impossible to see the camp from thirty yards off. To go outside for a moment entailed getting covered all over with fine powdery snow, which required a great deal of brushing off before one could enter again.

As the blizzard eased up, the temperature dropped and it became bitterly cold. In our weak condition, with torn, greasy clothes, we felt these sudden variations in temperature much more than we otherwise would have done. A calm, clear, magnificently warm day followed, and next day came a strong southerly blizzard. Drifts four feet deep covered everything, and we had to be continually digging up our scanty stock of meat to prevent its being lost altogether. We had taken advantage of the previous fine day to attempt to thaw out our blankets, which were frozen stiff and could be held out like pieces of sheet-iron; but on this day, and for the next two or three also, it was impossible to do anything but get right inside one's frozen sleeping-bag to try and get warm. Too cold to read or sew, we had to keep our hands well inside, and pass the time in conversation with each other.

'The temperature was not strikingly low as temperatures go down here, but the terrific winds penetrate the flimsy fabric of our fragile tents and create so much draught that it is impossible to keep warm within. At supper last night our drinking-water froze over in the tin in the tent before we could drink it. It is curious how thirsty we all are.'

Two days of brilliant warm sunshine succeeded these cold times, and on March 29 we experienced, to us, the most amazing weather. It began to rain hard, and it was the first rain that we had seen since we left South Georgia sixteen months ago. We regarded it as our first touch with civilisation, and many of the men longed for the rain and fogs of London.

Strong south winds with dull, overcast skies and occasional high temperatures were now our lot till April 7, when the mist lifted and we could make out what appeared to be land to the north.

Although the general drift of our ice-floe had indicated to us that we must eventually drift north, our progress in that direction was not by any means uninterrupted. We were at the mercy of the wind, and could no more control our drift than we could control the weather.

A long spell of calm, still weather at the beginning of January caused us some anxiety by keeping us at about the latitude that we were in at the beginning of December. Towards the end of January, however, a long drift of eighty-four miles in a blizzard cheered us all up. This soon stopped and we began a slight drift to the east. Our general drift now slowed up considerably, and by February 22 we were still eighty miles from Paulet Island, which now was our objective. There was a hut there and some stores which had been taken down by the ship which went to the rescue of Nordenskjold's Expedition in 1904, and whose fitting out and equipment I had charge of. We remarked amongst ourselves what a strange turn of fate it would be if the very cases of provisions which I had ordered and sent out so many years before were now to support us during the coming winter. But this was not to be. March 5 found us about forty miles south of the longitude of Paulet Island, but well to the east of it; and as the ice was still too much broken up to sledge over, it appeared as if we should be carried past it. By March 17 we were exactly on a level with Paulet Island but sixty miles to the east. It might have been six hundred for all the chance that we had of reaching it by sledging across the broken sea-ice in its present condition.

Our thoughts now turned to the Danger Islands, thirty-five miles away. 'It seems that we are likely to drift up and down this coast from south-west to north-east and back again for some time yet before we finally clear the point of Joinville Island; until we do we cannot hope for much opening up, as the ice must be very congested against the south-east coast of the island, otherwise our failure to respond to the recent south-easterly gale cannot be well accounted for. In support of this there has been some very heavy pressure on the north-east side of our floe, one immense block being up-ended to a height of 25 ft. We saw a Dominican gull fly over today, the first we have seen since leaving South Georgia; it is another sign of our proximity to land. We cut steps in this 25-ft. slab, and it makes a fine look-out. When the weather clears we confidently expect to see land.'

A heavy blizzard obscured our view till March 23. '"Land in sight" was reported this morning. We were sceptical, but this afternoon it showed up unmistakably to the west, and there can be no further doubt about it. It is Joinville Island, and its serrated mountain ranges, all snow-clad, are just visible on the horizon. This barren, inhospitable-looking land would be a haven of refuge to us if we could but reach it. It would be ridiculous to make the attempt though, with the ice all broken up as it is. It is too loose and broken to march over, yet not open enough to be able to launch the boats.' For the next two or three days we saw ourselves slowly drifting past the land, longing to reach it yet prevented from doing so by the ice between, and towards the end of March we saw Mount Haddington fade away into the distance.

Our hopes were now centred on Elephant Island or Clarence Island, which lay 100 miles almost due north of us.

If we failed to reach either of them we might try for South Georgia, but our chances of reaching it would be very small.

CHAPTER 8

Escape from the ice

On April 7 at daylight the long-desired peak of Clarence Island came into view, bearing nearly north from our camp. At first it had the appearance of a huge berg, but with the growing light we could see plainly the black lines of scree and the high, precipitous cliffs of the island, which were miraged up to some extent. The dark rocks in the white snow were a pleasant sight. So long had our eyes looked on icebergs that apparently grew or dwindled according to the angles at which the shadows were cast by the sun; so often had we discovered rocky islands and brought in sight the peaks of Joinville Land, only to find them, after some change of wind or temperature, floating away as nebulous cloud or ordinary berg, that not until Worsley, Wild, and Hurley had unanimously confirmed my observation was I satisfied that I was really looking at Clarence Island. The land was still more than sixty miles away, but it had to our eyes something of the appearance of home, since we expected to find there our first solid footing after all the long months of drifting on the unstable ice. We had adjusted ourselves to the life on the floe, but our hopes had been fixed all the time on some possible landing-place. As one hope failed to materialise, our anticipations fed themselves on another. Our drifting home had no rudder to guide it, no sail to give it speed. We were dependent upon the caprice of wind and current; we went whither those irresponsible forces listed. The longing to feel solid earth under our feet filled our hearts.

In the full daylight Clarence Island ceased to look like land and had the appearance of a berg of more than eight or ten miles away, so deceptive are distances in the clear air of the Antarctic. The sharp white peaks of Elephant Island showed to the west of north a little later in the day.

'I have stopped issuing sugar now, and our meals consist of seal meat and blubber only, with 7 ozs. of dried milk per day for the party,' I wrote. 'Each man receives a pinch of salt, and the milk is boiled up to make hot drinks for all hands. The diet suits us, since we cannot get much exercise on the floe and the blubber supplies heat. Fried slices of blubber seem to our taste to resemble crisp bacon. It certainly is no hardship to eat it, though persons living under civilised conditions probably would shudder at it. The hardship would come if we were unable to get it.'

I think that the palate of the human animal can adjust itself to anything. Some creatures will die before accepting a strange diet if deprived of their natural food. The Yaks of the Himalayan uplands must feed from the growing grass, scanty and dry though it may be, and would starve even if allowed the best oats and corn.

'We still have the dark water-sky of the last week with us to the south-west and west, round to the north-east. We are leaving all the bergs to the west and there are few within our range of vision now. The swell is more marked today, and I feel sure we are at the verge of the floe-ice. One strong gale followed by a calm would scatter the pack, I think, and then we could push through. I have been thinking much of our prospects. The appearance of Clarence Island after our long drift seems, somehow, to convey an ultimatum. The island is the last outpost of the south and our final chance of a landing-place. Beyond it lies the broad Atlantic. Our little boats may be compelled any day now to sail unsheltered over the open sea with a thousand leagues of ocean separating them from the land to the north and east. It seems vital that we shall land on Clarence Island or its neighbour, Elephant Island. The latter island has attraction for us, although as far as I know nobody has ever landed there. Its name suggests the presence of the plump and succulent sea-elephant. We have an increasing desire in any case to get firm ground under our feet. The floe has been a good friend to us, but it is reaching the end of its journey, and it is liable at any time now to break up and fling us into the unplumbed sea.'

A little later, after reviewing the whole situation in the light of our circumstances, I made up my mind that we should try to reach Deception Island. The relative positions of Clarence, Elephant, and Deception Islands can be seen on the chart. The two islands first named lay comparatively near to us and were separated by some eighty miles of water from Prince George Island, which was about 160 miles away from our camp on the berg. From this island a chain of similar islands extends westward, terminating in Deception Island. The channels separating these desolate patches of rock and ice are from ten to fifteen miles wide. But we knew from the Admiralty sailing directions that there were stores for the use of shipwrecked mariners on Deception Island, and it was possible that the summer whalers had not yet deserted its harbour. Also we had learned from our scanty records that a small church had been erected there for the benefit of the transient whalers. The existence of this building would mean to us a supply of timber, from which, if dire necessity urged us, we could construct a reasonably seaworthy boat. We had discussed this point during our drift on the floe. Two of our boats were fairly strong, but the third, the *James Caird*, was light, although a little longer than the others. All of them were small for the navigation of these notoriously stormy seas, and they would be heavily loaded, so a voyage in open water would be a serious undertaking. I fear that the carpenter's fingers were already itching to convert pews into topsides and decks. In any case, the worst that could befall us when we had reached Deception Island would be a wait until the whalers returned about the middle of November.

Another bit of information gathered from the records of the west side of the Weddell Sea related to Prince George Island. The Admiralty 'Sailing Directions', referring to the South Shetlands, mentioned a cave on this island. None of us had seen that cave or could say if it was large or small, wet or dry; but as we drifted on our floe and later, when navigating the treacherous leads and making our uneasy night camps, that cave seemed to my fancy to be a palace which in contrast would dim the splendours of Versailles.

The swell increased that night, and the movement of the ice became more pronounced. Occasionally a neighbouring floe would hammer against the ice on which we were camped, and the lesson of these blows was plain to read. We must get solid ground under our feet quickly. When the vibration ceased after a heavy surge, my thoughts flew round to the problem ahead. If the party had not numbered more than six men a solution would not have been so hard to find; but obviously the transportation of the whole party to a place of safety, with the limited means at our disposal, was going to be a matter of extreme difficulty. There were twenty-eight men on our floating cake of ice, which was steadily dwindling under the influence of wind, weather, charging floes, and heavy swell. I confess that I felt the burden of responsibility sit heavily on my shoulders; but, on the other hand, I was stimulated and cheered by the attitude of the men. Loneliness is the penalty of leadership, but the man who has to make the decisions is assisted greatly if he feels that there is no uncertainty in the minds of those who follow him, and that his orders will be carried out confidently and in expectation of success.

The sun was shining in the blue sky on the following morning (April 8). Clarence Island showed clearly on the horizon, and Elephant Island could also be distinguished. The single snow-clad peak of Clarence Island stood up as a beacon of safety, though the most optimistic imagination could not make an easy path of the ice and ocean that separated us from that giant, white and austere. 'The pack was much looser this morning, and the long rolling swell from the north-east is more pronounced than it was yester-day. The floes rise and fall with the surge of the sea. We evidently are drifting with the surface current, for all the heavier masses of floe, bergs, and hummocks are being left behind. There has been some discussion in the camp as to the advisability of making one of the bergs our home for the time being and drifting with it to the west. The idea is not sound. I cannot be sure that the berg would drift in the right direction. If it did move west and carried us into the open water, what would be our fate when we tried to launch the boats-down the steep sides of the berg in the sea-swell after the surrounding floes had left us? One must reckon, too, the chance of the berg splitting or even overturning during our stay. It is not possible to gauge the condition of a big mass of ice by surface appearance. The ice may have a fault, and when the wind, current, and swell set up strains and tensions, the line of weakness may reveal itself suddenly and disastrously. No, I do not like the idea of drifting on a berg. We must stay on our floe till conditions improve and then make another attempt to advance towards the land.'

At 6.30 p.m. a particularly heavy shock went through our floe. The watchman and other members of the party made an immed-iate inspection and found a crack right under the *James Baird* and between the other two boats and the main camp. Within five minutes the boats were over the crack and close to the tents. The trouble was not caused by a blow from another floe. We could see that the piece of ice we occupied had slewed and now presented its long axis towards the oncoming swell. The floe, therefore, was pitching in the manner of a ship, and it had cracked across when the swell lifted the centre, leaving the two ends comparatively unsupported. We were now on a triangular raft of ice, the three sides measuring, roughly, 90, 100, and 120 yds. Night came down dull and overcast, and before midnight the wind had freshened from the west. We could see that the pack was opening under the influence of wind, wave, and current; and I felt that the time for launching the boats was near at hand. Indeed, it was obvious that even if the conditions were unfavourable for a start during the coming day, we could not safely stay on the floe many hours longer. The movement of the ice in the swell was increasing, and the floe might split right under our camp. We had made preparations for quick action if anything of the kind occurred. Our case would be desperate if the ice broke into small pieces not large enough to support our party and not loose enough to permit the use of the boats.

The following day was Sunday (April 9), but it proved no day of rest for us. Many of the important events of our Expedition occurred on Sundays, and this particular day was to see our forced departure from the floe on which we had lived for nearly six months, and the start of our journeyings in the boats. This has been an eventful day. The morning was fine, though somewhat overcast by stratus and cumulus clouds; moderate south-south-westerly and south-easterly breezes. We hoped that with this wind the ice would drift nearer to Clarence Island. At 7 a.m. lanes of water and leads could be seen on the horizon to the west. The ice separating us from the lanes was loose, but did not appear to be workable for the boats. The long swell from the north-west was coming in more freely than on the previous day and was driving the floes together in the utmost confusion. The loose brash between the masses of ice was being churned to mudlike consistency, and no boat could have lived in the channels that opened and closed around us. Our own floe was suffering in the general disturbance, and after breakfast I ordered the tents to be struck and everything prepared for an immediate start when the boats could be launched.'

I had decided to take the *James Caird* myself, with Wild and eleven men. This was the largest of our boats, and in addition to her human complement she carried the major portion of the stores. Worsley had charge of the *Dudley Docker* with nine men, and Hudson and Crean were the senior men on the *Stancomb Wills*.

Soon after breakfast the ice closed again. We were standing by, with our preparations as complete as they could be made, when at 11 a.m. our floe suddenly split right across under the boats. We rushed our gear on to the larger of the two pieces and watched with strained attention for the next development. The crack had cut through the site of my tent. I stood on the edge of the new fracture, and, looking across the widening channel of water, could see the spot where for many months my head and shoulders had rested when I was in my sleeping bag. The depression formed by my body and legs was on our side of the crack. The ice had sunk under my weight during the months of waiting in the tent, and I had many times put snow under the bag to fill the hollow. The lines of stratification showed clearly the different layers of snow. How fragile and precarious had been our resting-place! Yet usage had dulled our sense of danger. The floe had become our home, and during the early months of the drift we had almost ceased to realise that it was but a sheet of ice floating on unfathomed seas. Now our home was being shattered under our feet, and we had a sense of loss and incompleteness hard to describe.

The fragments of our floe came together again a little later, and we had our lunch of seal meat, all hands eating their fill. I thought that a good meal would be the best possible preparation for the journey that now seemed imminent, and as we would not be able to take all our meat with us when we finally moved, we could regard every pound eaten as a pound rescued. The call to action came at 1 p.m. The pack opened well and the channels became navigable. The conditions were not all one could have desired, but it was best not to wait any longer. The *Dudley Docker* and the *Stancomb Wills* were launched quickly. Stores were thrown in, and the two boats were pulled clear of the immediate floes towards a pool of open water three miles broad, in which floated a lone and mighty berg. The *James Caird* was the last boat to leave, heavily

loaded with stores and odds and ends of camp equipment. Many
things regarded by us as essentials at that time were to be discarded
a little later as the pressure of the primitive became more severe.
Man can sustain life with very scanty means. The trappings of
civilisation are soon cast aside in the face of stern realities, and
given the barest opportunity of winning food and shelter, man can
live and even find his laughter ringing true.

The three boats were a mile away from our floe home at 2 p.m.
We had made our way through the channels and had entered the
big pool when we saw a rush of foam-clad water and tossing ice
approaching us, like the tidal bore of a river. The pack was being
impelled to the east by a tide-rip, and two huge masses of ice
were driving down upon us on converging courses. The *James
Caird* was leading. Starboarding the helm and bending strongly to
the oars, we managed to get clear. The two other boats followed
us, though from their position astern at first they had not realised
the immediate danger. The *Stancomb Wills* was the last boat and
she was very nearly caught; but by great exertion she was kept
just ahead of the driving ice. It was an unusual and startling
experience. The effect of tidal action on ice is not often as marked
as it was that day. The advancing ice, accompanied by a large
wave, appeared to be travelling at about three knots; and if
we had not succeeded in pulling clear we would certainly have
been swamped.

We pulled hard for an hour to windward of the berg that lay
in the open water. The swell was crashing on its perpendicular
sides and throwing spray to a height of sixty feet. Evidently there
was an ice-foot at the east end, for the swell broke before it
reached the berg-face and flung its white spray on to the blue
ice-wall. We might have paused to have admired the spectacle
under other conditions; but night was coming on apace, and we
needed a camping-place. As we steered north-west, still amid
the ice-floes, the *Dudley Docker* got jammed between two masses
while attempting to make a short cut. The old adage about a
short cut being the longest way round is often as true in the
Antarctic as it is in the peaceful countryside. The *James Caird*
got a line aboard the *Dudley Docker*, and after some hauling the
boat was brought clear of the ice again. We hastened forward
in the twilight in search of a flat, old floe, and presently found

a fairly large piece rocking in the swell. It was not an ideal camping-place by any means, but darkness had overtaken us. We hauled the boats up, and by 8 p.m. had the tents pitched and the blubber-stove burning cheerily. Soon all hands were well fed and happy in their tents, and snatches of song came to me as I wrote up my log.

Some intangible feeling of uneasiness made me leave my tent about 11 p.m. that night and glance around the quiet camp. The stars between the snow-flurries showed that the floe had swung round and was end on to the swell, a position exposing it to sudden strains. I started to walk across the floe in order to warn the watchman to look carefully for cracks, and as I was passing the men's tent the floe lifted on the crest of a swell and cracked right under my feet. The men were in one of the dome-shaped tents, and it began to stretch apart as the ice opened. A muffled sound, suggestive of suffocation, came from beneath the stretching tent. I rushed forward, helped some emerging men from under the canvas, and called out, 'Are you all right?'

'There are two in the water,' somebody answered. The crack had widened to about four feet, and as I threw myself down at the edge, I saw a whitish object floating in the water. It was a sleeping-bag with a man inside. I was able to grasp it, and with a heave lifted man and bag on to the floe. A few seconds later the ice-edges came together again with tremendous force. Fortunately, there had been but one man in the water, or the incident might have been a tragedy. The rescued bag contained Holness, who was wet down to the waist but otherwise unscathed. The crack was now opening again. The *James Caird* and my tent were on one side of the opening and the remaining two boats and the rest of the camp on the other side. With two or three men to help me I struck my tent; then all hands manned the painter and rushed the *James Caird* across the opening crack. We held to the rope while, one by one, the men left on our side of the floe jumped the channel or scrambled over by means of the boat. Finally I was left alone. The night had swallowed all the others and the rapid movement of the ice forced me to let go the painter. For a moment I felt that my piece of rocking floe was the loneliest place in the world. Peering into the darkness; I could just see the dark figures on the other floe. I hailed Wild, ordering him to launch the *Stancomb Wills*, but I need not have troubled. His quick brain had anticipated the order and already the boat was being manned and hauled to the ice-edge. Two or three minutes later she reached me, and I was ferried across to the Camp.

We were now on a piece of flat ice about 200 ft. long and 100 ft. wide. There was no more sleep for any of us that night. The killers were blowing in the lanes around, and we waited for daylight and watched for signs of another crack in the ice. The hours passed with laggard feet as we stood huddled together or walked to and fro in the effort to keep some warmth in our bodies. We lit the blubber-stove at 3 a.m., and with pipes going and a cup of hot milk for each man, we were able to discover some bright spots in our outlook. At any rate, we were on the move at last, and if dangers and difficulties lay ahead we could meet and overcome them. No longer were we drifting helplessly at the mercy of wind and current.

The first glimmerings of dawn came at 6 a.m., and I waited anxiously for the full daylight. The swell was growing, and at times our ice was surrounded closely by similar pieces. At 6.30 a.m. we had hot hoosh, and then stood by waiting for the pack to open. Our chance came at 8, when we launched the boats, loaded them, and started to make our way through the lanes in a northerly direction; The *James Caird* was in the lead, with the *Stancomb Wills* next and the *Dudley Docker* bringing up the rear. In order to make the boats more seaworthy we had left some of our shovels, picks, and dried vegetables on the floe, and for a long time we could see the abandoned stores forming a dark spot on the ice. The boats were still heavily loaded. We got out of the lanes, and entered a stretch of open water at 11 a.m. A strong easterly breeze was blowing, but the fringe of pack lying outside protected us from the full force of the swell, just as the coral-reef of a tropical island checks the rollers of the Pacific. Our way was across the open sea, and soon after noon we swung round the north end of the pack and laid a course to the westward, the *James Caird* still in the lead. Immediately our deeply laden boats began to make heavy weather. They shipped sprays, which, freezing as they fell, covered men and gear with ice, and soon it was clear that we could not safely proceed. I put the *James Caird* round and ran for the shelter of the pack again, the other boats following. Back inside the outer line of ice the sea was not breaking. This was at 3 p.m., and all hands were tired and cold. A big floe-berg resting peacefully ahead caught my eye, and half an hour later we had hauled up the boats and pitched camp for the night. It was a fine, big, blue berg with an attractively solid appearance, and from our camp we could get a good view of the surrounding sea and ice. The highest point was about 15 ft. above sea-level. After a hot meal all hands, except the watchman, turned in. Everyone was in need of rest after the troubles of the previous night and the unaccustomed strain of the last thirty-six hours at the oars. The berg appeared well able to withstand the battering of the sea, and too deep and massive to be seriously affected by the swell; but it was not as safe as it looked. About midnight the watchman called me and showed me that the heavy north-westerly swell was undermining the ice. A great piece had broken off within eight feet of my tent. We made what inspection was possible in the darkness, and found that on the westward side of the berg the thick snow covering was yielding rapidly to the attacks of the sea. An ice-foot had formed just under the surface of the water. I decided that there was no immediate danger and did not call the men. The north-westerly wind strengthened during the night.

The morning of April 11 was overcast and misty. There was a haze on the horizon, and daylight showed that the pack had closed round our berg, making it impossible in the heavy swell to launch the boats. We could see no sign of the water. Numerous whales and killers were blowing between the floes, and Cape pigeons, petrels, and fulmars were circling round our berg. The scene from our camp as the daylight brightened was magnificent beyond description, though I must admit that we viewed it with anxiety. Heaving hills of pack and floe were sweeping towards us in long undulations, later to be broken here and there by the dark lines that indicated open water. As each swell lifted around our rapidly dissolving berg it drove floe-ice on to the ice-foot, shearing off more of the top snow-covering and reducing the size of our camp. When the floes retreated to attack again the water swirled over the ice-foot, which was rapidly increasing in width. The launching of the boats under such conditions would be difficult. Time after time, so often that a track was formed, Worsley, Wild, and I, climbed to the highest point of the berg and stared out to the horizon in search of a break in the pack. After long hours had dragged past, far away on the lift of the swell there appeared a dark break in the tossing field of ice. Aeons seemed to pass, so slowly it approached. I noticed enviously the calm peaceful attitudes of two seals which lolled lazily on a rocking floe. They were at home and had no reason for worry or cause for fear. If they thought at all, I suppose they counted it an ideal day for a joyous journey on the tumbling ice. To us it was a day that seemed likely to lead to no more days. I do not think I had ever before felt the anxiety that belongs to leadership quite so keenly. When I looked down at the camp to rest my eyes from the strain of watching the wide white expanse broken by that one black ribbon of open water, I could see that my companions were waiting with more than ordinary interest to learn what I thought about it all. After one particularly heavy collision somebody shouted sharply, 'She has cracked in the middle.' I jumped off the look-out station and ran to the place the men were examining. There was a crack, but investigation showed it to be a mere surface-break in the snow with no indication of a split in the berg itself. The carpenter mentioned calmly that earlier in the day he had actually gone adrift on a fragment of ice. He was standing near the edge of our camping-ground when the ice under his feet parted from the parent mass. A quick jump over the widening gap saved him.

The hours dragged on. One of the anxieties in my mind was the possibility that we would be driven by the current through the eighty-mile gap between Clarence Island and Prince George Island into the open Atlantic; but slowly the open water came nearer, and at noon it had almost reached us. A long lane, narrow but navigable, stretched out to the south-west horizon. Our chance came a little later. We rushed our boats over the edge of the reeling berg and swung them clear of the ice-foot as it rose beneath them. The *James Caird* was nearly capsized by a blow from below as the berg rolled away, but she got into deep water. We flung stores and gear aboard and within a few minutes were away. The *James Caird* and *Dudley Docker* had good sails and with a favourable breeze could make progress along the lane, with the rolling fields of ice on either side. The swell was heavy and spray was breaking over the ice-floes. An attempt to set a little rag of sail on the *Stancomb Wills* resulted in serious delay. The area of sail was too small to be of much assistance, and while the men were engaged in this work the boat drifted down towards the ice-floe, where her position was likely to be perilous. Seeing her plight, I sent the *Dudley Docker* back for her and tied the *James Caird* up to a piece of ice. The *Dudley Docker* had to tow the *Stancomb Wills*, and the delay cost us two hours of valuable daylight. When I had the three boats together again we continued down the lane, and soon saw a wider stretch of water to the west; it appeared to offer us release from the grip of the pack. At the head of an ice-tongue that nearly closed the gap through which we might enter the open space was a wave-worn berg shaped like some curious antediluvian monster, an icy Cerberus guarding the way. It had head and eyes and rolled so heavily that it almost overturned. Its sides dipped deep in the sea, and as it rose again the water seemed to be streaming from its eyes, as though it were weeping at our escape from the clutch of the floes. This may seem fanciful to the reader, but the impression was real to us at the time. People living under civilised conditions, surrounded by Nature's varied forms of life and by all the familiar work of their own hands, may scarcely realise how quickly the mind, influenced by the eyes, responds to the unusual and weaves about it curious imaginings like the firelight fancies of our childhood days. We had lived long amid the ice, and we half-unconsciously strove to see resemblances to human faces and living forms in the fantastic contours and massively uncouth shapes of berg and floe.

At dusk we made fast to a heavy floe, each boat having its painter fastened to a separate hummock in order to avoid collisions in the swell. We landed the blubber-stove, boiled some water in order to provide hot milk, and served cold rations. I also landed the dome tents and stripped the coverings from the hoops. Our experience of the previous day in the open sea had shown us that the tents must be packed tightly. The spray had dashed over the bows and turned to ice on the cloth, which had soon grown dangerously heavy. Other articles of our scanty equipment had to go that night. We were carrying only the things that had seemed essential, but we stripped now to the barest limit of safety. We had hoped for a quiet night, but presently we were forced to cast off, since pieces of loose ice began to work round the floe. Drift-ice is always attracted to the lee side of a heavy floe, where it bumps and presses under the influence of the current. I had determined not to risk a repetition of the last night's experience and so had not pulled the boats up. We spent the hours of darkness keeping an offing from the main line of pack under the lee of the smaller pieces. Constant rain and snow squalls blotted out the stars and soaked us through, and at times it was only by shouting to each other that we managed to keep the boats together. There was no sleep for anybody owing to the severe cold, and we dare not pull fast enough to keep ourselves warm since we were unable to see more than a few yards ahead. Occasionally the ghostly shadows of silver, snow, and fulmar petrels flashed close to us, and all around we could hear the killers blowing, their short, sharp hisses sounding like sudden escapes of steam. The killers were a source of anxiety, for a boat could easily have been capsized by one of them coming up to blow. They would throw aside in a nonchalant fashion pieces of ice much bigger than our boats when they rose to the surface, and we had an uneasy feeling that the white bottoms of the boats would look like ice from below. Shipwrecked mariners drifting in the Antarctic seas would be things not dreamed of in the killers' philosophy, and might appear on closer examination to be tasty substitutes for seal and penguin. We certainly regarded the killers with misgivings.

Early in the morning of April 12 the weather improved and the wind dropped. Dawn came with a clear sky, cold and fearless. I looked around at the faces of my companions in the *James Caird* and saw pinched and drawn features. The strain was beginning to tell. Wild sat at the rudder with the same calm, confident expression that he would have worn under happier conditions; his steel-blue eyes looked out to the day ahead. All the people, though evidently suffering, were doing their best to be cheerful, and the prospect of a hot breakfast was inspiriting. I told all the boats that immediately we could find a suitable floe the cooker would be started and hot milk and Bovril would soon fix everybody up. Away we rowed to the westward through open pack, floes of all shapes and sizes on every side of us, and every man not engaged in pulling looking eagerly for a suitable camping-place. I could gauge the desire for food of the different members by the eagerness they displayed in pointing out to me the floes they considered exactly suited to our purpose. The temperature was about 10 degrees

Fahr., and the Burberry suits of the rowers crackled as the men bent to the oars. I noticed little fragments of ice and frost falling from arms and bodies. At eight o'clock a decent floe appeared ahead and we pulled up to it. The galley was landed, and soon the welcome steam rose from the cooking food as the blubber-stove flared and smoked. Never did a cook work under more anxious scrutiny. Worsley, Crean, and I stayed in our respective boats to keep them steady and prevent collisions with the floe, since the swell was still running strong, but the other men were able to stretch their cramped limbs and run to and fro 'in the kitchen', as somebody put it. The sun was now rising gloriously. The Burberry suits were drying and the ice was melting off our beards. The steaming food gave us new vigour, and within three-quarters of an hour we were off again to the west with all sails set. We had given an additional sail to the *Stancomb Wills* and she was able to keep up pretty well. We could see that we were on the true pack-edge, with the blue, rolling sea just outside the fringe of ice to the north. White-capped waves vied with the glittering floes in the setting of blue water, and countless seals basked and rolled on every piece of ice big enough to form a raft.

We had been making westward with oars and sails since April 9, and fair easterly winds had prevailed. Hopes were running high as to the noon observation for position. The optimists thought that we had done sixty miles towards our goal, and the most cautious guess gave us at least thirty miles. The bright sunshine and the brilliant scene around us may have influenced our anticipations. As noon approached I saw Worsley, as navigating officer, balancing himself on the gunwale of the *Dudley Docker* with his arm around the mast, ready to snap the sun. He got his observation and we waited eagerly while he worked out the sight. Then the *Dudley Docker* ranged up alongside the *James Caird* and I jumped into Worsley's boat in order to see the result. It was a grievous disappointment. Instead of making a good run to the westward we had made a big drift to the south-east. We were actually thirty miles to the east of the position we had occupied when we left the floe on the 9th. It has been noted by sealers operating in this area that there are often heavy sets to the east in the Belgica Straits, and no doubt it was one of these sets that we had experienced. The originating cause would be a north-westerly gale off Cape

Horn, producing the swell that had already caused us so much trouble. After a whispered consultation with Worsley, and Wild I announced that we had not made as much progress as we expected, but I did not inform the hands of our retrograde movement.

The question of our course now demanded further consideration. Deception Island seemed to be beyond our reach. The wind was foul for Elephant Island, and as the sea was clear to the southwest, I discussed with Worsley and Wild the advisability of proceeding to Hope Bay on the mainland of the Antarctic Continent, now only eighty miles distant. Elephant Island was the nearest land, but it lay outside the main body of pack, and even if the wind had been fair we would have hesitated at that particular time to face the high sea that was running in the open. We laid a course roughly for Hope Bay, and the boats moved on again. I gave Worsley a line for a berg ahead and told him, if possible, to make fast before darkness set in. This was about three o'clock in the afternoon. We had set sail, and as the *Stancomb Wills* could not keep up with the other two boats I took her in tow, not being anxious to repeat the experience of the day we left the reeling berg. The *Dudley Docker* went ahead, but came beating down towards us at dusk. Worsley had been close to the berg, and he reported that it was unapproachable. It was rolling in the swell and displaying an ugly ice-foot. The news was bad. In the failing light we turned towards a line of pack, and found it so tossed and churned by the sea that no fragment remained big enough to give us an anchorage and shelter. Two miles away we could see a larger piece of ice, and to it we managed, after some trouble, to secure the boats. I brought my boat bow on to the floe, whilst Howe, with the painter in his hand, stood ready to jump. Standing up to watch our chance, while the oars were held ready to back the moment Howe had made his leap, I could see that there would be no possibility of getting the galley ashore that night. Howe just managed to get a footing on the edge of the floe, and then made the painter fast to a hummock. The other two boats were fastened alongside the *James Caird*. They could not lie astern of us in a line, since cakes of ice came drifting round the floe and gathering under its lee. As it was we spent the next two hours poling off the drifting ice that surged towards us. The blubber-stove could not be used, so we started the Primus lamps. There was a rough, choppy sea, and the *Dudley Docker* could not get her Primus under way, something being adrift. The men in that boat had to wait until the cook on the *James Caird* had boiled up the first pot of milk.

The boats were bumping so heavily that I had to slack away the painter of the *Stancomb Wills* and put her astern. Much ice was coming round the floe and had to be poled off. Then the *Dudley Docker*, being the heavier boat, began to damage the *James Caird*, and I slacked the *Dudley Docker* away. The *James Caird* remained moored to the ice, with the *Dudley Docker* and the *Stancomb Wills* in line behind her. The darkness had become complete, and we strained our eye to see the fragments of ice that threatened us. Presently we thought we saw a great berg bearing down upon us, its form outlined against the sky, but this startling spectacle resolved itself into a low-lying cloud in front of the rising moon. The moon appeared in a clear sky. The wind shifted to the south-east as the light improved and drove the boats broadside on towards the jagged edge of the floe. We had to cut the painter of the *James Caird* and pole her off, thus losing much valuable rope. There was no time to cast off. Then we pushed away from the floe, and all night long we lay in the open, freezing sea, the *Dudley Docker* now ahead, the *James Caird* astern of her, and the *Stancomb Wills* third in the line. The boats were attached to one another by their painters. Most of the time the *Dudley Docker* kept the *James Caird* and the *Stancomb Wills* up to the swell, and the men who were rowing were in better pass than those in the other boats, waiting inactive for the dawn. The temperature was down to 4 degrees below zero, and a film of ice formed on the surface of the sea. When we were not on watch we lay in each other's arms for warmth. Our frozen suits thawed where our bodies met, and as the slightest movement exposed these comparatively warm spots to the biting air, we clung motionless, whispering each to his companion our hopes and thoughts. Occasionally from an almost clear sky came snowshowers, falling silently on the sea and laying a thin shroud of white over our bodies and our boats.

The dawn of April 13 came clear and bright, with occasional passing clouds. Most of the men were now looking seriously worn and strained. Their lips were cracked and their eyes and eyelids showed red in their salt-encrusted faces. The beards even of the younger men might have been those of patriarchs, for the frost and the salt spray had made them white. I called the *Dudley Docker* alongside and found the condition of the people there was no better than in the *James Caird*. Obviously we must make land quickly, and I decided to run for Elephant Island. The wind had shifted fair for that rocky isle, then about one hundred miles away, and the pack that separated us from Hope Bay had closed up during the night from the south. At 6 p.m. we made a distribution of stores among the three boats, in view of the possibility of their being separated. The preparation of a hot breakfast was out of the question. The breeze was strong and the sea was running high in the loose pack around us. We had a cold meal, and I gave orders that all hands might eat as much as they pleased, this concession being due partly to a realisation that we would have to jettison some of our stores when we reached open sea in order to lighten the boats. I hoped, moreover, that a full meal of cold rations would compensate to some extent for the lack of warm food and shelter. Unfortunately, some of the men were unable to take advantage of the extra food owing to sea-sickness. Poor fellows, it was bad enough to be huddled in the deeply laden, spray-swept boats, frost-bitten and half-frozen, without having the pangs of sea-sickness added to the list of their woes. But some smiles were caused even then by the plight of one man, who had a habit of accumulating bits of food against the day of starvation that he seemed always to think was at hand, and who was condemned now to watch impotently while hungry comrades with undisturbed stomachs made biscuits, rations, and sugar disappear with extraordinary rapidity.

We ran before the wind through the loose pack, a man in the bow of each boat trying to pole off with a broken oar the lumps of ice that could not be avoided. I regarded speed as essential. Sometimes collisions were not averted. The *James Caird* was in the lead, where she bore the brunt of the encounter with lurking fragments, and she was holed above the water-line by a sharp spur of ice, but this mishap did not stay us. Later the wind became stronger and we had to reef sails, so as not to strike the ice too heavily. The *Dudley Docker* came next to the *James Caird* and the *Stancomb Wills* followed. I had given order that the boats should keep 30 or 40 yds. apart, so as to reduce the danger of a collision if one boat was checked by the ice. The pack was thinning, and we came to occasional open areas where thin ice had formed during the night. When we encountered this new ice we had to shake the reef out of the sails in order to force a way through. Outside of the pack the wind must have been of hurricane force. Thousands of small dead fish were to be seen, killed probably by a cold current and the heavy weather. They floated in the water and lay on the ice, where they had been cast by the waves. The petrels and skua-gulls were swooping down and picking them up like sardines off toast.

We made our way through the lanes till at noon we were suddenly spewed out of the pack into the open ocean. Dark blue and sapphire green ran the seas. Our sails were soon up; and with a fair wind we moved over the waves like three Viking ships on the quest of a lost Atlantis. With the sheet well out and the sun shining bright above, we enjoyed for a few hours a sense of the freedom and magic of the sea, compensating us for pain and trouble in the days that had passed. At last we were free from the ice, in water that our boats could navigate. Thoughts of home, stifled by the deadening weight of anxious days and nights, came to birth once more, and the difficulties that had still to be overcome dwindled in fancy almost to nothing.

During the afternoon we had to take a second reef in the sails, for the wind freshened and the deeply laden boats were shipping much water and steering badly in the rising sea. I had laid the course for Elephant Island and we were making good progress. The *Dudley Docker* ran down to me at dusk and Worsley suggested that we should stand on all night; but already the *Stancomb Wills* was barely discernible among the rollers in the gathering dusk, and I decided that it would be safer to heave to and wait for the daylight. It would never have done for the boats to have become separated from one another during the night. The party must be kept together, and, moreover, I thought it possible that we might overrun our goal in the darkness and not be able to return. So we made a sea-anchor of oars and hove to, the *Dudley Docker* in the lead, since she had the longest painter. The *James Caird* swung astern of the *Dudley Docker* and the *Stancomb Wills* again had the third place. We ate a cold meal and did what little we could to make things comfortable for the hours of darkness. Rest was not for us. During the greater part of the night the sprays broke over the boats and froze in masses of ice, especially at the stern and bows. This ice had to be broken away in order to prevent the boats growing too heavy. The temperature was below zero and the wind penetrated our clothes and chilled us almost unbearably. I doubted if all the men would survive that night. One of our troubles was lack of water. We had emerged so suddenly from the pack into the open sea that we had not had time to take aboard ice for melting in the cookers, and without ice we could not have hot food. The *Dudley Docker* had one lump of ice weighing about ten pounds, and this was shared out among all hands. We sucked small pieces and got a little relief from thirst engendered by the salt spray, but at the same time we reduced our bodily heat. The condition of most of the men was pitiable. All of us had swollen mouths and we could hardly touch the food. I longed intensely for the dawn. I called out to the other boats at intervals during the night, asking how things were with them. The men always managed to reply cheerfully. One of the people on the *Stancomb Wills* shouted, 'We are doing all right, but I would like some dry mitts.' The jest brought a smile to cracked lips. He might as well have asked for the moon. The only dry things aboard the boats were swollen mouths and burning tongues. Thirst is one of the troubles that confront the traveller in polar regions. Ice may be plentiful on every hand, but it does not become drinkable until it is melted, and the amount that may be dissolved in the mouth is limited. We had been thirsty during the days of heavy pulling in the pack, and our condition was aggravated quickly by the salt spray. Our sleeping-bags would have given us some warmth, but they were not within our reach. They were packed under the tents in the bows, where a mail-like coating of ice enclosed them, and we were so cramped that we could not pull them out.

At last daylight came, and with the dawn the weather cleared and the wind fell to a gentle south-westerly breeze. A magnificent sunrise heralded in what we hoped would be our last day in the boats. Rose-pink in the growing light, the lofty peak of Clarence Island told of the coming glory of the sun. The sky grew blue above us and the crests of the waves sparkled cheerfully. As soon as it was light enough we chipped and scraped the ice off the bows and sterns. The rudders had been unshipped during the night in order to avoid the painters catching them. We cast off our ice-anchor and pulled the oars aboard. They had grown during the night to the thickness of telegraph-poles while rising and falling in the freezing seas, and had to be chipped clear before they could be brought inboard.

We were dreadfully thirsty now. We found that we could get momentary relief by chewing pieces of raw seal meat and swallowing the blood, but thirst came back with redoubled force owing to the saltness of the flesh. I gave orders, therefore, that meat was to be served out only at stated intervals during the day or when thirst seemed to threaten the reason of any particular individual. In the full daylight Elephant Island showed cold and severe to the north-north-west. The island was on the bearings that Worsley had laid down, and I congratulated him on the accuracy of his navigation under difficult circumstances, with two days dead reckoning while following a devious course through the pack-ice and after drifting during two nights at the mercy of wind and waves. The *Stancomb Wills* came up and McIlroy reported that Blackborrow's feet were very badly frost-bitten. This was unfortunate, but nothing could be done. Most of the people were frost-bitten to some extent, and it was interesting to notice that the 'oldtimers', Wild, Crean, Hurley, and I, were all right. Apparently we were acclimatised to ordinary Antarctic temperature, though we learned later that we were not immune.

All day, with a gentle breeze on our port bow, we sailed and pulled through a clear sea. We would have given all the tea in China for a lump of ice to melt into water, but no ice was within our reach. Three bergs were in sight and we pulled towards them; hoping that a trail of brash would be floating on the sea to leeward; but they were hard and blue, devoid of any sign of cleavage, and the swell that surged around them as they rose and fell made it impossible for us to approach closely. The wind was gradually hauling ahead, and as the day wore on the rays of the sun beat fiercely down from a cloudless sky on pain-racked men. Progress was slow, but gradually Elephant Island came nearer. Always while I attended to the other boats, signalling and ordering, Wild sat at the tiller of the *James Caird*. He seemed unmoved by fatigue and unshaken by privation. About four o'clock in the afternoon a stiff breeze came up ahead and, blowing against the current, soon produced a choppy sea. During the next hour of hard pulling we seemed to make no progress at all. The *James Caird* and the

Dudley Docker had been towing the *Stancomb Wills* in turn, but my boat now took the *Stancomb Wills* in tow permanently, as the *James Caird* could carry more sail than the *Dudley Docker* in the freshening wind.

We were making up for the south-east side of Elephant Island, the wind being between north-west and west. The boats, held as close to the wind as possible, moved slowly, and when darkness set in our goal was still some miles away. A heavy sea was running. We soon lost sight of the *Stancomb Wills*, astern of the *James Caird* at the length of the painter, but occasionally the white gleam of broken water revealed her presence. When the darkness was complete I sat in the stern with my hand on the painter, so that I might know if the other boat broke away, and I kept that position during the night. The rope grew heavy with the ice as the unseen seas surged past us and our little craft tossed to the motion of the waters. Just at dusk I had told the men on the *Stancomb Wills* that if their boat broke away during the night and they were unable to pull against the wind, they could run for the east side of Clarence Island and await our coming there. Even though we could not land on Elephant Island, it would not do to have the third boat adrift.

It was a stern night. The men, except the watch, crouched and huddled in the bottom of the boat, getting what little warmth they could from the soaking sleeping-bags and each other's bodies. Harder and harder blew the wind and fiercer and fiercer grew the sea. The boat plunged heavily through the squalls and came up to the wind, the sail shaking in the stiffest gusts. Every now and then, as the night wore on, the moon would shine down through a rift in the driving clouds, and in the momentary light I could see the ghostly faces of men, sitting up to trim the boat as she heeled over to the wind. When the moon was hidden its presence was revealed still by the light reflected on the streaming glaciers of the island. The temperature had fallen very low, and it seemed that the general discomfort of our situation could scarcely have been increased; but the land looming ahead was a beacon of safety, and I think we were all buoyed up by the hope that the coming day would see the end of our immediate troubles. At least we would get firm land under our feet. While the painter of the *Stancomb Wills* tightened and drooped under my hand, my thoughts were busy with plans for the future.

Towards midnight the wind shifted to the south-west, and this change enabled us to bear up closer to the island. A little later the *Dudley Docker* ran down to the *James Caird*, and Worsley shouted a suggestion that he should go ahead and search for a landing-place. His boat had the heels of the *James Caird*, with the *Stancomb Wills* in tow. I told him he could try, but he must not lose sight of the *James Caird*. Just as he left me a heavy snow-squall came down, and in the darkness the boats parted. I saw the *Dudley Docker* no more. This separation caused me some anxiety during the remaining hours of the night. A cross-sea was running and I could not feel sure that all was well with the missing boat. The waves could not be seen in the darkness, though the direction and force of the wind could be felt, and under such conditions, in an open boat, disaster might overtake the most experienced navigator. I flashed our compass-lamp on the sail in the hope that the signal would be visible on board the *Dudley Docker*, but could see no reply. We strained our eyes to windward in the darkness in the hope of catching a return signal and repeated our flashes at intervals.

My anxiety, as a matter of fact, was groundless. I will quote Worsley's own account of what happened to the *Dudley Docker*. 'About midnight we lost sight of the *James Caird* with the *Stancomb Wills* in tow, but not long after saw the light of the *James Caird*'s compass-lamp, which Sir Ernest was flashing on their sail as a guide to us. We answered by lighting our candle under the tent and letting the light shine through. At the same time we got the direction of the wind and how we were hauling from my little pocket-compass, the boat's compass being smashed. With this candle our poor fellows lit their pipes, their only solace, as our raging thirst prevented us from eating anything. By this time we had got into a bad tide-rip, which, combined with the heavy, lumpy sea, made it almost impossible to keep the *Dudley Docker* from swamping. As it was we shipped several bad seas over the stern as well as abeam and over the bows, although we were "on a wind". Lees, who owned himself to be a rotten oarsman, made good here by strenuous baling, in which he was well seconded by Cheetham. Greenstreet, a splendid fellow, relieved me at the tiller and helped generally. He and Macklin were my right and left bowers as stroke-oars throughout. McLeod and Cheetham were two good sailors and oars, the former a typical old deep-sea salt and growler, the latter a pirate to his finger-tips. In the height of the gale that night Cheetham was buying matches from me for bottles of champagne, one bottle per match (too cheap; I should have charged him two bottles). The champagne is to be paid when he opens his pub in Hull and I am able to call that way . . . We had now had one hundred and eight hours of toil, tumbling, freezing, and soaking, with little or no sleep. I think Sir Ernest, Wild, Greenstreet, and I could say that we had no sleep at all. Although it was sixteen months since we had been in a rough sea, only four men were actually sea-sick, but several others were off colour.

'The temperature was 20 degrees below freezing-point; fortunately, we were spared the bitterly low temperature of the previous night. Greenstreet's right foot got badly frost-bitten, but Lees restored it by holding it in his sweater against his stomach. Other men had minor frostbites, due principally to the fact that their clothes were soaked through with salt water . . . We were close to the land as the morning approached, but could see nothing of it through the snow and spindrift. My eyes began to fail me. Constant peering to windward, watching for seas to strike us, appeared to have given me a cold in the eyes. I could not see or judge distance properly, and found myself falling asleep momentarily at the tiller. At 3 a.m. Greenstreet relieved me there. I was so cramped from long hours, cold, and wet, in the constrained position one was forced to assume on top of the gear and stores at the tiller, that the other men had to pull me amidships and straighten me out like a jack-knife, first rubbing my thighs, groin, and stomach.

'At daylight we found ourselves close alongside the land, but the weather was so thick that we could not see where to make for a landing. Having taken the tiller again after an hour's rest under the shelter (save the mark!) of the dripping tent, I ran the *Dudley Docker* off before the gale, following the coast around to the north. This course for the first hour was fairly risky, the heavy sea before which we were running threatening to swamp the boat, but by 8 a.m. we had obtained a slight lee from the land. Then I was able to keep her very close in, along a glacier front, with the object of picking up lumps of fresh-water ice as we sailed through them. Our thirst was intense. We soon had some ice aboard, and for

the next hour and a half we sucked and chewed fragments of ice
with greedy relish.

'All this time we were coasting along beneath towering rocky
cliffs and sheer glacier-faces, which offered not the slightest possibility of landing anywhere. At 9:30 a.m. we spied a narrow, rocky
beach at the base of some very high crags and cliff, and made for
it. To our joy, we sighted the *James Caird* and the *Stancomb Wills*
sailing into the same haven just ahead of us. We were so delighted
that we gave three cheers, which were not heard aboard the other
boats owing to the roar of the surf. However, we soon joined
them and were able to exchange experiences on the beach.'

Our experiences on the *James Caird* had been similar, although
we had not been able to keep up to windward as well as the *Dudley
Docker* had done. This was fortunate as events proved, for the *James
Caird* and Stancamb Wills went to leeward of the big bight the
Dudley Docker entered and from which she had to turn out with
the sea astern. We thus avoided the risk of having the *Stancomb
Wills* swamped in the following sea. The weather was very thick
in the morning. Indeed at 7 a.m. we were right under the cliffs,
which plunged sheer into the sea, before we saw them. We followed the coast towards the north, and ever the precipitous cliffs
and glacier-faces presented themselves to our searching eyes. The
sea broke heavily against these walls and a landing would have
been impossible under any conditions. We picked up pieces of ice
and sucked them eagerly. At 9 a.m. at the north-west end of the
island we saw a narrow beach at the foot of the cliffs. Outside lay a
fringe of rocks heavily beaten by the surf but with a narrow
channel showing as a break in the foaming water. I decided that
we must face the hazards of this unattractive landing-place. Two
days and nights without drink or hot food had played havoc with
most of the men, and we could not assume that any safer haven lay
within our reach. The *Stancomb Wills* was the lighter and handier
boat – and I called her alongside with the intention of taking her
through the gap first and ascertaining the possibilities of a landing
before the *James Caird* made the venture. I was just climbing into
the *Stancomb Wills* when I saw the *Dudley Docker* coming up astern
under sail. The sight took a great load off my mind.

Rowing carefully and avoiding the blind rollers which showed
where sunken rocks lay, we brought the *Stancomb Wills* towards

the opening in the reef. Then, with a few strong strokes we shot through on the top of a swell and ran the boat on to a stony beach. The next swell lifted her a little farther. This was the first landing ever made on Elephant Island, and a thought came to me that the honour should belong to the youngest member of the Expedition, so I told Blackborrow to jump over. He seemed to be in a state almost of coma, and in order to avoid delay I helped him, perhaps a little roughly, over the side of the boat. He promptly sat down in the surf and did not move. Then I suddenly realised what I had forgotten, that both his feet were frost-bitten badly. Some of us jumped over and pulled him into a dry place. It was a rather rough experience for Blackborrow, but, anyhow, he is now able to say that he was the first man to sit on Elephant Island. Possibly at the time he would have been willing to forgo any distinction of the kind. We landed the cook with his blubber-stove, a supply of fuel and some packets of dried milk, and also several of the men. Then the rest of us pulled out again to pilot the other boats through the channel. The *James Caird* was too heavy to be beached directly, so after landing most of the men from the *Dudley Docker* and the *Stancomb Wills* I superintended the transhipment of the *James Caird*'s gear outside the reef. Then we all made the passage, and within a few minutes the three boats were aground. A curious spectacle met my eyes when I landed the second time. Some of the men were reeling about the beach as if they had found an unlimited supply of alcoholic liquor on the desolate shore. They were laughing uproariously, picking up stones and letting handfuls of pebbles trickle between their fingers like misers gloating over hoarded gold. The smiles and laughter, which caused cracked lips to bleed afresh, and the gleeful exclamations at the sight of two live seals on the beach made me think for a moment of that glittering hour of childhood when the door is open at last and the Christmas tree in all its wonder bursts upon the vision. I remember that Wild, who always rose superior to fortune, bad and good, came ashore as I was looking at the men and stood beside me as easy and unconcerned as if he had stepped out of his car for a stroll in the park.

Soon half a dozen of us had the stores ashore. Our strength was nearly exhausted and it was heavy work carrying our goods over the rough pebbles and rocks to the foot of the cliff, but we dare not leave anything within reach of the tide. We had to wade knee-deep in the icy water in order to lift the gear from the boats. When the work was done we pulled the three boats a little higher on the beach and turned gratefully to enjoy the hot drink the cook had prepared. Those of us who were comparatively fit had to wait until the weaker members of the party had been supplied; but every man had his pannikin of hot milk in the end, and never did anything taste better. Seal steak and blubber followed, for the seals that had been careless enough to await our arrival on the beach had already given up their lives. There was no rest for the cook. The blubber-stove flared and spluttered fiercely as he cooked, not one meal, but many meals, which merged into a day-long bout of eating. We drank water and ate seal meat until every man had reached the limit of his capacity.

The tents were pitched with oars for supports, and by 3 p.m. our camp was in order. The original framework of the tents had been cast adrift on one of the floes in order to save weight. Most of the men turned in early for a safe and glorious sleep, to be broken only by the call to take a turn on watch. The chief duty of the watchman was to keep the blubber-stove alight, and each man on duty appeared to find it necessary to cook himself a meal during his watch, and a supper before he turned in again.

Wild, Worsley, and Hurley accompanied me on an inspection of our beach before getting into the tents. I almost wished then that I had postponed the examination until after sleep, but the sense of caution that the uncertainties of polar travel implant in one's mind had made me uneasy. The outlook we found to be anything but cheering. Obvious signs showed that at spring tides the little beach would be covered by the water right up to the foot of the cliffs. In a strong north-easterly gale, such as we might expect to experience at any time, the waves would pound over the scant barrier of the reef and break against the sheer sides of the rocky wall behind us. Well-marked terraces showed the effect of other gales, and right at the back of the beach was a small bit of wreckage not more than three feet long, rounded by the constant chafing it had endured. Obviously we must find some better resting-place. I decided not to share with the men the knowledge of the uncertainties of our situation until they had enjoyed the full sweetness of rest untroubled by the thought that at any minute they might be called to face peril again. The threat of the sea had been our portion during many, many days, and a respite meant much to weary bodies and jaded minds.

The accompanying plan* will indicate our exact position more clearly than I can describe it. The cliffs at the back of the beach were inaccessible except at two points where there were steep snow-slopes. We were not worried now about food, for, apart from our own rations, there were seals on the beach and we could see others in the water outside the reef. Every now and then one of the animals would rise in the shallows and crawl up on the beach, which evidently was a recognised place of resort for its kind. A small rocky island which protected us to some extent from the north-westerly wind carried a ringed-penguin rookery. These birds were of migratory habit and might be expected to leave us before the winter set in fully, but in the meantime they were within our reach. These attractions, however, were overridden by the fact that the beach was open to the attack of wind and sea from the north-east and east. Easterly gales are more prevalent than western in that area of the Antarctic during the winter. Before turning in that night I studied the whole position and weighed every chance of getting the boats and our stores into a place of safety out of reach of the water. We ourselves might have clambered a little way up the snow-slopes, but we could not have taken the boats with us. The interior of the island was quite inaccessible. We climbed up one of the slopes and found ourselves stopped soon by overhanging cliffs. The rocks behind the camp were much weathered, and we noticed the sharp, unworn boulders that had fallen from above. Clearly there was a danger from overhead if we camped at the back of the beach. We must move on. With that thought in mind I reached my tent and fell asleep on the rubbly ground, which gave a comforting sense of stability. The fairy princess who would not rest on her seven downy mattresses because a pea lay underneath the pile might not have understood the pleasure we all derived from the irregularities of the stones, which could not possibly break beneath us or drift away; the very searching lumps were sweet reminders of our safety.

Early next morning (April 15) all hands were astir. The sun soon shone brightly and we spread out our wet gear to dry, till the

* Not shown in this edition

beach looked like a particularly disreputable gipsy camp. The boots
and clothing had suffered considerably during our travels. I had
decided to send Wild along the coast in the *Stancomb Wills* to look
for a new camping-ground, and he and I discussed the details of the
journey while eating our breakfast of hot seal steak and blubber.
The camp I wished to find was one where the party could live for
weeks or even months in safety, without danger from sea or wind
in the heaviest winter gale. Wild was to proceed westwards along
the coast and was to take with him four of the fittest men, Marston,
Crean, Vincent, and McCarthy. If he did not return before dark we
were to light a flare, which would serve him as a guide to the
entrance of the channel. The *Stancomb Wills* pushed off at 11 a.m.
and quickly passed out of sight around the island. Then Hurley and
I walked along the beach towards the west, climbing through a gap
between the cliff and a great detached pillar of basalt. The narrow
strip of beach was cumbered with masses of rock that had fallen
from the cliffs. We struggled along for two miles or more in the
search for a place where we could get the boats ashore and make a
permanent camp in the event of Wild's search proving fruitless, but
after three hours' vain toil we had to turn back. We had found on
the far side of the pillar of basalt a crevice in the rocks beyond the
reach of all but the heaviest gales. Rounded pebbles showed that
the seas reached the spot on occasions. Here I decided to depot
ten cases of Bovril sledging ration in case of our having to move
away quickly. We could come back for the food at a later date if
opportunity offered.

Returning to the camp, we found the men resting or attending
to their gear. Clark had tried angling in the shallows off the rocks
and had secured one or two small fish. The day passed quietly.
Rusty needles were rubbed bright on the rocks and clothes were
mended and darned. A feeling of tiredness – due, I suppose, to
reaction after the strain of the preceding days – overtook us, but
the rising tide, coming farther up the beach than it had done on
the day before, forced us to labour at the boats, which we hauled
slowly to a higher ledge. We found it necessary to move our
makeshift camp nearer the cliff. I portioned out the available
ground for the tents, the galley, and other purposes, as every foot
was of value. When night arrived the *Stancomb Wills* was still away,
so I had a blubber-flare lit at the head of the channel.

About 8 p.m. we heard a hail in the distance. We could see nothing, but soon like a pale ghost out of the darkness came the boat, the faces of the men showing white in the glare of the fire. Wild ran her on the beach with the swell, and within a couple of minutes we had dragged her to a place of safety. I was waiting Wild's report with keen anxiety, and my relief was great when he told me that he had discovered a sandy spit seven miles to the west, about 200 yds. long, running out at right angles to the coast and terminating at the seaward end in a mass of rock. A long snow-slope joined the spit at the shore end, and it seemed possible that a 'dugout' could be made in the snow. The spit, in any case, would be a great improvement on our narrow beach. Wild added that the place he described was the only possible camping-ground he had seen. Beyond, to the west and south-west, lay a frowning line of cliffs and glaciers, sheer to the water's edge. He thought that in very heavy gales either from the south-west or east the spit would be spray-blown, but that the seas would not actually break over it. The boats could be run up on a shelving beach.

After hearing this good news I was eager to get away from the beach camp. The wind when blowing was favourable for the run along the coast. The weather had been fine for two days and a change might come at any hour. I told all hands that we would make a start early on the following morning. A newly killed seal provided a luxurious supper of steak and blubber, and then we slept comfortably till the dawn.

The morning of April 17 came fine and clear. The sea was smooth, but in the offing we could see a line of pack, which seemed to be approaching. We had noticed already pack and bergs being driven by the current to the east and then sometimes coming back with a rush to the west. The current ran as fast as five miles an hour, and it was a set of this kind that had delayed Wild on his return from the spit. The rise and fall of the tide was only about five feet at this time, but the moon was making for full and the tides were increasing. The appearance of ice emphasised the importance of getting away promptly. It would be a serious matter to be prisoned on the beach by the pack. The boats were soon afloat in the shallows, and after a hurried breakfast all hands worked hard getting our gear and stores aboard. A mishap befell us when we were launching the boats. We were using oars as rollers, and three of these were broken, leaving us short for the journey that had still to be undertaken. The preparations took longer than I had expected; indeed, there seemed to be some reluctance on the part of several men to leave the barren safety of the little beach and venture once more on the ocean. But the move was imperative, and by 11 a.m. we were away, the *James Caird* leading. Just as we rounded the small island occupied by the ringed penguins the 'willywaw' swooped down from the 2000-ft. cliffs behind us, a herald of the southerly gale that was to spring up within half an hour.

Soon we were straining at the oars with the gale on our bows. Never had we found a more severe task. The wind shifted from the south to the south-west, and the shortage of oars became a serious matter. The *James Caird*, being the heaviest boat, had to keep a full complement of rowers, while the *Dudley Docker* and the *Stancomb Wills* went short and took turns using the odd oar. A big swell was thundering against the cliffs and at times we were almost driven on to the rocks by swirling green waters. We had to keep close inshore in order to avoid being embroiled in the raging sea, which was lashed snow-white and quickened by the furious squalls into a living mass of sprays. After two hours of strenuous labour we were almost exhausted, but we were fortunate enough to find comparative shelter behind a point of rock. Overhead towered the sheer cliffs for hundreds of feet, the sea-birds that fluttered from the crannies of the rock dwarfed by the height. The boats rose and fell in the big swell, but the sea was not breaking in our little haven, and we rested there while we ate our cold ration. Some of the men had to stand by the oars in order to pole the boats off the cliff-face.

After half an hour's pause I gave the order to start again. The *Dudley Docker* was pulling with three oars, as the *Stancomb Wills* had the odd one, and she fell away to leeward in a particularly heavy squall. I anxiously watched her battling up against wind and sea. It would have been useless to take the *James Caird* back to the assistance of the *Dudley Docker* since we were hard pressed to make any progress ourselves in the heavier boat. The only thing was to go ahead and hope for the best. All hands were wet to the skin again and many men were feeling the cold severely. We forged on slowly and passed inside a great pillar of rock standing out to sea and towering to a height of about 2400 ft. A line of reef stretched between the shore and this pillar, and I thought as we approached that we would have to face the raging sea outside; but a break in the white surf revealed a gap in the reef and we laboured through, with the wind driving clouds of spray on our port beam. The *Stancomb Wills* followed safely. In the stinging spray I lost sight of the *Dudley Docker* altogether. It was obvious she would have to go outside the pillar as she was making so much leeway, but I could not see what happened to her and I dared not pause. It was a bad time. At last, about 5 p.m., the *James Caird* and the *Stancomb Wills* reached comparatively calm water and we saw Wild's beach just ahead of us. I looked back vainly for the *Dudley Docker*.

Rocks studded the shallow water round the spit and the sea surged amongst them. I ordered the *Stancomb Wills* to run on to the beach at the place that looked smoothest, and in a few moments the first boat was ashore, the men jumping out and holding her against the receding wave. Immediately I saw she was safe I ran the *James Caird* in. Some of us scrambled up the beach through the fringe of the surf and slipped the painter round a rock, so as to hold the boat against the backwash. Then we began to get the stores and gear out, working like men possessed, for the boats could not be pulled up till they had been emptied. The blubber-stove was quickly alight and the cook began to prepare a hot drink. We were labouring at the boats when I noticed Rickenson turn white and stagger in the surf. I pulled him out of reach of the water and sent him up to the stove, which had been placed in the shelter of some rocks. McIlroy went to him and found that his heart had been temporarily unequal to the strain placed upon it. He was in a bad way and needed prompt medical attention. There are some men who will do more than their share of work and who will attempt more than they are physically able to accomplish. Rickenson was one of these eager souls. He was suffering, like many other members of the Expedition, from bad salt-water boils. Our wrists, arms, and legs were attacked. Apparently this infliction was due to constant soaking with sea-water, the chafing of wet clothes, and exposure.

I was very anxious about the *Dudley Docker*, and my eyes as well as my thoughts were turned eastward as we carried the stores ashore; but within half an hour the missing boat appeared, labouring through the spume-white sea, and presently she reached the comparative calm of the bay. We watched her coming with that sense of relief that the mariner feels when he crosses the harbour-bar. The tide was going out rapidly, and Worsley lightened the *Dudley Docker* by placing some cases on an outer rock, where they were retrieved subsequently. Then he beached his boat, and with many hands at work we soon had our belongings ashore and our three craft above high-water mark. The spit was by no means an ideal camping-ground; it was rough, bleak, and inhospitable – just an acre or two of rock and shingle, with the sea foaming around it except where the snow-slope, running up to a glacier, formed the landward boundary. But some of the larger rocks provided a measure of shelter from the wind, and as we clustered round the blubber-stove, with the acrid smoke blowing into our faces, we were quite a cheerful company. After all, another stage of the homeward journey had been accomplished and we could afford to forget for an hour the problems of the future. Life was not so bad. We ate our evening meal while the snow drifted down from the surface of the glacier, and our chilled bodies grew warm. Then we dried a little tobacco at the stove and enjoyed our pipes before we crawled into our tents. The snow had made it impossible for us to find the tide-line and we were uncertain how far the sea was going to encroach upon our beach. I pitched my tent on the seaward side of the camp so that I might have early warning of danger, and, sure enough, about 2 a.m. a little wave forced its way under the tent-cloth. This was a practical demonstration that we had not gone far enough back from the sea, but in the semi-darkness it was difficult to see where we could find safety. Perhaps it was fortunate that experience had inured us to the unpleasantness of sudden forced changes of camp. We took down the tents and re-pitched them close against the high rocks at the seaward end of the spit, where large boulders made an uncomfortable resting-place. Snow was falling heavily. Then all hands had to assist in pulling the boats farther up the beach, and at this task we suffered a serious misfortune. Two of our four bags of clothing had been placed under the bilge of the *James Caird*, and before we realised the danger a wave had lifted the boat and carried the two bags back into the surf. We had no chance of recovering them. This accident did not complete the tale of the night's misfortunes. The big eight-man tent was blown to pieces in the early morning. Some of the men who had occupied it took refuge in other tents, but several remained in their sleeping-bags under the fragments of cloth until it was time to turn out.

A southerly gale was blowing on the morning of April 18 and the drifting snow was covering everything. The outlook was cheerless indeed, but much work had to be done and we could not yield to the desire to remain in the sleeping-bags. Some sea-elephants were lying about the beach above high-water mark, and we killed several of the younger ones for their meat and blubber. The big tent could not be replaced, and in order to provide shelter for the men we turned the *Dudley Docker* upside down and wedged up the weather side with boulders. We also lashed the painter and stern-rope round the heaviest rocks we could find, so as to guard against the danger of the boat being moved by the wind. The two bags of clothing were bobbing about amid the brash and glacier-ice to the windward side of the spit, and it did not seem possible to reach them. The gale continued all day, and the fine drift from the surface of the glacier was added to the big flakes of snow falling from the sky. I made a careful examination of the spit with the object of ascertaining its possibilities as a camping-ground. Apparently, some of the beach lay above high-water mark and the rocks that stood above the shingle gave a measure of shelter. It would be possible to mount the snow-slope towards the glacier in fine weather, but I did not push my exploration in that direction during the gale. At the seaward end of the spit was the mass of rock already mentioned. A few thousand ringed penguins, with some gentoos, were on these rocks, and we had noted this fact with a great deal of satisfaction at the time of our landing. The ringed penguin is by no means the best of the penguins from the point of view of the hungry traveller, but it represents food. At 8 a.m. that morning I noticed the ringed penguins mustering in orderly fashion close to the water's edge, and thought that they were preparing for the daily fishing excursion; but presently it became apparent that some important move was on foot. They were going to migrate, and with their departure much valuable food would pass beyond our reach. Hurriedly we armed ourselves with pieces of sledge-runner and other improvised clubs, and started towards the rookery. We were too late. The leaders gave their squawk of command and the columns took to the sea in unbroken ranks. Following their leaders, the penguins dived through the surf and reappeared in the heaving water beyond. A very few of the weaker birds took fright and made their way back to the beach, where they fell victims later to our needs; but the main army went northwards and we saw them no more. We feared that the gentoo penguins might follow the example of their ringed cousins, but they stayed with us; apparently they had not the migratory habit. They were comparatively few in number, but from time to time they would come in from the sea and walk up our beach. The gentoo is the most strongly marked of all the smaller varieties of penguins as far as colouring is concerned, and it far surpasses the adelie in weight of legs and breast, the points that particularly appealed to us.

The deserted rookery was sure to be above high-water mark at all times; and we mounted the rocky ledge in search of a place to pitch our tents. The penguins knew better than to rest where the sea could reach them even when the highest tide was supported by the strongest gale. The disadvantages of a camp on the rookery were obvious. The smell was strong, to put it mildly, and was not likely to grow less pronounced when the warmth of our bodies thawed the surface. But our choice of places was not wide, and that afternoon we dug out a site for two tents in the debris of the rookery, levelling it off with snow and rocks. My tent, No. 1, was pitched close under the cliff, and there during my stay on Elephant Island I lived. Crean's tent was close by, and the other three tents, which had fairly clean snow under them, were some yards away. The fifth tent was a ramshackle affair. The material of the torn eight-man tent had been drawn over a rough framework of oars, and shelter of a kind provided for the men who occupied it.

The arrangement of our camp, the checking of our gear, the killing and skinning of seals and sea-elephants occupied us during the day, and we took to our sleeping-bags early. I and my companions in No. 1 tent were not destined to spend a pleasant night. The heat of our bodies soon melted the snow and refuse beneath us and the floor of the tent became an evil-smelling yellow mud. The snow drifting from the cliff above us weighted the sides of the tent, and during the night a particularly stormy gust brought our little home down on top of us. We stayed underneath the snow-laden cloth till the morning, for it seemed a hopeless business to set about re-pitching the tent amid the storm that was raging in the darkness of the night.

The weather was still bad on the morning of April 19. Some of the men were showing signs of demoralisation. They were disinclined to leave the tents when the hour came for turning out, and it was apparent they were thinking more of the discomforts of the moment than of the good fortune that had brought us to sound ground and comparative safety. The condition of the gloves and headgear shown me by some discouraged men illustrated the proverbial carelessness of the sailor. The articles had frozen stiff during the night, and the owners considered, it appeared, that this state of affairs provided them with a grievance, or at any rate gave them the right to grumble. They said they wanted dry clothes and that their health would not admit of their doing any work. Only by rather drastic methods were they induced to turn to. Frozen gloves and helmets undoubtedly are very uncomfortable, and the proper thing is to keep these articles thawed by placing them inside one's shirt during the night.

The southerly gale, bringing with it much snow, was so severe that as I went along the beach to kill a seal I was blown down by a gust. The cooking-pots from No. 2 tent took a flying run into the sea at the same moment. A case of provisions which had been placed on them to keep them safe had been capsized by a squall. These pots, fortunately, were not essential, since nearly all our cooking was done over the blubberstove. The galley was set up by the rocks close to my tent, in a hole we had dug through the debris of the penguin rookery. Cases of stores gave some shelter from the wind and a spread sail kept some of the snow off the cook when he was at work. He had not much idle time. The amount of seal and sea-elephant steak and blubber consumed by our hungry party was almost incredible. He did not lack assistance – the neighbourhood of the blubber-stove had attractions for every member of the party; but he earned everybody's gratitude by his unflagging energy in preparing meals that to us at least were savoury and satisfying. Frankly, we needed all the comfort that the hot food could give us. The icy fingers of the gale searched every cranny of our beach and pushed relentlessly through our worn garments and tattered tents.

The snow, drifting from the glacier and falling from the skies, swathed us and our gear and set traps for our stumbling feet. The rising sea beat against the rocks and shingle and tossed fragments of floe-ice within a few feet of our boats. Once during the morning the sun shone through the racing clouds and we had a glimpse of blue sky; but the promise of fair weather was not redeemed. The consoling feature of the situation was that our camp was safe. We could endure the discomforts, and I felt that all hands would be benefited by the opportunity for rest and recuperation.

CHAPTER 9

The boat journey

The increasing sea made it necessary for us to drag the boats farther up the beach. This was a task for all hands, and after much labour we got the boats into safe positions among the rocks and made fast the painters to big boulders. Then I discussed with Wild and Worsley the chances of reaching South Georgia before the winter locked the seas against us. Some effort had to be made to secure relief. Privation and exposure had left their mark on the party, and the health and mental condition of several men were causing me serious anxiety. Blackborrow's feet, which had been frost-bitten during the boat journey, were in a bad way, and the two doctors feared that an operation would be necessary. They told me that the toes would have to be amputated unless animation could be restored within a short period. Then the food-supply was a vital consideration. We had left ten cases of provisions in the crevice of the rocks at our first camping-place on the island. An examination of our stores showed that we had full rations for the whole party for a period of five weeks. The rations could be spread over three months on a reduced allowance and probably would be supplemented by seals and sea-elephants to some extent. I did not dare to count with full confidence on supplies of meat and blubber, for the animals seemed to have deserted the beach and the winter was near. Our stocks included three seals and two and a half skins (with blubber attached). We were mainly dependent on the blubber for fuel, and, after making a preliminary survey of the situation, I decided that the party must be limited to one hot meal a day.

A boat journey in search of relief was necessary and must not be delayed. That conclusion was forced upon me. The nearest port where assistance could certainly be secured was Port Stanley, in the Falkland Islands, 540 miles away, but we could scarcely hope to beat up against the prevailing northwesterly wind in a frail and weakened boat with a small sail area. South Georgia was over 800 miles away, but lay in the area of the west winds, and I could count upon finding whalers at any of the whaling-stations on the east coast. A boat party might make the voyage and be back with relief within a month, provided that the sea was clear of ice and the boat survived the great seas. It was not difficult to decide that South Georgia must be the objective, and I proceeded to plan ways and means. The hazards of a boat journey across 800 miles of stormy sub-Antarctic ocean were obvious, but I calculated that at worst the venture would add nothing to the risks of the men left on the island. There would be fewer mouths to feed during the winter and the boat would not require to take more than one month's provisions for six men, for if we did not make South Georgia in that time we were sure to go under. A consideration that had weight with me was that there was no chance at all of any search being made for us on Elephant Island.

The case required to be argued in some detail, since all hands knew that the perils of the proposed journey were extreme. The risk was justified solely by our urgent need of assistance. The ocean south of Cape Horn in the middle of May is known to be the most tempestuous storm-swept area of water in the world. The weather then is unsettled, the skies are dull and overcast, and the gales are almost unceasing. We had to face these conditions in a small and weather-beaten boat, already strained by the work of the months that had passed. Worsley and Wild realised that the attempt must be made, and they both asked to be allowed to accompany me on the voyage. I told Wild at once that he would have to stay behind. I relied upon him to hold the party together while I was away and to make the best of his way to Deception Island with the men in the spring in the event of our failure to bring help. Worsley I would take with me, for I had a very high opinion of his accuracy and quickness as a navigator, and especially in the snapping and working out of positions in difficult circumstances – an opinion that was only enhanced during the actual journey. Four other men would be required, and I decided to call for volunteers, although, as a matter of fact, I pretty well knew which of the people I would select. Crean I proposed to leave on the island as a right-hand man for Wild, but he begged so hard to be allowed to come in the boat that, after consulation with Wild, I promised to take him. I called the men together, explained my plan, and asked for volunteers. Many came forward at once. Some were not fit enough for the work that would have to be done, and others would not have been much use in the boat since they were not seasoned sailors, though the experiences of recent months entitled them to some consideration as seafaring men. McIlroy and Macklin were both anxious to go but realised that their duty lay on the island with the sick men. They suggested that I should take Blackborrow in order that he might have shelter and warmth as quickly as possible, but I had to veto this idea. It would be hard enough for fit men to live in the boat. Indeed, I did not see how a sick man, lying helpless in the bottom of the boat, could possibly survive in the heavy weather we were sure to encounter. I finally selected McNeish, McCarthy, and Vincent in addition to Worsley and Crean. The crew seemed a strong one, and as I looked at the men I felt confidence increasing.

The decision made, I walked through the blizzard with Worsley and Wild to examine the *James Caird*. The 20-ft. boat had never looked big; she appeared to have shrunk in some mysterious way when I viewed her in the light of our new undertaking. She was an ordinary ship's whaler, fairly strong, but showing signs of the strains she had endured since the crushing of the *Endurance*. Where she was holed in leaving the pack was, fortunately, about the water-line and easily patched. Standing beside her, we glanced at the fringe of the storm-swept, tumultuous sea that formed our path. Clearly, our voyage would be a big adventure. I called the carpenter and asked him if he could do anything to make the boat more seaworthy. He first inquired if he was to go with me, and seemed quite pleased when I said 'Yes'. He was over fifty years of age and not altogether fit, but he had a good knowledge of sailing-boats and was very quick. McCarthy said that he could contrive some sort of covering for the *James Caird* if he might use the lids of the cases and the four sledge-runners that we had lashed inside the boat for use in the event of a landing on Graham Land at Wilhelmina Bay. This bay, at one time the goal of our desire, had been left behind in the course of our drift, but we had retained the runners. The carpenter proposed to complete the covering with some of our canvas; and he set about making his plans at once.

Noon had passed and the gale was more severe than ever. We could not proceed with our preparations that day. The tents were suffering in the wind and the sea was rising. We made our way to the snow-slope at the shoreward end of the spit, with the intention of digging a hole in the snow large enough to provide shelter for the party. I had an idea that Wild and his men might camp there during my absence, since it seemed impossible that the tents could hold together for many more days against the attacks of the wind; but an examination of the spot indicated that any hole we could dig probably would be filled quickly by the drift. At dark, about 5 p.m., we all turned in, after a supper consisting of a pannikin of hot milk, one of our precious biscuits, and a cold penguin leg each.

The gale was stronger than ever on the following morning (April 20). No work could be done. Blizzard and snow, snow and blizzard, sudden lulls and fierce returns. During the lulls we could see on the far horizon to the north-east bergs of all shapes and sizes driving along before the gale, and the sinister appearance of the swift-moving masses made us thankful indeed that, instead of battling with the storm amid the ice, we were required only to face the drift from the glaciers and the inland heights. The gusts might throw us off our feet, but at least we fell on solid ground and not on the rocking floes. Two seals came up on the beach that day, one of them within ten yards of my tent. So urgent was our need of food and blubber that I called all hands and organised a line of beaters instead of simply walking up to the seal and hitting it on the nose. We were prepared to fall upon this seal en masse if it attempted to escape. The kill was made with a pick-handle, and in a few minutes five days' food and six days' fuel were stowed in a place of safety among the boulders above high-water mark. During this day the cook, who had worked well on the floe and throughout the boat journey, suddenly collapsed. I happened to be at the galley at the moment and saw him fall. I pulled him down the slope to his tent and pushed him into its shelter with orders to his tent-mates to keep him in his sleeping-bag until I allowed him to come out or the doctors said he was fit enough. Then I took out to replace the cook one of the men who had expressed a desire to lie down and die. The task of keeping the galley fire alight was both difficult and strenuous, and it took his thoughts away from the chances of immediate dissolution. In fact, I found him a little later gravely concerned over the drying of a naturally not over-clean pair of socks which were hung up in close proximity to our evening milk. Occupation had brought his thoughts back to the ordinary cares of life.

There was a lull in the bad weather on April 21, and the carpenter started to collect material for the decking of the *James Caird*. He fitted the mast of the *Stancomb Wills* fore and aft inside the *James Caird* as a hog-back and thus strengthened the keel with the object of preventing our boat 'hogging' – that is, buckling in heavy seas. He had not sufficient wood to provide a deck, but by using the sledge-runners and box-lids he made a framework extending from the forecastle aft to a well. It was a patched-up affair, but it provided a base for a canvas covering. We had a bolt of canvas frozen stiff, and this material had to be cut and then thawed out over the blubber-stove, foot by foot, in order that it might be sewn into the form of a cover. When it had been nailed and screwed into position it certainly gave an appearance of safety to the boat, though I had an uneasy feeling that it bore a strong likeness to stage scenery, which may look like a granite wall and is in fact nothing better than canvas and lath. As events proved, the covering served its purpose well. We certainly could not have lived through the voyage without it.

Another fierce gale was blowing on April 22, interfering with our preparations for the voyage. The cooker from No. 5 tent came adrift in a gust, and, although it was chased to the water's edge, it disappeared for good. Blackborrow's feet were giving him much pain, and McIlroy and Macklin thought it would be necessary for them to operate soon. They were under the impression then that they had no chloroform, but they found some subsequently in the medicine-chest after we had left. Some cases of stores left on a rock off the spit on the day of our arrival were retrieved during this day. We were setting aside stores for the boat journey and choosing the essential equipment from the scanty stock at our disposal. Two ten-gallon casks had to be filled with water melted down from ice collected at the foot of the glacier. This was a rather slow business. The blubber-stove was kept going all night, and the watchmen emptied the water into the casks from the pot in which the ice was melted. A working party started to dig a hole in the snow-slope about forty feet above sea-level with the object of providing a site for a camp. They made fairly good progress at first, but the snow drifted down unceasingly from the inland ice, and in the end the party had to give up the project.

The weather was fine on April 23, and we hurried forward our preparations. It was on this day I decided finally that the crew for the *James Caird* should consist of Worsley, Crean, McNeish, McCarthy, Vincent, and myself. A storm came on about noon, with driving snow and heavy squalls. Occasionally the air would clear for a few minutes, and we could see a line of pack-ice, five miles out, driving across from west to east. This sight increased my anxiety to get away quickly. Winter was advancing, and soon the pack might close completely round the island and stay our departure for days or even for weeks, I did not think that ice would remain around Elephant Island continuously during the winter, since the strong winds and fast currents would keep it in motion. We had noticed ice and bergs, going past at the rate of four or five knots. A certain amount of ice was held up about the end of our spit, but the sea was clear where the boat would have to be launched.

Worsley, Wild, and I climbed to the summit of the seaward rocks and examined the ice from a better vantage-point than the beach offered. The belt of pack outside appeared to be sufficiently broken for our purposes, and I decided that, unless the conditions forbade it, we would make a start in the *James Caird* on the following morning. Obviously the pack might close at any time. This decision made, I spent the rest of the day looking over the boat, gear, and stores, and discussing plans with Worsley and Wild.

Our last night on the solid ground of Elephant Island was cold and uncomfortable. We turned out at dawn and had breakfast. Then we launched the *Stancomb Wills* and loaded her with stores, gear, and ballast, which would be transferred to the *James Caird* when the heavier boat had been launched. The ballast consisted of bags made from blankets and filled with sand, making a total weight of about 1000 lb. In addition we had gathered a number of round boulders and about 250 lb. of ice, which would supplement our two casks of water.

The stores taken in the *James Caird*, which would last six men for one month, were as follows:

    30 boxes of matches.
    6½ gallons paraffin.
    1 tin methylated spirit.
    10 boxes of flamers.
    1 box of blue lights.
    2 Primus stoves with spare parts and prickers.
    1 Nansen aluminium cooker.
    6 sleeping-bags.
    A few spare socks.
    A few candles and some blubber-oil in an oil-bag.

Food:
    3 cases sledging rations = 300 rations.
    2 cases nut food = 200 ditto.
    2 cases biscuits = 600 biscuits.
    1 case lump sugar.
    30 packets of Trumilk.
    1 tin of Bovril cubes.
    1 tin of Cerebos salt.
    36 gallons of water.
    112 lb. of ice.

Instruments:
    Sextant.
    Sea-anchor.
    Binoculars.
    Charts.
    Prismatic compass.
    Aneroid.

The swell was slight when the *Stancomb Wills* was launched and the boat got under way without any difficulty; but half an hour later, when we were pulling down the *James Caird*, the swell increased suddenly. Apparently the movement of the ice outside had made an opening and allowed the sea to run in without being blanketed by the line of pack. The swell made things difficult. Many of us got wet to the waist while dragging the boat out – a serious matter in that climate. When the *James Caird* was afloat in the surf she nearly capsized among the rocks before we could get her clear, and Vincent and the carpenter, who were on the deck, were thrown into the water. This was really bad luck, for the two men would have small chance of drying their clothes after we had got under way. Hurley, who had the eye of the professional photographer for 'incidents', secured a picture of the upset, and I firmly believe that he would have liked the two unfortunate men to remain in the water until he could get a 'snap' at close quarters; but we hauled them out immediately, regardless of his feelings.

The *James Caird* was soon clear of the breakers. We used all the available ropes as a long painter to prevent her drifting away to the north-east, and then the *Stancomb Wills* came alongside, transferred her load, and went back to the shore for more. As she was being beached this time the sea took her stern and half filled her with water. She had to be turned over and emptied before the return journey could be made. Every member of the crew of the *Stancomb Wills* was wet to the skin. The water-casks were towed behind the *Stancomb Wills* on this second journey, and the swell, which was increasing rapidly, drove the boat on to the rocks, where one of the casks was slightly stove in. This accident proved later to be a serious one, since some sea-water had entered the cask and the contents were now brackish.

By midday the *James Caird* was ready for the voyage. Vincent and the carpenter had secured some dry clothes by exchange with members of the shore party (I heard afterwards that it was a full fortnight before the soaked garments were finally dried), and the boat's crew was standing by waiting for the order to cast off. A moderate westerly breeze was blowing. I went ashore in the *Stancomb Wills* and had a last word with Wild, who was remaining in full command, with directions as to his course of action in the event of our failure to bring relief, but I practically left the whole situation and scope of action and decision to his own judgment, secure in the knowledge that he would act wisely. I told him that I trusted the party to him and said goodbye to the men. Then we pushed off for the last time, and within a few minutes I was aboard the *James Caird*. The crew of the *Stancomb Wills* shook hands with us as the boats bumped together and offered us the last good wishes. Then, setting our jib, we cut the painter and moved away to the north-east. The men who were staying behind made a pathetic little group on the beach, with the grim heights of the island behind them and the sea seething at their feet, but they waved to us and gave three hearty cheers. There was hope in their hearts and they trusted us to bring the help that they needed.

I had all sails set, and the *James Caird* quickly dipped the beach and its line of dark figures. The westerly wind took us rapidly to the line of pack, and as we entered it I stood up with my arm around the mast, directing the steering, so as to avoid the great lumps of ice that were flung about in the heave of the sea. The pack thickened and we were forced to turn almost due east, running before the wind towards a gap I had seen in the morning from the high ground. I could not see the gap now, but we had come out on its bearing and I was prepared to find that it had been influenced by the easterly drift. At four o'clock in the afternoon we found the channel, much narrower than it had seemed in the morning but still navigable. Dropping sail, we rowed through without touching the ice anywhere, and by 5.30 p.m. we were clear of the pack with open water before us. We passed one more piece of ice in the darkness an hour later, but the pack lay behind, and with a fair wind swelling the sails we steered our little craft through the night, our hopes centred on our distant goal. The swell was very heavy now, and when the time came for our first evening meal we found great difficulty in keeping the Primus lamp alight and preventing the hoosh splashing out of the pot. Three men were needed to attend to the cooking, one man holding the lamp and two men guarding the aluminium cooking-pot, which had to be lifted clear of the Primus whenever the movement of the boat threatened to cause a disaster. Then the lamp had to be protected from water, for sprays were coming over the bows and our flimsy decking was by no means water-tight. All these operations were conducted in the confined space under the decking, where the men lay or knelt and adjusted themselves as best they could to the angles of our cases and ballast. It was uncomfortable, but we found consolation in the reflection that without the decking we could not have used the cooker at all.

The tale of the next sixteen days is one of supreme strife amid heaving waters. The sub-Antarctic Ocean lived up to its evil winter reputation. I decided to run north for at least two days while the wind held and so get into warmer weather before turning to the east and laying a course for South Georgia. We took two-hourly spells at the tiller. The men who were not on watch crawled into the sodden sleeping-bags and tried to forget their troubles for a period; but there was no comfort in the boat. The bags and cases seemed to be alive in their unfailing knack of presenting their most uncomfortable angles to our rest-seeking bodies. A man might imagine for a moment that he had found a position of ease, but always discovered quickly that some un-yielding point was impinging on muscle or bone. The first night aboard the boat was one of acute discomfort for us all, and we were heartily glad when the dawn came and we could set about the preparation of a hot breakfast.

This record of the voyage to South Georgia is based upon scanty notes made day by day. The notes dealt usually with the bare facts of distances, positions, and weather, but our memories retained the incidents of the passing days in a period never to be forgotten. By running north for the first two days I hoped to get warmer weather and also to avoid lines of pack that might be extending beyond the main body. We needed all the advantage that we could obtain from the higher latitude for sailing on the great circle, but we had to be cautious regarding possible ice-streams. Cramped in our narrow quarters and continually wet by the spray, we suffered severely from cold throughout the journey. We fought the seas and the winds and at the same time had a daily struggle to keep ourselves alive. At times we were in dire peril. Generally we were upheld by the knowledge that we were making progress towards the land where we would be, but there were days and nights when we lay hove to, drifting across the storm-whitened seas and watching, with eyes interested rather than apprehensive, the uprearing masses of water, flung to and fro by Nature in the pride of her strength. Deep seemed the valleys when we lay between the reeling seas. High were the hills when we perched momentarily on the tops of giant combers. Nearly always there were gales. So small was our boat and so great were the seas that often our sail flapped idly in the calm between the crests of two waves. Then we would climb the next slope and catch the full fury of the gale where the wool-like whiteness of the breaking water surged around us. We had our moments of laughter – rare, it is true, but hearty enough. Even when cracked lips and swollen mouths checked the outward and visible signs of amusement we could see a joke of the primitive kind. Man's sense of humour is always most easily stirred by the petty misfortunes of his neighbours, and I shall never forget Worsley's efforts on one occasion to place the hot aluminium stand on top of the Primus stove after it had fallen off in an extra heavy roll. With his frost-bitten fingers he picked it up, dropped it, picked it up again, and toyed with it gingerly as though it were some fragile article of lady's wear. We laughed, or rather gurgled with laughter.

The wind came up strong and worked into a gale from the north-west on the third day out. We stood away to the east. The increasing seas discovered the weaknesses of our decking. The continuous blows shifted the box-lids and sledge-runners so that the canvas sagged down and accumulated water. Then icy trickles, distinct from the driving sprays, poured fore and aft into the boat. The nails that the carpenter had extracted from cases at Elephant Island and used to fasten down the battens were too short to make firm the decking. We did what we could to secure it, but our means were very limited, and the water continued to enter the boat at a dozen points. Much baling was necessary, and nothing that we could do prevented our gear from becoming sodden. The searching runnels from the canvas were really more unpleasant than the sudden definite douches of the sprays. Lying under the thwarts during watches below, we tried vainly to avoid them. There were no dry places in the boat, and at last we simply covered our heads with our Burberrys and endured the all-pervading water. The baling was work for the watch. Real rest we had none. The perpetual motion of the boat made repose impossible; we were cold, sore, and anxious. We moved on hands and knees in the semi-darkness of the day under the decking. The darkness was complete by 6 p.m., and not until 7 a.m. of the following day could we see one another under the thwarts. We had a few scraps of candle, and they were preserved carefully in order that we might have light at meal-times. There was one fairly dry spot in the boat, under the solid original decking at the bows, and we managed to protect some of our biscuit from the salt water; but I do not think any of us got the taste of salt out of our mouths during the voyage.

The difficulty of movement in the boat would have had its humorous side if it had not involved us in so many aches and pains.

We had to crawl under the thwarts in order to move along the boat, and our knees suffered considerably. When watch turned out it was necessary for me to direct each man by name when and where to move, since if all hands had crawled about at the same time the result would have been dire confusion and many bruises. Then there was the trim of the boat to be considered. The order of the watch was four hours on and four hours off, three men to the watch. One man had the tiller-ropes, the second man attended to the sail, and the third baled for all he was worth. Sometimes when the water in the boat had been reduced to reasonable proportions, our pump could be used. This pump, which Hurley had made from the Flinders bar case of our ship's standard compass, was quite effective, though its capacity was not large. The man who was attending the sail could pump into the big outer cooker, which was lifted and emptied overboard when filled. We had a device by which the water could go direct from the pump into the sea through a hole in the gunwale, but this hole had to be blocked at an early stage of the voyage, since we found that it admitted water when the boat rolled.

While a new watch was shivering in the wind and spray, the men who had been relieved groped hurriedly among the soaked sleeping-bags and tried to steal a little of the warmth created by the last occupants; but it was not always possible for us to find even this comfort when we went off watch. The boulders that we had taken aboard for ballast had to be shifted continually in order to trim the boat and give access to the pump, which became choked with hairs from the moulting sleeping-bags and finneskoe. The four reindeer-skin sleeping-bags shed their hair freely owing to the continuous wetting, and soon became quite bald in appearance. The moving of the boulders was weary and painful work. We came to know every one of the stones by sight and touch, and I have vivid memories of their angular peculiarities even today. They might have been of considerable interest as geological specimens to a scientific man under happier conditions. As ballast they were useful. As weights to be moved about in cramped quarters they were simply appalling. They spared no portion of our poor bodies. Another of our troubles, worth mention here, was the chafing of our legs by our wet clothes, which had not been changed now for seven months. The insides of our thighs were rubbed raw, and the one tube of Hazeline cream in our medicine-chest did not go far in alleviating our pain, which was increased by the bite of the salt water. We thought at the time that we never slept. The fact was that we would doze off uncomfortably, to be aroused quickly by some new ache or another call to effort. My own share of the general unpleasantness was accentuated by a finely developed bout of sciatica. I had become possessor of this originally on the floe several months earlier.

Our meals were regular in spite of the gales. Attention to this point was essential, since the conditions of the voyage made increasing calls upon our vitality. Breakfast, at 8 a.m., consisted of a pannikin of hot hoosh made from Bovril sledging ration, two biscuits, and some lumps of sugar. Lunch came at 1 p.m., and comprised Bovril sledging ration, eaten raw, and a pannikin of hot milk for each man. Tea, at 5 p.m., had the same menu. Then during the night we had a hot drink, generally of milk. The meals were the bright beacons in those cold and stormy days. The glow of warmth and comfort produced by the food and drink made optimists of us all. We had two tins of Virol, which we were keeping for an emergency; but, finding ourselves in need of an oil-lamp to eke out our supply of candles, we emptied one of the tins in the manner that most appealed to us, and fitted it with a wick made by shredding a bit of canvas. When this lamp was filled with oil it gave a certain amount of light, though it was easily blown out, and was of great assistance to us at night. We were fairly well off as regarded fuel, since we had 6½ gallons of petroleum.

A severe south-westerly gale on the fourth day out forced us to heave to. I would have liked to have run before the wind, but the sea was very high and the *James Caird* was in danger of broaching to and swamping. The delay was vexatious, since up to that time we had been making sixty or seventy miles a day; good going with our limited sail area. We hove to under double-reefed mainsail and our little jigger, and waited for the gale to blow itself out. During that afternoon we saw bits of wreckage, the remains probably of some unfortunate vessel that had failed to weather the strong gales south of Cape Horn. The weather conditions did not improve, and on the fifth day out the gale was so fierce that we were compelled to take in the double-reefed mainsail and hoist our small jib instead. We put out a sea-anchor to keep the *James Caird*s' head up to the sea. This anchor consisted of a triangular canvas bag fastened to the end of the painter and allowed to stream out from the bows. The boat was high enough to catch the wind, and, as she drifted to leeward, the drag of the anchor kept her head to windward. Thus our boat took most of the seas more or less end on. Even then the crests of the waves often would curl right over us and we shipped a great deal of water, which necessitated unceasing baling and pumping. Looking out abeam, we would see a hollow like a tunnel formed as the crest of a big wave toppled over on to the swelling body of water. A thousand times it appeared as though the *James Caird* must be engulfed; but the boat lived. The south-westerly gale had its birthplace above the Antarctic Continent, and its freezing breath lowered the temperature far towards zero. The sprays froze upon the boat and gave bows, sides, and decking a heavy coat of mail. This accumulation of ice reduced the buoyancy of the boat, and to that extent was an added peril; but it possessed a notable advantage from one point of view. The water ceased to drop and trickle from the canvas, and the spray came in solely at the well in the after part of the boat. We could not allow the load of ice to grow beyond a certain point, and in turns we crawled about the decking forward, chipping and picking at it with the available tools.

When daylight came on the morning of the sixth day out we saw and felt that the *James Caird* had lost her resiliency. She was not rising to the oncoming seas. The weight of the ice that had formed in her and upon her during the night was having its effect, and she was becoming more like a log than a boat. The situation called for immediate action. We first broke away the spare oars, which were encased in ice and frozen to the sides of the boat, and threw them overboard. We retained two oars for use when we got inshore. Two of the fur sleeping-bags went over the side; they were thoroughly wet, weighing probably 40 lb. each, and they had frozen stiff during the night. Three men constituted the watch below, and when a man went down it was better to turn into the wet bag just vacated by another man than to thaw out a frozen bag with the heat of his unfortunate body. We now had four bags, three in use and one for emergency use in case a member of the party should break down permanently. The reduction of weight relieved the boat to some extent, and vigorous chipping and scraping did more. We had to be very careful not to put axe or knife through the frozen canvas of the decking as we crawled over it, but gradually we got rid of a lot of ice. The *James Caird* lifted to the endless waves as though she lived again.

About 11 a.m. the boat suddenly fell off into the trough of the sea. The painter had parted and the sea-anchor had gone. This was serious. The *James Caird* went away to leeward, and we had no chance at all of recovering the anchor and our valuable rope, which had been our only means of keeping the boat's head up to the seas without the risk of hoisting sail in a gale. Now we had to set the sail and trust to its holding. While the *James Caird* rolled heavily in the trough, we beat the frozen canvas until the bulk of the ice had cracked off it and then hoisted it. The frozen gear worked protestingly, but after a struggle our little craft came up to the wind again, and we breathed more freely. Skin frostbites were troubling us, and we had developed large blisters on our fingers and hands. I shall always carry the scar of one of these frostbites on my left hand, which became badly inflamed after the skin had burst and the cold had bitten deeply.

We held the boat up to the gale during that day, enduring as best we could discomforts that amounted to pain. The boat tossed interminably on the big waves under grey, threatening skies. Our thoughts did not embrace much more than the necessities of the hour. Every surge of the sea was an enemy to be watched and circumvented. We ate our scanty meals, treated our frostbites, and hoped for the improved conditions that the morrow might bring. Night fell early, and in the lagging hours of darkness we were cheered by a change for the better in the weather. The wind dropped, the snow-squalls became less frequent, and the sea moderated. When the morning of the seventh day dawned there was not much wind. We shook the reef out of the sail and laid our course once more for South Georgia. The sun came out bright and clear, and presently Worsley got a snap for longitude. We hoped that the sky would remain clear until noon, so that we could get the latitude. We had been six days out without an observation, and our dead reckoning naturally was uncertain. The boat must have presented a strange appearance that morning. All hands basked in the sun. We hung our sleeping-bags to the mast and spread our socks and other gear all over the deck. Some of the ice bad melted off the *James Caird* in the early morning after the gale began to slacken; and dry patches were appearing in the decking. Porpoises came blowing round the boat, and Cape pigeons wheeled and swooped within a few feet of us. These little black-and-white birds have an air of friendliness that is not possessed by the great circling albatross. They had looked grey against the swaying sea during the storm as they darted about over our heads and uttered their plaintive cries. The albatrosses, of the black or sooty variety, had watched with hard, bright eyes, and seemed to have a quite impersonal interest in our struggle to keep afloat amid the battering seas. In addition to the Cape pigeons an occasional stormy petrel flashed overhead. Then there was a small bird, unknown to me, that appeared always to be in a fussy, bustling state, quite out of keeping with the surroundings. It irritated me. It had practically no tail, and it flitted about vaguely as though in search of the lost member. I used to find myself wishing it would find its tail and have done with the silly fluttering.

We revelled in the warmth of the sun that day. Life was not so bad, after all. We felt we were well on our way. Our gear was drying, and we could have a hot meal in comparative comfort. The swell was still heavy, but it was not breaking and the boat rode easily. At noon Worsley balanced himself on the gunwale and clung with one hand to the stay of the mainmast while he got a snap of the sun. The result was more than encouraging. We had done over 380 miles and were getting on for half-way to South Georgia. It looked as though we were going to get through.

The wind freshened to a good stiff breeze during the afternoon, and the *James Caird* made satisfactory progress. I had not realised until the sunlight came how small our boat really was. There was some influence in the light and warmth, some hint of happier days, that made us revive memories of other voyages, when we had stout decks beneath our feet, unlimited food at our command, and pleasant cabins for our ease. Now we clung to a battered little boat, 'alone, alone, all, all alone, alone on a wide, wide sea'. So low in the water were we that each succeeding swell cut off our view of the sky-line. We were a tiny speck in the vast vista of the sea – the ocean that is open to all and merciful to none, that threatens even when it seems to yield, and that is pitiless always to weakness. For a moment the consciousness of the forces arrayed against us would be almost overwhelming. Then hope and confidence would rise again as our boat rose to a wave and tossed aside the crest in a sparkling shower like the play of prismatic colours at the foot of a waterfall. My double-barrelled gun and some cartridges had been stowed aboard the boat as an emergency precaution against a shortage of food, but we were not disposed to destroy our little neighbours, the Cape pigeons, even for the sake of fresh meat. We might have shot an albatross, but the wandering king of the ocean aroused in us something of the feeling that inspired, too late, the Ancient Mariner. So the gun remained among the stores and sleeping-bags in the narrow quarters beneath our leaking deck, and the birds followed us unmolested.

The eighth, ninth, and tenth days of the voyage had few features worthy of special note. The wind blew hard during those days, and the strain of navigating the boat was unceasing, but always we made some advance towards our goal. No bergs showed on our horizon, and we knew that we were clear of the ice-fields. Each day brought its little round of troubles, but also compensation in the form of food and growing hope. We felt that we were going to succeed. The odds against us had been great, but we were winning through. We still suffered severely from the cold, for, though the temperature was rising, our vitality was declining owing to shortage of food, exposure, and the necessity of main-taining our cramped positions day and night. I found that it was now absolutely necessary to prepare hot milk for all hands during the night, in order to sustain life till dawn. This meant lighting the Primus lamp in the darkness and involved an increased drain on our small store of matches. It was the rule that one match must serve when the Primus was being lit. We had no lamp for the compass and during the early days of the voyage we would strike a match when the steersman wanted to see the course at night; but later the necessity for strict economy impressed itself upon us, and the practice of striking matches at night was stopped. We had one water-tight tin of matches. I had stowed away in a pocket, in readiness for a sunny day, a lens from one of the telescopes, but this was of no use during the voyage. The sun seldom shone upon us. The glass of the compass got broken one night, and we contrived to mend it with adhesive tape from the medicine-chest. One of the memories that comes to me from those days is of Crean singing at the tiller. He always sang while he was steering, and nobody ever discovered what the song was. It was devoid of tune and as monotonous as the chanting of a Buddhist monk at his prayers; yet somehow it was cheerful. In moments of inspiration Crean would attempt 'The Wearing of the Green'.

On the tenth night Worsley could not straighten his body after his spell at the tiller. He was thoroughly cramped, and we had to drag him beneath the decking and massage him before he could unbend himself and get into a sleeping-bag. A hard north-westerly gale came up on the eleventh day (May 5) and shifted to the south-west in the late afternoon. The sky was overcast and occasional snow-squalls added to the discomfort produced by a tremendous cross-sea – the worst, I thought, that we had experienced. At midnight I was at the tiller and suddenly noticed a line of clear sky between the south and south-west. I called to the other men that the sky was clearing, and then a moment later I realised that what I had seen was not a rift in the clouds but the white crest of an enormous wave. During twenty-six years' experience of the ocean in all its moods I had not encountered a wave so gigantic. It was a mighty upheaval of the ocean, a thing quite apart from the big white-capped seas that had been our tireless enemies for many days. I shouted, 'For God's sake, hold on! It's got us!' Then came a moment of suspense that seemed drawn out into hours. White surged the foam of the breaking sea around us. We felt our boat lifted and flung forward like a cork in breaking surf. We were in a seething chaos of tortured water; but somehow the boat lived through it, half-full of water, sagging to the dead weight and shuddering under the blow. We baled with the energy of men fighting for life, flinging the water over the sides with every receptacle that came to our hands, and after ten minutes of uncertainty we felt the boat renew her life beneath us. She floated again and ceased to lurch drunkenly as though dazed by the attack of the sea. Earnestly we hoped that never again would we encounter such a wave.

The conditions in the boat, uncomfortable before, had been made worse by the deluge of water. All our gear was thoroughly wet again. Our cooking-stove had been floating about in the bottom of the boat, and portions of our last hoosh seemed to have permeated everything. Not until 3 a.m., when we were all chilled almost to the limit of endurance, did we manage to get the stove alight and make ourselves hot drinks. The carpenter was suffering particularly, but he showed grit and spirit. Vincent had for the past week ceased to be an active member of the crew, and I could not easily account for his collapse. Physically he was one of the strongest men in the boat. He was a young man, he had served on North Sea trawlers, and he should have been able to bear hardships better than McCarthy, who, not so strong, was always happy.

The weather was better on the following day (May 6), and we got a glimpse of the sun. Worsley's observation showed that we were not more than a hundred miles from the north-west corner of South Georgia. Two more days with a favourable wind and we would sight the promised land. I hoped that there would be no delay, for our supply of water was running very low. The hot drink at night was essential, but I decided that the daily allowance of water must be cut down to half a pint per man. The lumps of ice we had taken aboard had gone long ago. We were dependent upon the water we had brought from Elephant Island, and our thirst was increased by the fact that we were now using the brackish water in the breaker that had been slightly stove in in the surf when the boat was being loaded. Some sea-water had entered at that time. Thirst took possession of us. I dared not permit the allowance of water to be increased since an unfavourable wind might drive us away from the island and lengthen our voyage by many days. Lack of water is always the most severe privation that men can be condemned to endure, and we found, as during our earlier boat voyage, that the salt water in our clothing and the salt spray that lashed our faces made our thirst grow quickly to a burning pain. I had to be very firm in refusing to allow anyone to anticipate the morrow's allowance, which I was sometimes begged to do. We did the necessary work dully and hoped for the land. I had altered the course to the east so as to make sure of our striking the island, which would have been impossible to regain if we had run past the northern end. The course was laid on our scrap of chart for a point some thirty miles down the coast. That day and the following day passed for us in a sort of nightmare. Our mouths were dry and our tongues were swollen. The wind was still strong and the heavy sea forced us to navigate carefully, but any thought of our peril from the waves was buried beneath the consciousness of our raging thirst. The bright moments were those when we each received our one mug of hot milk during the long, bitter watches of the night. Things were bad for us in those days, but the end was coming. The morning of May 8 broke thick and stormy, with squalls from the north-west. We searched the waters ahead for a sign of land, and though we could see nothing more than had met our eyes for many days, we were cheered by a sense that the goal was near at hand. About ten o'clock that morning we passed a little bit of kelp, a glad signal of the proximity of land. An hour later we saw two shags sitting on a big mass of kelp, and knew then that we must be within ten or fifteen miles of the shore. These birds are as sure an indication of the proximity of land as a lighthouse is, for they never venture far to sea. We gazed ahead with increasing eagerness, and at 12.30 p.m., through a rift in the clouds, McCarthy caught a glimpse of the black cliffs of South Georgia, just fourteen days after our departure from Elephant Island. It was a glad moment. Thirst-ridden, chilled, and weak as we were, happiness irradiated us. The job was nearly done.

We stood in towards the shore to look for a landing-place, and presently we could see the green tussock-grass on the ledges above the surf-beaten rocks. Ahead of us and to the south, blind rollers showed the presence of uncharted reefs along the coast. Here and there the hungry rocks were close to the surface, and over them the great waves broke, swirling viciously and spouting thirty and forty feet into the air. The rocky coast appeared to descend sheer to the sea. Our need of water and rest was wellnigh desperate, but to have attempted a landing at that time would have been suicidal. Night was drawing near, and the weather indications were not favourable. There was nothing for it but to haul off till the following morning, so we stood away on the starboard tack until we had made what appeared to be a safe offing. Then we hove to in the high westerly swell. The hours passed slowly as we waited the dawn, which would herald, we fondly hoped, the last stage of our journey. Our thirst was a torment and we could scarcely touch our food; the cold seemed to strike right through our weakened bodies. At 5 a.m. the wind shifted to the north-west and quickly increased to one of the worst hurricanes any of us had ever experienced. A great cross-sea was running and the wind simply shrieked as it tore the tops off the waves and converted the whole seascape into a haze of driving spray. Down into valleys, up to tossing heights, straining until her seams opened, swung our little boat, brave still but labouring heavily. We knew that the wind and set of the sea was driving us ashore, but we could do nothing. The dawn showed us a storm-torn ocean, and the morning passed without bringing us a sight of the land; but at 1 p.m., through a rift in the flying mists, we got a glimpse of the huge crags of the island and realised that our position had become desperate. We were on a dead lee shore, and we could gauge our approach to the unseen cliffs by the roar of the breakers against the sheer walls of rock. I ordered the double-reefed mainsail to be set in the hope that we might claw off, and this attempt increased the strain upon the boat. The *James Caird* was bumping heavily, and the water was pouring in everywhere. Our thirst was forgotten in the realisation of our imminent danger, as we baled unceasingly, and adjusted our weights from time to time; occasional glimpses showed that the shore was nearer. I knew that Annewkow Island lay to the south of us, but our small and badly marked chart showed uncertain reefs in the passage between the island and the mainland, and I dared not trust it, though as a last resort we could try to lie under the lee of the island. The afternoon wore away as we edged down the coast, with the thunder of the breakers in our ears. The approach of evening found us still some distance from Annewkow Island, and, dimly in the twilight, we could see a snow-capped mountain looming above us. The chance of surviving the night, with the driving gale and the implacable sea forcing us on to the lee shore, seemed small. I think most of us had a feeling that the end was very near. Just after 6 p.m., in the dark, as the boat was in the yeasty backwash from the seas flung from this iron-bound coast, then, just when things looked their worst, they changed for the best. I have marvelled often at the thin line that divides success from failure and the sudden turn that leads from apparently certain disaster to comparative safety. The wind suddenly shifted, and we were free once more to make an offing. Almost as soon as the gale eased, the pin that locked the mast to the thwart fell out. It must have been on the point of doing this throughout the hurricane, and if it had gone nothing could have saved us; the mast would have snapped like a carrot. Our backstays had carried away once before when iced up and were not too strongly fastened now. We were thankful indeed for the mercy that had held that pin in its place throughout the hurricane.

We stood off shore again, tired almost to the point of apathy. Our water had long been finished. The last was about a pint of hairy liquid, which we strained through a bit of gauze from the medicine-chest. The pangs of thirst attacked us with redoubled intensity, and I felt that we must make a landing on the following day at almost any hazard. The night wore on. We were very tired. We longed for day. When at last the dawn came on the morning of May 10 there was practically no wind, but a high cross-sea was running. We made slow progress towards the shore. About 8 a.m. the wind backed to the north-west and threatened another blow. We had sighted in the meantime a big indentation which I thought must be King Haakon Bay, and I decided that we must land there. We set the bows of the boat towards the bay and ran before the freshening gale. Soon we had angry reefs on either side. Great glaciers came down to the sea and offered no landing-place. The sea spouted on the reefs and thundered against the shore. About noon we sighted a line of jagged reef, like blackened teeth, that seemed to bar the entrance to the bay. Inside, comparatively smooth water stretched eight or nine miles to the head of the bay. A gap in the reef appeared, and we made for it. But the fates had another rebuff for us. The wind shifted and blew from the east right out of the bay. We could see the way through the reef, but we could not approach it directly. That afternoon we bore up, tacking five times in the strong wind. The last tack enabled us to get through, and at last we were in the wide mouth of the bay. Dusk was approaching. A small cove, with a boulder-strewn beach guarded by a reef, made a break in the cliffs on the south side of the bay, and we turned in that direction. I stood in the bows directing the steering as we ran through the kelp and made the passage of the reef. The entrance was so narrow that we had to take in the oars, and the swell was piling itself right over the reef into the cove; but in a minute or two we were inside, and in the gathering darkness the *James Caird* ran in on a swell and touched the beach. I sprang ashore with the short painter and held on when the boat went out with the backward surge. When the *James Caird* came in again three of the men got ashore, and they held the painter while I climbed some rocks with another line. A slip on the wet rocks twenty feet up nearly closed my part of the story just at the moment when we were achieving safety. A jagged piece of rock held me and at the same time bruised me sorely. However, I made fast the line, and in a few minutes we were all safe on the beach, with the boat floating in the surging water just off the shore. We heard a gurgling sound that was sweet music in our ears, and, peering around, found a stream of fresh water almost at our feet. A moment later we were down on our knees drinking the pure, ice-cold water in long draughts that put new life into us. It was a splendid moment.

The next thing was to get the stores and ballast out of the boat, in order that we might secure her for the night. We carried the stores and gear above high-water mark and threw out the bags of sand and the boulders that we knew so well. Then we attempted to pull the empty boat up the beach, and discovered by this effort how weak we had become. Our united strength was not sufficient to get the *James Caird* clear of the water. Time after time we pulled together, but without avail. I saw that it would be necessary to have food and rest before we beached the boat. We made fast a line to a heavy boulder and set a watch to fend the *James Caird* off the rocks of the beach. Then I sent Crean round to the left side of the cove, about thirty yards away, where I had noticed a little cave as we were running in. He could not see much in the darkness, but reported that the place certainly promised some shelter. We carried the sleeping-bags round and found a mere hollow in the rock-face, with a shingle floor sloping at a steep angle to the sea. There we prepared a hot meal, and when the food was finished I ordered the men to turn in. The time was now about 8 p.m., and I took the first watch beside the *James Caird*, which was still afloat in the tossing water just off the beach.

Fending the *James Caird* off the rocks in the darkness was awkward work. The boat would have bumped dangerously if allowed to ride in with the waves that drove into the cove. I found a flat rock for my feet, which were in a bad way owing to cold, wetness, and lack of exercise in the boat, and during the next few hours I laboured to keep the *James Caird* clear of the beach. Occasionally I had to rush into the seething water. Then, as a wave receded, I let the boat out on the alpine rope so as to avoid a sudden jerk. The heavy painter had been lost when the sea-anchor went adrift. The *James Caird* could be seen but dimly in the cove, where the high black cliffs made the darkness almost complete, and the strain upon one's attention was great. After several hours had passed I found that my desire for sleep was becoming irresistible, and at 1 a.m. I called Crean. I could hear him groaning as he stumbled over the sharp rocks on his way down the beach. While he was taking charge of the *James Caird* she got adrift, and we had some anxious moments. Fortunately, she went across towards the cave and we secured her, unharmed. The loss or destruction of the boat at this stage would have been a very serious matter, since we probably would have found it impossible to leave the cove except by sea. The cliffs and glaciers around offered no practicable path towards the head of the bay. I arranged for one-hour watches during the remainder of the night and then took Crean's place among the sleeping men and got some sleep before the dawn came.

The sea went down in the early hours of the morning (May 11), and after sunrise we were able to set about getting the boat ashore, first bracing ourselves for the task with another meal. We were all weak still. We cut off the topsides and took out all the movable gear. Then we waited for Byron's 'great ninth wave', and when it lifted the *James Caird* in we held her and, by dint of great exertion, worked her round broadside to the sea. Inch by inch we dragged her up until we reached the fringe of the tussock-grass and knew that the boat was above high-water mark. The rise of the tide was about five feet, and at spring tide the water must have reached almost to the edge of the tussock-grass. The completion of this job removed our immediate anxieties, and we were free to examine our surroundings and plan the next move. The day was bright and clear.

King Haakon Bay is an eight-mile sound penetrating the coast of South Georgia in an easterly direction. We had noticed that the northern and southern sides of the sound were formed by steep mountain-ranges, their flanks furrowed by mighty glaciers, the outlets of the great ice-sheet of the interior. It was obvious that these glaciers and the precipitous slopes of the mountains barred our way inland from the cove. We must sail to the head of the sound. Swirling clouds and mist-wreaths had obscured our view of the sound when we were entering, but glimpses of snow-slopes had given us hope that an overland journey could be begun from that point. A few patches of very rough, tussocky land, dotted with little tarns, lay between the glaciers along the foot of the mountains, which were heavily scarred with scree-slopes. Several magnificent peaks and crags gazed out across their snowy domains to the sparkling waters of the sound.

Our cove lay a little inside the southern headland of King Haakon Bay. A narrow break in the cliffs, which were about a hundred feet high at this point, formed the entrance to the cove. The cliffs continued inside the cove on each side and merged into a hill which descended at a steep slope to the boulder beach. The slope, which carried tussock-grass, was not continuous. It eased at two points into little peaty swamp terraces dotted with frozen pools and drained by two small streams. Our cave was a recess in the cliff on the left-hand end of the beach. The rocky face of the cliff was undercut at this point, and the shingle thrown up by the waves formed a steep slope, which we reduced to about one in six by scraping the stones away from the inside. Later we strewed the rough floor with the dead, nearly dry underleaves of the tussock-grass, so as to form a slightly soft bed for our sleeping-bags. Water had trickled down the face of the cliff and formed long icicles, which hung down in front of the cave to the length of about fifteen feet. These icicles provided shelter, and when we had spread our sails below them, with the assistance of oars, we had quarters that, in the circumstances, had to be regarded as reasonably comfortable. The camp at least was dry, and we moved our gear there with confidence. We built a fireplace and arranged our sleeping-bags and blankets around it. The cave was about 8 ft. deep and 12 ft. wide at the entrance.

While the camp was being arranged Crean and I climbed the tussock slope behind the beach and reached the top of a headland overlooking the sound. There we found the nests of albatrosses, and, much to our delight, the nests contained young birds. The fledgelings were fat and lusty, and we had no hesitation about deciding that they were destined to die at an early age. Our most pressing anxiety at this stage was a shortage of fuel for the cooker. We had rations for ten more days, and we knew now that we could get birds for food; but if we were to have hot meals we must secure fuel. The store of petroleum carried in the boat was running

very low, and it seemed necessary to keep some quantity for use on
the overland journey that lay ahead of us. A sea-elephant or a seal
would have provided fuel as well as food, but we could see none in
the neighbourhood. During the morning we started a fire in the
cave with wood from the top-sides of the boat, and though the
dense smoke from the damp sticks inflamed our tired eyes, the
warmth and the prospect of hot food were ample compensation.
Crean was cook that day, and I suggested to him that he should
wear his goggles, which he happened to have brought with him.
The goggles helped him a great deal as he bent over the fire and
tended the stew. And what a stew it was! The young albatrosses
weighed about fourteen pounds each fresh-killed, and we estimated that they weighed at least six pounds each when cleaned and
dressed for the pot. Four birds went into the pot for six men, with
a Bovril ration for thickening. The flesh was white and succulent,
and the bones, not fully formed, almost melted in our mouths.
That was a memorable meal. When we had eaten our fill, we dried
our tobacco in the embers of the fire and smoked contentedly. We
made an attempt to dry our clothes, which were soaked with salt
water, but did not meet with much success. We could not afford
to have a fire except for cooking purposes until blubber or drift-
wood had come our way.

The final stage of the journey had still to be attempted. I realised
that the condition of the party generally, and particularly of
McNeish and Vincent, would prevent us putting to sea again
except under pressure of dire necessity. Our boat, moreover, had
been weakened by the cutting away of the topsides, and I doubted
if we could weather the island. We were still 150 miles away from
Stromness whaling-station by sea. The alternative was to attempt
the crossing of the island. If we could not get over, then we
must try to secure enough food and fuel to keep us alive through
the winter, but this possibility was scarcely thinkable. Over on
Elephant Island twenty-two men were waiting for the relief that
we alone could secure for them. Their plight was worse than ours.
We must push on somehow. Several days must elapse before our
strength would be sufficiently recovered to allow us to row or sail
the last nine miles up to the head of the bay. In the meantime we
could make what preparations were possible and dry our clothes
by taking advantage of every scrap of heat from the fires we lit

for the cooking of our meals. We turned in early that night, and I remember that I dreamed of the great wave and aroused my companions with a shout of warning as I saw with half-awakened eyes the towering cliff on the opposite side of the cove. Shortly before midnight a gale sprang up suddenly from the north-east with rain and sleet showers. It brought quantities of glacier-ice into the cove, and by 2 a.m. (May 12) our little harbour was filled with ice, which surged to and fro in the swell and pushed its way on to the beach. We had solid rock beneath our feet and could watch without anxiety. When daylight came rain was falling heavily, and the temperature was the highest we had experienced for many months. The icicles overhanging our cave were melting down in streams and we had to move smartly when passing in and out lest we should be struck by falling lumps. A fragment weighing fifteen or twenty pounds crashed down while we were having breakfast. We found that a big hole had been burned in the bottom of Worsley's reindeer sleeping-bag during the night. Worsley had been awakened by a burning sensation in his feet, and had asked the men near him if his bag was all right; they looked and could see nothing wrong. We were all superficially frostbitten about the feet, and this condition caused the extremities to burn painfully, while at the same time sensation was lost in the skin. Worsley thought that the uncomfortable heat of his feet was due to the frostbites, and he stayed in his bag and presently went to sleep again. He discovered when he turned out in the morning that the tussock-grass which we had laid on the floor of the cave had smouldered outwards from the fire and had actually burned a large hole in the bag beneath his feet. Fortunately, his feet were not harmed.

Our party spent a quiet day, attending to clothing and gear, checking stores, eating and resting. Some more of the young albatrosses made a noble end in our pot. The birds were nesting on a small plateau above the right-hand end of our beach. We had previously discovered that when we were landing from the boat on the night of May 10 we had lost the rudder. The *James Caird* had been bumping heavily astern as we were scrambling ashore, and evidently the rudder was then knocked off. A careful search of the beach and the rocks within our reach failed to reveal the missing article. This was a serious loss, even if the voyage to the head of the sound could be made in good weather. At dusk the ice in the cove was rearing and crashing on the beach. It had forced up a ridge of stones close to where the *James Caird* lay at the edge of the tussock-grass. Some pieces of ice were driven right up to the canvas wall at the front of our cave. Fragments lodged within two feet of Vincent, who had the lowest sleeping-place, and within four feet of our fire. Crean and McCarthy had brought down six more of the young albatrosses in the afternoon, so we were well supplied with fresh food. The air temperature that night probably was not lower than 38 or 40 degrees Fahr., and we were rendered uncomfortable in our cramped sleeping quarters by the unaccustomed warmth. Our feelings towards our neighbours underwent a change. When the temperature was below 20 deg. Fahr, we could not get too close to one another – every man wanted to cuddle against his neighbour; but let the temperature rise a few degrees and the warmth of another man's body ceased to be a blessing. The ice and the waves had a voice of menace that night, but I heard it only in my dreams.

The bay was still filled with ice on the morning of Saturday, May 13, but the tide took it all away in the afternoon. Then a strange thing happened. The rudder, with all the broad Atlantic to sail in and the coasts of two continents to search for a resting-place, came bobbing back into our cove. With anxious eyes we watched it as it advanced, receded again, and then advanced once more under the capricious influence of wind and wave. Nearer and nearer it came as we waited on the shore, oars in hand, and at last we were able to seize it. Surely a remarkable salvage! The day was bright and clear; our clothes were drying and our strength was returning. Running water made a musical sound down the tussock slope and among the boulders. We carried our blankets up the hill and tried to dry them in the breeze 300 ft. above sea-level. In the afternoon we began to prepare the *James Caird* for the journey to the head of King Haakon Bay. A noon observation on this day gave our latitude as 54 degrees 10' 47" S., but according to the German chart the position should have been 54 deg. 12' S. Probably Worsley's observation was the more accurate. We were able to keep the fire alight until we went to sleep that night, for while climbing the rocks above the cove I had seen at the foot of a cliff a broken spar, which had been thrown up by the waves. We could reach this spar by climbing down the cliff, and with a reserve supply of fuel thus in sight we could afford to burn the fragments of the *James Caird*'s topsides more freely.

During the morning of this day (May 13) Worsley and I tramped across the hills in a north-easterly direction with the object of getting a view of the sound and possibly gathering some inform-ation that would be useful to us in the next stage of our journey. It was exhausting work, but after covering about 2½ miles in two hours, we were able to look east, up the bay. We could not see very much of the country that we would have to cross in order to reach the whaling-station on the other side of the island. We had passed several brooks and frozen tarns, and at a point where we had to take to the beach on the shore of the sound we found some wreckage – an 18-ft. pine-spar (probably part of a ship's topmast), several pieces of timber, and a little model of a ship's hull, evid-ently a child's toy. We wondered what tragedy that pitiful little plaything indicated. We encountered also some gentoo penguins and a young sea-elephant, which Worsley killed.

When we got back to the cave at 3 p.m., tired, hungry, but rather pleased with ourselves, we found a splendid meal of stewed albatross chicken waiting for us. We had carried a quantity of blubber and the sea-elephant's liver in our blouses, and we produced our treasures as a surprise for the men. Rough climbing on the way back to camp had nearly persuaded us to throw the stuff away, but we had held on (regardless of the condition of our already sorely tried clothing), and had our reward at the camp. The long bay had been a magnificent sight, even to eyes that had dwelt on grandeur long enough and were hungry for the simple, familiar things of everyday life. Its green-blue waters were being beaten to fury by the north-westerly gale. The mountains, 'stern peaks that dared the stars', peered through the mists, and between them huge glaciers poured down from the great ice-slopes and -fields that lay behind. We counted twelve glaciers and heard every few minutes the reverberating roar caused by masses of ice calving from the parent streams.

On May 14 we made our preparations for an early start on the following day if the weather held fair. We expected to be able to pick up the remains of the sea-elephant on our way up the sound. All hands were recovering from the chafing caused by our wet clothes during the boat journey. The insides of our legs had suffered severely, and for some time after landing in the cove we found movement extremely uncomfortable. We paid our last visit to the nests of the albatrosses, which were situated on a little undulating plateau above the cave amid tussocks, snow-patches, and little frozen tarns. Each nest consisted of a mound over a foot high of tussock-grass, roots, and a little earth. The albatross lays one egg and very rarely two. The chicks, which are hatched in January, are fed on the nest by the parent birds for almost seven months before they take to the sea and fend for themselves. Up to four months of age the chicks are beautiful white masses of downy fluff, but when we arrived on the scene their plumage was almost complete. Very often one of the parent birds was on guard near the nest. We did not enjoy attacking these birds, but our hunger knew no law. They tasted so very good and assisted our recuperation to such an extent that each time we killed one of them we felt a little less remorseful.

May 15 was a great day. We made our hoosh at 7.30 a.m. Then we loaded up the boat and gave her a flying launch down the steep beach into the surf. Heavy rain had fallen in the night and a gusty north-westerly wind was now blowing, with misty showers. The *James Caird* headed to the sea as if anxious to face the battle of the waves once more. We passed through the narrow mouth of the cove with the ugly rocks and waving kelp close on either side, turned to the east, and sailed merrily up the bay as the sun broke through the mists and made the tossing waters sparkle around us. We were a curious-looking party on that bright morning, but we were feeling happy. We even broke into song, and, but for our Robinson Crusoe appearance, a casual observer might have taken us for a picnic party sailing in a Norwegian fiord or one of the beautiful sounds of the west coast of New Zealand. The wind blew fresh and strong, and a small sea broke on the coast as we advanced. The surf was sufficient to have endangered the boat if we had attempted to land where the carcass of the sea-elephant was lying, so we decided to go on to the head of the bay without risking anything, particularly as we were likely to find sea-elephants on the upper beaches. The big creatures have a habit of seeking peaceful quarters protected from the waves. We had hopes, too, of finding penguins. Our expectation as far as the sea-elephants were concerned was not at fault. We heard the roar of the bulls as we neared the head of the bay, and soon afterwards saw the great unwieldy forms of the beasts lying on a shelving beach towards the bay-head. We rounded a high, glacier-worn bluff on the north side, and at 12.30 p.m. we ran the boat ashore on a low beach of sand and pebbles, with tussock growing above high-water mark. There were hundreds of sea-elephants lying about, and our anxieties with regard to food disappeared. Meat and blubber enough to feed our party for years was in sight. Our landing-place was about a mile and a half west of the north-east corner of the bay. Just east of us was a glacier-snout ending on the beach but giving a passage towards the head of the bay, except at high water or when a very heavy surf was running. A cold, drizzling rain had begun to fall, and we provided ourselves with shelter as quickly as possible. We hauled the *James Caird* up above high-water mark and turned her over just to the lee or east side of the bluff. The spot was separated from the mountain-side by a low morainic bank, rising twenty or thirty feet above sea-level. Soon we had converted the boat into a very comfortable cabin *à la* Peggotty, turfing it round with tussocks, which we dug up with knives. One side of the *James Caird* rested on stones so as to afford a low entrance, and when we had finished she looked as though she had grown there. McCarthy entered into this work with great spirit. A sea-elephant provided us with fuel and meat, and that evening found a well-fed and fairly contented party at rest in Peggotty Camp.

Our camp, as I have said, lay on the north side of King Haakon Bay near the head. Our path towards the whaling-stations led round the seaward end of the snouted glacier on the east side of the camp and up a snow-slope that appeared to lead to a pass in the great Allardyce Range, which runs north-west and south-east and forms the main backbone of South Georgia. The range dipped opposite the bay into a well-defined pass from east to west. An ice-sheet covered most of the interior, filling the valleys and disguising the configurations of the land, which, indeed, showed only in big rocky ridges, peaks, and nunataks. When we looked up the pass from Peggotty Camp the country to the left appeared to offer two easy paths through to the opposite coast, but we knew that the island was uninhabited at that point (Possession Bay). We had to turn our attention farther east, and it was impossible from the camp to learn much of the conditions that would confront us on the overland journey. I planned to climb to the pass and then be guided by the configuration of the country in the selection of a route eastward to Stromness Bay, where the whaling-stations were established in the minor bays, Leith, Husvik, and Stromness. A range of mountains with precipitous slopes, forbidding peaks, and large glaciers lay immediately to the south of King Haakon Bay and seemed to form a continuation of the main range. Between this secondary range and the pass above our camp a great snow-upland sloped up to the inland ice-sheet and reached a rocky ridge that stretched athwart our path and seemed to bar the way. This ridge was a right-angled offshoot from the main ridge. Its chief features were four rocky peaks with spaces between that looked from a distance as though they might prove to be passes.

The weather was bad on Tuesday, May 16, and we stayed under the boat nearly all day. The quarters were cramped but gave full protection from the weather, and we regarded our little cabin with a great deal of satisfaction. Abundant meals of sea-elephant steak and liver increased our contentment. McNeish reported during the day that he had seen rats feeding on the scraps, but this interesting statement was not verified. One would not expect to find rats at such a spot, but there was a bare possibility that they had landed from a wreck and managed to survive the very rigorous conditions.

A fresh west-south-westerly breeze was blowing on the following morning (Wednesday, May 17), with misty squalls, sleet, and rain. I took Worsley with me on a pioneer journey to the west with the object of examining the country to be traversed at the beginning of the overland journey. We went round the seaward end of the snouted glacier, and after tramping about a mile over stony ground and snow-coated debris, we crossed some big ridges of scree and moraines. We found that there was good going for a sledge as far as the north-east corner of the bay, but did not get much information regarding the conditions farther on owing to the view becoming obscured by a snow-squall. We waited a quarter of an hour for the weather to clear but were forced to turn back without having seen more of the country. I had satisfied myself, however, that we could reach a good snow-slope leading apparently to the inland ice. Worsley reckoned from the chart that the distance from our camp to Husvik, on an east magnetic course, was seventeen geographical miles, but we could not expect to follow a direct line. The carpenter started making a sledge for use on the overland journey. The materials at his disposal were limited in quantity and scarcely suitable in quality.

We overhauled our gear on Thursday, May 18; and hauled our sledge to the lower edge of the snouted glacier. The vehicle proved heavy and cumbrous. We had to lift it empty over bare patches of rock along the shore, and I realised that it would be too heavy for three men to manage amid the snow-plains, glaciers, and peaks of the interior. Worsley and Crean were coming with me, and after consultation we decided to leave the sleeping-bags behind us and make the journey in very light marching order. We would take three days' provisions for each man in the form of sledging ration and biscuit. The food was to be packed in three sacks, so that each member of the party could carry his own supply. Then we were to take the Primus lamp filled with oil, the small cooker, the carpenter's adze (for use as an ice-axe), and the alpine rope, which made a total length of fifty feet when knotted. We might have to lower ourselves down steep slopes or cross crevassed glaciers. The filled lamp would provide six hot meals, which would consist of sledging ration boiled up with biscuit. There were two boxes of matches left, one full and the other partially used. We left the full box with the men at the camp and took the second box, which contained forty-eight matches. I was unfortunate as regarded footgear, since I had given away my heavy Burberry boots on the floe, and had now a comparatively light pair in poor condition. The carpenter assisted me by putting several screws in the sole of each boot with the object of providing a grip on the ice. The screws came out of the *James Caird*.

We turned in early that night, but sleep did not come to me. My mind was busy with the task of the following day. The weather was clear and the outlook for an early start in the morning was good. We were going to leave a weak party behind us in the camp. Vincent was still in the same condition, and he could not march. McNeish was pretty well broken up. The two men were not capable of managing for themselves and McCarthy must stay to look after them. He might have a difficult task if we failed to reach the whaling station. The distance to Husvik, according to the chart, was no more than seventeen geographical miles in a direct line, but we had very scanty knowledge of the conditions of the interior. No man had ever penetrated a mile from the coast of South Georgia at any point, and the whalers I knew regarded the country as inaccessible. During that day, while we were walking to the snouted glacier, we had seen three wild duck flying towards the head of the bay from the eastward. I hoped that the presence of these birds indicated tussock-land and not snow-fields and glaciers in the interior, but the hope was not a very bright one.

We turned out at 2 a.m. on the Friday morning and had our hoosh ready an hour later. The full moon was shining in a practically cloudless sky, its rays reflected gloriously from the pinnacles and crevassed ice of the adjacent glaciers. The huge peaks of the mountains stood in bold relief against the sky and threw dark shadows on the waters of the sound. There was no need for delay, and we made a start as soon as we had eaten our meal. McNeish walked about 200 yds with us; he could do no more. Then we said goodbye and he turned back to the camp. The first task was to get round the edge of the snouted glacier, which had points like fingers projecting towards the sea. The waves were reaching the points of these fingers, and we had to rush from one recess to another when the waters receded. We soon reached the east side of the glacier and noticed its great activity at this point. Changes had occurred within the preceding twenty-four hours. Some huge pieces had broken off, and the masses of mud and stone that were being driven before the advancing ice showed movement. The glacier was like a gigantic plough driving irresistibly towards the sea.

Lying on the beach beyond the glacier was wreckage that told of many ill-fated ships. We noticed stanchions of teakwood, liberally carved, that must have come from ships of the older type; iron-bound timbers with the iron almost rusted through; battered barrels and all the usual debris of the ocean. We had difficulties and anxieties of our own, but as we passed that graveyard of the sea we thought of the many tragedies written in the wave-worn fragments of lost vessels. We did not pause, and soon we were ascending a snow-slope heading due east on the last lap of our long trail.

The snow-surface was disappointing. Two days before we had

been able to move rapidly on hard, packed snow; now we sank over our ankles at each step and progress was slow. After two hours' steady climbing we were 2500 ft. above sea-level. The weather continued fine and calm, and as the ridges drew nearer and the western coast of the island spread out below, the bright moonlight showed us that the interior was broken tremendously. High peaks, impassable cliffs, steep snow-slopes, and sharply descending glaciers were prominent features in all directions, with stretches of snow-plain overlaying the ice-sheet of the interior. The slope we were ascending mounted to a ridge and our course lay direct to the top. The moon, which proved a good friend during this journey, threw a long shadow at one point and told us that the surface was broken in our path. Warned in time, we avoided a huge hole capable of swallowing an army. The bay was now about three miles away, and the continued roaring of a big glacier at the head of the bay came to our ears. This glacier, which we had noticed during the stay at Peggotty Camp, seemed to be calving almost continuously.

I had hoped to get a view of the country ahead of us from the top of the slope, but as the surface became more level beneath our feet, a thick fog drifted down. The moon became obscured and produced a diffused light that was more trying than darkness, since it illuminated the fog without guiding our steps. We roped ourselves together as a precaution against holes, crevasses, and precipices, and I broke trail through the soft snow. With almost the full length of the rope between myself and the last man we were able to steer an approximately straight course, since, if I veered to the right or the left when marching into the blank wall of the fog, the last man on the rope could shout a direction. So, like a ship with its 'port', 'starboard', 'steady', we tramped through the fog for the next two hours.

Then, as daylight came, the fog thinned and lifted, and from an elevation of about 3000 ft. we looked down on what seemed to be a huge frozen lake with its farther shores still obscured by the fog. We halted there to eat a bit of biscuit while we discussed whether we would go down and cross the flat surface of the lake, or keep on the ridge we had already reached. I decided to go down, since the lake lay on our course. After an hour of comparatively easy travel through the snow we noticed the thin beginnings of crevasses. Soon they were increasing in size and showing fractures, indicating that we were travelling on a glacier. As the daylight brightened the fog dissipated; the lake could be seen more clearly, but still we could not discover its east shore. A little later the fog lifted completely, and then we saw that our lake stretched to the horizon, and realised suddenly that we were looking down upon the open sea on the east coast of the island. The slight pulsation at the shore showed that the sea was not even frozen; it was the bad light that had deceived us. Evidently we were at the top of Possession Bay, and the island at that point could not be more than five miles across from the head of King Haakon Bay. Our rough chart was inaccurate. There was nothing for it but to start up the glacier again. That was about seven o'clock in the morning, and by nine o'clock we had more than recovered our lost ground. We regained the ridge and then struck southeast, for the chart showed that two more bays indented the coast before Stromness. It was comforting to realise that we would have the eastern water in sight during our journey, although we could see there was no way around the shore line owing to steep cliffs and glaciers. Men lived in houses lit by electric light on the east coast. News of the outside world waited us there, and, above all, the east coast meant for us the means of rescuing the twenty-two men we had left on Elephant Island.

CHAPTER 10

Across South Georgia

The sun rose in the sky with every appearance of a fine day, and we grew warmer as we toiled through the soft snow. Ahead of us lay the ridges and spurs of a range of mountains, the transverse range that we had noticed from the bay. We were travelling over a gently rising plateau, and at the end of an hour we found ourselves growing uncomfortably hot. Years before, on an earlier expedition, I had declared that I would never again growl at the heat of the sun, and my resolution had been strengthened during the boat journey. I called it to mind as the sun beat fiercely on the blinding white snow-slope. After passing an area of crevasses we paused for our first meal. We dug a hole in the snow about three feet deep with the adze and put the Primus into it. There was no wind at the moment, but a gust might come suddenly. A hot hoosh was soon eaten and we plodded on towards a sharp ridge between two of the peaks already mentioned. By 11 a.m. we were almost at the crest. The slope had become precipitous and it was necessary to cut steps as we advanced. The adze proved an excellent instrument for this purpose, a blow sufficing to provide a foothold. Anxiously but hopefully I cut the last few steps and stood upon the razor-back, while the other men held the rope and waited for my news. The outlook was disappointing. I looked down a sheer precipice to a chaos of crumpled ice 1,500 ft. below. There was no way down for us. The country to the east was a great snow upland, sloping upwards for a distance of seven or eight miles to a height of over 4000 ft. To the north it fell away steeply in glaciers into the bays, and to the south it was broken by huge outfalls from the inland ice-sheet. Our path lay between the glaciers and the outfalls, but first we had to descend from the ridge on which we stood. Cutting steps with the adze, we moved in a lateral direction round the base of a dolomite, which blocked our view to the north. The same precipice confronted us. Away to the north-east there appeared to be a snow-slope that might give a path to the lower country, and so we retraced our steps down the long slope that had taken us three hours to climb. We were at the bottom in an hour. We were now feeling the strain of the unaccustomed marching. We had done little walking since January and our muscles were out of tune. Skirting the base of the mountain above us, we came to a gigantic *bergschrund*, a mile and a half long and 1000 ft. deep. This tremendous gully, cut in the snow and ice by the fierce winds blowing round the mountain, was semicircular in form, and it ended in a gentle incline. We passed through it, under the towering precipice of ice, and at the far end we had another meal and a short rest. This was at 12:30 p.m. Half a pot of steaming Bovril ration warmed us up, and when we marched again ice-inclines at angles of 45 degrees did not look quite as formidable as before.

Once more we started for the crest. After another weary climb we reached the top. The snow lay thinly on blue ice at the ridge, and we had to cut steps over the last fifty yards. The same precipice lay below, and my eyes searched vainly for a way down. The hot sun had loosened the snow, which was now in a treacherous condition, and we had to pick our way carefully. Looking back, we could see that a fog was rolling up behind us and meeting in the valleys a fog that was coming up from the east. The creeping grey clouds were a plain warning that we must get down to lower levels before becoming enveloped.

The ridge was studded with peaks, which prevented us getting a clear view either to the right or to the left. The situation in this respect seemed no better at other points within our reach, and I had to decide that our course lay back the way we had come. The afternoon was wearing on and the fog was rolling up ominously from the west. It was of the utmost importance for us to get down into the next valley before dark. We were now up 4500 ft. and the night temperature at that elevation would be very low. We had no tent and no sleeping-bags, and our clothes had endured much rough usage and had weathered many storms during the last ten months. In the distance, down the valley below us, we could see tussock-grass close to the shore, and if we could get down it might be possible to dig out a hole in one of the lower snow-banks, line it with dry grass, and make ourselves fairly comfortable for the night. Back we went, and after a detour we reached the top of another ridge in the fading light. After a glance over the top I turned to the anxious faces of the two men behind me and said, 'Come on, boys.' Within a minute they stood beside me on the ice-ridge. The surface fell away at a sharp incline in front of us, but it merged into a snow-slope. We could not see the bottom clearly owing to mist and bad light, and the possibility of the slope ending in a sheer fall occurred to us; but the fog that was creeping up behind allowed no time for hesitation. We descended slowly at first, cutting steps in the hard snow; then the surface became softer, indicating that the gradient was less severe. There could be no turning back now, so we unroped and slid in the fashion of youthful days. When we stopped on a snow-bank at the foot of the slope we found that we had descended at least 900 ft. in two or three minutes. We looked back and saw the grey fingers of the fog appearing on the ridge, as though reaching after the intruders into untrodden wilds. But we had escaped.

The country to the east was an ascending snow upland dividing the glaciers of the north coast from the outfalls of the south. We had seen from the top that our course lay between two huge masses of crevasses, and we thought that the road ahead lay clear. This belief and the increasing cold made us abandon the idea of camping. We had another meal at 6 p.m. A little breeze made cooking difficult in spite of the shelter provided for the cooker by a hole. Crean was the cook, and Worsley and I lay on the snow to windward of the lamp so as to break the wind with our bodies. The meal over, we started up the long, gentle ascent. Night was upon us, and for an hour we plodded along in almost complete darkness, watching warily for signs of crevasses. Then about 8 p.m. a glow which we had seen behind the jagged peaks resolved itself into the full moon, which rose ahead of us and made a silver pathway for our feet. Along that pathway in the wake of the moon we advanced in safety, with the shadows cast by the edges of crevasses showing black on either side of us. Onwards and upwards through soft snow we marched, resting now and then on hard patches which had revealed themselves by glittering ahead of us in the white light. By midnight we were again at an elevation of about 4000 ft. Still we were following the light, for as the moon swung round towards the north-east our path curved in that direction. The friendly moon seemed to pilot our weary feet. We could have had no better guide. If in bright daylight we had made that march we would have followed the course that was traced for us that night.

Midnight found us approaching the edge of a great snowfield, pierced by isolated nunataks which cast long shadows like black rivers across the white expanse. A gentle slope to the north-east lured our all-too-willing feet in that direction. We thought that at the base of the slope lay Stromness Bay. After we had descended about 300 ft. a thin wind began to attack us. We had now been on the march for over twenty hours, only halting for our occasional meals. Wisps of cloud drove over the high peaks to the southward, warning us that wind and snow were likely to come. After 1 a.m. we cut a pit in the snow, piled up loose snow around it, and started the Primus again. The hot food gave us another renewal of energy. Worsley and Crean sang their old songs when the Primus was going merrily. Laughter was in our hearts, though not on our parched and cracked lips.

We were up and away again within half an hour, still downward to the coast. We felt almost sure now that we were above Stromness Bay. A dark object down at the foot of the slope looked like Mutton Island, which lies off Husvik. I suppose our desires were giving wings to our fancies, for we pointed out joyfully various landmarks revealed by the now vagrant light of the moon, whose friendly face was cloud-swept. Our high hopes were soon shattered. Crevasses warned us that we were on another glacier, and soon we looked down almost to the seaward edge of the great riven ice-mass. I knew there was no glacier in Stromness and realised that this must be Fortuna Glacier. The disappointment was severe. Back we turned and tramped up the glacier again, not directly tracing our steps but working at a tangent to the south-east. We were very tired.

At 5 a.m. we were at the foot of the rocky spurs of the range. We were tired, and the wind that blew down from the heights was chilling us. We decided to get down under the lee of a rock for a rest. We put our sticks and the adze on the snow, sat down on them as close to one another as possible, and put our arms round each other. The wind was bringing a little drift with it and the white dust lay on our clothes. I thought that we might be able to keep warm and have half an hour's rest this way. Within a minute my two companions were fast asleep. I realised that it would be disastrous if we all slumbered together, for sleep under such conditions merges into death. After five minutes I shook them into consciousness again, told them that they had slept for half an hour, and gave the word for a fresh start. We were so stiff that for the first two or three hundred yards we marched with our knees bent. A jagged line of peaks with a gap like a broken tooth confronted us. This was the ridge that runs in a southerly direction from Fortuna Bay, and our course eastward to Stromness lay across it. A very steep slope led up to the ridge and an icy wind burst through the gap.

We went through the gap at 6 a.m. with anxious hearts as well as weary bodies. If the farther slope had proved impassable our situation would have been almost desperate; but the worst was turning to the best for us. The twisted, wavelike rock-formations of Husvik Harbour appeared right ahead in the opening of dawn. Without a word we shook hands with one another. To our minds the journey was over, though as a matter of fact twelve miles of difficult country had still to be traversed. A gentle snow-slope descended at our feet towards a valley that separated our ridge from the hills immediately behind Husvik, and as we stood gazing Worsley said solemnly, 'Boss, it looks too good to be true!' Down we went, to be checked presently by the sight of water 2500 ft. below. We could see the little wave-ripples on the black beach, penguins strutting to and fro, and dark objects that looked like seals lolling lazily on the sand. This was an eastern arm of Fortuna Bay, separated by the ridge from the arm we had seen below us during the night. The slope we were traversing appeared to end in a precipice above this beach. But our revived spirits were not to be damped by difficulties on the last stage of the journey, and we camped cheerfully for breakfast. Whilst Worsley and Crean were digging a hole for the lamp and starting the cooker I climbed a ridge above us, cutting steps with the adze, in order to secure an extended view of the country below. At 6.30 a.m. I thought I heard the sound of a steam-whistle. I dared not be certain, but I knew that the men at the whaling-station would be called from their beds about that time. Descending to the camp I told the

others, and in intense excitement we watched the chronometer for
seven o'clock, when the whalers would be summoned to work.
Right to the minute the steam-whistle came to us, borne clearly on
the wind across the intervening miles of rock and snow. Never had
any one of us heard sweeter music. It was the first sound created
by outside human agency that had come to our ears since we left
Stromness Bay in December 1914. That whistle told us that men
were living near, that ships were ready, and that within a few hours
we should be on our way back to Elephant Island to the rescue of
the men waiting there under the watch and ward of Wild. It was a
moment hard to describe. Pain and ache, boat journeys, marches,
hunger and fatigue seemed to belong to the limbo of forgotten
things, and there remained only the perfect contentment that
comes of work accomplished.

My examination of the country from a higher point had not
provided definite information, and after descending I put the situation before Worsley and Crean. Our obvious course lay down
a snow-slope in the direction of Husvik. 'Boys,' I said, 'this
snow-slope seems to end in a precipice, but perhaps there is no
precipice. If we don't go down we shall have to make a detour of
at least five miles before we reach level going What shall it be?'
They both replied at once, 'Try the slope.' So we started away
again downwards. We abandoned the Primus lamp, now empty,
at the breakfast camp and carried with us one ration and a biscuit
each. The deepest snow we had yet encountered clogged our feet,
but we plodded downward, and after descending about 500 ft.,
reducing our altitude to 2000 ft. above sea-level, we thought we
saw the way clear ahead. A steep gradient of blue ice was the next
obstacle. Worsley and Crean got a firm footing in a hole excav-
ated with the adze and then lowered me as I cut steps until the full
50 ft. of our alpine rope was out. Then I made a hole big enough
for the three of us, and the other two men came down the steps.
My end of the rope was was anchored to the adze and I had settled
myself in the hole braced for a strain in case they slipped. When
we all stood in the second hole I went down again to make more
steps, and in this laborious fashion we spent two hours descending
about 500 ft. Halfway down we had to strike away diagonally to
the left, for we noticed that the fragments of ice loosened by the
adze were taking a leap into space at the bottom of the slope.

Eventually we got off the steep ice, very gratefully, at a point where some rocks protruded, and we could see then that there was a perilous precipice directly below the point where we had started to cut steps. A slide down a slippery slope, with the adze and our cooker going ahead, completed this descent, and incidentally did considerable damage to our much-tried trousers.

When we picked ourselves up at the bottom we were not more than 1500 ft. above the sea. The slope was comparatively easy. Water was running beneath the snow, making 'pockets' between the rocks that protruded above the white surface. The shells of snow over these pockets were traps for our feet; but we scrambled down, and presently came to patches of tussock. A few minutes later we reached the sandy beach. The tracks of some animals were to be seen, and we were puzzled until I remembered that reindeer, brought from Norway, had been placed on the island and now ranged along the lower land of the eastern coast. We did not pause to investigate. Our minds were set upon reaching the haunts of man, and at our best speed we went along the beach to another rising ridge of tussock. Here we saw the first evidence of the proximity of man, whose work, as is so often the ease, was one of destruction. A recently killed seal was lying there, and presently we saw several other bodies bearing the marks of bullet-wounds. I learned later that men from the whaling-station at Stromness sometimes go round to Fortuna Bay by boat to shoot seals.

Noon found us well up the slope on the other side of the bay working east-south-east, and half an hour later we were on a flat plateau, with one more ridge to cross before we descended into Husvik. I was leading the way over this plateau when I suddenly found myself up to my knees in water and quickly sinking deeper through the snow-crust. I flung myself down and called to the others to do the same, so as to distribute our weight on the treacherous surface. We were on top of a small lake, snow-covered. After lying still for a few moments we got to our feet and walked delicately, like Agag, for 200 yds., until a rise in the surface showed us that we were clear of the lake.

At 1.30 p.m. we climbed round a final ridge and saw a little steamer, a whaling-boat, entering the bay 2500 ft below. A few moments later, as we hurried forward, the masts of a sailing-ship lying at a wharf came in sight. Minute figures moving to and fro about the boats caught our gaze, and then we saw the sheds and factory of Stromness whaling-station. We paused and shook hands, a form of mutual congratulation that had seemed necessary on four other occasions in the course of the expedition. The first time was when we landed on Elephant Island, the second when we reached South Georgia, and the third when we reached the ridge and saw the snow-slope stretching below on the first day of the overland journey, then when we saw Husvik rocks.

Cautiously we started down the slope that led to warmth and comfort. The last lap of the journey proved extraordinarily difficult. Vainly we searched for a safe, or a reasonably safe, way down the steep ice-clad mountain-side. The sole possible pathway seemed to be a channel cut by water running from the upland. Down through icy water we followed the course of this stream. We were wet to the waist, shivering, cold, and tired. Presently our ears detected an unwelcome sound that might have been musical under other conditions. It was the splashing of a waterfall, and we were at the wrong end. When we reached the top of this fall we peered over cautiously and discovered that there was a drop of 25 or 30 ft., with impassable ice-cliffs on both sides. To go up again was scarcely thinkable in our utterly wearied condition. The way down was through the waterfall itself. We made fast one end of our rope to a boulder with some difficulty, due to the fact that the rocks had been worn smooth by the running water. Then Worsley and I lowered Crean, who was the heaviest man. He disappeared altogether in the falling water and came out gasping at the bottom. I went next, sliding down the rope, and Worsley, who was the lightest and most nimble member of the party, came last. At the bottom of the fall we were able to stand again on dry land. The rope could not be recovered. We had flung down the adze from the top of the fall and also the logbook and the cooker wrapped in one of our blouses. That was all, except our wet clothes, that we brought out of the Antarctic, which we had entered a year and a half before with well-found ship, full equipment, and high hopes. That was all of tangible things; but in memories we were rich. We had pierced the veneer of outside things. We had 'suffered, starved, and triumphed, grovelled down yet grasped at glory, grown bigger in the bigness of the whole.' We had seen God in his splendours, heard the text that Nature renders. We had reached the naked soul of man.

Shivering with cold, yet with hearts light and happy, we set off towards the whaling-station, now not more than a mile and a half distant. The difficulties of the journey lay behind us. We tried to straighten ourselves up a bit, for the thought that there might be women at the station made us painfully conscious of our uncivilised appearance. Our beards were long and our hair was matted. We were unwashed and the garments that we had worn for nearly a year without a change were tattered and stained. Three more unpleasant-looking ruffians could hardly have been imagined. Worsley produced several safety-pins from some corner of his garments and effected some temporary repairs that really emphasised his general disrepair. Down we hurried, and when quite close to the station we met two small boys ten or twelve years of age. I asked these lads where the manager's house was situated. They did not answer. They gave us one look – a comprehensive look that did not need to be repeated. Then they ran from us as fast as their legs would carry them. We reached the outskirts of the station and passed through the 'digesting-house', which was dark inside. Emerging at the other end, we met an old man, who started as if he had seen the Devil himself and gave us no time to ask any question. He hurried away. This greeting was not friendly. Then we came to the wharf, where the man in charge stuck to his station. I asked him if Mr Sorlle (the manager) was in the house.

'Yes,' he said as he stared at us.

'We would like to see him,' said I.

'Who are you?' he asked.

'We have lost our ship and come over the island,' I replied.

'You have come over the island?' he said in a tone of entire disbelief.

The man went towards the manager's house and we followed him. I learned afterwards that he said to Mr Sorlle: 'There are three funny-looking men outside, who say they have come over the island and they know you. I have left them outside.' A very necessary precaution from his point of view.

Mr Sorlle came out to the door and said, 'Well?'

'Don't you know me?" I said.

'I know your voice,' he replied doubtfully. 'You're the mate of the *Daisy*.'

'My name is Shackleton,' I said.

Immediately he put out his hand and said, 'Come in. Come in.'
'Tell me, when was the war over?' I asked.

'The war is not over,' he answered. 'Millions are being killed. Europe is mad. The world is mad.'

Mr Sorlle's hospitality had no bounds. He would scarcely let us wait to remove our freezing boots before he took us into his house and gave us seats in a warm and comfortable room. We were in no condition to sit in anybody's house until we had washed and got into clean clothes, but the kindness of the station-manager was proof even against the unpleasantness of being in a room with us. He gave us coffee and cakes in the Norwegian fashion, and then showed us upstairs to the bathroom, where we shed our rags and scrubbed ourselves luxuriously.

Mr Sorlle's kindness did not end with his personal care for the three wayfarers who had come to his door. While we were washing he gave orders for one of the whaling-vessels to be prepared at once in order that it might leave that night for the other side of the island and pick up the three men there. The whalers knew King Haakon Bay, though they never worked on that side of the island. Soon we were clean again. Then we put on delightful new clothes supplied from the station stores and got rid of our superfluous hair. Within an hour or two we had ceased to be savages and had become civilised men again. Then came a splendid meal, while Mr Sorlle told us of the arrangements he had made and we discussed plans for the rescue of the main party on Elephant Island.

I arranged that Worsley should go with the relief ship to show the exact spot where the carpenter and his two companions were camped, while I started to prepare for the relief of the party on Elephant Island. The whaling-vessel that was going round to King Haakon Bay was expected back on the Monday morning, and was to call at Grytviken Harbour, the port from which we had sailed in December 1914, in order that the magistrate resident there might be informed of the fate of the *Endurance*. It was possible that letters were awaiting us there. Worsley went aboard the whaler at ten o'clock that night and turned in. The next day the relief ship entered King Haakon Bay and he reached Peggotty Camp in a boat. The three men were delighted beyond measure to know that we had made the crossing in safety and that their wait under the upturned *James Caird* was ended. Curiously enough, they did not recognise Worsley, who had left them a hairy, dirty ruffian and had returned his spruce and shaven self. They thought he was one of the whalers. When one of them asked why no member of the party had come round with the relief, Worsley said, 'What do you mean?' 'We thought the Boss or one of the others would come round,' they explained. 'What's the matter with you?' said Worsley. Then it suddenly dawned upon them that they were talking to the man who had been their close companion for a year and a half. Within a few minutes the whalers had moved our bits of gear into their boat. They towed off the *James Caird* and hoisted her to the deck of their ship. Then they started on the return voyage. Just at dusk on Monday afternoon they entered Stromness Bay, where the men of the whaling-station mustered on the beach to receive the rescued party and to examine with professional interest the boat we had navigated across 800 miles of the stormy ocean they knew so well.

When I look back at those days I have no doubt that Providence guided us, not only across those snowfields, but across the storm-white sea that separated Elephant Island from our landing-place on South Georgia. I know that during that long and racking march of thirty-six hours over the unnamed mountains and glaciers of South Georgia it seemed to me often that we were four, not three. I said nothing to my companions on the point, but afterwards Worsley said to me, 'Boss, I had a curious feeling on the march that there was another person with us.' Crean confessed to the same idea. One feels 'the dearth of human words, the roughness of mortal speech' in trying to describe things intangible, but a record of our journeys would be incomplete without a reference to a subject very near to our hearts.

CHAPTER II

The rescue

Our first night at the whaling-station was blissful. Crean and I shared a beautiful room in Mr Sorlle's house, with electric light and two beds, warm and soft. We were so comfortable that we were unable to sleep. Late at night a steward brought us tea, bread and butter and cakes, and we lay in bed revelling in the luxury of it all. Outside a dense snow-storm, which started two hours after our arrival and lasted until the following day, was swirling and driving about the mountain-slopes. We were thankful indeed that we had made a place of safety, for it would have gone hard with us if we had been out on the mountains that night. Deep snow lay everywhere when we got up the following morning.

After breakfast Mr Sorlle took us round to Husvik in a motor-launch. We were listening avidly to his account of the war and of all that had happened while we were out of the world of men. We were like men arisen from the dead to a world gone mad. Our minds accustomed themselves gradually to the tales of nations in arms, of deathless courage and unimagined slaughter, of a world-conflict that had grown beyond all conceptions, of vast red battlefields in grimmest contrast with the frigid whiteness we had left behind us. The reader may not realise quite how difficult it was for us to envisage nearly two years of the most stupendous war of history. The locking of the armies in the trenches, the sinking of the Lusitania, the murder of Nurse Cavell, the use of poison-gas and liquid fire, the submarine warfare, the Gallipoli campaign, the hundred other incidents of the war, almost stunned us at first, and then our minds began to compass the train of events and develop a perspective. I suppose our experience was unique. No other civilised men could have been as blankly ignorant of world-shaking happenings as we were when we reached Stromness Whaling Station.

I heard the first rumour of the *Aurora*'s misadventures in the Ross Sea from Mr Sorlle. Our host could tell me very little. He had been informed that the *Aurora* had broken away from winter quarters in McMurdo Sound and reached New Zealand after a long drift, and that there was no news of the shore party. His information was indefinite as to details, and I had to wait until I reached the Falkland Islands some time later before getting a definite report concerning the *Aurora*. The rumour that had reached South Georgia, however, made it more than ever important that I should bring out the rest of the Weddell Sea party quickly, so as to free myself for whatever effort was required on the Ross Sea side.

When we reached Husvik that Sunday morning we were warmly greeted by the magistrate (Mr Bernsten), whom I knew of old, and the other members of the little community. Moored in the harbour was one of the largest of the whalers, the *Southern Sky*, owned by an English company but now laid up for the winter. I had no means of getting into communication with the owners without dangerous delay, and on my accepting all responsibility Mr Bernsten made arrangements for me to take this ship down to Elephant Island. I wrote out an agreement with Lloyd's for the insurance of the ship. Captain Thom, an old friend of the Expedition, happened to be in Husvik with his ship, the *Orwell*, loading oil for use in Britain's munition works, and he at once volunteered to come with us in any capacity. I asked him to come as captain of the *Southern Sky*. There was no difficulty about getting a crew. The whalers were eager to assist in the rescue of men in distress. They started work that Sunday to prepare and stow the ship. Parts of the engines were ashore, but willing hands made light labour. I purchased from the station stores all the stores and equipment required, including special comforts for the men we hoped to rescue, and by Tuesday morning the *Southern Sky* was ready to sail. I feel it is my duty as well as my pleasure to thank here the Norwegian whalers of South Georgia for the sympathetic hands they stretched out to us in our need. Among memories of kindness received in many lands sundered by the seas, the recollection of the hospitality and help given to me in South Georgia ranks high. There is a brotherhood of the sea. The men who go down to the sea in ships, serving and suffering, fighting their endless battle against the caprice of wind and ocean, bring into their own horizons the perils and troubles of their brother sailormen.

The *Southern Sky* was ready on Tuesday morning, and at nine o'clock we steamed out of the bay, while the whistles of the whaling-station sounded a friendly farewell. We had forgathered aboard Captain Thom's ship on the Monday night with several whaling captains who were bringing up their sons to their own profession. They were 'old stagers' with faces lined and seamed by the storms of half a century, and they were even more interested in the story of our voyage from Elephant Island than the younger generation was. They congratulated us on having accomplished a remarkable boat journey. I do not wish to belittle our success with the pride that apes humility. Under Providence we had overcome great difficulties and dangers, and it was pleasant to tell the tale to men who knew those sullen and treacherous southern seas.

McCarthy, McNeish, and Vincent had been landed on the Monday afternoon. They were already showing some signs of increasing strength under a regime of warm quarters and abundant food. The carpenter looked woefully thin after he had emerged from a bath. He must have worn a lot of clothes when he landed from the boat, and I did not realise how he had wasted till I saw him washed and changed. He was a man over fifty years of age, and the strain had told upon him more than upon the rest of us. The rescue came just in time for him.

The early part of the voyage down to Elephant Island in the Southern Sky was uneventful. At noon on Tuesday, May 23, we were at sea and steaming at ten knots on a south-westerly course. We made good progress, but the temperature fell very low, and the signs gave me some cause for anxiety as to the probability of encountering ice. On the third night out the sea seemed to grow silent. I looked over the side and saw a thin film of ice. The sea was freezing around us and the ice gradually grew thicker, reducing our speed to about five knots. Then lumps of old pack began to appear among the new ice. I realised that an advance through pack-ice was out of the question. The *Southern Sky* was a steel-built steamer, and her structure, while strong to resist the waves, would not endure the blows of masses of ice. So I took the ship north, and at daylight on Friday we got clear of the pancake-ice. We skirted westward, awaiting favourable conditions. The morning of the 28th was dull and overcast, with little wind. Again the ship's head was turned to the south-west, but at 3 p.m. a definite line of pack showed up on the horizon. We were about 70 miles from Elephant Island, but there was no possibility of taking the steamer through the ice that barred the way. Northwest again we turned. We were directly north of the island on the following day, and I made another move south. Heavy pack formed an impenetrable barrier.

To admit failure at this stage was hard, but the facts had to be faced. The *Southern Sky* could not enter ice of even moderate thickness. The season was late, and we could not be sure that the ice would open for many months, though my opinion was that the pack would not become fast in that quarter even in the winter, owing to the strong winds and currents. The *Southern Sky* could carry coal for ten days only, and we had been out six days. We were 500 miles from the Falkland Islands and about 600 miles from South Georgia. So I determined that, since we could not wait about for an opening, I would proceed to the Falklands, get a more suitable vessel either locally or from England, and make a second attempt to reach Elephant Island from that point.

We encountered very bad weather on the way up, but in the early afternoon of May 31 we arrived at Port Stanley, where the cable provided a link with the outer world. The harbour-master came out to meet us, and after we had dropped anchor I went ashore and met the Governor, Mr Douglas Young. He offered me his assistance at once. He telephoned to Mr Harding, the manager of the Falkland Islands station, and I learned, to my keen regret, that no ship of the type required was available at the islands. That evening I cabled to London a message to His Majesty the King, the first account of the loss of the *Endurance* and the subsequent adventures of the Expedition. The next day I received the following message from the King:

> Rejoice to hear of your safe arrival in the Falkland Islands and trust your comrades on Elephant Island may soon be rescued.
> GEORGE R. I.

The events of the days that followed our arrival at the Falkland Islands I will not attempt to describe in detail. My mind was bent upon the rescue of the party on Elephant Island at the earliest possible moment. Winter was advancing, and I was fully conscious that the lives of some of my comrades might be the price of unnecessary delay. A proposal had been made to send a relief ship from England, but she could not reach the southern seas for many weeks. In the meantime I got into communication with the Governments of the South American Republics by wireless and cable and asked if they had any suitable ship I could use for a rescue. I wanted a wooden ship capable of pushing into loose ice, with fair speed and a reasonable coal capacity. Messages of congratulation and goodwill were reaching me from all parts of the world, and the kindness of hundreds of friends in many lands was a very real comfort in a time of anxiety and stress.

The British Admiralty informed me that no suitable vessel was available in England and that no relief could be expected before October. I replied that October would be too late. Then the British Minister in Montevideo telegraphed me regarding a trawler named *Instituto de Pesca No. 1*, belonging to the Uruguayan Government. She was a stout little vessel, and the Government had generously offered to equip her with coal, provisions, clothing, etc., and send her across to the Falkland Islands for me to take down to Elephant Island. I accepted this offer gladly, and the trawler was in Port Stanley on June 10. We started south at once.

The weather was bad but the trawler made good progress, steaming steadily at about six knots, and in the bright, clear dawn of the third day we sighted the peaks of Elephant Island. Hope ran high; but our ancient enemy the pack was lying in wait, and within twenty miles of the island the trawler was stopped by an impenetrable barrier of ice. The pack lay in the form of a crescent, with a horn to the west of the ship stretching north. Steaming north-east, we reached another horn and saw that the pack, heavy and dense, then trended away to the east. We made an attempt to push into the ice, but it was so heavy that the trawler was held up at once and began to grind in the small thick floes, so we cautiously backed out. The propeller, going slowly, was not damaged, though any moment I feared we might strip the blades. The island lay on our starboard quarter, but there was no possibility of approaching it. The Uruguayan engineer reported to me that he had three days' coal left, and I had to give the order to turn back. A screen of fog hid the lower slopes of the island, and the men watching from the camp on the beach could not have seen the ship. Northward we steamed again, with the engines knocking badly, and after encountering a new gale, made Port Stanley with the bunkers nearly empty and the engines almost broken down. H.M.S. Glasgow was in the port, and the British sailors gave us a hearty welcome as we steamed in.

The Uruguayan Government offered to send the trawler to Punta Arenas and have her dry-docked there and made ready for another effort. One of the troubles on the voyage was that according to estimate the trawler could do ten knots on six tons of coal a day, which would have given us a good margin to allow for lying off the ice; but in reality, owing to the fact that she had not been in dock for a year, she only developed a speed of six knots on a consumption of ten tons a day. Time was precious and these preparations would have taken too long. I thanked the Government then for its very generous offer, and I want to say now that the kindness of the Uruguayans at this time earned my warmest gratitude. I ought to mention also the assistance given me by Lieut. Ryan, a Naval Reserve officer who navigated the trawler to the Falklands and came south on the attempt at relief. The *Instituto de Pesca* went off to Montevideo and I looked around for another ship.

A British mail-boat, the *Orita*, called at Port Stanley opportunely, and I boarded her with Worsley and Cretin and crossed to Punta Arenas in the Magellan Straits. The reception we received there was heartening. The members of the British Association of Magellanes took us to their hearts. Mr Allan McDonald was especially prominent in his untiring efforts to assist in the rescue of our twenty-two companions on Elephant Island. He worked day and night, and it was mainly due to him that within three days they had raised a sum of £1500 amongst themselves, chartered the schooner *Emma* and equipped her for our use. She was a forty-year-old oak schooner, strong and seaworthy, with an auxiliary oil-engine.

Out of the complement of ten men all told who were manning the ship, there were eight different nationalities; but they were all good fellows and understood perfectly what was wanted. The Chilean Government lent us a small steamer, the *Yelcho*, to tow us part of the way. She could not touch ice though, as she was built of steel. However, on July 12 we passed her our tow-rope and proceeded on our way. In bad weather we anchored next day, and

although the wind increased to a gale I could delay no longer, so
we hove up anchor in the early morning of the 14th. The strain on
the tow-rope was too great. With the crack of a gun the rope
broke. Next day the gale continued, and I will quote from the log
of the *Emma*, which Worsley kept as navigating officer.

> 9 a.m. – Fresh, increasing gale; very rough, lumpy sea.
>
> 10 a.m. – Tow-rope parted.
>
> 12 noon. – Similar weather.
>
> 1 p.m. – Tow-rope parted again. Set foresail and forestay-sail
> and steered south-east by south.
>
> 3 p.m. – *Yelcho* hailed us and said that the ship's bilges were full
> of water (so were our decks) and they were short of coal. Sir
> Ernest told them that they could return to harbour. After this
> the *Yelcho* steamed into San Sebastian Bay.

After three days of continuous bad weather we were left alone to
attempt once more to rescue the twenty-two men on Elephant
Island, for whom by this time I entertained very grave fears.

At dawn of Friday, July 21 we: were within a hundred miles of
the island; and we encountered the ice in the half-light. I waited
for the full day and then tried to push through. The little craft was
tossing in the heavy swell, and before she had been in the pack
for ten minutes she came down on a cake of ice and broke the
bobstay. Then the water-inlet of the motor choked with ice. The
schooner was tossing like a cork in the swell, and I saw after a few
bumps that she was actually lighter than the fragments of ice
around her. Progress under such conditions was out of the question. I worked the schooner out of the pack and stood to the east.
I ran her through a line of pack towards the south that night, but
was forced to turn to the north-east, for the ice trended in that
direction as far as I could see. We hove to for the night, which was
now sixteen hours long. The winter was well advanced and the
weather conditions were thoroughly bad. The ice to the southward was moving north rapidly. The motor-engine had broken
down and we were entirely dependent on the sails. We managed
to make a little southing during the next day, but noon found us
108 miles from the island. That night we lay off the ice in a gale,
hove to, and morning found the schooner iced up. The ropes,
cased in frozen spray, were as thick as a man's arm, and if the wind

had increased much we would have had to cut away the sails, since there was no possibility of lowering them. Some members of the scratch crew were played out by the cold and the violent tossing. The schooner was about seventy feet long, and she responded to the motions of the storm-racked sea in a manner that might have disconcerted the most seasoned sailors.

I took the schooner south at every chance, but always the line of ice blocked the way. The engineer, who happened to be an American, did things to the engines occasionally, but he could not keep them running, and, the persistent south winds were dead ahead. It was hard to turn back a third time, but I realised we could not reach the island under those conditions, and we must turn north in order to clear the ship of heavy masses of ice. So we set a northerly course, and after a tempestuous passage reached Port Stanley once more. This was the third reverse, but I did not abandon my belief that the ice would not remain fast around Elephant Island during the winter, whatever the armchair experts at home might say. We reached Port Stanley in the schooner on August 8, and I learned there that the ship *Discovery* was to leave England at once and would be at the Falkland Islands about the middle of September. My good friend the Governor said I could settle down at Port Stanley and take things quietly for a few weeks. The street of that port is about a mile and a half long. It has the slaughter-house at one end and the graveyard at the other. The chief distraction is to walk from the slaughter-house to the graveyard. For a change one may walk from the graveyard to the slaughter-house. Ellaline Terriss was born at Port Stanley – a fact not forgotten by the residents, but she has not lived there much since. I could not content myself to wait for six or seven weeks, knowing that six hundred miles away my comrades were in dire need. I asked the Chilean Government to send the *Yelcho*, the steamer that had towed us before, to take the schooner across to Punta Arenas, and they consented promptly, as they had done to every other request of mine. So in a north-west gale we went across, narrowly escaping disaster on the way, and reached Punta Arenas on August 14.

There was no suitable ship to be obtained. The weather was showing some signs of improvement, and I begged the Chilean Government to let me have the *Yelcho* for a last attempt to reach the island. She was a small steel-built steamer, quite unsuitable for work in the pack, but I promised that I would not touch the ice. The Government was willing to give me another chance, and on August 25 I started south on the fourth attempt at relief. This time Providence favoured us. The little steamer made a quick run down in comparatively fine weather, and I found as we neared Elephant Island that the ice was open. A southerly gale had sent it northward temporarily, and the *Yelcho* had her chance to slip through. We approached the island in a thick fog. I did not dare to wait for this to clear, and at 10 a.m. on August 30 we passed some stranded bergs. Then we saw the sea breaking on a reef, and I knew that we were just outside the island. It was an anxious moment, for we had still to locate the camp and the pack could not be trusted to allow time for a prolonged search in thick weather; but presently the fog lifted and revealed the cliffs and glaciers of Elephant Island. I proceeded to the east, and at 11.40 a.m. Worsley's keen eyes detected the camp, almost invisible under its covering of snow. The men ashore saw us at the same time, and we saw tiny black figures hurry to the beach and wave signals to us. We were about a mile and a half away from the camp. I turned the *Yelcho* in, and within half an hour reached the beach with Crean and some of the Chilean sailors. I saw a little figure on a surf-beaten rock and recognised Wild. As I came nearer I called out, 'Are you all well?' and he answered, 'We are all well, boss,' and then I heard three cheers. As I drew close to the rock I flung packets of cigarettes ashore; they fell on them like hungry tigers, for well I knew that for months tobacco was dreamed of and talked of. Some of the hands were in a rather bad way, but Wild had held the party together and kept hope alive in their hearts. There was no time then to exchange news or congratulations. I did not even go up the beach to see the camp, which Wild assured me had been much improved. A heavy sea was running and a change of wind might bring the ice back at any time. I hurried the party aboard with all possible speed, taking also the records of the Expedition and essential portions of equipment. Everybody was aboard the *Yelcho* within an hour, and we steamed north at the little steamer's best speed. The ice was open still, and nothing worse than an expanse of stormy ocean separated us from the South American coast.

During the run up to Punta Arenas I heard Wild's story, and blessed again the cheerfulness and resource that had served the party so well during four and a half months of privation. The twenty-two men on Elephant Island were just at the end of their resources when the *Yelcho* reached them. Wild had husbanded the scanty stock of food as far as possible and had fought off the devils of despondency and despair on that little sand-spit, where the party had a precarious foothold between the grim ice-fields and the treacherous, ice-strewn sea. The pack had opened occasionally, but much of the time the way to the north had been barred. The *Yelcho* had arrived at the right moment. Two days earlier she could not have reached the island, and a few hours later the pack may have been impenetrable again. Wild had reckoned that help would come in August, and every morning he had packed his kit, in cheerful anticipation that proved infectious, as I have no doubt it was meant to be. One of the party to whom I had said 'Well, you all were packed up ready,' replied, 'You see, boss, Wild never gave up hope, and whenever the sea was at all clear of ice he rolled up his sleeping-bag and said to all hands, "Roll up your sleeping-bags, boys; the boss may come today."' And so it came to pass that we suddenly came out of the fog, and, from a black outlook, in an hour all were in safety homeward bound. The food was eked out with seal and penguin meat, limpets, and seaweed. Seals had been scarce, but the supply of penguins had held out fairly well during the first three months. The men were down to the last Bovril ration, the only form of hot drink they had, and had scarcely four days' food in hand at the time of the rescue. The camp was in constant danger of being buried by the snow, which drifted heavily from the heights behind, and the men moved the accumulations with what implements they could provide. There was danger that the camp would become completely invisible from the sea, so that a rescue party might look for it in vain.

'It had been arranged that a gun should be fired from the relief ship when she got near the island,' said Wild. 'Many times when the glaciers were "calving", and chunks fell off with a report like a gun, we thought that it was the real thing, and after a time we got to distrust these signals. As a matter of fact, we saw the *Yelcho* before we heard any gun. It was an occasion one will not easily forget. We were just assembling for lunch to the call of

"Lunch O!" and I was serving out the soup, which was particularly good that day, consisting of boiled seal's backbone, limpets, and seaweed, when there was another hail from Marston of "Ship O!" Some of the men thought it was "Lunch O!" over again but when there was another yell from Marston lunch had no further attractions. The ship was about a mile and a half away and steaming past us. A smoke-signal was the agreed sign from the shore, and, catching up somebody's coat that was lying about, I struck a pick into a tin of kerosene kept for the purpose, poured it over the coat, and set it alight. It flared instead of smoking; but that didn't matter, for you had already recognised the spot where you had left us and the *Yelcho* was turning in.'

We encountered bad weather on the way back to Punta Arenas, and the little *Yelcho* laboured heavily; but she had light hearts aboard. We entered the Straits of Magellan on September 3 and reached Rio Secco at 8 a.m. I went ashore, found a telephone, and told the Governor and my friends at Punta Arenas that the men were safe. Two hours later we were at Punta Arenas, where we were given a welcome none of us is likely to forget. The Chilean people were no less enthusiastic than the British residents. The police had been instructed to spread the news that the *Yelcho* was coming with the rescued men, and lest the message should fail to reach some people, the fire-alarm had been rung. The whole populace appeared to be in the streets. It was a great reception, and with the strain of long, anxious months lifted at last, we were in a mood to enjoy it.

The next few weeks were crowded ones, but I will not attempt here to record their history in detail. I received congratulations and messages of friendship and good cheer from all over the world, and my heart went out to the good people who had remembered my men and myself in the press of terrible events on the battlefields. The Chilean Government placed the *Yelcho* at my disposal to take the men up to Valparaiso and Santiago. We reached Valparaiso on September 27. Everything that could swim in the way of a boat was out to meet us, the crews of Chilean warships were lined up, and at least thirty thousand thronged the streets. I lectured in Santiago on the following evening for the British Red Cross and a Chilean naval charity. The Chilean flag and the Union Jack were draped together, the band played the Chilean national anthem, 'God Save the King', and the 'Marseillaise', and the Chilean Minister for Foreign Affairs spoke from the platform and pinned an Order on my coat. I saw the President and thanked him for the help that he had given a British expedition. His Government had spent 4000 pounds on coal alone. In reply he recalled the part that British sailors had taken in the making of the Chilean Navy.

The Chilean Railway Department provided a special train to take us across the Andes, and I proceeded to Montevideo in order to thank personally the President and Government of Uruguay for the help they had given generously in the earlier relief voyages. We were entertained royally at various spots en route. We went also to Buenos Ayres on a brief call. Then we crossed the Andes again. I had made arrangements by this time for the men and the staff to go to England. All hands were keen to take their places in the Empire's fighting forces. My own immediate task was the relief of the marooned Ross Sea party, for news had come to me of the *Aurora*'s long drift in the Ross Sea and of her return in a damaged condition to New Zealand. Worsley was to come with me. We hurried northwards via Panama, steamship and train companies giving us everywhere the most cordial and generous assistance, and caught at San Francisco a steamer that would get us to New Zealand at the end of November. I had been informed that the New Zealand Government was making arrangements for the relief of the Ross Sea party, but my information was incomplete, and I was very anxious to be on the spot myself as quickly as possible.

CHAPTER 12

Elephant Island

The twenty-two men who had been left behind on Elephant Island were under the command of Wild, in whom I had absolute confidence, and the account of their experiences during the long four and a half months' wait while I was trying to get help to them, I have secured from their various diaries, supplemented by details which I obtained in conversation on the voyage back to civilisation.

The first consideration, which was even more important than that of food, was to provide shelter. The semi-starvation during the drift on the ice-floe, added to the exposure in the boats, and the inclemencies of the weather encountered after our landing on Elephant Island, had left its mark on a good many of them. Rickenson, who bore up gamely to the last, collapsed from heart-failure. Blackborrow and Hudson could not move. All were frost-bitten in varying degrees and their clothes, which had been worn continuously for six months, were much the worse for wear. The blizzard which sprang up the day that we landed at Cape Wild lasted for a fortnight, often blowing at the rate of seventy to ninety miles an hour, and occasionally reaching even higher figures. The tents which had lasted so well and endured so much were torn to ribbons, with the exception of the square tent occupied by Hurley, James, and Hudson. Sleeping-bags and clothes were wringing wet, and the physical discomforts were tending to produce acute mental depression. The two remaining boats had been turned upside down with one gunwale resting on the snow, and the other raised about two feet on rocks and cases, and under these the sailors and some of the scientists, with the two invalids, Rickenson and Blackborrow, found head-cover at least. Shelter from the weather and warmth to dry their clothes was imperative, so Wild hastened the excavation of the ice-cave in the slope which had been started before I left.

The high temperature, however, caused a continuous stream of water to drip from the roof and sides of the ice-cave, and as with twenty-two men living in it the temperature would be practically always above freezing, there would have been no hope of dry quarters for them there. Under the direction of Wild they therefore collected some big flat stones, having in many cases to dig down under the snow which was covering the beach, and with these they erected two substantial walls four feet high and nineteen feet apart.

'We are all ridiculously weak, and this part of the work was exceedingly laborious and took us more than twice as long as it would have done had we been in normal health. Stones that we could easily have lifted at other times we found quite beyond our capacity, and it needed two or three of us to carry some that would otherwise have been one man's load. Our difficulties were added to by the fact that most of the more suitable stones lay at the farther end of the spit, some one hundred and fifty yards away. Our weakness is best compared with that which one experiences on getting up from a long illness; one "feels" well, but physically enervated.

'The site chosen for the hut was the spot where the stove had been originally erected on the night of our arrival. It lay between two large boulders, which, if they would not actually form the walls of the hut, would at least provide a valuable protection from the wind. Further protection was provided to the north by a hill called Penguin Hill at the end of the spit. As soon as the walls were completed and squared off, the two boats were laid upside down on them side by side. The exact adjustment of the boats took some time, but was of paramount importance if our structure was to be the permanent affair that we hoped it would be. Once in place they were securely chocked up and lashed down to the rocks. The few pieces of wood that we had were laid across from keel to keel, and over this the material of one of the torn tents was spread and secured with guys to the rocks. The walls were ingeniously contrived and fixed up by Marston. First he cut the now useless tents into suitable lengths; then he cut the legs of a pair of seaboots into narrow strips, and using these in much the same way that the leather binding is put round the edge of upholstered chairs, he nailed the tent-cloth all round the insides of the outer gunwales of the two boats in such a way that it hung down like a valance to the ground, where it was secured with spars and oars. A couple of overlapping blankets made the door, superseded later by a sack-mouth door cut from one of the tents. This consisted of a sort of tube of canvas sewn on to the tent-cloth, through which the men crawled in or out, tying it up as one would the mouth of a sack as soon as the man had passed through. It is certainly the most convenient and efficient door for these conditions that has ever been invented.

'Whilst the side walls of the hut were being fixed, others proceeded to fill the interstices between the stones of the end walls with snow. As this was very powdery and would not bind well, we eventually had to supplement it with the only spare blanket and an overcoat. All this work was very hard on our frost-bitten fingers, and materials were very limited.

'At last all was completed and we were invited to bring in our sodden bags, which had been lying out in the drizzling rain for several hours; for the tents and boats that had previously sheltered them had all been requisitioned to form our new residence.

'We took our places under Wild's direction. There was no squabbling for best places, but it was noticeable that there was something in the nature of a rush for the billets up on the thwarts of the boats.

'Rickenson, who was still very weak and ill, but very cheery, obtained a place in the boat directly above the stove, and the sailors having lived under the *Stancomb Wills* for a few days while she was upside down on the beach, tacitly claimed it as their own, and flocked up on to its thwarts as one man. There was one 'upstair' billet left in this boat, which Wild offered to Hussey and Lees simultaneously, saying that the first man that got his bag up could have the billet. Whilst Lees was calculating the pros and cons Hussey got his bag, and had it up just as Lees had determined that the pros had it. There were now four men up on the thwarts of the *Dudley Docker*, and the five sailors and Hussey on those of the *Stancomb Wills*, the remainder disposing themselves on the floor.'

The floor was at first covered with snow and ice, frozen in amongst the pebbles. This was cleared out, and the remainder of the tents spread out over the stones. Within the shelter of these cramped but comparatively palatial quarters cheerfulness once more reigned amongst the party. The blizzard, however, soon discovered the flaws in the architecture of their hut, and the fine drift-snow forced its way through the crevices between the stones forming the end walls. Jaeger sleeping-bags and coats were spread over the outside of these walls, packed over with snow and securely frozen up, effectively keeping out this drift.

At first all the cooking was done outside under the lee of some rocks, further protection being provided by a wall of provision-cases. There were two blubber-stoves made from old oil-drums, and one day, when the blizzard was unusually severe, an attempt was made to cook the meals inside the hut. There being no means of escape for the pungent blubber-smoke, the inmates had rather a bad time, some being affected with a form of smoke-blindness similar to snow-blindness, very painful and requiring medical attention.

A chimney was soon fitted, made by Kerr out of the tin lining of one of the biscuit-cases, and passed through a close-fitting tin grummet sewn into the canvas of the roof just between the keels of the two boats, and the smoke nuisance was soon a thing of the past. Later on, another old oil-drum was made to surround this chimney, so that two pots could be cooked at once on the one stove. Those whose billets were near the stove suffered from the effects of the local thaw caused by its heat, but they were repaid by being able to warm up portions of steak and hooshes left over from previous meals, and even to warm up those of the less fortunate ones, for a consideration. This consisted generally of part of the hoosh or one or two pieces of sugar.

The cook and his assistant, which latter job was taken by each man in turn, were called about 7 a.m., and breakfast was generally ready by about 10 a.m.

Provision-cases were then arranged in a wide circle round the stove, and those who were fortunate enough to be next to it could dry their gear. So that all should benefit equally by this, a sort of 'General Post' was carried out, each man occupying his place at meal-times for one day only, moving up one the succeeding day. In this way eventually every man managed to dry his clothes, and life began to assume a much brighter aspect.

The great trouble in the hut was the absence of light. The canvas walls were covered with blubber-soot, and with the snow-drifts accumulating round the but its inhabitants were living in a state of perpetual night. Lamps were fashioned out of sardine-tins, with bits of surgical bandage for wicks; but as the oil consisted of seal-oil rendered down from the blubber, the remaining fibrous tissue being issued very sparingly at lunch, by the by, and being considered a great delicacy, they were more a means of conserving the scanty store of matches than of serving as illuminants.

Wild was the first to overcome this difficulty by sewing into the canvas wall the glass lid of a chronometer box. Later on three other windows were added, the material in this case being some celluloid panels from a photograph case of mine which I had left behind in a bag. This enabled the occupants of the floor billets who were near enough to read and sew, which relieved the monotony of the situation considerably.

'Our reading material consisted at this time of two books of poetry, one book of *Nordenskjold's Expedition*, one or two torn volumes of the *Encyclopaedia Britannica*, and a penny cookery book, owned by Marston. Our clothes, though never presentable, as they bore the scars of nearly ten months of rough usage, had to be continually patched to keep them together at all.'

As the floor of the hut had been raised by the addition of loads of clean pebbles, from which most of the snow had been removed, during the cold weather it was kept comparatively dry. When, however, the temperature rose to just above freezing-point, as occasionally happened, the hut became the drainage-pool of all the surrounding hills. Wild was the first to notice it by remarking one morning that his sleeping-bag was practically afloat. Other men examined theirs with a like result, so baling operations commenced forthwith. Stones were removed from the floor and a large hole dug, and in its gloomy depths the water could be seen rapidly rising. Using a saucepan for a baler, they baled out over 100 gallons of dirty water. The next day gallons were removed, the men taking it in turns to bale at intervals during the night; 160 more gallons were baled out during the next twenty-four hours, till one man rather pathetically remarked in his diary, 'This is what nice, mild, high temperatures mean to us: no wonder we prefer the cold.' Eventually, by removing a portion of one wall a long channel was dug nearly down to the sea, completely solving the problem. Additional precautions were taken by digging away the snow which surrounded the hut after each blizzard, sometimes entirely obscuring it.

A huge glacier across the bay behind the hut nearly put an end to the party. Enormous blocks of ice weighing many tons would break off and fall into the sea, the disturbance thus caused giving rise to great waves. One day Marston was outside the hut digging up the frozen seal for lunch with a pick, when a noise 'like an artillery barrage' startled him. Looking up he saw that one of these tremendous waves, over thirty feet high, was advancing rapidly across the bay, threatening to sweep hut and inhabitants into the sea. A hastily shouted warning brought the men tumbling out, but fortunately the loose ice which filled the bay damped the wave down so much that, though it flowed right under the hut, nothing was carried away. It was a narrow escape, though, as had they been washed into the sea nothing could have saved them.

Although they themselves gradually became accustomed to the darkness and the dirt, some entries in their diaries show that occasionally they could realise the conditions under which they were living.

'The hut grows more grimy every day. Everything is a sooty black. We have arrived at the limit where further increments from the smoking stove, blubber-lamps, and cooking-gear are unnoticed. It is at least comforting to feel that we can become no filthier. Our shingle floor will scarcely bear examination by strong light without causing even us to shudder and express our disapprobation at its state. Oil mixed with reindeer hair, bits of meat, sennegrass, and penguin feathers form a conglomeration which cements the stones together. From time to time we have a spring cleaning, but a fresh supply of flooring material is not always available, as all the shingle is frozen up and buried by deep rifts. Such is our Home Sweet Home.'

'All joints are aching through being compelled to lie on the hard, rubbly floor which forms our bedsteads.'

Again, later on, one writes: 'Now that Wild's window allows a shaft of light to enter our hut, one can begin to "see" things inside. Previously one relied upon one's sense of touch, assisted by the remarks from those whose faces were inadvertently trodden on, to guide one to the door. Looking down in the semi-darkness to the far end, one observes two very small smoky flares that dimly illuminate a row of five, endeavouring to make time pass by reading or argument. These are Macklin, Kerr, Wordie, Hudson, and Blackborrow – the last two being invalids.

'The centre of the hut is filled with the cases which do duty for the cook's bed, the meat and blubber boxes, and a mummified-looking object, which is Lees in his sleeping-bag. The near end of the floor space is taken up with the stove, with Wild and McIlroy on one side, and Hurley and James on the other. Marston occupies a hammock most of the night – and day – which is slung across the entrance. As he is large and the entrance very small, he invariably gets bumped by those passing in and out. His vocabulary at such times is interesting.

'In the attic, formed by the two upturned boats, live ten un-kempt and careless lodgers, who drop boots, mitts, and other articles of apparel on to the men below. Reindeer hairs rain down incessantly day and night, with every movement that they make in their moulting bags. These, with penguin feathers and a little grit from the floor, occasionally savour the hooshes. Thank heaven man is an adaptable brute! If we dwell sufficiently long in this hut, we are likely to alter our method of walking, for our ceiling, which is but four feet six inches high at its highest part, compels us to walk bent double or on all fours.

'Our doorway – Cheetham is just crawling in now, bringing a shower of snow with him – was originally a tent entrance. When one wishes to go out, one unties the cord securing the door, and crawls or wriggles out, at the same time exclaiming "Thank goodness I'm in the open air!" This should suffice to describe the atmosphere inside the hut, only pleasant when charged with the overpowering yet appetising smell of burning penguin steaks.

'From all parts there dangles an odd collection of blubbery garments, hung up to dry, through which one crawls, much as a chicken in an incubator. Our walls of tent-canvas admit as much light as might be expected from a closed Venetian blind. It is astonishing how we have grown accustomed to inconveniences, and tolerate, at least, habits which a little time back were regarded with repugnance. We have no forks, but each man has a sheath-knife and a spoon, the latter in many cases having been fashioned from a piece of box lid. The knife serves many purposes. With it we kill, skin, and cut up seals and penguins, cut blubber into strips for the fire, very carefully scrape the snow off our hut walls, and then after a perfunctory rub with an oily penguin-skin, use it at meals. We are as regardless of our grime and dirt as is the Esquimaux. We have been unable to wash since we left the ship, nearly ten months ago. For one thing we have no soap or towels, only bare necessities being brought with us; and, again, had we possessed these articles, our supply of fuel would only permit us to melt enough ice for drinking purposes. Had one man washed, half a dozen others would have had to go without a drink all day. One cannot suck ice to relieve the thirst, as at these low temperatures it cracks the lips and blisters the tongue. Still, we are all very cheerful.'

During the whole of their stay on Elephant Island the weather was described by Wild as 'simply appalling'. Stranded as they were on a narrow, sandy beach surrounded by high mountains, they saw little of the scanty sunshine during the brief intervals of clear sky. On most days the air was full of snow-drift blown from the adjacent heights. Elephant Island being practically on the outside edge of the pack, the winds which passed over the relatively warm ocean before reaching it clothed it in a 'constant pall of fog and snow'.

On April 25, the day after I left for South Georgia, the island was beset by heavy pack-ice, with snow and a wet mist. Next day was calmer, but on the 27th; to quote one of the diaries, they experienced 'the most wretched weather conceivable. Raining all night and day, and blowing hard. Wet to the skin.' The following day brought heavy fog and sleet, and a continuance of the blizzard. April ended with a terrific windstorm which nearly destroyed the hut. The one remaining tent had to be dismantled, the pole taken down, and the inhabitants had to lie flat all night under the icy canvas. This lasted well into May, and a typical May day is described as follows: 'A day of terrific winds, threatening to dislodge our shelter. The wind is a succession of hurricane gusts that sweep down the glacier immediately south-south-west of us. Each gust heralds its approach by a low rumbling which increases to a thunderous roar. Snow, stones, and gravel are flying about, and any gear left unweighted by very heavy stones is carried away to sea.'

Heavy bales of sennegrass, and boxes of cooking-gear, were lifted bodily in the air and carried away out of sight. Once the wind carried off the floor-cloth of a tent which six men were holding on to and shaking the snow off. These gusts often came with alarming suddenness; and without any warning. Hussey was outside in the blizzard digging up the day's meat, which had frozen to the ground, when a gust caught him and drove him down the spit towards the sea. Fortunately, when he reached the softer sand and shingle below high-water mark, he managed to stick his pick into the ground and hold on with both hands till the squall had passed.

On one or two rare occasions they had fine, calm, clear days. The glow of the dying sun on the mountains and glaciers filled even the most materialistic of them with wonder and admiration. These days were sometimes succeeded by calm, clear nights when, but for the cold, they would have stayed out on the sandy beach all night.

About the middle of May a terrific blizzard sprang up, blowing from sixty to ninety miles an hour, and Wild entertained grave fears for their hut. One curious feature noted in this blizzard was the fact that huge ice-sheets as big as window-panes, and about a quarter of an inch thick, were being hurled about by the wind, making it as dangerous to walk about outside as if one were in an avalanche of splintered glass. Still, these winds from the south and south-west, though invariably accompanied by snow and low temperatures, were welcome in that they drove the pack-ice away from the immediate vicinity of the island, and so gave rise on each occasion to hopes of relief. Northeast winds, on the other hand, by filling the bays with ice and bringing thick misty weather, made it impossible to hope for any ship to approach them.

Towards the end of May a period of dead calm set in, with ice closely packed all round the island. This gave place to north-east winds and mist, and at the beginning of June came another south-west blizzard, with cold driving snow. 'The blizzard increased to terrific gusts during the night, causing us much anxiety for the safety of our hut. There was little sleep, all being apprehensive of the canvas roof ripping off, and the boats being blown out to sea.'

Thus it continued, alternating between south-west blizzards, when they were all confined to the hut, and north-east winds, bringing cold, damp, misty weather.

On June 25 a severe storm from north-west was recorded, accompanied by strong winds and heavy seas, which encroached upon their little sandy beach up to within four yards of their hut.

Towards the end of July and the beginning of August they had a few fine, calm, clear days. Occasional glimpses of the sun, with high temperatures, were experienced, after south-west winds had blown all the ice away, and the party, their spirits cheered by Wild's unfailing optimism, again began to look eagerly for the rescue ship.

The first three attempts at their rescue unfortunately coincided with the times when the island was beset with ice, and though on the second occasion we approached close enough to fire a gun, in the hope that they would hear the sound and know that we were safe and well, yet so accustomed were they to the noise made by the calving of the adjacent glacier that either they did not hear or the sound passed unnoticed. On August 16 pack was observed on the horizon, and next day the bay was filled with loose ice, which soon consolidated. Soon afterwards huge old floes and many bergs drifted in. 'The pack appears as dense as we have ever seen it. No open water is visible, and "ice-blink" girdles the horizon. The weather is wretched – a stagnant calm of air and ocean alike, the latter obscured by dense pack through which no swell can penetrate, and a wet mist hangs like a pall over land and sea. The silence is oppressive. There is nothing to do but to stay in one's sleeping-bag, or else wander in the soft snow and become thoroughly wet.' Fifteen inches of snow fell in the next twenty-four hours, making over two feet between August 18 and 21. A slight swell next day from the north-east ground up the pack ice, but this soon subsided, and the pack became consolidated once more. On August 27 a strong west-south-west wind sprang up and drove all this ice out of the bay, and except for some stranded bergs left a clear ice-free sea through which we finally made our way from Punta Arenas to Elephant Island.

As soon as I had left the island to get help for the rest of the Expedition, Wild set all hands to collect as many seals and penguins as possible, in case their stay was longer than was at first anticipated. A sudden rise in temperature caused a whole lot to go bad and become unfit for food, so while a fair reserve was kept in hand too much was not accumulated.

At first the meals, consisting mostly of seal meat with one hot drink per day, were cooked on a stove in the open. The snow and wind, besides making it very unpleasant for the cook, filled all the cooking-pots with sand and grit, so during the winter the cooking was done inside the hut.

A little Cerebos salt had been saved, and this was issued out at the rate of three-quarters of an ounce per man per week. Some of the packets containing the salt had broken, so that all did not get the full ration. On the other hand, one man dropped his week's ration on the floor of the hut, amongst the stones and dirt. It was quickly collected, and he found to his delight that he had enough now to last him for three weeks. Of course it was not *all* salt. The hot drink consisted at first of milk made from milk-powder up to about one-quarter of its proper strength. This was later on diluted still more, and sometimes replaced by a drink made from a pea-soup-like packing from the Bovril sledging rations. For midwinter's day celebrations, a mixture of one tea-spoonful of methylated spirit in a pint of hot water, flavoured with a little ginger and sugar, served to remind some of cocktails and Veuve Cliquot.

At breakfast each had a piece of seal or half a penguin breast. Luncheon consisted of one biscuit on three days a week, nut-food on Thursdays, bits of blubber, from which most of the oil had been extracted for the lamps, on two days a week, and nothing on the remaining day. On this day breakfast consisted of a half-strength sledging ration. Supper was almost invariably seal and penguin, cut up very finely and fried with a little seal blubber.

There were occasionally very welcome variations from this menu. Some paddies – a little white bird not unlike a pigeon – were snared with a loop of string, and fried, with one water-sodden biscuit, for lunch. Enough barley and peas for one meal all round of each had been saved, and when this was issued it was a day of great celebration. Sometimes, by general consent, the luncheon biscuit would be saved, and, with the next serving of biscuit, was crushed in a canvas bag into a powder and boiled, with a little sugar, making a very satisfying pudding. When blubber was fairly plentiful there was always a saucepan of cold water, made from melting down the pieces of ice which had broken off from the glacier, fallen into the sea, and been washed ashore, for them to quench their thirst in. As the experience of Arctic explorers tended to show that sea-water produced a form of dysentery, Wild was rather diffident about using it. Penguin carcasses boiled in one part of sea-water to four of fresh were a great success though, and no ill-effects were felt by anybody.

The ringed penguins migrated north the day after we landed at Cape Wild, and though every effort was made to secure as large a stock of meat and blubber as possible, by the end of the month the supply was so low that only one hot meal a day could be served. Twice the usual number of penguin steaks were cooked at breakfast, and the ones intended for supper were kept hot in the pots by wrapping up in coats, etc. 'Clark put our saucepanful in his sleeping-bag today to keep it hot, and it really was a great success in spite of the extra helping of reindeer hairs that it contained. In this way we can make ten penguin skins do for one day.'

Some who were fortunate enough to catch penguins with fairly large undigested fish in their gullets used to warm these up in tins hung on bits of wire round the stove.

'All the meat intended for hooshes is cut up inside the hut, as it is too cold outside. As the boards which we use for the purpose are also used for cutting up tobacco, when we still have it, a definite flavour is sometimes imparted to the hoosh, which, if anything, improves it.'

Their diet was now practically all meat, and not too much of that, and all the diaries bear witness to their craving for carbohydrates, such as flour, oatmeal, etc. One man longingly speaks of the cabbages which grow on Kerguelen Island. By June 18 there were only nine hundred lumps of sugar left, i.e. just over forty pieces each. Even my readers know what shortage of sugar means at this very date, but from a different cause. Under these circumstances it is not surprising that all their thoughts and conversation should turn to food, past and future banquets, and second helpings that had been once refused.

A census was taken, each man being asked to state just what he would like to eat at that moment if he were allowed to have anything that he wanted. All, with but one exception, desired a suet pudding of some sort – the 'duff' beloved of sailors. Macklin asked for many returns of scrambled eggs on hot buttered toast. Several voted for 'a prodigious Devonshire dumpling', while Wild wished for 'any old dumpling so long as it was a large one.' The craving for carbohydrates, such as flour and sugar, and for fats was very real. Marston had with him a small penny cookery book. From this he would read out one recipe each night, so as to make them last. This would be discussed very seriously, and alterations and improvements suggested, and then they would turn into their bags to dream of wonderful meals that they could never reach. The following conversation was recorded in one diary:

WILD: Do you like doughnuts?
MCILROY: Rather!
WILD: Very easily made, too. I like them cold with a little jam.
MCILROY: Not bad; but how about a huge omelette?
WILD: Fine! [*with a deep sigh*]

'Overhead, two of the sailors are discussing some extraordinary mixture of hash, apple-sauce, beer, and cheese. Marston is in his hammock reading from his penny cookery book. Farther down, someone eulogises Scotch shortbread. Several of the sailors are talking of spotted dog, sea-pie, and Lockhart's with great feeling. Someone mentions nut-food, whereat the conversation becomes general, and we all decide to buy one pound's worth of it as soon as we get to civilisation, and retire to a country house to eat it undisturbed. At present we really mean it, too!'

Midwinter's day, the great Polar festival, was duly observed. A 'magnificent breakfast' of sledging ration hoosh, full strength and well boiled to thicken it, with hot milk was served. Luncheon consisted of a wonderful pudding, invented by Wild, made of powdered biscuit boiled with twelve pieces of mouldy nut-food. Supper was a very finely cut seal hooch flavoured with sugar.

After supper they had a concert, accompanied by Hussey on his 'indispensable banjo'. This banjo was the last thing to be saved off the ship before she sank, and I took it with us as a mental tonic. It was carried all the way through with us, and landed on Elephant Island practically unharmed, and did much to keep the men cheerful. Nearly every Saturday night such a concert was held, when each one sang a song about some other member of the party. If that other one objected to some of the remarks, a worse one was written for the next week.

The cook, who had carried on so well and for so long, was given a rest on August 9, and each man took it in turns to be cook for one week. As the cook and his 'mate' had the privilege of scraping out the saucepans, there was some anxiety to secure the job, especially amongst those with the larger appetites. 'The last of the methylated spirit was drunk on August 12, and from then onwards the King's health, "sweethearts and wives", and "the Boss and crew of the *Caird*", were drunk in hot water and ginger every Saturday night.'

The penguins and seals which had migrated north at the beginning of winter had not yet returned, or else the ice-foot, which surrounded the spit to a thickness of six feet, prevented them from coming ashore, so that food was getting short. Old seal-bones, that had been used once for a meal and then thrown away, were dug up and stewed down with sea-water. Penguin carcasses were treated likewise. Limpets were gathered from the pools disclosed between the rocks below high tide, after the pack-ice had been driven away. It was a cold job gathering these little shell-fish, as for each one the whole hand and arm had to be plunged into the icy water, and many score of these small creatures had to be collected to make anything of a meal. Seaweed boiled in sea-water was used to eke out the rapidly diminishing stock of seal and penguin meat. This did not agree with some of the party. Though it was acknowledged to be very tasty it only served to increase their appetite – a serious thing when there was nothing to satisfy it with! One man remarked in his diary: 'We had a sumptuous meal today – nearly five ounces of solid food each.'

It is largely due to Wild, and to his energy, initiative, and resource, that the whole party kept cheerful all along, and, indeed, came out alive and so well. Assisted by the two surgeons, Drs McIlroy and Macklin, he had ever a watchful eye for the health of each one. His cheery optimism never failed, even when food was very short and the prospect of relief seemed remote. Each one in his diary speaks with admiration of him. I think without doubt that all the party who were stranded on Elephant Island owe their lives to him. The demons of depression could find no foothold when he was around; and, not content with merely 'telling', he was 'doing' as much as, and very often more than, the rest. He showed wonderful capabilities of leadership and more than justified the absolute confidence that I placed in him. Hussey, with his cheeriness and his banjo, was another vital factor in chasing away any tendency to downheartedness.

Once they were settled in their hut, the health of the party was quite good. Of course, they were all a bit weak, some were light-headed, all were frost-bitten, and others, later, had attacks of heart failure. Blackborrow, whose toes were so badly frost-bitten in the boats, had to have all five amputated while on the island. With insufficient instruments and no proper means of sterilising them, the operation, carried out as it was in a dark, grimy hut, with only a blubber-stove to keep up the temperature and with an outside temperature well below freezing, speaks volumes for the skill and initiative of the surgeons. I am glad to be able to say that the operation was very successful, and after a little treatment ashore, very kindly given by the Chilean doctors at Punta Arenas, he has now completely recovered and walks with only a slight limp. Hudson, who developed bronchitis and hip disease, was practically well again when the party was rescued. All trace of the severe frostbites suffered in the boat journey had disappeared, though traces of recent superficial ones remained on some. All were naturally weak when rescued, owing to having been on such scanty rations for so long, but all were alive and very cheerful, thanks to Frank Wild.

August 30, 1916, is described in their diaries as a 'day of wonders'. Food was very short, only two days' seal and penguin meat being left, and no prospect of any more arriving. The whole party had been collecting limpets and seaweed to eat with the stewed seal bones. Lunch was being served by Wild, Hurley and Marston waiting outside to take a last long look at the direction from which they expected the ship to arrive. From a fortnight after I had left, Wild would roll up his sleeping-bag each day with the remark, 'Get your things ready, boys, the Boss may come today.' And sure enough, one day the mist opened and revealed the ship for which they had been waiting and longing and hoping for over four months. 'Marston was the first to notice it, and immediately yelled out "Ship O!" The inmates of the hut mistook it for a call of "Lunch O!" so took no notice at first. Soon, however, we heard him pattering along the snow as fast as he could run, and in a gasping, anxious voice, hoarse with excitement, he shouted, "Wild, there's a ship! Hadn't we better light a flare?" We all made one dive for our narrow door. Those who could not get through tore down the canvas walls in their hurry and excitement. The hooch-pot with our precious limpets and seaweed was kicked over in the rush. There, just rounding the island which had previously hidden her from our sight, we saw a little ship flying the Chilean flag.

Ernest H. Shackleton   Frank Wild
[*Scott Polar Research Institute*]

'We tried to cheer, but excitement had gripped our vocal chords. Macklin had made a rush for the flagstaff, previously placed in the most conspicuous position on the ice-slope. The running-gear would not work, and the flag was frozen into a solid, compact mass so he tied his jersey to the top of the pole for a signal.

'Wild put a pick through our last remaining tin of petrol, and soaking coats, mitts, and socks with it, carried them to the top of Penguin Hill at the end of our spit, and soon, they were ablaze.

'Meanwhile most of us had gathered on the foreshore watching with anxious eyes for any signs that the ship had seen us, or for any answering signals. As we stood and gazed she seemed to turn away as if she had not seen us. Again and again we cheered, though our feeble cries could certainly not have carried so far. Suddenly she stopped, a boat was lowered, and we could recognise Sir Ernest's figure as he climbed down the ladder. Simultaneously we burst into a cheer, and then one said to the other, "Thank God, the Boss is safe." For I think that his safety was of more concern to us than was our own.

'Soon the boat approached near enough for the Boss, who was standing up in the bows, to shout to Wild, "Are you all well?" To which he replied, "All safe, all well," and we could see a smile light up the Boss's face as he said, "Thank God!"

'Before he could land he threw ashore handsful of cigarettes and tobacco; and these the smokers, who for two months had been trying to find solace in such substitutes as seaweed, finely chopped pipe-bowls, seal meat, and sennegrass, grasped greedily.

'Blackborrow, who could not walk, had been carried to a high rock and propped up in his sleeping-bag, so that he could view the wonderful scene.

'Soon we were tumbling into the boat, and the Chilean sailors, laughing up at us, seemed as pleased at our rescue as we were. Twice more the boat returned, and within an hour of our first having sighted the boat we were heading northwards to the outer world from which we had had no news since October 1914, over twenty-two months before. We are like men awakened from a long sleep. We are trying to acquire suddenly the perspective which the rest of the world has acquired gradually through two years of war. There are many events which have happened of which we shall never know.

'Our first meal, owing to our weakness and the atrophied state of our stomachs, proved disastrous to a good many. They soon recovered though. Our beds were just shake-downs on cushions and settees, though the officer on watch very generously gave up his bunk to two of us. I think we got very little sleep that night. It was just heavenly to lie and listen to the throb of the engines, instead of to the crack of the breaking floe, the beat of the surf on the ice-strewn shore, or the howling of the blizzard.

'We intend to keep August 30 as a festival for the rest of our lives.'

You readers can imagine my feelings as I stood in the little cabin watching my rescued comrades feeding.

CHAPTER 13

The Ross Sea party

I now turn to the fortunes and misfortunes of the Ross Sea Party and the *Aurora*. In spite of extraordinary difficulties occasioned by the breaking out of the *Aurora* from her winter quarters before sufficient stores and equipment had been landed, Captain Aeneas Mackintosh and the party under his command achieved the object of this side of the Expedition. For the depot that was the main object of the Expedition was laid in the spot that I had indicated, and if the transcontinental party had been fortunate enough to have crossed they would have found the assistance, in the shape of stores, that would have been vital to the success of their undertaking. Owing to the dearth of stores, clothing, and sledging equipment, the depot party was forced to travel more slowly and with greater difficulty than would have otherwise been the case. The result was that in making this journey the greatest qualities of endurance, self-sacrifice, and patience were called for, and the call was not in vain, as you reading the following pages will realise. It is more than regrettable that after having gone through those many months of hardship and toil, Mackintosh and Hayward should have been lost. Spencer-Smith during those long days, dragged by his comrades on the sledge, suffering but never complaining, became an example to all men. Mackintosh and Hayward owed their lives on that journey to the unremitting care and strenuous endeavours of Joyce, Wild, and Richards, who, also scurvy-stricken but fitter than their comrades, dragged them through the deep snow and blizzards on the sledges. I think that no more remarkable story of human endeavour has been revealed than the tale of that long march which I have collated from various diaries. Unfortunately, the diary of the leader of this side of the Expedition was lost with him. The outstanding feature of the Ross Sea side was the journey made by these six men. The earlier journeys for the first year did not produce any sign of the qualities of leadership amongst the others. Mackintosh was fortunate for the long journey in that he had these three men with him: Ernest Wild, Richards, and Joyce.

Before proceeding with the adventures of this party I want to make clear in these pages how much I appreciate the assistance I received both in Australia and New Zealand, especially in the latter dominion. And amongst the many friends there it is not invidious on my part to lay special stress on the name of Leonard Tripp, who has been my mentor, counsellor, and friend for many years, and who, when the Expedition was in precarious and difficult circumstances, devoted his energy, thought, and gave his whole time and advice to the best interests of our cause. I also must thank Edward Saunders, who for the second time has greatly helped me in preparing an Expedition record for publication.

To the Dominion Government I tender my warmest thanks. To the people of New Zealand, and especially to those many friends – too numerous to mention here – who helped us when our fortunes were at a low ebb, I wish to say that their kindness is an ever-green memory to me. If ever a man had cause to be grateful for assistance in dark days, I am he.

The *Aurora*, under the command of Captain Aeneas Mackintosh, sailed from Hobart for the Ross Sea on December 24, 1914. The ship had refitted in Sydney, where the State and Federal Governments had given generous assistance, and would be able, if necessary, to spend two years in the Antarctic. My instructions to Captain Mackintosh, in brief, were to proceed to the Ross Sea, make a base at some convenient point in or near McMurdo Sound, land stores and equipment, and lay depots on the Great Ice Barrier in the direction of the Beardmore Glacier for the use of the party that I expected to bring overland from the Weddell Sea coast. This programme would involve some heavy sledging, but the ground to be covered was familiar, and I had not anticipated that the work would present any great difficulties. The *Aurora* carried materials for a hut, equipment for landing and sledging parties, stores and clothing of all the kinds required, and an ample supply of sledges. There were also dog teams and one of the motor-tractors. I had told Captain Mackintosh that it was possible the transcontinental journey would be attempted in the 1914-15 season in the event of the landing on the Weddell Sea coast proving unexpectedly easy, and it would be his duty, therefore, to lay out depots to the south immediately after his arrival at his base. I had directed him to place a depot of food and fuel-oil at lat. 84 degrees S. in 1914-15, with cairns and flags as guides to a sledging party approaching from the direction of the Pole. He would place depots farther south in the 1915-16 season.

The *Aurora* had an uneventful voyage southwards. She anchored off the sealing-huts at Macquarie Island on Christmas Day, December 25. The wireless station erected by Sir Douglas Mawson's Australian Antarctic Expedition could be seen on a hill to the north-west with the Expedition's hut at the base of the hill. This hut was still occupied by a meteorological staff, and later in the day the meteorologist, Mr Tulloch, came off to the ship and had dinner aboard. The *Aurora* had some stores for the Macquarie Island party, and these were sent ashore during succeeding days in the boats. The landing-place was a rough, kelp-guarded beach, where lay the remains of the New Zealand barque *Clyde*. Macquarie Island anchorages are treacherous, and several ships engaged in the sealing and whaling trade have left their bones on the rocky shores, where bask great herds of seals and sea-elephants. The *Aurora* sailed from the island on December 31, and three days later they sighted the first iceberg, a tabular berg rising 250 ft. above the sea. This was in lat. 62 degrees 44' S., long. 169 degrees 58' E. The next day, in lat. 64 degrees 27' 38" S., the *Aurora* passed through the first belt of pack-ice. At 9 a.m. on January 7, Mount Sabine, a mighty peak of the Admiralty Range, South Victoria Land, was sighted seventy-five miles distant.

It had been proposed that a party of three men should travel to Cape Crozier from winter quarters during the winter months in order to secure emperor penguins' eggs. The ship was to call at Cape Crozier, land provisions, and erect a small hut of fibro-concrete sheets for the use of this party. The ship was off the Cape on the afternoon of January 9, and a boat put off with Stenhouse, Cope, Joyce, Ninnis, Mauger, and Aitken to search for a landing-place. 'We steered in towards the Barrier,' wrote Stenhouse, 'and found an opening leading into a large bight which jutted back to eastward into the Barrier. We endeavoured without success to scale the steep ice-foot under the cliffs, and then proceeded up the bay. Pulling along the edge of perpendicular ice, we turned into a bay in the ice-cliff and came to a cul-de-sac, at the head of which was a grotto. At the head of the grotto and on a ledge of snow were perched some adelie penguins. The beautiful green and blue tints in the ice-colouring made a picture as unreal as a stage setting. Coming back along the edge of the bight towards the land, we caught and killed one penguin, much to the surprise of another, which ducked into a niche in the ice and, after much squawking, was extracted with a boat-hook and captured. We returned to our original landing, and were fortunate in our time, for no sooner had we cleared the ledge where Ninnis had been hanging in his endeavour to catch the penguin than the barrier calved and a piece weighing hundreds of tons toppled over into the sea.

'Since we left the ship a mist had blown up from the south, and when we arrived back at the entrance to the bay the ship could be but dimly seen. We found a slope on the ice-foot, and Joyce and I managed, by cutting steps, to climb up to a ledge of debris between the cliffs and the ice, which we thought might lead to the vicinity of the emperor penguin rookery. I sent the boat back to the ship to tell the captain of our failure to find a spot where we could depot the hut and stores, and then, with Joyce, set out to walk along the narrow land between the cliffs and the ice to the southward in hopes of finding the rookery. We walked for about a mile along the foot of the cliffs, over undulating paths, sometimes crawling carefully down a gully and then over rocks and debris which had fallen from the steep cliffs which towered above us, but we saw no signs of a rookery or any place where a rookery could be. Close to the cliffs and separated from them by the path on which we travelled, the Barrier in its movement towards the sea had broken and showed signs of pressure. Seeing a turn in the cliffs ahead, which we thought might lead to better prospects, we trudged on, and were rewarded by a sight which Joyce admitted as being the grandest he had ever witnessed. The Barrier had come into contact with the cliffs and, from where we viewed it, it looked as if icebergs had fallen into a tremendous cavern and lay jumbled together in wild disorder. Looking down into that wonderful picture one realised a little the 'eternalness' of things.

'We had not long to wait, and, much as we wished to go ahead, had to turn back. I went into a small crevasse; no damage. Arriving back at the place where we left the boat we found it had not returned, so sat down under an overhang and smoked and enjoyed the sense of loneliness. Soon the boat appeared out of the mist, and the crew had much news for us. After we left the ship the captain manoeuvred her in order to get close to the Barrier, but, unfortunately, the engines were loath to be reversed when required to go astern and the ship hit the Barrier end on. The Barrier here is about twenty feet high, and her jib-boom took the weight and snapped at the cap. When I returned Thompson was busy getting the broken boom and gear aboard. Luckily the cap was not broken and no damage was done aloft, but it was rather a bad introduction to the Antarctic. There is no place to land the Cape Crozier hut and stores, so we must build a hut in the winter here, which will mean so much extra sledging from winter quarters. Bad start, good finish! Joyce and I went aloft to the crow's-nest, but could see no opening in the Barrier to eastward where a ship might enter and get farther south.'

Mackintosh proceeded into McMurdo Sound. Heavy pack delayed the ship for three days, and it was not until January 16 that she reached a point off Cape Evans, where he landed ten tons of coal and ninety-eight cases of oil. During succeeding days Captain Mackintosh worked the *Aurora* southward, and by January 24 he was within nine miles of Hut Point. There he made the ship fast to sea-ice, then breaking up rapidly, and proceeded to arrange sledging parties. It was his intention to direct the laying of the depots himself and to leave his first officer, Lieut. J. R. Stenhouse, in command of the *Aurora*, with instructions to select a base and land a party.

The first objective was Hut Point, where stands the hut erected by the *Discovery* expedition in 1902. An advance party, consisting of Joyce (in charge), Jack, and Gaze, with dogs and fully loaded sledges, left the ship on January 24; Mackintosh, with Wild and Smith, followed the next day; and a supporting party, consisting of Cope (in charge), Stevens, Ninnis, Haywood, Hooke, and Richards, left the ship on January 30. The first two parties had dog teams. The third party took with it the motor-tractor, which does not appear to have given the good service that I had hoped to get from it. These parties had a strenuous time during the weeks that followed. The men, fresh from shipboard, were not in the best of training, and the same was true of the dogs. It was unfortunate that the dogs had to be worked so early after their arrival in the Antarctic. They were in poor condition and they had not learned to work together as teams. The result was the loss of many of the dogs, and this proved a serious matter in the following season. Captain Mackintosh's record of the sledging in the early months of 1915 is fairly full. It will not be necessary here to follow the fortunes of the various parties in detail, for although the men were facing difficulties and dangers, they were on well-travelled ground, which has been made familiar to most readers by the histories of earlier Expeditions.

Captain Mackintosh and his party left the *Aurora* on the evening of January 25. They had nine dogs and one heavily loaded sledge, and started off briskly to the accompaniment of a cheer from their shipmates. The dogs were so eager for exercise after their prolonged confinement aboard the ship that they dashed forward at their best speed, and it was necessary for one man to sit upon the sledge in order to moderate the pace. Mackintosh had hoped to get to Hut Point that night, but luck was against him. The weather broke after he had travelled about five miles, and snow, which completely obscured all landmarks, sent him into camp on the sea-ice. The weather was still thick on the following morning, and the party, making a start after breakfast, missed its way. 'We shaped a course where I imagined Hut Point to be,' wrote Captain Mackintosh in his diary, 'but when the sledge-meter showed thirteen miles fifty yards, which is four miles in excess of the distance from the slip to Hut Point, I decided to halt again. The surface was changing considerably and the land was still obscured. We have been travelling over a thick snow surface, in which we sink deeply, and the dogs are not too cheerful about it.' They started again at noon on January 27, when the weather had cleared sufficiently to reveal the land, and reached Hut Point at 4 p.m. The sledge-meter showed that the total distance travelled had been over seventeen miles. Mackintosh found in the hut a note from Joyce, who had been there on the 25th, and who reported that one of his dogs had been killed in a fight with its companions. The hut contained some stores left there by earlier Expeditions. The party stayed there for the night. Mackintosh left a note for Stenhouse directing him to place provisions in the hut in case the sledging parties did not return in time to be taken off by the ship. Early next morning Joyce reached the hut. He had encountered bad ice and had come back to consult with Mackintosh regarding the route to be followed. Mackintosh directed him to steer out towards Black Island in crossing the head of the Sound beyond Hut Point.

Mackintosh left Hut Point on January 28. He had taken some additional stores, and he mentions that the sledge now weighed 1200 lb. This was a heavy load, but the dogs were pulling well and he thought it practicable. He encountered difficulty almost at once after descending the slope from the point to the sea-ice, for the sledge stuck in soft snow and the party had to lighten the load and relay until they reached a better surface. They were having trouble with the dogs, which did not pull cheerfully, and the total distance covered in the day was under four miles. The weather was warm and the snow consequently was soft. Mackintosh had decided that it would be best to travel at night. A fall of snow held up the party throughout the following day, and they did not get away from their camp until shortly before midnight. 'The surface was abominably soft,' wrote Mackintosh. 'We harnessed ourselves on to the sledge and with the dogs made a start, but we had a struggle to get off. We had not gone very far when in deeper snow we stopped dead. Try as we would, no movement could be produced. Reluctantly we unloaded and began the tedious task of relaying. The work, in spite of the lighter load on the sledge, proved terrific for ourselves and for the dogs. We struggled for four hours, and then set camp to await the evening, when the sun would not be so fierce and the surface might be better. I must say I feel somewhat despondent, as we are not getting on as well as I expected, nor do we find it as easy as one would gather from reading.'

The two parties met again that day. Joyce also had been compelled to relay his load, and all hands laboured strenuously and advanced slowly. They reached the edge of the Barrier on the night of January 30 and climbed an easy slope to the Barrier surface, about thirty feet above the sea-ice. The dogs were showing signs of fatigue, and when Mackintosh camped at 6.30 a.m. on January 31, he reckoned that the distance covered in twelve and a half hours had been about two and a half miles. The men had killed a seal at the edge of the sea-ice and placed the meat on a cairn for future use. One dog, having refused to pull, had been left behind with a good feed of meat, and Mackintosh hoped the animal would follow. The experiences of the party during the days that followed can be indicated by some extracts from Mackintosh's diary.

'*Sunday, January 31.* – Started off this afternoon at 3 p.m. Surface too dreadful for words. We sink into snow at times up to our knees, the dogs struggling out of it panting and making great efforts. I think the soft snow must be accounted for by a phenomenally fine summer without much wind. After proceeding about 1000 yds I spotted some poles on our starboard side. We shaped course for these and found Captain Scott's Safety Camp. We unloaded a relay here and went back with empty sledge for the second relay. It took us four hours to do just this short distance. It is exasperating. After we had got the second load up we had lunch. Then we dug round the poles, while snow fell, and after getting down about three feet we came across, first, a bag of oats, lower down two cases of dog-biscuit – one with a complete week's ration, the other with seal-meat. A good find. About forty paces away we found a venesta-lid sticking out of the snow. Smith scraped round this with his ice-axe and presently discovered one of the motor-sledges Captain Scott used. Everything was just as it had been left, the petrol-tank partly filled and apparently undeteriorated. We marked the spot with a pole. The snow clearing, we proceeded with a relay. We got only half a mile, still struggling in deep snow; and then went back for the second load. We can still see the cairn erected at the Barrier edge and a black spot which we take to be the dog.

'*February 1.* – We turned out at 7.30 p.m., and after a meal broke camp. We made a relay of two and a half miles. The sledge-meter stopped during this relay. Perhaps that is the cause of our mileage not showing. We covered seven and a half miles in order to bring the load two and a half miles. After lunch we decided, as the surface was getting better, to make a shot at travelling with the whole load. It was a back-breaking job. Wild led the team, while Smith and I pulled in harness. The great trouble is to get the sledge started after the many unavoidable stops. We managed to cover one mile. This even is better than relaying. We then camped – the dogs being entirely done up, poor brutes.

'*February 2.* – We were awakened this afternoon, while in our bags, by hearing Joyce's dogs barking. They have done well and have caught us up. Joyce's voice was heard presently, asking us the time. He is managing the full load. We issued a challenge to race him to the Bluff, which he accepted. When we turned out at 6.30 p.m. his camp was seen about three miles ahead. About 8 p.m., after our hoosh, we made a start, and reached Joyce's camp at 1 a.m. The dogs had been pulling well, seeing the camp ahead, but when we arrived off it they were not inclined to go on. After a little persuasion and struggle we got off, but not for long. This starting business is terrible work. We have to shake the sledge and its big load while we shout to the dogs to start. If they do not pull together it is useless. When we get the sledge going we are on tenterhooks lest it stop again on the next soft slope, and this often occurs. Sledging is real hard work; but we are getting along:'

The surface was better on February 2, and the party covered six miles without relaying. They camped in soft snow, and when they started the next day they were two hours relaying over one hundred and fifty yards. Then they got into Joyce's track and found the going better. Mackintosh overtook Joyce on the morning of February 4 and went ahead, his party breaking trail during the next march. They covered ten miles on the night of the 4th. One dog had 'chucked his hand in' on the march, and Mackintosh mentions that he intended to increase the dogs' allowance of food. The surface was harder, and during the night of February 5 Mackintosh covered eleven miles twenty-five yards, but he finished with two dogs on the sledge. Joyce was travelling by day, so that the parties passed one another daily on the march.

A blizzard came from the south on February 10 and the parties were confined to their tents for over twenty-four hours. The weather moderated on the morning of the next day, and at 11 a.m. Mackintosh camped beside Joyce and proceeded to rearrange the parties. One of his dogs had died on the 9th, and several others had ceased to be worth much for pulling. He had decided to take the best dogs from the two teams and continue the march with Joyce and Wild, while Smith, Jack, and Gaze went back to Hut Point with the remaining dogs. This involved the adjustment of sledge-loads in order that the proper supplies might be available for the depots. He had eight dogs and Smith had five. A depot of oil and fuel was laid at this point and marked by a cairn with a bamboo pole rising ten feet above it. The change made for better progress.

Smith turned back at once, and the other party went ahead fairly rapidly, the dogs being able to haul the sledge without much assistance from the men. The party built a cairn of snow after each hour's travelling to serve as guides to the depot and as marks for the return journey. Another blizzard held the men up on February 13, and they had an uncomfortable time in their sleeping-bags owing to low temperature.

During succeeding days the party plodded forward. They were able to cover from five to twelve miles a day, according to the surface and weather. They built the cairns regularly and checked their route by taking bearings of the mountains to the west. They were able to cover from five to twelve miles a day, the dogs pulling fairly well. They reached lat. 80 degrees S. on the afternoon of February 20. Mackintosh had hoped to find a depot laid in that neighbourhood by Captain Scott, but no trace of it was seen. The surface had been very rough during the afternoon, and for that reason the depot to be laid there was named Rocky Mountain Depot. The stores were to be placed on a substantial cairn, and smaller cairns were to be built at right angles to the depot as a guide to the overland party. 'As soon as breakfast was over,' wrote Mackintosh the next day, 'Joyce and Wild went off with a light sledge and the dogs to lay out the cairns and place flags to the eastward, building them at every mile. The outer cairn had a large flag and a note indicating the position of the depot. I remained behind to get angles and fix our position with the theodolite. The temperature was very low this morning, and handling the theodolite was not too warm a job for the fingers. My whiskers froze to the metal while I was taking a sight. After five hours the others arrived back. They had covered ten miles, five miles out and five miles back. During the afternoon we finished the cairn, which we have built to a height of eight feet. It is a solid square erection which ought to stand a good deal of weathering, and on top we have placed a bamboo pole with a flag, making the total height twenty-five feet. Building the cairn was a fine warming jab, but the ice on our whiskers often took some ten minutes thawing out. Tomorrow we hope to lay out the cairns to the westward, and then to shape our course for the Bluff.'

The weather became bad again during the night. A blizzard kept the men in their sleeping-bags on February 21, and it was not until the afternoon of the 23rd that Mackintosh and Joyce made an attempt to lay out the cairns to the west. They found that two of the dogs had died during the storm, leaving seven dogs to haul the sledge. They marched a mile and a half to the westward and built a cairn, but the weather was very thick and they did not think it wise to proceed farther. They could not see more than a hundred yards and the tent was soon out of sight. They returned to the camp, and stayed there until the morning of February 24, when they started the return march with snow still falling. 'We did get off from our camp,' says Mackintosh, 'but had only proceeded about four hundred yards when the fog came on so thick that we could scarcely see a yard ahead, so we had to pitch the tent again, and are now sitting inside hoping the weather will clear. We are going back with only ten days' provisions, so it means pushing on for all we are worth. These stoppages are truly annoying. The poor dogs are feeling hungry; they eat their harness or any straps that may be about. We can give them nothing beyond their allowance of three biscuits each as we are on bare rations ourselves; but I feel sure they require more than one pound a day. That is what they are getting now . . . After lunch we found it a little clearer, but a very bad light. We decided to push on. It is weird travelling in this light. There is no contrast or outline; the sky and the surface are one, and we cannot discern undulations, which we encounter with disastrous results. We picked up the first of our outward cairns. This was most fortunate. After passing a second cairn everything became blotted out, and so we were forced to camp, after covering 4 miles 703 yds. The dogs are feeling the pangs of hunger and devouring everything they see. They will eat anything except rope. If we had not wasted those three days we might have been able to give them a good feed at the Bluff depot, but now that is impossible. It is snowing hard.'

The experiences of the next few days were unhappy. Another blizzard brought heavy snow and held the party up throughout the 25th and 26th. 'Outside is a scene of chaos. The snow, whirling along with the wind, obliterates everything. The dogs are completely buried, and only a mound with a ski sticking up indicates where the sledge is. We long to be off, but the howl of the wind shows how impossible it is. The sleeping-bags are damp and sticky, so are our clothes. Fortunately, the temperature is fairly high and

they do not freeze. One of the dogs gave a bark and Joyce went
out to investigate. He found that Major, feeling hungry, had
dragged his way to Joyce's ski and eaten off the leather binding.
Another dog has eaten all his harness, canvas, rope, leather, brass,
and rivets. I am afraid the dogs will not pull through; they all look
thin and these blizzards do not improve matters . . . We have a
week's provisions and one hundred and sixty miles to travel. It
appears that we will have to get another week's provisions from
the depot, but don't wish it. Will see what luck tomorrow. Of
course, at Bluff we can replenish.'

'We are now reduced to one meal in the twenty-four hours,'
wrote Mackintosh a day later. 'This going without food keeps us
colder. It is a rotten, miserable time. It is had enough having this
wait, but we have also the wretched thought of having to use the
provisions already depot-ed, for which we have had all this hard
struggle.' The weather cleared on the 27th, and in the afternoon
Mackintosh and Joyce went back to the depot, while Wild remained behind to build a cairn and attempt to dry the sleeping-
bags in the sun. The stores left at the depot had been two and a
quarter tins of biscuit (42 lb. to the tin), rations for three men for
three weeks in bags, each intended to last one week, and three tins
of oil. Mackintosh took one of the weekly bags from the depot and
returned to the camp. The party resumed the homeward journey
the next morning, and with a sail on the sledge to take advantage
of the southerly breeze, covered nine miles and a half during the
day. But the dogs had reached almost the limit of their endurance;
three of them fell out, unable to work longer, while on the march.
That evening, for the first time since leaving the *Aurora*, the men
saw the sun dip to the horizon in the south, a reminder that the
Antarctic summer was nearing its close.

The remaining four dogs collapsed on March 2. 'After lunch we
went off fairly well for half an hour. Then Nigger commenced to
wobble about, his legs eventually giving under him. We took him
out of his harness and let him travel along with us, but he has given
us all he can, and now can only lay down. After Nigger, my friend
Pompey collapsed. The drift, I think, accounts a good deal for this.
Pompey has been splendid of late, pulling steadily and well. Then
Scotty, the last dog but one, gave up. They are all lying down in
our tracks. They have a painless death, for they curl up in the snow

and fall into asleep from which they will never wake.' We are left with one dog, Pinkey. He has not been one of the pullers, but he is not despised. We can afford to give him plenty of biscuit. We must nurse him and see if we cannot return with one dog at least. We are now pulling ourselves, with the sail (the floor-cloth of the tent) set and Pinkey giving a hand. At one stage a terrific gust came along and capsized the sledge. The sail was blown off the sledge, out of its guys, and we prepared to camp, but the wind fell again to a moderate breeze, so we repaired the sledge and proceeded.

'It is blowing hard this evening, cold too. Another wonderful sunset. Golden colours illuminate the sky. The moon casts beautiful rays in combination with the more vivid ones from the dipping sun. If all was as beautiful as the scene we could consider ourselves in some paradise, but it is dark and cold in the tent and I shiver in a frozen sleeping-bag. The inside fur is a mass of ice, congealed from my breath. One creeps into the bag, toggles up with half-frozen fingers, and hears the crackling of the ice. Presently drops of thawing ice are falling on one's head. Then comes a fit of shivers. You rub yourself and turn over to warm the side of the bag which has been uppermost. A puddle of water forms under the body. After about two hours you may doze off, but I always wake with the feeling that I have not slept a wink.'

The party made only three and a half miles on March 3. They were finding the sledge exceedingly heavy to pull, and Mackintosh decided to remove the outer runners and scrape the bottom. These runners should have been taken off before the party started, and the lower runners polished smooth. He also left behind all spare gear, including dog-harness in order to reduce weight, and found the lighter sledge easier to pull. The temperature that night was −28 Fahr., the lowest recorded during the journey up to that time. 'We are struggling along at a mile an hour,' wrote Mackintosh on the 5th. 'It is a very hard pull, the surface being very sticky. Pinkey still accompanies us. We hope we can get him in. He is getting all he wants to eat. So he ought.' The conditions of travel changed the next day. A southerly wind made possible the use of the sail, and the trouble was to prevent the sledge bounding ahead over rough sastrugi and capsizing. The handling of ropes and the sail caused many frostbites, and occasionally the men were dragged along the surface by the sledge. The remaining dog collapsed

during the afternoon and had to be left behind. Mackintosh did
not feel that he could afford to reduce the pace. The sledge-meter
had got out of order, so the distance covered in the day was not
recorded. The wind increased during the night, and by the morning of the 7th was blowing with blizzard force. The party did not
move again until the morning of the 8th. They were still finding
the sledge very heavy and were disappointed at their slow progress,
their marches being six to eight miles a day. On the 10th they got
the Bluff Peak in line with Mount Discovery. My instructions had
been that the Bluff depot should be laid on this line, and as the
depot had been placed north of the line on the outward journey,
owing to thick weather making it impossible to pick up the
landmarks, Mackintosh intended now to move the stores to the
proper place. He sighted the depot flag about four miles away, and
after pitching camp at the new depot site, he went across with
Joyce and Wild and found the stores as he had left them.

'We loaded the sledge with the stores, placed the large mark flag
on the sledge, and proceeded back to our tent, which was now out
of sight. Indeed it was not wise to come out as we did without tent
or bag. We had taken the chance, as the weather had promised
fine. As we proceeded it grew darker and darker, and eventually
we were travelling by only the light of stars, the sun having
dipped. After four and a half hours we sighted the little green tent.
It was hard pulling the last two hours and weird travelling in the
dark. We have put in a good day, having had fourteen hours' solid
marching. We are now sitting in here enjoying a very excellent
thick hoosh. A light has been improvised out of an old tin with
methylated spirit.'

The party spent the next day in their sleeping-bags, while a
blizzard raged outside. The weather was fine again on March 12,
and they built a cairn for the depot. The stores placed on this cairn
comprised a six weeks' supply of biscuit and three weeks' full
ration for three men, and three tins of oil. Early in the afternoon
the men resumed their march northwards and made three miles
before camping. 'Our bags are getting into a bad state,' wrote
Mackintosh, 'as it is some time now since we have had an opportunity of drying them. We use our bodies for drying socks and
such-like clothing, which we place inside our jerseys and produce
when required. Wild carries a regular wardrobe in this position,

and it is amusing to see him searching round the back of his clothes for a pair of socks. Getting away in the mornings is our bitterest time. The putting on of the finneskoe is a nightmare, for they are always frozen stiff, and we have a great struggle to force our feet into them. The icy sennegrass round one's fingers is another punishment that causes much pain. We are miserable until we are actually on the move, then warmth returns with the work. Our conversation now is principally conjecture as to what can have happened to the other parties. We have various ideas.'

Saturday, March 13, was another day spent in the sleeping-bags. A blizzard was raging and everything was obscured. The men saved food by taking only one meal during the day, and they felt the effect of the short rations in lowered vitality. Both Joyce and Wild had toes frost-bitten while in their bags and found difficulty in getting the circulation restored. Wild suffered particularly in this way and his feet were very sore. The weather cleared a little the next morning, but the drift began again before the party could break camp, and another day had to be spent in the frozen bags.

The march was resumed on March 15. 'About 11 p.m. last night the temperature commenced to get lower and the gale also diminished. The lower temperature caused the bags, which were moist, to freeze hard. We had no sleep and spent the night twisting and turning. The morning brought sunshine and pleasure, for the hot hoosh warmed our bodies and gave a glow that was most comforting. The sun was out, the weather fine and clear but cold. At 8.30 a.m. we made a start. We take a long time putting on our finneskoe, although we get up earlier to allow for this. This morning we were over four hours' getting away. We had a fine surface this morning for marching, but we did not make much headway. We did the usual four miles before lunch. The temperature was −23 Fahr. A mirage made the sastrugi appear to be dancing like some ice-goblins. Joyce calls them "dancing jimmies". After lunch we travelled well, but the distance for the day was only 7 miles 400 yds. We are blaming our sledge-meter for the slow rate of progress. It is extraordinary that on the days when we consider we are making good speed we do no more than on days when we have a tussle.'

'*March 15.* – The air temperature this morning was −35 Fahr. Last night was one of the worst I have ever experienced. To cap everything, I developed toothache, presumably as a result of frost-bitten cheek. I was in positive agony. I groaned and moaned, got the medicine-chest, but could find nothing there to stop the pain. Joyce, who had wakened up, suggested methylated spirit, so I damped some cotton-wool, then placed it in the tooth, with the result that I burnt the inside of my mouth. All this time my fingers, being exposed (it must have been at least 50 deg. below zero), were continually having to be brought back. After putting on the methylated spirit I went back to the bag, which, of course, was frozen stiff. I wriggled and moaned till morning brought relief by enabling me to turn out. Joyce and Wild both had a bad night, their feet giving them trouble. My feet do not affect me so much as theirs. The skin has peeled off the inside of my mouth, exposing a raw sore, as the result of the methylated spirit. My tooth is better though. We have had to reduce our daily ration. Frostbites are frequent in consequence. The surface became very rough in the afternoon, and the light too was bad owing to cumulus clouds being massed over the sun. We are continually falling, for we are unable to distinguish the high and low parts of the sastrugi surface. We are travelling on our ski. We camped at 6 p.m. after travelling 6 miles 100 yds. I am writing this sitting up in the bag. This is the first occasion I have been able to do thus for some time, for usually the cold has penetrated through everything should one have the bag open. The temperature is a little higher tonight, but still it is −21 Fahr. (53 degrees of frost). Our matches, among other things, are running short, and we have given up using any except for lighting the Primus.'

The party found the light bad again the next day. After stumbling on ski among the sastrugi for two hours, the men discarded the ski and made better progress; but they still had many falls, owing to the impossibility of distinguishing slopes and irregularities in the grey, shadowless surface of the snow. They made over nine and a half miles that day, and managed to cover ten miles on the following day, March 18, one of the best marches of the journey. 'I look forward to seeing the ship. All of us bear marks of our tramp. Wild takes first place. His nose is a picture for Punch to be jealous of; his ears, too, are sore, and one big toe is a black sore. Joyce has a good nose and many minor sores. My jaw is swollen from the frostbite I got on the cheek, and I also have a bit of nose . . . We have discarded the ski, which we hitherto used, and travel in the finneskoe. This makes the sledge go better but it is not so comfortable travelling as on ski. We encountered a very high, rough sastrugi surface, most remarkably high, and had a cold breeze in our faces during the march. Our beards and moustaches are masses of ice. I will take care I am clean-shaven next time I come out. The frozen moustache makes the lobes of the nose freeze more easily than they would if there was no ice alongside them . . . I ask myself why on earth one comes to these parts of the earth. Here we are, frostbitten in the day, frozen at night. What a life!' The temperature at 1 p.m. that day was −23 Fahr., i.e. 55 degrees of frost.

The men camped abreast of 'Corner Camp', where they had been on February 1, on the evening of March 19. The next day, after being delayed for some hours by bad weather, they turned towards Castle Rock and proceeded across the disturbed area where the Barrier impinges upon the land. Joyce put his foot through the snow-covering of a fairly large crevasse, and the course had to be changed to avoid this danger. The march for the day was only 2 miles 900 yds. Mackintosh felt that the pace was too slow, but was unable to quicken it owing to the bad surfaces. The food had been cut down to close upon half-rations, and at this reduced rate the supply still in hand would be finished in two days. The party covered 7 miles 570 yds. on the 21st, and the hoosh that night was 'no thicker than tea'.

'The first thought this morning was that we must do a good march,' wrote Mackintosh on March 22. 'Once we can get to Safety Camp (at the junction of the Barrier with the sea-ice) we are right. Of course we can as a last resort abandon the sledge and take a run into Hut Point, about twenty-two miles away . . . We have managed quite a respectable forenoon march. The surface was hard, so we took full advantage of it. With our low food the cold is penetrating. We had lunch at 1 p.m., and then had left over one meal at full rations and a small quantity of biscuits. The temperature at lunch-time was −6 Fahr. Erebus is emitting large volumes of smoke, travelling in a south-easterly direction, and a red glare is also discernible. After lunch we again accomplished a good march, the wind favouring us for two hours. We are anxiously looking out for Safety Camp.' The distance for the day was 8 miles 1525 yds.

'*March 23, 1915.* – No sooner had we camped last night than a blizzard with drift came on and has continued ever since. This morning finds us prisoners. The drift is lashing into the sides of the tent and everything outside is obscured. This weather is rather alarming, for if it continues we are in a bad way. We have just made a meal of cocoa mixed with biscuit-crumbs. This has warmed us up a little, but on empty stomachs the cold is penetrating.'

The weather cleared in the afternoon, but too late for the men to move that day. They made a start at 7 a.m. on the 24th after a meal of cocoa and biscuit-crumbs.

'We have some biscuit-crumbs in the bag and that is all. Our start was made under most bitter circumstances, all of us being attacked by frostbites. It was an effort to bare hands for an instant. After much rubbing and "bringing back" of extremities we started. Wild is a mass of bites, and we are all in a bad way. We plugged on, but warmth would not come into our bodies. We had been pulling about two hours when Joyce's smart eyes picked up a flag. We shoved on for all we were worth, and as we got closer, sure enough, the cases of provisions loomed up. Then what feeds we promised to give ourselves. It was not long before we were putting our gastronomic capabilities to the test. Pemmican was brought down from the depot, with oatmeal to thicken it, as well as sugar. While Wild was getting the Primus lighted he called out to us that he believed his ear had gone. This was the last piece of his face left whole – nose, cheeks, and neck all having bites. I went into the tent and had a look. The ear was a pale green. I quickly put the palm of my hand to it and brought it round. Then his fingers went, and to stop this and bring back the circulation he put them over the lighted Primus, a terrible thing to do. As a result he was in agony. His ear was brought round all right, and soon the hot hoosh sent warmth tingling through us. We felt like new beings. We simply ate till we were full, mug after mug. After we had been well satisfied, we replaced the cases we had pulled down from the depot and proceeded towards the Gap. Just before leaving Joyce discovered a note left by Spencer-Smith and Richards. This told us that both the other parties had returned to the Hut and apparently all was well. So that is good. When we got to the Barrier-edge we found the ice-cliff on to the newly formed sea-ice not safe enough to bear us, so we had to make a detour along the Barrier-edge and, if the sea ice was not negotiable, find a way up by Castle Rock. At 7 p.m., not having found any suitable place to descend to the sea-ice, we camped. Tonight we have the Primus going and warming our frozen selves. I hope to make Hut Point tomorrow.'

Mackintosh and his companions broke camp on the morning of March 25, with the thermometer recording 55 degrees of frost, and, after another futile search for a way down the ice-cliff to the sea-ice, they proceeded towards Castle Rock. While in this course they picked up sledge-tracks, and, following these, they found a route down to the sea-ice. Mackintosh decided to depot the sledge on top of a well-marked undulation and proceed without gear. A short time later the three men, after a scramble over the cliffs of Hut Point, reached the door of the hut.

'We shouted. No sound. Shouted again, and presently a dark object appeared. This turned out to be Cope, who was by himself. The other members of the party had gone out to fetch the gear off their sledge, which they also had left. Cope had been laid up, so did not go with them. We soon were telling each other's adventures, and we heard then how the ship had called here on March 11 and picked up Spencer-Smith, Richards, Ninnis, Hooke, and Gaze, the present members here being Cope, Hayward, and Jack. A meal was soon prepared. We found here even a blubber-fire, luxurious, but what a state of dirt and grease! However, warmth and food are at present our principal objects. While we were having our meal Jack and Hayward appeared . . . Late in the evening we turned into dry bags. As there are only three bags here, we take it in turns to use them. Our party have the privilege . . . I got a letter here from Stenhouse giving a summary of his doings since we left him. The ship's party also have not had a rosy time.'

Mackintosh learned here that Spencer-Smith, Jack, and Gaze, who had turned back on February 10, had reached Hut Point without difficulty. The third party, headed by Cope, had also been out on the Barrier but had not done much. This party had attempted to use the motor-tractor, but had failed to get effective service from the machine and had not proceeded far afield. The motor was now lying at Hut Point. Spencer-Smith's party and Cope's party had both returned to Hut Point before the end of February.

The six men now at Hut Point were cut off from the winter quarters of the Expedition at Cape Evans by the open water of McMurdo Sound. Mackintosh naturally was anxious to make the crossing and get in touch with the ship and the other members of the shore party; but he could not make a move until the sea-ice became firm, and, as events occurred, he did not reach Cape Evans until the beginning of June. He went out with Cope and Hayward on March 29 to get his sledge and brought it as far as Pram Point, on the south side of Hut Point. He had to leave the sledge there owing to the condition of the sea-ice. He and his companions lived an uneventful life under primitive conditions at the hut. The weather was bad, and though the temperatures recorded were low, the young sea-ice continually broke away. The blubber-stove in use at the hut seemed to have produced soot and grease in the usual large quantities, and the men and their clothing suffered accordingly. The whites of their eyes contrasted vividly with the dense blackness of their skins. Wild and Joyce had a great deal of trouble with their frostbites. Joyce had both feet blistered, his knees were swollen, and his hands also were blistered. Jack devised some blubber-lamps, which produced an uncertain light and much additional smoke. Mackintosh records that the members of the party were contented enough but 'unspeakably dirty', and he writes longingly of baths and clean clothing. The store of seal-blubber ran low early in April, and all hands kept a sharp look-out for seals. On April 15 several seals were seen and killed. The operations of killing and skinning made worse the greasy and blackened clothes of the men. It is to be regretted that though there was a good deal of literature available, especially on this particular district, the leaders of the various parties had not taken advantage of it and so supplemented their knowledge. Joyce and Mackintosh of course had had previous Antarctic experience: but it was open to all to have carefully studied the detailed instructions published in the books of the three last Expeditions in this quarter.

CHAPTER 14

Wintering in McMurdo Sound

The *Aurora*, after picking up six men at Hut Point on March 11, had gone back to Cape Evans. The position chosen for the winter quarters of the *Aurora* was at Cape Evans, immediately off the hut erected by Captain Scott on his last Expedition. The ship on March 14 lay about forty yards off shore, bows seaward. Two anchors had been taken ashore and embedded in heavy stone rubble, and to these anchors were attached six steel hawsers. The hawsers held the stern, while the bow was secured by the ordinary ship's anchors. Later, when the new ice had formed round the *Aurora*, the cable was dragged ashore over the smooth surface and made fast. The final moorings thus were six hawsers and one cable astern, made fast to the shore anchors, and two anchors with about seventy fathoms of cable out forward. On March 23 Mr Stenhouse landed a party consisting of Stevens, Spencer-Smith, Gaze, and Richards in order that they might carry out routine observations ashore. These four men took up their quarters in Captain Scott's hut. They had been instructed to kill seals for meat and blubber. The landing of stores, gear, and coal did not proceed at all rapidly, it being assumed that the ship would remain at her moorings throughout the winter. Some tons of coal were taken ashore during April, but most of it stayed on the beach, and much of it was lost later when the sea-ice went out. This shore party was in the charge of Stevens, and his report, handed to me much later, gives a succinct account of what occurred, from the point of view of the men at the hut.

Cape Evans, Ross Island, July 30, 1915.

On the 23rd March, 1915, a party consisting of Spencer-Smith, Richards, and Gaze was landed at Cape Evans Hut in my charge. Spencer-Smith received independent instructions to devote his time exclusively to photography. I was verbally instructed that the main duty of the party was to obtain a supply of seals for food and fuel. Scientific work was also to be carried on.

Meteorological instruments were at once installed, and experiments were instituted on copper electrical thermometers in order to supplement our meagre supply of instruments and enable observations of earth, ice, and sea temperatures to be made. Other experimental work was carried on, and the whole of the time of the scientific members of the party was occupied. All seals seen were secured. On one or two occasions the members of the shore party were summoned to work on board ship.

In general the weather was unsettled, blizzards occurring frequently and interrupting communication with the ship across the ice. Only small, indispensable supplies of stores and no clothes were issued to the party on shore. Only part of the scientific equipment was able to be transferred to the shore, and the necessity to obtain that prevented some members of the party landing all their personal gear.

The ship was moored stern on to the shore, at first well over one hundred yards from it. There were two anchors out ahead and the vessel was made fast to two others sunk in the ground ashore by seven wires. The strain on the wires was kept constant by tightening up from time to time such as became slack, and easing cables forward, and in this way the ship was brought much closer inshore. A cable was now run out to the south anchor ashore, passed onboard through a fair-lead under the port end of the bridge, and made fast to bollards forward. Subsequent strain due to ice and wind pressure on the ship broke three of the wires. Though I believe it was considered on board that the ship was secure, there was still considerable anxiety felt. The anchors had held badly before, and the power of the ice-pressure on the ship was uncomfortably obvious.

Since the ship had been moored the bay had frequently frozen over, and the ice had as frequently gone out on account of blizzards. The ice does not always go out before the wind has passed its maximum. It depends on the state of tides and currents; for the sea-ice has been seen more than once to go out bodily when a blizzard had almost completely calmed down.

On the 6th May the ice was in and people passed freely between the shore and the ship. At 11 p.m. the wind was south, backing to south-east, and blew at forty miles per hour. The ship was still in her place. At 3 a.m. on the 7th the wind had not increased to any extent, but ice and ship had gone. As she was not seen to go we are unable to say whether the vessel was damaged. The shore end of the cable was bent twice sharply, and the wires were loose. On the afternoon of the 7th the weather cleared somewhat, but nothing was seen of the ship. The blizzard only lasted some twelve hours. Next day the wind became northerly, but on the 10th there was blowing the fiercest blizzard we have so far experienced from the south-east. Nothing has since been seen or heard of the ship, though a look-out was kept.

Immediately the ship went as accurate an inventory as possible of all stores ashore was made, and the rate of consumption of food-stuffs so regulated that they would last ten men for not less than one hundred weeks. Coal had already been used with the utmost economy. Little could be done to cut down the consumption, but the transference to the neighbourhood of the hut of such of the coal landed previously by the ship as was not lost was pushed on. Meat also was found to be very short; it was obvious that neither it nor coal could be made to last two years, but an evidently necessary step in the ensuing summer would be the ensuring of an adequate supply of meat and blubber, for obtaining which the winter presented little opportunity. Meat and coal were, therefore, used with this consideration in mind, as required but as carefully as possible.

A. Stevens

The men ashore did not at once abandon hope of the ship returning before the Sound froze firmly. New ice formed on the sea whenever the weather was calm, and it had been broken up and taken out many times by the blizzards. During the next few days eager eyes looked seaward through the dim twilight of noon, but the sea was covered with a dense black mist and nothing was visible. A northerly wind sprang up on May 8 and continued for a few hours, but it brought no sign of the ship, and when on May 10 the most violent blizzard yet experienced by the party commenced, hope grew slender. The gale continued for three days, the wind attaining a velocity of seventy miles an hour. The snow-drift was very thick and the temperature fell to −20 degrees Fahr. The shore party took a gloomy view of the ship's chances of safety among the ice-floes of the Ross Sea under such conditions.

Stevens and his companions made a careful survey of their position and realised that they had serious difficulties to face. No general provisions and no clothing of the kind required for sledging had been landed from the ship. Much of the sledging gear was also aboard. Fortunately, the hut contained both food and clothing, left there by Captain Scott's Expedition. The men killed as many seals as possible and stored the meat and blubber. June 2 brought a welcome addition to the party in the form of the men who had been forced to remain at Hut Point until the sea-ice became firm. Mackintosh and those with him had incurred some risk in making the crossing, since open water had been seen on their route by the Cape Evans party only a short time before. There were now ten men at Cape Evans – namely, Mackintosh, Spencer-Smith, Joyce, Wild, Cope, Stevens, Hayward, Gaze, Jack, and Richards. The winter had closed down upon the Antarctic and the party would not be able to make any move before the beginning of September. In the meantime they overhauled the available stores and gear, made plans for the work of the forthcoming spring and summer, and lived the severe but not altogether unhappy life of the polar explorer in winter quarters. Mackintosh, writing on June 5, surveyed his position:

'The decision of Stenhouse to make this bay the wintering place of the ship was not reached without much thought and consideration of all eventualities. Stenhouse had already tried the Glacier Tongue and other places, but at each of them the ship had been in an exposed and dangerous position. When this bay was tried the ship withstood several severe blizzards, in which the ice remained in on several occasions. When the ice did go out the moorings held. The ship was moored bows north. She had both anchors down forward and two anchors buried astern, to which the stern moorings were attached with seven lengths of wire. Taking all this into account, it was quite a fair judgment on his part to assume that the ship would be secure here. The blizzard that took the ship and the ice out of the bay was by no means as severe as others she had weathered. The accident proves again the uncertainty of conditions in these regions. I only pray and trust that the ship and those aboard are safe. I am sure they will have a thrilling story to tell when we see them.'

The *Aurora* could have found safe winter quarters farther up McMurdo Sound, towards Hut Point, but would have run the risk of being frozen in over the following summer, and I had given instructions to Mackintosh before he went south that this danger must be avoided.

'Meanwhile we are making all preparations here for a prolonged stay. The shortage of clothing is our principal hardship. The members of the party from Hut Point have the clothes we wore when we left the ship on January 25. We have been without a wash all that time, and I cannot imagine a dirtier set of people. We have been attempting to get a wash ever since we came back, but owing to the blow during the last two days no opportunity has offered. All is working smoothly here, and everyone is taking the situation very philosophically. Stevens is in charge of the scientific staff and is now the senior officer ashore. Joyce is in charge of the equipment and has undertaken to improvise clothes out of what canvas can be found here. Wild is working with Joyce. He is a cheerful, willing soul. Nothing ever worries or upsets him, and he is ever singing or making some joke or performing some amusing prank. Richards has taken over the keeping of the meteorological log. He is a young Australian, a hard, conscientious worker, and I look forward to good results from his endeavours. Jack, another young Australian, is his assistant. Hayward is the handy man, being responsible for the supply of blubber. Gaze, another Australian, is working in conjunction with Hayward. Spencer-Smith, the padre, is in charge of photography, and, of course, assists in the general routine work. Cope is the medical officer.

'The routine here is as follows: Four of us, myself, Stevens, Richards, and Spencer-Smith, have breakfast at 7 a.m. The others are called at 9 a.m., and their breakfast is served. Then the table is cleared, the floor is swept, and the ordinary work of the day is commenced. At 1 p.m. we have what we call "a counter lunch", that is, cold food and cocoa. We work from 2 p.m. till 5 p.m. After 5 p.m. people can do what they like. Dinner is at 7. The men play games, read, write up diaries. We turn in early, since we have to economise fuel and light. Night-watches are kept by the scientific men, who have the privilege of turning in during the day. The day after my arrival here I gave an outline of our situation and explained the necessity for economy in the use of fuel, light, and stores, in view of the possibility that we may have to stay here for two years . . . We are not going to commence work for the sledging operations until we know more definitely the fate of the *Aurora*. I dare not think any disaster has occurred.'

During the remaining days of June the men washed and mended clothes, killed seals, made minor excursions in the neighbourhood of the hut, and discussed plans for the future. They had six dogs, two being bitches without experience of sledging. One of these bitches had given birth to a litter of pups, but she proved a poor mother and the young ones died. The animals had plenty of seal meat and were tended carefully.

Mackintosh called a meeting of all hands on June 26 for the discussion of the plans he had made for the depot-laying exped-ition to be undertaken during the following spring and summer.

'I gave an outline of the position and invited discussion from the members. Several points were brought up. I had suggested that one of our party should remain behind for the purpose of keeping the meteorological records and laying in a supply of meat and blubber. This man would be able to hand my instructions to the ship and pilot a party to the Bluff. It had been arranged that Richards should do this. Several objected on the ground that the whole complement would be necessary, and, after the matter had been put to the vote, it was agreed that we should delay the decision until the parties had some practical work and we had seen how they fared. The shortage of clothing was discussed, and Joyce and Wild have agreed to do their best in this matter. October sledging (on the Barrier) was mentioned as being too early, but is to be given a trial. These were the most important points brought up, and it was mutually and unanimously agreed that we could do no more . . . I know we are doing our best.'

The party was anxious to visit Cape Royds, north of Cape Evans, but at the end of June open water remained right across the Sound and a crossing was impossible. At Cape Royds is the hut used by the Shackleton Expedition of 1907-1909, and the stores and supplies it contains might have proved very useful. Joyce and Wild made finneskoe (fur boots) from spare sleeping-bags. Mackintosh mentions that the necessity of economising clothing and footgear prevented the men taking as much exercise as they would otherwise have done. A fair supply of canvas and leather had been found in the hut, and some men tried their hands at making shoes. Many seals had been killed and brought in, and the supply of meat and blubber was ample for present needs.

During July Mackintosh made several trips northwards on the sea-ice, but found always that he could not get far. A crack stretched roughly from Inaccessible Island to the Barne Glacier, and the ice beyond looked weak and loose. The improving light told of the returning sun. Richards and Jack were weighing out stores in readiness for the sledging expeditions. Mackintosh, from the hill behind the hut, saw open water stretching westward from Inaccessible Island on August 1, and noted that probably McMurdo Sound was never completely frozen over. A week later the extent of the open water appeared to have increased, and the men began to despair of getting to Cape Royds. Blizzards were frequent and persistent. A few useful articles were found in the neighbourhood of the hut as the light improved, including some discarded socks and underwear, left by members of the Scott Expedition, and a case of candied peel, which was used for cakes. A small fire broke out in the hut on August 12. The acetylene-gas lighting plant installed in the hut by Captain Scott had been rigged, and one day it developed a leak. A member of the party searched for the leak with a lighted candle, and the explosion that resulted fired some woodwork. Fortunately the outbreak was extinguished quickly. The loss of the hut at this stage would have been a tragic incident.

Mackintosh and Stevens paid a visit to Cape Royds on August 13. They had decided to attempt the journey over the Barne Glacier, and after crossing a crevassed area they got to the slopes of Cape Barne and thence down to the sea-ice. They found this ice to be newly formed, but sufficiently strong for their purpose, and soon reached the Cape Royds hut.

'The outer door of the hut we found to be off,' wrote Mackintosh. 'A little snow had drifted into the porch, but with a shovel, which we found outside, this was soon cleared away. We then entered, and in the centre of the hut found a pile of snow and ice, which had come through the open ventilator in the roof of the hut. We soon closed this. Stevens prepared a meal while I cleared the ice and snow away from the middle of the hut. After our meal we commenced taking an inventory of the stores inside. Tobacco was our first thought. Of this we found one tin of Navy Cut and a box of cigars. Soap, too, which now ensures us a wash and clean clothes when we get back. We then began to look round for a sleeping-bag. No bags were here, however, but on the improvised beds of cases we found two mattresses, an old canvas screen, and two blankets. We took it in turns to turn in. Stevens started first, while I kept the fire going. No coal or blubber was here, so we had to use wood, which, while keeping the person alongside it warm, did not raise the temperature of the hut over freezing-point. Over the stove in a conspicuous place we found a notice by Scott's party that parties using the hut should leave the dishes clean.'

Mackintosh and Stevens stayed at the Cape Royds hut over the next day and made a thorough examination of the stores there. They found outside the hut a pile of cases containing meats, flour, dried vegetables, and sundries, at least a year's supply for a party of six. They found no new clothing, but made a collection of worn garments, which could be mended and made serviceable. Carrying loads of their spoils, they set out for Cape Evans on the morning of August 15 across the sea-ice. Very weak ice barred the way and they had to travel round the coast. They got back to Cape Evans in two hours. During their absence Wild and Gaze had climbed Inaccessible Island, Gaze having an ear badly frost-bitten on the journey. The tobacco was divided among the members of the party. A blizzard was raging the next day, and Mackintosh congratulated himself on having chosen the time for his trip fortunately.

The record of the remaining part of August is not eventful. All hands were making preparations for the sledging, and were rejoicing in the increasing daylight. The party tried the special sledging ration prepared under my own direction, and 'all agreed it was excellent both in bulk and taste.' Three emperor penguins, the first seen since the landing, were caught on August 19. By that time the returning sun was touching with gold the peaks of the

Western Mountains and throwing into bold relief the massive form of Erebus. The volcano was emitting a great deal of smoke, and the glow of its internal fires showed occasionally against the smoke-clouds above the crater. Stevens, Spencer-Smith, and Cope went to Cape Royds on the 20th, and were still there when the sun made its first appearance over Erebus on the 26th. Preceding days had been cloudy, and the sun, although above the horizon, had not been visible.

'The morning broke clear and fine,' wrote Mackintosh. 'Over Erebus the sun's rays peeped through the massed cumulus and produced the most gorgeous cloud effects. The light made us all blink and at the same time caused the greatest exuberance of spirits. We felt like men released from prison. I stood outside the hut and looked at the truly wonderful scenery all round. The West Mountains were superb in their wild grandeur. The whole outline of peaks, some eighty or ninety miles distant, showed up, stencilled in delicate contrast to the sky-line. The immense ice-slopes shone white as alabaster against dark shadows. The sky to the west over the mountains was clear, except for low-lying banks at the foot of the slopes round about Mount Discovery. To the south hard streaks of stratus lay heaped up to 30 degrees above the horizon . . . Then Erebus commenced to emit volumes of smoke, which rose hundreds of feet and trailed away in a north-westerly direction. The southern slopes of Erebus were enveloped in a mass of cloud.' The party from Cape Royds returned that afternoon, and there was disappointment at their report that no more tobacco had been found.

The sledging of stores to Hut Point, in preparation for the depot-laying journeys on the Barrier, was to begin on September 1. Mackintosh, before that date, had discussed plans fully with the members of his party. He considered that sufficient sledging provisions were available at Cape Evans, the supply landed from the ship being supplemented by the stores left by the Scott Expedition of 1912-13 and the Shackleton Expedition of 1907-09. The supply of clothing and tents was more difficult. Garments brought from the ship could be supplemented by old clothing found at Hut Point and Cape Evans. The Burberry wind-proof outer garments were old and in poor order for the start of a season's sledging. Old sleeping-bags had been cut up to make finneskoe (fur boots) and mend other sleeping-bags. Three tents were available, one sound one landed from the *Aurora*, and two old ones left by Captain Scott. Mackintosh had enough sledges, but the experience of the first journey with the dogs had been unfortunate, and there were now only four useful dogs left. They did not make a full team and would have to be used merely as an auxiliary to man-haulage.

The scheme adopted by Mackintosh, after discussion with the members of his party, was that nine men, divided into three parties of three each, should undertake the sledging. One man would be left at Cape Evans to continue the meteorological observations during the summer. The motor-tractor, which had been left at Hut Point, was to be brought to Cape Evans and, if possible, put into working order. Mackintosh estimated that the provisions required for the consumption of the depot parties, and for the depots to be placed southward to the foot of the Beardmore Glacier, would amount to 4000 lb; The first depot was to be placed off Minna Bluff, and from there southward a depot was to be placed on each degree of latitude. The final depot would be made at the foot of the Beardmore Glacier. The initial task would be the haulage of stores from Cape Evans to Hut Point, a distance of 13 miles. All the sledging stores had to be taken across, and Mackintosh proposed to place additional supplies there in case a party, returning late from the Barrier, had to spend winter months at Hut Point.

The first party, consisting of Mackintosh, Richards, and Spencer-Smith, left Cape Evans on September 1 with 600 lb. of stores on one sledge, and had an uneventful journey to Hut Point. They pitched a tent half-way across the bay, on the sea-ice, and left it there for the use of the various parties during the month. At Hut Point they cleared the snow from the motor-tractor and made some preliminary efforts to get it into working order. They returned to Cape Evans on the 3rd. The second trip to Hut Point was made by a party of nine, with three sledges. Two sledges, man-hauled, were loaded with 1278 lb. of stores, and a smaller sledge, drawn by the dogs, carried the sleeping-bags. This party encountered a stiff southerly breeze, with low temperature, and, as the men were still in rather soft condition, they suffered much from frostbites. Joyce and Gaze both had their heels badly blistered. Mackintosh's face suffered, and other men had fingers and ears 'bitten'. When they returned Gaze had to travel on a sledge, since he could not set foot to the ground. They tried to haul the motor to Cape Evans on this occasion, but left it for another time after covering a mile or so. The motor was not working and was heavy to pull.

Eight men made the third journey to Hut Point, Gaze and Jack remaining behind. They took 660 lb. of oil and 630 lb. of stores. From Hut Point the next day (September 14) the party proceeded with loaded sledges to Safety Camp, on the edge of the Barrier. This camp would be the starting-point for the march over the Barrier to the Minna Bluff depot. They left the two sledges, with 660 lb. of oil and 500 lb. of oatmeal, sugar, and sundries, at Safety Camp and returned to Hut Point. The dogs shared the work on this journey. The next day Mackintosh and his companions took the motor to Cape Evans, hauling it with its grip-wheels mounted on a sledge. After a pause due to bad weather, a party of eight men took another load to Hut Point on September 24, and on to Safety Camp the next day. They got back to Cape Evans on the 26th. Richards meanwhile had overhauled the motor and given it some trial runs on the sea-ice. But he reported that the machine was not working satisfactorily, and Mackintosh decided not to persevere with it.

'Everybody is up to his eyes in work,' runs the last entry in the journal left by Mackintosh at Cape Evans. 'All gear is being overhauled, and personal clothing is having the last stitches. We have been improvising shoes to replace the finneskoe, of which we are badly short. Wild has made an excellent shoe out of an old horse-rug he found here, and this is being copied by other men. I have made myself a pair of mits out of an old sleeping-bag. Last night I had a bath, the second since being here . . . I close this journal today (September 30) and am packing it with my papers here. Tomorrow we start for Hut Point. Nine of us are going on the sledge party for laying depots – namely, Stevens, Spencer-Smith, Joyce, Wild, Cope, Hayward, Jack, Richards, and myself. Gaze, who is still suffering from bad feet, is remaining behind and will probably be relieved by Stevens after our first trip. With us we take three months' provisions to leave at Hut Point. I continue this journal in another book, which I keep with me.'

The nine men reached Hut Point on October 1. They took the last loads with them. Three sledges and three tents were to be taken on to the Barrier; and the parties were as follows:

No. 1: Mackintosh, Spencer-Smith, and Wild;

No. 2: Joyce, Cope, and Richards;

No. 3: Jack, Hayward, and Gaze.

On October 3 and 4 some stores left at Half Way Camp were brought in, and other stores were moved on to Safety Camp. Bad weather delayed the start of the depot-laying expedition from Hut Point until October 9.

CHAPTER 15

Laying the depots

Mackintosh's account of the depot-laying journeys undertaken by his parties in the summer of 1915-16 unfortunately is not available. The leader of the parties kept a diary, but he had the book with him when he was lost on the sea-ice in the following winter. The narrative of the journeys has been compiled from the notes kept by Joyce, Richards, and other members of the parties, and I may say here that it is a record of dogged endeavour in the face of great difficulties and serious dangers. It is always easy to be wise after the event, and one may realise now that the use of the dogs, untrained and soft from shipboard inactivity, on the comparatively short journey undertaken immediately after the landing in 1915 was a mistake. The result was the loss of nearly all the dogs before the longer and more important journeys of 1915-16 were undertaken. The men were sledging almost continuously during a period of six months; they suffered from frostbite, scurvy, snow-blindness, and the utter weariness of overtaxed bodies. But they placed the depots in the required positions, and if the Weddell Sea party had been able to make the crossing of the Antarctic continent, the stores and fuel would have been waiting for us where we expected to find them.

The position on October 9 was that the nine men at Hut Point had with them the stores required for the depots and for their own maintenance throughout the summer. The remaining dogs were at Cape Evans with Gaze, who had a sore heel and had been replaced temporarily by Stevens in the sledging party. A small quantity of stores had been conveyed already to Safety Camp on the edge of the Barrier beyond Hut Point. Mackintosh intended to form a large depot off Minna Bluff, seventy miles out from Hut Point. This would necessitate several trips with heavy loads. Then he would use the Bluff depot as a base for the journey to Mount

Hope, at the foot of the Beardmore Glacier, where the final depot was to be laid.

The party left Hut Point on the morning of October 9, the nine men hauling on one rope and trailing three loaded sledges. They reached Safety Camp in the early afternoon, and, after repacking the sledges with a load of about 2000 lb., they began the journey over the Barrier. The pulling proved exceedingly heavy, and they camped at the end of half a mile. It was decided next day to separate the sledges, three men to haul each sledge. Mackintosh hoped that better progress could be made in this way. The distance for the day was only four miles, and the next day's journey was no better. Joyce mentions that he had never done harder pulling, the surface being soft, and the load amounting to 220 lb. per man. The new arrangement was not a success, owing to differences in hauling capacity and inequalities in the loading of the sledges; and on the morning of the 12th, Mackintosh, after consultation, decided to push forward with Wild and Spencer-Smith, hauling one sledge and a relatively light load, and leave Joyce and the remaining five men to bring two sledges and the rest of the stores at their best pace. This arrangement was maintained on the later journeys. The temperatures were falling below −30 degrees Fahr. at some hours, and, as the men perspired freely while hauling their heavy loads in the sun, they suffered a great deal of discomfort in the damp and freezing clothes at night. Joyce cut down his load on the 13th by depot-ing some rations and spare clothing, and made better progress. He was building snow-cairns as guide-posts for use on the return journey. He mentions passing some large crevasses during succeeding days. Persistent head winds with occasional drift made the conditions unpleasant and caused many frostbites. When the surface was hard, and the pulling comparatively easy, the men slipped and fell continually, 'looking much like classical dancers'.

On the 20th a northerly wind made possible the use of a sail, and Joyce's party made rapid progress. Jack sighted a bamboo pole during the afternoon; and Joyce found that it marked a depot he had laid for my own 'Farthest South' party in 1908. He dug down in the hope of finding some stores, but the depot had been cleared. The party reached the Bluff depot on the evening of the 21st and found that Mackintosh had been there on the 19th. Mackintosh had left 178lb. of provisions, and Joyce left one sledge and 273 lb.

of stores. The most interesting incident of the return journey was the discovery of a note left by Mr Cherry Garrard for Captain Scott on March 19, 1912, only a few days before the latter perished at his camp farther south. An upturned sledge at this point was found to mark a depot of dog-biscuit and motor oil, laid by one of Captain Scott's parties. Joyce reached Safety Camp on the afternoon of the 27th, and, after dumping all spare gear, pushed on to Hut Point in a blizzard. The sledges nearly went over a big drop at the edge of the Barrier, and a few moments later Stevens dropped down a crevasse to the length of his harness.

'Had a tough job getting him up, as we had no alpine rope and had to use harness,' wrote Joyce. 'Got over all right and had a very hard pull against wind and snow, my face getting frost-bitten as I had to keep looking up to steer. We arrived at the hut about 7.30 p.m. after a very hard struggle. We found the Captain and his party there. They had been in for three days. Gaze was also there with the dogs. We soon had a good feed and forgot our hard day's work.'

Mackintosh decided to make use of the dogs on the second journey to the Bluff depot. He thought that with the aid of the dogs heavier loads might be hauled. This plan involved the dispatch of a party to Cape Evans to get dog-pemmican. Mackintosh himself, with Wild and Spencer-Smith, started south again on October 29. Their sledge overturned on the slope down to the sea-ice, and the rim of their tent-spread was broken. The damage did not appear serious, and the party soon disappeared round Cape Armitage. Joyce remained in charge at Hut Point, with instructions to get dog-food from Cape Evans and make a start south as soon as possible. He sent Stevens, Hayward, and Cope to Cape Evans the next day, and busied himself with the repair of sledging-gear. Cope, Hayward, and Gaze arrived back from Cape Evans on November 1, Stevens having stayed at the base. A blizzard delayed the start southward, and the party did not get away until November 5. The men pulled in harness with the four dogs, and, as the surface was soft and the loads on the two sledges were heavy, the advance was slow. The party covered 5 miles 700 yards on the 6th, 4 miles 300 yards on the 7th, and 8 miles 1300 yards on the 9th, with the aid of a light northerly wind. They passed on the 9th a huge *bergstrom*, with a drop of about 70 feet from the flat surface of the Barrier. Joyce thought that a big crevasse bad caved in. 'We took some photographs,' wrote Joyce. 'It is a really extraordinary fill-in of ice, with cliffs of blue ice about 70 feet high, and heavily crevassed, with overhanging snow-curtains. One could easily walk over the edge coming from the north in thick weather.' Another *bergstrom*, with crevassed ice around it, was encountered on the 11th. Joyce reached the Bluff depot on the evening of the 14th and found that he could leave 624 lb. of provisions. Mackintosh had been there several days earlier and had left 188 lb. of stores.

Joyce made Hut Point again on November 20 after an adventurous day. The surface was good in the morning and he pushed forward rapidly. About 10.30 a.m. the party encountered heavy pressure-ice with crevasses, and had many narrow escapes. 'After lunch we came on four crevasses quite suddenly. Jack fell through. We could not alter course, or else we should have been steering among them, so galloped right across. We were going so fast that the dogs that went through were jerked out. It came on very thick at 2 p.m. Every bit of land was obscured, and it was hard to steer. Decided to make for Hut Point, and arrived at 6.30 p.m., after doing twenty-two miles, a very good performance. I had a bad attack of snow-blindness and had to use cocaine. Hayward also had a bad time. I was laid up and had to keep my eyes bandaged for three days. Hayward, too.' The two men were about again on November 24, and the party started south on its third journey to the Bluff on the 25th. Mackintosh was some distance ahead, but the two parties met on the 28th and had some discussion as to plans. Mackintosh was proceeding to the Bluff depot with the intention of taking a load of stores to the depot placed on lat. 80 degrees S. in the first season's sledging. Joyce, after depositing his third load at the Bluff, would return to Hut Point for a fourth and last load, and the parties would then join forces for the journey southward to Mount Hope.

Joyce left 729 lb. at the Bluff depot on December 2, reached Hut Point on December 7, and, after allowing dogs and men a good rest, he moved southward again on December 13. This proved to be the worst journey the party had made. The men had much trouble with crevasses, and they were held up by blizzards on December 16, 18, 19, 22, 23, 26, and 27. They spent Christmas Day struggling through soft snow against an icy wind and drift.

The party reached the Bluff depot on December 28, and found that Mackintosh, who had been much delayed by the bad weather, had gone south two days earlier on his way to the 80 degrees S. depot. He had not made much progress and his camp was in sight. He had left instructions for Joyce to follow him. The Bluff depot was now well stocked. Between 2800 and 2900 lb. of provisions had been dragged to the depot for the use of parties working to the south of this point. This quantity was in addition to stores placed there earlier in the year.

Joyce left the Bluff depot on December 29, and the parties were together two days later. Mackintosh handed Joyce instructions to proceed with his party to lat. 81 degrees S and place a depot there. He was then to send three men back to Hut Point and proceed to lat. 82 degrees S., where he would lay another depot. Then if provisions permitted he would push south as far as lat. 83 degrees. Mackintosh himself was reinforcing the depot at lat. 80 degrees S. and would then carry on southward. Apparently his instructions to Joyce were intended to guard against the contingency of the parties failing to meet. The dogs were hauling well, and though their number was small they were of very great assistance. The parties were now ninety days out from Cape Evans, and 'all hands were feeling fit.'

The next incident of importance was the appearance of a defect in one of the two Primus lamps used by Joyce's party. The lamps had all seen service with one or other of Captain Scott's parties, and they had not been in first-class condition when the sledging commenced. The threatened failure of a lamp was a matter of grave moment, since a party could not travel without the means of melting snow and preparing hot food. If Joyce took a faulty lamp past the 80 degrees S. depot, his whole party might have to turn back at lat. 81 degrees S., and this would imperil the success of the season's sledging. He decided, therefore, to send three men back from the 80 degrees S. depot, which he reached on January 6, 1916. Cope, Gaze, and Jack were the men to return. They took the defective Primus and a light load, and by dint of hard travelling, without the aid of dogs, they reached Cape Evans on January 16.

Joyce, Richards, and Hayward went forward with a load of 1280 lb., comprising twelve weeks' sledging rations, dog-food and depot supplies, in addition to the sledging-gear. They built cairns at short intervals as guides to the depots. Joyce was feeding the dogs well and giving them a hot hoosh every third night. 'It is worth it for the wonderful amount of work they are doing. If we can keep them to 82 degrees S. I can honestly say it is through their work we have got through.' On January 8 Mackintosh joined Joyce, and from that point the parties, six men strong, went forward together. They marched in thick weather during January 10, 11, and 12, keeping the course by means of cairns, with a scrap of black cloth on top of each one. It was possible, by keeping the cairns in line behind the sledges and building new ones as old ones disappeared, to march on an approximately straight line. On the evening of the 12th they reached lat. 81 degrees S., and built a large cairn for the depot. The stores left here were three weeks' rations for the ordinary sledging unit of three men. This quantity would provide five days' rations for twelve men, half for the use of the overland party, and half for the depot party on its return journey.

The party moved southwards again on January 13 in bad weather.

'After a little consultation we decided to get under way,' wrote Joyce. 'Although the weather is thick, and snow is falling, it is worth while to make the effort. A little patience with the direction and the cairns, even if one has to put them up 200 yds. apart, enables us to advance, and it seems that this weather will never break. We have cut up an old pair of trousers belonging to Richards to place on the sides of the cairns, so as to make them more prominent. It was really surprising to find how we got on in spite of the snow and the pie-crust surface. We did 5 miles 75 yds. before lunch. The dogs are doing splendidly. I really don't know how we should manage if it were not for them . . . The distance for the day was 10 miles 720 yds., a splendid performance considering surface and weather.'

The weather cleared on the 14th; and the men were able to get bearings from the mountains to the westward. They advanced fairly rapidly during succeeding days, the daily distances being from ten to twelve miles, and reached lat. 82 degrees S. on the morning of January 18. The depot here, like the depot at 81 degrees S., contained five days' provisions for twelve men. Mackintosh was having trouble with the Primus lamp in his tent, and this made it inadvisable to divide the party again. It was decided, therefore, that all should proceed, and that the next and last depot should be placed on the base of Mount Hope, at the foot of the Beardmore Glacier, in lat. 83 degrees 30' S. The party proceeded at once and advanced five miles beyond the depot before camping on the evening of the 18th.

The sledge loads were now comparatively light, and on the 19th the party covered 13 miles 700 yds. A new trouble was developing, for Spencer-Smith was suffering from swollen and painful legs, and was unable to do much pulling. Joyce wrote on the 21st that Smith was worse, and that Mackintosh was showing signs of exhaustion. A mountain that he believed to be Mount Hope could be seen right ahead, over thirty miles away. Spencer-Smith, who had struggled forward gamely and made no unnecessary complaints, started with the party the next morning and kept going until shortly before noon. Then he reported his inability to proceed, and Mackintosh called a halt. Spencer-Smith suggested that he should be left with provisions and a tent while the other members of the party pushed on to Mount Hope, and pluckily assured Mackintosh that the rest would put him right and that he would be ready to march when they returned. The party agreed, after a brief consultation, to adopt this plan. Mackintosh felt that the depot must be laid, and that delay would be dangerous. Spencer-Smith was left with a tent, one sledge, and provisions, and told to expect the returning party in about a week. The tent was made as comfortable as possible inside, and food was placed within the sick man's reach. Spencer-Smith bade his companions a cheery good-bye after lunch, and the party was six or seven miles away before evening. Five men had to squeeze into one tent that night, but with a minus temperature they did not object to being crowded.

On January 23 a thick fog obscured all landmarks, and as bearings of the mountains were now necessary the party had to camp at 11 a.m., after travelling only four miles. The thick weather continued over the 24th, and the men did not move again until the morning of the 25th. They did 17¾ miles that day, and camped at 6 p.m. on the edge of 'the biggest ice-pressure' Joyce had ever seen. They were steering in towards the mountains and were encountering the tremendous congestion created by the flow of the Beardmore Glacier into the barrier ice.

'We decided to keep the camp up,' ran Joyce's account of the work done on January 26. 'Skipper, Richards, and myself roped ourselves together, I taking the lead, to try and find a course through this pressure. We came across very wide crevasses, went down several, came on top of a very high ridge, and such a scene! Imagine thousands of tons of ice churned up to a depth of about 300 ft. We took a couple of photographs, then carried on to the east. At last we found a passage through, and carried on through smaller crevasses to Mount Hope, or we hoped it was the mountain by that name. We can see a great glacier ahead which we take for the Beardmore, which this mountain is on, but the position on the chart seems wrong. [It was not. – E.H.S.] We nearly arrived at the ice-foot when Richards saw something to the right, which turned out to be two of Captain Scott's sledges, upright, but three-quarters buried in snow. Then we knew for certain this was the place we had struggled to get to. So we climbed the glacier on the slope and went up about one and a quarter miles, and saw the great Beardmore Glacier stretching to the south. It is about twenty-five miles wide – a most wonderful sight. Then we returned to our camp, which we found to be six miles away. We left at 8 a.m. and arrived back at 3 p.m., a good morning's work. We then had lunch. About 4 p.m. we got under way and proceeded with the two sledges and camped about 7 o'clock. Wild, Hayward and myself then took the depot up the Glacier, a fortnight's provisions. We left it lashed to a broken sledge and put up a large flag. I took two photographs of it. We did not arrive back until 10.30 p.m. It was rather a heavy pull up. I was very pleased to see our work completed at last . . . Turned in 12 o'clock. The distance done during day 22 miles.'

The party remained in camp until 3.30 p.m. on the 27th, owing to a blizzard with heavy snow. Then they made a start in clearer weather and got through the crevassed area before camping at 7 p.m. Joyce was suffering from snow-blindness. They were now homeward bound, with 365 miles to go. They covered 16½ miles on the 28th, with Joyce absolutely blind and hanging to the harness for guidance, 'but still pulling his whack'. They reached Spencer-Smith's camp the next after noon and found him in his sleeping-bag, quite unable to walk. Joyce's diary of this date contains a rather gloomy reference to the outlook, since he guessed that Mackintosh also would be unable to make the homeward march. 'The dogs are still keeping fit,' he added. 'If they will only last to 80 degrees S. we shall then have enough food to take them in, and then if the ship is in I guarantee they will live in comfort the remainder of their lives.'

No march could be made on the 30th, since a blizzard was raging. The party made 8 miles on the 31st, with Spencer-Smith on one of the sledges in his sleeping-bag. The sufferer was quite helpless, and had to be lifted and carried about, but his courage did not fail him. His words were cheerful even when his physical suffering and weakness were most pronounced. The distance for February 1 was 13 miles. The next morning the party abandoned one sledge in order to lighten the load, and proceeded with a single sledge, Spencer-Smith lying on top of the stores and gear. The distance for the day was 15½ miles. They picked up the 82 degrees S. depot on February 3, and took one week's provisions, leaving two weeks' rations for the overland party. Joyce, Wild, Richards, and Hayward were feeling fit. Mackintosh was lame and weak; Spencer-Smith's condition was alarming. The party was being helped by strong southerly winds, and the distances covered were decidedly good. The sledge-meter recorded 15 miles 1700 yds. on February 4, 17 miles 1400 yds. on the 5th, 18 miles 1200 yds. on the 6th, and 13 miles 1000 yds. on the 7th, when the 81 degrees S. depot was picked up at 10.30 a.m., and one week's stores taken, two weeks' rations being left.

The march to the next depot, at 80 degrees S., was uneventful. The party made good marches in spite of bad surfaces and thick weather, and reached the depot late in the afternoon of February 12. The supply of stores at this depot was ample, and the men took a fortnight's rations (calculated on a three-man basis), leaving nearly four weeks' rations. Spencer-Smith seemed a little better, and all hands were cheered by the rapid advance. February 14, 15, and 16 were bad days, the soft surface allowing the men to sink to their knees at times. The dogs had a rough time, and the daily distances fell to about eight miles. Mackintosh's weakness was increasing. Then on the 18th, when the party was within twelve miles of the Bluff depot, a furious blizzard made travelling impossible. This blizzard raged for five days. Rations were reduced on the second day, and the party went on half-rations the third day.

'Still blizzarding,' wrote Joyce on the 20th. 'Things are serious, what with our patient and provisions running short. Dog provisions are nearly out, and we have to halve their rations. We are now on one cup of hooch among the three of us, with one biscuit and six lumps of sugar. The most serious of calamities is that our oil is running out. We have plenty of tea, but no fuel to cook it with.' The men in Mackintosh's tent were in no better plight. Mackintosh himself was in a bad way. He was uncertain about his ability to resume the march, but was determined to try.

'Still blizzarding,' wrote Joyce again on the 21st. 'We are lying in pools of water made by our bodies through staying in the same place for such a long time. I don't know what we shall do if this does not ease. It has been blowing continuously without a lull. The food for today was one cup of pemmican amongst three of us, one biscuit each, and two cups of tea among the three.' The kerosene was exhausted, but Richards improvised a lamp by pouring some spirit (intended for priming the oil-lamp) into a mug, lighting it, and holding another mug over it. It took half an hour to heat a mug of melted snow in this way. 'Same old thing, no ceasing of this blizzard,' was Joyce's note twenty-four hours later. 'Hardly any food left except tea and sugar. Richards, Hayward, and I, after a long talk, decided to get under way tomorrow in any case, or else we shall be sharing the fate of Captain Scott and his party. The other tent seems to be very quiet, but now and again we hear a burst of song from Wild, so they are in the land of the living. We gave the dogs the last of their food tonight, so we shall have to push, as a great deal depends on them.' Further quotations from Joyce's diary tell their own story.

'*February 23, Wednesday.* – About 11 o'clock saw a break in the clouds and the sun showing. Decided to have the meal we kept for getting under way. Sang out to the Skipper's party that we should shift as soon as we had a meal. I asked Wild, and found they had a bag of oatmeal, some Bovril cubes, one bag of chocolate, and eighteen biscuits, so they are much better off than we are. After we had our meal we started to dig out our sledge, which we found right under. It took us two hours, and one would hardly credit how weak we were. Two digs of the shovel and we were out of breath. This was caused through our lying up on practically no food. After getting sledge out we took it around to the Skipper's tent on account of the heavy sastrugi, which was very high. Got under way about 2.20. Had to stop very often on account of sail, etc. About 3.20 the Skipper, who had tied himself to the rear of the sledge, found it impossible to proceed. So after a consultation with Wild and party, decided to pitch their tent, leaving Wild to look after the Skipper and Spencer-Smith, and make the best of our way to the depot, which is anything up to twelve miles away. So we made them comfortable and left them about 3.40. I told Wild I should leave as much as possible and get back 26th or 27th, weather permitting, but just as we left them it came on to snow pretty hard, sun going in, and we found even with the four dogs we could not make more than one-half to three-quarters of a mile an hour. The surface is so bad that sometimes you go in up to your waist; still in spite of all this we carried on until 6.35. Camped in a howling blizzard. I found my left foot badly frost-bitten. Now after this march we came in to our banquet – one cup of tea and half a biscuit. Turned in at 9 o'clock. Situation does not look very cheerful. This is really the worst surface I have ever come across in all my journeys here.'

Mackintosh had stayed on his feet as long as was humanly possible. The records of the outward journey show clearly that he was really unfit to continue beyond the 82 degrees S. depot, and other members of the party would have liked him to have stayed with Spencer-Smith at lat. 83 degrees S. But the responsibility for the work to be done was primarily his, and he would not give in. He had been suffering for several weeks from what he cheerfully called 'a sprained leg', owing to scurvy. He marched for half an hour on the 23rd before breaking down, but had to be supported partly by Richards. Spencer-Smith was sinking. Wild, who stayed in charge of the two invalids, was in fairly good condition. Joyce, Richards, and Hayward, who had undertaken the relief journey, were all showing symptoms of scurvy, though in varying degrees. Their legs were weak, their gums swollen. The decision that the invalids, with Wild, should stay in camp from February 24, while Joyce's party pushed forward to Bluff depot, was justified fully by the circumstances. Joyce, Richards, and Hayward had difficulty in reaching the depot with a nearly empty sledge. An attempt to make their journey with two helpless men might have involved the loss of the whole party.

'*February 24, Thursday.* – Up at 4:30; had one cup of tea, half biscuit; under way after 7. Weather, snowing and blowing like yesterday. Richards, laying the cairns, had great trouble in getting the compass within 10 degrees on account of wind. During the forenoon had to stop every quarter of an hour on account of our breath. Every time the sledge struck a drift she stuck in (although only 200 lb.), and in spite of three men and four dogs we could only shift her with the 1 –2 –3 haul. I wonder if this weather will ever clear up. Camped in an exhausted condition about 12.10. Lunch, half cup of weak tea and quarter biscuit, which took over half an hour to make. Richards and Hayward went out of tent to prepare for getting under way, but the force of wind and snow drove them back. The force of wind is about seventy to eighty miles per hour. We decided to get the sleeping-bags in, which took some considerable time. The worst of camping is the poor dogs and our weak condition, which means we have to get out of our wet sleeping-bags and have another half cup of tea without working for it. With scrapings from dog-tank it is a very scanty meal. This is the second day the dogs have been without food, and if we cannot soon pick up depot and save the dogs it will be almost impossible to drag our two invalids back the one hundred miles which we have to go. The wind carried on with unabating fury until 7 o'clock, and then came a lull. We at once turned out, but found it snowing so thickly that it was impossible to proceed on account of our weakness. No chance must we miss. Turned in again. Wind sprang up again with heavy drift 8.30. In spite of everything my tentmates are very cheerful and look on the bright side of everything. After a talk we decided to wait and turned in. It is really wonderful what dreams we have, especially of food. Trusting in Providence for fine weather tomorrow.

'*February 25, Friday.* – Turned out 4.45. Richards prepared our usual banquet, half cup of tea, quarter biscuit, which we relished. Under way at 7, carried on, halting every ten minutes or quarter of an hour. Weather, snowing and blowing same as yesterday. We are in a very weak state, but we cannot give in. We often talk about poor Captain Scott and the blizzard that finished him and party. If we had stayed in our tent another day I don't think we should have got under way at all, and we would have shared the same fate. But if the worst comes we have made up our minds to carry on and die in harness. If any one were to see us on trek they would be surprised: three men staggering on with four dogs, very weak; practically empty sledge with fair wind and just crawling along; our clothes are all worn out, finneskoe and sleeping bags torn. Tent is our worst point, all torn in front, and we are afraid to camp on account of it, as it is too cold to mend it. We camped for our grand lunch at noon. After five hours' struggling I think we did about three miles. After lunch sat in our tent talking over the situation. Decided to get under way again as soon as there is any clearance. Snowing and blowing, force about fifty or sixty miles an hour.

'*February 26, Saturday.* – Richards went out 1.10 a.m. and found it clearing a bit, so we got under way as soon as possible, which was 2.10 a.m. About 2.35 Richards sighted depot, which seemed to be right on top of us. I suppose we camped no more than three-quarters of a mile from it. The dogs sighted it, which seemed to electrify them. They had new life and started to run, but we were so weak that we could not go more than 200 yds. and then spell. I think another day would have seen us off. Arrived at depot 3.25; found it in a dilapidated condition, cases all about the place. I don't suppose there has ever been a weaker party arrive at any depot, either north or south. After a hard struggle got our tent up and made camp. Then gave the dogs a good feed of pemmican. If ever dogs saved the lives of anyone they have saved ours. Let us hope they will continue in good health, so that we can get out to our comrades. I started on our cooking. Not one of us had any appetite, although we were in the land of plenty, as we call this depot; plenty of biscuit, etc., but we could not eat. I think it is the reaction, not only in arriving here, but also finding no news of the ship, which was arranged before we left. We all think there has been a calamity there. Let us hope for the best. We decided to have rolled-oats and milk for a start, which went down very well, and then a cup of tea. How cheery the Primus sounds. It seems like coming out of a thick London fog into a drawing-room. After a consultation we decided to have a meal of pemmican in four hours, and so on, until our weakness was gone. Later. – Still the same weather. We shall get under way and make a forced march back as soon as possible. I think we shall get stronger travelling and feeding well. Later. – Weather will not permit us to travel yet. Mended our torn tent with food-bags. This took four hours. Feeding the dogs every four hours, and Richards and Hayward built up depot. It is really surprising to find it takes two men to lift a 50-lb. case; it only shows our weakness. Weather still the same; force of wind at times about seventy to ninety miles an hour; really surprising how this can keep on so long.

'*February 27, Sunday.* – Wind continued with fury the whole night. Expecting every minute to have the tent blown off us. Up 5 o'clock; found it so thick one could not get out of the tent. We are still very weak, but think we can do the twelve miles to our comrades in one long march. If only it would clear up for just one day we would not mind. This is the longest continuous blizzard I have ever been in. We have not had a travelling day for eleven days, and the amount of snow that has fallen is astonishing. Later. – Had a meal 10.30 and decided to get under way in spite of the wind and snow. Under way 12 o'clock. We have three weeks' food on sledge, about 160 lb., and one week's dog-food, 50 lb. The whole weight, all told, about 600 lb., and also taking an extra sledge to bring back Captain Mackintosh. To our surprise we could not shift the sledges. After half an hour we got about ten yards. We turned the sledge up and scraped runners; it went a little better after. I am afraid our weakness is much more than we think. Hayward is in rather a bad way about his knees, which are giving him trouble and are very painful; we will give him a good massage when we camp. The dogs have lost all heart in pulling; they seem to think that going south again is no good to them; they seem to just jog along, and one cannot do more. I don't suppose our pace is more than one-half or three-quarters of a mile per hour. The surface is rotten, snow up to one's knees, and what with wind and drift a very bad outlook. Lunched about 4.30. Carried on until 11.20, when we camped. It was very dark making our dinner, but soon got through the process. Then Richards spent an hour or so in rubbing Hayward with methylated spirits, which did him a world of good. If he were to break up now I should not know what to do. Turned in about 1.30. It is now calm, but overcast with light falling snow.

'*February 28, Monday.* – Up at 6 o'clock; can just see a little skyline. Under way at 9 o'clock. The reason of delay, had to mend finneskoe, which are in a very dilapidated condition. I got my feet badly frost-bitten yesterday. About 11 o'clock came on to snow, everything overcast. We ought to reach our poor boys in three or four hours, but Fate wills otherwise, as it came on again to blizzard force about 11.45. Camped at noon. I think the party must be within a very short distance, but we cannot go on as we might pass them, and as we have not got any position to go on except compass. Later. – Kept on blizzarding all afternoon and night.

'*February 29, Tuesday.* – Up at 5 o'clock; still very thick. It cleared up a little to the south about 8 o'clock, when Richards sighted something black to the north of us, but could not see properly what it was. After looking round sighted camp to the south, so we got under way as soon as possible. Got up to the camp about 12.45, when Wild came out to meet us. We gave him a cheer, as we fully expected to find all down. He said he had taken a little exercise every day; they had not any food left. The Skipper then came out of the tent, very weak and as much as he could do to walk. He said, "I want to thank you for saving our lives." I told Wild to go and give them a feed and not to eat too much at first in case of reaction, as I am going to get under way as soon as they have had a feed. So we had lunch, and the Skipper went ahead to get some exercise, and after an hour's digging out got everything ready for leaving. When we lifted Smith we found he was in a great hole which he had melted through. This party had been in one camp for twelve days. We got under way and picked the Skipper up; he had fallen down, too weak to walk. We put him on the sledge we had brought out, and we camped about 8 o'clock. I think we did about three miles – rather good with two men on the sledges and Hayward in a very bad way. I don't think there has been a party, either north or south, in such straits, three men down and three of us very weak; but the dogs seem to have new life since we turned north. I think they realise they are homeward bound. I am glad we kept them, even when we were starving. I knew they would have to come in at the finish. We have now to look forward to southerly winds for help, which I think we shall get at this time of year. Let us hope the temperature will keep up, as our sleeping-bags are wet through and worn out, and all our clothes full of holes, and finneskoe in a dilapidated condition; in fact, one would not be out on a cold day in civilisation with the rotten clothes we have on. Turned in 11 o'clock, wet through, but in a better frame of mind. Hope to try and reach the depot tomorrow, even if we have to march overtime.

'*March 1, Wednesday.* – Turned out usual time; a good south wind, but, worse luck, heavy drift. Set sail; put the Skipper on rear sledge. The temperature has gone down and it is very cold. Bluff in sight. We are making good progress, doing a good mileage before lunch. After lunch a little stronger wind. Hayward still hanging on to sledge; Skipper fell off twice. Reached depot 5.45. When camping found we had dropped our tent-poles, so Richards went back a little way and spotted them through the binoculars about half a mile off, and brought them back. Hayward and I were very cold by that time, the drift very bad. Moral: See everything properly secured. We soon had our tent up, cooked our dinner in the dark, and turned in about 10 o'clock.

'*March 2, Thursday.* – Up as usual. Strong south-west wind with heavy drift. Took two weeks' provisions from the depot. I think that will last us through, as there is another depot about fifty miles north from here; I am taking the outside course on account of the crevasses, and one cannot take too many chances with two men on sledges and one crippled. Under way about 10 o'clock; lunched noon in a heavy drift; took an hour to get the tents up, etc., the wind being so heavy. Found sledges buried under snow after lunch, took some time to get under way. Wind and drift very heavy; set half-sail on the first sledge and under way about 3.30. The going is perfect; sometimes sledges overtaking us. Carried on until 8 o'clock, doing an excellent journey for the day; distance about eleven or twelve miles. Gives one a bit of heart to carry on like this; only hope we can do this all the way. Had to cook our meals in the dark, but still we did not mind. Turned in about 11 o'clock, pleased with ourselves, although we were wet through with snow, as it got through all the holes in our clothes, and the sleeping-bags are worse than awful.

'*March 3, Friday.* – Up the usual time. It has been blowing a raging blizzard all night. Found to our disgust utterly impossible to carry on. Another few hours of agony in these rotten bags. Later. – Blizzard much heavier. Amused myself mending finneskoe and Burberrys, mits and socks. Had the Primus while this operation was in force. Hoping for a fine day tomorrow.

'*March 4, Saturday*. – Up 5.20. Still blizzarding, but have decided to get under way as we will have to try and travel through everything, as Hayward is getting worse, and one doesn't know who is the next. No mistake it is scurvy, and the only possible cure is fresh food. I sincerely hope the ship is in; if not we shall get over the hills by Castle Rock, which is rather difficult and will delay another couple of days. Smith is still cheerful; he has hardly moved for weeks and he has to have everything done for him. Got under way 9.35. It took some two hours to dig out dogs and sledges, as they were completely buried. It is the same every morning now. Set sail, going along pretty fair. Hayward gets on sledge now and again. Lunched as usual; sledges got buried again at lunch-time. It takes some time to camp now, and in this drift it is awful. In the afternoon wind eased a bit and drift went down. Found it very hard pulling with the third man on sledge, as Hayward has been on all the afternoon. Wind veered two points to south, so we had a fair wind. An hour before we camped Erebus and Terror showing up, a welcome sight. Only hope wind will continue. Drift is worst thing to contend with as it gets into our clothes, which are wet through now. Camped 8 o'clock. Cooked in the dark, and turned in in our wet sleeping-bags about 10 o'clock. Distance about eight or nine miles.

'*March 5, Sunday*. – Turned out 6.15. Overslept a little; very tired after yesterday. Sun shining brightly and no wind. It seemed strange last night, no flapping of tent in one's ears. About 8.30 came on to drift again. Under way 9.20, both sails set. Sledge going hard, especially in soft places. If Hayward had not broken down we should not feel the weight so much. Lunch 12.45. Under way at 3. Wind and drift very heavy. A good job it is blowing some, or else we should have to relay. All land obscured. Distance about ten or eleven miles, a very good performance. Camped 7.10 in the dark. Patients not in the best of trim. I hope to get in, bar accidents, in four days.

'*March 6, Monday*. – Under way 9.20. Picked up third two-mile depot 11 o'clock. Going with a fair wind in the forenoon, which eased somewhat after lunch and so caused very heavy work in pulling. It seems to me we shall have to depot someone if the wind eases at all. Distance during day about eight miles.

'*March 7, Tuesday*. – Under way 9 o'clock. Although we turn out at 5 it seems a long time to get under way. There is double as much work to do now with our invalids. This is the calmest day we have had for weeks. The sun is shining and all land in sight. It is very hard going. Had a little breeze about 11 o'clock, set sail, but work still very, very heavy. Hayward and Skipper going on ahead with sticks, very slow pace, but it will buck them up and do them good. If one could only get some fresh food! About 11 o'clock decided to camp and overhaul sledges and depot all gear except what is actually required. Under way again at 2, but surface being so sticky did not make any difference. After a consultation the Skipper decided to stay behind in a tent with three weeks' provisions whilst we pushed on with Smith and Hayward. It seems hard, only about thirty miles away, and yet cannot get any assistance. Our gear is absolutely rotten, no sleep last night, shivering all night in wet bags. I wonder what will be the outcome of it all after our struggle. Trust in Providence. Distance about three and a half miles.

'*March 8, Wednesday*. – Under way 9.20. Wished the Skipper goodbye; took Smith and Hayward on. Had a fair wind, going pretty good. Hope to arrive in Hut Point in four days. Lunched at No. 2 depot. Distance about four and a half miles. Under way as usual after lunch; head wind, going very heavy. Carried on until 6.30. Distance about eight or nine miles.

'*March 9, Thursday*. – Had a very bad night, cold intense. Temperature down to −29 degrees all night. At 4 a.m. Spencer–Smith called out that he was feeling queer. Wild spoke to him. Then at 5.45 Richards suddenly said, "I think he has gone." Poor Smith, for forty days in pain he had been dragged on the sledge, but never grumbled or complained. He had a strenuous time in his wet bag, and the jolting of the sledge on a very weak heart was not too good for him. Sometimes when we lifted him on the sledge he would nearly faint, but during the whole time he never complained. Wild looked after him from the start. We buried him in his bag at 9 o'clock at the following position: Ereb. 184 degrees – Obs. Hill 149 degrees. We made a cross of bamboos, and built a mound and cairn, with particulars. After that got under way with Hayward on sledge. Found going very hard, as we had a northerly wind in our faces, with a temperature below 20 degrees. What with frostbites, etc., we are all suffering. Even the dogs seem like giving in; they do not seem to take any interest in their work. We have been out much too long, and nothing ahead to cheer us up but a cold, cheerless hut. We did about two and a half miles in the forenoon, Hayward toddling ahead every time we had a spell. During lunch the wind veered to the south with drift, just right to set sail. We carried on with Hayward on sledge and camped in the dark about 8 o'clock. Turned in at 10, weary, worn, and sad. Hoping to reach depot tomorrow.

'*March 10, Friday*. – Turned out as usual. Beam wind, going pretty fair, very cold. Came into very soft snow about 3; arrived at Safety Camp 5 o'clock. Got to edge of Ice Barrier; found passage over in a bay full of seals. Dogs got very excited; had a job to keep them away. By the glass it looked clear right to Cape Armitage, which is four and a half miles away. Arrived there 8 o'clock, very dark and bad light. Found open water. Turned to climb slopes against a strong north-easterly breeze with drift. Found a place about a mile away, but we were so done up that it took until 11.30 to get gear up. This slope was about 150 yds. up, and every three paces we had to stop and get breath. Eventually camped and turned in about 2 o'clock. I think this is the worst day I ever spent. What with the disappointment of not getting round the Point, and the long day and the thought of getting Hayward over the slopes, it is not very entertaining for sleep.

'*March 11, Saturday*. – Up at 7 o'clock; took binoculars and went over the slope to look around the Cape. To my surprise found the open water and pack at the Cape only extended for about a mile. Came down and gave the boys the good news. I think it would take another two hard days to get over the hills, and we are too weak to do much of that, as I am afraid of another collapsing. Richards and Wild climbed up to look at the back of the bay and found the ice secure. Got under way 10.30, went round the Cape and found ice; very slushy, but continued on. No turning now; got into hard ice shortly after, eventually arriving at Hut Point about 3 o'clock. It seems strange after our adventures to arrive back at the old hut. This place has been standing since we built it in 1901, and has been the starting-point of a few expeditions since. When we were coming down the bay I could fancy the *Discovery* there when Scott arrived from his Farthest South in 1902, the ship decorated rainbow fashion, and Lieutenant Armitage giving out the news that Captain Scott had got to 82 degrees 17' S. We went wild that day. But now our homecoming is quite different. Hut half-full of snow through a window being left open and drift getting in; but we soon got it shipshape and Hayward in. I had the fire going and plenty of vegetables on, as there was a fair supply of dried vegetables. Then after we had had a feed, Richards and Wild went down the bay, and killed a couple of seals. I gave a good menu of seal meat at night, and we turned in about 11 o'clock, full – too full in fact. As there is no news here of the ship, and we cannot see her, we surmise she has gone down with all hands. I cannot see there is any chance of her being afloat or she would be here. I don't know how the Skipper will take it.

'*March 12, Sunday.* – Heard groans proceeding from the sleeping-bags all night; all hands suffering from over-eating. Hayward not very well. Turned out 8 o'clock. Good breakfast – porridge, seal, vegetables, and coffee; more like a banquet to us. After breakfast Richards and Wild killed a couple of seals whilst I made the hut a bit comfy. Hayward can hardly move. All of us in a very bad state, but we must keep up exercise. My ankles and knees badly swollen, gums prominent. Wild, very black around joints, and gums very black. Richards about the best off. After digging hut out I prepared food which I think will keep the scurvy down. The dogs have lost their lassitude and are quite frisky, except Oscar, who is suffering from over-feeding. After a strenuous day's work turned in 10 o'clock.

'*March 13, Monday.* – Turned out 7 o'clock. Carried on much the same as yesterday, bringing in seal blubber and meat. Preparing for departure tomorrow; hope everyone will be all right. Made new dog harness and prepared sledges. In afternoon cooked sufficient seal meat for our journey out and back, and same for dogs. Turned in 10 o'clock, feeling much better.

'*March 14, Tuesday.* – A beautiful day. Under way after lunch. One would think, looking at our party, that we were the most ragged lot one could meet in a day's march; all our clothes past mending, our faces as black as niggers' – a sort of crowd one would run away from. Going pretty good. As soon as we rounded Cape Armitage a dead head wind with a temperature of −18 degrees Fahr., so we are not in for a pleasant time. Arrived at Safety Camp 6 o'clock, turned in 8.30, after getting everything ready.

'*March 15, Wednesday*. – Under way as usual. Nice calm day. Had a very cold night, temperature going down to −30 degrees Fahr. Going along at a rattling good rate; in spite of our swollen limbs we did about fifteen miles. Very cold when we camped; temperature −20 degrees Fahr. Turned in 9 o'clock.

'*March 16, Thursday*. – Up before the sun, 4.45 a.m. Had a very cold night, not much sleep. Under way early. Going good. Passed Smith's grave 10.45 a.m. and had lunch at depot. Saw Skipper's camp just after, and looking through glass found him outside tent, much to the joy of all hands, as we expected him to be down. Picked him up 4.15 p.m. Broke the news of Smith's death and no ship. I gave him the date of the 17th to look out for our returning, so he had a surprise. We struck his camp and went north for about a mile and camped. We gave the Skipper a banquet of seal, vegetables, and blackcurrant jam, the feed of his life. He seems in a bad way. I hope to get him in in three days, and I think fresh food will improve him. We turned in 8 o'clock. Distance done during day sixteen miles.

'*March 17, Friday*. – Up at 5 o'clock. Under way 8 a.m. Skipper feeling much better after feeding him up. Lunched a few yards past Smith's grave. Had a good afternoon, going fair. Distance about sixteen miles. Very cold night, temperature −30 degrees Fahr. What with wet bags and clothes, rotten.

'*March 18, Saturday*. – Turned out 5 o'clock. Had rather a cold night. Temperature −29 degrees Fahr. Surface very good. The Skipper walked for a little way, which did him good. Lunched as usual. Pace good. After lunch going good. Arrived at Safety Camp 4.10 p.m. To our delight found the sea-ice in the same condition and arrived at Hut Point at 7 o'clock. Found Hayward still about same. Set to, made a good dinner, and all hands seem in the best of spirits. Now we have arrived and got the party in, it remains to themselves to get better. Plenty of exercise and fresh food ought to do miracles. We have been out 160 days, and done a distance of 1561 miles, a good record. I think the irony of fate was poor Smith going under a day before we got in. I think we shall all soon be well. Turned in 10.30 p.m. Before turning in Skipper shook us by the hand with great emotion, thanking us for saving his life.'

Richards, summarising the work of the parties, says that the journeys made between September 1 and March 18, a period of

160 days, totalled 1561 miles. The main journey, from Hut Point to Mount Hope and return, was 830 miles.

'The equipment,' he adds, 'was old at the commencement of the season, and this told severely at the later stages of the journey. Three Primus lamps gave out on the journeys, and the old tent brought back by one of the last parties showed rents several feet in length. This hampered the travelling in the long blizzards. Finneskoe were also in pieces at the end, and time had frequently to be lost through repairs to clothing becoming imperative. This account would not be complete without some mention of the unselfish service rendered by Wild to his two ill tent-mates. From the time he remained behind at the long blizzard till the death of Spencer-Smith he had two helpless men to attend to, and despite his own condition he was ever ready, night or day, to minister to their wants. This, in a temperature of −30 degrees Fahr. at times, was no light task.

'Without the aid of four faithful friends, Oscar, Con, Gunner, and Towser, the party could never have arrived back. These dogs from November 5 accompanied the sledging parties, and, although the pace was often very slow, they adapted themselves well to it. Their endurance was fine. For three whole days at one time they had not a scrap of food, and this after a period on short rations. Though they were feeble towards the end of the trip, their condition usually was good, and those who returned with them will ever remember the remarkable service they rendered.

'The first indication of anything wrong with the general health of the party occurred at about lat. 82 degrees 30' S., when Spencer-Smith complained of stiffness in the legs and discoloration. He attributed this to holes in his windproof clothing. At lat. 83 degrees S., when he gave way, it was thought that the rest would do him good. About the end of January Captain Mackintosh showed very serious signs of lameness. At this time his party had been absent from Hut Point, and consequently from fresh food, about three months.

'On the journey back Spencer-Smith gradually became weaker, and for some time before the end was in a very weak condition indeed. Captain Mackintosh, by great efforts, managed to keep his feet until the long blizzard was encountered. Here it was that Hayward was first found to be affected with the scurvy, his knees being stiff. In his case the disease took him off his feet very suddenly, apparently causing the muscles of his legs to contract till they could be straightened hardly more than a right angle. He had slight touches in the joints of the arms. In the cases of Joyce, Wild, and Richards, joints became stiff and black in the rear, but general weakness was the worst symptom experienced. Captain Mackintosh's legs looked the worst in the party.'

The five men who were now at Hut Point found quickly that some of the winter months must be spent there. They had no news of the ship, and were justified in assuming that she had not returned to the Sound, since if she had some message would have been awaiting them at Hut Point, if not farther south. The sea-ice had broken and gone north within a mile of the point, and the party must wait until the new ice became firm as far as Cape Evans. Plenty of seal meat was available, as well as dried vegetables, and the fresh food improved the condition of the patients very rapidly. Richards massaged the swollen joints and found that this treatment helped a good deal. Before the end of March Mackintosh and Hayward, the worst sufferers, were able to take exercise. By the second week of April Mackintosh was free of pain, though the backs of his legs were still discoloured.

A tally of the stores at the hut showed that on a reasonable allowance the supply would last till the middle of June. Richards and Wild killed many seals, so that there was no scarcity of meat and blubber. A few penguins were also secured. The sole means of cooking food and heating the hut was an improvised stove of brick, covered with two sheets of iron. This had been used by the former Expedition. The stove emitted dense smoke and often made the hut very uncomfortable, while at the same time it covered the men and all their gear with clinging and penetrating soot. Cleanliness was out of the question, and this increased the desire of the men to get across to Cape Evans. During April the sea froze in calm weather, but winds took the ice out again. On April 23 Joyce walked four miles to the north, partly on young ice two inches thick, and he thought then that the party might be able to reach Cape Evans within a few days. But a prolonged blizzard took the ice out right up to the Point, so that the open water extended at the end of April right up to the foot of Vinie's Hill. Then came a spell of calm weather, and during the first

week of May the sea-ice formed rapidly. The men made several
short trips over it to the north. The sun had disappeared below
the horizon in the middle of April, and would not appear again
for over four months.

The disaster that followed is described by both Richards and
Joyce. 'And now a most regrettable incident occurred,' wrote
Richards. 'On the morning of May 8, before breakfast, Captain
Mackintosh asked Joyce what he thought of his going to Cape
Evans with Hayward. Captain Mackintosh considered the ice
quite safe, and the fine morning no doubt tempted him to
exchange the quarters at the hut for the greater comfort and
better food at Cape Evans.' (Mackintosh naturally would be
anxious to know if the men at Cape Evans were well and had
any news of the ship.) 'He was strongly urged at the time not
to take the risk, as it was pointed out that the ice, although firm,
was very young, and that a blizzard was almost sure to take part
of it out to sea.'

However, at about 1 p.m., with the weather apparently changing for the worse, Mackintosh and Hayward left, after promising
to turn back if the weather grew worse. The last sight the watching
party on the hill gained of them was when they were about a
mile away, close to the shore, but apparently making straight for
Cape Evans. At 3 p.m. a moderate blizzard was raging, which later
increased in fury, and the party in the hut had many misgivings for
the safety of the absent men.

On May 10, the first day possible, the three men left behind
walked over new ice to the north to try and discover some trace as
to the fate of the others. The footmarks were seen clearly enough
raised up on the ice, and the track was followed for about two
miles in a direction leading to Cape Evans. Here they ended
abruptly, and in the dim light a wide stretch of water, very lightly
covered with ice, was seen as far as the eye could reach. It was at
once evident that part of the ice over which they had travelled had
gone out to sea.'

The whole party had intended, if the weather had held good, to
have attempted the passage across with the full moon about May
16. On the date on which Mackintosh and Hayward left it was
impossible that a sledge should travel the distance over the sea-ice
owing to the sticky nature of the surface. Hence their decision to

go alone and leave the others to follow with the sledge and equipment when the surface should improve. That they had actually been lost was learned only on July 15, on which date the party from Hut Point arrived at Cape Evans.

The entry in Joyce's diary shows that he had very strong forebodings of disaster when Mackintosh and Hayward left. He warned them not to go, as the ice was still thin and the weather was uncertain. Mackintosh seems to have believed that he and Hayward, travelling light, could get across to Cape Evans quickly before the weather broke, and if the blizzard had come two or three hours later they probably would have been safe. The two men carried no sleeping-bags and only a small meal of chocolate and seal meat.

The weather during June was persistently bad. No move had been possible on May 16, the sea-ice being out, and Joyce decided to wait until the next full moon. When this came the weather was boisterous, and so it was not until the full moon of July that the journey to Cape Evans was made. During June and July seals got very scarce, and the supply of blubber ran short.

Meals consisted of little but seal meat and porridge. The small stock of salt was exhausted, but the men procured two and a half pounds by boiling down snow taken from the bottom layer next to the sea-ice. The dogs recovered condition rapidly and did some hunting on their own account among the seals.

The party started for Cape Evans on July 15. They had expected to take advantage of the full moon, but by a strange chance they had chosen the period of an eclipse, and the moon was shadowed most of the time they were crossing the sea-ice. The ice was firm, and the three men reached Cape Evans without difficulty. They found Stevens, Cope, Gaze, and Jack at the Cape Evans Hut, and learned that nothing had been seen of Captain Mackintosh and Hayward. The conclusion that these men had perished was accepted reluctantly. The party at the base consisted now of Stevens, Cope, Joyce, Richards, Gaze, Wild, and Jack.

The men settled down now to wait for relief. When opportunity offered Joyce led search-parties to look for the bodies or any trace of the missing men, and he subsequently handed me the following report:

I beg to report that the following steps were taken to try and discover the bodies of Captain Mackintosh and Mr Hayward. After our party's return to the hut at Cape Evans, July 15, 1916, it was learned that Captain Mackintosh and Mr Hayward had not arrived; and, being aware of the conditions under which they were last seen, all the members of the wintering party were absolutely convinced that these two men were totally lost and dead – that they could not have lived for more than a few hours at the outside in the blizzard that they had encountered, they being entirely unprovided with equipment of any sort.

There was the barest chance that after the return of the sun some trace of their bodies might be found, so during the spring – that is, August and September 1916 – and in the summer – December and January 1916–17 – the following searches were carried out:

(1) Wild and I thoroughly searched Inaccessible Island at the end of August 1916.

(2) Various parties in September searched along the shore to the vicinity of Turk's Head.

(3) In company with Messrs. Wild and Gaze I started from Hut Point, December 31, 1916, at 8 a.m., and a course was steered inshore as close as possible to the cliffs in order to search for any possible means of ascent. At a distance of half a mile from Hut Point we passed a snow slope which I had already ascended in June 1916; three and a half miles farther on was another snow slope, which ended in Blue Ice Glacier slope, which we found impossible to climb, snow slope being formed by heavy winter snowfall. These were the only two places accessible. Distance on this day, 10 miles 1710 yds covered. On January 1 search was continued round the south side of Glacier Tongue from the base towards the seaward end. There was much heavy pressure; it was impossible to reach the summit owing to the wide crack. Distance covered 4 miles 100 yds. On January 2 thick weather caused party to lay up. On 3rd, glacier was further examined, and several slopes formed by snow led to top of glacier, but crevasses between slope and the tongue prevented crossing. The party then proceeded round the Tongue to Tent Island, which was also

searched, a complete tour of the island being made. It was decided to make for Cape Evans, as thick weather was approaching. We arrived at 8 p.m. Distance 8 miles 490 yds.

I remain, etc.,

ERNEST E. JOYCE

To Sir ERNEST SHACKLETON, C.V.O.,
Commander, I.T.A.E.

In September Richards was forced to lay up at the hut owing to a strained heart, due presumably to stress of work on the sledging journeys. Early in October a party consisting of Joyce, Gaze, and Wild spent several days at Cape Royds, where they skinned specimens. They sledged stores back to Cape Evans in case it should be found necessary to remain there over another winter. In September, Joyce, Gaze, and Wild went out to Spencer-Smith's grave with a wooden cross, which they erected firmly. Relief arrived on January 10, 1917, but it is necessary now to turn back to the events of May 1915, when the *Aurora* was driven from her moorings off Cape Evans.

CHAPTER 16

The *Aurora*'s drift

After Mackintosh left the *Aurora* on January 25, 1915, Stenhouse kept the ship with difficulty off Tent Island. The ice-anchors would not hold, owing to the continual breaking away of the pack, and he found it necessary much of the time to steam slow ahead against the floes. The third sledging party, under Cope, left the ship on the afternoon of the 31st, with the motor-tractor towing two sledges, and disappeared towards Hut Point. Cope's party returned to the ship on February 2 and left again on February 5, after a delay caused by the loose condition of the ice. Two days later, after more trouble with drifting floes, Stenhouse proceeded to Cape Evans, where he took a line of soundings for the winter quarters. During the next month the *Aurora* occupied various positions in the neighbourhood of Cape Evans. No secure moorings were available. The ship had to keep clear of threatening floes, dodge 'growlers' and drifting bergs, and find shelter from the blizzards. A sudden shift of wind on February 24, when the ship was sheltering in the lee of Glacier Tongue, caused her to be jammed hard against the low ice off the glacier, but no damage was done. Early in March Stenhouse sent moorings ashore at Cape Evans, and on March 11 he proceeded to Hut Point, where he dropped anchor in Discovery Bay. Here he landed stores, amounting to about two months' full rations for twelve men, and embarked Spencer-Smith, Stevens, Hook, Richards, Ninnis, and Gaze, with two dogs. He returned to Cape Evans that evening.

'We had a bad time when we were "sculling" about the Sound, first endeavouring to make Hut Point to land provisions, and then looking for winter quarters in the neighbourhood of Glacier Tongue,' wrote Stenhouse afterwards. 'The ice kept breaking away in small floes, and we were apparently no nearer to anywhere than when the sledges left; we were frustrated in every move. The ship broke away from the fast ice in blizzards, and then we went dodging about the Sound from the Ross Island side to the western pack, avoiding and clearing floes and growlers in heavy drift when we could see nothing, our compasses unreliable and the ship short-handed. In that homeless time I kept watch and watch with the second officer, and was hard pressed to know what to do. Was ever ship in such predicament? To the northward of Cape Royds was taboo, as also was the coast south of Glacier Tongue. In a small stretch of ice-bound coast we had to find winter quarters. The ice lingered on, and all this time we could find nowhere to drop anchor, but had to keep steam handy for emergencies. Once I tried the North Bay of Cape Evans, as it apparently was the only ice-free spot. I called all hands, and making up a boat's crew with one of the firemen sent the whaler away with the second officer in charge to sound. No sooner had the boat left ship than the wind freshened from the northward, and large bergs and growlers, setting into the bay, made the place untenable. The anchorage I eventually selected seemed the best available – and here we are drifting, with all plans upset, when we ought to be lying in winter quarters.'

A heavy gale came up on March 12, and the *Aurora*, then moored off Cape Evans, dragged her anchor and drifted out of the bay. She went northward past Cape Barne and Cape Royds in a driving mist, with a heavy storm-sea running. This gale was a particularly heavy one. The ship and gear were covered with ice, owing to the freezing of spray, and Stenhouse had anxious hours amid the heavy, ice-encumbered waters before the gale moderated. The young ice, which was continually forming in the very low temperature, helped to reduce the sea as soon as the gale moderated, and the *Aurora* got back to Cape Evans on the evening of the 13th. Ice was forming in the bay, and on the morning of the 14th Stenhouse took the ship into position for winter moorings. He got three steel hawsers out and made fast to the shore anchors. These hawsers were hove tight, and the *Aurora* rested then, with her stern to the shore, in seven fathoms. Two more wires were taken ashore the next day. Young ice was forming around the ship, and under the influence of wind and tide this ice began early to put severe strains upon the moorings. Stenhouse had the fires drawn and the boiler blown down on the 20th, and the engineer reported at that time that the bunkers contained still 118 tons of coal.

The ice broke away between Cape Evans and Cape Barne on the 23rd, and pressure around the ship shattered the bay ice and placed heavy strains on the stern moorings. The young ice, about four inches thick, went out eventually and left a lead along the shore. The ship had set in towards the shore, owing to the pressure, and the stern was now in four-and-a-half fathoms. Stenhouse tightened the moorings and ran out an extra wire to the shore anchor. The nature of the ice movements is illustrated by a few extracts from the log:

'*March 27, 5 p.m.* – Ice broke away from shore and started to go out. *8 p.m.* – Light southerly airs; fine; ice setting out to northwest; heavy pressure of ice on starboard side and great strain on moorings. *10 p.m.* – Ice clear of ship.

'*March 28.* – New ice forming over bay. *3 a.m.* – Ice which went out last watch set in towards bay. *5 a.m.* – Ice coming in and overriding newly formed bay-ice; heavy pressure on port side of ship; wires frozen into ice. *8 a.m.* – Calm and fine; new ice setting out of bay. *5 p.m.* – New ice formed since morning cleared from bay except area on port side of ship and stretching abeam and ahead for about 200 yds., which is held by bights of wire; new ice forming.

'*March 29, 1.30 p.m.* – New ice going out. *2 p.m.* – Hands on floe on port quarter clearing wires; stern in three fathoms; hauled wires tight, bringing stern more to eastward and in four fathoms; hove in about one fathom of starboard cable, which had dragged during recent pressure.

'*April 10, 1.30 p.m.* – Ice breaking from shore under influence of south-east wind. Two starboard quarter wires parted; all bights of stern wires frozen in ice; chain taking weight. *2 p.m.* – Ice opened, leaving ice in bay in line from Cape to landward of glacier. *8 p.m.* – Fresh wind; ship holding ice in bay; ice in Sound wind-driven to north-west.

'*April 17, 1 am.* – Pressure increased and wind shifted to northwest. Ice continued to override and press into shore until 5 o'clock; during this time pressure into bay was very heavy; movement of ice in straits causing noise like heavy surf. Ship took ground gently at rudder-post during pressure; bottom under stern shallows very quickly. *10 p.m.* – Ice moving out of bay to westward; heavy strain on after moorings and cables, which are cutting the floe.'

Stenhouse continued to nurse his moorings against the onslaughts of the ice during the rest of April and the early days of May. The break-away from the shore came suddenly and unexpectedly on the evening of May 6:

'*May 6, 1915.* – Fine morning with light breezes from east-south-east. . . . *3.30 p.m.* – Ice nearly finished. Sent hands ashore for sledge-load. *4 p.m.* – Wind freshening with blizzardy appearance of sky. *8 p.m.* – . . . Heavy strain on after-moorings. *9.45 p.m.* – The ice parted from the shore; all moorings parted. Most fascinating to listen to waves and chain breaking. In the thick haze I saw the ice astern breaking up and the shore receding. I called all hands and clapped relieving tackles (4-in. Manila luff tackles) on to the cables on the forepart of the windlass. The bos'n had rushed along with his hurricane lamp, and shouted, "She's away wi' it!" He is a good fellow and very conscientious. I ordered steam on main engines, and the engine-room staff, with Hooke and Ninnis, turned to. Grady, fireman, was laid up with a broken rib. As the ship, in the solid floe, set to the northwest, the cables rattled and tore at the hawse-pipes; luckily the anchors, lying as they were on a strip-sloping bottom, came away easily, without damage to windlass or hawse-pipes. Slowly as we disappeared into Sound, the light in the hut died away. At 11.30 p.m. the ice around us started to break up, the floes playing tattoo on the ship's sides. We were out in the Sound and catching the full force of the wind. The moon broke through the clouds after midnight and showed us the pack, stretching continuously to northward, and about one mile to the south. As the pack from the southward came up and closed in on the ship, the swell lessened and the banging of floes alongside eased a little.

'*May 7, 8 a.m.* – Wind east-south-east. Moderate gale with thick drift. The ice around ship is packing up and forming ridges about two feet high. The ship is lying with head to the eastward, Cape Bird showing to north-east. When steam is raised I have hopes of getting back to the fast ice near the Glacier Tongue. Since we have been in winter quarters the ice has formed and, held by the islands and land at Cape Evans, has remained north of the Tongue. If we can return we should be able now to moor to the fast ice. The engineers are having great difficulty with the sea connections, which are frozen. The main bow-down cock, from which the

boiler is "run up", has been tapped and a screw plug put into it
to allow of a hot iron rod being inserted to thaw out the ice
between the cock and the ship's side – about two feet of hard
ice. *4.30 p.m.* – The hot iron has been successful. Donolly (second
engineer) had the pleasure of stopping the first spurt of water
through the pipe; he got it in the eye. Fires were lit in furnaces,
and water commenced to blow in the boiler – the first blow in
our defence against the terrific forces of Nature in the Antarctic.
8 p.m. – The gale has freshened, accompanied by thick drift.'

The *Aurora* drifted helplessly throughout May 7. On the morning
of May 8 the weather cleared a little and the Western Mountains
became indistinctly visible. Cape Bird could also be seen. The ship
was moving northwards with the ice. The daylight was no more
than a short twilight of about two hours' duration. The boiler was
being filled with ice, which had to be lifted aboard, broken up,
passed through a small porthole to a man inside, and then carried
to the manhole on top of the boiler. Stenhouse had the wireless
aerial rigged during the afternoon, and at 5 p.m. was informed that
the watering of the boiler was complete. The wind freshened to
a moderate southerly gale, with thick drift, in the night, and this
gale continued during the following day, the 9th. The engineer
reported at noon that he had 40 lb. pressure in the boiler and was
commencing the thawing of the auxiliary sea-connection pump
by means of a steam-pipe.

'Cape Bird is the only land visible, bearing north-east true about
eight miles distant,' wrote, Stenhouse on the afternoon of the 9th.
'So this is the end of our attempt to winter in McMurdo Sound.
Hard luck after four months' buffeting, for the last seven weeks of
which we nursed our moorings. Our present situation calls for
increasing vigilance. It is five weeks to the middle of winter. There
is no sun, the light is little and uncertain, and we may expect many
blizzards. We have no immediate water-supply, as only a small
quantity of fresh ice was aboard when we broke drift.

'The *Aurora* is fast in the pack and drifting God knows where.
Well, there are prospects of a most interesting winter drift. We
are all in good health, except Grady, whose rib is mending
rapidly; we have good spirits and we will get through. But what
of the poor beggars at Cape Evans, and the Southern Party? It is a
dismal prospect for them. There are sufficient provisions at Cape

Evans, Hut Point, and, I suppose, Cape Royds, but we have the remaining Burberrys, clothing, etc., for next year's sledging still on board. I see little prospect of getting back to Cape Evans or anywhere in the Sound. We are short of coal and held firmly in the ice. I hope she drifts quickly to the north-east. Then we can endeavour to push through the pack and make for New Zealand, coal and return to the Barrier eastward of Cape Crozier. This could be done, I think, in the early spring, September. We must get back to aid the depot-laying next season.'

A violent blizzard raged on May 10 and 11. 'I never remember such wind-force,' said Stenhouse. 'It was difficult to get along the deck.' The weather moderated on the 12th, and a survey of the ship's position was possible. 'We are lying in a field of ice with our anchors and seventy-five fathoms of cable on each hanging at the bows. The after-moorings were frozen into the ice astern of us at Cape Evans. Previous to the date of our leaving our winter berth four small wires had parted. When we broke away the chain two of the heavy (4-in.) wires parted close to shore; the other wire went at the butts. The chain and two wires are still fast in the ice and will have to be dug out. This morning we cleared the ice around the cables, but had to abandon the heaving-in, as the steam froze in the return pipes from the windlass exhaust, and the joints had to be broken and the pipe thawed out. Hooke was "listening in" from 8.30 p.m. to 12.30 a.m. for the Macquarie Island wireless station (1340 miles away) or the Bluff (New Zealand) station (1860 miles away), but had no luck.'

The anchors were hove in by dint of much effort on the 13th and 14th, ice forming on the cable as it was hoisted through a hole cut in the floe. Both anchors had broken, so the *Aurora* had now one small kedge-anchor left aboard. The ship's position on May 14 was approximately forty-five miles north, thirty-four west of Cape Evans. 'In one week we have drifted forty-five miles (geographical). Most of this distance was covered during the first two days of the drift. We appear to be nearly stationary. What movement there is in the ice seems to be to the northwest towards the ice-bound coast. Hands who were after penguins yesterday reported much noise in the ice about one mile from the ship. I hope the floe around the ship is large enough to take its own pressure. We cannot expect much pressure from the south, as McMurdo Sound should soon be frozen over and the ice holding. North-east winds would drive the pack in from the Ross Sea. I hope for the best. Plans for future development are ready, but probably will be checkmated again . . . I took the anchors aboard. They are of no further use as separate anchors, but they ornament the forecastle head, so we put them in their places . . . The supply of fresh water is a problem. The engineer turned steam from the boiler into the main water-tank (starboard) through a pipe leading from the main winch-pipe to the tank top. The steam condenses before reaching the tank. I hope freezing does not burst the tank. A large tabular iceberg, calved from the Barrier, is silhouetted against the twilight glow in the sky about ten miles away. The sight of millions of tons of fresh ice is most tantalising. It would be a week's journey to the berg and back over pack and pressure, and probably we could bring enough ice to last two days.'

The record of the early months of the *Aurora*'s long drift in the Ross Sea is not eventful. The galley condenser was rigged, but the supply of fresh water remained a problem. The men collected fresh-fallen snow when possible and hoped to get within reach of fresh ice. Hooke and Ninnis worked hard at the wireless plant with the object of getting into touch with Macquarie Island, and possibly sending news of the ship's movements to Cape Evans. They got the wireless motor running and made many adjustments of the instruments and aerials, but their efforts were not successful. Emperor penguins approached the ship occasionally, and the birds were captured whenever possible for the fresh meat they afforded. The *Aurora* was quite helpless in the grip of the ice, and after the engine-room bilges had been thawed and pumped out the boilers were blown down. The pressure had been raised to sixty pounds, but there was no chance of moving the ship, and the supply of coal was limited. The story of the *Aurora*'s drift during long months can be told briefly by means of extracts from Stenhouse's log:

'*May 21.* – Early this morning there appeared to be movements in the ice. The grating and grinding noise makes one feel the unimportance of man in circumstances like ours. Twilight towards noon showed several narrow, open leads about two cables from ship and in all directions. Unable to get bearing, but imagine that there is little or no alteration in ship's position, as ship's head is same, and Western Mountains appear the same . . . Hope all is well at Cape Evans and that the other parties have returned safely. Wish we could relieve their anxiety.

'*May 22*. – Obtained good bearings of Beaufort Island, Cape Ross, and Dunlop Island, which put the ship in a position eighteen miles south 75 degrees east (true) from Cape Ross. Since the 14th, when reliable bearings were last obtained, we have drifted north-west by north seven miles.

'*May 24*. – Blizzard from south-south-east continued until 9 p.m., when it moderated, and at 11.45 p.m. wind shifted to north-west, light, with snow. Quite a lot of havoc has been caused during this blow, and the ship has made much northing. In the morning the crack south of the ship opened to about three feet. At 2 p.m. felt heavy shock and the ship heeled to port about 70 degrees. Found ice had cracked from port gangway to north-west, and parted from ship from gangway along to stern. Crack extended from stern to south-east. *7.35 p.m.* – Ice cracked from port fore chains, in line parallel to previous crack. The ice broke again between the cracks and drifted to north-west for about ten yards. The ice to southward then commenced to break up, causing heavy strain on ship, and setting apparently north in large broken fields. Ship badly jammed in. *9.15 p.m.* – Ice closed in again around ship. Two heavy windsqualls with a short interval between followed by cessation of wind. We are in a labyrinth of large rectangular floes (some with their points pressing heavily against ship) and high-pressure ridges.

May 25. – In middle watch felt pressure occasionally. Twilight showed a scene of chaos all around; one floe about three feet in thickness had upended, driven under ship on port quarter. As far as can be seen there are heavy blocks of ice screwed up on end, and the scene is like a graveyard. I think swell must have come up under ice from seaward (north-east), McMurdo Sound, and broken the ice, which afterwards started to move under the influence of the blizzard. Hardly think swell came from the Sound, as the cracks were wending from north-west to south-east, and also as the Sound should be getting icebound by now. If swell came from north-east then there is open water not far away. I should like to know. I believe the Ross Sea is rarely entirely ice-covered. Have bright moonlight now, which accentuates everything – the beauty and loneliness of our surroundings, and uselessness of ourselves, while in this prison: so near to Cape Evans and yet we might as well be anywhere as here. Have made our sledging-ration scales, and crew are busy making harness and getting sledging equipment ready for emergencies. Temperature −30 degrees Fahr.

'*May 26.* − If the ship is nipped in the ice, the ship's company (eighteen hands) will take to four sledges with one month's rations and make for nearest land. Six men and one sledge will endeavour to make Cape Evans via the western land, Butler Point, Hut Point, etc. The remaining twelve will come along with all possible speed, but no forced marches, killing and depot-ing penguins and seals for emergency retreats. If the ship remains here and makes no further drift to the north, towards latter end of July light will be making. The sun returns August 23. The sea-ice should be fairly safe, and a party of three, with one month's rations, will proceed to Cape Evans. If the ice sets north and takes the ship clear of land, we will proceed to New Zealand, bunker, get extra officer and four volunteers, provisions, etc., push south with all speed to the Barrier, put party on to the Barrier, about two miles east of Cape Crozier, and land all necessary stores and requirements. The ship will stand off until able to reach Cape Evans. If necessary, party will depot all stores possible at Corner Camp and go on to Cape Evans. If worst has happened my party will lay out the depot at the Beardmore for Shackleton. If the ship is released from the ice after September we must endeavour to reach Cape Evans before going north to bunker. We have not enough coal to hang about the Sound for many days.

'*May 28.* − By the position obtained by meridian altitude of stars and bearing of Mount Melbourne, we have drifted thirty-six miles north-east from last bearings taken on 23rd inst. The most of this must have been during the blizzard of the 24th. Mount Melbourne is one hundred and eleven miles due north of us, and there is some doubt in my mind as to whether the peak which we can see is this mountain. There may be a mirage . . . In the evening had the football out on the ice by the light of a beautiful moon. The exercise and break from routine are a splendid tonic. Ice-noises sent all hands on board.

'*June 1.* − Thick, hazy weather. In the afternoon a black streak appeared in the ice about a cable's length to the westward and stretching north and south. *8 p.m.* – The black line widened and showed long lane of open water. Apparently we are fast in a floe which has broken from the main field. With thick weather we are uncertain of our position and drift. It will be interesting to find out what this crack in the ice signifies. I am convinced that there is open water, not far distant, in the Ross Sea . . . Tonight Hooke is trying to call up Cape Evans. If the people at the hut have rigged the set which was left there, they will hear "All well" from the *Aurora*. I hope they have. [The messages were not received.]

'*June 8.* – Made our latitude 75 degrees 59' S. by altitude of Sirius. This is a very monotonous life, but all hands appear to be happy and contented. Find that we are not too well off for meals and will have to cut rations a little. Grady is taking exercise now and should soon be well again.. He seems very anxious to get to work again, and is a good man. No wireless calls tonight, as there is a temporary breakdown – condenser jar broken. There is a very faint display of aurora in northern sky. It comes and goes almost imperceptibly, a most fascinating sight. The temperature is –20 degrees Fahr.; 52 degrees of frost is much too cold to allow one to stand for long.

'*June 11.* – Walked over to a very high pressure-ridge about a quarter of a mile north-north-west of the ship. In the dim light walking over the ice is far from being monotonous, as it is almost impossible to see obstacles, such as small, snowed-up ridges, which makes us wary and cautious. A dip in the sea would be the grand finale, but there is little risk of this as the water freezes as soon as a lane opens in the ice. The pressure-ridge is about fifteen to twenty feet high for several hundred feet, and the ice all about it is bent up in a most extraordinary manner. At 9 p.m. Hooke called Cape Evans, "All well – *Aurora*", etc.; *10 p.m.*, weather reports for 8 p.m. sent to Wellington, New Zealand, and Melbourne, via Macquarie Island. [The dispatch of messages from the *Aurora* was continued, but it was learned afterwards that none of them had been received by any station.]

'*June 13.* – The temperature in the chart-room ranges from zero to a little above freezing-point. This is a very disturbing factor in rates of the chronometers (five in number, 3 G.M.T. and 2 Sid.T.), which are kept in cases in a padded bag, each case covered by a piece of blanket, and the box covered by a heavy coat. In any enclosed place where people pass their time, the niches and places where no heat penetrates are covered with frozen breath. There will be a big thaw-out when the temperature rises.

'*June 14.* – Mount Melbourne is bearing north 14 degrees W (true). Our approximate position is forty miles east-north-east of Nordenskjold Ice Tongue. At 9 p.m. Hooke called Cape Evans and sent weather reports to Wellington and Melbourne via Macquarie Island. Hooke and Ninnis on several evenings at about 11 o'clock have heard what appeared to be faint messages, but unreadable. He sent word to Macquarie Island of this in hopes that they would hear and increase the power.

'*June 20.* – During this last blow with its accompanying drift-snow there has been much leakage of current from the aerial during the sending of reports. This is apparently due to induction caused by the snow accumulating on the insulators aloft, and thus rendering them useless, and probably to increased inductive force of the current in a body of snow-drift. Hooke appears to be somewhat downhearted over it, and, after discussing the matter, gave me a written report on the non-success (up to the present time) of his endeavours to establish communication. He thinks that the proximity of the Magnetic Pole and *Aurora Australis* might affect things. The radiation is good and sufficient for normal conditions. His suggestion to lead the down lead wires out to the ahead and astern would increase scope, but I cannot countenance it owing to unsettled state of ice and our too lofty poles.

'*June 21.* – Blowing gale from south-west throughout day, but for short spell of westerly breeze about 5 *p.m.* Light drift at frequent intervals, very hazy, and consequently no land in sight during short twilight. Very hard up for mitts and clothing. What little we have on board I have put to one side for the people at the hut. Have given Thompson instructions to turn crew to making pair mitts and helmet out of Jaeger fleece for all hands forward. With strict economy we should make things spin out; cannot help worrying over our people at the hut. Although worrying does no good, one cannot do otherwise in this present impotent state. *11 p.m.* – Wind howling and whistling through rigging. Outside, in glare of moon, flying drift and expanse of icefield. Desolation!

'*June 22.* – Today the sun has reached the limit of his northern declination and now he will start to come south. Observed this day

as holiday, and in the evening had hands aft to drink to the health
of the King and the Expedition. All hands are happy, but miss the
others at Cape Evans. I pray to God we may soon be clear of this
prison and in a position to help them. We can live now for sunlight and activity.

'*July 1.* – The 1st of July! Thank God. The days pass quickly.
Through all my waking hours one long thought of the people at
Cape Evans, but one must appear to be happy and take interest in
the small happenings of shipboard.

'*July 3.* – Rather hazy with very little light. Moderate west-
north-west to south-west winds until noon, when wind veered to
south and freshened. No apparent change in ship's position; the
berg is on the same bearing (1 point on the port quarter) and
apparently the same distance off. Mount Melbourne was hidden
behind a bank of clouds. This is our only landmark now, as
Franklin Island is towered in perpetual gloom. Although we have
had the berg in sight during all the time of our drift from the
entrance to McMurdo Sound, we have not yet seen it in a
favourable light, and, were it not for its movement, we might
mistake it for a tabular island. It will be interesting to view our
companion in the returning light – unless we are too close to it!

'*July 5.* – Dull grey day (during twilight) with light, variable,
westerly breezes. All around hangs a heavy curtain of haze, and,
although very light snow is falling, overhead is black and clear with
stars shining. As soon as the faint noon light fades away the heavy
low haze intensifies the darkness and makes one thankful that one
has a good firm "berth" in the ice. I don't care to contemplate the
scene if the ice should break up at the present time.

'*July 6.* – Last night I thought I saw open water in the shape of a
long black lane to the southward of the ship and extending in an
easterly and westerly direction, but owing to the haze and light
snow I could not be sure; this morning the lane was distinctly
visible and appeared to be two or three hundred yards wide and
two miles long . . . At 6 p.m. loud pressure-noises could be heard
from the direction of the open lane and continued throughout the
night. Shortly after 8 o'clock the grinding and hissing spread to our
starboard bow (west-south-west), and the vibration caused by the
pressure could be felt intermittently on board the ship . . . The
incessant grinding and grating of the ice to the southward, with

seething noises, as of water rushing under the ship's bottom, and ominous sounds, kept me on the *qui vive* all night, and the prospect of a break-up of the ice would have racked my nerves had I not had them numbed by previous experiences.

'*July 9.* – At noon the sky to the northward had cleared sufficiently to allow of seeing Mount Melbourne, which appears now as a low peak to the north-west. Ship's position is twenty-eight miles north-north-east of Franklin Island. On the port bow and ahead of the ship there are some enormous pressure-ridges; they seem to be the results of the recent and present ice-movements. Pressure heard from the southward all day.

'*July 13.* – At 5 p.m. very heavy pressure was heard on the port beam and bow (south) and very close to the ship. This occurred again at irregular intervals. Quite close to the ship the ice could be seen bending upwards, and occasional jars were felt on board. I am inclined to think that we have set into a cul-de-sac and that we will now experience the full force of pressure from the south. We have prepared for the worst and can only hope for the best – a release from the ice with a seaworthy vessel under us.

'*July 18.* – This has been a day of events. About 8 a.m. the horizon to the north became clear and, as the light grew, the more westerly land showed up. This is the first clear day that we have had since the 9th of the month, and we have set a considerable distance to the north-east in the meantime. By meridian altitudes of stars and bearings of the land, which proved to be Coulman Islands, Mount Murchison, and Mount Melbourne, our position shows seventy-eight miles (geographical) north-east by north of Franklin Island. During the last three days we have drifted forty miles (geographical), so there has been ample reason for all the grinding and growling of pressure lately. The ship endured some severe squeezes this day.

'*July 20.* – Shortly before breakfast the raucous voice of the emperor penguin was heard, and afterwards two were seen some distance from the ship . . . The nearest mainland (in vicinity of Cape Washington) is ninety miles distant, as also is Coulman Island. Franklin Island is eighty miles south-east by south, and the pack is in motion. This is the emperor's hatching season, and here we meet them out in the cheerless desert of ice . . . *10.45 p.m.* – Heavy pressure around ship, lanes opened and ship worked astern about twenty feet. The wires in the ice took the strain (lashings at mizzen chains carried away) and carried away fair-lead bollard on port side of forecastle head.

'*July 21, 1 a.m.* – Lanes opened to about 40 ft. wide. Ship in open pool about 100 ft. wide. Heavy pressure in vicinity of ship. Called all hands and cut wires at the forecastle head. [These wires had remained frozen in the ice after the ship broke away from her moorings, and they had served a useful purpose at some times by checking ice-movements close to the ship.] *2 a.m.* – Ship swung athwart lane as the ice opened, and the floes on the port side pressed her stern round. *11.30 a.m.* – Pack of killer whales came up in the lane around the ship. Some broke soft ice (about one inch thick) and pushed their heads through, rising to five or six feet perpendicularly out of the water. They were apparently having a look round. It is strange to see killers in this immense field of ice; open water must be near, I think. *5.15 p.m.* – New ice of lanes cracked and opened. Floes on port side pushed stern on to ice (of floe); floes then closed in and nipped the ship fore and aft. The rudder was bent over to starboard and smashed. The solid oak and iron went like matchwood. *8 p.m.* – Moderate south–south-west gale with drift. Much straining of timbers with pressure. *10 p.m.* – Extra hard nip fore and aft; ship visibly hogged. Heavy pressure.

'*July 22.* – Ship in bad position in newly frozen lane, with bow and stern jammed against heavy floes; heavy strain with much creaking and groaning. *8 a.m.* – Called all hands to stations for sledges, and made final preparations for abandoning ship. Allotted special duties to several hands to facilitate quickness in getting clear should ship be crushed. Am afraid the ship's back will be broken if the pressure continues, but cannot relieve her. *2 p.m.* – Ship lying easier. Poured Sulphuric acid on the ice astern in hopes of rotting crack and relieving pressure on stern-post, but unsuccessfully. Very heavy pressure on and around ship (taking strain fore and aft and on starboard quarter). Ship jumping and straining and listing badly. *10 p.m.* – Ship has crushed her way into new ice on starboard side and slewed aslant lane with stern-post clear of land-ice. *12 p.m.* – Ship is in safer position; lanes opening in every direction.

'*July 23.* – Caught glimpse of Coulman Island through haze. Position of ship south 14 degrees east (true), eighty miles off Coulman Island. Pressure continued intermittently throughout the day and night, with occasional very heavy squeezes to the ship which made timbers crack and groan. The ship's stern is now in a more or less soft bed, formed of recently frozen ice of about one foot in thickness. I thank God that we have been spared through this fearful nightmare. I shall never forget the concertina motions of the ship during yesterday's and Wednesday's fore and aft nips.

'*July 24.* – Compared with previous days this is a quiet one. The lanes have been opening and closing, and occasionally the ship gets a nasty squeeze against the solid floe on our starboard quarter. The more lanes that open the better, as they form "springs" (when covered with thin ice, which makes to a thickness of three or four inches in a few hours) between the solid and heavier floes and fields. Surely we have been guided by the hands of Providence to have come in heavy grinding pack for over two hundred miles (geographical), skirting the ice-bound western shore, around and to the north of Franklin Island, and now into what appears a clear path to the open sea! In view of our precarious position and the lives of men in jeopardy, I sent this evening an aerogram to H.M. King George asking for a relief ship. I hope the wireless gets through. I have sent this message after much consideration, and know that in the event of our non-arrival in New Zealand on the specified date (November 1) a relief ship will be sent to aid the Southern Party.

'*July 25.* – Very heavy pressure about the ship. During the early hours a large field on the port quarter came charging up, and on meeting our floe tossed up a ridge from ten to fifteen feet high. The blocks of ice as they broke off crumbled and piled over each other to the accompaniment of a thunderous roar. Throughout the day the pressure continued, the floes alternately opening and closing, and the ship creaking and groaning during the nips between floes.

'*August 4.* – For nine days we have had southerly winds, and the last four we have experienced howling blizzards. I am sick of the sound of the infernal wind. Din! din! din! and darkness. We should have seen the sun today, but a bank of cumulus effectually hid him, although the daylight is a never-ending joy.

'*August 6.* – The wind moderated towards 6 a.m., and about breakfast-time, with a clear atmosphere, the land from near Cape Cotter to Cape Adare was visible. What a day of delights! After four days of thick weather we find ourselves in sight of Cape Adare in a position about forty-five miles east of Possession Isles; in this time we have been set one hundred miles. Good going. Mount Sabine, the first land seen by us when coming south, lies away to the westward, forming the highest peak (10,000 ft.) of a majestic range of mountains covered in eternal snow. Due west we can see the Possession Islands, lying under the stupendous bluff of Cape Downshire, which shows large patches of black rock. The land slopes down to the north-west of Cape Downshire, and rises again into the high peninsula about Cape Adare. We felt excited this morning in anticipation of seeing the sun, which rose about nine-thirty (local time). It was a glorious, joyful sight. We drank to something, and with very light hearts gave cheers for the sun.

'*August 9.* – Donolly got to work on the rudder again. It is a long job cutting through the iron sheathing-plates of the rudder, and not too safe at present, as the ice is treacherous. Hooke says that the conditions are normal now. I wish for his sake that he could get through. He is a good sportsman and keeps on trying, although, I am convinced, he has little hope with this inadequate aerial.

'*August 10.* – The ship's position is lat. 70 degrees 40' S., forty miles north 29 degrees east of Cape Adare. The distance drifted from August 2 to 6 was one hundred miles, and from the 6th to the 10th eighty-eight miles.

'*August 12.* – By observation and bearings of land we are forty-five miles north-east of Cape Adare, in lat. 70 degrees 42' S. This position is a little to the eastward of the position on the 10th. The bearings as laid off on a small scale chart of gnomonic projection are very inaccurate, and here we are handicapped, as our chronometers have lost all regularity. Donolly and Grade are having quite a job with the iron platings on the rudder, but should finish the cutting tomorrow. A jury-rudder is nearly completed. This afternoon we mixed some concrete for the lower part, and had to use boiling water, as the water froze in the mixing. The carpenter has made a good job of the rudder, although he has had to construct it on the quarterdeck in low temperatures and exposed to biting blasts.

'*August 16.* – We are "backing and filling" about forty miles north-east of Cape Adare. This is where we expected to have made much mileage. However, we cannot grumble and must be patient. There was much mirage to the northward, and from the crow's-nest a distinct appearance of open water could be seen stretching from north-north-west to north-east.

'*August 17.* – A glorious day! Land is distinctly visible, and to the northward the black fringe of water-sky over the horizon hangs continuously. Hooke heard Macquarie Island "speaking" Hobart. The message heard was the finish of the weather reports. We have hopes now of news in the near future.

'*August 23.* – Saw the land in the vicinity of Cape North. To the south-south-west the white cliffs and peaks of the inland ranges were very distinct, and away in the distance to the south-west could be seen a low stretch of undulating land. At times Mount Sabine was visible through the gloom. The latitude is 69 degrees 44½' S. We are fifty-eight miles north, forty miles east of Cape North.

'*August 24.* – We lifted the rudder out of the ice and placed it clear of the stern, athwart the fore-and-aft line of the ship. We had quite a job with it (weight, four and a half tons), using treble-and-double-sheaved blocks purchase, but with the endless-chain tackle from the engine-room, and plenty of "beef" and leverage, we dragged it clear. All the pintles are gone at the fore part of the rudder; it is a clean break and bears witness to the terrific force exerted on the ship during the nip. I am glad to see the rudder upon the ice and clear of the propeller. The blade itself (which is solid oak and sheathed on two sides and after part halfway down, with three-quarter-inch iron plating) is undamaged, save for the broken pintles; the twisted portion is in the rudder trunk.

'*August 25, 11 p.m.* – Hooke has just been in with the good tidings that he has heard Macquarie and the Bluff (New Zealand) sending their weather reports and exchanging signals. Can this mean that they have heard our recent signals and are trying to get us now? Our motor has been out of order.

'*August 26.* – The carpenter has finished the jury-rudder and is now at work on the lower end of the rudder-truck, where the rudder burst into the stern timbers. We are lucky in having this opportunity to repair these minor damages, which might prove serious in a seaway.

'*August 31, 6.30 a.m.* – Very loud pressure-noises to the south-east. I went aloft after breakfast and had the pleasure of seeing many open lanes in all directions. The lanes of yesterday are frozen over, showing what little chance there is of a general and continued break-up of the ice until the temperature rises. Land was visible, but far too distant for even approximate bearings. The berg still hangs to the north-west of the ship. We seem to have pivoted outwards from the land. We cannot get out of this too quickly, and although everyone has plenty of work, and is cheerful, the uselessness of the ship in her present position palls.

'*September 5.* – The mizzen wireless mast came down in a raging blizzard today. In the forenoon I managed to crawl to windward on the top of the bridge-house, and under the lee of the charthouse watched the mast bending over with the wind and swaying like the branch of a tree, but after the aerial had stood throughout the winter I hardly thought the mast would carry away. Luckily, as it is dangerous to life to be on deck in this weather (food is brought from the galley in relays through blinding drift and over big heaps of snow), no one was about when the mast carried away.

'*September 8.* – This is dull, miserable weather. Blow, snow, and calm for an hour or two. Sometimes it blows in this neighbourhood without snow and sometimes with – this seems to be the only difference. I have two patients now, Larkman and Mugridge. Larkman was frost-bitten on the great and second toes of the left foot some time ago, and has so far taken little notice of them. Now they are causing him some alarm as gangrene has set in. Mugridge is suffering from an intermittent rash, with red, inflamed skin and large, short-lived blisters. I don't know what the deuce it is, but the nearest description to it in a *Materia Medica*, etc., is *pemphigus*, so pemphigus it is, and he has been "tonic-ed" and massaged.

'*September 9.* – This is the first day for a long time that we have registered a minimum temperature above zero for the twenty-four hours. It is pleasant to think that from noon to noon throughout the night the temperature never fell below +4 deg. (28 degrees frost), and with the increase of daylight it makes one feel that summer really is approaching.

'*September 13.* – All around the northern horizon there is the appearance of an open-water sky, but around the ship the prospect is dreary. The sun rose at 6.20 a.m. and set at 5.25 p.m. Ship's time eleven hours five minutes of sunlight and seventeen hours light. Three hours twilight morning and evening. The carpenter is dismantling the taffrail (to facilitate the landing and, if necessary, the boarding of the jury-rudder) and will construct a temporary, removable rail.

'*September 16.* – There has been much mirage all around the horizon, and to the eastward through south to south-west heavy frost-smoke has been rising. Over the northern horizon a low bank of white fog hangs as though over the sea. I do not like these continued low temperatures. I am beginning to have doubts as to our release until the sun starts to rot the ice.

'*September 17.* – This is the anniversary of our departure from London. There are only four of the original eleven on board – Larkman, Ninnis, Mauger, and I. Much has happened since Friday, September 18, 1914, and I can recall the scene as we passed down the Thames with submarines and cruisers, in commission and bent on business, crossing our course. I can also remember the regret at leaving it all and the consequent "fedup-ness".

'*September 21.* – The sun is making rapid progress south, and we have had today over seventeen hours' light and twelve hours' sunlight. Oh for a release! The monotony and worry of our helpless position is deadly. I suppose Shackleton and his party will have started depot-laying now and will be full of hopes for the future. I wonder whether the *Endurance* wintered in the ice or went north. I cannot help thinking that if she wintered in the Weddell Sea she will be worse off than the *Aurora*. What a lot we have to look for in the next six months – news of Shackleton and the *Endurance*, the party at Cape Evans, and the war.

'*September 22.* – Lat. 69 degrees 12' S.; long. 165 degrees 00' E. Sturge Island (Balleny Group) is bearing north (true) ninety miles distant. Light north-west airs with clear, fine weather. Sighted Sturge Island in the morning, bearing due north of us and appearing like a faint low shadow on the horizon. It is good to get a good landmark for fixing positions again, and it is good to see that we are making northerly progress, however small. Since breaking away from Cape Evans we have drifted roughly seven hundred and five miles around islands and past formidable obstacles, a wonderful drift! It is good to think that it has not been in vain, and that the knowledge of the set and drill of the pack will be a valuable addition to the sum of human knowledge. The distance from Cape Evans to our present position is seven hundred and five miles (geographical).

'*September 27*. – The temperature in my room last night was round about zero, rather chilly, but warm enough under the blankets. Hooke has dismantled his wireless gear. He feels rather sick about not getting communication, although he does not show it.

'*September 30*. – Ninnis has been busy now for the week on the construction of a new tractor. He is building the body and will assemble the motor in the fore 'tween-deck where it can be lashed securely when we are released from the ice. I can see leads of open water from the masthead, but we are still held firmly. How long?

'*October 7*. – As time wears on the possibility of getting back to the Barrier to land a party deserves consideration; if we do not get clear until late in the season we will have to turn south first, although we have no anchors and little moorings, no rudder and a short supply of coal. To leave a party on the Barrier would make us very short-handed; still, it can be done, and anything is preferable to the delay in assisting the people at Cape Evans. At 5 a.m. a beautiful parhelion formed around the sun. The sight so impressed the bos'n that he roused me out to see it.'

During the month of October the *Aurora* drifted uneventfully. Stenhouse mentions that there was often an appearance of open water on the northern and eastern horizon. But anxious eyes were strained in vain for indications that the day of the ship's release was near at hand. Hooke had the wireless plant running again and was trying daily to get into touch with Macquarie Island, now about eight hundred and fifty miles distant. The request for a relief ship was to be renewed if communication could be established, for by this time, if all had gone well with the *Endurance*, the overland party from the Weddell Sea would have been starting. There was considerable movement of the ice towards the end of the month, lanes opening and closing, but the floe, some acres in area, into which the *Aurora* was frozen, remained firm until the early days of November. The cracks appeared close to the ship, due apparently to heavy drift causing the floe to sink. The temperatures were higher now, under the influence of the sun, and the ice was softer. Thawing was causing discomfort in the quarters aboard. The position on November 12 was reckoned to be lat. 66 degrees 9' S., long. 155 degrees 17' 45" E. Stenhouse made a sounding on November 17, in lat. 66 degrees 40' S., long. 154 degrees 45' E., and found bottom at 194 fathoms. The bottom sample was mud and a few small stones. The sounding-line showed a fairly strong under-current to the north-west. 'We panned out some of the mud,' says Stenhouse, 'and in the remaining grit found several specks of gold.' Two days later the trend of the current was south-easterly. There was a pronounced thaw on the 22nd. The cabins were in a dripping state, and recently fallen snow was running off the ship in little streams. All hands were delighted, for the present discomfort offered promise of an early break-up of the pack.

'*November 23.* – At 3 a.m. Young Island, Balleny Group, was seen bearing north 54 degrees east (true). The island, which showed up clearly on the horizon, under a heavy stratus-covered sky, appeared to be very far distant. By latitude at noon we are in 66 degrees 26' S. As this is the charted latitude of Peak Foreman, Young Island, the bearing does not agree. Land was seen at 8 a.m. bearing south 60 degrees west (true). This, which would appear to be Cape Hudson, loomed up through the mists in the form of a high, bold headland, with low undulating land stretching away to the south-south-east and to the westward of it. The appearance of this headland has been foretold for the last two days, by masses of black fog, but it seems strange that land so high should not have been seen before, as there is little change in the atmospheric conditions.

'*November 24.* – Overcast and hazy during forenoon. Cloudy, clear, and fine in afternoon and evening. Not a vestige of land can be seen, so Cape Hudson is really "Cape Flyaway". This is most weird. All hands saw the headland to the south-west, and some of us sketched it. Now (afternoon), although the sky is beautifully clear to the south-west, nothing can be seen. We cannot have drifted far from yesterday's position. No wonder Wilkes reported land. *9 p.m.* – A low fringe of land appears on the horizon bearing south-west, but in no way resembles our Cape of yesterday. This afternoon we took a cast of the lead through the crack 200 yds. west of the ship, but found no bottom at 700 fathoms.'

An interesting incident on November 26 was the discovery of an emperor penguin rookery. Ninnis and Kavenagh took a long walk to the north-west, and found the deserted rookery. The depressions in the ice, made by the birds, were about eighteen inches long and contained a greyish residue. The rookery was in a hollow surrounded by pressure ridges six feet high. Apparently about twenty birds had been there. No pieces of egg-shell were seen, but the petrels and skuas had been there in force and probably would have taken all scraps of this kind. The floes were becoming soft and 'rotten', and walking was increasingly difficult. Deep pools of slush and water covered with thin snow made traps for the men. Stenhouse thought that a stiff blizzard would break up the pack. His anxiety was increasing with the advance of the season, and his log is a record of deep yearning to be free and active again. But the grip of the pack was inexorable. The hands had plenty of work on the *Aurora*, which was being made ship-shape after the buffeting of the winter storms. Seals and penguins were seen frequently, and the supply of fresh meat was maintained. The jury-rudder was ready to be shipped when the ship was released, but in the meantime it was not being exposed to the attacks of the ice. 'No appreciable change in our surroundings', was the note for December 17. 'Every day past now reduces our chance of getting out in time to go north for rudder, anchors, and coal. If we break out before January 15 we might get north to New Zealand and down to Cape Evans again in time to pick up the parties. After that date we can only attempt to go south in our crippled state, and short of fuel. With only nine days' coal on board we would have little chance of working through any Ross Sea pack, or of getting south at all if we encountered many blizzards. Still there is a sporting chance and luck may be with us . . . Shackleton may be past the Pole now. I wish our wireless calls had got through.'

Christmas Day, with its special dinner and mild festivities, came and passed, and still the ice remained firm. The men were finding some interest in watching the moulting of emperor penguins, who were stationed at various points in the neighbourhood of the ship. They had taken station to leeward of hummocks, and appeared to move only when the wind changed or the snow around them had become foul. They covered but a few yards on these journeys, and even then stumbled in their weakness. One Emperor was brought on board alive, and the crew were greatly amused to see the bird balancing himself on heels and tail, with upturned toes, the position adopted when the egg is resting on the feet during the incubation period. The threat of a stiff 'blow' aroused hopes of release several times, but the blizzard – probably the first Antarctic blizzard that was ever longed for – did not arrive. New Year's Day found Stenhouse and other men just recovering from an attack of snow-blindness, contracted by making an excursion across the floes without snow-goggles.

At the end of the first week in January the ship was in lat. 65 degrees 45' S. The pack was well broken a mile from the ship, and the ice was rolling fast. Under the bows and stern the pools were growing and stretching away in long lanes to the west. A seal came up to blow under the stern on the 6th, proving that there was an opening in the sunken ice there. Stenhouse was economising in food. No breakfast was served on the ship, and seal or penguin meat was used for at least one of the two meals later in the day. All hands were short of clothing, but Stenhouse was keeping intact the sledging gear intended for the use of the shore party. Strong, variable winds on the 9th raised hopes again, and on the morning of the 10th the ice appeared to be well broken from half a mile to a mile distant from the ship in all directions. 'It seems extraordinary that the ship should be held in an almost unbroken floe of about a mile square, the more so as this patch was completely screwed and broken during the smash in July, and contains many faults. In almost any direction at a distance of half a mile from the ship there are pressure ridges of eight-inch ice piled twenty feet high. It was provident that although so near these ridges were escaped.'

The middle of January was passed and the *Aurora* lay still in the ice. The period of continuous day was drawing towards its close, and there was an appreciable twilight at midnight. A dark water-sky could be seen on the northern horizon. The latitude on January 24 was 65 degrees 39½' S. Towards the end of the month Stenhouse ordered a thorough overhaul of the stores and general preparations for a move. The supply of flour and butter was ample. Other stores were running low, and the crew lost no opportunity of capturing seals and penguins. Adelies were travelling to the east-south-east in considerable numbers, but they could not be taken unless they approached the ship closely, owing to the soft condition of the ice. The wireless plant, which had been idle during the months of daylight, had been rigged again, and Hooke resumed his calls to Macquarie Island on February 2. He listened in vain for any indication that he had been heard. The pack was showing much movement, but the large floe containing the ship remained firm.

The break-up of the floe came on February 12. Strong north-east to south-east winds put the ice in motion and brought a perceptible swell. The ship was making some water, a foretaste of a trouble to come, and all hands spent the day at the pumps, reducing the water from three feet eight and a half inches in the well to twelve inches, in spite of frozen pipes and other difficulties. Work had just finished for the night when the ice broke astern and quickly split in all directions under the influence of the swell. The men managed to save some seal meat which had been cached in a drift near the gangway. They lost the flagstaff, which had been rigged as a wireless mast out on the floe, but drew in the aerial. The ship was floating now amid fragments of floe, and bumping considerably in the swell. A fresh southerly wind blew during the night, and the ship started to forge ahead gradually without sail. At 8.30 a.m. on the 13th Stenhouse set the foresail and foretopmast staysail, and the *Aurora* moved northward slowly, being brought up occasionally by large floes. Navigation under such conditions, without steam and without a rudder, was exceedingly difficult, but Stenhouse wished if possible to save his small remaining stock of coal until he cleared the pack, so that a quick run might be made to McMurdo Sound. The jury-rudder could not be rigged in the pack. The ship was making about three and a half feet of water in the twenty-four hours, a quantity easily kept in check by the pumps.

During the 14th the *Aurora* worked very slowly northward through heavy pack. Occasionally the yards were backed or an ice-anchor put into a floe to help her out of difficult places, but much of the time she steered herself. The jury-rudder boom was topped into position in the afternoon, but the rudder was not to be shipped until open pack or open water was reached. The ship was held up all day on the 15th in lat. 64 degrees 38' S. Heavy floes barred progress in every direction. Attempts were made to work the ship by trimming sails and warping with ice-anchors, but she could not be manoeuvred smartly enough to take advantage of leads that opened and closed. This state of affairs continued throughout the 16th. That night a heavy swell was rolling under the ice and the ship had a rough time. One pointed floe ten or twelve feet thick was steadily battering, with a three-feet send, against the starboard side, and fenders only partially deadened the shock. 'It is no use butting against this pack with steam-power,' wrote Stenhouse. 'We would use all our meagre supply of coal in reaching the limit of the ice in sight, and then we would be in a hole, with neither ballast nor fuel . . . But if this stagnation lasts another week we will have to raise steam and consume our coal in an endeavour to get into navigable waters. I am afraid our chances of getting south are very small now.'

The pack remained close, and on the 21st a heavy swell made the situation dangerous. The ship bumped heavily that night and fenders were of little avail. With each 'send' of the swell the ship would bang her bows on the floe ahead, then bounce back and smash into another floe across her stern-post. This floe, about six feet thick and 100 ft. across, was eventually split and smashed by the impacts. The pack was jammed close on the 23rd, when the noon latitude was 64 degrees 361' S. The next change was for the worse. The pack loosened on the night of the 25th, and a heavy north-west swell caused the ship to bump heavily. This state of affairs recurred at intervals in succeeding days. 'The battering and ramming of the floes increased in the early hours [of February 29] until it seemed as if some sharp floe or jagged underfoot must go through the ship's hull. At 6 a.m. we converted a large coir-spring into a fender, and slipped it under the port quarter, where a pressured floe with a twenty to thirty feet underfoot was threatening to try and knock the propeller and stern-post off altogether. At 9 a.m., after pumping ship, the engineer reported a leak in the way of the propeller-shaft aft near the stern-post on the port side. The carpenter cut part of the lining and filled the space between the timbers with Stockholm tar, cement, and oakum. He could not get at the actual leak, but his makeshift made a little difference.

I am anxious about the propeller. This pack is a dangerous place for a ship now; it seems miraculous that the old Barky still floats.'

The ice opened out a little on March 1. It was imperative to get the ship out of her dangerous situation quickly, as winter was approaching, and Stenhouse therefore ordered steam to be raised. Next morning he had the spanker gaff rigged over the stern for use as a temporary rudder while in the heavy pack. Steam had been raised to working pressure at 5.15 p.m. on the 2nd, and the *Aurora* began to work ahead to the westward. Progress was very slow owing to heavy floes and deep underfoots, which necessitated frequent stoppages of the engines. Open water was in sight to the north and north-west the next morning, after a restless night spent among the rocking floes. But progress was very slow. The *Aurora* went to leeward under the influence of a west-south-west breeze, and steering by means of the yards and a warp-anchor was a ticklish business. The ship came to a full stop among heavy floes before noon on the 3rd, and three hours later, after vain attempts to warp ahead by means of ice-anchors, Stenhouse had the fires partially drawn (to save coal) and banked.

No advance was made on March 4 and 5. A moderate gale from the east-north-east closed the ice and set it in motion, and the *Aurora*, with banked fires, rolled and bumped, heavily. Seventeen bergs were in sight, and one of them was working southwards into the pack and threatening to approach the ship. During the night the engines were turned repeatedly by the action of ice on the propeller-blades. 'All theories about the swell being non-existent in the pack are false,' wrote the anxious master. 'Here we are with a suggestion only of open water-sky, and the ship rolling her scuppers under and sitting down bodily on the floes.' The ice opened when the wind moderated, and on the afternoon of the 6th the *Aurora* moved northward again. 'Without a rudder (no jury-rudder can yet be used amongst these swirling, rolling floes) the ship requires a lot of attention. Her head must be pointed between floes by means of ice-anchors and warps, or by mooring to a floe and steaming round it. We kept a fairly good course between two bergs to our northward and made about five miles northing before, darkness coming on, the men could no longer venture on the floes with safety to fix the anchors.'

The next three days were full of anxiety. The *Aurora* was held by the ice, and subjected to severe buffeting, while two bergs approached from the north. On the morning of the 10th the nearest berg was within three cables of the ship. But the pack had opened and by 9.30 a.m. the ship was out of the danger zone and headed north-north-east. The pack continued to open during the afternoon, and the *Aurora* passed through wide stretches of small loose floes and brash. Progress was good until darkness made a stop necessary. The next morning the pack was denser. Stenhouse shipped a preventer jury-rudder (the weighted spanker gaff), but could not get steerage way. Broad leads were sighted to the north-west in the afternoon, and the ship got within a quarter of a mile of the nearest lead before being held up by heavy pack. She again bumped severely during the night, and the watch stood by with fenders to ease the more dangerous blows.

Early next morning Stenhouse lowered a jury-rudder, with steering-pennants to drag through the water, and moved north to north-west through heavy pack. He made sixteen miles that day on an erratic course, and then spent an anxious night with the ship setting back into the pack and being pounded heavily. Attempts to work forward to an open lead on the morning of the 13th were unsuccessful. Early in the afternoon a little progress was made, with all hands standing by to fend off high ice, and at 4.50 p.m. the *Aurora* cleared the main pack. An hour was spent shipping the jury-rudder under the counter, and then the ship moved slowly northward. There was pack still ahead, and the bergs and growlers were a constant menace in the hours of darkness. Some anxious work remained to be done, since bergs and scattered ice extended in all directions, but at 2 p.m. on March 14 the *Aurora* cleared the last belt of pack in lat. 62 degrees 27.5' S., long. 157 degrees 32' E. 'We "spliced the mainbrace",' says Stenhouse, 'and blew three blasts of farewell to the pack with the whistle.'

The *Aurora* was not at the end of her troubles, but the voyage up to New Zealand need not be described in detail. Any attempt to reach McMurdo Sound was now out of the question. Stenhouse had a battered, rudderless ship, with only a few tons of coal left in the bunkers, and he struggled northward in heavy weather against persistent adverse winds and head seas. The jury-rudder needed constant nursing, and the shortage of coal made it impossible to get the best service from the engines. There were times when the ship could make no progress and fell about helplessly in a confused swell or lay hove to amid mountainous seas. She was short-handed, and one or two of the men were creating additional difficulties. But Stenhouse displayed throughout fine seamanship and dogged perseverance. He accomplished successfully one of the most difficult voyages on record, in an ocean area notoriously stormy and treacherous. On March 23 he established wireless communication with Bluff Station, New Zealand, and the next day was in touch with Wellington and Hobart. The naval officer in New Zealand waters offered assistance, and eventually it was arranged that the Otago Harbour Board's tug *Plucky* should meet the *Aurora* outside Port Chalmers. There were still bad days to be endured. The jury-rudder partially carried away and had to be unshipped in a heavy sea. Stenhouse carried on, and in the early morning of April 2 the *Aurora* picked up the tug and was taken in tow. She reached Port Chalmers the following morning, and was welcomed with the warm hospitality that New Zealand has always shown towards Antarctic explorers.

CHAPTER 17

The last relief

When I reached New Zealand at the beginning of December 1916 I found that the arrangements for the relief were complete. The New Zealand Government had taken the task in hand earlier in the year, before I had got into touch with the outside world. The British and Australian Governments were giving financial assistance. The *Aurora* had been repaired and refitted at Port Chalmers during the year at considerable cost, and had been provisioned and coaled for the voyage to McMurdo Sound. My old friend Captain John K. Davis, who was a member of my first Antarctic Expedition in 1907-1909, and who subsequently commanded Dr Mawson's ship in the Australian Antarctic Expedition, had been placed in command of the *Aurora* by the Governments, and he had engaged officers, engineers, and crew. Captain Davis came to Wellington to see me on my arrival there, and I heard his account of the position. I had interviews also with the Minister for Marine, the late Dr Robert McNab, a kindly and sympathetic Scotsman who took a deep personal interest in the Expedition. Stenhouse also was in Wellington, and I may say again here that his account of his voyage and drift in the *Aurora* filled me with admiration for his pluck, seamanship, and resourcefulness.

After discussing the situation fully with Dr McNab, I agreed that the arrangements already made for the Relief Expedition should stand. Time was important and there were difficulties about making any change of plans or control at the last moment. After Captain Davis had been at work for some months the Government agreed to hand the *Aurora* over to me free of liability on her return to New Zealand. It was decided, therefore, that Captain Davis should take the ship down to McMurdo Sound, and that I should go with him to take charge of any shore operations that might be necessary. I 'signed on' at a salary of 1s. a month, and we sailed from Port Chalmers on December 20, 1916. A week later we sighted ice again. The *Aurora* made a fairly quick passage through the pack and entered the open water of the Ross Sea on January 7, 1917.

Captain Davis brought the *Aurora* alongside the ice edge off Cape Royds on the morning of January 10, and I went ashore with a party to look for some record in the hut erected there by my Expedition in 1907. I found a letter stating that the Ross Sea party was housed at Cape Evans, and was on my way back to the ship when six men, with dogs and sledge, were sighted coming from the direction of Cape Evans. At 1 p.m. this party arrived on board, and we learned that of the ten members of the Expedition left behind when the *Aurora* broke away on May 6, 1915, seven had survived, namely, A. Stevens, E. Joyce, H. E. Wild, J. L. Cope, R. W. Richards, A. K. Jack, I. O. Gaze. These seven men were all well, though they showed traces of the ordeal through which they had passed. They told us of the deaths of Mackintosh, Spencer-Smith, and Hayward, and of their own anxious wait for relief.

All that remained to be done was to make a final search for the bodies of Mackintosh and Hayward. There was no possibility of either man being alive. They had been without equipment when the blizzard broke the ice they were crossing. It would have been impossible for them to have survived more than a few days, and eight months had now elapsed without news of them. Joyce had already searched south of Glacier Tongue. I considered that further search should be made in two directions, the area north of Glacier Tongue, and the old depot off Butler Point, and I made a report to Captain Davis to this effect.

On January 12 the ship reached a point five and a half miles east of Butler Point. I took a party across rubbly and waterlogged ice to within thirty yards of the piedmont ice, but owing to high cliffs and loose slushy ice could not make a landing. The land-ice had broken away at the point cut by the cross-bearings of the depot, but was visible in the form of two large bergs grounded to the north of Cape Bernacchi. There was no sign of the depot or of any person having visited the vicinity. We returned to the ship and proceeded across the Sound to Cape Bernacchi.

The next day I took a party ashore with the object of searching the area north of Glacier Tongue, including Razorback Island, for traces of the two missing men. We reached the Cape Evans Hut at 1.30 p.m., and Joyce and I left at 3 p.m. for the Razorbacks. We conducted a search round both islands, returning to the hut at 7 p.m. The search had been fruitless. On the 14th I started with Joyce to search the north side of Glacier Tongue, but the surface drift, with wind from south-east, decided me not to continue, as the ice was moving rapidly at the end of Cape Evans, and the pool between the hut and Inaccessible Island was growing larger. The wind increased in the afternoon. The next day a south-east blizzard was blowing, with drift half up the islands. I considered it unsafe to sledge that day, especially as the ice was breaking away from the south side of Cape Evans into the pool. We spent the day putting the hut in order.

We got up at 3 a.m. on the 16th. The weather was fine and calm. I started at 4.20 with Joyce to the south at the greatest possible speed. We reached Glacier Tongue about one and a half miles from the seaward end. Wherever there were not precipitous cliffs there was an even snow-slope to the top. From the top we searched with glasses; there was nothing to be seen but blue ice, crevassed, showing no protuberances. We came down and, half running, half walking, worked about three miles towards the root of the glacier; but I could see there was not the slightest chance of finding any remains owing to the enormous snow-drifts wherever the cliffs were accessible. The base of the steep cliffs had drifts ten to fifteen feet high. We arrived back at the hut at 9.40, and left almost immediately for the ship. I considered that all places likely to hold the bodies of Mackintosh and Hayward had now been searched. There was no doubt to my mind that they met their deaths on the breaking of the thin ice when the blizzard arose on May 8, 1916. During my absence from the hut Wild and Jack had erected a cross to the memory of the three men who had lost their lives in the service of the Expedition.

Captain Davis took the ship northward on January 17. The ice conditions were unfavourable and pack barred the way. We stood over to the western coast towards Dunlop Island and foll-owed it to Granite Harbour. No mark or depot of any kind was seen. The *Aurora* reached the main pack, about sixty miles from Cape Adare, on January 22. The ice was closed ahead, and Davis went south in open water to wait for better conditions.

A north-west gale on January 28 enabled the ship to pass between the pack and the land off Cape Adare, and we crossed the Antarctic Circle on the last day of the month. On February 4 Davis sent a formal report to the New Zealand Government by wireless, and on February 9 the *Aurora* was berthed at Wellington. We were welcomed like returned brothers by the New Zealand people.

CHAPTER 18

The final phase

The foregoing chapters of this book represent the general narrative of our Expedition. That we failed in accomplishing the object we set out for was due, I venture to assert, not to any neglect or lack of organisation, but to the overwhelming natural obstacles, especially the unprecedented severe summer conditions on the Weddell Sea side. But though the Expedition was a failure in one respect, I think it was successful in many others. A large amount of important scientific work was carried out. The meteorological observations in particular have an economic bearing. The hydrographical work in the Weddell Sea has done much to clear up the mystery of this, the least known of all the seas. I have appended a short scientific memorandum to this volume, but the more detailed scientific results must wait until a more suitable time arrives, when more stable conditions prevail. Then results will be worked out.

To the credit side of the Expedition one can safely say that the comradeship and resource of the members of the Expedition was worthy of the highest traditions of Polar service; and it was a privilege to me to have had under my command men who, through dark days and the stress and strain of continuous danger, kept up their spirits and carried out their work regardless of themselves and heedless of the limelight. The same energy and endurance that they showed in the Antarctic they brought to the greater war in the Old World. And having followed our fortunes in the South you may be interested to know that practically every member of the Expedition was employed in one or other branches of the active fighting forces during the war. Several are still abroad, and for this very reason it has been impossible for me to obtain certain details for this book.

Of the fifty-three men who returned out of the fifty-six who left for the South, three have since been killed and five wounded. Four decorations have been won, and several members of the

Expedition have been mentioned in dispatches. McCarthy, the best and most efficient of the sailors, always cheerful under the most trying circumstances, and who for these very reasons I chose to accompany me on the boat journey to South Georgia, was killed at his gun in the Channel. Cheetham, the veteran of the Antarctic, who had been more often south of the Antarctic circle than any man, was drowned when the vessel he was serving in was torpedoed, a few weeks before the Armistice. Ernest Wild, Frank Wild's brother, was killed while mine-sweeping in the Mediterranean. Mauger, the carpenter on the *Aurora*, was badly wounded while serving with the New Zealand Infantry, so that he is unable to follow his trade again. He is now employed by the New Zealand Government. The two surgeons, Macklin and McIlroy, served in France and Italy, McIlroy being badly wounded at Ypres. Frank Wild, in view of his unique experi-ence of ice and ice conditions, was at once sent to the North Russian front, where his zeal and ability won him the highest praise.

Macklin served first with the Yorks and later transferred as medical officer to the Tanks, where he did much good work. Going to the Italian front with his battalion, he won the Military Cross for bravery in tending wounded under fire.

James joined the Royal Engineers, Sound-Ranging Section, and after much front-line work was given charge of a Sound-Ranging School to teach other officers this latest and most scientific addition to the art of war.

Wordie went to France with the Royal Field Artillery and was badly wounded at Armentières.

Hussey was in France for eighteen months with the Royal Garrison Artillery, serving in every big battle from Dixmude to Saint-Quentin.

Worsley, known to his intimates as Depth-Charge Bill, owing to his success with that particular method of destroying German submarines, has the Distinguished Service Order and three submarines to his credit.

Stenhouse, who commanded the *Aurora* after Mackintosh landed, was with Worsley as his second-in-command when one of the German submarines was rammed and sunk, and received the D.S.C. for his share in the fight. He was afterwards given command of a Mystery Ship, and fought several actions with enemy submarines.

Clark served on a minesweeper. Greenstreet was employed with the barges on the Tigris. Rickenson was commissioned as Engineer-Lieutenant, R.N. Kerr returned to the Merchant Service as an engineer.

Most of the crew of the *Endurance* served on minesweepers.

Of the Ross Sea Party, Mackintosh, Hayward, and Spencer-Smith died for their country as surely as any who gave up their lives on the fields of France and Flanders. Hooke, the wireless operator, now navigates an airship.

Nearly all of the crew of the *Aurora* joined the New Zealand Field Forces and saw active service in one or other of the many theatres of war. Several have been wounded, but it has been impossible to obtain details.

On my return, after the rescue of the survivors of the Ross Sea Party, I offered my services to the Government, and was sent on a mission to South America. When this was concluded I was commissioned as Major and went to North Russia in charge of Arctic Equipment and Transport, having with me Worsley, Stenhouse, Hussey, Macklin, and Brocklehurst, who was to have come South with us, but who, as a regular officer, rejoined his unit on the outbreak of war. He has been wounded three times and was in the retreat from Mons. Worsley was sent across to the Archangel front, where he did excellent work, and the others served with me on the Murmansk front. The mobile columns there had exactly the same clothing, equipment, and sledging food as we had on the Expedition. No expense was spared to obtain the best of everything for them, and as a result not a single case of avoidable frostbite was reported.

Taking the Expedition as a unit, out of fifty-six men three died in the Antarctic, three were killed in action, and five have been wounded, so that our casualties have been fairly high.

Though some have gone there are enough left to rally round and form a nucleus for the next Expedition, when troublous times are over and scientific exploration can once more be legitimately undertaken.

APPENDIX I

Scientific work
by J. M. Wordie, M. A. (Cantab.), Lieut. R. F. A.

The research undertaken by the Expedition was originally planned for a shore party working from a fixed base on land, but it was only in South Georgia that this condition of affairs was fully realised. On this island, where a full month was spent, the geologist made very extensive collections, and began the mapping of the country; the magnetician had some of his instruments in working order for a short while; and the meteorologist was able to co—operate with the Argentine observer stationed at Grytviken. It had been realised how important the meteorological observations were going to be to the Argentine Government, and they accordingly did all in their power to help, both before and at the end of the Expedition. The biologist devoted most of his time, meanwhile, to the whaling industry, there being no less than seven stations on the island; he also made collections of the neritic fauna, and, accompanied by the photographer, studied the bird life and the habits of the sea-elephants along the east coast.

By the time the actual southern voyage commenced, each individual had his own particular line of work which he was prepared to follow out. The biologist at first confined himself to collecting the plankton, and a start was made in securing water samples for temperature and salinity. In this, from the beginning, he had the help of the geologist, who also gave instructions for the taking of a line of soundings under the charge of the ship's officers. This period of the southward voyage was a very busy time so far as the scientists were concerned, for, besides their own particular work, they took their full share of looking after the dogs and working the ship watch by watch. At the same time, moreover, the biologist had to try and avoid being too lavish with his preserving material at the expense of the shore station collections which were yet to make.

When it was finally known that the ship had no longer any chance of getting free of the ice in the 1914–1915 season, a radical change was made in the arrangements. The scientists were freed, as far as possible, from ship's duties, and were thus able to devote themselves almost entirely to their own particular spheres. The meteorological investigations took on a more definite shape; the instruments intended for the land base were set up on board ship, including self-recording barographs, thermometers, and a Dines anemometer, with which very satisfactory results were got. The physicist set up his quadrant electrometer after a good deal of trouble, but throughout the winter had to struggle constantly with rime forming on the parts of his apparatus exposed to the outer air. Good runs were being thus continually spoilt. The determination of the magnetic constants also took up a good part of his time.

Besides collecting plankton the biologist was now able to put down one or other of his dredges at more frequent intervals, always taking care, however, not to exhaust his store of preserving material, which was limited. The taking of water samples was established on a better system, so that the series should be about equally spaced out over the ship's course. The geologist suppressed all thought of rocks, though occasionally they were met with in bottom samples; his work became almost entirely oceanographical, and included a study of the sea-ice, of the physiography of the sea-floor as shown by daily soundings, and of the bottom deposits; besides this he helped the biologist in the temperature and salinity observations.

The work undertaken and accomplished by each member was as wide as possible; but it was only in keeping with the spirit of the times that more attention should be paid to work from which practical and economic results were likely to accrue. The meteorologist had always in view the effect of Antarctic climate on the other southern continents, the geologist looked on ice from a seaman's point of view, and the biologist not unwillingly put whales in the forefront of his programme. The accounts which follow on these very practical points show how closely scientific work in the Antarctica is in touch with, and helps on the economic development of, the inhabited lands to the north.

Sea-ice nomenclature

by J. M. Wordie, M. A. (Cantab.), Lieut. R. F. A.

During the voyage of the *Endurance* it was soon noticed that the terms being used to describe different forms of ice were not always in agreement with those given in Markham's and Mill's glossary, in *The Antarctic Manual*, 1901. It was the custom, of course, to follow implicitly the terminology used by those of the party whose experience of ice dated back to Captain Scott's first voyage, so that the terms used may be said to be common to all Antarctic voyages of the present century. The principal changes, therefore, in nomenclature must date from the last quarter of the nineteenth century, when there was no one to pass on the traditional usage from the last naval Arctic Expedition in 1875 to the *Discovery* Expedition of 1901. On the latter ship Markham's and Mill's glossary was, of course, used, but apparently not slavishly; founded, as far as sea-ice went, on Scoresby's, made in 1820, it might well have been adopted in its entirety, for no writer could have carried more weight than Scoresby the younger, combining as he did more than ten years' whaling experience with high scientific attainments. Above all others he could be accepted both by practical seamen and also by students of ice forms.

That the old terms of Scoresby did not all survive the period of indifference to Polar work, in spite of Markham and Mill, is an indication either that their usefulness has ceased or that the original usage has changed once and for all. A restatement of terms is, therefore, now necessary. Where possible the actual phrases of Scoresby and of his successors, Markham and Mill, are still used. The principle adopted, however, is to give preference to the words actually used by the Polar seamen themselves.

The following authorities have been followed as closely as possible:

W. Scoresby, Jun., *An Account of the Arctic Regions*, 1820, vol. i, pp. 225–233, 238–241.

C. R. Markham and H. R. Mill in *The Antarctic Manual*, 1901, pp. xiv–xvi.

J. Payer, *New Lands within the Arctic Circle*, 1876, vol. i, pp. 3–14.

W. S. Bruce, 'Polar Exploration' in *Home University Library*, c. 1911, pp. 54–71.

Reference should also be made to the annual publication of the Danish Meteorological Institute showing the Arctic ice conditions of the previous summer. This is published in both Danish and English, so that the terms used there are bound to have a very wide acceptance; it is hoped, therefore, that they may be the means of preventing the Antarctic terminology following a different line of evolution; for but seldom is a seaman found nowadays who knows both Polar regions. On the Danish charts six different kinds of sea-ice are marked – namely, unbroken polar ice; land-floe; great ice-fields; tight pack-ice; open ice; bay-ice and brash. With the exception of bay-ice, which is more generally known as young ice, all these terms pass current in the Antarctic.

Slush or *Sludge*. The initial stages in the freezing of sea-water, when its consistency becomes gluey or soupy. The term is also used (but not commonly) for brash-ice still further broken down.

Pancake-ice. Small circular floes with raised rims; due to the break-up in a gently ruffled sea of the newly formed ice into pieces which strike against each other, and so form turned-up edges.

Young ice. Applied to all unhummocked ice up to about a foot in thickness. Owing to the fibrous or platy structure, the floes crack easily, and where the ice is not over-thick a ship under steam cuts a passage without much difficulty. Young ice may originate from the coalescence of 'pancakes', where the water is slightly ruffled, or else be a sheet of 'black ice', covered maybe with 'ice-flowers', formed by the freezing of a smooth sheet of sea-water.

In the Arctic it has been the custom to call this form of ice 'bay-ice'; in the Antarctic, however, the latter term is wrongly used for land-floes (fast ice, etc.), and has been so misapplied consistently for fifteen years. The term bay-ice should possibly, therefore, be dropped altogether, especially since, even in the Arctic, its meaning is not altogether a rigid one, as it may denote, first, the gluey 'slush' which forms when sea-water freezes, and, secondly, the firm level sheet ultimately produced.

Land floes. Heavy but not necessarily hummocked ice, with generally a deep snow covering, which has remained held up in the position of growth by the enclosing nature of some feature of the coast, or by grounded bergs throughout the summer season when most of the ice breaks out. Its thickness is, therefore, above the average. Has been called at various times 'fast ice', 'coast-ice', 'land-ice', 'bay-ice' by Shackleton and David and the Charcot Expedition; and possibly what Drygalski calls '*Schelfeis*' is not very different.

Floe. An area of ice, level or hummocked, whose limits are with in sight. Includes all sizes between brash on the one hand and fields on the other. 'Light floes' are between one and two feet in thickness (anything thinner being 'young ice'). Those exceeding two feet in thickness are termed 'heavy floes', being generally hummocked, and in the Antarctic, at any rate, covered by fairly deep snow.

Field. A sheet of ice of such extent that its limits cannot be seen from the masthead.

Hummocking. Includes all the processes of pressure formation whereby level young ice becomes broken up and built up into

Hummocky floes. The most suitable term for what has also been called 'old pack' and 'screwed pack' by David and '*Scholleneis*' by German writers. In contrast to young ice, the structure is no longer fibrous, but becomes spotted or bubbly, a certain percentage of salt drains away, and the ice becomes almost translucent.

The pack. Is a term very often used in a wide sense to include any area of sea-ice, no matter what form it takes or how disposed. The French term is *banquise de dérive*.

Pack-ice. A more restricted use than the above, to include hummocky floes or close areas of young ice and light floes. Pack-ice is 'close' or 'tight' if the floes constituting it are in contact; 'open' if, for the most part, they do not touch. In both cases it hinders, but does not necessarily check, navigation; the contrary holds for

Drift-ice. Loose open ice, where the area of water exceeds that of ice. Generally drift-ice is within reach of the swell, and is a stage in the breaking down of pack-ice, the size of the floes being much smaller than in the latter. (Scoresby's use of the term drift-ice for pieces of ice intermediate in size between floes and brash has, however, quite died out). The Antarctic or Arctic pack usually has a girdle or fringe of drift-ice.

Brash. Small fragments and roundish nodules; the wreck of other kinds of ice.

Bergy bits. Pieces, about the size of a cottage, of glacier-ice or of hummocky pack washed clear of snow.

Growlers. Still smaller pieces of sea-ice than the above, greenish in colour, and barely showing above water-level.

Crack. Any sort of fracture or rift in the sea–ice covering.

Lead or *Lane.* Where a crack opens out to such a width as to be navigable. In the Antarctic it is customary to speak of these as leads, even when frozen over to constitute areas of young ice.

Pods. Any enclosed water areas in the pack, where length and breadth are about equal.

Meteorology
By L. D. A. Hussey, B.Sc. (Lond.), Capt. R. G. A.

The meteorological results of the Expedition, when properly worked out and correlated with those from other stations in the southern hemisphere, will be extremely valuable, both for their bearing on the science of meteorology in general, and for their practical and economic applications.

South America is, perhaps, more intimately concerned than any other country, but Australia, New Zealand, and South Africa are all affected by the weather conditions of the Antarctic. Researches are now being carried on which tend to show that the meteorology of the two hemispheres is more interdependent than was hitherto believed, so that a meteorological disturbance in one part of the world makes its presence felt, more or less remotely perhaps, all over the world.

It is evident, therefore, that a complete knowledge of the weather conditions in any part of the world, which it is understood carries with it the ability to make correct forecasts, can never be obtained unless the weather conditions in every other part are known. This makes the need for purely scientific Polar Expeditions so imperative, since our present knowledge of Arctic and Antarctic meteorology is very meagre, and to a certain extent unsystematic. What is wanted is a chain of observing stations well equipped with instruments and trained observers stretching across the Antarctic Continent. A series of exploring ships could supplement these observations with others made by them while cruising in the Antarctic Seas. It would pay to do this, even for the benefit accruing to farmers, sailors, and others who are so dependent on the weather.

As an instance of the value of a knowledge of Antarctic weather conditions, it may be mentioned that, as the result of observations and researches carried out at the South Orkneys – a group of sub-Antarctic islands at the entrance to the Weddell Sea – it has been found that a cold winter in that sea is a sure precursor of a drought over the maize- and cereal-bearing area of Argentina three and a half years later. To the farmers the value of this knowledge so far in advance is enormous, and since England has some three hundred million pounds sterling invested in Argentine interests, Antarctic Expeditions have proved, and will prove, their worth even from a purely commercial point of view.

I have given just this one instance to satisfy those who question the utility of Polar Expeditions, but many more could be cited.

As soon as it was apparent that no landing could be made, and that we should have to spend a winter in the ship drifting round with the pack, instruments were set up and observations taken just as if we had been ashore.

A meteorological screen or box was erected on a platform over the stern, right away from the living quarters, and in it were placed the maximum and minimum thermometers, the recording barograph, and thermograph – an instrument which writes every variation of the temperature and pressure on a sheet of paper on a revolving drum – and the standard thermometer, a very carefully manufactured thermometer, with all its errors determined and tabulated. The other thermometers were all checked from this one. On top of the screen a Robinson's anemometer was screwed. This consisted of an upright rod, to the top of which were pivoted four arms free to revolve in a plane at right angles to it. At the end of these arms hemispherical cups were screwed. These were caught by the wind and the arms revolved at a speed varying with the force of the wind. The speed of the wind could be read off on a dial below the arms.

In addition there was an instrument called a Dines anemometer which supplied interesting tracings of the force, duration, and direction of the wind. There was an added advantage in the fact that the drum on which these results were recorded was comfortably housed down below, so that one could sit in a comparatively warm room and follow all the varying phases of the blizzard which was raging without. The barometer used was of the Kew standard pattern. When the ship was crushed, all the monthly records were saved, but the detailed tracings, which had been packed up in the hold, were lost. Though interesting they were not really essential. Continuous observations were made during the long drift on the floe and while on Elephant Island the temperature was taken at midday each day as long as the thermometers lasted. The mortality amongst these instruments, especially those which were tied to string and swung round, was very high.

A few extracts from the observations taken during 1915 – the series for that year being practically complete—may be of interest. January was dull and overcast, only 7 per cent. of the observations recording a clear blue sky, 71 per cent being completely overcast.

The percentage of clear sky increased steadily up till June and July, these months showing respectively 42 per cent. and 45-47 per cent. In August 40 per cent. of the observations were clear sky, while September showed a sudden drop to 27 per cent. October weather was much the same, and November was practically overcast the whole time, clear sky showing at only 8 per cent. of the observations. In December the sky was completely overcast for nearly 90 per cent. of the time.

Temperatures on the whole were fairly high; though a sudden unexpected drop in February, after a series of heavy north-easterly gales, caused the ship to be frozen in, and effectually put an end to any hopes of landing that year. The lowest temperature experienced was in July, when −35 degrees Fahr., i.e. 67 degrees below freezing, was reached. Fortunately, as the sea was one mass of consolidated pack, the air was dry, and many days of fine bright sunshine occurred. Later on, as the pack drifted northwards and broke up, wide lanes of water were formed, causing fogs and mist and dull overcast weather generally. In short, it may be said that in the Weddell Sea the best weather comes in winter. Unfortunately during that season the sun also disappears, so that one cannot enjoy it as much as one would like.

As a rule, too, southerly winds brought fine clear weather, with marked fall in the temperature, and those from the north were accompanied by mist, fog, and overcast skies, with comparatively high temperatures. In the Antarctic a temperature of 30 degrees, i.e. 2 degrees *below* freezing, is considered unbearably hot.

The greatest difficulty that was experienced was due to the accumulation of rime on the instruments. In low temperatures everything became covered with ice-crystals, deposited from the air, which eventually grew into huge blocks. Sometimes these blocks became dislodged and fell, making it dangerous to walk along the decks. The rime collected on the thermometers, the glass bowl of the sunshine recorder, and the bearings of the anemometer, necessitating the frequent use of a brush to remove it, and sometimes effectively preventing the instruments from recording at all.

One of our worst blizzards occurred on August 1, 1915, which was, for the ship, the beginning of the end. It lasted for four days, with cloudy and overcast weather for the three following days, and from that time onwards we enjoyed very little sun.

The weather that we experienced on Elephant Island can only be described as appalling. Situated as we were at the mouth of a gully, down which a huge glacier was slowly moving, with the open sea in front and to the left, and towering, snow-covered mountains on our right, the air was hardly ever free from snow-drift, and the winds increased to terrific violence through being forced over the glacier and through the narrow gully. Huge blocks of ice were hurled about like pebbles, and cases of clothing and cooking utensils were whisked out of our hands and carried away to sea. For the first fortnight after our landing there, the gale blew, at times, at over one hundred miles an hour. Fortunately it never again quite reached that intensity, but on several occasions violent squalls made us very fearful for the safety of our hut. The island was almost continuously covered with a pall of fog and snow, clear weather obtaining occasionally when pack-ice surrounded us. Fortunately a series of south-westerly gales had blown all the ice away to the north-east two days before the rescue ship arrived, leaving a comparatively clear sea for her to approach the island.

Being one solitary moving station in the vast expanse of the Weddell Sea, with no knowledge of what was happening anywhere around us, forecasting was very difficult and at times impossible.

Great assistance in this direction was afforded by copies of Mr R. C. Mossmann's researches and papers on Antarctic meteorology, which he kindly supplied to us.

I have tried to make this very brief account of the meteorological side of the Expedition rather more 'popular' than scientific, since the publication and scientific discussion of the observations will be carried out elsewhere; but if, while showing the difficulties under which we had to work, it emphasises the value of Antarctic Expeditions from a purely utilitarian point of view, and the need for further continuous research into the conditions obtaining in the immediate neighbourhood of the Pole, it will have achieved its object.

Physics
By R. W. James, M.A. (Cantab.), B.Sc. (Fond.), Capt. R.E.

Owing to the continued drift of the ship with the ice, the programme of physical observations originally made out had to be considerably modified. It had been intended to set up recording magnetic instruments at the base, and to take a continuous series of records throughout the whole period of residence there, absolute measurements of the earth's horizontal magnetic force, of the dip and declination being taken at frequent intervals for purposes of calibration. With the ice continually drifting, and the possibility of the floe cracking at any time, it proved impracticable to set up the recording instruments, and the magnetic observations were confined to a series of absolute measurements taken whenever opportunity occurred. These measurements, owing to the drift of the ship, extend over a considerable distance, and give a chain of values along a line stretching, roughly from 77 degrees S. lat. to 69 degrees S. lat. This is not the place to give the actual results; it is quite enough to state that, as might have been expected from the position of the magnetic pole, the values obtained correspond to a comparatively low magnetic latitude, the value of the dip ranging from 63 degrees to 68 degrees.

So far as possible, continuous records of the electric potential gradient in the atmosphere were taken, a form of quadrant electrometer with a boom and ink recorder, made by the Cambridge Scientific Instrument Company, being employed. Here again, the somewhat peculiar conditions made work difficult, as the instrument was very susceptible to small changes of level, such as occurred from time to time owing to the pressure of the ice on the ship. An ionium collector, for which the radioactive material was kindly supplied by Mr. F. H. Glew, was used. The chief difficulty to contend with was the constant formation of thick deposits of rime, which either grew over the insulation and spoiled it, or covered up the collector so that it could no longer act. Nevertheless, a considerable number of good records were obtained, which have not yet been properly worked out. Conditions during the Expedition were very favourable for observations on the physical properties and natural history of sea-ice, and a considerable number of results were obtained, which are, however, discussed elsewhere, mention of them being made here since they really come under the heading of physics.

In addition to these main lines of work, many observations of a miscellaneous character were made, including those on the occurrence and nature of parhelia or 'mock suns', which were very common, and generally finely developed, and observations of the auroral displays, which were few and rather poor owing to the comparatively low magnetic latitude. Since most of the observations made are of little value without a knowledge of the place where they were made, and since a very complete set of soundings were also taken, the daily determination of the ship's position was a matter of some importance. The drift of the ship throws considerable light on at least one geographical problem, that of the existence of Morrell Land. The remainder of this appendix will therefore be devoted to a discussion of the methods used to determine the positions of the ship from day to day.

The latitude and longitude were determined astronomically every day when the sun or stars were visible, the position thus determined serving as the fixed points between which the position on days when the sky was overcast could be interpolated by the process known as 'dead reckoning', that is to say, by estimating the speed and course of the ship, taking into account the various causes affecting it. The sky was often overcast for several days at a stretch, and it was worth while to take a certain amount of care in the matter. Captain Worsley constructed an apparatus which gave a good idea of the direction of drift at any time. This consisted of an iron rod, which passed through an iron tube, frozen vertically into the ice, into the water below. At the lower end of the rod, in the water, was a vane. The rod being free to turn, the vane took up the direction of the current, the direction being shown by an indicator attached to the top of the rod. The direction shown depended, of course, on the drift of the ice relative to the water, and did not take into account any actual current which may have been carrying the ice with it, but the true current seems never to have been large, and the direction of the vane probably gave fairly accurately the direction of the drift of the ice. No exact idea of the rate of drift could be obtained from the apparatus, although one could get an estimate of it by displacing the vane from its position of rest and noticing how quickly it returned to it, the speed of return being greater the more rapid the drift. Another means of estimating the speed and direction of the drift was from the trend of the wire when a sounding was being taken. The rate and direction of drift appeared to depend almost entirely on the wind-velocity and direction at the time. If any true current-effect existed, it is not obvious from a rough comparison of the drift with the prevailing wind, but a closer investigation of the figures may show some outstanding effect due to current.[*] The drift was always to the left of the actual wind-direction. This effect is due to the rotation of the earth, a corresponding deviation to the right of the wind direction being noted by Nansen during the drift of the *Fram*. A change in the direction of the wind was often preceded by some hours by a change in the reading of the drift vane. This is no doubt due to the ice to windward being set in motion, the resulting disturbance travelling through the ice more rapidly than the approaching wind.

For the astronomical observations either the sextant or a theodolite was used. The theodolite employed was a light 3″ Vernier instrument by Casey Porter, intended for sledging work. This instrument was fairly satisfactory, although possibly rigidity had been sacrificed to lightness to rather too great an extent. Another point which appears worth mentioning is the following: the foot-screws

---

[*] cf. *Scientific results of Norwegian North Polar Expedition, 1893–96*, vol. iii p. 357.

were of brass, the tribrach, into which they fitted, was made of aluminium for the sake of lightness. The two metals have a different coefficient of expansion, and while the feet fitted the tribrach at ordinary temperatures, they were quite loose at temperatures in the region of 20 degrees Fahr. below zero. In any instrument designed for use at low temperatures, care should be taken that parts which have to fit together are made of the same material.

For determining the position in drifting pack-ice, the theodolite proved to be a more generally useful instrument than the sextant. The ice-floes are quite steady in really thick pack-ice, and the theodolite can be set up and levelled as well as on dry land. The observations, both for latitude and longitude, consist in measuring altitude of the sun or of a star. The chief uncertainty in this measurement is that introduced by the refraction of light by the air. At very low temperatures the correction to be applied on this account is uncertain, and, if possible, observations should always be made in pairs with a north star and a south star for a latitude, and an east star and a west star for a longitude. The refraction error will then usually mean out. This error affects observations both with the theodolite and the sextant, but in the case of the sextant another cause of error occurs. In using the sextant, the angle between the heavenly body and the visible horizon is measured directly. Even in dense pack-ice, if the observations are taken from the deck of the ship or from a hummock or a low berg, the apparent horizon is usually sharp enough for the purpose. In very cold weather, however, and particularly if there are open leads and pools between the observer and the horizon, there is frequently a great deal of mirage, and the visible horizon may be miraged up several minutes. This will reduce the altitude observed, and corrections on this account are practically impossible to apply. This error may be counterbalanced to some extent by pairing observations as described above, but it by no means follows that the mirage effect will be the same in the two directions. Then again, during the summer months, no stars will be visible, and observations for latitude will have to depend on a single noon sight of the sun. If the sun is visible at midnight its altitude will be too low for accurate observations, and in any case atmospheric conditions will be quite different from those prevailing at noon. In the Antarctic, therefore, conditions are peculiarly difficult for getting really accurate observations, and it is necessary to reduce the probability of error in a single observation as much as possible. When possible, observations of the altitude of a star or of the sun should be taken with the theodolite, since the altitude is referred to the spirit-level of the instrument, and is independent of any apparent horizon. During the drift of the *Endurance* both means of observation were generally employed. A comparison of the results showed an agreement between sextant and theodolite, within the errors of the instrument if the temperature was above about 20 degrees. Fahr. At lower temperatures there were frequently discrepancies which could generally be attributed to the mirage effects described above.

As the *Endurance* was carried by the ice-drift well to the west of the Weddell Sea, towards the position of the supposed Morrell Land, the accurate determination of longitude became a matter of moment in view of the controversy as to the existence of this land. During a long voyage latitude can always be determined with about the same accuracy, the accuracy merely depending on the closeness with which altitudes can be measured. In the case of longitude matters are rather different. The usual method employed consists in the determination of the local time by astronomical observations, and the comparison of this time with Greenwich time, as shown by the ship's chronometer, an accurate knowledge of the errors and rate of the chronometer being required. During the voyage of the *Endurance* about fifteen months elapsed during which no check on the chronometers could be obtained by the observation of known land, and had no other check been applied there would have been the probability of large errors in the longitudes. For the purpose of checking the chronometers a number of observations of occultations were observed during the winter of 1915. An occultation is really the eclipse of a star by the moon. A number of such eclipses occur monthly, and are tabulated in the *Nautical Almanac*. From the data given there it is possible to compute the Greenwich time at which the phenomenon ought to occur for an observer situated at any place on the earth, provided his position is known within a few miles, which will always be the case. The time of disappearance of the star by the chronometer to be corrected is noted. The actual Greenwich time of the occurrence is calculated, and the error of the chronometer is thus determined. With ordinary care the chronometer error can be determined in this way to within a few seconds, which is accurate enough for purposes of navigation. The principal difficulties of this method lie in the fact that comparatively few occultations occur, and those which do occur are usually of stars of the fifth magnitude or lower. In the Antarctic, conditions for observing occultation are rather favourable during the winter, since fifth-magnitude stars can be seen with a small telescope at any time during the twenty-four hours if the sky is clear, and the moon is also often above the horizon for a large fraction of the time. In the summer, however, the method is quite impossible, since, for some months, stars are not to be seen.

No chronometer check could be applied until June 1915. On June 24 a series of four occultations were observed; and the results of the observations showed an error in longitude of a whole degree. In July, August, and September further occultations were observed, and a fairly reliable rate was worked out for the chronometers and watches. After the crushing of the ship on October 27, 1915, no further occultations were observed, but the calculated rates for the watches were employed, and the longitude deduced, using these rates on March 23, 1916, was only about 10' of arc in error, judging by the observations of Joinville Land made on that day. It is thus fairly certain that no large error can have been made in the determination of the position of the *Endurance* at any time during the drift, and her course can be taken as known with greater certainty than is usually the case in a voyage of such length.

South Atlantic whales and whaling
By Robert S. Cry, M.A., B.Sc., Lieut. R.N.V.R.

Modern whaling methods were introduced into sub-Antarctic seas in 1904, and operations commenced in the following year at South Georgia. So successful was the initial venture that several companies were floated, and the fishing area was extended to the South Shetlands, the South Orkneys, and as far as 67 degrees S along the western coast of Graham Land. This area lies within the Dependencies of the Falkland Islands, and is under the control of the British Government, and its geographical position offers exceptional opportunities for the successful prosecution of the industry by providing a sufficient number of safe anchorages and widely separated islands, where shore stations have been established. The Dependencies of the Falkland Islands lie roughly within latitude 50 degrees and 65 degrees S. and longitude 25 degrees and 70 degrees W., and include the Falkland Islands, South Georgia, South Sandwich, South Orkney, and South Shetland Islands, and part of Graham Land.

The industry is prosperous, and the products always find a ready market. In this sub-Antarctic area alone, the resulting products more than doubled the world's supply. The total value of the Falkland Island Dependencies in 1913 amounted to £1,252,432, in 1914 to £1,300,978, in 1915 to £1,333,401, and in 1916 to £1,774,570. This has resulted chiefly from the marketing of whale-oil and the by-product guano, and represents for each total a season's capture of several thousand whales. In 1916 the number of whales captured in this area was 11,860, which included 6000 for South Georgia alone. Whale-oil, which is now the product of most economic value in the whaling industry, is produced in four grades (some companies adding a fifth). These are Nos. 0, i, ii, iii, iv, which in 1913 sold at £24, £22, £20, and £18 respectively per ton, net weight, barrels included (there are six barrels to a ton). The 1919 prices have increased to:

72 pounds 10s. per ton (barrels included) less 2½ per cent.
68 pounds per ton (barrels included) less 2½ per cent.
65 pounds per ton (barrels included) less 2½ per cent.
63 pounds per ton (barrels included) less 2½ per cent.

Whale-oil can be readily transformed into glycerine: it is used in the manufacture of soap, and quite recently, both in this country and in Norway, it has been refined by means of a simple hardening process into a highly palatable and nutritious margarine. Wartime conditions emphasised the importance of the whale-oil, and fortunately the supply was fairly constant for the production of the enormous quantities of glycerine required by the country in the manufacture of explosives. In relation to the food-supply it was no less important in saving the country from a 'fat' famine when the country was confronted with the shortage of vegetable and other animal oils. The production of guano, bone-meal, and flesh-meal may pay off the running expenses of a whaling-station, but their value lies, perhaps, more in their individual properties. Flesh-meal makes up into cattle-cake, which forms an excellent fattening food for cattle, while bone-meal and guano are very effective fertilisers. Guano is the meat – generally the residue of distillation – which goes through a process of drying and disintegration, and is mixed with the crushed bone in the proportion of two parts flesh to one part bone. This is done chiefly at the shore stations, and, to a less extent on floating factories, though so far on the latter it has not proved very profitable. Whale flesh, though slightly greasy perhaps and of strong flavour, is quite palatable, and at South Georgia, it made a welcome addition to our bill of fare – the flesh of the hump back being used. A large supply of whale flesh was 'shipped' as food for the dogs on the journey South, and this was eaten ravenously. It is interesting to note also the successful rearing of pigs at South Georgia – chiefly, if not entirely, on the whale products. The whalebone or baleen plates, which at one time formed the most valuable article of the Arctic fishery, may here be regarded as of secondary importance. The baleen plates of the southern right whale reach only a length of about 7 ft., and have been valued at 750 pounds per ton, but the number of these whales captured is very small indeed. In the case of the other whale-bone whales, the baleen plates are much smaller and of inferior quality – the baleen of the sei-whale probably excepted, and this only makes about £85 per ton, Sperm-whales have been taken at South Georgia and the South Shetlands, but never in any quantity, being more numerous in warmer areas. The products and their value are too well known to be repeated.

The *Endurance* reached South Georgia on November 5, 1914, and anchored in King Edward Cove, Cumberland Bay, off Gryt-viken, the shore station of the Argentina Pesca Company. During the month's stay at the island a considerable amount of time was devoted to a study of the whales and the whaling industry, in the intervals of the general routine of expedition work, and simul-taneously with other studies on the general life of this interesting sub-Antarctic island. Visits were made to six of the seven existing stations, observations were made on the whales landed, and useful insight was gathered as to the general working of the industry.

From South Georgia the track of the *Endurance* lay in a direct line to the South Sandwich Group, between Saunders and Candlemas Islands. Then south-easterly and southerly courses were steered to the Coats' Land barrier, along which we steamed for a few hundred miles until forced westward, when we were unfortunately held up in about lat. 76 degrees 34' S. and long. 37 degrees 30' W. on January 19, 1915, by enormous masses of heavy pack-ice. The ship drifted to lat. 76 degrees 59' S., long. 37 degrees 47' W. on March 19, 1915, and then west and north until crushed in lat. 69 degrees 5' S. and long. 51 degrees 30' W. on October 26, 1915. We continued drifting gradually north, afloat on ice-floes, past Graham Land and Joinville Island, and finally took to the boats on April 9, 1916, and reached Elephant Island on April 15. The Falkland Island Dependencies were thus practically circumnavigated, and it may be interesting to compare the records of whales seen in the region outside and to the south of this area with the records and the percentage of each species captured in the intensive fishing area.

The most productive part of the South Atlantic lies south of latitude 50 degrees S., where active operations extend to and even beyond the Antarctic circle. It appears to be the general rule in Antarctic waters that whales are more numerous the closer the association with ice conditions, and there seems to be reasonable grounds for supposing that this may explain the comparatively few whales sighted by expeditions which have explored the more northerly and more open seas, while the whalers themselves have even asserted that their poor seasons have nearly always coincided with the absence of ice, or with poor ice conditions. At all events, those expeditions which have penetrated far south and well into the pack-ice have, without exception, reported the presence of whales in large numbers, even in the farthest south latitudes, so that our knowledge of the occurrence of whales in the Antarctic has been largely derived from these expeditions, whose main object was either the discovery of new land or the Pole itself. The largest number of Antarctic expeditions has concentrated on the two areas of the South Atlantic and the Ross Sea, and the records of the occurrences of whales have, in consequence, been concentrated in these two localities. In the intervening areas, however, expeditions, notably the *Belgica* on the western side and the *Gauss* on the eastern side of the Antartic continent, have reported whales in moderately large numbers, so that the stock is by no means confined to the two areas above mentioned.

The effective fishing area may be assumed to lie within a radius of a hundred miles from each shore station and floating-factory anchorage, and a rough estimate of all the Falkland stations works out at 160,000 square miles. The total for the whole Falkland area is about 2,000,000 square miles, which is roughly less than a sixth of the total Antarctic sea area. The question then arises as to how far the 'catch percentage' during the short fishing season affects the total stock, but so far one can only conjecture as to the actual results from a comparison of the numbers seen, chiefly by scientific and other expeditions, in areas outside the intensive fishing area with the numbers and percentage of each species captured in the intensive fishing area. Sufficient evidence, however, seems to point quite definitely to one species – the humpback – being in danger of extermination, but the blue and fin whales – the other two species of rorquals which form the bulk of the captures – appear to be as frequent now as they have ever been.

The whales captured at the various whaling-stations of the Falkland area are confined largely to three species – blue whale (*Balaenoptera musculus*), fin whale (*Balaenoptera physalus*), and humpback (*Megaptera nodosa*); sperm-whales (*Physeter catodon*) and right whales (*Balaena glacialis*) being only occasional and rare captures, while the sei-whale (*Balaenoptera borealis*) appeared in the captures at South Georgia in 1913, and now forms a large percentage of the captures at the Falkland Islands. During the earlier years of whaling at South Georgia, and up to the fishing season 1910–11, humpbacks formed practically the total catch. In 1912–13 the following were the percentages for the three rorquals in the captures at South Georgia and South Shetlands.

Humpback 38 per cent., fin whale 36 per cent., blue whale 20 per cent. Of late years the percentages have altered considerably, blue whales and fin whales predominating, humpbacks decreasing rapidly. In 1915 the South Georgia Whaling Company (Messrs. Salvesen, Leith) captured 1085 whales, consisting of 15 per cent. humpback, 25 per cent. fin whales, 58 per cent. blue whales, and 2 right whales. In the same year the captures of three companies at the South Shetlands gave 1512 whales, and the percentages worked out at 12 per cent. humpbacks, 42 per cent. fin whales, and 45 per cent. blue whales. In 1919 the Southern Whaling and Sealing Company captured (at Stromness, South Georgia) 529 whales, of which 2 per cent. were humpbacks, 51 per cent. fin whales, and 45 per cent. blue whales. These captures do not represent the total catch, but are sufficiently reliable to show how the species are affected. The reduction in numbers of the humpback is very noticeable, and even allowing for the possible increase in size of gear for the capture of the larger and more lucrative blue and fin whales, there is sufficient evidence to warrant the fears that the humpback stock is threatened with extinction.

In the immediate northern areas – in the region from latitude 50 degrees S. northward to the equator, which is regarded as next in importance quantitatively to the sub-Antarctic, though nothing like being so productive, the captures are useful for a comparative study in distribution. At Saldanha Bay, Cape Colony, in 1912, 131 whales were captured and the percentages were as follows: 35 per cent. humpback, 13 per cent. fin whale, 4 per cent. blue whale, 46 per cent. sei-whale; while nearer the equator, at Port Alexander, the total capture was 322 whales, and the percentages gave 98 per cent. humpback, and only 2 captures each of fin and sei whales. In 1914, at South Africa (chiefly Saldanha Bay and Durban), out of a total of 839 whales 60 per cent. were humpback, 25 per cent. fin whales, and 13 per cent. blue whales. In 1916, out of a total of 853 whales 10 per cent. were humpback, 13 per cent. fin whales, 6 per cent. blue whales, 68 per cent. sperm-whales, and 1 per cent. sei whales. In Chilean waters, in 1916, a total of 327 whales gave 31 per cent. humpbacks, 24 per cent. fin whales, 26 per cent. blue whales, 12 per cent. sperm-whales, and 5 right whales. There seems then to be a definite interrelation between the two areas. The same species of whales are captured, and the periods of capture alternate with perfect regularity, the fishing season occurring from the end of November to April in the sub-Antarctic and from May to November in the sub-tropics. A few of the companies, however, carry on operations to a limited extent at South Georgia and at the Falkland islands during the southern winter, but the fishing is by no means a profitable undertaking, though proving the presence of whales in this area during the winter months.

The migrations of whales are influenced by two causes:
  (1) The distribution of their food–supply;
  (2) The position of their breeding–grounds.

In the Antarctic, during the summer months, there is present in the sea an abundance of plant and animal life, and whales which feed on the small *plankton* organisms are correspondingly numerous, but in winter this state of things is reversed, and whales are poorly represented or absent, at least in the higher latitudes. During the drift of the *Endurance* samples of plankton were taken almost daily during an Antarctic summer and winter. From December to March, a few minutes haul of a tow-net at the surface was sufficient to choke up the meshes with the plant and animal life, but this abundance of surface life broke off abruptly in April, and subsequent hauls contained very small organisms until the return of daylight and the opening up of the pack-ice. The lower water strata, down to about 100 fathoms, were only a little more productive, and *Euphausiae* were taken in the hauls – though sparingly. During the winter spent at Elephant Island, our total catch of gentoo penguins amounted to 1436 for the period April 15 to August 30, 1916. All these birds were cut up, the livers and hearts were extracted for food, and the skins were used as fuel. At the same time the stomachs were invariably examined, and a record kept of the contents. The largest proportion of these contained the small crustacean *Euphausiae*, and this generally to the exclusion of other forms. Occasionally, however, small fish were recorded. The quantity of *Euphausiae* present in most of the stomachs was enormous for the size of the birds. These penguins were migrating, and came ashore only when the bays were clear of ice, as there were several periods of fourteen consecutive days when the bays and the surrounding sea were covered over with a thick compact mass of ice-floes, and then penguins were entirely absent. *Euphausiae*, then, seem to be present in sufficient quantity in certain, if not in all, sub-Antarctic waters during the southern winter. We may assume then that the migration to the south, during the Antarctic summer, is definitely in search of food. Observations have proved the existence of a northern migration, and it seems highly improbable that this should also be in search of food, but rather for breeding purposes, and it seems that the whales select the more temperate regions for the bringing forth of their young. This view is strengthened by the statistical foetal records, which show that pairing takes place in the northern areas, that the foetus is carried by the mother during the southern migration to the Antarctic, and that the calves are born in the more congenial waters north of the sub-Antarctic area. We have still to prove, however, the possibility of a circumpolar migration, and we are quite in the dark as to the number of whales that remain in sub-Antarctic areas during the Southern winter.

The following is a rough classification of whales, with special reference to those known to occur in the South Atlantic

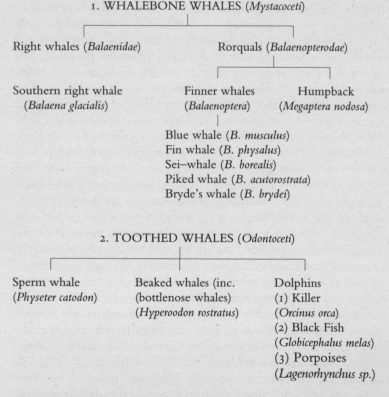

1. WHALEBONE WHALES (*Mystacoceti*)

Right whales (*Balaenidae*)   Rorquals (*Balaenopterodae*)

Southern right whale   Finner whales   Humpback
  (*Balaena glacialis*)   (*Balaenoptera*)   (*Megaptera nodosa*)

Blue whale (*B. musculus*)
Fin whale (*B. physalus*)
Sei–whale (*B. borealis*)
Piked whale (*B. acutorostrata*)
Bryde's whale (*B. brydei*)

2. TOOTHED WHALES (*Odontoceti*)

Sperm whale   Beaked whales (inc.   Dolphins
(*Physeter catodon*)   (bottlenose whales)   (1) Killer
            (*Hyperoodon rostratus*)   (*Orcinus orca*)
                                   (2) Black Fish
                                   (*Globicephalus melas*)
                                   (3) Porpoises
                                   (*Lagenorhynchus sp.*)

The subdivision of whalebone whales is one of degree in the size of the whalebone. These whales have enormously muscular tongues, which press the water through the whalebone lamellae and thus, by a filtering process, retain the small food organisms. The food of the whalebone whales is largely the small crustacea which occur in the plankton, though some whales (humpback, fin whales, and sei-whales) feed also on fish. The stomachs examined at South Georgia, during December 1914, belonged to the three species, humpbacks, fin whales, and blue whales, and all contained small crustacean – *Euphausiae*, with a mixture of *Amphipods*. The toothed whale – sperms and bottlenoses – are known to live on squids, and that there is an abundance of this type of food in the Weddell Sea was proved by an examination of penguin and seal stomachs. Emperor penguins (and hundreds of these were examined) were invariably found to contain Cephalopod 'beaks', while large, partly-digested squids were often observed in Weddell seals. A dorsal fin is present in the rorquals but absent in right whales. With other characters, notably the size of the animal, it serves as a ready mark of identification, but is occasionally confusing owing to the variation in shape in some of the species.

With the exception of several schools of porpoises very few whales were seen during the outward voyage. Not till we approached the Falkland area did they appear in any numbers. Four small schools of fin whales and a few humpbacks were sighted on October 28 and 29, 1914, in lat. 38 degrees 01' S., long. 55 degrees 03' W. and in lat. 40 degrees 35' S., long. 53 degrees 11' W., while *Globicephalus melas* was seen only once, in lat. 45 degrees 17' S., long. 48 degrees 58' W., on October 31, 1914. At South Georgia the whales captured at the various stations in December 1914 were blue whales, fin whales, and humpbacks (arranged respectively according to numbers captured). During the fishing season 1914–15 (from December to March) in the area covered – South Georgia to the South Sandwich Islands and along Coats' Land to the head of the Weddell Sea – the records of whales were by no means numerous. Two records only could with certainty be assigned to the humpback, and these were in the neighbourhood of the South Sandwich Islands. Pack-ice was entered in lat. 59 degrees 55' S., long. 18 degrees 28' W., and blue whales were recorded daily until about 65 degrees S. Between lat. 65 degrees 43' S., long. 17 degrees 30' W., on December 27, 1914, and lat. 69 degrees 59' S., long. 17 degrees 31' W., on January 3, 1915, no whales were seen. On January 4, however, in lat. 69 degrees 59' S., long. 17 degrees 36' W., two large sperm-whales appeared close ahead of the ship in fairly open water, and were making westward. They remained sufficiently long on the surface to render their identification easy. Farther south, blue whales were only seen occasionally, and fin whales could only be identified in one or two cases. Killers, however, were numerous, and the lesser piked whale was quite frequent. There was no doubt about the identity of this latter species as it often came close alongside the ship. From April to September (inclusive) the sea was frozen over (with the exception of local 'leads'), and whales were found to be absent. In October whales again made their appearance, and from then onwards they were a daily occurrence. Identification of the species, however, was a difficult matter, for the *Endurance* was crushed and had sunk, and observations were only possible from the ice-floe, or later on from the boats. The high vertical 'spout' opening out into a dense spray was often visible, and denoted the presence of blue and fin whales. The lesser piked whale again appeared in the 'leads' close to our 'camp' floe, and was easily identified. An exceptional opportunity was presented to us on December 6, 1915, when a school of eight bottlenose whales (*Hyperoodon rostratus*) appeared in small 'pool' alongside 'Ocean' Camp in lat. 67 degrees 47' S., long. 52 degrees 18' W. These ranged from about 20 ft. to a little over 30 ft. in length, and were of a uniform dark dun colour – the large specimens having a dull yellow appearance. There were no white spots. At the edge of the pack-ice during the first half of April 1916, about lat. 62 degrees S. and long. 54 degrees W. (entrance to Bransfield Strait), whales were exceedingly numerous, and these were chiefly fin whales, though a few seemed to be sei-whales. It is interesting to note that the fishing season 1915–1916 was exceptionally productive – no less than 11,860 whales having been captured in the Falkland area alone.

The South Atlantic whaling industry, then, has reached a critical stage in development. It is now dependent on the captures of the large fin and blue whales, humpbacks having been rapidly reduced in numbers, so that the total stock appears to have been affected. With regard to the other species, the southern right whale has never been abundant in the captures, the sperm-whale and the sei-whale have shown a good deal of seasonal variation, though never

numerous, and the bottlenose and lesser piked whale have so far
not been hunted, except in the case of the latter for human food.
The vigorous slaughter of whales both in the sub-Antarctic and in
the sub-tropics, for the one area reacts on the other, calls for
universal legislation to protect the whales from early commercial
extinction, and the industry, which is of world-wide economic
importance, from having to be abandoned. The British Government, with the control of the world's best fisheries, is thoroughly
alive to the situation, and an Inter-departmental Committee,
under the direction of the Colonial Office, is at present devising a
workable scheme for suitable legislation for the protection of the
whales and for the welfare of the industry.

The Expedition huts at McMurdo Sound
by Sir E. H. Shackleton

The following notes are designed for the benefit of future explorers who may make McMurdo Sound a base for inland operations, and to clear any inaccuracies or ambiguities concerning the history, occupation, and state of these huts.

(1) *The National Antarctic Expedition's hut at Hut Point – the head of McMurdo Sound*

This hut was constructed by Captain Scott in 1902, by the Expedition sent out by the Royal Geographical Society, the Royal Society, the Government, and by private subscription. Captain Robert F. Scott was appointed to the command of the Expedition. I served as Third Lieutenant until February 1903, when I was invalided home through a broken blood-vessel in the lungs, the direct result of scurvy contracted on the Southern journey. The *Discovery* hut was a large strong building, but was so draughty and cold in comparison with the ship, which was moored one hundred yards away, that it was, during the first year, never used for living quarters. Its sole use was as a storehouse, and a large supply of rough stores, such as flour, cocoa, coffee, biscuit, and tinned meat, was left there in the event of its being used as a place of retreat should any disaster overtake the ship. During the second year occasional parties camped inside the hut, but no bunks or permanent sleeping quarters were ever erected. The discomfort of the hut was a byword on the Expedition, but it formed an excellent depot and starting–point for all parties proceeding to the south.

When the *Discovery* finally left McMurdo Sound, the hut was stripped of all gear, including the stove, but there was left behind a large depot of the stores mentioned above. I was not aware of this until I returned to McMurdo Sound in February 1908, when I sent Adams, Joyce, and Wild across to the hut whilst the *Nimrod* was lying off the ice.

On the return of the party they reported that the door had been burst open, evidently by a southerly blizzard, and was jammed by snow outside and in, so they made an entrance through one of the lee windows. They found the hut practically clear of snow, and the structure quite intact. I used the hut in the spring, i.e. September and October 1908, as a storehouse for the large amount of equipment, food, and oil that we were to take on the Southern journey. We built a sort of living-room out of the cases of provisions, and swept out the debris. The Southern Party elected to sleep there before the start, but the supporting party slept outside in the tents, as they considered it warmer.

We still continued to use the lee window as means of ingress and egress to avoid continual shovelling away of the snow, which would be necessary as every southerly blizzard blocked up the main entrance. The various depot parties made use of the hut for replenishing their stores, which had been sledged from my own hut to Hut Point. On the night of March 3, 1909, I arrived with the Southern Party, with a sick man, having been absent on the march 128 days. Our position was bad, as the ship was north of us. We tried to burn the Magnetic Hut in the hope of attracting attention from the ship, but were not able to get it to light. We finally managed to light a flare of carbide, and the ship came down to us in a blizzard, and all were safely aboard at 1 a.m. on March 4, 1909. Before leaving the hut we jammed the window up with baulks of timber, to the best of our ability in the storm and darkness. The hut was used again by the Ross Sea Section of this last Expedition. The snow was cleared out and extra stores were placed in it. From reports I have received the *Discovery* Hut was in as good condition in 1917 as it was in 1902.

The stores placed there in 1902 are intact. There are a few cases of extra provisions and oil in the hut, but no sleeping gear or accommodation, nor stoves, and it must not be looked upon as anything else than a shelter and a most useful *pied-à-terre* for the start of any Southern journey. No stores nor any equipment have been taken from it during either of my two Expeditions.

(2) *Cape Royds hut*

For several reasons, when I went into McMurdo Sound in 1908 in command of my own Expedition, known as the British Antarctic Expedition, after having failed to land on King Edward VII Land, I decided to build our hut at Cape Royds – a small promontory twenty-three miles north of Hut Point. Here the whole shore party lived in comfort through the winter of 1908. When spring came stores were sledged to Hut Point, so that should the sea-ice break up early between these two places we might not be left in an awkward position. After the return of the Southern Party we went direct north to civilisation, so I never visited my hut again. I had left, however, full instructions with Professor David as to the care of the hut, and before the whole Expedition left the hut was put in order. A letter was pinned in a conspicuous place inside, stating that there were sufficient provisions and equipment to last fifteen men for one year, indicating also the details of these provisions and the position of the coal store. The stove was in good condition, and the letter ended with an invitation for any succeeding party to make what use they required of stores and hut. The hut was then locked and the key nailed on the door in a conspicuous place. From the report of Captain Scott's last Expedition the hut was in good condition, and from a still later report from the Ross Sea side of this present Expedition the hut was still intact.

(3) *Cape Evans hut*

This large and commodious hut was constructed by Captain Scott at Cape Evans on his last Expedition. The party lived in it in comfort, and it was left well supplied with stores in the way of food and oil and a certain amount of coal. Several of the scientific staff of this present Expedition were ashore in it, when the *Aurora*, which was to have been the permanent winter quarters, broke adrift in May 1915 and went north with the ice. The hut became the permanent living quarters for the ten marooned men, and thanks to the stores they were able to sustain life in comparative comfort, supplementing these stores from my hut at Cape Royds. In January 1917, after I had rescued the survivors, I had the hut put in order and locked up.

To sum up, there are three available huts in McMurdo Sound:

(a) The *Discovery* Hut, with a certain amount of rough stores, and only of use as a point of departure for the South.

(b) Cape Royds Hut, with a large amount of general stores but no clothing or equipment now.

(c) Cape Evans Hut, with a large amount of stores but no clothing or equipment and only a few sledges.

(4) *Depots south of Hut Point*

In spite of the fact that several depots have been laid to the south of Hut Point on the Barrier, the last being at the Gap (the entrance to the Beardmore Glacier), no future Expedition should depend on them as the heavy snowfall obliterates them completely. There is no record of the depots of any Expedition being made use of by any subsequent Expedition. No party in any of my Expeditions has used any depot laid down by a previous Expedition.